In the footsteps of the Six Wives of Henry VIII

SARAH MORRIS & NATALIE GRUENINGER

AMBERLEY

This book is dedicated to six remarkable women whose lives have deeply touched our hearts and souls: Katherine of Aragon, Anne Boleyn, Jane Seymour, Anne of Cleves, Catherine Howard and Katherine Parr. Thank you for enriching our lives and for being an endless source of inspiration.

Natalie and Sarah

This edition published 2017
First published 2016

Amberley Publishing
The Hill, Stroud
Gloucestershire, GL5 4EP

www.amberley-books.com

British Library Cataloguing in Publication Data.
A catalogue record for this book is available from the British Library.

ISBN 978 1 4456 7114 7 (paperback)
ISBN 978 1 4456 4304 5 (ebook)

Typesetting and Origination by Amberley Publishing.
Printed in the UK.

Contents

Acknowledgements

The authors would like to thank the following people most sincerely for their contribution towards making this book possible:

Katherine of Aragon

Alcala de Henares: Abraham Consuegra Gandullo, BlogTURISTAlcalá.
Javier Lerma, Tourism Office Alcala de Henares.
Medina del Campo: Antonio Sánchez del Barrio, director, Fundación Museo de las Ferias.
Santiago de Compostela: Ramón Yzquierdo Peiró, director, Cathedral Museum, Santiago de Compostela.
Buckden Palace: The Friends of Buckden Towers, in particular Christine Laurence and Peter Ibbett.
The St Claret Centre.
Kimbolton Castle: Kimbolton Castle School, in particular Jonathan Belbin, headmaster, and Nora Butler, castle historian.
Leeds Castle: Tori Reeve, curator, Leeds Castle.

Anne Boleyn

Hever Castle: Anna Spender, castle co-ordinator; Ashley Collins, retail manager; Jan Ryan, guide; Susanne Moller, guide; Heath Pye.
Mechelen: Jessica Van Humbeeck and Nathalie Van Humbeeck. Maurits Delbaere, JS.
Château d'Amboise: Marc Metay, director; Aline Colin, guide.
Haseley Court: Mr and Mrs Heyward, owners.
Chertsey Abbey: Emma Warren, curator, Chertsey Museum.
Berkeley Castle: Eleanor Taylor.
Buckingham: Ed Grimsdale, local historian/outreach officer, The Old Gaol Museum, Buckingham.
Hunsdon: Sandra Vasoli.

Jane Seymour

Wolfhall: Graham Bathe, historian.
Mercer's Hall: Jane Ruddell, archivist.
Chester Place: Graham Bathe, historian.
Professor Nicolas Orme, University of Exeter.

Anne of Cleves

Before addressing individual locations, we would like to express our heartfelt thanks to a number of individuals who helped with the translation of a number of German and Dutch texts during the research process. Their assistance has been invaluable in the research and writing of this section: Nancy Claeys, Michael Glaeser, Sindy Hombach, Ursula Madel, Beatrix Grueninger, Huberta Barber and Carmen Parrado.

For the Anne of Cleves Panels: Christine Hill, local historian and author of *Old Warden: Tales of Tenants and Squires*.
Dr Jonathan Folye, architectural historian.
John Scott and the Old Warden Parochial Church Council.
Swiss Garden and Old Warden Social History Project, sponsored by the Heritage Lottery Fund.
For Düsseldorf: City Marketing of Düsseldorf.
For Schloss Düren: Eheleute Ilse and Martin Müller, owners of Schloss Hambach.
For Schloss Burg: Schlossbauverein Burg an der Wupper e.V.
Cevin Conrad, castle guide.
For Schwanenburg: Helga Ullrich-Scheyda – local historian and castle guide.
For Antwerp: Nancy Claeys, local historian.
Annemie De Vos, Conservator Collectie Stadhuis en MAS.
For Bruges: Carmen Parrado, local historian.
Jan Anseeuw, archivist, Bruges City Archives.
For Deal: Judith Gaunt, researcher and writer.
For Dover: Gordon Higgott, an independent architectural historian.
For Rochester: The Kent Archaeological Society.
For Dartford: Mike Still, curator of Dartford Museum.
Peter Boreham, author and retired curator of Dartford Museum.
For Bletchingley: Rod Wild, data secretary of the Domestic Buildings Research Group (Surrey).
Research by Dennis Turner and Richard Greening.

Catherine Howard

For Pontefract: Rosalind Buck, Historic Environment Record Information Officer, West Yorkshire Archaeology Advisory Service.

Ian Roberts FSA MIfA, Principal Archaeologist, Archaeological Services WYAS. Pontefract Museum.
The Hepworth Gallery.
Wakefield City Council.
For Cawood: Jill Forster-Walmsley, author of *Cawood*.
Alastair Oswald, Landscape Archaeologist, the University of York.
Ms Audrey Thorstad, member of the West Yorkshire Archaeological Society.
The Landmark Trust.
For the King's Manor, York: J. P. D. Cooper, MA, D.Phil., FRHistS, Senior Lecturer in History at the University of York.
Ms Audrey Thorstad, member of the West Yorkshire Archaeological Society.
Sally-Anne Shearn, Archive Assistant, The Borthwick Insitute, York.
Professor Christopher Norton, Centre for Medieval Studies, University of York.
   With special thanks to the *The West Yorkshire Archaeological Society* for their assistance with our research regarding Cawood and Pontefract castles, particularly, Kirtsy McHugh, archivist.

Katherine Parr

For Rye House: Ronnie Garside, President of the Stanstead Abbots Local History Society and Sue Dale.
For Sizergh Castle: Georgina Gates, National Trust and the Strickland family.
For Snape Castle: John Knopp and Peter Smith, Snape Local History Group.
For Church Stowe Manor: Carol and Geoff Wood, current owners.
For Charterhouse Square: Stephen Porter, Charterhouse archivist and author of *The London Charterhouse* and *Charterhouse: The Official Guide*.
For Woking Palace: The Friends of Woking Palace, in particular Jean Follet.
For Sudeley Castle: Derek Maddock, archivist.
For Otford Palace: Rod Shelton, author and historian.
For Nonsuch Palace: Marguerite de Bohun, Secretary for Friends of Nonsuch.

To the love of my life, my husband, Chris, my deepest gratitude for your support, love and encouragement, and for so patiently enduring my extended sojourns in the sixteenth century. To the two brightest lights in my life, Isabel and Tristan, thank you for putting a smile on mummy's face each and every day. Thank you to my parents for gifting me their love of words and writing, for which I am eternally grateful. To my sister (and best friend), Karina, words can never truly express how grateful I am for your support and encouragement, and for taking the time to read and offer feedback on every word that I penned. Gratitude also to my brother-in-law Anibal and my niece and nephew Jasmin and Tabare for keeping my husband and children entertained while my sister and I talked Tudor and pondered the mysteries of the universe. I am also grateful to my dear friends Shelly, Sam and Kate, for knowing exactly when laughs and bubbles were required, and to my friend

Debbie Fenton, for believing in me and cheering me along the way. Thank you, too, to Sarah Bryson and James Peacock for their generous support of our work. A special thanks to Claire and Tim Ridgway for their willingness to share their expertise and guide my family and I around the Alhambra in Granada. A huge thank you to the visitors to my website (www.onthetudortrail.com) and the online Tudor community on Facebook, Instagram and Twitter, for their contributions and endless enthusiasm. And finally, to my soul sister and co-author Sarah Morris, thank you, thank you, thank you! My most sincere gratitude and appreciation for your friendship, hard work and unwavering dedication to this project. I can't wait until the next time we walk the cobbled paths of history together.

Natalie

To my dear friend and fellow time traveller, Natalie Grueninger; every step, both real and virtual, has been one of sheer pleasure. Thank you for your patience, kindness and enthusiasm. Your companionship on our adventures has once again been a joy, and the memories we have created together, I will treasure for a lifetime.

Sarah

Introduction

Afterward she was carried to her tomb, [where] she lies with a herse-cloth of gold, the which lies [over her]; and there all her head officers brake their staffs, [and all] her ushers brake their rods, and all they cast them into her tomb.

Henry Machyn, diarist, describing the interment of
Anne of Cleves in Westminster Abbey

On 4 August 1557, the body of Anne of Cleves, the last surviving wife of Henry VIII, was sealed within its marble tomb. The Tudors would live on for a little over forty years more, but Anne's demise heralded the end of an era which had been dominated by the omnipotent figure of the late king. Over thirty years, Henry's very personal dynastic struggles, and ever-changing passions, would reshape the religious landscape of a country and utterly define the lives of six remarkable women: Katherine of Aragon, Anne Boleyn, Jane Seymour, Anne of Cleves, Catherine Howard and Katherine Parr.

Five hundred years on and their lives continue to intrigue us endlessly. From foreign courts and the aristocratic families of Henry's green England, the destinies of each of these six women drew them to London and eventually into Henry's bed. All suffered one way or another as a result, with five of Henry's queens in time tasting the bitter fruit of their husband's capricious moods and paranoia. The price of glory for Katherine of Aragon and Anne of Cleves was exile and humiliation; Anne Boleyn and Catherine Howard paid for it with their blood. Even Jane Seymour in her hour of triumph was not spared, although in this instance she perished from natural causes. Nevertheless, it could be argued that in doing her duty Jane became the sacrificial goat on the altar of Henry's dynastic aspirations. Perhaps only Katherine Parr, through a combination of circumstance, luck and character, steered a safe course through the dangerous waters of the king's court – although only just.

The lives of the six wives of Henry VIII were entwined. Several of Henry's queens knew each other; some were bound in ties of blood, such as Anne Boleyn and Catherine Howard. Others served as ladies-in-waiting to the mistress they would eventually replace, as was the case with Anne Boleyn, Jane Seymour and Catherine Howard. But in taking their place as queen consort of England, each of them also physically shared many of the same lodgings, particularly in Henry's Great Houses, situated along the Thames Valley, in and around London. Although heraldic devices painted and carved into the fabric of these buildings changed to honour the current incumbent, in contemporary inventories it is easy to find examples of soft furnishings that remained *in situ* as the transition took place between one of Henry's wives and the next. One can only imagine the thoughts and memories these items must have evoked as each of these ladies pondered, however briefly, upon the fate of their predecessor(s).

And so it is, then as now, the power of artefacts and places to powerfully connect us to the presence of those who have gone before. It is something that is keenly felt by any time traveller and originally drew us to write our first *In the Footsteps* book, *In the Footsteps of Anne Boleyn*. This comprehensive guide to the artefacts and places associated with Henry's second wife was enjoyed by many who shared our passion for this most enigmatic and influential of women. We followed Anne from her early years in modern-day Belgium and France through her rise to power and subsequent fall as she travelled across great swathes of southern England. Through the places we visited, more keenly than ever we felt connected to the cultural milieu which forged her character; through the veil of time, the bricks and mortar we touched and the landscapes we travelled across seemed to reveal just a little more of her extraordinary life.

With this book we returned to extend our odyssey, hoping that our travels would similarly open up new insights into, and a deeper appreciation of, the lives of each of Henry's other consorts. So in this second instalment of the *In the Footsteps* series, our aim is to explore the key locations associated with all six of Henry VIII's wives. It has been a truly fascinating pilgrimage that has taken us even further afield in our search for answers, from the sun-baked plains of Spain in the south, through the lush mountains of the Rhine Valley in Germany to the east, via the great abbeys of England's West Country to the medieval cities of northern England.

The Research Process

In our quest to make real the lost Tudor landscape of sixteenth-century Europe, we once again sought out contemporary accounts, inventories, drawings and floor plans of lost towns and buildings; we spoke to archivists, curators, local historians, architectural historians and archaeologists – and held artefacts in our hands; we visited all the locations in Spain, Germany, France and the Low Countries and almost all those in England. As we painstakingly retraced their footsteps, little by little, each woman emerged afresh, the buildings reconnecting us to a past which in some cases has been overlooked and almost forgotten. Thankfully, once more our enquiries were most often greeted warmly and with equal enthusiasm; sadly, we were occasionally met with deafening silence. However, we are both excited and delighted to now be able to present to you, the reader, around seventy locations, many of which we imagine you will be reading about in detail for the first time.

There is much to share, and so without further ado we will describe how to make the most of this book.

Layout and How to Use This Guidebook

In writing the book, we decided to concentrate on a handful of the most interesting, controversial or revealing locations connected to each of the women. In particular, we have focused, where possible, on locations which are still standing and can be visited by the time traveller. Therefore, unlike *In the Footsteps of Anne Boleyn*, this book is not meant to be a comprehensive guide to all the places known to each queen consort.

In the first section, Principal Royal Residences, we cover familiar territory, revisiting some of the key locations situated along the Thames Valley: Eltham Palace, Greenwich Palace, Whitehall Palace, Hampton Court Palace, Richmond Palace and Windsor Castle. Of course, London was Henry's capital. The king based himself in or around the city for much of the year, lodging in so-called Great Houses that were large enough to accommodate the entire court. Naturally, all but one of these, the Tower of London, became home to Henry's consorts in turn until they fell from fashion or were gifted as part of a divorce settlement. Such was the case with Eltham and Richmond respectively. In revisiting these locations, we have adapted each entry to account for this shared occupancy. Events associated with each queen at each location are presented on a timeline for ease of reference.

The remaining five sections are dedicated to covering those locations associated with each of Henry's wives in turn: Katherine of Aragon, Anne Boleyn, Jane Seymour, Anne of Cleves, Catherine Howard and Katherine Parr. Each section is presented chronologically. Every location acts as a stepping stone, creating touchpoints that lead us through each of their fascinating lives from cradle to grave. Of the seventy or so locations included here, the number is roughly divided equally between each consort; although as we soon found out during our research, the scarcity of information on Jane Seymour's early life and her brief reign has meant that fewer locations are included in her section. Nevertheless, we are delighted to be presenting to a wider audience the very recent research by historian Graham Bathe into the appearance of the Seymours' ancestral home, Wolfhall. Bathe is an expert on the Seymours and in collaboration with him we were also able to review some of the original Seymour Papers, held today at Longleat. These revealed some interesting details on Edward Seymour's first London home, Chester Place, and the christening attended there by Jane Seymour in February 1537.

Having already penned a comprehensive guide to the palaces, castles and houses associated with Anne Boleyn, by necessity we have reproduced here some of the most pivotal or interesting locations associated with Henry's second wife. However, having continued our research into Anne's life and travels since the publication of the first book, we are now in a position to include a further four new locations this time around: Haseley Court, Buckingham, Hunsdon House and Chertsey Abbey.

Looking further afield, we are particularly thrilled to be bringing to an English-speaking audience the palaces, castles and houses associated with the early years of Katherine of Aragon and Anne of Cleves. Just as with the locations associated with the formative years of Anne Boleyn, the language barrier has hitherto meant that these places were largely known by little more than name only outside of local interest. However, in working with local historians and native speakers, little by little we have unlocked the secrets of the places that shaped the early lives of the ladies in question. Because of the paucity of information accessible to the English-speaking reader currently, we have decided to place a particular emphasis on the early-years locations for the aforementioned women.

Finally, we are honoured to be presenting a newly acknowledged, nationally important historic collection of carved wooden panels linked to one of our key protagonists – Anne of Cleves. During the course of writing this book, our research led us to commission an extensive research project with architectural historian Jonathan Foyle, directed at investigating the provenance of a much-debated artefact linked with Henry's s fourth wife: the so-called 'Anne of Cleves panels', sited in Old Warden church, Bedfordshire. It has turned out to be an intriguing story and we present, for the first time, the results of a comprehensive, scientific, physical and historical analysis of the panels which finally place them as being contemporaneous to Anne's lifetime.

In general, each entry describes the location as it would have appeared in the sixteenth century, alongside the background for its inclusion and the events which took place there. Wherever possible, we highlight how our understanding of the location creates a richer context for the appreciation of each of our protagonists. Although we hope you will enjoy reading the entire book cover to cover, each entry is also meant to stand alone. Thus, certain information may be repeated, or revisited, across more than one entry. A 'Visitor Information' section concludes each entry. For those of you who wish to physically travel in the footsteps of these remarkable women, we have provided a wealth of handy tips about what to see, where to take rest and refreshment, opening times (where relevant) and postcodes to help you locate each place.

As with *In the Footsteps of Anne Boleyn*, a series of maps inserted at the front of the book will help those of you who are less familiar with European geography to orientate yourself, particularly if you are looking to combine visits to multiple locations. Inside, ninety-five colour and around forty black-and-white images, including photographs, etchings, paintings and floor plans, are included to illustrate the text.

We hope that our selection of locations will bring you closer to each of the ladies in question and that by focusing upon the locations themselves the journey across Europe in their footsteps will open up new insights and understanding for those who are fascinated by this period. So, once again, whether you are snuggling into your favourite armchair, or packing your bags and heading out of your front door, it is time to turn back the clock and let your imagination recreate six exceptional lives through the buildings they have left behind. Bon voyage!

Sarah Morris and Natalie Grueninger

2015

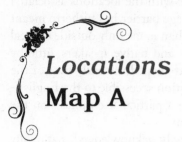

Locations
Map A

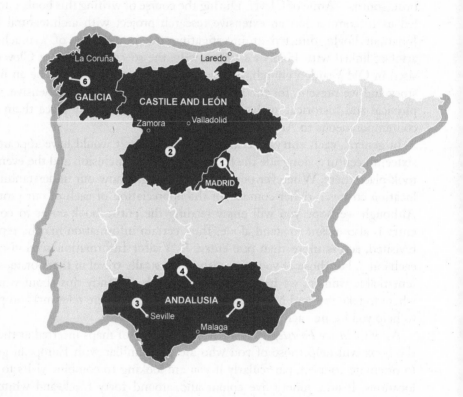

Madrid
1. Archbishop's Palace, Alcalá de Henares

Castile and León
2. Medina del Campo

Andalusia
3. Alcazar of Seville
4. Alcazar of Cordoba
5. The Alhambra & Capilla Real

Galicia
6. Santiago de Compostela

Map A: Locations in Spain

Locations
Map B

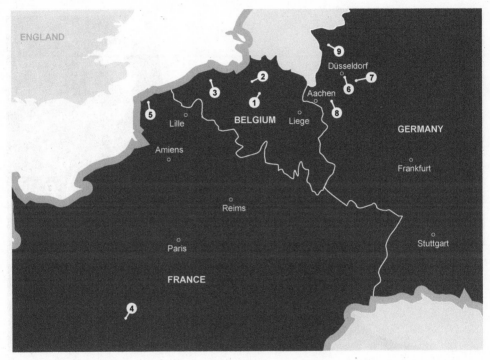

Belgium
1. Mechelen
2. The English House, Antwerp
3. Bruges

France
4. The Loire Valley
5. Calais

Germany
6. The City Palace of Düsseldorf
7. Burg Castle, Solingen
8. Castle of Düren (Castle Hambach)
9. Schwanenburg Castle, Kleve

Map B: Locations in France, Belgium and Germany

Locations
Map C

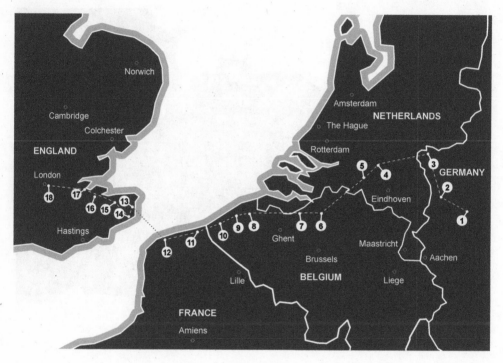

Germany
1. Düsseldorf
2. Duisberg
3. Kleve

Netherlands
4. S'Hertogenbosch
5. Tilburg

Belgium
6. Antwerp
7. Stekene
8. Bruges
9. Oudenburg
10. Newport *(Nieuwport)*

France
11. Dunkerque
12. Calais

England
13. Deal
14. Dover
15. Canterbury
16. Sittingbourne
17. Rochester
18. Greenwich

Map C: The Journey of Anne of Cleves from Germany to England in 1539/40

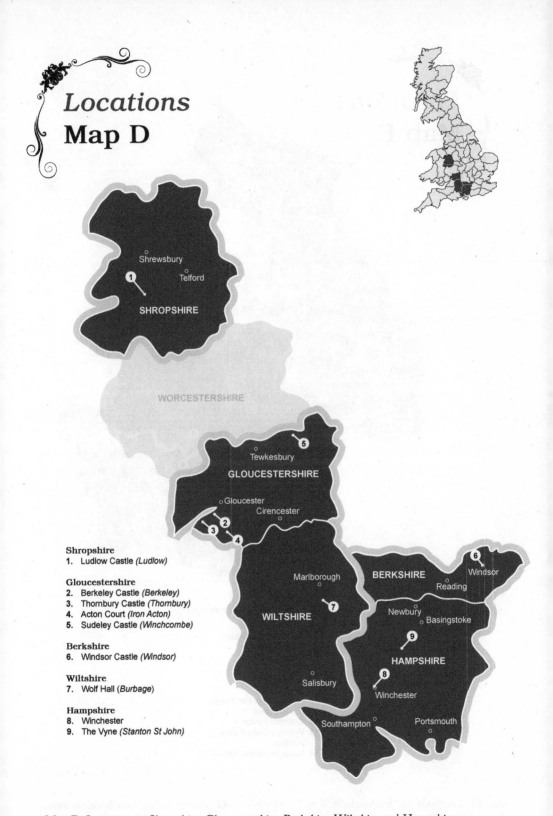

Locations
Map D

Shrewsbury
○

Telford
○

1

SHROPSHIRE

WORCESTERSHIRE

5

Tewkesbury
○

GLOUCESTERSHIRE

Gloucester
○

Cirencester
○

2
3
4

Marlborough
○

BERKSHIRE

Windsor
○

Reading
○

WILTSHIRE

7

Newbury
○

Basingstoke
○

9

HAMPSHIRE

Salisbury
○

8

Winchester
○

Southampton
○

Portsmouth
○

Shropshire
1. Ludlow Castle *(Ludlow)*

Gloucestershire
2. Berkeley Castle *(Berkeley)*
3. Thornbury Castle *(Thornbury)*
4. Acton Court *(Iron Acton)*
5. Sudeley Castle *(Winchcombe)*

Berkshire
6. Windsor Castle *(Windsor)*

Wiltshire
7. Wolf Hall *(Burbage)*

Hampshire
8. Winchester
9. The Vyne *(Stanton St John)*

Map D: Locations in Shropshire, Gloucestershire, Berkshire, Wiltshire and Hampshire

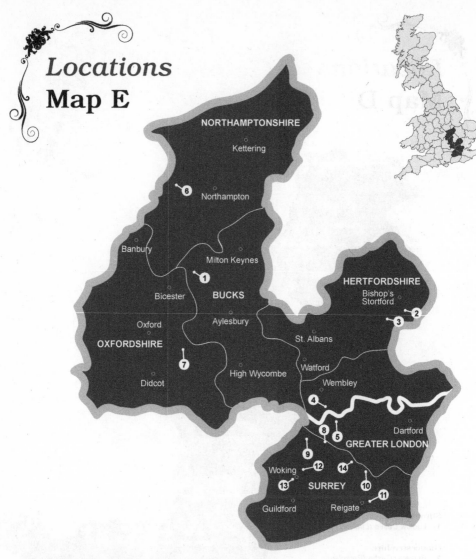

Locations
Map E

NORTHAMPTONSHIRE

Kettering

6 Northampton

Banbury

Milton Keynes

1

Bicester **BUCKS**

Oxford Aylesbury

OXFORDSHIRE

7

Didcot High Wycombe

HERTFORDSHIRE
Bishop's
Stortford

2

3

St. Albans

Watford

Wembley

4

8 5

9 Dartford

GREATER LONDON

12

14

Woking 13 **SURREY** 10

11

Guildford Reigate

Buckinghamshire (Bucks)	Oxfordshire
1. Buckingham	7. Haseley Court (Little Haseley)

Buckinghamshire (Bucks)
1. Buckingham

Hertfordshire
2. Hunsdon House *(Hunsdon)*
3. Rye House *(Hoddesdon)*

Greater London
4. Syon Abbey
5. Richmond Palace
   (Richmond, Surrey)

Northamptonshire
6. Church Stowe Manor
   (Stowe-Nine-Churches)

Oxfordshire
7. Haseley Court (Little Haseley)

Surrey
8. Hampton Court Palace
   (East Moseley)
9. Chertsey Abbey
   (Chertsey)
10. Beddington Place
    (Beddington)
11. The Manor of Bletchingley
    (Bletchingley)
12. Oatlands Palace
13. Woking / Oking Palace
    (Woking)
14. Nonsuch Palace *(Sutton)*

Map E: Locations in Buckinghamshire, Hertfordshire, Greater London, Northamptonshire, Oxfordshire and Surrey

Locations
Map F

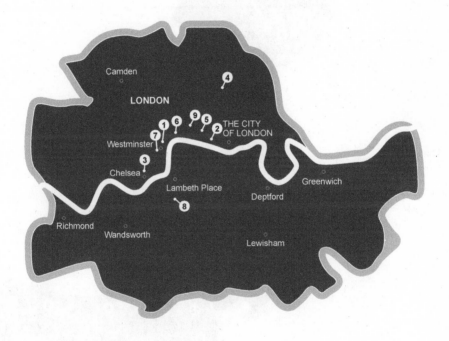

London

1. Whitehall Palace
2. The Tower of London
3. Chelsea Place *(Chelsea)*
4. King's Place (Brooke House) *(Hackney)*
5. Mercers' Hall *(Cheapside)*
6. Chester Place *(The Strand)*
7. Westminster Abbey
8. Norfolk House *(Lambeth)*
9. Charterhouse *(Charterhouse Square)*

Map F: Locations in London

Locations
Map G

CAMBRIDGESHIRE

Chatteris

Huntingdon

④ ③

Cambridge

HERTFORDSHIRE

BUCKS

ESSEX

①
②

GREATER LONDON

⑪

⑩

KENT

⑫ Maidstone ⑤

⑨

Canterbury

⑦
⑧

Ashford

Dover

⑥ Tonbridge

Folkestone

SURREY

Greater London
1. Greenwich Palace
2. Eltham Palace

Cambridgeshire
3. Bishop of Lincoln's Palace *(Buckden)*
4. Kimbolton Castle *(Kimbolton)*

Kent
5. Leeds Castle *(Maidstone)*
6. Hever and St Peter's Church *(Hever)*
7. Deal Castle *(Deal)*
8. Dover Castle *(Dover)*
9. St Austin's Priory *(Canterbury)*
10. St Andrew's Priory *(Rochester)*
11. The King's Manor *(Dartford)*
12. Otford Palace *(Otford)*

Map G: Cambridgeshire, Greater London and Kent

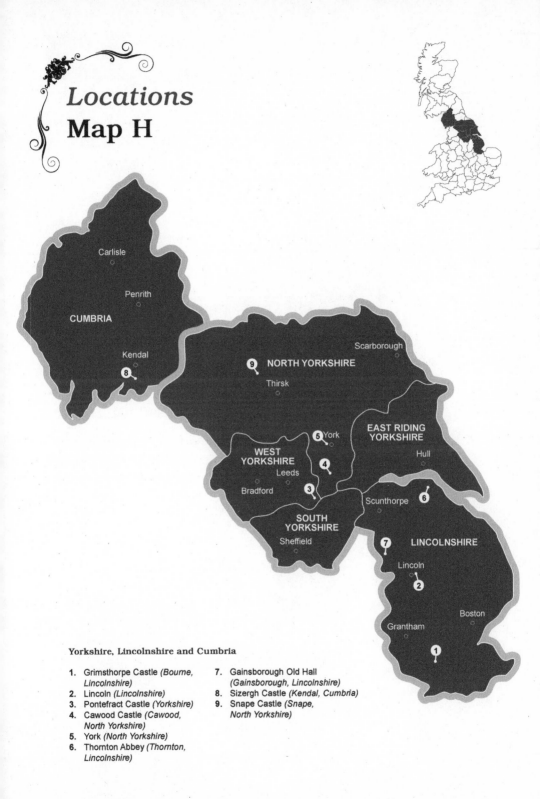

Locations
Map H

Carlisle

Penrith

CUMBRIA

Kendal

8

NORTH YORKSHIRE

9

Scarborough

Thirsk

5 York

EAST RIDING YORKSHIRE

WEST YORKSHIRE

4

Leeds

Hull

Bradford

3

Scunthorpe

6

SOUTH YORKSHIRE

Sheffield

7

LINCOLNSHIRE

Lincoln

2

Boston

Grantham

1

Yorkshire, Lincolnshire and Cumbria

1. Grimsthorpe Castle *(Bourne, Lincolnshire)*
2. Lincoln *(Lincolnshire)*
3. Pontefract Castle *(Yorkshire)*
4. Cawood Castle *(Cawood, North Yorkshire)*
5. York *(North Yorkshire)*
6. Thornton Abbey *(Thornton, Lincolnshire)*
7. Gainsborough Old Hall *(Gainsborough, Lincolnshire)*
8. Sizergh Castle *(Kendal, Cumbria)*
9. Snape Castle *(Snape, North Yorkshire)*

Map H: Yorkshire, Lincolnshire and Cumbria

Part One
Principal Royal Residences

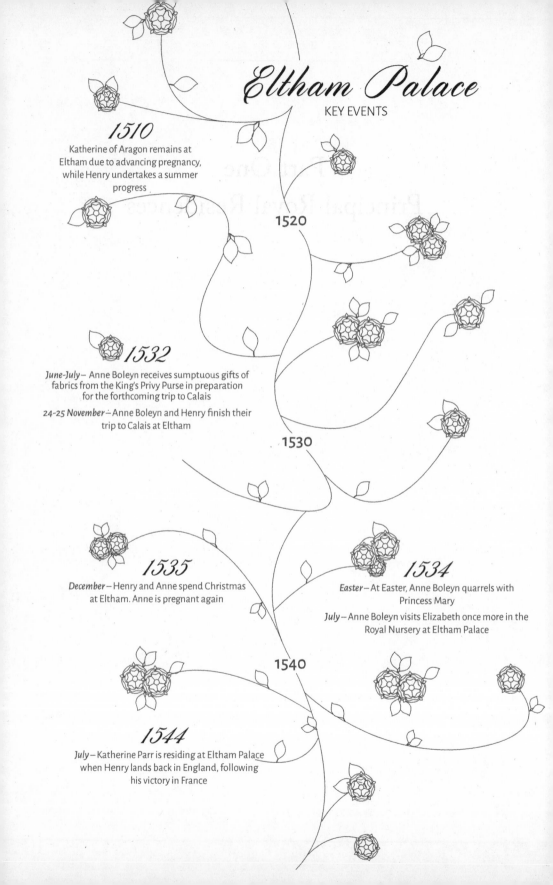

Eltham Palace

KEY EVENTS

1510

Katherine of Aragon remains at Eltham due to advancing pregnancy, while Henry undertakes a summer progress

1520

1532

June-July – Anne Boleyn receives sumptuous gifts of fabrics from the King's Privy Purse in preparation for the forthcoming trip to Calais

24-25 November – Anne Boleyn and Henry finish their trip to Calais at Eltham

1530

1535

December – Henry and Anne spend Christmas at Eltham. Anne is pregnant again

1534

Easter – At Easter, Anne Boleyn quarrels with Princess Mary

July – Anne Boleyn visits Elizabeth once more in the Royal Nursery at Eltham Palace

1540

1544

July – Katherine Parr is residing at Eltham Palace when Henry lands back in England, following his victory in France

Eltham Palace, Greater London

I went to see his Majesty's house at Eltham, both palace and chapel in miserable ruins, the noble woods and park destroyed.

J. Evelyn, diary entry for 26 April 1656

Eltham Palace has its origins in a manor house owned by Odo, who was Bishop of Bayeux, Earl of Kent and younger brother of William the Conqueror; it was first mentioned in the Domesday Book of 1086.

Early in the fourteenth century the manor passed into royal hands, and it soon became a favoured residence of the king and court. During its glory days in the fourteenth and fifteenth centuries, Eltham witnessed much of England's turbulent history, and was treasured by its royal owners as a palace of pleasure, nestled among some of the finest hunting ground in the country. Successive monarchs subsequently enlarged the buildings so that Eltham's importance grew, until by the reign of Henry VIII the Palace of Eltham, as it was by then known, was considered one of the king's five 'Great Houses', comparable in size to Windsor Castle, Greenwich or Hampton Court.

Early in his reign the king commissioned new works at the palace, including the building of a permanent tilt yard to the east of the palace moat and the construction of new privy apartments for himself in the western range, while also making alterations to the queen's lodgings. Finally, he commanded the construction of a new brick-built chapel in the central courtyard. However, despite this large investment in the fabric of the building, its use as a palace was already in decline, for lying just 2 miles to the west was Greenwich Palace, constructed by Henry VII at the turn of the sixteenth century. When Henry VIII succeeded his father in 1509, Greenwich quickly assumed far greater importance than its medieval, royal cousin. As a consequence, Eltham was increasingly confined to being used as a nursery for royal children, a place of entertainment for important visitors or a simple hunting lodge.

In the 1530s, its decline accelerated; with the development of Hampton Court and Whitehall, the court began to move evermore westwards, leaving Eltham to slip further into decay. By the seventeenth century the palace was falling into ruin, and for two hundred years after the English Civil War it was used as a farm. In the 1930s, Virginia and Stephen Courtauld saved the building from complete collapse. Thanks to their efforts, fans of Tudor history are today able to visit the salvaged great hall, originally built by Edward IV in the 1470s, which had almost been lost to the ravages of time.

Touring Eltham Palace
When making a pilgrimage to the remains of Eltham Palace today, the street names around the main gate whisper to visitors of its ancient past, names such as 'Court Yard' and 'Tilt Yard Approach'. The former alludes to the fact that the area

lying outside of the moat directly in front of the main gates was once occupied by a huge outer courtyard called the Green Court, which was flanked on its north, east and west sides by service buildings. The second refers to the aforementioned tilt yard, lying to the east of Green Court. Note that just before you cross the bridge to your right is an extant building from the earlier palace. This building is called 'The Chancellor's Lodgings', where Chaucer, Wolsey and Thomas More are known to have stayed in their time.

The north stone bridge, built originally by Richard II in 1396 and enhanced in brick by Edward IV in the fifteenth century, is enchanting and conveys a sense of the lost grandeur of the palace. Its four stone arches once spanned one of the widest moats in England, reaching nearly 100 feet across on the south side.

Many people come to Eltham to visit one of the finest art deco houses in the country. These buildings sit roughly on top of what was once a vast range of courtier lodgings running around the north-east edge of the original Great Court. You might want to start here, and although the art deco house is interesting, as a Tudor enthusiast you will no doubt be making a beeline for the restored great hall. While not quite as grand, it is certainly reminiscent of the great hall at Hampton Court Palace. Many a king and queen have feasted here, and you might imagine Erasmus arriving to be greeted by the young and precocious Prince Henry in 1499.

Once back outside, make your way to the Courtauld's turning circle outside the house, which roughly marks the centre of the original inner court. In front of you lies the great hall. While facing the hall, turn to your right; close to where you are standing would have been the east end of the chapel in which the famous quarrel between Anne Boleyn and the Lady Mary took place in 1534. According to *The Life of Jane Dormer, Duchess of Feria* by Henry Clifford, Anne and Mary found themselves in the chapel at the same time. Afterward, one of Anne's maids reported to the queen that Mary had made a reverence to her as she departed the chapel – a thing of some note, since Mary had yet to acquiesce to Anne as premier lady of the land. Anne duly sent a message to the Lady Mary saying, 'If we had seen it, we would have done as much to her' and that she would embrace Mary's love 'with the kindness of a true friend'. Mary impertinently replied that it was not possible

> that the queen can send me such a message; nor is it fit she should, nor can it be so sudden, her majesty being so far from this place. You should have said that the Lady Anne Boleyn had sent it for I can acknowledge no other queen but my mother, nor esteem them as friends who are not hers. And for the reverence I made, it was to the altar, to Her maker and mine.

Needless to say, Anne was furious, replying that 'one day she would pull down this high sprit'. A tree now stands on the lawn over the site of its remains.

If you walk over to your right, you will come upon the exposed remains of the west range, which once contained the queen's privy apartments to the north (the end of the range closest to where you entered the turning circle from the main entrance), and the king's to the south. Therefore, standing in the north-west of the inner courtyard means we are looking down on the remains of the queen's apartments. Certainly, Katherine of Aragon, Anne Boleyn and Katherine Parr all stayed at Eltham. We know something of Anne Boleyn's taste in decor, for in 1534, we hear of preparations being made 'against the coming of a Prince' with the redecoration of the suite in yellow ochre, mirroring the decoration seen in the French palaces of Anne's youth.

As you stand there, you will notice that the palace stood proudly atop of some of the highest ground in the neighbourhood – excepting nearby Shooter's Hill. Views from the royal apartments must have been magnificent, looking down across a broad and beautiful landscape that stretched out to the west. Just 2 miles away in the distance would have once been the bold and finely wooded outline of Greenwich Park, while beyond that it was possible to trace out the spire of the Gothic cathedral of St Paul's and the lofty roof of Westminster Abbey.

Eltham Palace has a genial charm. It is delightful to imagine Katherine of Aragon whiling away some of her pregnancy there in 1510 while the king conducted a short summer progress, or Anne Boleyn spending treasured time with Elizabeth in the royal nursery. Somehow, even though London stands silhouetted against the horizon just a mile or so away, it is easy to feel that you are tucked away in a peaceful idyll that somehow, despite the neglect and abandonment by its former royal patrons, still speaks easily of happier times at the centre of English sovereign power.

Visitor Information
Eltham Palace is managed by English Heritage. For more information on how to reach Eltham Palace and its opening hours, which are seasonal, visit the English Heritage website at http://www.english-heritage.org.uk/daysout/properties/eltham-palace-and-gardens/, or telephone +44 (0) 208 294 2548.

Postcode for Eltham Palace: SE9 5QE.

Greenwich Palace

KEY EVENTS

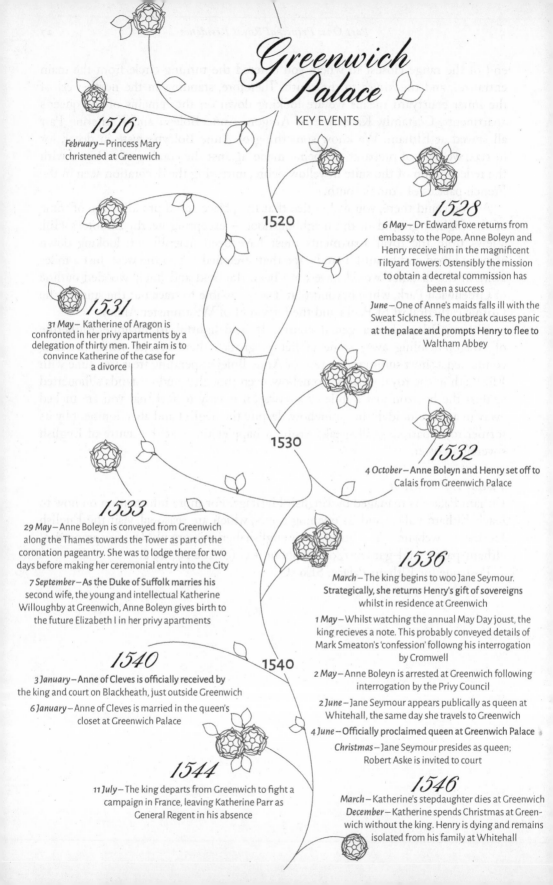

1516
February – Princess Mary christened at Greenwich

1520

1528
6 May – Dr Edward Foxe returns from embassy to the Pope. Anne Boleyn and Henry receive him in the magnificent Tiltyard Towers. Ostensibly the mission to obtain a decretal commission has been a success

June – One of Anne's maids falls ill with the Sweat Sickness. The outbreak causes panic at the palace and prompts Henry to flee to Waltham Abbey

1531
31 May – Katherine of Aragon is confronted in her privy apartments by a delegation of thirty men. Their aim is to convince Katherine of the case for a divorce

1530

1532
4 October – Anne Boleyn and Henry set off to Calais from Greenwich Palace

1533
29 May – Anne Boleyn is conveyed from Greenwich along the Thames towards the Tower as part of the coronation pageantry. She was to lodge there for two days before making her ceremonial entry into the City

7 September – As the Duke of Suffolk marries his second wife, the young and intellectual Katherine Willoughby at Greenwich, Anne Boleyn gives birth to the future Elizabeth I in her privy apartments

1536
March – The king begins to woo Jane Seymour. Strategically, she returns Henry's gift of sovereigns whilst in residence at Greenwich

1 May – Whilst watching the annual May Day joust, the king recieves a note. This probably conveyed details of Mark Smeaton's 'confession' followng his interrogation by Cromwell

2 May – Anne Boleyn is arrested at Greenwich following interrogation by the Privy Council

2 June – Jane Seymour appears publically as queen at Whitehall, the same day she travels to Greenwich

4 June – Officially proclaimed queen at Greenwich Palace

Christmas – Jane Seymour presides as queen; Robert Aske is invited to court

1540
3 January – Anne of Cleves is officially received by the king and court on Blackheath, just outside Greenwich

6 January – Anne of Cleves is married in the queen's closet at Greenwich Palace

1540

1544
11 July – The king departs from Greenwich to fight a campaign in France, leaving Katherine Parr as General Regent in his absence

1546
March – Katherine's stepdaughter dies at Greenwich

December – Katherine spends Christmas at Greenwich without the king. Henry is dying and remains isolated from his family at Whitehall

Greenwich Palace (The Palace of Placentia), Greater London

Behold the glories of the place,
Bedeckt with each celestial grace,
Fit seat of Gods! The roofs how gay
The painted windows' rich array,
The lofty tow'rs that kiss the skies;
The bow'rs a ceaseless spring supplies,
The gardens trim, that Flora court
To make this spot her lov'd resort,
And willing yield their royal lords
The richest bounties she affords.
What skill these varied beauties plann'd
That thus adorn old Thames's strand,
And, conscious of its future fame,
Devis'd Placentia for its name?

John Leland, Tudor antiquarian

In around 1501, the old Manor of Pleasaunce, or Placentia, which had originally been built by Duke Humphrey of Gloucester, was demolished by King Henry VII. In its place a fine red-brick palace rose up on the southern banks of the Thames at Greenwich. In time, this new palace would become one of Henry VIII's most favoured 'Great Houses', particularly during the early years of his reign.

Sadly, nothing at all remains of Greenwich Palace today, except ghosts and the imprint of the historic events that unfolded upon its glittering stage. On account of all this, the site of Greenwich Palace is a 'must see' for anybody wanting to follow in the footsteps of Henry's six wives. Just remember to take your imagination with you!

The Palace Buildings

Greenwich Palace was highly innovative in design, being a courtyard house, built of brick and without a moat. A seventeenth-century painting of the palace by an anonymous painter shows the fine river frontage, which comprised the kitchens to the west; the king's lodgings, including the magnificent five-storey donjon containing the king's privy bedroom, library and study in the centre; and, to the east, the Chapel Royal. Running parallel to this range on the opposite side of a grand courtyard were the queen's apartments, which looked out over the Great Garden, an orchard and Greenwich Park beyond.

The complete arrangement of the west wing is not entirely known. However, it seems that a privy gallery connected the king's and queen's sides, and the queen's bedroom seems to have been accessed from this gallery. To the east were the king and queen's great watching chambers – the most public rooms of the royal apartments after the great hall. These chambers were connected to the hall via a central staircase.

Touring the Site of the Lost Palace of Greenwich
One of the best ways to arrive at Greenwich is to follow in the footsteps of the
Tudor court and arrive by boat. Take a river cruiser from Westminster Pier past
the sites of the Palace of Whitehall, Durham House, Chester Place (see entry on
Chester Place), Bridewell and Baynard's Palace. Travelling further downstream
past the Tower of London, you will eventually arrive at Greenwich to be greeted
by the sight of the eighteenth-century Royal Naval College. This stands squarely
on the site of the now lost Palace of Greenwich.

With this guide in hand, take a walk through the grounds of what is now a college
of music. Head first for the riverfront; adjacent to the Thames once stood the north
wing of the palace. This contained the king's apartments to the west, while the
chapel in which both Anne Boleyn and Jane Seymour were first presented publicly
as queen lay at the east end of the same range. With your back to the river, face into
a large courtyard. This roughly marks the spot of the original Tudor courtyard, once
adorned with a central conduit. The far side of the courtyard roughly marks the spot
of the original south wing of the palace, also running parallel to the river. This wing
contained the queen's apartments. Keep walking southwards toward Greenwich
Park. The modern-day Romney Road bisects an area that once separated the
queen's apartments from the orchard and Great Garden of the palace. Today those
gardens, called the National Maritime Museum Gardens, are laid to lawn. As you
walk along the path cutting across the park, toward the Queen's House, look to
your left and imagine the two elaborate Tiltyard Towers rising up from the ground
and looking down on the tilt yard that lay to the east. A car park now covers most
of the area once given over to the tilt. Of course, it was here that Anne Boleyn last
presided over the court as queen at the annual May Day joust, on 1 May 1536.

Several notable events of Henry's reign took place at Greenwich, including the
christening of Princess Mary in 1516, the birth of Princess Elizabeth in September
1533, Anne Boleyn's arrest in 1536 and the marriage of Anne of Cleves in January
1540. Yet as the king's reign progressed, the court increasingly moved westwards,
favouring the likes of Hampton Court and Whitehall, and the new palaces that
were built by Henry himself, such as Oatlands.

Sadly, the palace at Greenwich fell into serious decay during the English Civil
War and was demolished shortly thereafter.

Visitor Information
We highly recommended starting your visit by heading for the Discover Greenwich
Visitor Centre, part of the old Naval College, and near to Greenwich Pier. There
are excellent models of both Henry's palace and tilt yard. These will help fire your
imagination before your wander round the site of the old palace itself. There is also
a section that includes several artefacts from the original palace, such as the green
and yellow tiles that were excavated from the site of the Chapel Royal in the 1970s.
There is also a replica of Anne Boleyn's coat of arms, fashioned from the stained
glass that would have decorated many of the palace's fine mullioned windows
during her short tenure as queen.

However, one of our favourite things is to make our way through Greenwich Park, which lies to the south of the old palace. Climb up to the top of Castle Hill, where the Greenwich Observatory now stands. In the exact same spot once stood Duke Humphrey's Tower, a miniature castle where Henry is said to have kept his fine wine and mistresses, including Mary (and possibly Anne) Boleyn. Look back down upon the old Naval College and take a moment to imagine the pitched roofs, barley-twist chimneys and pleasant gardens of the sixteenth-century palace laid out below you.

You are welcome to roam the grounds of the current music college, upon which the palace once stood, at any time. Discover Greenwich, part of the National Maritime Museum, is open 10 a.m. to 5 p.m. daily. Entrance is free. For further information, visit the following web sites: http://www.rmg.co.uk/visit or http://www.ornc.org/visit/getting-here/opening-times.

If arriving by car, you might wish to park in the large public car park at the top of Castle Hill, adjacent to the observatory. From here, you can walk down the hill to the site of the old palace.

Postcode for the site of Greenwich Palace: SE10 9NN.

Postcode for Greenwich Park car park: SE10 8QY.

Whitehall
KEY EVENTS

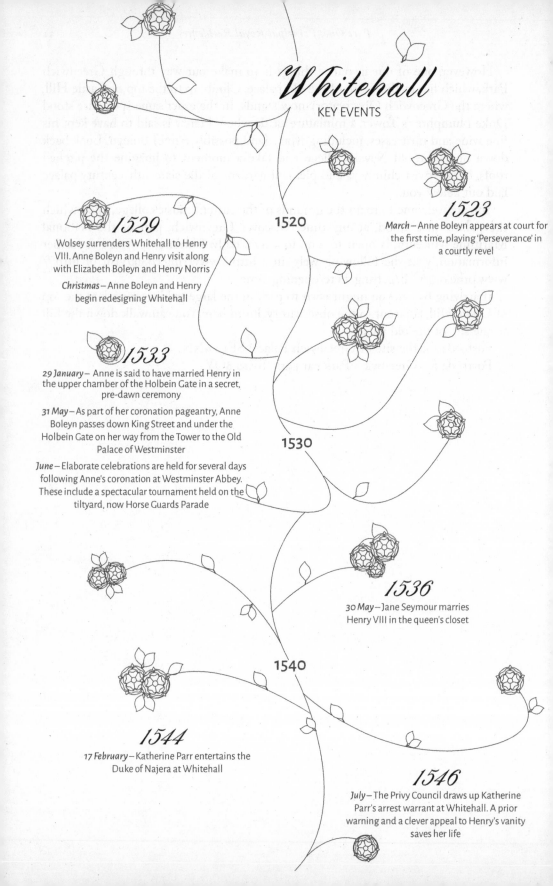

1520

1523

March – Anne Boleyn appears at court for the first time, playing 'Perseverance' in a courtly revel

1529

Wolsey surrenders Whitehall to Henry VIII. Anne Boleyn and Henry visit along with Elizabeth Boleyn and Henry Norris

Christmas – Anne Boleyn and Henry begin redesigning Whitehall

1533

29 January – Anne is said to have married Henry in the upper chamber of the Holbein Gate in a secret, pre-dawn ceremony

31 May – As part of her coronation pageantry, Anne Boleyn passes down King Street and under the Holbein Gate on her way from the Tower to the Old Palace of Westminster

June – Elaborate celebrations are held for several days following Anne's coronation at Westminster Abbey. These include a spectacular tournament held on the tiltyard, now Horse Guards Parade

1530

1536

30 May – Jane Seymour marries Henry VIII in the queen's closet

1540

1544

17 February – Katherine Parr entertains the Duke of Najera at Whitehall

1546

July – The Privy Council draws up Katherine Parr's arrest warrant at Whitehall. A prior warning and a clever appeal to Henry's vanity saves her life

Whitehall Palace (York Place), London

... to please the lady [Anne Boleyn] who prefers that place for the King's residence to any other.

The Spanish ambassador writing about Whitehall Palace,
Christmas/New Year 1529/30

From our point of view, the story of Whitehall begins with Anne Boleyn. For it was here that we saw the twenty-one-year-old Anne, who was newly returned from France, make her first recorded appearance at the English court, taking part in a masque called the Château Vert during which she rather prophetically played the part of Perseverance.

At the time, the palace was part of the Archdiocese of York and was occupied by the king's powerful and wealthy first minister, Cardinal Wolsey. However, by 1526 Henry had fallen head over heels in love with the captivating Mistress Boleyn, and Wolsey's world was about to be turned upside down. Unable to secure the king his divorce, Wolsey fell into disgrace after the collapse of the Blackfriars trial of 1529. Then, on 22 October 1529, he pleaded guilty to charges of *praemunire*. In an effort to gain mercy from the king, Thomas Wolsey surrendered all his property and goods into the king's hands. Among the spoils was the fabulous York Place, a sumptuous palace positioned conveniently on the western bank of the Thames, just half a mile north of Thorney Island, which formed the old city of Westminster, then the seat of government in England.

We know that just two days later, Anne Boleyn accompanied the king from Greenwich, along with her mother, Elizabeth, and Sir Henry Norris. The king found the present 'more valuable than even he expected', including as it did a glittering array of silver-gilt and gold plate, some encrusted with precious stones, much of it laid out in the eponymous Gilt Chamber, Wolsey's private study that overlooked the Thames.

Henry and Anne were by this time at the centre of the storm that was the king's 'Great Matter', with the king utterly resolved to set Katherine of Aragon aside and take Anne as his new wife. York Place, as it was still known, soon became the favoured residence of the two lovers; having no queen's side, Henry could lodge Anne at the palace away from the withering disapproval of his discarded wife. York Place, or Whitehall as it was later to be known, was to be a glittering new Renaissance palace, which Anne and Henry set about designing together over the Christmas of 1529.

Whitehall was to be much enlarged, encompassing the buildings of York Place within its core. Added to the existing kitchens, service buildings, great hall, watching, presence and privy chambers and long gallery would be an entirely remodelled and augmented queen's side incorporating many of Wolsey's original rooms; a 100-foot-long privy stair that projected out into the Thames for private use by the king and queen; an entire privy gallery range containing the king's most private apartments; and the Holbein Gate, which marked the entry and exit point from the royal enclave of Whitehall and Westminster. It also connected the palace's lodgings to its new leisure complex, which lay on the far side of King Street, now the site of the modern-day Whitehall. Land was also reclaimed to the south of the palace in order to augment the gardens, making a vast orchard/garden, and to the north of the new privy gallery an additional privy garden with surrounding loggia was also created.

While sadly the palace is entirely lost, with the exception of some underground corridors and fireplaces that are not accessible to the public, a number of contemporary descriptions and illustrations survive to give us a good idea of its external and internal decoration in the sixteenth century.

The complex itself was truly enormous, a staggering 23 acres compared to the rather paltry 6 acres which defined the footprint of Hampton Court. At the same time, its edifice extended 200 feet along the western bank of the Thames. The palace was bisected by King Street, a busy thoroughfare which allowed Londoners to pass from Charing Cross at its northern end down to old Westminster Palace. To the west of King Street Henry and Anne planned a marvellous recreation complex, including a tilt yard and viewing gallery, four tennis courts, a bowling alley and cockpit, all backing onto the pleasant park of St James, which provided the couple with excellent hunting.

The east side of the palace contained the state and privy chambers; here very little brickwork was visible. Instead, the timber framing was left exposed throughout, producing a grid-like pattern extending across the whole face of the building. Between these grids, plaster panels were painted decoratively with grotesque work. In contrast to this, the great hall was painted in chequer work, while the privy kitchen was inlaid with bands of galleting. All this gave Whitehall an entirely distinctive appearance. Henry had been keen that in every way it should embody the best of Renaissance architecture; all about it were symbols of chivalry and heraldry, creating forms which were painted in bright colours and which cast strong silhouettes against the London skyline.

Inside, there are records of the giant fresco depicting Henry VIII's coronation painted along one wall of the long gallery overlooking the Great Orchard; also of a wide, newly built processional vice-stair which led up to the queen's apartments from a cloister connecting this stair to the great hall. Then there was the 150-foot queen's privy gallery, which so impressed Sir Thomas More that he is said to have told Wolsey of his distinct preference for it over that of the privy gallery at Hampton Court. And if you want a visual impression of the interior of Whitehall, then look at Henry VIII's dynastic portrait, *The Family of Henry VIII*, painted retrospectively around 1545. This probably depicted both the interior and exterior aspects of design at Whitehall. You can see the richness of the grotesque work and the elaborate carving of heraldic symbols of the Tudor dynasty on the ceiling and get a sense of the vivid colours that adorned every great Tudor palace.

Visitor Information

There is nothing above ground to be seen of the old Tudor palace, and we admit that busy traffic roaring incessantly along modern-day Whitehall makes it difficult to find the inner space to imagine Henry's magnificent palace sprawled across both sides of the road. However, taking a trip down Whitehall from Charing Cross takes you in Anne Boleyn's footsteps as she processed in a fabulous litter draped in white cloth of gold to the City to Westminster on Saturday 31 May 1533. Jane Seymour would make her way along the same route but in the opposite direction, in December 1536, when the king and queen progressed from Whitehall, through the city, to spend Christmas at Greenwich.

Just before the Banqueting House is Horse Guards Avenue; this roughly marks the spot of the main-street-side entrance to the palace. Beyond Banqueting House, but on the same side of the road, a hideous concrete building called Gwydr House stands roughly over the original site of the Great Orchard. Then, on the other side of the road is the arch that leads through to Horse Guards Parade ground, the original site of the palace's tilt yard, while the statue of George, Duke of Cambridge, on horseback is the original position of the Holbein Gate.

Whitehall is always accessible to the public, except during exceptional state occasions (e.g. royal weddings, funerals, etc.) and on Remembrance Sunday, when it is closed for the morning.

Postcode for Whitehall: SW1A 2ER.

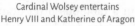

Hampton Court Palace

KEY EVENTS

1516
Cardinal Wolsey entertains
Henry VIII and Katherine of Aragon

1520

1522
Katherine of Aragon's nephew,
the emperor Charles V, is
entertained at the palace

1528
November – Katherine of Aragon
is in residence

1533
2 July – Henry and Anne Boleyn arrive at the
palace to inspect the new building work

December – The royal couple make another brief visit

1529
January – Katherine of Aragon
and Henry stay at the palace

1530

1534
Summer – Henry and Anne Boleyn make a number
of short visits to the palace and twice entertain
ambassadors from Lubeck

Late June/early July – It's possible that Queen Anne
was delivered of a stillborn child at the palace

1535
Mid-March – Henry and Anne Boleyn stay at the palace,
unaware that this would be the queen's last visit

1539
October – A treaty of marriage between King Henry VIII
and Anne of Cleves is signed in the Council Chamber

1537
8 May – Henry and Jane Seymour arrive at the palace.
The king had not spent a night there since mid-March 1535

12 October – Jane Seymour gives birth to Prince Edward

15 October – Prince Edward is baptised in the Chapel Royal

24 October – Jane Seymour dies of puerperal fever

1541
3 January – Anne of Cleves visits and exchanges New Year's gifts
with her former husband and his new queen, Catherine Howard

2 November – Archbishop Thomas Cranmer leaves a letter for
King Henry VIII in the Holy Day Closet, revealing Catherine Howard's
earlier sexual liaisons

6 November – Henry VIII orders his dinner to be served in a field near
Hampton Court, on the pretext of a hunting trip. He departs by river,
without returning to Hampton Court and never sees his young wife again

13 November – Sir Thomas Wriothesley summons Queen Catherine
Howard's household to the 'Great Chamber', (possibly the Great
Watching Chamber that survives today), and dismisses them, and also
orders the queen's removal from the palace to house arrest at Syon House

14 November – Catherine Howard is moved from Hampton Court
Palace to Syon House

1540

1540
Henry VIII's divorce from Anne of Cleves
is signed, 'in a lofty and ornate chamber'

1544
Late July-August – Queen Katherine Parr and the
king's three children spend part of the summer
at the palace, while the king is away in France

December-January – The Royal family celebrates
Christmas, New Year, Epiphany and
Candlemas at the palace

Hampton Court Palace, Surrey

This is the most splendid and magnificent royal palace that may be found in England or indeed in any other kingdom.

Jacob Rathgeb, 1592

To walk the grounds and corridors of Hampton Court Palace is to walk in the footsteps of all of the Tudor kings and queens. Within the Tudor palace's russet-coloured walls, the present fades into the brickwork and the past emerges to greet us.

Although much of the Tudor palace has, over the years, been modified or demolished and replaced with William III and Mary II's baroque palace, the buildings that survive propel us back through the years to a time when Hampton Court was one of Henry VIII's most beloved palaces, at the centre of court life and politics.

A Brief History of Hampton Court

Originally built for Cardinal Wolsey as a house for entertaining royalty, foreign ambassadors and dignitaries, its magnificence reflected his status as cardinal and Lord Chancellor of England. Wolsey built new kitchens, courtyards, lodgings, galleries and gardens, and began work on the chapel. He also built luxurious apartments for Henry VIII, Katherine of Aragon and Princess Mary on the site of the present-day east range of Clock Court, which faces the astronomical clock.

Henry VIII took full possession of Hampton Court in 1529, and embarked on an enormous building campaign attested to by the 6,500 pages of building accounts that survive in the Public Record Office.

Visiting Hampton Court Palace Today

The main entrance is via the west front, begun by Cardinal Wolsey and completed for Henry VIII. Wolsey's gatehouse was originally five-stories high, rather than the three that we see today, but was found to be unstable and so reduced in the eighteenth century.

On the turrets either side of the gatehouse are terracotta roundels with the heads of the Roman emperors Tiberius and Nero. These were found in a cottage in Windsor Park by the Victorian surveyor Edward Jesse, and were probably originally from the Holbein Gate at Whitehall.

The bridge leading to the central gateway is lined with ten heraldic beasts supporting the royal arms, including the Tudor dragon and the queen's lion. These are modern replacements of the originals that once stood here. Look up above the central gateway and on a carved panel are the arms of Henry VIII.

Stepping into Base Court feels very much like time travel. It is much as it was when Wolsey built it as a place to house his guests and large household; all of Henry's queens would certainly recognise it today. Each of the thirty double-guest lodgings had an outer room and an inner room with garderobe (toilet) and fireplace. The epitome of sixteenth-century luxury! A visiting French dignitary mentions the rooms when describing his visit to the palace in 1527:

> ... they returned again to Hampton Court, and every of them conveyed to his chamber severally, having in them great fires and wine ready to refresh them, remaining there until their supper was ready, and the chambers where they should sup were ordered in due form ... and whilst they were in communion and other pastimes, all their liveries were served to their chambers. Every chamber had a bason and a ewer of silver, some gilt and some parcel gilt, and some two great pots of silver in like manner, and one pot at the least with wine and beer, a bowl or goblet, and a silver pot to drink beer in; a silver candlestick or two, with both white lights and yellow lights of three sized of wax; and a staff torch; a fine manchet, and a loaf of bread. Thus was every chamber furnished throughout the house ...

The four-metre-high recreated Tudor wine fountain that you see in this courtyard is built on the very spot where Henry VIII's octagonal fountain once stood and testifies to Hampton Court's role as a pleasure palace. The design is based on the fountain visible in the *Field of Cloth of Gold* painting that hangs in the 'Young Henry VIII' exhibition and is actually engineered to serve real wine on special occasions.

Anne Boleyn's Gatehouse
This name dates from the nineteenth century, when the vault beneath the gateway was reconstructed. The ceiling is decorated with Henry and Anne's entwined initials and Anne's falcon badge; sadly these are not original, rather Victorian replicas. The good news is that there is a stone falcon badge from the original vault on display in the great hall, where you should head next.

The entry to Henry VIII's state apartments is up the staircase under Anne Boleyn's Gateway, which takes you into the magnificent great hall. The doorway leading into the buttery, just before the hall, is decorated with Tudor roses for Henry VIII and Spanish pomegranates – Katherine of Aragon's personal badge.

The Great Hall
The great hall is majestic and breathtaking. The splendid hammer-beam roof is decorated with royal arms and badges and a series of carved and painted heads. In Tudor times, the floor would have been paved with tiles and the roof painted blue, red and gold.

The hall today is hung with priceless Flemish tapestries of the *Story of Abraham* commissioned by Henry VIII and woven in the 1540s with real silver and gold thread. A series of six hangs in the great hall, one of which – *The Oath and Departure of Eliezer* – was hung in Westminster Abbey for the coronation of Elizabeth I. The tapestries have faded over time, but you can still get a sense of how vibrant and splendid they would have been when first woven.

Anne Boleyn took a great interest in the building works at Hampton Court, and on the ceiling you can still see Henry and Anne's entwined initials and Anne's falcon badge. The wooden screen behind you as you enter the hall is carved with Anne and Henry's interlocking initials – all serving as a poignant reminder of her brief reign. After Anne's arrest and execution, Henry ordered all of her badges removed and replaced them with those of Jane Seymour. Luckily for us, in the frenzy to eradicate all memory of Henry's fallen queen, those less accessible were overlooked.

The great watching chamber was originally the first of Henry VIII's state apartments and its principal function in Henry's reign was as a dining room for household officials. The door at the 'high' end of the room (directly to your right as you enter from the great hall) once led to the king's presence chamber and state apartments, sadly, now lost. This door would have been heavily guarded and only those close to the king would have been permitted entry.

The stained-glass window in this chamber, although beautiful, is not original, and the Tudor fireplace and great heraldic frieze that once decorated the walls above the tapestries are long gone. However, the splendid ceiling, decorated with the arms of Henry VIII and Jane Seymour, and the tapestries, are original.

The Horn Room, the Council Chamber and the Haunted Gallery

The Horn Room was originally used as a waiting area for servants bringing food up to the great hall and great watching chamber from the Tudor kitchens directly below. The balustrade is Victorian; however, the original Tudor oak steps survive.

Further down the gallery is King Henry VIII's council chamber, opened to the public for the first time in April 2009. It is worth pausing here for a moment to consider that in this very room Henry VIII discussed and debated important matters of state, making many historic decisions within its four walls. Like so many of the chambers at Hampton Court, the energetic imprint of those who have passed through here – Norfolk, Suffolk, Cromwell, Thomas Boleyn and Henry himself – is tangible; you can almost hear their voices speaking to you across time. When we were there, a brief glimpse out of the window into the courtyard below catapulted us back in time. For there, walking through the gardens, were two Tudor noble ladies. It was quite disorientating, but a wonderful snapshot of a lost era.

From here proceed to the upper chapel cloister, better known as the Haunted Gallery (see visitor information below). It was built by Cardinal Wolsey to connect the chapel to the rest of the palace and is home to some wonderful tapestries and paintings, including *The Family of Henry VIII* by an unknown artist around 1545. Look closely at the 'A' necklace adorning the neck of the Princess Elizabeth, as it's said to have belonged to her mother. From the Haunted Gallery you can access the royal pew; here all Tudor queens would have sat and looked down into the body of the chapel.

In the sixteenth century, the king and queen had separate rooms in the royal pew, with windows looking down into the choir of the chapel. Henry VIII installed the magnificent vaulted ceiling that you see today in 1535–6, replacing an earlier ceiling added by Cardinal Wolsey, who built the body of the chapel. Originally, there would have been a great double window at the east end filled with stained glass. In October 1536, the window was re-glazed to remove the figure of St Anne, the mother of Mary, originally installed as a way of linking Anne Boleyn with the Virgin. In the eighteenth century, all the glass was removed and the window hidden behind the current mahogany reredos. It is in this chapel that Prince Edward, Henry VIII's long-awaited son, was christened in October 1537. In the king's closet, within the chapel royal, Henry married his sixth and final wife, Katherine Parr, in the presence of his two daughters, the Princesses Elizabeth and Mary. If only walls could talk!

As you exit the chapel into the north cloister, take note of Henry VIII and Jane Seymour's coat of arms flanking the chapel door. Although almost certainly moved from another part of the palace, these two heraldic plaques once held Cardinal Wolsey's arms and hat, which were repainted by Henry VIII after 1530.

Henry's Lost Privy Apartments – The Cumberland Suite

The Georgian rooms may seem like they have nothing to offer the Tudor enthusiast, but as mentioned earlier, it is precisely on the site of the present-day Cumberland Suite that Wolsey built Henry's most private rooms, including his bedchamber. Remember the door at the far end of the great watching chamber? This once opened into Henry's presence chamber, which in turn led through to the king's inner sanctum. Sadly, Henry's presence chamber, once one of the grandest rooms in the palace, has been greatly remodelled over time and has subsequently lost all of its earlier grandeur. It is not accessible to the general public.

The queen's apartments were originally positioned directly above the king's, on the second floor. In 1533, Henry VIII ordered that new lodgings be built for his then queen, Anne Boleyn. These lavish apartments were to be constructed on the east side of a new courtyard, overlooking the park. The external appearance of these new rooms can be seen on a number of early views of the east front of the palace; they stood in the area now known as Fountain Court but were demolished in the late seventeenth century to make way for Sir Christopher Wren's baroque palace. However, given that the apartments were not completed until early 1536, in the meantime it was necessary for Anne to stay in Wolsey's original lodgings facing onto Clock Court.

This three-storey range was originally designed to house the Princess Mary on the lower level, Henry on the first floor and Katherine of Aragon directly above him. The queen's apartments contained three large rooms, the entrance to which still survives, although it too is not accessible to the public. A surviving doorway on this level depicts Wolsey's arms on one spandrel and the royal arms on the other. Within, a few more remnants of its Tudor past survive: a large chimneypiece containing Wolsey's badges and mottoes and a door leading to a closet.

In 1537, Jane Seymour occupied the same 'old lodgings' as her two predecessors while awaiting the remodelling of the newly built queen's apartments. Here she gave birth to Prince Edward in one of the rooms. She would never recover, dying twelve days later. It's possible that in this same room, Anne Boleyn was delivered of a stillborn baby in late June/early July 1534. So, in the end, neither Anne nor Jane were able to enjoy the luxurious new apartments built expressly for their pleasure. Interestingly, a visitor to the palace in 1600 recorded seeing, in one of the chambers, a bed, 'gilt all over', which belonged to Henry VIII and 'in this bed his Queen [Jane] gave birth to Edward VI'.

Within the Cumberland Suite, make your way into the room which contains a large bed set back into an alcove. Over in the far corner is a bricked-up doorway that once connected the king's privy chambers directly with Wolsey's gallery and apartments. Another doorway on your right, just before you enter the room, opens onto a Tudor spiral staircase. This once led down to Henry VIII's wardrobe. Every morning, Henry's clothes would be brought up these stairs and handed to a gentleman of the privy chamber responsible for dressing the king. There is no access through this doorway at the current time.

The Wolsey Closet and Rooms
The Wolsey Closet, beyond the Cumberland Suite, gives visitors a good idea of what a small closet might have looked like during Henry's reign. Although heavily restored in the nineteenth century, conservation revealed that part of the ceiling dating from the late 1530s has remained *in situ*. The ceiling is decorated with gilded Renaissance motifs and badges incorporating the Tudor rose.

Further evidence of Hampton Court's Tudor past can be found in the Wolsey Rooms, believed to have been Wolsey's private lodgings in the 1520s. It is also thought that Princess Mary and Katherine Parr may have also stayed, or entertained, here.

Like so much of Hampton Court Palace the rooms have been modified and altered over time, but some original Tudor features have survived: sixteenth-century linenfold panelling lines the walls of the two smaller rooms, the plain Tudor fireplaces date from Wolsey's time, the ribbed ceilings in the two main rooms incorporate early Renaissance motifs, and the ceiling of the end room incorporates Wolsey's badges.

The Renaissance Picture Gallery and the Wolsey Rooms house many sixteenth- and seventeenth-century paintings, including a portrait of Anne Boleyn said to be 'a copy of a contemporary portrait, probably painted in the late 1500s'.

The Palace Kitchens and the Tilt Yard
No visit to Hampton Court Palace is complete without a tour of the Tudor kitchens. They were built partly by Lord Daubeney, who owned Hampton Court before Wolsey, and extended by Henry VIII in 1529. The kitchens were designed to feed the royal household, which in the wintertime could number up to eight hundred people, who dined in the great hall and the great watching chamber twice a day.

Today, the smell of woodsmoke from the fire burning in the great kitchens awakens memories of a distant past. The throngs of tourists that pack the kitchens during peak times evoke a sense of the hustle and bustle of the two-hundred-strong staff that manned this vast operation during Henry's reign.

Royal dishes were prepared in a separate, or privy, kitchen by the king and queen's own cook and personnel. From 1529 until 1537, Henry's private kitchen was situated beneath his lodgings and survives, albeit in a much-altered state, on the ground floor below the Wolsey Closet.

And while on the topic of food ... the Privy Kitchen (a café) is housed in what was once Elizabeth I's private kitchen. It's easy to miss this gem, home to some interesting artefacts, including a large plate marked with the crowned ostrich feathers of Arthur, Prince of Wales.

The Tiltyard Café is the only surviving tower of five that were built by Henry VIII as viewing platforms where dignitaries and courtiers could watch tournaments in the tilt yard below.

The Gardens

There are also over 60 acres of stunning gardens waiting to be explored at Hampton Court Palace. Cardinal Wolsey was probably the first to build ornamental gardens on-site, but it was Henry who established the magnificent gardens for which the palace would subsequently become renowned; gardens that surpassed in beauty and size those of all other royal residences. Baron Waldstein, writing in the early seventeenth century, noted,

> This [the garden] is especially interesting because of its many avenues and also for the large number of growing plants shaped into animals, in fact they even had sirens, centaurs, sphinxes, and other fabulous poetic creatures portrayed here in topiary work.

The sunken pond gardens, once Wolsey's fishponds, look and smell exquisite in early summer, when they are bursting with blossom and overrun with flowers. In March 1528, Anne Boleyn dined with Thomas Heneage at Windsor and commented on these very fishponds, saying how pleasing it would be during Lent to have some freshwater shrimps or carp from Wolsey's famous ponds.

To get a sense of what the gardens were like in the sixteenth century, be sure to visit the recreated gardens in Chapel Court, inspired by those visible in the background of *The Family of Henry VIII*, which hangs in the Haunted Gallery. The gardens are planted with flowers and herbs that would have been available in the sixteenth century, enclosed by green-and-white-striped low fencing and guarded by heraldic beasts on poles.

Apart from the impressive gardens, when completed, Hampton Court Palace boasted tennis courts, bowling alleys, a hunting park and even a multiple garderobe. All of Henry's children spent time indulging in Hampton Court's splendour, both as heirs to the throne and in their own right as Tudor kings and queens.

Elizabeth I, like her mother, visited Hampton Court Palace not long after her coronation. It is here that her first official summer progress concluded in 1559. One wonders whether Elizabeth took note of her parents' entwined initials in the great hall, or thought about her mother's first triumphant visit to the palace as queen, when she – and not the expected male heir – was safely cradled in her womb.

For those of us wanting to follow in the footsteps of the Tudor queens, Hampton Court has no equal. So much of Henry VIII's private drama, from heartbreak to triumph, played out within its walls. Listen closely, as they echo with the footsteps of its past inhabitants and play back the memories of those distant, cataclysmic events.

Visitor Information

Hampton Court Palace is by far one of our favourite places in the world. Not only does more survive of Hampton Court than of any other Tudor palace, it is also home to some incredibly authentic costumed live interpretations that help bring the palace, and its stories, vividly to life.

Don't forget to try and find a quiet moment in the Haunted Gallery, said to be rife with ghostly goings-on. The palace is home to a myriad of ghost stories, but perhaps the most famous is that of Catherine Howard's screaming spectre.

On 2 November 1541, Archbishop Cranmer informed the king of Catherine's extramarital dalliances while he was at Mass in his Privy Closet. Legend tells that Catherine, knowing that her husband was at Mass, escaped her captors and ran screaming through the gallery in a final attempt to plead for her life. She was quickly restrained and dragged back to her apartments, only to face the executioner's block on 13 February 1542 at the Tower of London.

Tradition has it that her ghost replays, again and again, this final desperate dash for mercy in the gallery at Hampton Court. We love a good ghost story, but there is no documentary evidence to confirm that the original event ever took place. In fact, after hearing the devastating news, Henry left Hampton Court and his young wife was confined to her apartments, where she remained until she was moved to Syon House on 14 November. However, the truth doesn't detract from the eerie atmosphere of the gallery, as no doubt you'll find out …

From its beginnings as a palace built to impress to its present-day role as a magnificent time capsule, Hampton Court remains, after almost five hundred years, a wonder without peer.

Hampton Court Palace is managed by Historic Royal Palaces. For more information on how to reach Hampton Court and its opening hours, visit the Historic Royal Palaces website at http://www.hrp.org.uk/hamptoncourtpalace, or telephone +44 (0) 203 166 6000.

Postcode for Hampton Court Palace: KT8 9AU.

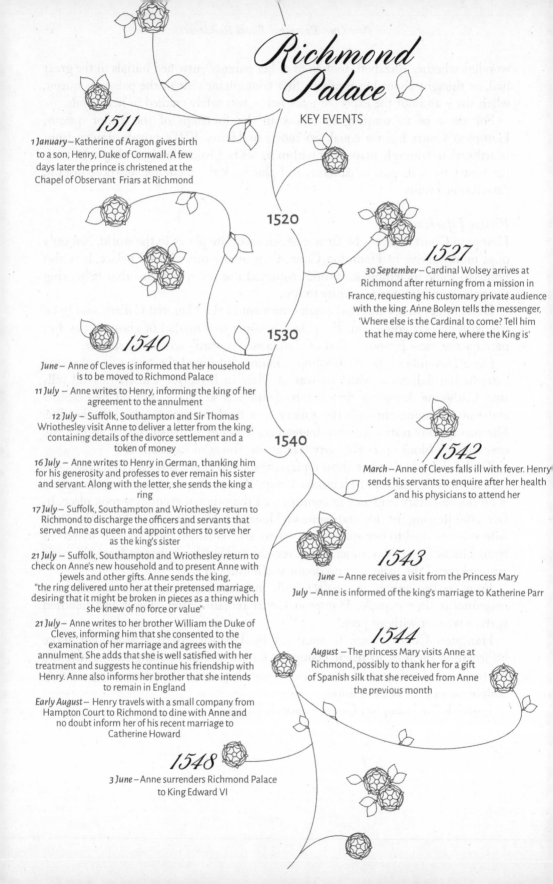

Richmond Palace
KEY EVENTS

1511

1 January – Katherine of Aragon gives birth to a son, Henry, Duke of Cornwall. A few days later the prince is christened at the Chapel of Observant Friars at Richmond

1520

1527

30 September – Cardinal Wolsey arrives at Richmond after returning from a mission in France, requesting his customary private audience with the king. Anne Boleyn tells the messenger, 'Where else is the Cardinal to come? Tell him that he may come here, where the King is'

1530

1540

June – Anne of Cleves is informed that her household is to be moved to Richmond Palace

11 July – Anne writes to Henry, informing the king of her agreement to the annulment

12 July – Suffolk, Southampton and Sir Thomas Wriothesley visit Anne to deliver a letter from the king, containing details of the divorce settlement and a token of money

16 July – Anne writes to Henry in German, thanking him for his generosity and professes to ever remain his sister and servant. Along with the letter, she sends the king a ring

17 July – Suffolk, Southampton and Wriothesley return to Richmond to discharge the officers and servants that served Anne as queen and appoint others to serve her as the king's sister

21 July – Suffolk, Southampton and Wriothesley return to check on Anne's new household and to present Anne with jewels and other gifts. Anne sends the king, "the ring delivered unto her at their pretensed marriage, desiring that it might be broken in pieces as a thing which she knew of no force or value"

21 July – Anne writes to her brother William the Duke of Cleves, informing him that she consented to the examination of her marriage and agrees with the annulment. She adds that she is well satisfied with her treatment and suggests he continue his friendship with Henry. Anne also informs her brother that she intends to remain in England

Early August – Henry travels with a small company from Hampton Court to Richmond to dine with Anne and no doubt inform her of his recent marriage to Catherine Howard

1540

1542

March – Anne of Cleves falls ill with fever. Henry sends his servants to enquire after her health and his physicians to attend her

1543

June – Anne receives a visit from the Princess Mary

July – Anne is informed of the king's marriage to Katherine Parr

1544

August – The princess Mary visits Anne at Richmond, possibly to thank her for a gift of Spanish silk that she received from Anne the previous month

1548

3 June – Anne surrenders Richmond Palace to King Edward VI

Richmond Palace, Greater London

The King's goodly manour of Richemond, is sett and bullid betwene dyvers highe and pleasunt mountayns in a valley and goodly playnys felds, where the most holsem eyerys [wholesome air is] ...

Tudor herald, *c.* 1501

Richmond Palace is perhaps best known to the Tudor enthusiast as the place where the first and last Tudor monarchs – Henry VII and Elizabeth I – took their last breaths, but it was also well known to Henry's queens, in particular Anne of Cleves, whose primary residence it was from June 1540 until June 1548, when she was forced to surrender it to Edward VI.

Rediscovering the Lost Palace of Richmond

The palace where Anne spent long periods of time after her separation from Henry stood on the south bank of the River Thames, on a site formerly occupied by the Palace of Sheen. It was constructed by Henry V between 1414 and 1422, and largely destroyed by fire on the night of 22 December 1497. Henry VII rebuilt and renovated the palace, which dominated the surrounding countryside, as a monument to the Tudor dynasty. In 1501, when the main building works were complete, he renamed it 'Rich mount'.

Approaching the house from the river, rising from the banks of the Thames, visitors would have seen the elegant facade of the royal apartments, which according to Simon Thurley 'were built within the shell of the early fifteenth-century donjon of the manor of Sheen'. The privy lodgings were three storeys high and built of white stone, enlivened by many octagonal and round towers, topped with cupolas and decorated with weathervanes. Each of the three floors contained twelve rooms built around an internal courtyard; the ground floor housed the household officials, while the second and third floors were the king and queen's richly furnished private apartments.

North of the lodgings, and accessible via a bridge over an inner moat, was a paved courtyard. In the centre stood a water fountain decorated with lions, Tudor dragons and other 'goodly beasts'. The courtyard was enclosed by the chapel on the east, a great hall on the west, an inner gatehouse in the north and a two-storey 'passage building', which connected the hall and the chapel, on the south. The stone chapel, which stood above the wine cellars, was 96 feet long and 30 feet wide. It was lavishly decorated and had a ceiling 'checkeryd with tymber' and embellished with roses and portcullis badges. On the west side was the king's privy closet, sumptuously furnished with silk hangings, carpets and cushions, and on the opposite side was the queen's closet.

The equally impressive hall was also made of stone and was 100 feet long by 40 feet wide. Its timber ceiling was embellished with carved pendants and the interior adorned with statues depicting famous rulers of England, including Henry VII. To the west of the hall stood household offices, such as the pantry and larders and a freestanding kitchen, with a pyramidal roof that can be seen in Wyngaerde's view of the palace.

The inner gatehouse opened into the outer courtyard, surrounded by red-brick ranges to the east, west and north that contained additional lodgings for officials and courtiers. The main gateway was in the north range, and opened on to Richmond Green. The privy gardens and privy orchard lay to the east of the palace, surrounded by timber-framed two-storey galleries, the first of their kind in England. Here, important guests undoubtedly perambulated, admiring the knot gardens from above. There was also a 'housis of pleasure', where visitors could pass the time playing chess, dice and cards. The galleries linked the palace to the church of the Observant Friars that stood to the east. A Tudor herald described the gardens as 'most faire and pleasaunt' and noted that they contained 'many marvelous beasts, as lyons, dragons, and such othre of dyvers kynde'.

The palace, which also boasted a bowling alley, tennis courts and archery butts, was rarely visited by the court after 1530, as Henry preferred the comforts of Whitehall and Hampton Court Palace. Despite this, we find Henry and Anne Boleyn in residence in early December 1535, and in December 1536 the court returned with Queen Jane by Henry's side. As previously mentioned, in 1540 Richmond was given to Anne of Cleves as part of her divorce settlement and it enjoyed something of a revival under Elizabeth I. She visited Richmond often and appears to have been genuinely fond of it.

All that is now left to see of Richmond Palace is the main gateway and part of the outer range facing the Green.

Visitor Information

Today, Richmond is a much-sought-after residential location for well-heeled Londoners, and subsequently is one of the wealthiest areas in the United Kingdom. Although now part of suburban London, a little like Greenwich, it maintains a 'village' feel with its own sophisticated style. Consequently, you will find plenty of restaurants, bars and boutique shops to indulge in once you have finished your Tudor adventure.

To begin this, make your way to Richmond Green. There is parking by pay and display around the Green, although many locals and visitors to London will come to Richmond via the Tube (station: Richmond, District line).

All that survives above ground of Henry VII's palace is the main gateway and part of what was once the palace wardrobe. Make your way to the west side of the park to view the typical red-brick Tudor architecture that we have so come to associate with the period. A nearby notice board, opposite the gateway, helpfully provides an illustration of how the palace appeared in its heyday. Passing under this same structure, as Henry's queens undoubtedly did on several occasions, notice Henry VIII's coat of arms above your head. You are now entering Old Palace Yard, originally part of the palace's outer court. In the sixteenth century, it was bounded by ranges of lodgings connected by galleries. Directly opposite the main gateway would have stood the middle gate building, which led through to the inner courtyard and the privy lodgings. This magnificent building once stood about halfway between the eighteenth-century Trumpeter's House, now a private residence, and the riverfront, its foundations buried beneath immaculately manicured lawns. Finally, you cannot miss the range of Tudor buildings lying to your left, originally part of Henry VIII's wardrobe.

Sadly, you can go no further here. However, if you retrace your steps and turn left, you can follow the road as it becomes Old Palace Lane. This brings you down to the river; five hundred years ago, the river frontage of the palace, containing the king's lodgings, would have stretched away in front of you. You might even imagine Katherine of Aragon, Anne Boleyn or Jane Seymour arriving at the palace with Henry by barge, brightly coloured flags bearing heraldry of the Tudor dynasty fluttering gently in the river breeze.

Before you leave Richmond behind you, consider heading to Richmond Park, situated about a mile away from the site of the old palace. This was originally part of the royal hunting park, a park that Henry's queens would have known well. It still remains in royal hands today and forms the largest royal park in London, containing over six hundred fallow and red deer. As you can imagine, it is very popular with locals, particularly when the sun is shining. You too can enjoy its charms. Of particular interest is King Henry's Mound, the highest point in the park. Legend has it that it is here that Henry heard the cannon of the Tower roar on the morning of 19 May 1536, a signal that Anne Boleyn had been executed within the Tower precinct and that their extraordinary story was over. This is an interesting legend, but almost certainly untrue. Most modern historians agree that Henry VIII was at Whitehall Palace when he received news of Anne's execution, at which time he set off to visit Jane Seymour, whom he had lodged 'within a mile of his lodging'.

Postcode for Richmond Green: TW9 1QQ.

Postcode for Richmond Park: TW10 5HS.

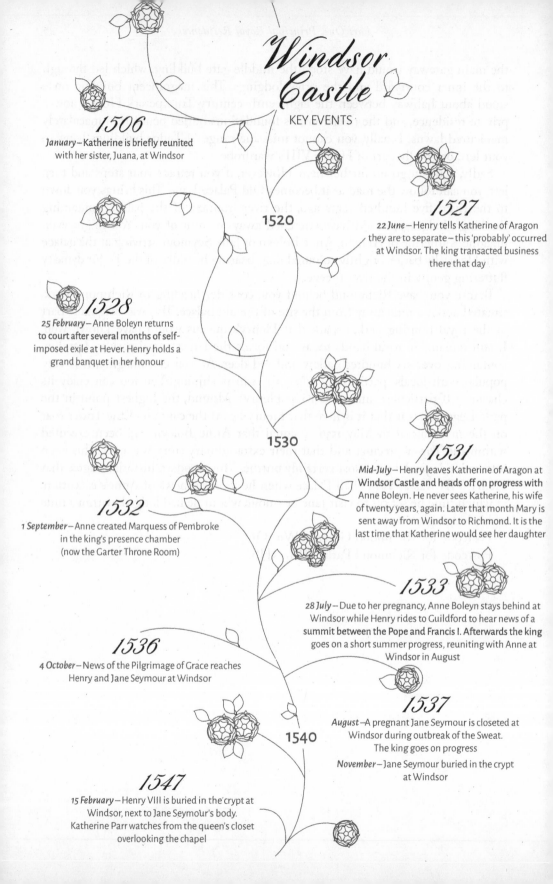

Windsor Castle

KEY EVENTS

1506
January – Katherine is briefly reunited with her sister, Juana, at Windsor

1520

1527
22 June – Henry tells Katherine of Aragon they are to separate – this 'probably' occurred at Windsor. The king transacted business there that day

1528
25 February – Anne Boleyn returns to court after several months of self-imposed exile at Hever. Henry holds a grand banquet in her honour

1530

1531
Mid-July – Henry leaves Katherine of Aragon at Windsor Castle and heads off on progress with Anne Boleyn. He never sees Katherine, his wife of twenty years, again. Later that month Mary is sent away from Windsor to Richmond. It is the last time that Katherine would see her daughter

1532
1 September – Anne created Marquess of Pembroke in the king's presence chamber (now the Garter Throne Room)

1533
28 July – Due to her pregnancy, Anne Boleyn stays behind at Windsor while Henry rides to Guildford to hear news of a summit between the Pope and Francis I. Afterwards the king goes on a short summer progress, reuniting with Anne at Windsor in August

1536
4 October – News of the Pilgrimage of Grace reaches Henry and Jane Seymour at Windsor

1540

1537
August – A pregnant Jane Seymour is closeted at Windsor during outbreak of the Sweat. The king goes on progress
November – Jane Seymour buried in the crypt at Windsor

1547
15 February – Henry VIII is buried in the crypt at Windsor, next to Jane Seymour's body. Katherine Parr watches from the queen's closet overlooking the chapel

Windsor Castle, Berkshire

> Calmly, from its hill-top, it enjoys the most delightful view in the world. It gazes down over the prospect of a wide and far-reaching vale, patterned with ploughland, green with meadows, clad here and there with woodlands, and watered by the softly flowing Thames. Behind it the hills rise all round ... crowned with woods as though Nature herself has dedicated them to the chase.
>
> William Camden, Elizabethan antiquarian and topographer

Windsor Castle was originally built by William the Conqueror as part of a ring of strategically defensive castles constructed around London, shortly after the Norman invasion of England in 1066. Some 20 miles upstream from Hampton Court Palace, the mighty castle perches high on a chalky outcrop of the Chiltern Hills, almost 30 metres above the River Thames; it dominates the surrounding skyline.

Although the interior has been greatly altered over the centuries, its basic footprint remains almost completely unchanged since the original motte-and-bailey castle was established in 1070. Within easy reach of London, and surrounded by a royal hunting forest, Windsor quickly established itself as a popular royal abode.

In external appearance, Windsor Castle certainly would be recognisable to each of Henry's queens today, with only one or two notable differences. For example, the central round tower was squatter in the sixteenth century; the main exit on the southern side of the Upper Ward was from the south-west corner, via a bridge crossing the original defensive ditch, while a tennis court clung to the foot of the central mound within the Upper Ward, close to the modern-day Engine Court.

Sadly, however, the Tudor interiors have been decimated in the remodelling/refurbishment carried out by successive monarchs in the seventeenth, eighteenth and nineteenth centuries. To the uninitiated and unprepared, all trace of the Tudor apartments appears to have vanished, and it is easy to dismiss the interior rooms as irrelevant to our story. Do not despair! Beneath the gaudy baroque grandeur are hidden gems of an earlier time, just waiting to be uncovered by the determined time traveller. So, with this book to hand, get ready to rediscover the lost treasures of Tudor Windsor.

For ease, we have arranged our tour to follow the sequence of rooms you will pass through on your visit to Windsor Castle (correct at the time of writing this book). Our aim is to help you orientate yourself to the lost chambers of the Tudor palace. In taking the tour, we would recommend that you refer to the plan of the Tudor apartments outlined in the image section of this book. This shows the castle as it was in the sixteenth century, with the royal apartments on the north side of the Upper Ward, basically on the same footprint as the current State Apartments. The key difference between then and now was the existence of three internal courtyards that have since been internalised within the structure of the modern-day building.

The Grand Staircase

At the beginning of your tour, you will soon find yourself climbing the Grand Staircase. In the sixteenth century this was the first open courtyard of the castle, known as Brick Court. Thus five hundred years ago, you would have been standing in the open air. Once at the top of the staircase, you are now inside a wing of the Tudor building that ran perpendicular to the staircase on a north–south axis. Part of this wing was once occupied by the queen's watching chamber, and it is within this chamber that you are now standing. However, as most of the walls have been taken down, it is unrecognisable as such.

The Waterloo Chamber

This was the second open courtyard of the Tudor royal apartments. Understand that you are now standing at first-floor level. At the entrance to the Waterloo Chamber, you might well have been looking out of a window and down onto the courtyard below you. As with Brick Court, this second courtyard was later covered and a first floor inserted. Enter the chamber and imagine that running along the wall to your right was a gallery linking the queen's watching chamber to the king's watching chamber at the far end. To your left would have been two enormous oriel windows, which looked out from the king's presence chamber.

The King's Drawing Room

This modern-day room was once Henry's privy chamber, the first of the private rooms to make up the king's privy lodgings. As you follow the modern-day tour of the apartments, you will pass through the king's bedchamber (once Henry's state bedchamber), dressing room and closet. All these rooms were originally part of Henry's privy chamber suite. Here, Henry would have been attended only by his close personal friends and male members of the king's privy chamber.

The Queen's Drawing Room and the Queen's Ballroom

These rooms have been extensively remodelled since the sixteenth century. During that time, the northern end of the queen's drawing room was occupied by a chamber on the king's side, while the far end of the room (from where you enter) was once part of the queen's bedchamber. So, in other words, this single room was once split into two. Some iconic Tudor portraits are not to be missed here. Once you are through into the current Queen's Ballroom, you find yourself in the main part of what was once the queen's privy suite. The northern part of the room, which you enter first, was occupied by the remainder of the bedchamber, and the southern end of the room comprised the queen's privy chamber.

The Queen's Audience and Presence Chambers

These two rooms originally made up a much larger, single presence chamber on the queen's side. Here the queen would formally receive guests or hear petitions. If she were dining in public, she would do so in her presence chamber.

St George's Hall
This huge space was once divided in two. In Tudor times, the part that you enter on the modern-day tour would have been the chapel royal, while the second half of the room was occupied by the great hall; originally the main public space of the royal apartments.

The Grand Reception Room
This was once the site of the great staircase of Edward III's medieval palace. The chamber was later to become Henry's great watching chamber and, as you can see, was much bigger than its cousin at Hampton Court Palace.

The Garter Throne Room
So many lovers of Tudor history pass through this room blissfully unaware that it witnessed a defining moment in Tudor history. Here, on 1 September 1532, Anne Boleyn came before Henry and the court to be ennobled as Marquess of Pembroke. This elevation in her status was in preparation for the historic trip to Calais, when Henry and Anne would meet the French king, Francis I, in order to gain Francis' support for their anticipated, and imminent, marriage.

Visitor Information
Windsor Castle is still owned by the Crown and very much a royal family home to this day. Therefore, only some of the parts in which we are interested, including the state chambers, are open to the public. It is a popular tourist destination and so the castle and town can get very busy in the height of summer. If you want to avoid some of the queues, get there at opening time, or book tickets in advance via the website, http://www.royalcollection.org.uk/visit/windsorcastle, or telephone +44 (0)207 766 7304.

While at Windsor, do visit the Chapel of St George and see the simple tombstone of Henry VIII himself, set into the floor of the chancel. He is buried beneath your feet in the crypt below, alongside Jane Seymour. On the north side of the choir, above eye level and adjacent to the altar, is the Queen's Closet, named after Katherine of Aragon. It is from inside this closet that Katherine Parr watched the burial of her third, and most illustrious, husband.

Don't forget to also locate the plain tombstone marking the burial site of Charles Brandon, Duke of Suffolk, toward the south door of the chapel. The plain black marble gravestone carries the simple inscription, 'Charles Brandon, Duke of Suffolk, K.G. Died August 24 1545. Married Mary, daughter of Henry VII. Widow of Louis XII, King of France.'

Postcode for Windsor Castle: SL4 1NJ.

Part Two
Katherine of Aragon
[Catalina de Aragón]

'HUMBLE AND LOYAL'

Introduction

A small cluster of loyal courtiers spoke in hushed tones inside a chamber of Kimbolton Castle. It was 7 January 1536, and Katherine of Aragon lay just hours from death. Outside, the English winter raged, mirroring, perhaps, the tempest inside the ousted queen's heart. What thoughts might have swirled like snowflakes around her mind as her tired body succumbed to illness? She left us a clue … but other than that, we can safely surmise that this proudest of monarchs never entertained regret.

Not for a moment did Katherine of Aragon ever doubt the legitimacy of her marriage to Henry. She never once wavered from the belief that she was the king's one and only true wife, even when it meant virtual exile and separation from her beloved daughter Mary. Through the many years of heartache, she stood firm and weathered every storm, risking her own life, and even that of her only daughter's, by obstinately refusing to obey her husband and king. Regardless of Henry's threats, Katherine would not renounce her title as queen, nor step aside for any man or woman. Her steadfast determination won her many admirers but enraged Henry – and those who supported his marriage to Anne Boleyn.

Almost five hundred years later, it's easy to condemn Katherine for her apparent willingness to sacrifice Mary. Some might wonder how any mother could risk such a thing for religion, or a crown, but as Hilary Mantel once said, 'the essence of the thing is not to judge with hindsight, not to pass judgment from the lofty perch of the twenty-first century when we know what happened'. It's to immerse ourselves in their world, to be there at the pivotal moments and the quiet ones too, and to share in their hopes and dreams, and in the uncertainty of the future. If we want to know Katherine, to understand why she fought until her dying day, we must follow her into her past, and walk by her side from the very beginning.

The Spanish Years

Katherine was born in the Archbishop's Palace of Alcala de Henares, near Madrid, on 15 or 16 December 1485, just four months after a Welshman by the name of Henry Tudor seized the English crown. She was the youngest child of Queen Isabella I of Castile and King Ferdinand II of Aragon – the Catholic Monarchs – an appellation formally conferred on them by Pope Alexander VI in 1494, in recognition of their reconquest of Granada from the Moors. Katherine's engagement to Arthur Tudor, heir to the newly established Tudor dynasty, was negotiated at Medina del Campo in March 1489, when she was just three years old. So for as long as Katherine could remember, she'd been a Spanish princess and a Princess of Wales, raised to one day be England's queen.

Her childhood was spent largely on the move, criss-crossing the country from one end to the other, sometimes staying in as many as a dozen different towns and cities in a month, some of which, like Seville and Cordoba, we explore in this chapter of the book. Katherine travelled with her parents as they asserted their authority in every corner of the land, listening to petitions and administering justice wherever they went. She watched as each spring they embarked on a military campaign against the Emirate of Granada, and on occasions even stayed with her parents at army camps close to the front line. While it was the joint military forces of Isabella and Ferdinand that finally defeated the Moors in Granada, it was Isabella's kingdom that was the more powerful. An impressionable Katherine must have noted her mother's authority and influence, and seen how her father often sought his wife's advice.

On her travels, Katherine would have seen the great variety of people who inhabited her parents' land, from Jews, who were expelled from Spain in 1492 when Katherine was just six years old, to the large population of Muslims, known as Mudejars, who remained in Spain after the Christian reconquest. From birth, she was exposed to her parents' anti-semitism and raised to share their ardent abhorrence of heresy. One wonders if whispers ever reached the young Infanta (princess) of her mother's fervent implementation of the Spanish Inquisition and of the barbarous punishments inflicted on those found guilty of heresy. While Katherine would have been sheltered from the worst of the religious turmoil, this is the world in which she was born and raised.

Unlike the English court, where royal children were often established in their own households from a very young age, Isabella kept her daughters close, and personally oversaw their education and upbringing. Katherine learnt to read and write Spanish at around six, and learnt Latin from Beatriz Galindo, the same woman who'd taught her mother. Isabella hired noted Italian tutors for her children and ensured that they were all adept at the courtly skills of music, dance, falconry and hunting, while also instructing her daughters in the more domestic pursuits of sewing and needlework. In 1518, the Dutch humanist Erasmus commented, 'The Queen [Katherine] is well instructed – not merely in comparison with her own sex – and is no less to be respected for her piety than her erudition.' Surprisingly, though, Katherine was not taught English before leaving Spain to marry Arthur. In July 1498, the Spanish ambassador de Puebla wrote to his monarchs with some advice for the twelve-year-old Katherine from her future mother-in-law, Elizabeth of York:

> The Queen and the mother of the King wish that the Princess of Wales should always speak French with the Princess Margaret, who is now in Spain, in order to learn the language, and to be able to converse in it when she comes to England. This is necessary, because these ladies do not understand Latin, and much less, Spanish. They also wish that the Princess of Wales should accustom herself to drink wine. The water of England is not drinkable, and even if it were, the climate would not allow the drinking of it.

When Katherine arrived in England in 1501, she spoke a little French and so it appears that she heeded the advice and learnt from her sister-in-law, Margaret of Austria, who lived for a time in Spain after the death of her first husband, Prince John, Katherine's elder brother.

Princess of Wales and Queen of England

After travelling around Spain, we cross the Bay of Biscay with Katherine, and set foot on English soil for the first time on 2 October 1501, where 'she could not have been received with greater rejoicings, if she had been the Saviour of the world'. Immediately after landing in Plymouth Harbour, Katherine went in procession to the church to give thanks for her safe arrival – religion, of course, dictating the rhythm of Katherine's daily life. In Henry Clifford's *The Life of Jane Dormer, Duchess of Feria*, chronicling the experiences of a lady-in-waiting to Mary I, we learn that as queen Katherine 'rose at midnight to be present at the Matins of the Religious, after which she heard Mass at five o'clock in the morning', a ritual she may have followed in her early years too.

From Plymouth, the Spanish princess travelled in stages to London, passing through Dogmersfield, where she first met her future father-in-law and husband, to Chertsey, Kingston upon Thames and Lambeth. On 12 November 1501 Katherine made her formal entry into London, and two days later, after more than a decade of negotiations and waiting, she married her prince at Old St Paul's Cathedral. A fortnight after the wedding, Arthur wrote to his in-laws from Richmond Palace, expressing the joy he felt when he 'beheld the sweet face of his bride' and promising 'to make a good husband'.

Tragically, after only four and a half months of marriage, Arthur Tudor died, leaving sixteen-year-old Katherine a widow, and plunging her into seven long years of hardship and uncertainty, punctuated by numerous episodes of illness, where all she dreamed of was returning home to Spain. After Elizabeth of York's death in February 1503, a bereaved Henry VII considered marrying his daughter-in-law himself, a union that Katherine's mother found repulsive. So instead, on 23 June 1503, Katherine was betrothed to Arthur's younger brother, Henry, now heir to the Tudor throne. The marriage, though, did not take place until 11 June 1509, almost two months after the death of Henry VII, who had done his best to delay the nuptials.

Immediately after the private ceremony held at Greenwich Palace, plans were put in place for a magnificent double coronation, which took place at Westminster Abbey on 24 June 1509. A month later, from his palace at Greenwich, Henry wrote to his father-in-law of his marriage to Katherine and his affection for his new queen:

> ... and, regards that sincere love, which we have to the most serene queen our consort, – her eminent virtues daily more and more shine forth, blossom, and increase so much, that, if we were still free, we would yet choose her for our wife before all other.

Katherine had fulfilled her destiny and was now an anointed Queen of England, set above all others. In her eyes, only death could remove her.

As Katherine's English years are heavily documented elsewhere, we've chosen to only include four locations from her time as Princess of Wales and Queen of England. These are Ludlow Castle, Leeds Castle, the Bishop of Lincoln's Palace in Buckden and Kimbolton Castle, all of which bore witness to pivotal moments in Katherine's life, the latter two playing host to Katherine's darkest days when, after more than twenty years of marriage, Henry VIII discarded his first wife with little more than a second thought.

Despite the years of mistreatment that Katherine endured at the hands of her fickle and often heartless husband, despite the tragedy of her enforced separation from her daughter, it was to Henry that her dying heart leaned towards on 7 January 1536 when with her last breath she vowed 'that mine eyes desire thou aboufe all things'. Yet she followed this declaration of love and fealty with one final act of defiance: she signed her letter, 'Katharine the Quene'.

Authors' Note: As we refer to Katherine by her English name throughout the book, rather than the Spanish Catalina, we've chose, for clarity's sake, to also use the English translations for the names of Katherine's parents and siblings.

Archbishop's Palace, Alcalá de Henares, Madrid

> Recently arrived to Alcalá, the queen gave birth to the Princess Catalina, Thursday 15 December of the year 1485.
> Hernando del Pulgar, *Crónica de los Señores Reyes Católicos Don Fernando y Doña Isabel de Castilla y de Aragón*

In the great fortified palace of Alcalá de Henares, one of history's mightiest queens took her first breath. It was Thursday 15 December, or the early hours of 16 December 1485, and Isabella, the thirty-four-year-old Queen of Castile, had just given birth to her last child. The *Infanta*, as Spanish princesses are known, was named Catalina (Katherine), possibly after her English great-grandmother, Catherine of Lancaster. The baby was the last of seven children born to Isabella and her husband, Ferdinand II of Aragon, two of which had been stillbirths. Katherine's seven-year-old brother John, or *Juan*, was the royal family's only surviving male heir.

While one chronicler reported that, with only one son, *los Reyes Católicos* (the Catholic Monarchs) would have been happier with a boy, Katherine's birth was still welcome and marked by celebrations. The chronicler Hernando del Pulgar recorded that Cardinal Pedro González de Mendoza, who had recently refurbished the palace – situated about 35 kilometres north-east of Madrid – where the royal family was lodged, gave a lavish party for the nobles and ladies of the court and, despite the cold and rain, organised jousts to celebrate.

Most of what we know about Katherine's infancy comes from the meticulous records of Isabella's treasurer, Gonzalo de Baeza, from whom we learn that Elena de Carmona was one of baby Katherine's first maids. She watched over the princess as she slept in her crib, on a newly made mattress stuffed with fresh cotton and fitted with sheets of fine linen from Holland, which was also used to make her nightshirts and bibs. Katherine was bathed in a small brass basin and dressed in beautiful tunics, including ones made of scarlet Florentine cloth. Giles Tremlett, Katherine's biographer, notes that one of her first possessions was a small perfume sprinkler. There was also a wet nurse, whose job it was to breastfeed the newborn princess and help raise her once she was weaned. Other expenses recorded by Baeza include an exquisite christening gown made of white brocade, lined with green velvet and edged with gold lace, worn by Katherine at her christening.

While Isabella had spent the months preceding her daughter's birth overseeing the campaign against the Nasrid kingdom of Granada, winter was a time of rest. The war against the Moors would not resume until the weather had improved, and so Katherine's family was free to enjoy the Christmas festivities in peace.

Birthplace of a Queen

The palace where Katherine was born had begun its life in the thirteenth century as a fortress built to house the archbishops of Toledo, who'd acquired the land from King Alfonso VII in the twelfth century. Probably quadrangular in plan and with four square corner towers, it resembled the still-standing Alcazar of Toledo, constructed around the same time. It was not until the fourteenth and fifteenth centuries that the medieval castle was greatly enlarged and transformed into a luxurious palace, reflecting the growing power and wealth of the archbishops of Toledo. By the sixteenth century, the palace was at its zenith. With the establishment of the University of Alcalá, founded by Cardinal Jiménez de Cisneros (Cardinal Mendoza's successor) at the turn of the sixteenth century, the town quickly became one of the most important intellectual centres of its time and the world's first planned university city, serving as a model for other hubs of learning across Europe and the world.

At the time of Katherine's birth in 1485, the palace was the residence of Cardinal Mendoza. It was the crux of political and religious life in the city, where Christians, Moors and Jews lived harmoniously side by side. This was reflected in the palace's architecture, which combined different styles, from Gothic to Mudejar – a fusion of Christian and Islamic styles of architecture and decoration, building materials and techniques prevalent in Spain in the twelfth to fifteenth centuries – and later Renaissance.

The palace was a vast complex of buildings, gardens and courtyards, more than double the size of the original fortress. It comprised several *patios* (courtyards), towers, galleries and chambers, including *la sala de la Reyna*, the queen's chamber, elaborately decorated in Gothic-Mudejar style, and on the floor above, *el Salon de Concilios,* or Council Wing. This was the principal chamber of the palace, and the most spectacular, where many important events were held. The room was 40 metres in length and boasted seven large windows and a magnificent coffered ceiling and richly decorated plaster frieze. It may have been where Queen Isabella met with the explorer Christopher Columbus for the first time in February 1486.

As for the rooms that witnessed the birth of Katherine of Aragon, it's possible that these once stood around the main cloister (see reconstruction in the colour image section), in the southwest of the palace complex, overlooking the *Jardin de Bosque,* or Forest Garden. This was the original nucleus of the palace, and so probably housed the apartments that the royal family, the archbishop and other important guests occupied during their visits.

In the sixteenth century, further alterations were made to the palace, including a new Renaissance-style facade designed by the architect Alonso de Covarrubias, who was also responsible for the design of the most beautiful courtyard of the palace: the *Patio de Fonseca* or Fonseca Courtyard, a rectangular courtyard bordered by a two-storey arcade of seventy-six stone columns built on the site of its medieval predecessor.

Over the next four hundred years, the palace was further modified and suffered significant damage during the Peninsular War, when it was used as a barracks for French and Spanish soldiers. It went on to become the state's central archives, and by 1930 contained around 1,000,000 state documents and an impressive library that housed more than 8,000 books.

Tragically, on the afternoon of 11 August 1939, a fire swept through the palace buildings, destroying virtually the entire complex, with the exception of a small section of the facade, which was later incorporated into a new building. In a matter of hours, around eight hundred years of history, including the chamber where Katherine of Aragon's story began, was lost.

Visitor Information
There is much for the history enthusiast to see and do in Alcalá de Henares, declared a World Heritage Site in 1998 on account of its rich cultural and built heritage. We recommend arriving early and parking in the free car park on Calle [street] Cardenal Sandoval y Rojas. If you're visiting between mid-October and the beginning of August, you're in for a treat: nesting on almost all of the city's towers and historical buildings, you'll find a large number of white storks. At the time of writing, there were more than 111 breeding couples registered, hence why Alcalá is known as 'the city of the storks'.

Turn left out of the entrance to the car park and head towards Plaza Palacio, keeping an eye out for a bronze statue of Katherine's mother, Isabella, along the way. Just beyond the statue you'll find the reconstructed facade of the Archbishop's

Palace, as designed by Covarrubias in the sixteenth century. This new building, which incorporates remains of the original palace, is today home to the bishopric of Alcalá and not open to the public. However, it is possible to arrange a guided tour (in Spanish) of two of the medieval towers that formed part of the defensive wall surrounding the palace. As part of this tour, arranged through the tourism office in nearby Santos Niños Square, visitors also gain access to an open-air exhibition area called 'Antiquarian', where archaeological remains of the old palace are on display.

Continue walking along, past the Torreón de Tenorio (Tenorio Tower), a remnant of the palace Katherine would have known, towards the beautiful Plaza de las Bernardas, where you'll find another exquisite bronze statue, this time of a young Katherine of Aragon, installed in 2007. This plaza is also home to the Regional Archaeological Museum, located in the former seventeenth-century Augustinian Convent-College of the Mother of God and home to many important archaeological remains of the province of Madrid, including mosaics from the old Roman city of Complutum. From the plaza you can also access the Cistercian Convent of Saint Bernard, built around 1618.

Just a short walk away in the Santos Niños Square you will find the Magisterial Cathedral of St Justus and St Pastor, which was constructed on the site of an earlier church, where it's possible the infant Katherine was baptised by Cardinal Mendoza just days after her birth. The present cathedral was built between 1497 and 1515, and from its tower offers visitors uninterrupted views of the city and its surroundings. Both the palace and the church are clearly visible in Antony van den Wyngaerde's view of the city painted in 1565.

With so much to see in Alcalá, we recommend that before you visit you download a tourist guide from http://www.turismoalcala.es/guia-turistica-alcaladehenares.html, which includes, among other things, a list of monuments and museums open to the public and suggested walking trails depending on your interests, including the 'Route of Cervantes', which will help guide you to all the sites associated with Miguel de Cervantes, who was born in Alcalá de Henares and authored the universally acclaimed novel *Don Quixote*. We also recommend downloading a tourist map from http://www.turismoalcala.es/plano-de-alcalá. html and watching a short video by 'Dream! Alcala' on YouTube that will help you visualise what the Archbishop's Palace looked like before the blaze. It is a brilliant digital reconstruction of the palace as it stood in the spring of 1936. While it had, by then, been greatly altered to serve its new function as an archive (namely the walls of shelving), and reflects more the layout of the sixteenth-century palace rather than the palace Katherine was born in, it does allow us a glimpse into the chamber of Queen Isabella and the *Salon de Concilios* with its breathtaking Mudejar decoration. (Search on YouTube: Un Paseo virtual por el Palacio Arzobispal de Alcalá de Henares.)

While there may not be much left to see of the buildings that witnessed the birth of a future Queen of England, the Archbishop's Palace remains a powerful and evocative place. It's a space where, rather than imagining a stout middle-aged matron, rejected and abandoned by her husband and living unhappily in virtual isolation, we are free to imagine a youthful and exuberant Katherine, beloved by her family and people, a girl with a glittering future spread before her.

To book a tour of the surviving medieval towers of the Archbishop's Palace and gain access to the open-air museum, contact or visit the tourist information office at Santos Niños Square or email otssnn@ayto-alcaladehenares.es.

For information on how to reach the Magisterial Cathedral and its opening hours, visit http://www.catedraldealcala.org.

The Royal Palace of Medina del Campo, Valladolid, Castile and Leon

On the 24th day of March the kings sent for the said ambassadors. It was the eve of Our Lady of March, and they went to the complines. And afterwards they went with the kings into a gallery hung with fine tapestry. There they found the young princesses, these were Donna Maria and our princess of England Donna Catherine.

Journals of Roger Machado

On 12 March 1489, the English ambassadors Thomas Savage and Richard Nanfan arrived in the Castilian market town of Medina del Campo, a bustling cosmopolitan community of around 20,000 inhabitants, south of Valladolid and the centre of international trade fairs. Merchants from all over the Iberian Peninsula and Europe flocked to its two annual fairs, held in the main square in May and October, to trade in a great variety of products, including wool, livestock and wine.

Savage and Nanfan had been sent to meet with the Catholic Monarchs, Queen Isabella of Castile and her husband King Ferdinand II of Aragon, to, among other things, negotiate the marriage of Prince Arthur Tudor, heir to the Tudor throne, and Princess Katherine of Aragon. Isabella and Ferdinand, intent on unifying the kingdoms of the peninsula under one central government, were rapidly becoming one of the most powerful royal couples in Europe, and Henry Tudor desperately needed influential friends and allies to help solidify his still shaky hold on the English crown. The Catholic Monarchs, too, welcomed an alliance that might help ward off any threat from the French on their northern border, and so agreed to receive an embassy from England.

The meetings took place in the royal palace of Medina del Campo, during which time the English ambassadors laid eyes on Katherine, their future queen, for the first time. As Katherine's biographer Giles Tremlett reminds us, 'this encounter is one of only a handful of childhood sightings of Catherine in the chronicles of the time', making Medina del Campo an important location in Katherine's story.

An Embassy to Spain

In December 1488, the English ambassadors took leave of their king and made their way to Southampton, where at midday on 19 January they boarded a Spanish ship in the company of several Spanish ambassadors, to begin a gruelling journey over sea and land. Twice, violent storms and strong winds forced them to return to the safety of the English ports of Plymouth and Falmouth respectively, before finally landing in the town of Laredo on 16 February. However, this was not before they had encountered a raging tempest in the Bay of Biscay that almost ended in catastrophe. According to the herald Roger Machado, a member of the English ambassadors' party, they were comforted and saved, 'by God's grace, and by the prayers and pilgrimages promised to the good Saints', and so, with grateful hearts, all on board disembarked the battered ships as the sun set over the Spanish port town in the kingdom of Castile.

There, once more, the weather wreaked havoc. A great snowstorm prevented the party from leaving Laredo for a week. Finally, on 23 February they began their journey overland, staying with merchants along the way and, for the most part, being warmly received and well looked after. However, Machado records one instance where they 'were very ill lodged'; their Spanish landlady first reprimanded them for 'being so bold as to come into her house without her leave', and then tried to expel them from her house, accusing them of being 'bawdy villains'! Needless to say, 'they rose very early' and fled.

The ambassadors made their way to the city of Valladolid and then on to Medina del Campo, where the royal family presided. The English visitors were lodged very comfortably in town, in well-furnished chambers hung with fine tapestries, and there, they awaited the royal summons. It came on 14 March, two days after their arrival.

Daylight was fading as the torchlit procession of bishops, counts and 'other lords, knights and great persons in great number' conducted the ambassadors to the royal palace where 'the kings', Isabella and Ferdinand, were seated in a 'great room … under a rich cloth of gold of state; and in the middle of this great cloth of state was an escutcheon quartered with the arms of Castile and Aragon'. The monarchs, seated side by side, shone like suns in robes 'woven entirely of gold'. Ferdinand's was lined with fine sable fur, but it was Isabella's spectacular clothing and jewels that so dazzled Machado, he recorded the moment in great detail, a description worth reproducing here in full. Over her robe, the herald noted, the queen wore

> … a riding hood of black velvet, all slashed in large holes, so as to show under the said velvet the cloth of gold in which she was dressed. And on the said hood a line [of trimming], not extended, but a sort of [broken] line, composed of oblong parts about a finger's length, and half a finger in width, all of solid gold; and each oblong part decorated with fine and valuable jewels, so rich that no one has ever seen the like. The said queen wore around her waist a girdle of white leather made in the style that men usually wear; [of] which girdle the pouch was decorated with a large balass ruby the size of a tennis ball, between five rich diamonds and other precious stones the size of a bean. And the rest of the girdle was decorated with a great number of other precious stones. She wore on her neck a rich gold necklace composed entirely of white and red roses, each rose being adorned with

a large jewel. Besides this she had two ribbons suspended on each side of her breast, adorned with large diamonds, balass and other rubies, pearls, and various other jewels of great value to the number of a hundred or more. Over all this dress she wore a short cloak of fine crimson satin furred with ermine, very handsome in appearance and very brilliant. It was thrown on [negligently] cross-wise over her left side. Her head was uncovered, excepting only a little coiffe de plaisance at the back of her head without anything else.

Machado estimated that the queen's attire was worth 'two hundred thousand crowns of gold', an ostentatious display of the Spanish monarchy's wealth and power. Giles Tremlett called it 'blatant power-dressing' and a reinforcement 'of Isabel's absolute superiority over all those who surrounded her'. There was no room left for error – in Castile, Isabella was not to be outshone.

After the formal introductions and speeches – including an almost incomprehensible one made by the elderly and toothless Diego de Muros, Bishop of Cuidad Rodrigo – the ambassadors were escorted back to their accommodation.

The following day, they were again taken to see 'the kings'. In his account Machado quotes Dr Rodrigo Gonzalez de Puebla's explanation for why he referred to them in plural form:

And because perhaps some may blame me that I speak of 'kings' and some people may be astonished, and say, 'How! Are there two kings in Castile?' No, [I say] but I write 'kings' because the king is king on account of the queen, by right of marriage, and because they call themselves 'kings', and superscribe their letters 'By the King and Queen', for she is the heiress [of the throne].

After an hour of negotiations, they requested to meet the prince and princesses, obviously eager to catch their first glimpse of the young girl who would one day become England's queen, but were told that they 'should willingly be allowed to see' the prince and his older sister at this time, 'and that another day they should see the other princesses'.

What followed was twelve days of negotiations and entertainment, including dancing, feasting, jousting and bullfighting, where the queen continued to impress her visitors with her sumptuous wardrobe. On one occasion, she wore a robe of cloth of gold, with a 'mantilla spangled with lozenges of crimson and black velvet, and on each lozenge a large pearl', and alongside each pearl a fine balas ruby the size of a beechnut. Machado, overawed, recorded that it was 'the richest thing that could be seen, no man ever saw anything equal to it'.

While they had now twice seen the prince and the eldest of the princesses, Isabella, they were yet to see the younger *Infantas*, Maria and three-year-old Katherine. This took place on 24 March, in a gallery hung with fine tapestries. Machado relates:

There they [the ambassadors] found the young princesses, these were Donna Maria and our princess of England Donna Catherine. The king and queen entered and went and sat down, the prince sat on the ground before him, and the eldest daughter before him, afterwards the other daughters. And I must say that the Queen was very richly dressed. And all her daughters were similarly dressed, and the said two daughters, the Infanta donna Maria, and the Infanta donna Catherine, princess of England, had fourteen maidens, all noble ladies [attending upon them] all of them dressed in cloth of gold, and all of them daughters of noblemen. The eldest of them was not more than fourteen years old.

The maidens danced for the ambassadors, as did the six-year-old Maria, but Katherine was still too young to dance for her English visitors.

The following day, the ambassadors were introduced to the Spanish bullfight. Katherine was with her family for the occasion. There, Machado saw a more relaxed side to the queen: 'It was beautiful to see how the queen held up her youngest daughter, who was the Infanta donna Catherine, princess of Wales.'

Two days later, and after further negotiating, the Treaty of Medina del Campo was signed and the ambassadors said their goodbyes. However, it was the peripatetic Spanish royal family that departed Medina del Campo first. Machado recalled, 'The said ambassadors took their leaves again, and kissed the hands of the King, the Queen, the prince, and all the princesses the King's daughters.' The following day, the ambassadors received a number of gifts from the royal family, including a Spanish warhorse, a Moorish jennet, two mules, ten yards of silk and sixty marks of silver each. Machado concluded,

> Indeed I believe that no ambassadors ever went [on an embassy] who had more honor done them than was done to the said ambassadors in everything. People speak of the honor done to ambassadors in England; certainly it is not to be compared to the honor which is done to ambassadors in the kingdom of Castile, and especially in the time of this noble king and queen.

Isabella and Ferdinand had charmed and dazzled their visitors, and proven themselves powerful and wealthy allies, and suitable future in-laws for the heir to the Tudor throne.

A Short History of the Palace

The palace that bore witness to this momentous meeting was constructed in the fourteenth century and was home to the kings of Castile up until the end of the fifteenth century. It had been the birthplace of two kings: Alfonso V of Aragon in 1394 and Juan II of Navarra and Aragon, Katherine's paternal grandfather in 1397. On 26 November 1504, Queen Isabella of Castile took her final breath within its walls.

At the end of the fourteenth century and the beginning of the fifteenth century, it underwent an important transformation through Fernando de Antequera, King of Aragon, and in 1465 was described by Leon de Rosmithal in his travel diary as a very large house, magnificently and richly decorated, and indeed it was.

Constructed mainly of brick, timber and *tapial*, or rammed earth, its internal decoration was luxurious and consisted of Mudejar ceilings, tiles and plasterwork. Its rooms were hung with fine tapestries and important works of art, and in 1468 the palace complex contained, among other things, a number of 'houses', a tower and various courtyards.

The sixteenth century, though, brought with it the palace's demise, in part as a result of the decline of the aforementioned fairs and a loss of royal favour. By 1524, it was in need of significant repairs and in 1601 the second floor was entirely demolished. The next three hundred years saw further modifications and deterioration, and all that remains today is a small and much-modified part of what, in its heyday, was one of the most important royal palaces of the kingdom of Castile.

Visitor Information

The *Palacio Testamentario* or Testamentary Palace is situated in the Plaza Mayor de la Hispanidad, where the medieval fairs were held. It is thus named because it stands on the remains of the former royal palace in which Isabella I lived, dictated her will and died on 26 November 1504. The principal facade of the palace, where the English ambassadors first laid eyes on a three-year-old Katherine, faced the western corner of the Plaza Mayor, as seen in a panoramic sketch of the area made by Anton van den Wyngaerde in 1565. It covered much of the area today delineated by the following streets: Almirante, la de Cerradilla and la del Rey. Today, the Testamentary Palace is home to the museum of *Isabel la Católica* where visitors can learn more about the life of this remarkable woman and see the famous painting by Eduardo Rosales of Isabella dictating her will, recreated in one of the rooms. For opening times and other visitor information please visit http://www.palaciorealtestamentario.com.

Just a ten- to fifteen-minute walk from the main square, you'll find the reconstructed medieval fortress, *Castillo de la Mota*, which over the centuries has had many uses, including a royal archives, an arsenal and a prison of the state. Visit the tourism office in the Plaza Mayor to obtain a map of the local area.

For castle opening times and other visitor information please visit http://www.castillodelamota.es.

A short walk from the Plaza Mayor is the Museo de las Ferias, which houses artefacts found on the site of the lost palace, including fragments of Moorish art, tiling and plasterwork.

For opening times and other visitor information please visit http://www.museoferias.net/.

Alcazar of Seville, Andalusia

A city which looks up at the sun, so beautiful for its wealth, nobility and majesty, manners and courtesy; the port of and gateway to the Indies through which it can be said that the whole of Spain's sustenance enters twice a year.

Lope de Vega, *The Pilgrim in His Own Country*, 1604

According to Giles Tremlett, the sixteen Christmases Katherine spent in Spain were celebrated in thirteen different cities, including in Seville, situated on the banks of the Guadalquivir River. By the end of the fifteenth century, Seville was one of Castile's major ports, and rapidly growing in prestige and importance as a result of the discovery of the 'New World' in 1492. The bustling and cosmopolitan city was the European gateway to the Americas and home to many foreign merchants, traders and artists. In its royal fortress, or alcazar, Katherine spent the Christmas festivities of 1499, and almost certainly her fourteenth birthday as well. While the Catholic Monarchs put on a brave face in public, the grief of the past few years was beginning to seep through their regal facade: in October 1497, their son and heir, John, had died, possibly of tuberculosis, followed shortly by the death of his posthumous child at birth. The pain of losing their only son was still rugged and raw when their eldest daughter, Isabella, perished in August 1498, within hours of giving birth to her only son Miguel, on whose tiny shoulders now rested the hopes of his grandparents' kingdoms. Sadly, death had not yet delivered its final blow, and in the New Year tragedy would strike again (see entry for The Alhambra).

Despite the family's private grief, preparations for Katherine's wedding and upcoming voyage to England continued. On 20 December 1499, from Seville, Katherine ratified the act of marriage with Arthur, Prince of Wales, performed in her name by De Puebla 'in the chapel of the manor of Bewdley on the 19th of May 1499'. No doubt she hoped and prayed that Arthur would prove a more loyal and kind husband than her sister Joanna's husband, Philip the Handsome of Burgundy, who was fast becoming known for his cruel treatment of his young wife, and his philandering ways.

In the New Year, Isabella paid for two ounces of Florentine gold; eight ounces of black and white silk; a white hat; black velvet for two bonnets; and a black velvet cap for her two youngest daughters, Katherine and Maria, the heartache and loss of the past few years – and Queen Isabella's increasingly troubled and dark moods – reflected in the sombre palette. The once vibrant and happy court of Katherine's childhood was slowly becoming devoid of joy; however, the palaces where Katherine's life was unfurling remained as beautiful as ever.

Touring the Alcazar

The Royal Alcazar of Seville is a magnificent complex of courtyards and buildings in different architectural styles, from Mudejar to Gothic. Construction began in the thirteenth century, on the site of an Almohad palace. Alfonso X initiated the first works, but subsequent monarchs added to it, adapting and renovating the buildings over the centuries.

The main entrance to the alcazar today is via the *Puerta del Leon* or Lion's Gate. It's believed to have been built in the fourteenth century, when the Mudejar palace was constructed by order of Peter I of Castile, and takes its name from the nineteenth-century tilework, depicting a crowned lion rampant, seen above the entranceway. From here visitors proceed into the *Patio del Leon*, Lion's Courtyard.

The wall with three arches that separates this courtyard from the *Patio de la Monteria* (Courtyard of the Hunt) beyond was also built in the reign of Peter I, as was the magnificent Mudejar palace whose facade can be seen through the central arch.

To the left of the Lion's Courtyard is the *Sala de Justicia*, or Hall of Justice, built by Alfonso XI in the mid-fourteenth century. This beautiful room, with its octagonal coffered ceiling and intricate stuccowork depicting Castilian emblems, was the first example of Mudejar architecture in the palace and probably formed part of a series of rooms where Alfonso's successor, Peter I, may have resided until his new Mudejar palace was completed. The adjacent courtyard, *Patio del Yeso*, contains a pool and the only surviving section of the twelfth-century Almohad palace.

Returning through the Lion's Courtyard, and passing under the old wall, we are now standing in the alcazar's main courtyard, the Courtyard of the Hunt, which links all the palace buildings: the Mudejar Palace, the Gothic Palace and the House of Trade. When facing the Mudejar palace, on the right stands the *Casa de la Contratacion*, or House of Trade, an institution created by Katherine's parents in 1503 to regulate trade between Spain and the New World. The buildings have undergone many changes over the centuries, with the present facade dating to 1755. While exploring these rooms, keep an eye out for the sixteenth-century ceilings in the *Cuarto del Almirante* and the Chapter House, along with the outstanding sixteenth-century altarpiece in the latter room. One of the main highlights, though, for those of us following in Katherine's footsteps, is the Mudejar palace of Peter I, today home to the *Cuarto Real Alto*, the official residence of Their Majesties the King and Queen of Spain in Seville, and only accessible on a guided tour.

The Cuarto Real Alto or Upper Royal Apartments

These apartments have housed many important figures over the centuries, including Peter I, the Catholic Monarchs and their children, and Katherine's nephew, the Emperor Charles V. While the rooms have undergone many changes and extensions since Katherine and her family called the palace home, with a little imagination one can sweep away the modern interiors and furnishings and call forth images of a teenaged Katherine and her sister Maria on their last visit, excitedly discussing what the future had in store for them. Before long, the sisters would be separated; Maria would be sent to Portugal to marry her late sister's widow, Manuel I, and Katherine would venture to England to wed her young Tudor prince. Could she ever have imagined that, like her brother-in-law Manuel, she too would end up marrying her first spouse's sibling? Let's now briefly visit the rooms associated with Katherine's family on the upper floor of the palace.

The Vestibule

Built in the reign of Katherine's parents, this room once formed part of Queen Isabella's private apartments, and functioned as a reception room. The staircase that now connects the royal apartments on the first floor with the alcazar's main courtyard below was constructed in the sixteenth century, at which time this room became a vestibule. Note the heraldic emblems on the frieze beneath the coffered ceiling: *Tanto Monta* was Ferdinand II's personal emblem, and the coat of arms with the yoke and arrows represented the Catholic Monarchs.

The Ante-Oratory and Oratory of the Catholic Monarchs

The ante-oratory was built in the fifteenth century as a bedchamber for Isabella I. The small chapel, although constructed in the fifteenth century, was refurbished in the sixteenth. The beautiful altarpiece that dominates the space was made for Isabella in 1504. However, the queen never saw it finished as she died before its completion.

The Antecomedor and Comedor de Gala

These splendid rooms are still used for banquets and state events by the Spanish royal family today. It's believed their construction dates back to the birth of Katherine's older brother, Prince John, at the alcazar in 1478.

The King's Private Apartments

In the south wing of the palace once stood the private apartments of Ferdinand II, today occupied by the *Comedor de Ayudantes, Antecomedor de Familia* and *Comedor de Familia.* These rooms were modified during the reign of Charles V, as evidenced by the Renaissance elements and imperial emblems that adorn the plaster friezes.

The Mirador of the Catholic Monarchs

This room was built in the reign of the Catholic Monarchs and on one side overlooks the main courtyard of the Mudejar palace, the *Patio de las Doncellas*, or Courtyard of the Damsels, and on the other the charming gardens. Like much of this wing, Charles V had the rooms redesigned for his personal use.

The Mudejar Palace

The ground floor of the Mudejar palace can be explored at your leisure. It is a space that Katherine would have known well, and one of the finest examples of Mudejar architecture and decoration in Spain. This distinctive style, unique to the Iberian Peninsula, represents a fusion of two artistic traditions, Christian and Islamic, characterised by an inventive use of brick, ceramic, wood and plaster. Peter I ordered the construction of the palace in the fourteenth century, calling upon the best master builders and architects from Granada and Toledo to bring his plan to fruition. Christian builders worked side by side with local Mudejar artists, and the result is a striking feast for the senses.

Wandering through the various rooms and courtyards of the palace today, you are struck by the airiness and brightness of the rooms, afforded by the high ceilings, large doorways and arrangement around an open courtyard. Notable too is the emphasis placed on water throughout the palace, which is soothing and refreshing, not to mention the wonderful optical effect created by the intricate stuccowork reflected in the still waters.

Other highlights include the *Sala del Principe*, Room of the Prince, said to be where Isabella I gave birth to Prince John on 30 June 1478; the *Sala Del Los Reyes Catolicos*, home to a superb coffered ceiling that dates from the reign of Katherine's parents, and again features the monarchs' emblems – the yoke, arrows and the motto *Tanto Monta*; the *Salas de los Infantes*, where it's possible Katherine and her siblings stayed during their visits; and finally, perhaps the most spectacular room of the Mudejar palace, the *Salon de Embajadores* (the Ambassadors' Hall).

The Ambassadors' Hall

This magnificent room, with its golden dome and breathtaking decoration, was the main hall of the Mudejar palace, and hence a room with which Katherine would have been familiar. It was used as the main reception room, where important guests were received, and where large court gatherings were held. The density and splendour of the decoration must have dazzled any foreign visitor and continues to do so to this day. Encircling the entire room are sixteenth-century portraits of the Spanish monarchs from Chindasuinth to Philip III, above which are a series of portraits of unknown ladies, who are thought to have been courtiers.

Beyond the hall, is the *Salon del Techo de Carlos V*, Charles V Ceiling Room, renowned for its beautiful sixteenth-century panelled ceiling.

The Gothic Palace

In the thirteenth century, Alfonso X constructed the Gothic Palace on the site of the old Almohad palace. These rooms, known from the sixteenth century onwards as the rooms of Charles V, have been much remodelled over the centuries. They lost much of their medieval appearance when they were redesigned after being damaged in an earthquake in 1755.

A Touch of Paradise

A visit to the alcazar is not complete without a wander through the enchanting and diverse gardens, where beautiful courtyards, pools and fountains abound. The gentle murmur of the fountains is background music in this calming space where visitors can sit and enjoy the peace and tranquillity. The seemingly endless gardens, bursting with aromatic plants, blooming flowers, palms and orange trees, were designed and planted at different times. Some features, like the Pavilion of Charles V and the Prince's Garden, dating back to the sixteenth century.

After spending time exploring the glorious Mudejar palace and the paradisiacal gardens, one can only conclude that winters in England must have been particularly hard for Katherine, especially her first English winter, spent at Ludlow Castle in the Welsh Marches. As she sat by the roaring fire, desperately seeking warmth, did she lose herself in thoughts of the magical palaces of her homeland, and wrap the sunny memories of her childhood around herself like a blanket against the dampness of the stone walls and icy Shropshire winds?

Visitor Information
Seville's alcazar was without doubt one of the highlights of our travels through Spain; no words can justly describe its beauty. Be sure to book a place on the guided tour of the Upper Royal Apartments first thing in the morning, as these fill up very quickly, and if you don't fancy waiting in long queues, book your tickets to the alcazar online prior to your visit.

Remember to allow enough time to visit Seville's immense cathedral, said to be the third-largest in Europe and home to the tomb of Christopher Columbus, which may or may not contain the famous explorer's remains – but that's another story! If you're feeling energetic, why not climb to the top of the Giralda Tower, originally built in the twelfth century, for a bird's-eye view of the city?

With so much to see and do, we recommend downloading a tourist guide from http://www.visitasevilla.es/ or visiting the tourist information office in the Plaza del Triunfo on arrival.

For opening times and other visitor information please visit the Alcazar of Seville's website at http://www.alcazarsevilla.org/.

For cathedral opening times and other visitor information visit http://www.catedraldesevilla.es/.

Alcazar of Cordoba, Andalusia

Cordoba is the Bride of all Al Andaluz. To her belong all the beauty and ornaments that delight the eye or dazzle the sight. Her long line of Sultans form her crown of glory; her necklace is strung with the pearls which her poets have gathered from the ocean of language; her dress is of the banners of learning, well-knit together by her men of science; and the masters of every art and industry are the hem of her garments.
A description of Cordoba in the tenth century by an unknown Arab writer, quoted in Stanley Lane-Poole's *The Moors in Spain*, 1888

The court of Isabella and Ferdinand was constantly on the move; as a result, Katherine's childhood was spent travelling from one end of the country to the other, by horse or mule. Just months after Katherine's birth, the royal family was in Cordoba, situated on the banks of the Guadalquivir River. The former capital of Islamic Spain, Cordoba was a famed centre of learning and at its zenith was praised for its architectural beauty, paved streets and cleanliness. Queen Isabella and family arrived first, followed by King Ferdinand a short time after. The royal chronicler, Hernando del Pulgar, recorded that Ferdinand came to the city under a cloth of gold, and was met by his son 'Don Juan' and other gentlemen of the court. They travelled in procession to the *Iglesia Mayor*, the principal church, where the Bishop of Cordoba blessed Ferdinand. The king and his entourage then returned in procession to the palace, where Queen Isabella, their eldest daughter Isabel and all the ladies of the court were sumptuously dressed and waiting to greet him.

This family reunion took place at the Royal Palace of Cordoba, today known as the Alcazar of Cordoba. While previous kings and queens had made it their temporary home, The Catholic Monarchs were the first to spend long periods of time there and directed the last military operations of the Reconquest from within its sturdy walls.

The alcazar was constructed in the early fourteenth century by King Alfonso XI on the site of a former Caliphal fortress, itself built on the foundations of a Roman structure. Alfonso's new fortified palace was built on a square plan, consisting of four main towers at the corners and two intermediate towers. To the west of the enclosed area stood the palace's vegetable gardens, irrigated by the Albolafia watermill, dismantled in the fifteenth century because Isabella disliked the noise it made.

Towards the end of the fifteenth century the alcazar became the seat of the Court of the Holy Inquisition, necessitating significant changes to its layout, including the repurposing of a number of chambers as cells, the destruction of corridors to make way for courtyards and the adaptation of halls into living spaces for the inquisitors.

In 1821 it became the city's public prison, which led to further alterations, before finally being declared a Historic-Artistic Monument in 1931.

The Alcazar Today

Despite its many alterations, and a twentieth-century restoration, the alcazar remains one of the most important and popular tourist attractions in Cordoba, renowned for its delightful gardens and fascinating array of Roman artefacts, including a collection of mosaics and a beautifully carved sarcophagus.

Remnants of the original fourteenth-century fortress can be found in the area enclosed by the four corner towers, of which only the Tower of Lions, which forms the principal entrance to the alcazar in the north-west corner, and the Tower of Homage, in the north-east corner, date from King Alfonso's reign, and are open to the public. The latter, refurbished in the fifteenth century, was where royal audiences and other court ceremonies were held during the reign of Katherine's parents.

The Tower of the Inquisition, in the south-west corner, dates from the reign of Henry IV of Castile, Isabella's predecessor, while the Tower of the Candle, also known as The Tower of the Doves, which once stood in the south-east corner, was demolished in 1856 and replaced with the small rectangular concrete tower we see today.

Katherine would have seen the Moorish-style baths, built by King Alfonso XI for his beloved long-term mistress Eleanor, although it's believed that they were not in use in the fifteenth century. The rectangular Mudejar Courtyard, with a fountain at its centre and two small ponds at its shorter ends, is the only area in the alcazar that retains its original layout. For a breathtaking view of the alcazar and its enchanting gardens, and a panoramic view over Cordoba's old quarter, be sure to walk the north wall connecting the Tower of Homage with the Tower of Lions.

The alcazar's splendid terraced gardens occupy the site of the former vegetable gardens and orchards of the palace and were designed in the twentieth century. Visitors can wander the tree-lined paths at their leisure, and take in the outstanding beauty of the pools and fountains, interspersed with fruit trees, cypresses and palms. The gardens are also home to several sculptures, including one representing the meeting between Isabella, Ferdinand and Christopher Columbus, which took place in 1486.

In this tranquil and quiet space, it's easy to imagine a young Katherine playing with her sister Maria under the watchful eye of their maid, their growing retinue of servants and ladies-in-waiting trailing behind. While the centuries may separate us, the soothing sound of tinkling water falling from the fountains and the scent of oranges and lemons, both so familiar to Katherine, connect us.

Visitor Information

We recommend parking on the south side of the Guadalquivir River, where there is ample parking, and walking over the Roman bridge, which has stood on this site for more than two thousand years! It has, of course, undergone many reconstructions since it was first built, and probably reflects little of its Roman roots. Interestingly, until the early 1950s it was the only way to cross the river at Cordoba, and so you can be certain that Katherine and her family used it when arriving from the south. Pause for a moment on the bridge and compare the view we see today with that immortalised by Anton van den Wyngaerde in his drawing of Cordoba made in 1567. The fortified gate, seen in the foreground, is Calahorra Tower, which to this day stands sentinel over the ancient city, and presently houses the Al-Andalus Living Museum.

Once over the bridge, pick up a tourist map from the visitor centre, located in the Plaza del Triunfo, to help you navigate the labyrinth of charming cobbled streets. Head back towards the river and turn right towards the alcazar, keeping an eye out for the *Molino de Albolafia*, or Albolafia watermill, that so annoyed Queen Isabella!

Do not dream of leaving Cordoba without visiting the extraordinary 'Mosque-Cathedral', a symbol of the many religious changes the city has undergone over the centuries, and a building sure to leave you utterly speechless! It is the same *Iglesia Mayor* that Ferdinand visited on arrival to Cordoba in 1486, and can be clearly seen in Wyngaerde's drawing, just beyond the bridge and marked by the letter 'A'.

For information on how to reach the Alcazar of Cordoba and its opening hours, visit their website at www.alcazardelosreyescristianos.cordoba.es.

For more information about visiting the Calahorra Tower, visit their website at http://www.torrecalahorra.es/.

For opening times and other visitor information for *La Catedral de Cordoba* (Mosque-Cathedral), visit http://www.catedraldecordoba.es/.

Alhambra, Andalusia

I do not believe there is the like in all Europe ... everything was made in different ways so splendidly, so brilliantly and so elegantly that you would think it was Paradise.

From the diaries of Hieronymus Munzer, who visited the Alhambra in 1494

Perched high above the city of Granada, and set against the backdrop of the Sierra Nevada, the Alhambra must be seen to be believed. It is a sprawling and breathtaking palace and fortress complex built by the Nasrid kings in the thirteenth century and added to in later centuries by subsequent rulers, including Charles V. With the exception of a couple of sojourns in Seville, the last two years of Katherine's life in Spain were spent within the Alhambra's rust-coloured walls, from where she penned love letters to her betrothed, Prince Arthur.

The Surrender

After spending the Christmas festivities of 1499 in Seville, Katherine's family returned to Granada, the city they'd conquered eight years earlier. The formal surrender had taken place on 2 January 1492, in a staged ceremony that saw Boabdil, the last Nasrid ruler of Granada, hand over the keys to the opulent city to the triumphant Catholic Monarchs. While it has been postulated that a six-year-old Katherine may have been by her parents' side on this momentous occasion, Isabella I's biographer, Peggy K. Liss, asserts that it was in fact Prince John and 'an unspecified *Infanta* – either Isabel or Juana' that witnessed the surrender. With the banners of Castile and Leon flying high above the Tower of Comares, a jubilant Isabella and Ferdinand entered the Alhambra for the first time. They had often gazed at it from afar and marvelled at its magnificence, and now it was theirs. After a short stay, the court had resumed its travels, not returning to Granada until that summer of 1499.

A 'Third Stab of Pain'

Not long after the court had settled back at the Alhambra, tragedy struck Katherine's family once again. After the death of Isabella and Ferdinand's eldest daughter, Isabella, in August 1498, her infant son, Miguel, now heir to the crowns of Castile, Aragon and Portugal, was raised at the court of his maternal grandparents, alongside his teenaged aunts Katherine and Maria. Isabella and Ferdinand pinned their hopes for a united Iberia on this little boy. However, as they well knew, the first couple of years of life were particularly dangerous.

It must have been a heartbreaking scene when, on 19 July 1500, Miguel succumbed to illness, dying in the arms of his grandmother. The chronicler Andres Bernaldez wrote that 'it was the third stab of pain to pierce the queen's soul', and it was one that she found difficult to bear. The equanimous queen fell into a dark abyss. From this moment, as Bernaldez noted, she 'lived without joy'.

We don't know for certain how Katherine reacted to her nephew's death, but it's not too much of a stretch to imagine that she too was suffering. She'd lived with Miguel since her sister's passing and probably loved him like a brother, and now he was gone. Katherine and Maria must have been a great comfort to each other, and to their mother, during this trying time, but even this was destined to end.

In October 1500, Maria left her family to travel to Portugal to wed little Miguel's father, Manuel I. Only Katherine now remained with her parents at court, and they were in no rush to say goodbye.

Postponement of the Coming of the Princess of Wales

Henry VII had been expecting Katherine to arrive in England in September 1500, around the time of her future husband's fourteenth birthday. However, in April of that year the Spanish diplomat Don Pedro de Ayala wrote to the Catholic Monarchs to inform them that he'd received their letter telling him that Katherine's departure would be delayed because a 'revolution of the Moors' had broken out and needed to be supressed before Katherine could depart.

In June 1500, they were still promising Henry that the Princess of Wales' departure was imminent, to which the Spanish ambassador reported that 'the king and the whole nation are delighted at this news'. This missive included an interesting note about the ladies who should accompany Katherine to England: 'The King and Queen wish very much that the ladies who are to accompany the Princess of Wales should be of gentle birth and beautiful, or at least that none of them should be ugly.'

By late June, news reached Spain that some English doubted whether Katherine would ever come to England, to which the Catholic Monarchs responded, 'tell the king of England that we would not in any circumstances, or for any cause, dissolve the union which we have concluded with him', and assured him in a letter written from Granada on 25 July 1500 that 'we are already preparing the fleet and the other things necessary for the departure of the Princess'. However, by August it had been agreed that Katherine would remain in Spain until the 'Feast of St John next [24 June 1501] as her voyage during the stormy season would be dangerous'.

Preparations and Farewells

When the king and queen had run out of excuses, there was nothing left to do but prepare for their youngest daughter's departure. In late March 1501, from her palace in the Alhambra, Isabella ordered white, black and purple satin to adorn a number of Katherine's gowns. She also paid to have a black velvet robe made and fifteen pairs of slippers. With Katherine's wardrobe refreshed, it was time to say goodbye.

Katherine drank in the sights and sounds of the Alhambra one final time, etching the memories onto her heart, before riding out into the spring morning. Her parents accompanied her as far as Santa Fe, like they'd done with Maria, and there they said their emotional goodbyes. How often did Katherine think of this moment over the course of her life? Did there come a point when she could no longer recall her parents' faces, so worn and hardened by grief and the business of kingship? With Katherine's departure, what spark remained in Isabella's eyes vanished. She would never see her beautiful daughter again.

Granada in 1494

The detailed travel diaries of Hieronymus Munzer, a German who travelled through Spain and Portugal in 1494–5, offer us a rare glimpse into life in Granada at this time, and a first-hand account of the Alhambra, a walled city of palaces, parks and gardens that in its heyday covered an approximate area of 104,000 square metres, the equivalent of about twenty football fields! The city, which was completely separate to Granada, was protected by around thirty towers and completely encircled by a defensive wall. According to Rafael Hierro Calleja, author of *Granada and the Alhambra*, before the arrival of the Catholic Monarchs, it boasted

> at least seven palaces, residences for completely diverse social categories, all kinds of offices, the royal mint, private and public mosques, workshops of different trades, shops, public and private baths, a royal cemetery and a fortress with barracks and prisons.

After Boabdil surrendered the city in 1492, the royal family occupied the Alcazaba, the original thirteenth-century fortress, and the Royal Nasrid residence, a complex of three independent palaces that they renamed the Royal Residence of the Alhambra, and divided up the rest of the vast complex among their court. The new rulers of Granada were so delighted with the beauty of the palace complex that they made only small modifications, preserving the buildings almost in their entirety. Over the next fifty or so years, a number of churches, convents and monasteries were built in Granada to reassert Christian authority, including the still extant Monastery of St Isabella the Royal, Monastery of St Jerome and the Royal Chapel. However, it wasn't until 1581 that building commenced on the Church of Santa Maria, constructed on the site of the Alhambra's great mosque.

For a few years after the Reconquest, Boabdil's former subjects were permitted to keep their way of life and worship freely, in exchange for paying a tax. Munzer recalled that on arrival to the city in October 1494, he passed 'countless Saracens' and noted that there were over two hundred mosques in the city, albeit some only small prayer rooms. The call to prayer echoed throughout the city: 'That night seemed to last 36 hours till dawn, so great was the clamour from the towers of the mosques that it is difficult to believe,' he said.

However, as time went on, the Catholic Monarchs adopted a less moderate position, until eventually the Muslim residents of Granada were forced to convert to Catholicism or be imprisoned or expelled. These new converts, known as *Moriscos*, were closely watched, as it soon became obvious to the Christian authorities that their conversion had been superficial, and in secret they continued practicing Islam. This stricter policy led to much discord and some open rebellions.

The sturdy walls of the Alhambra would have sheltered Katherine from the worst of the religious turmoil. She would have had little need to venture out of the enclosed city, because, as Munzer relates, within lay a paradise.

> There [at the Alhambra] we saw many courtyards paved with white marble, beautiful gardens ornamented with lemons and myrtles, with pools and paved with marble round the sides, and four other halls full of weapons, lances, catapults, swords, breastplates, arrows and other things, fine bedrooms and assembly rooms. In every courtyard so many wide, white marble vases, bigger than Saint Augustine's vase, and all full of fresh water; a marvellous vaulted bath with couches outside; so many tall marble columns that there are none more so;

in the middle of one courtyard a huge marble vase resting on 13 carved white marble lions, and water flowed out of each lion's mouth as if from a canal … There is so much beauty in all the courtyards, with artfully made water channels … in every place, that nothing could be finer.

Like those who had come before him and many that would follow him, Munzer had fallen under the Alhambra's enticing spell, 'I do not believe there is the like in all Europe,' he wrote, 'everything was made in different ways so splendidly, so brilliantly and so elegantly that you would think it was paradise.'

The Alhambra Today

The palace and fortress complex we see today is considerably smaller than the one Katherine, and the German traveller, experienced in the late fifteenth century. Rafael Hierro Calleja states that only about a third of its buildings and palaces survive. These include the Alcazaba, the Nasrid Palaces, the Partal and the Towers, the Palace of Charles V and the Generalife. It is not our intention to look at each of these monuments in detail, as that is beyond the scope of this book. However, let us briefly visit each, making note of the highlights.

The Alcazaba

This was the first of the Alhambra's constructions, built in the thirteenth century by Al-Ahmar, the first of the Nasrid kings. The glorious view from the top of the Watch Tower is not to be missed. At 27 metres high, it's the tallest of all the towers in the Alcazaba, and offers uninterrupted views of Granada, the Sierra Nevada and Albaycin, the city's old Muslim quarter.

The Nasrid Palaces

Katherine's family's apartments were in the Nasrid Palaces, a complex of three independent palaces – the Mexuar, Comares Palace and the Palace of the Lions – all of which are of unsurpassed beauty and particularly magical when toured at twilight; when bathed in a golden light, they appear almost ethereal.

During the reign of the Nasrid kings, each palace had its own purpose. The Mexuar, the oldest of the three palaces, was used for public audiences and the administering of justice; the Comares was the king's official residence; and the Palace of the Lions was the inner sanctum, the royal family's private residence, where only those closest to the king could enter. The Catholic Monarchs joined the three buildings, using them as one palace.

While some of the buildings may look quite simple from the outside, once inside you are left speechless by how profusely and beautifully decorated the rooms are. Sometimes there is not a single space left unadorned, like in the Ambassador's Hall in the Comares Tower. Notable also throughout the Alhambra, and in the aforementioned room, are the writings in plasterwork that decorate many of the walls. Calligraphy was a very important decorative motif in Islamic civilisation, Rafael Hierro Calleja explains:

Calligraphy in Islamic buildings not only fulfils a decorative function, but also an iconographic one, comparable to and substituting the function images have in the Christian world. It serves to preserve and manifest the word of God ... Most of the contents of the calligraphy decorating the walls of the buildings are passages from the Koran.

Another striking feature of the Nasrid Palaces is the way the light filters in through the large windows, positioned low, like doorways. Since it was customary for the Moors to recline on cushions on the floor, the Alhambra was designed to be appreciated from the floor.

The Courtyard of the Lions, with its central fountain consisting of twelve marble lions spouting jets of water, and the splendid Hall of the Kings, where the Catholic Monarchs first heard Mass after conquering Granada, are must-sees. However, one of the most spectacular of all the rooms is the Hall of the Two Sisters, with its breathtaking *muqarnas*, or honeycomb cupola, and poetry adorning its walls, and the adjoining Lindaraja Mirador that once looked out over the city of Granada.

The Nasrid Palaces are the jewel of the Alhambra, a masterpiece of Islamic architecture so exquisitely beautiful they defy imagination. Its golden rooms, majestic outlook and splendid courtyards, dappled in light and shadow, are not easily forgotten.

The Partal and the Towers

Originally this part of the Alhambra was home to a number of splendid houses and beautiful palaces, where the court's most distinguished families lived. Unfortunately, time has robbed us of most of these buildings. However, part of the Partal Palace survives, along with a small oratory and the ruins of a second palace, that of Yusuf III.

The Partal Palace, also known as the Tower of the Ladies, is the oldest of the Alhambra's palaces, dating from the first decade of the fourteenth century. Its most outstanding architectural feature is its magnificent portico, after which it is named (*partal* in Arabic meaning portico).

From the ruins of the Palace of Yusuf III, visitors can access the Promenade of the Towers, a route which follows the main wall of the Alhambra from the Partal to the Generalife, passing by many towers along the way, including the Tower of the Captive Lady and the Tower of the Princesses, which are among the most beautifully and richly decorated in the Alhambra.

The Palace of Charles V

Work on this Renaissance palace started in 1527 and thus post-dates Katherine's time at the Alhambra. It was financed with money collected from the *Moriscos* and was unfinished at the time of the emperor's death in 1558.

The enormous open-air courtyard, circular in the Roman style, is its most striking feature and since the late nineteenth century has played host to the symphony concerts of Granada's International Festival of Music and Dance, which takes place yearly in late June and early July. The palace also houses two important museums: the Alhambra Museum, home to a wonderful collection of Nasrid and Spanish-Moorish art and artefacts, and the Fine Arts Museum.

The Generalife

The garden and palace complex above the Alhambra was used as a place of retreat and rest by the Nasrid kings and contained decorative gardens, fruit and vegetable patches, water features and other garden structures. In the surrounding meadows, animals grazed and the sultan hunted. There were also orchards and cultivated fields aplenty. It was totally independent of the Alhambra and originally covered a much larger area than it does today. The Venetian ambassador to the Imperial court, Andrea Navagero, visited the Alhambra in 1526, and in a letter to his friend recorded his impressions of the Generalife:

> You leave this palace from a secret door in the back, outside the surrounding wall, and you enter a beautiful garden of a palace higher on the mountain; [the palace is] called the Generalife. The Generalife is not a very big palace, but it is very well built and beautiful, and the splendor of its gardens and waters makes it the most beautiful thing that I have seen in Spain; it has more spaces, all with abundant water, but one has water flowing in a channel, and is full of beautiful myrtles, and orange trees in the middle, in which there is a loggia ... the water flows everywhere in the palace, and also in the rooms when you want, in a few of which it would be very pleasant to stay in the summer.

Today you are free to explore the palace, courtyards and gardens that occupy the site of the recreational estate that so impressed Navagero. It's located high up on the Cerro del Sol (Sun Hill) overlooking the Alhambra and Granada, and while the palace has been much reformed in the last five hundred years it retains much of its beauty and charm. The abundance of water features, framed by hedges and flowers, and large variety of trees and aromatic plants, including magnolias, fir trees, cypresses, myrtles, jasmines and rose bushes, make this a real treat for the senses. Don't even bother putting your camera away!

Navagero summed up his visit like this: 'This place lacks nothing pleasing or beautiful, except someone to appreciate it, and enjoy it, living in quiet and tranquil pursuit of studies.' Katherine had been that someone. After years spent criss-crossing the country from one end to the other, the Alhambra became her home. Later, when she finally fulfilled her destiny of becoming England's queen, she adopted the pomegranate as her personal heraldic symbol. The fruit, with its abundance of reddish seeds, had long been a symbol of fertility, but it was also the symbol of Granada. It was a city that Katherine carried with her in her heart until her dying day.

Visitor Information

As we toured the site and explored the extensive grounds, with its fragrant gardens, water features and glorious courtyards, yet again, it dawned on us just how difficult those first few years in England must have been for the young Spanish princess. She spent the last months of her Spanish life at the sunlit Alhambra, intentionally designed to reflect paradise, and the first few months of her married life to Arthur at Ludlow Castle in Shropshire, beneath a cold and leaden sky. Having visited both, we cannot think of two more contrasting places.

When planning your visit, be sure to pre-book tickets online well ahead of your visit and don't forget to book a time slot to tour the Nasrid Palaces, as these fill up quickly. Also, remember to arrive ten to fifteen minutes before your allocated time slot.

If time permits, we recommend enjoying a drink in the courtyard of the Parador Hotel, the former Convent of San Francisco, where Isabella I and Ferdinand II were buried before being moved to the Royal Chapel, where they now lie.

Another wonderful place to visit is the Royal Chapel of Granada, close to the Plaza de Isabel la Catolica in Granada – not only is it the final resting place of Katherine's parents, but there also rest her nephew Miguel and sister Joanna. Do not miss the Sacristy Museum, which houses Isabella's crown and sceptre and Ferdinand's sword, along with some other of their personal belongings.

To book tickets to the Alhambra and for other visitor information, please visit the Alhambra's website at http://www.alhambra-patronato.es/.

For information on visiting the Royal Chapel in Granada, visit http://www. capillarealgranada.com.

For information on the Parador Granada, please visit http://www.paradores-spain.com/spain/pgranada.html.

Santiago de Compostela Cathedral, Galicia

Her indisposition and the absence of the King are the reasons why the departure of the Princess of Wales has been hitherto delayed. But as soon as the King arrives, the Princess will start by way of Santiago in Galicia, in order to embark at Coruña.
'By the Queen [Isabella]. To Doctor De Puebla,
her ambassador in England, and of her Council', 7 May 1501

Fifteen-year-old Katherine and her parents stood together under a blazing Castilian sun. While they'd always known this moment would come, it didn't make the pain any easier to bear. On the morning of 21 May 1501, Isabella embraced her auburn-haired daughter one final time, and breathed in the familiar scent of her last-born, who was poised to begin her new life in England. The previous five years had brought with it much heartache for the Catholic Monarchs: the death of their only son and heir, John, and that of their eldest daughter Isabella and their grandson, Miguel, along with the departure of their daughters Joanna and Maria to Flanders and Portugal. And now, it was time to say goodbye once again.

Isabella and Ferdinand had ridden with Katherine from Granada to Santa Fe but would not accompany her any further, because, as the queen explained, Katherine was already late and would 'travel quicker if left alone'. The losses and suffering of recent years had obviously taken their toll on the fifty-year-old queen, who now lacked the energy to traipse across the country in the punishing heat. With grief etched across their faces, the Spanish monarchs waved the small party off. Katherine would never see her parents again.

The entourage of around sixty people began the arduous journey across the sun-drenched country, stopping in various villages and cities along the way, including Santiago de Compostela, before arriving at the port town of La Coruña in north-western Spain. There, Katherine would board the ship that would take her to England, to begin her new life as Prince Arthur Tudor's wife, a role she had been waiting to fulfil since she was three years old. The Catholic Monarchs had placed their youngest daughter in the care of the formidable Doña Elvira Manuel, who together with her husband, Pedro Manrique, held the leading positions in Katherine's new household.

The Journey of the Princess of Wales

For several months now, Queen Isabella had been promising the English king that his new daughter-in-law would be leaving Spain 'as soon as possible', however, Katherine's departure had been delayed time and time again. If it wasn't illness preventing the bride-to-be from travelling, it was affairs of state; in April 1501, a rebellion had broken out in the Sierra de Ronda, calling for Ferdinand's intervention to 'subdue the rebels ... the last converts to Christianity', and Katherine could not depart until her father had returned. When the king did finally arrive back at the Alhambra, the Spanish queen reported that the princess had fallen ill with a 'low fever', and would need time to recover her strength. These may have been legitimate reasons to keep the already anxious English waiting, or perhaps the Catholic Monarchs were simply making excuses, in order to keep their youngest daughter by their side for a little while longer. Regardless, the parting was inevitable.

The trip across land was expected to take a couple of months at the most, Isabella and Ferdinand confident that their daughter would reach the north coast of Spain by mid-July. Instead, the journey took a lengthy and exhausting three months, the intense Spanish heat forcing Katherine's party to make regular stops. On 5 July, Katherine arrived at the monastery in Guadalupe, where the young princess rested and paid homage at the shrine of the Virgin of Guadalupe, home to a Black Madonna, a statue said to have been crafted by Saint Luke the Evangelist and given by Pope Gregory I to Saint Leander, Bishop of Seville in the late sixth century. Following the Moorish conquest in around 712, the statue, which is still extant, was hidden and forgotten for hundreds of years, until it was supposedly rediscovered by a shepherd and priests in the fourteenth century, from which time a chapel built on the site of the discovery became an important pilgrimage destination.

Staying at inns and villages along the way, Katherine's entourage continued its slow progress northward, finally arriving in Santiago de Compostela sometime in late July or early August 1501. Earlier that year, Isabella had written to De Puebla, the Spanish ambassador in London, confirming that Katherine would sail from La Coruña, as this was the shortest passage from Spain to England, and, 'where, moreover, the Princess and all her companions can obtain the indulgence of the jubilee'.

Santiago and Its Cathedral

In the ninth century, King Alfonso II built a small church in Santiago de Compostela, on the site of the supposed burial of St James, one of the twelve apostles of Jesus. Pilgrims began to flock to the site in their hundreds and so a larger church was built and consecrated in 899. The city was invaded and sacked in 997, before being completely rebuilt in the eleventh and twelfth centuries. On 2 April 1211, Bishop Pedro Muniz, with King Alfonso IX, consecrated the Romanesque cathedral. The new city included defensive walls, an archbishop's palace, several churches and the impressive cathedral that was expanded and embellished over the centuries.

To cater for the growing numbers of pilgrims who descended on Santiago, many convent hospices sprang up on the outskirts of the city, and as the population grew, an urban fabric was formed around the cathedral.

The Story of Katherine and the Botafumeiro

As 1501 was a jubilee year, Katherine – and all other pilgrims arriving at the cathedral – gained a plenary indulgence. To obtain the jubilee they would have needed to follow the three traditions: visit the cathedral where the mortal remains of St James the Apostle were reputedly buried; pray in the cathedral and attend Holy Mass; and receive the sacraments of penance and communion. Local tradition tells us that during Katherine's visit to the cathedral, the *botafumeiro*, an enormous censer hung from the ceiling at the crossing, originally used to dispel the bad odours that flooded the cathedral when large crowds of pilgrims gathered there, came flying off as it was being swung and flew out of one of the cathedral's windows! The story is mentioned in Antonio Lopez Ferreiro's *Historia de la Santa A. M. Iglesia de Santiago de Compostela*, published in 1898. The author states that the source of the story is an 'ancient document' found in the Colombina Library of Seville by José Villaamil y Castro, in the nineteenth century, and published for the first time in volume 4 of *Galicia Diplomatica* (1882–93).

Unfortunately, we have been unable to locate this 'ancient document' and so must view the tale with a dose of scepticism. Furthermore, the event is often cited as having taken place on St James's Day in 1499, when Katherine and her family were staying at the Alhambra in Granada, around 1,000 kilometres away.

If this did indeed did take place during Katherine's visit in 1501, then one can only imagine that all present would have seen it as a bad omen. Storm clouds were indeed gathering around Katherine, and heartache and hardship loomed.

On 25 August 1501, Katherine boarded a ship at La Coruña bound for England, but after a week, a violent storm forced the vessel to return to Spain, landing in Laredo on 2 September. There they sought refuge for three weeks while the ship was repaired, before finally setting sail once more. On 27 September 1501, as daylight faded, a nervous Katherine caught her final glimpse of her beloved Spain. She would carry memories of her homeland with her for the rest of her life but would only ever see it again in her dreams.

Visitor Information

Santiago remains one of the most important centres of pilgrimage in the world and each year welcomes millions of visitors who come from around the globe to admire its magnificent cathedral and explore the city's rich tapestry of historic sites, including convents, monasteries, churches, *pazos* (great Galician houses) and museums. Many of those who descend on this beautiful city have walked the Camino de Santiago, one of a number of pilgrimage routes with starting points all over Europe, to the tomb of St James. A Pilgrim's Mass takes place at noon each day, after which visitors can ascend the steps beside the altar to embrace a thirteenth-century sculpture of St James. Did Katherine do the same during her visit in 1501? Perhaps.

The vast cathedral occupies an area of around 8,000 square metres and combines various architectural styles: Gothic, Renaissance, baroque and neoclassical. It's fair to say that much of the exterior of the cathedral would be unrecognisable to Katherine today, as it has undergone significant remodelling over the years. However, the Platerias Facade is the church's oldest, and most accurately reflects the Romanesque church that Katherine would have seen.

Once inside the cathedral, keep an eye out for the famous *botafumeiro*. If you're lucky, you may see one of two giant censers in action. The oldest, made in 1851 of silver-plated brass, is 160 centimetres high and weighs up to 100 kilograms when filled with incense and coal. It can reach speeds of up to 68 kilometres per hour and requires eight people to operate it.

Make your way to the Portico of Glory, one of the most striking features of the cathedral and one that Katherine would have seen and admired. This amazing work of art took twenty years to complete and is considered one of the finest examples of medieval sculpture in the world.

Before exploring the rest of the cathedral, we recommend you request an audio guide from the visitors reception centre near the Portico of Glory, which will guide you through the interior of the cathedral and the different rooms of the museum's permanent collection. Be sure to visit the Chapel of La Corticela, originally a Benedictine church, demolished and rebuilt in the thirteenth century, since when it has formed part of the fabric of the cathedral. This is a lovely space and offers visitors a real sense of what the original Romanesque church would have been like.

We recommend purchasing a combined cathedral/museum ticket, which gives you access to the cathedral, the museum's permanent collection, and entry into the Palace of Gelmirez, which adjoins the cathedral in the north. Constructed by Diego Gelmirez, the first Archbishop of Santiago de Compostela, in the twelfth century, it once formed part of a larger archbishop's palace, where it's possible Katherine and her entourage stayed during their visit in 1501. Today, it houses temporary exhibitions.

You may also like to visit the nearby Museo das Peregrinacións e de Santiago that, among other things, houses a scale model of the cathedral and a model of what the city of Santiago would have looked like in the Middle Ages.

For cathedral opening times and other visitor information, including details of when the *botafumeiro* will be in use, visit http://www.catedraldesantiago.es/en.

For museum opening times and other visitor information visit http://museoperegrinacions.xunta.gal.

Ludlow Castle, Shropshire

The town of Ludlow is very propre, welle walled and gated, and standeth every way eminent from a Botom. In the side of the Town, as a Peace of the Enclosing of the Walle, is a fair Castel.

John Leland, *Leland's Itinerary*

A Brief History of the Castle at Ludlow

In January 1502, teenage newlyweds Prince Arthur Tudor and Katherine of Aragon arrived at Ludlow Castle in Shropshire, on the Welsh borders. Perched on a rocky promontory overlooking the River Teme, the ancient fortress must have appeared both imposing and intimidating to a foreign princess more accustomed to the pretty palaces and sunny, orange-scented courtyards of home.

Originally built in Norman times by the de Lacy family, the castle became royal property in 1461, when Arthur's maternal grandfather, Edward IV, ascended the throne. Edward's young son and heir had been sent to live at Ludlow, away from the foul air and machinations of London, with a council of nobles and gentlemen formed to rule on his behalf. What began as the Prince's Council later became known as the Council of the Marches, and from its inception gradually assumed responsibility for the government of Wales and the border counties. From around the age of seven, Arthur too had resided at the castle at Ludlow with his council, where his tutors and advisors worked to prepare him for kingship. Now, he would return with his wife to, as one chronicler noted, 'keep liberal hospitality and to minister to the rude Welshman indifferent justice' and continue his schooling in the art of government.

Honeymoon and Heartbreak at Ludlow

The royal couple departed London in December 1501, just weeks after their extravagant and long-awaited wedding had been celebrated in Old St Paul's Cathedral. Henry VII had worked tirelessly towards this union for thirteen years, betrothing his eldest son and heir to Isabella of Castile and Ferdinand of Aragon's fourth daughter when Arthur was just two years of age and his future wife a year older. It was hoped that the match would cement England's alliance with Spain and bring peace and prosperity to the kingdom. For fifteen-year-old Katherine, it was just a step away from fulfilling her God-given destiny of becoming England's queen.

Despite the biting cold, the Prince and Princess of Wales must have approached

Ludlow with a sense of hope and anticipation. Their future looked bright and there was no reason to suspect that theirs would be anything other than a happy and fruitful marriage. No doubt the streets were lined with many of Ludlow's two thousand citizens, eager to pay their respects and catch a glimpse of the newlyweds.

The party would have wound its way down the narrow and twisting side streets of Ludlow, heavy with the tang of woodsmoke, through the bustling marketplace and under the twelfth-century gatehouse, which formed the principal entrance to the castle and allowed access to the vast outer bailey. Occupying an area of almost 4 acres, and surrounded by the castle's curtain wall, this huge space housed stables, storehouses and workshops.

Passing through an arched entrance next to the original Norman keep, the royal party – which included Sir Richard Pole, a relation of Henry VII, and presumably his wife Margaret, the niece of kings Edward IV and Richard III – would then have entered the oldest part of the castle, and one of the most important: the inner bailey. Surrounded by curtain walls 5–6 feet thick and flanked by imposing towers that offered uninterrupted views of the undulating countryside, Katherine must have felt well protected, even in this traditionally troublesome border county.

Situated on the north side, along the curved curtain wall, were the residential apartments where Arthur and Katherine would be housed during their stay. Begun in the late thirteenth century and completed in the fourteenth century, these high-status buildings were palace-like in their magnificence and comprised a series of interconnected buildings that, from left to right, included a three-storey solar block which extended into the northwest Norman tower and an adjoining Closet Tower; a magnificent great hall, which in 1684 was said to be 'very fair'; and another three-storey residential block, sometimes referred to as the Great Chamber Block. Prince Arthur's rooms on the upper storey of the solar block were accessed directly from the adjacent great hall by a spiral staircase or by a staircase on the ground floor.

We do not know for certain which rooms Katherine occupied during her stay at Ludlow, but it's likely that she too resided in a suite of rooms on the upper floors of the solar block, possibly occupying the floor directly below Arthur's. We can surmise that, like her husband's lodgings, Katherine's would have been luxurious, well lit and warmed by a fine fireplace. The walls would have been plastered, or panelled, and hung with splendid tapestries – all worthy of a future Queen of England.

There are no extant records detailing how Katherine spent her time at Ludlow, but it's likely that while her husband attended council meetings and, as one chronicler recalled, ruled with 'moost and rightuous ordre and wisdam ... uppholdyng and defending the pore', Katherine tended to her devotions and when not in the chapel likely whiled away the hours with her ladies, sewing, reading and talking. On Sundays and holy days prayers and services were held in the Norman chapel of St Mary Magdalene, situated in the inner bailey, no doubt in the presence of the devoutly religious Katherine, who, according to the recollections of Jane Dormer, 'fasted on bread and water every Friday and Saturday, and all the eves of our Blessed Lady, whose Office she read daily'.

It was probably during her months at Ludlow that the future queen formed a friendship with Margaret Pole, the wife of her husband's chamberlain. She would become Katherine's steadfast supporter and lifelong friend. Unfortunately for Margaret, her Plantagenet blood eventually led an increasingly paranoid Henry VIII to order her execution for treason in 1541, at the age of sixty-seven.

Ludlow afforded the newlyweds more privacy than at Henry VII's court. One of Arthur's gentlemen, William Thomas, would later recall how he conducted Arthur 'in his nightgown unto the princess's bedchamber … whereupon he [Arthur] entered and there continued all night'. In the morning he would receive his master 'at the said doors'. Katherine would later swear that her marriage to Arthur Tudor was never consummated, a statement which the ever-vigilant Doña Elvira, head of Katherine's household, who accompanied the princess to Ludlow, would fervently stand by.

It should have been the first of many winters for the royal couple, an unfurling of decades promising joy, prosperity and heirs to secure the stability of the realm. Instead, it ended in tragedy only months into their marriage, when on Saturday 2 April 1502, fifteen-year-old Prince Arthur Tudor succumbed to a short illness. Katherine too was struck down, leading some historians to suggest that the cause of Arthur's death was something highly infectious, like the 'sweating sickness'. However, other authorities have suggested testicular cancer. Whatever eventually claimed the life of this young man, it is fair to say that his death was unexpected and a shock to the royal family, who were devastated by the loss of their beloved eldest son and heir.

Arthur embodied the hopes of a still vulnerable Tudor dynasty; his was supposed to be a golden rule, a return to the legendary days of Camelot. Instead, his embalmed body now lay in state in his chambers, surrounded by burning tapers, and watched over by a group of poor men, paid to sit by Arthur's side holding torches day and night. Their prayers filled the otherwise silent room, while the residents of Ludlow went about their days in quiet reverence. At the same time, Katherine, uncertain of what the future now held, recovered her strength.

Three weeks later, on 23 April, St George's Day, amid torrential rain and howling winds, the funeral cortege finally left the ancient grey castle and began its bleak, muddy journey; first to Ludlow's parish church, where Arthur's coffin remained for two days, and then, via the town of Bewdley, on to Worcester Cathedral, where the prince was buried on 25 April. A contemporary chronicler tells us of the weather that day, recalling the 'foulest, cold, windy, and rainy day … that I have seen'; so foul, in fact, that between Ludlow and Bewdley oxen were sometimes needed to pull the hearse. Mother Nature, it seemed, was grieving.

As custom dictated, Henry VII and Elizabeth of York were not present at their son's funeral, and illness, or perhaps despair, prevented Katherine from attending. Instead, she remained at Ludlow Castle, where the dismal weather made afternoon appear as night. While the people genuinely mourned the loss of their noble Arthur, Katherine was left in an unenviable position – a young widow in a foreign country, and at the mercy of her avaricious father-in-law.

Visiting Ludlow Today

Today, the view that greets visitors to Ludlow is not unlike that which welcomed Katherine all those centuries ago; the now ruined but picturesque castle and the Church of St Lawrence, where Arthur's coffin rested on its way to Worcester, continue to dominate the town's skyline, while the town plan established in the fourteenth century remains largely unaltered.

Approaching the castle from the market square, we pass through the remains of the twelfth-century gatehouse that witnessed Katherine and Arthur's arrival. The Tudor buildings to your left were constructed from the mid-sixteenth century onwards and served as a porter's lodge (current castle entrance and shop) and prison, while the building on your right, Castle House, was constructed in the nineteenth century on the site of a Tudor tennis court; the southern end today houses the castle's tea room.

To the left as you cross the grassy outer bailey, note the remains of the original curtain wall and the fourteenth-century Chapel of St Peter. On the west side are the remains of Mortimer's Tower. It was built in the thirteenth century, possibly as a gatehouse controlling a rear exit from the castle. It is thought that Richard, Duke of York, and his son Edward, the future King Edward IV, escaped through here after their forces were routed at Ludford in 1459.

Make your way across the bridge that spans the old castle ditch, and walk towards the arched entrance. The arms of Sir Henry Sidney, Lord President of the Council of the Marches from 1559 to 1586, can be seen over the gatehouse, surmounted by the royal arms of Elizabeth I. The upper arch was cut through the curtain wall in the twelfth century, when the castle's original entrance, a gatehouse in the Norman keep, was blocked up. Look carefully at the facade of the keep (on your left as you face the arched entrance) and you'll notice that the stones in the blocked arch contrast with the surrounding masonry. The keen-eyed among us may even be able to identify the ledge where the original drawbridge rested.

The lower, narrower arch, which now serves as the entry to the inner bailey, was made in the fourteenth century and leads to the evocative ruins of the buildings Katherine and Arthur would have known.

From the moment you set foot in the castle's inner sanctum, it's clear that you have arrived somewhere important. A sense of significance, tinged with the ghost of reverent sadness, pervades the air.

Wander over to the Norman Chapel of St Mary Magdalene, which is one of only a handful of round churches to survive in Britain today. Like other round naves, its circular nave (much of which remains standing) was built in imitation of the church of the Holy Sepulchre in Jerusalem, which is said to have been built on the site of Christ's tomb. While the church was extensively remodelled in the late sixteenth century, there are surviving features that Katherine would have seen, including the impressive chancel arch that originally led to a square chancel and polygonal apse (now demolished), an arcade of seven arches, carved decorative heads and a stone bench that runs all the way around the nave.

As you explore the 'Tudor Lodgings' on the far right of the north range, spare a thought for Prince Edward and Prince Richard, sons of King Edward IV, known to history as the doomed Princes in the Tower, who are traditionally said to have lived in the building that occupied the site before the current building was erected in the sixteenth century.

Keep an eye out for the splendid hooded fireplace in the Great Chamber block, with its foliage and figure carving, and the many arched doorways and traceried windows that now stand as stalwart reminders of Ludlow's past magnificence.

In the great hall, visitors stand on a newly constructed timber platform at the original floor level. Note the three doors at the service end of the hall. In most great halls of the time, the main central door opened into the kitchen and the flanking doors into the buttery and pantry, but since Ludlow's kitchen was housed in a separate building in the courtyard (unusual for the time), there was no need for a kitchen door. Instead, the door closest to the main curtain wall opened on to a spiral staircase that led to Prince Arthur's chamber and to the battlements; the next door, which led into the adjacent block, may have been a service hatch for the pantry and buttery; the third, larger, door probably accessed the adjacent solar wing.

On the opposite end of the hall there was a raised dais, where Katherine and Arthur would have dined, warmed by an open stone hearth, the base of which can still be seen today. The smoke escaped through a louvre in the roof. However, this was not always an efficient system, as demonstrated by an outbreak of fire in 1579; a stone chimney replaced the hearth in 1580. Behind the dais was a wooden staircase that led to an upper gallery and a richly decorated doorway that gave access to the Great Chamber block. It's tempting to picture the young newlyweds stealing a quiet moment in the window embrasures on either side of the hall, which were originally furnished with facing stone seats, still partly visible today.

In the Solar Wing, where Katherine and Arthur lodged, weeds grow from the broken walls where love once blossomed, but despite the passage of time it's still possible to imagine a teenaged Katherine looking out over the gently sloping hills of the surrounding countryside, her thoughts with the family and land she'd so recently left behind. Perhaps she sought refuge from the cold, damp days by losing herself in memories of the sun-kissed walls of the Alhambra, from where she'd written love letters to her then fiancé, Arthur. The enamoured young prince penned his responses from his chambers at Ludlow:

> Truly those your letters, traced by your own hand, have so delighted me, and have rendered me so cheerful and jocund, that I fancied I beheld your highness and conversed with and embraced my dearest wife. I cannot tell you what an earnest desire I feel to see your highness, and how vexatious to me is this procrastination about your coming. I owe eternal thanks to your excellence that you so lovingly correspond to this my so ardent love. Let it continue, I entreat, as it has begun; and, like as I cherish your sweet remembrance night and day, so do you preserve my name ever fresh in your breast.

As you explore the grounds it's difficult to keep your own thoughts from wandering. What if Arthur had not fallen ill and died so young? What if he'd ascended the Tudor throne and lived to father many children, many sons, with Katherine? How remarkably different world history would be.

There is something undeniably alluring about this ancient fortress, something almost magical that will etch itself onto your heart and draw you back to its gates time and time again.

Visitor Information

A visit to Ludlow would not be complete without visiting the medieval parish church of St Laurence, where Arthur's funeral cortège stopped on its way to Worcester and where his 'heart' (more likely the prince's internal organs, removed during the embalming process) is said to have been buried in the chancel. In the north aisle, note the beautiful Victorian stained-glass windows depicting many of Ludlow's famous residents, including Richard, Duke of York, King Edward IV, his son Edward V and Prince Arthur. The church is located off King Street, the main thoroughfare, just a short stroll from the castle entrance.

We also recommend a visit to Castle Lodge, situated next to the castle. This fascinating building probably dates from the fifteenth century and is home to some exquisite linenfold panelling, beautifully carved fireplaces and a selection of modern reproductions of well-known Tudor portraits. There is also an extraordinary plaster ceiling said to date from the sixteenth century. Although privately owned, the lodge is opened to the public for a small fee. Just knock on the front door! While the house is certainly worth visiting, a sense of sadness lingers in the large, sparsely furnished rooms, many of which are in need of restoration. You're not likely to forget the house, nor the owner, in a hurry.

Remember to leave plenty of time to explore the many artisan shops and historic buildings that line Ludlow's streets and perhaps consider planning your visit to coincide with Ludlow's open-air market, which takes place every Monday, Friday and Saturday throughout the year, with an additional Wednesday market from April to September. In addition to the regular market, the Sunday flea market is also worth exploring.

To find out more about the parish church of St Laurence, please visit their website at http://www.stlaurences.org.uk/.

For castle opening times and other visitor information, please visit the Ludlow Castle website at http://www.ludlowcastle.com, or telephone +44 (0) 158 487 3355.

Postcode for Ludlow Castle: SY8 1AY.

Leeds Castle, Kent

Wonderful in manifold glories are the great castle visions of Europe; Windsor from the Thames, Warwick or Ludlow from their riversides, Conway or Caernarvon from the sea, Amboise from the Loire, Aigues Mortes from the lagoons, Carcassonne, Coucy, Falaise and Chateau Gaillard – beautiful as they are and crowned with praise, they are not comparable in beauty with Leeds, beheld among the waters on an autumnal evening when the bracken is golden and there is faint blue mist among the trees – the loveliest castle, as thus beheld, in the whole world.

Lord Conway, *Country Life*, December 1913

A Royal Visit to Leeds Castle

On the afternoon of 22 May 1520, a cavalcade of around six thousand people and over 3,200 horses descended on Leeds Castle in Kent. Towards the front of the huge procession was England's twenty-eight-year-old charismatic ruler, Henry VIII, and not far behind was his wife of almost eleven years, Katherine of Aragon.

After the death of Katherine's first husband, Arthur Tudor, in 1502, the Spanish princess had lived at the mercy of her miserly father-in-law, King Henry VII, who, reluctant to allow her – and her dowry – to return to Spain, had eventually agreed to a marriage between Katherine and his younger son, Henry Tudor. However, it wasn't until the king's death in 1509 that Henry and Katherine finally wed and were crowned as England's new monarchs in a magnificent double coronation ceremony at Westminster Abbey. While, by all accounts, their first decade of marriage had been a happy one, it had been marred by the tragic loss of at least five children, who were either stillborn or died not long after birth, including a son, Henry, who was just fifty-two days old when he died on 22 February 1511. The royal couple's only surviving daughter was the Princess Mary, born on 18 February 1516 at Greenwich. The loss of so many children undoubtedly strained Henry and Katherine's relationship; however, they presented a united front when they arrived at Leeds Castle at the head of the royal procession.

This vast assembly would stay overnight at the castle, en route to meet Francis I, King of France, near Calais. It was a reunion arranged to improve relations between England and France and cement a bond of friendship between the two long-standing rivals. The historic meeting between the two young Renaissance princes took place between 7 and 24 June 1520, and became known for its opulence: the Field of Cloth of Gold.

According to contemporary records, the queen had 1,260 people in her retinue; these included an earl, bishops, barons, knights, chaplains, a duchess, countesses, baronesses, wives of knights, gentlewomen, chamberers, yeomen, stablehands and other attendants. Among those who attended the queen were Eleanor Percy, the Duchess of Buckingham; Lady Boleyn, the mother of Henry VIII's future wife Anne Boleyn; Mistress Carey, wife of William Carey and sister of Anne Boleyn; and Maud Green, Lady Parr, widow of Sir Thomas Parr and mother of Katherine Parr, who would become Henry VIII's sixth wife.

Among those listed in the king's 4,500-strong retinue were Cardinal Wolsey, the dukes of Suffolk and Buckingham, and Thomas More. Also of interest: Sir Thomas Boleyn, Sir John Seymour and Lord Edmund Howard, fathers of Henry VIII's second, third and fifth queen consorts respectively.

Henry and Katherine and their closest attendants would have been lodged in the castle, while the rest of the party were likely accommodated in tents and pavilions erected on the grounds. As constable of the castle, it was Sir Henry Guildford's job to ensure that all was prepared for the king's stay. He was paid the handsome sum of £66 13s 4d, approximately £25,500 in today's money, for accommodating and feeding the vast entourage.

Apart from this injection of funds, between 1518 and 1522 Henry VIII paid over £1,300 to Sir Henry Guildford, 'to be bestowed about the repair of the castle of Leeds'. Further repairs were carried out in 1536, when Gaylon Hone, the king's glazier, reset 27 feet of 'old glass of Image work' in the king's chapel. In 1544, Hone was again called upon to repair the glass in various windows in preparation for a visit by Katherine Parr, who spent time at the castle with Henry VIII after his return from the Siege of Boulogne.

In an inventory of Sir Henry Guildford's goods at Leeds Castle, made after his death in 1532, the king's breakfast and dining chambers and the queen's dining, bedroom and inner chambers are mentioned. Unfortunately, little else is known for certain about the layout of the castle in the sixteenth century, and much of the Tudor fabric was lost in subsequent alterations. The modern visitor can, though, find evidence of Henry VIII's expenditure and Katherine of Aragon's visit in the Gloriette, the castle's original keep.

Visiting Leeds Castle Today

The historian Lord Conway described Leeds Castle as the 'loveliest castle in the world' and it's hard to disagree. Set on two small, linked islands in the middle of a still lake where swans glide elegantly across the water, and surrounded by 500 acres of beautiful parkland and formal gardens, Leeds Castle is truly breathtaking.

Originally built as a Norman stronghold, the castle came into royal possession in 1278, when Edward I purchased it as a home for his wife, Eleanor of Castile. For the next three hundred years it remained a royal residence and became home to six medieval queens of England, including Anne of Bohemia, Joan of Navarre and Catherine of Valois, whose grandson by her second marriage would in 1485 ascend the throne as Henry VII.

The principal apartments at the time of Katherine's visit were in the Gloriette. As you wander around this area of the castle today, keep an eye out for the decorative spandrels in the fireplace in the Queen's Gallery, which are decorated with the castle of Castile and pomegranates of Aragon. The fireplace was originally located on the upper floor of the Gloriette, which was added during the reign of Henry VIII for the exclusive use of his first wife. The marble busts of Henry VIII, Mary I, Elizabeth I and Edward VI date from Elizabeth's reign and the central courtyard, although heavily altered, dates from the thirteenth century. In the Henry VIII Banqueting Hall, note the large Tudor bay window and the magnificent sixteenth-century French Caen stone fireplace installed during renovations in the twentieth century. Take your time admiring the beautiful paintings and furniture, notably the sixteenth-century painting *The Embarkation at Dover*, which depicts Henry VIII's fleet setting sail from Dover on its way to the Field of Cloth of Gold. If you're lucky, you may also get to see a Latin service book said to have once belonged to Katherine, and an early Tudor missal box reputed to have once belonged to Anne Boleyn. At the time of writing, the latter was on display in the Gatehouse Exhibition.

While the upper floor was refurbished for Lady Baillie, the last private owner of Leeds Castle, who lived there for almost half a century until her death in 1974, the area would have originally formed Katherine of Aragon's private apartments. The Catherine of Aragon Bedroom is believed to be the site of Katherine's bedchamber.

While time and alterations have robbed us of the majority of the buildings that Katherine would have known, the castle's illustrious past and sheer beauty make it well worth the visit.

Visitor Information

For those of you wishing to follow in the footsteps of Katherine and Henry by staying overnight at the castle, we recommend booking a room in the sixteenth-century Maiden's Tower. Standing apart from both the Gloriette and the New Castle, this Tudor structure was reputedly constructed during Henry VIII's reign as lodgings for the queen's ladies-in-waiting. Today it forms part of the conference and wedding facilities.

If you're more the adventurous type and looking for something different, why not do as Henry and Katherine's courtiers did and stay in a pavilion for the night!

For accommodation at Leeds Castle, please visit http://www.leeds-castle.com/Accommodation.

For castle opening times and other visitor information, please visit the Leeds Castle website at http://www.leeds-castle.com, or telephone +44 (0) 166 276 5400.

Postcode for Leeds Castle: ME17 1PL.

Buckden Palace, Cambridgeshire

Find Katharine the most obstinate woman that may be. There is no other remedy but to convey her by force to Somersham ... Bugden [Buckden], Friday, 19 Dec.
Excerpt from a letter written by Charles, Duke of Suffolk,
to the Duke of Norfolk from Buckden Palace, 1533

The year is 1533. A sharp frost gradually gives way to the feeble warmth of the winter's sun. From a distance, villagers watch as a handful of elegant gentlemen, clad in opulent fur and fine clothes, ride their mounts across a two-span brick-bridge. The bridge traverses a wide moat that connects the outer gatehouse to the inner courtyard of the eponymously named bishop's palace. On the other side of that bridge and out of sight, the forty-eight-year-old Katherine of Aragon looks down on men arriving below the window of her privy chamber. She sees the familiar figure of the Duke of Suffolk as he dismounts from his horse. Unaware that he is being watched, Charles Brandon secretly wishes some calamity had befallen him en route from London, for he has little appetite to carry out the orders entrusted to him by the king; the duke has been 'commissioned to bring the queen by force to a house surrounded with deep water and marshes, which is ... the most unhealthy and pestilential house in England' (described as such by Chapuys in a letter dated 23 December 1533). Ahead lies one of the most well-documented and theatrical episodes in Katherine's life.

By this time, the king had cast aside his wife of over twenty years and taken the vivacious and controversial Anne Boleyn as his bride and queen. His adoration of Anne and quest for a male Tudor heir had culminated in a titanic battle between the king, Katherine of Aragon and Rome, known as the 'King's Great Matter'. When Rome failed to deliver Henry his divorce, the king had taken matters into his own hands. Henry banished Katherine from court in the summer of 1531, and headed off on summer progress with Anne, leaving Katherine behind at Windsor Castle. After being removed from Windsor to The More in Hertfordshire, Katherine was subsequently transferred first to Ampthill in Bedfordshire before being removed to Buckden (known in the sixteenth century as 'Bugden') in midsummer 1533. Records of letters and gifts sent to the princess dowager in *The Letters and Papers of Henry VIII* (dated 15 December 1533) record that certainly by the 16 July, she had left Ampthill, travelling 25 miles in a north-easterly direction to her new lodgings. She would only reside there for ten months, but typical of Katherine, those months would not be without their fair share of high drama.

An Episcopal Palace on the Edge of the Fens

There had been a permanent episcopal residence of the bishops of Lincoln at Buckden since the twelfth century. Sited adjacent to the Great North Road (today the A1), Buckden Palace proved a convenient stopping-off point between Lincoln and London; this was essential as many of its medieval bishops were involved with state affairs. Given Katherine's plaintive complaints about the unhealthy situation of Buckden echoing across time, we might be tempted to think of her imprisoned in some dreary, outdated medieval fortress. The truth is that Buckden Palace, although near the dreaded damp of the Cambridgeshire Fens, was a fine residence, with large parts of it having been constructed and redeveloped in the late fifteenth century, just fifty or so years earlier. According to *British History Online,* the original palace consisted of 'an inner walled and moated enclosure, containing the main buildings of the house and entered by the Inner Gatehouse on the W[est] side, and an outer walled enclosure on the W[est], entered by the Outer Gate-house'. The outer gateway was connected to the inner one by way of the brick-built bridge described above. This indeed spanned a wide moat.

After many, if not all, of the inner courtyard buildings were burnt down in 1291, the great hall was almost immediately reconstructed. Emery's *Greater Medieval Houses of England and Wales, Volume II* states that 'probably then rather than later, a detached chamber block and chapel were erected south of the hall, separated from it by a small garth, or courtyard'.

The palace was extended again two centuries later by Bishops Rotherham and Russell. As successive holders of the office, they built between them the lofty Tower House that came to contain the bishop's principal private chambers, refurbished the great hall and built the inner and outer gatehouses. The chapel was also replaced by Russell's successor at the turn of the sixteenth century. The key aforementioned buildings of the hall, chapel and great chamber, were arranged around the (probably) cloistered garth to the north, east and south respectively; all the principal chambers were sited at first-floor level.

The Great Chamber

> On Wednesday last, after dinner, we declared your pleasure to the Princess Dowager in her great chamber before all the servants of the house.

On Friday 19 December 1533, Suffolk put pen to paper. He wrote first to the king, then more bluntly to both Norfolk and Cromwell. In those missives, he recalled the tense encounter between himself and the newly titled 'Princess Dowager'. The meeting took place just two days previously, in her 'Great Chamber' at Buckden. As the quill moved quickly across the parchment, Suffolk went on to describe Katherine's response to the king's insistence that she refrain from using the title 'queen' and that she was to remove herself to nearby Somersham:

> She protested with open voice that she was your Queen, and would rather be hewn in pieces than depart from this assertion. She refuses the name of Princess Dowager, and resists her removal to Somersham because of her health; and for all the persuasions that could be made by us or lord Mountjoy, or Dymock, her almoner, who urged her to remove, however she might order herself in her cause, she refuses to take any person into her service sworn to her as Princess Dowager.

Unfortunately, the chamber in which this audience took place is lost to time. Only its foundations remain in outline on the ground. Yet, due to the Commonwealth Survey of 1647, we know something of the appearance of the said building and its interior. Lying to the south of the garth, directly across from the great hall, it measured 49 feet by 23.5 feet. Embedded in the south wall was a large projecting fireplace. Opposite the high end of the chamber, a large oriel window with a stone canopy was inset into the east wall, with thirteenth- and fifteenth-century windows built into the north and south walls respectively.

According to Chapuys, Suffolk and the other commissioners stayed at Buckden for six days, pressuring Katherine and her household to submit. As the princess dowager always preferred such audiences to take place in the open, in front of witnesses, one assumes that much of this titanic struggle played out in this Great Chamber – that is with the documented exception of the events that unfolded on the final morning of Suffolk's stay in Buckden.

As the duke directed the packing up of the dowager princess' household, Katherine raised the ante by barring herself in her privy chamber. In our opinion, it is highly likely that what followed next took place in The Tower House.

The Tower House

The Tower House was a fine three-storey building, set above a semi-basement. As previously mentioned, it contained the bishop's principal private apartments. As such, the rooms would have been the most luxurious in the palace and one imagines they must have been used by Katherine for the same purposes during her tenure at Buckden, particularly since there are no other obvious contenders for the role within the palace complex. The internal arrangement of the rooms has been changed since the sixteenth century. At some point the building was entirely gutted (leaving only a single chamber per floor) and the vaulting of the basement removed. However, according to *British History Online*,

> the principal floor had been occupied as the king's dining room, the northern end cut off by a screen, the walls panelled and the ceiling supported upon heavy moulded beams with large carved bosses at the intersections – one of which had Bishop Russell's rebus, a thrush or throstle with the motto 'Verus celluy je sui,' the other had the bishop's arms. The upper stories were divided into several rooms (of which there were ten in total).

Notably, the original staircase survives in the north-east turret of the tower. Emery states that the stair is 'complete with its stone handrail sunk into the wall and [with] internal evidence of a doorway from the great chamber midway between the [current] ground and first-floor level'.

Given the contemporary accounts of Katherine's ferocious encounter with the Duke of Suffolk in December 1533, it is quite plausible that it was through this door and up this staircase that the enraged princess dowager fled, only to lock herself into her chamber, refusing to yield to Suffolk's threats or reasoning. As ever, it is the wily ambassador Chapuys who has left behind an account of the encounter, with Charles Brandon resorting to addressing Katherine through a hole in the wall:

> The said Commissioners [Suffolk, Sussex, Paulet and Sampson] stopped six days, as well to close the house as to see if the Queen, through the loss of her servants and their rough menaces, would change her purpose. But seeing that she was constant, they proceeded at length to load the baggage, and get a litter and horses in order to mount the Queen thereon. She had locked herself in her chamber since the morning, and when the Commissioners came to take her away, she told them through a hole in the wall that they must break down the doors if they wished to remove her.

The commissioners left without achieving their primary aim. Katherine remained at Buckden, albeit with a hugely reduced household. Many of her servants had refused to swear an oath to refrain from calling Katherine 'queen' as they considered to do so would amount to perjury. As a result, a significant number were 'driven away with great harshness' and others were imprisoned. According to Chapuys in a letter dated 27 December 1533, they debated on taking away her confessor, a Spanish bishop; but on the Queen saying that she never confessed, nor knew how to do it, except in Spanish, they left him, and said nothing to her physician and apothecary, who are Spaniards. They took away almost all her femmes de chambre; but as the Queen affirmed she would not have any others, and would sleep in her clothes, and lock the gate herself, they returned two of them, but not those that the Queen wished. All her present servants, except the confessor, physician, and apothecary, who cannot speak English, have been sworn not to address her as Queen; and for this she has protested before the Commissioners that she will not regard them as her servants, but only her guards, as she is a prisoner.

A Life of Unhappy Obscurity

As the dust settled, Katherine's life slipped back into an unhappy obscurity. According to Nicolas Harpsfield, who wrote an account in defence of the validity of the marriage between Henry VIII and Katherine, she 'spent her solitary life much in prayer, great alms and abstinence, and when she was not this way occupied, then was she, and her gentlewomen, working with their own hands something wrought in needlework, which she intended to the honour of God, to bestow on some of the churches'.

This 'solitary life much in prayer' is also attested to in a retrospective account of Katherine, recorded by Henry Clifford from the recollections of Jane Dormer, later Duchess of Feria, a close friend and confidante of Mary I. From this source we have already heard a little of Katherine's daily routine in the introduction to this section, and also in the entry for Ludlow. Over and above this, we know that at some point Katherine had taken the Third Order of St Francis; this order (which still exists today) allows married men and women to follow a rule 'animated by the spirit of St Francis' while living a lay existence. On account of this, she wore the habit of St Francis under her royal attire. In addition, 'on every Sunday she received the Blessed Sacrament of the Altar. Most part of the morning was spent in the church at holy service, and after dinner she read the life of the saint of the day to her maids. And then she returned to the church.'

According to Harpsfield, Katherine also 'regained some of her cheerfulness and peace of mind at Bugden, where the country people began to love her exceedingly. They visited her frequently out of pure respect and she received the daily tokens of regard [with which] they showered her most sweetly and graciously.'

Despite this greater peace of mind, by this time Katherine had been afflicted for some months by a malady that was first noted by Henry's commissioners when they visited her at Ampthill the year before. The princess dowager had developed a troublesome cough and general frailty of health, which is commented upon here and there in the *Letters and Papers of Henry VIII* from this point until her death in early January 1536. It seems that the life force had gradually begun to depart from a soul weary of war. In May 1534, Katherine's time at Buckden Palace came to an end, moving to a place that would be witness to the final saga in her long and sorry tale – Kimbolton Castle.

Visitor Information

In 1962, the old Great North Road was diverted away from Buckden. This left the little village to rest peacefully, undisturbed by the increasingly heavy flow of traffic that now streams incessantly north to south along this ancient highway. However, we should bear in mind that in Katherine's day the old road ran straight past the entrance to the outer gatehouse of the palace.

In 1974, the somewhat ruinous site was gifted to a Catholic order, the Claretian Missionary. Together with the Friends of Buckden Palace, the surviving Tudor buildings were renovated in the 1980s. The site is now used as a conference and retreat centre.

Although almost all the Tudor interiors have disappeared, the extant sixteenth-century buildings have been secured for the foreseeable future. Today, the principal features of interest to the Tudor time traveller are the outer and inner gatehouse, the range of buildings to the right of the inner gatehouse (as approached across the now in-filled moat) and the Great Tower. This latter building once contained Katherine's privy apartments. The great hall, chapel and Great Chamber are lost. However, as you tour the grounds, you will see their imprint outlined in the grass. The small stone-built chapel appended to the rear of the modern church was reconstructed to mark the site of the original chapel.

A car park is accessed close to the outer gatehouse. Signs clearly point out that anybody is free to roam around the grounds, although only assistance dogs are permitted on-site if you usually travel with your four-legged friend. As you pass beneath the inner gatehouse, note that the list of illustrious visitors to Buckden include Henry VIII and Catherine Howard. They are noted to have visited in 1541 as part of the northern progress, although we have been unable to find any collaborating evidence in the contemporary geists or other accounts to validate this claim.

Do feel free to explore inside the courtyard and on either side of the current church, where you will see the imprints of the great hall and chamber, as described above. If the tower is not in use, it may be possible to gain access to what was once Katherine's principal dining chamber. Inside, the spiral staircase takes you up to the upper floor. Both these floors have been completely stripped of all original features and are currently used as dormitories for delegates. There is little to see there. However, between the ground and first floor is a bricked-up doorway, its outline still clearly visible in the wall. This once gave Katherine access from her private apartments directly to the Great Chamber. When you run your hand up the remnants of the stone handrail, carved into the wall of the staircase, you can be sure that you really are treading in the footsteps of Henry's once proud Spanish queen.

The Friends of Buckden Palace has a small refectory on-site. Two main events are held during the year, including the Heritage Open Day in September. At these times the refectory is open and there is access to Queen Katherine's Garden. This Tudor knot garden did not exist in Katherine's day, but has been recreated in her honour. Indeed, the village of Buckden seems to have remained loyal to Katherine over time. A window that is only accessible via the modern-day chapel is known as Queen Katherine's window. It is a twentieth-century tribute, in stained glass, to Katherine's memory and depicts some of the key events in her life, including the showdown between the princess dowager and Charles Brandon in the winter of 1533.

If you want to be sure to access this, then please support the Friends of Buckden Palace and arrange a guided tour. You will be met by one of their very helpful guides and given your own exclusive tour of the grounds (and interiors if they are not in use by the mission), all for the very reasonable price of £4 per person. If you wish to arrange a tour, please email admin@fobt.org.uk. Please check on their website for current information regarding events held on-site at http://www.fobt.org.uk/events.htm.

Postcode: PE19 5TA.

Kimbolton Castle, Cambridgeshire

Kimbolton Castle, Hunts, 'is a right goodly lodging contained in little room, within a moat well and compendiously trussed together in due and convenient proportion'.

From the Inventory of the Duke of Buckingham's Lands,
Letters and Papers of Henry VIII, May 1521

On 23 March 1534, a new Act of Succession was passed in England. This effectively placed the Princess Elizabeth as heir to the throne, and declared Katherine's daughter, Mary, a bastard. For those who had stoically stood firm in Katherine's support, these were increasingly dangerous times, for a proclamation issued on 30 March stated that

concerning the King's divorce from the lady Katharine, princess Dowager, late wife to prince Arthur, and his marriage with princess lady Aune [Anne], who has been crowned; which have taken place with the assent of Parliament and Convocation. Any person doing anything to the hindrance or derogation of the proceedings, &c. in the said divorce and marriage will incur the penalties of the statute of provision and præmunire made 16 Ric[hard]. II.

It was now a treasonable offence to assert Katherine's title of queen. In addition, just to drive the point home, Henry had decreed that all faithful subjects swear an oath to recognise this Act, as well as acknowledging the king's supremacy. Those who refused to do so would pay for it with their life, forfeiting their goods to the Crown. As these dramatic events unfolded in London, Katherine arrived at Kimbolton Castle.

A History of Kimbolton Castle

Situated about 6 miles west of Buckden, and therefore further from the Fens, Kimbolton was a preferable location for the woman who was, by that time, battling constant ill health. Although termed 'castle', by the 1530s, the thirteenth-century medieval fortress that we might associate with the term had long been abandoned. In its place, a rectangular courtyard house had been built by the Bohun family in the mid- to late fourteenth century. The site of this new house was, according to Emery's *Greater Medieval Houses of England and Wales*, 'considerably to the west' of the original 'fortlet'. In the fifteenth century the property passed into the hands of the mighty Buckingham family. Anne Neville, wife of the 1st Duke of Buckingham, lived there after her husband's death in 1460, doing much to rebuild the inner court. However, it is from the inventory of the castle at the time of the 3rd Duke of Buckingham's attainder in May 1521 (listed in the *Letters and Papers of Henry VIII*) that we have most of our information about the appearance of the house Katherine would have known. In addition to the opening quote, the entry in *Letters and Papers* goes onto say,

> There are lodgings and offices for keeping a duke's house in stately manner; but, 'by occasion of the old maintill [mantle] wall, the hall there well builded is likely to perish; and through the said castle is and will be great decay, by occasion there is no reparations done'. Outside the moat is a 'convenient room for a bace [base] court, used now like a gresse [grass] close'; in it are a fair barn and goodly houses fit for stables.

Thus, it seems the house needed repair. This was duly attended to by Sir Richard Wingfield, who was granted the castle upon Buckingham's execution. He remodelled part of it before dying prematurely in Toledo in 1525. In the 1530s, John Leland described the house as 'double dyked and the building of it metely strong' and that Sir Richard Wingfield had 'built fair new galleries and lodgyns upon the foundation of the old castle'.

In spite of these changes, in the years preceding Katherine's residence at Kimbolton, the house remained essentially unchanged in design: a central courtyard, surrounded by four wings. The entrance was from the west, which in turn was positioned directly opposite the great hall. Katherine's apartments were contained within the south range, and so one imagines were flooded with sunlight. Off the great hall was a 'withdrawing chamber'; this in turn led into a large gallery that occupied the central part of the south range. Katherine's most private apartments were situated beyond this, in the south-west corner of the castle. *The History of Huntingdon, Volume 3* states,

> Next to it (the gallery) were Queen Katharine's bedchamber and closet, which are said to have survived unaltered, but it is obvious that they had new windows and doors inserted in 1707, and apparently other alterations have been made. The chapel and the archway adjoining it doubtless still occupy their original positions.

However, if Simon Thurley is correct, there must have been some alteration to Katherine's apartments, for he states in a 2006 article written for *Country Life* that 'in the southwest corner there was a round tower, possibly dating from the time of Geoffrey Fitzpiers, the founder of the castle on the present site'. If this assertion is correct, then this round tower no longer exists. So if the bedchamber and closet survives, the queen's former chambers seem to have extended into this tower.

Two inventories taken in 1642 and 1687 tell us that there were many other rooms associated with the castle: a gatehouse, stables, 'the Castle Court', 'the Dyall [Dial] Court', 'the Great Garden' and the 'Little Fountain Garden'. Indirectly, through Chapuys, we are left with the impression that Katherine preferred this new residence to her previous one at Buckden. In a letter dated 14 May 1534, he states, 'She is better lodged than she was, although the house is small.'

Kimbolton: Katherine's Last Stand

On the very same day the Act of Succession was confirmed by Parliament in England, Rome finally passed sentence in Katherine's favour with regard to the King of England's 'Great Matter'. In her eyes, the highest court in Christendom had spoken and Katherine was vindicated. She was the king's 'true wife', as she had always maintained. Undoubtedly, this only served to augment her resolve to stand firm in the face of pressure from the king and his 'whore', Anne Boleyn. As her biographer Giles Tremlett writes, 'It should have been a monumental victory. In practice, however, it was almost worthless. Justice had arrived too late and, by doing so, became injustice … For Katherine, however, the moral and ideological victory was as important as the practical one. God was the real judge.'

Her resolve was soon put to the test – yet again. Determined to exact a submission from his thus far intransigent wife, Henry sent archbishops Lee and Tunstall north in an attempt to bring Katherine to heel. Some sources state this happened at Buckden. However, unless there are errors in the dating of the primary source letters, this cannot be the case. The audience must have taken place at her new lodgings in Kimbolton Castle. The letter reporting on the event is dated 21 May 1534, the same day the meeting took place, and a week after Chapuys reports that Katherine had been moved to her new lodgings. The Archbishop of York was there, he said,

> to declare to her the effect of our commission, [that] – 1, that you had often sent me and others of her council to declare to her the invalidity of your marriage with her; 2, that carnal knowledge, which is the great key of the matter, is sufficiently proved in the law, and admitted by some of her council; 3, that on proof of this you and she were divorced; 4, that she was thereupon admonished to give up the name of queen and not account herself your wife; 5, that you had contracted a new marriage with your dearest wife queen Anne; 6, that as fair issue is already sprung of this marriage, and more likely to follow, Parliament has made acts for the succession, and against all that would impugn it.

Katherine was incandescent as she batted away each article with self-righteous indignation, 'being therewith in great choler and agony, and always interrupting our words' according to the commissioners. Stalemate prevailed.

The Prisoner of Kimbolton

While at Kimbolton, it seems that Katherine remained, by choice, largely confined to her rooms, much as she had been while at Buckden following the Duke of Suffolk's visit four months earlier. Tremlett states that while at Kimbolton 'she was attended by a handful of servants, some ladies and her trio of faithful Spanish men – the confessor, the doctor and the apothecary'. Although increasingly frail, Katherine's behaviour remained unyielding and increasingly self-sacrificing. With so little left to lose, the idea of playing out some kind of martyrdom, in which she seemed willing to also sacrifice her daughter, increasingly drove the Dowager Princess of Wales to lock herself away in the 'delights and dangers' of virtuous suffering. Tremlett goes onto say that if Katherine was going to be treated like a prisoner, she was determined to live like one – and make sure people knew about it. Her room could serve as her cell, even if she had the key.'

Yet amid all this suffering, there comes one final moment of light-hearted pageantry associated with Henry's first wife. Aware of the decline in Katherine's health, two of her oldest friends and staunchest allies sought the required licence to visit the 'queen' at Kimbolton during 1534 – Maria de Salinas and Eustace Chapuys. Both were denied access. However, this did not deter the latter from making a very public display of Katherine's plight. Let us allow Chapuys to speak for himself as he describes the set-piece of Renaissance propaganda that he so ably orchestrated in July 1534:

> I set out with about 60 horses, both of my own men and of certain Spanish merchants here, to visit the Queen; and it happened most conveniently for my purpose that the way lay through the whole length of this town [London]. On the second day a messenger on horseback riding at full speed went before us and returned afterwards to where I lay, accompanied by an honest man sent by the Queen's chamberlain and steward to inform me that they had received commands by the said messenger not to let me enter where the Queen was or speak with her. My answer was that I did not intend to displease the King, either in this or in anything else, but that considering the solicitations I had made to know the King's intentions in this matter, and that I had come to within five miles of where the Queen was, I would not return so lightly ... Next day early in the morning another man came to us of more authority than the first ... [saying] that they did not think it advisable that I should come to the house, or even pass through the village ... One of her [Katherine's] chamber gave me to understand that, although she did not dare to declare it, he knew well she would have great pleasure if part of the company were to present themselves before the place; which they did next day, to the great consolation, as it seemed, of the ladies with the Queen, who spoke to them from the battlements and windows; and it seemed to the country people about that Messiah had come.

According to the *Spanish Chronicle*, when Katherine's ladies appeared at the windows and battlements of the castle, a 'very funny, young fellow', a fool, jumped down from his horse and waded waist-deep into the moat, crying out that he longed to reach them. When he feigned drowning, he was pulled from the water, ripping a padlock off his hood and hurling it toward the ladies, crying out in Spanish, 'Take this and the next time, I will bring the key!' Much hilarity ensued, with all the Spanish entourage being offered food within the 'lower hall' before returning to debrief the Spanish ambassador. There is no indication in the accounts that Katherine showed her face, but nevertheless, she must have derived enormous satisfaction and comfort from the devoted efforts of her long-time servant in highlighting her cause.

All of this must have taken place on the lawns that now surround the current building on the south side of the building, the side of Katherine's apartments, although the moat has long since been filled in. If the 'lower hall' refers to the great hall, the only known 'hall' in the castle, then according to the *History of the County of Huntingdon, Volume 3* this would have been sited where the current 'White Hall' stands but also 'included the site of the present drawing room (once the billiard room)'.

The Death of a Spanish Queen

By December 1535, Katherine lay dying in her bedchamber. According to Chapuys, writing to Charles V two days after her death, the 'queen's' final illness 'began about five weeks ago, as I then wrote to your Majesty, and the attack was renewed on the morrow of Christmas day. It was a pain in the stomach, so violent that she could retain no food.' He went on to explain that she was 'unable to eat or sleep, except so little that it might be called nothing. She was so wasted that she could not support herself either on her feet or sitting in bed.'

Chapuys informed King Henry that she 'was in great danger of life'. In reply to the king's letters enquiring about Katherine's health, her chief steward, Sir Edmund Bedingfield, wrote to Cromwell on the 31 December 1535, saying, 'Considering her weakness, she cannot long continue, if the sickness remains. The doctor moved her to take other advice, but she answered that she would in no wise have any other physician, but only commit herself to the pleasure of God.'

Chapuys had finally been given leave to go to Katherine and was at her side for four days, arriving on New Year's Eve, the same day the above letter was dispatched. Seeing her recover somewhat, the Spanish ambassador wrote retrospectively that 'I therefore took leave of her on Tuesday evening (4th January), leaving her very cheerful; and that evening I saw her laugh two or three times, and about half an hour after I left her she desired to have some pastime with one of my men "que fait du plaisant".'

Just days earlier, Maria de Salinas had also finally forced her way into the castle by employing a potent cocktail of charm and the ability to evoke pity in Katherine's custodians. She attended her former mistress, passing time as the two friends conversed for many hours in Katherine's native Castilian tongue. Knowing that the end was fast drawing near, Katherine summoned one of her ladies and dictated her final letter to Henry. Here it is in full:

My most dear lord, King and husband,
The hour of my death now drawing on, the tender love I ouge [owe] thou
forceth me, my case being such, to commend myselv to thou, and to put thou in
remembrance with a few words of the healthe and safeguard of thine allm [soul]
which thou ougte to preferce before all worldley matters, and before the care and
pampering of thy body, for the which thoust have cast me into many calamities
and thineselv into many troubles. For my part, I pardon thou everything, and I
desire to devoutly pray God that He will pardon thou also. For the rest, I commend
unto thou our doughtere Mary, beseeching thou to be a good father unto her, as I
have heretofore desired. I entreat thou also, on behalve of my maides, to give them
marriage portions, which is not much, they being but three. For all mine other
servants I solicit the wages due them, and a year more, lest they be unprovided
for. Lastly, I makest this vouge [vow], that mine eyes desire thou aboufe all things.
Katharine the Quene.

'Katharine the Quene'; Katherine, just as Anne Boleyn once said, always had the
final word in her quarrels with Henry, this time asserting her God-given place as
Henry's real wife and consort in her last letter to him. Katherine of Aragon died
in Maria's arms at 2 p.m. on Friday 7 January 1536. Eight hours later, her body was
opened in a secret autopsy, before provision was made for the 'bowelling, coring,
and enclosing [of] the corpse in lead'. *Letters and Papers* also states that 'lights and
other things [should be put] about the corpse, in the house, or the next church
or chapel'. As Katherine's body rested at Kimbolton for around three weeks, it is
likely that the leaded coffin was kept by candlelight in the chapel of the castle, next
to Katherine's privy chambers. The chapel still survives to this day, although greatly
altered in the sweeping remodelling of Kimbolton undertaken by the architect
John Vanbrugh at the turn of the eighteenth century.

And so ended a life of great struggle. According to Nicolas Harpsfield's
romantic notions of Katherine,

she changed this woeful, troublesome existence for the serenity of a celestial
life and her terrestrial ingrate husband for that heavenly spouse who will never
divorce her, and with whom she will reign in glory forever.

Visitor Information
Although the external appearance of Kimbolton Castle has changed out of all
recognition from the sixteenth century, its footprint essentially remains unchanged.
In fact, the imposing view of the castle from the end of the High Street, near the
church, has been essentially unaltered since the medieval period. Today the castle
is home to a private school and generally is not accessible to the general public.
Happily, though, the school has two open days a year; the first on the first Sunday
in March and the second on the first Sunday in November. During that time there
is access to all parts of the castle relevant to Katherine's story, including to the
room in which she died.

Passing through the current outer gatehouse, you will find yourself fronting onto a large, grassy area. However, this was not the position of the Tudor gateway. In Katherine's day, the outer gatehouse was positioned to the left of the castle, a bridge, spanning the 'double-dyked' (figure-of-eight) moat. The outer courtyard likely contained some service buildings, while a second bridge crossed the moat again to connect with the main entrance to the castle (the side that faces you as you pass through the modern gatehouse).

The inner courtyard is somewhat smaller than the one Katherine would have known. It was diminished when a few metres were shaved off all sides during later remodelling, aimed at creating a series of internal corridors that linked rooms inside the building. Today, the entrance to the great hall is positioned centrally. However, in the sixteenth century the hall's lower end was probably accessed to the left of the existing staircase. The hall in which Chapuys' servants were most probably received and fed occupied the site of the current White Hall, although the original chamber was somewhat larger than it is today. At some point, an additional chamber was created by partitioning off part of the hall at the high end.

Of the original Tudor house only two internal carved stone windows and a single door frame remain from the building that Katherine would have known. These are sited on the ground floor in what is aptly now called the Tudor Corridor. The south wing, once home to Katherine's privy chambers survives (although the round tower which existed into the seventeenth century has long since gone). However, there is no recognisable semblance of the earlier Tudor interiors. These were entirely dismantled at the hands of John Vanbrugh and Nicolas Hawksmoor during the years 1690–1720. Particularly poignant, though, is the Queen's Chamber (now the headmaster's office) and the adjacent closet. In the former room Katherine finally ended her earthly struggle with Henry and his English nation. According to Mackenzie's *Castles of England*, from 1896, 'the chamber in which she expired is shown in the castle; it is hung with tapestry and covers a little door leading to a closet, still called after the queen whose ghost is said to haunt the structure. One of her portmanteaux is shown also, covered with red velvet and having the letters K.R. with the queen's crown upon it.'

This portmanteau has since left the castle and been reattributed to Katherine of Braganza, queen of Charles II. Thankfully, we did not bump into Katherine's ghost! However, more real and moving is the chapel in which Katherine's body probably laid in state for three weeks prior to her burial at Peterborough Cathedral. Although now completely gutted of its fine Tudor interiors, the intimate space felt alive with her presence. It was easy to picture her coffin in the central aisle, before the altar, draped in the colours of the Princess Dowager of Wales, four tapers continually lighted, burning through the day and night at each corner of the casket. As you stand in the chapel, note that above your eyeline is a simple gallery. There is evidence that this was once a separate chamber overlooking the body of the chapel. Here Katherine would have heard Mass in privacy, away from the rest of the household. It connected directly to her privy chambers.

Once finished with your time travelling, the high street has a couple of cafés to cater to your refreshment needs. They provide a welcome break to take stock of the place in which Katherine's long struggle finally reached its sorry end. Perhaps as you sit sipping your tea, looking out onto the High Street, you might remember the fresh-faced princess we have followed from Spain, as Katherine's ghostly funeral cortege makes its way unnoticed down Kimbolton's busy high street, finding its way quietly to her final place of rest.

Postcode: PE28 0EA.

Part Three
Anne Boleyn

'THE MOSTE HAPPI'

Introduction

On 19 May 1536, a French sword stilled the beating heart of an English queen. Her name was Anne Boleyn and she would become one of the most controversial and iconic queens in English history. In her lifetime, Anne was a force of nature; she captivated the heart and soul of a king, divided a court and ignited the Reformation on English soil, beginning a process that would transform the religious and social landscape of the country.

While after her death her enemies continued to defile her name 'full sore', her legacy lived on in her daughter, perhaps the greatest monarch that England has ever known – Elizabeth I. But more than that, in her own right Anne Boleyn was an intelligent, powerful and influential woman who refused to be intimidated by those who sought her destruction. Her sense of destiny and purpose for religious reform carried her all the way to the scaffold with characteristic temerity, courage and grace.

Almost five hundred years later, Anne's memory burns as brightly as ever. In recent times, the tireless work of historians like the late Professor Eric Ives has done much to rehabilitate the slandered reputation of Anne as the archetypal harlot, whore and homewrecker. She is now largely recognised as ultimately being the victim of court faction; of a deadly power struggle with a man that the Boleyns had once so ardently supported – Thomas Cromwell; and of a powder keg of unfortunate circumstances that made her vulnerable to the machinations of her enemies during the first few months of 1536. Yet, when the twelve-year-old Anne Boleyn left English shores, bound for the royal court of Margaret of Austria in the Low Countries in 1513, she could not have conceived of such a meteoric rise to power, nor such a traumatic end.

In this section, we start our journey in Anne's iconic childhood home, the impossibly romantic and atmospheric Hever Castle in Kent. Some of that romanticism is of early twentieth-century design, thanks to its wealthy benefactors, the Astors. The family saved the castle from ruin, although its interiors were much remodelled from its original Tudor design. The home that Anne would have known is represented here, as we roll back the centuries to discover the moated medieval manor house that became home to the Boleyns in 1505.

From here, we follow Anne across the English Channel on the journey that would transform her from an innocent child of precocious talent to a formidable woman, self-assured, cultured and, as it turned out, fatally charismatic. There are several locations we could have chosen to include from this period of Anne's life, but perhaps two of the most formative in our opinion are Mechelen, in modern-day Belgium, and the Chateau d'Amboise, located in the heart of the Loire Valley, France. Here Anne's bright, impressionable mind was exposed to inspiring female role models – powerful women who managed not only their affairs independently of men, but managed the business of nations; women of fierce intellect and disarming charm who were embracing some of the most radical and emergent ideas of the epoch. At this tender age, Anne was thrown into the heart of the greatest Renaissance court of the age and her natural creative flair embraced the words and music of some of the keenest minds of the time. It is here that we can almost touch Anne's joyful youth as the woman who would become queen finally emerges and returns to England.

The next four locations, back on English soil, have been freshly researched for this second instalment of the *In the Footsteps* series. We present these for the first time: Hunsdon House, Haseley Court, Buckingham and Chertsey Abbey. All were visited by Anne in the years prior to her marriage to Henry VIII.

The year 1529 saw Anne and Henry visit first Haseley, and then the county town of Buckingham (the latter on two separate occasions in the same month). Contemporary records record that the royal couple stayed at the house of little Henry Carey, Anne's nephew and ward. We postulate that the visit, coming the year following the fatal outbreak of the 'sweat' which killed Master Carey's father, was orchestrated by Anne, who was keen to see her young ward and her sister, Mary.

Hunsdon became a regular stop on the court's summer progress in the early 1530s, and Anne was at the king's side when he lodged there in 1530, 1531 and 1532. In the same year, Hunsdon House was granted to Anne as part of her elevation to the title of Marquess of Pembroke.

The final of these four entries, Chertsey Abbey, played host to Anne on two occasions, both moments of triumph for the soon-to-be Queen of England. In the summer of 1531, Chertsey was the first location in which the royal couple lodged after Henry finally left Katherine behind at Windsor Castle. He would never see her again. One can only imagine Anne's sense of jubilation at finally being freed of their ever-present and irksome *ménage a trois*. Yet, perhaps even these feelings paled into insignificance against those associated with Anne's second visit in September 1532. She had just been created Marquess of Pembroke, and Anne Boleyn was at the zenith of her power and influence with Henry, her soon-to-be lover and husband. As she rode from Windsor to London via Chertsey, did she finally sense that all she had longed for, all that she had so patiently waited for, for six interminable years, was finally about to come to pass?

The remaining entries largely cover some of the most notable and interesting locations visited by Anne as part of the lengthy summer progress of 1535. It was Anne's last summer on earth, and the torch of passion which had once blazed so brightly between the royal couple now flickered precariously. Yet, Anne was still the king's 'beloved wife' – on paper at least – and a three-month progress honoured men of the reformed faith whom Anne had so ardently championed. The progress culminated toward the end of October with a longed-for child in the queen's belly. The 1535 progress was covered in full in our *In the Footsteps of Anne Boleyn*. Here we have included five extant locations from the progress, providing the time traveller with destinations that have either significant remains, or intact property, to visit.

We complete this section in the place where Anne's life was cut short in an act of judicial murder – the Tower of London. While also acknowledging the fate of Anne's cousin Catherine Howard in that same grisly fortress, we have decided to include the Tower in this section as it played host to Anne during her coronation (where Henry had had new apartments constructed to honour his queen), as well as her incarceration and execution three years later. It was a pivotal place in Anne's life. As her body lies beneath the altar in the chapel of St Peter ad Vincula, it also remains a place of pilgrimage for those who can never forget the life of this most beguiling of women.

Hever Castle, Kent

Remember me when you do pray, that hope doth spring from day to day.

Anne Boleyn

Two of Henry VIII's wives are associated with Hever Castle. In 1540, Anne of Cleves was allowed to take a lease on the castle as a part of her handsome divorce settlement. However, it is Anne Boleyn whom we most associate with the place that has since become known as her childhood home. So for anyone who loves Anne Boleyn, Hever Castle, in the heart of 'England's Garden' of Kent, is a natural place of pilgrimage.

As the name suggests, it is located in the village of Hever and began as a country house, built in the thirteenth century. From 1462 to 1539 it was the seat of the Boleyn family. Sir Thomas Boleyn inherited the property upon the death of his father in 1505, and subsequently set about making the rather outdated moated medieval castle into a fine contemporary English manor house fit for an aspiring courtier. This he did by carrying out a number of redevelopments to the building, including the addition of the fabulous staircase gallery, which remains intact to this day.

Anne spent a good deal of her childhood at Hever before being sent to the Low Countries in 1513 to receive an education at the court of the Archduchess Margaret of Austria. Later, during the early days of Anne's romance with Henry VIII, she would again spend periods of time at the castle, including a long sojourn there over the winter of 1527/8, when Katherine still held precedence at court over the Christmas celebrations. During this time, in February 1528, Anne received Dr

Edward Foxe and Dr Stephen Gardiner on their way to visit the Pope in exile, their embassy being to obtain a decretal commission from the Holy Father allowing the divorce case to be heard in England. Then again, she returned in June of the same year. During that fateful summer, the 'sweat' returned to England, forcing Henry to flee to Waltham Abbey, while Anne sought refuge at Hever. She was probably with her mother and father at the time. Anne, and possibly Thomas, fell ill there in late June/July. Fortunately, both made a full recovery and Anne returned to court sometime around early December 1528.

This quintessential fortified medieval manor house, nestled at the bottom of an idyllic, gently sloping valley, is utterly beguiling and catches your heart in an instant. The setting makes a picture-perfect English postcard; there are sculpted lawns with pretty lily covered moats, and all around you immaculately tended flower and herb gardens abound. However, do not be fooled by modern-day appearances. If you want to get a feel for how the castle looked in Anne's day, you have to think rather differently about it. So let's go back in time, to see the castle as Anne would have known it.

Touring Hever Castle: Rediscovering Its Lost Past
The first difference you would notice as you approach the castle is the setting. It was much more wild and rugged than the cultivated gardens you see today. The original Norman castle had its origins in the classic motte-and-bailey design with a central timber-framed hall defended by a surrounding ditch and palisade. Later, in the thirteenth century, a stone gatehouse was erected which contained its own hall; this for a time became the heart of the castle. To the west of the castle was the tiny village of Hever, consisting of a scattering of modest dwellings. It was the original village before it was moved by Lord Astor to its current position in the early twentieth century, thereby providing the Astor family with greater privacy.

In the sixteenth century, the area which lay in front of the building was covered in boggy marshland and was surrounded by dense forest. In Norman times, this was given the name *Andredswald*, which roughly translates to 'the woodland where no man dwells'. Even the royal map-makers of medieval England knew of its reputation as being notoriously lawless and dared not enter it.

Rather than the picturesque double moat that we see today, during the Tudor period the front entrance to the castle was guarded only by a single moat, which was traversed by a stone bridge. The main body of the castle consisted of only two floors; the third floor was added by William Astor. However, the gatehouse has remained unchanged since it was built in the thirteenth century.

If the setting of Hever Castle is much changed, so too is its interior, which in Anne's day would have been far less elaborate. This was last extensively renovated by the wealthy Astor family in the early twentieth century. As a result, many of its rooms are now sumptuously clad in oak panelling; the staircase and minstrels' gallery in the great hall are both intricately carved in the grotesque style so popular in Henry VIII's palaces. The ceilings are ornately moulded in traditional designs, and the rooms stuffed full of beautiful antiques – although not all are contemporary to the sixteenth century. Finally, its collection of Tudor portraits makes for a Who's Who of the Tudor court, and has been described by David Starkey as second only to that of the National Portrait Gallery in London.

As you wander round this charming little home, it is not hard to imagine Sir Thomas, or Lady Elizabeth, or indeed any of the Boleyn children, moving about its rooms, perhaps even receiving the King of England as he visited Hever in passionate pursuit of Anne. There is serenity about the castle and it sucks you in, leaving space for the walls to whisper their secrets to you. Let's now look at each of the rooms in turn.

The Great Hall

There would have been no fine oak panelling. Rather, the walls were covered in plain, light-coloured plaster and simple terracotta floor tiles. The fireplace had no ornate stone carving; it would have been fashioned into the simple shape of the iconic Tudor arch that we now associate with the period. Also there was no ornate minstrels' gallery, which so dominates the modern-day room. As a result, the hall would have looked much more plain and open.

The two windows that we see today would have had no glass in them, just shutters closed at night in order to keep out the worst of the weather. The Boleyn family, like any family of the time, tended to live their life mainly outdoors. They came in only to shelter in the foulest weather, to eat, sleep or entertain guests. At the top of the hall would have stood a dais, upon which rested a grand table. Here, during the day, when Thomas Boleyn was at home, he would work on his documents and attend to family business. This place is also reserved for the lord, his family and any honoured guests to eat.

The Inner Hall

In Anne's day, this hallway did not exist. Instead this part of the castle was occupied by the kitchen, larder and buttery. In the early twentieth century, these rooms were replaced by the grand and sumptuously decorated inner hall that we see today.

The Library and the Parlour

On the ground floor of the west wing at Hever Castle is the elegant library created by W. W. Astor, its walls crammed with precious books in fine oak cases. However, this wing of the Boleyn family home was not always so grand. Nor is it likely that an extensive library existed. Books were far too rare and precious and such libraries were probably the preserve of only the king himself. Instead, the library and the room beyond that, which is not open to the public, would have formed the main administrative, or *châtelaine's*, office where Elizabeth Boleyn would have run the estate in her husband's absence.

The retiring room, or parlour, was the main private reception room for the family in Anne's time. Here you would be entertained in the presence of a roaring fire and offered a drink to quench your thirst. Originally, it is likely that a doorway connected the upper end of the great hall directly with this room.

The Staircase

Another of the major differences in the layout of the castle between the sixteenth century and now is in the position of the main staircase leading to the upper floors. The original staircase probably originated just to the right of the short gallery that separated the great hall from the kitchen, almost opposite the main front door. When William Astor undertook his renovations, this staircase was flipped around to its current position.

Anne Boleyn's Bedroom, the Book of Hours Room and the Tudor Portrait Room

This part of the castle yet again looked entirely different to how we have come to know it in our modern-day life. In the twenty-first century, it is divided into distinct and separate rooms: Anne Boleyn's bedroom in the north-west; a large, central room which houses two of Anne's prayer books (the Book of Hours Room); and finally, overlooking the moat to the south, the room containing numerous fine Tudor portraits. Nobody quite knows the arrangement of rooms on the first floor of the west wing during the sixteenth century. However, broadly speaking, it seems that these three rooms once made up the so called solar, or main family room. Thus, it was a large room that extended across the entire length of the west wing. Here the family would relax and sleep. In the early sixteenth century this room was probably open, only screens at its southern end walling off the area where Thomas and Elizabeth Boleyn might have slept in a fine oak bed.

The Staircase Gallery

On the first floor you will come across the magnificent Staircase Gallery, added by Thomas Boleyn in 1506, when the family first moved into the castle. It was created to connect both wings of the house on the first floor and the then newly created long gallery upstairs. At the time it would have undoubtedly been the epitome of sixteenth-century fashion. Even today it is a broad, light and airy space, and during Anne's day it would have also been the only place in the castle to sport expensive glass windows. Unlike the plain windows of today, it is likely that they would have been inlaid with brightly coloured heraldic emblems of the Boleyn family tree.

The Waldegrave Room and the Henry VIII Room

When the Boleyns occupied Hever, the rooms in the east wing of the castle were probably used by servants and never used by the family themselves. In truth, the magnificent Henry VIII Bedroom, which currently occupies part of this wing, is sadly only named in honour of the king; it is unlikely that he ever used this room. What is more likely, however, is that when the king visited the Boleyn family would have decamped to Polbrooke Manor, located just a few hundred metres from the castle (today in private ownership and not open to the public), thus allowing the king to take sole occupancy of the Boleyn family home during his visits.

The Long Gallery

This particular room was created in 1506 by Thomas Boleyn, who did so by putting a ceiling over the great hall below and thereby reducing its height. At one point, the hall would have been open to the rafters, as was the fashion of the day. A hole in the roof allowed smoke to escape from a central hearth. Once again, the sixteenth-century gallery appeared much simpler than the sumptuously wainscoted room that we see today. Although there would have been a pretty ceiling which was highly decorative and much stuccoed with foliage. Of course, the long gallery served several purposes; a number of pieces of art could be displayed along its walls, while its size provided the perfect space in which to take exercise when the weather kept the family indoors.

These Bloody Days: Hever Castle after 1536

These bloody days have broken my heart. My lust, my youth did them depart.

The above words, taken from a poem written by Sir Thomas Wyatt, capture perfectly the heart-wrenching sadness and shock that surely shook those close to the queen as her blood (and that of the men who died with her) ran cold across the scaffold. Of course, nobody must have been more broken than the families of those who died so unjustly. We do not know what happened to the Earl and Countess of Wiltshire immediately after their children were arrested. All that we know is that Elizabeth Boleyn died in London on 3 April 1538, and was buried in the Howard family vault in St Mary's Church, Lambeth. As we shall hear shortly, Thomas himself departed this earthly realm at Hever on 12 March 1539. He remained in royal service after the death of his children, although stripped of the great offices which he had held during their lifetime. One can only begin to imagine that the house, once so filled with laughter and hope for the brightest of futures, must have been unbearably draped in the most bittersweet memories. How painful it must have been for Anne and George's parents to return there.

After Thomas's death, the house was granted to Anne of Cleves as part of her divorce settlement. She was allowed to lease the property at an annual rent of £9 13s 3½d. It is not known how often, or for how long, Anne resided at Hever. However, we do know that she was there during the summer of 1554, as it was from Hever that 'Anna, Daughter of Cleves' penned the following letter to Queen Mary:

It may please you Highness that I have been informed of your Grace's return to London again, being desirous to do my duty to see your Majesty and the King, if it may so stand with your Highness' pleasure and that I may know when and where I may wait upon your Majesty and his.
From my poor house at Hever, 4th August. Your Highness' to command, Anna, Daughter of Cleves.

Mary had married the King of Spain at Winchester around one week earlier. There is no indication that the request to pay her respects to the new monarchs was granted, and Anne was never again received at court. (See also the entry for the King's Manor, Dartford, for more information on this.)

St Peter's Church, Hever

> My good lord and master is dead [Thomas Boleyn]. He made the end of a good Christian man. Hever, 13 March.

St Peter's church dates back to the twelfth century and is located in the centre of Hever next to Hever Castle. Built on the site of an earlier Norman church, it has been a house of worship for the last nine hundred years and is a place that Anne would have known well.

Although little documentary evidence exists about the Boleyns' links with the church, they would have undoubtedly attended, especially considering the absence of a private chapel at Hever Castle. The tranquil atmosphere of the chapel is a haven from thoughts of the tumultuous – and tragic – final years of the Boleyns. Within its walls we are free to let our thoughts wander, imagining a young Anne, before her move to the court of the Archduchess Margaret of Austria in 1513, arriving to the church with her siblings, George and Mary, under the watchful eye of their parents, Elizabeth and Thomas. Perhaps they warmed themselves by the fireplace and talked with other local families before tending to their religious devotions.

Today the church is best known for being the final resting place of Anne's father, Sir Thomas Boleyn, who on 12 March 1539 passed away at Hever Castle, leaving his worldly troubles behind. On the day after Sir Thomas's death, Robert Cranewell, his auditor, wrote to Thomas Cromwell to inform him of the death of 'his good lord and master' and to assert that he had 'made the end of a good Christian man'.

His worn Purbeck marble tomb is located in the Boleyn Chapel, added to the original church in the middle of the fifteenth century or early in the sixteenth. On the tomb is a fine brass showing Thomas in the robes of a Knight of the Garter, the badge of the Garter on his left breast and above his right shoulder the falcon, the Boleyn family crest. This is said to be one of only two brasses in England depicting the full robes and insignia of the Order of the Garter.

The fireplace in the Boleyn Chapel is Tudor, as is the parish chest, believed to have originally been the alms box for the church, as indicated by the slit on the top. The fine, flattened, barrel-vaulted ceiling in the nave would also have been *in situ* during Anne's visits. At some point the floor in the chapel was raised; notice how Sir Thomas's tomb stands on the original (lower) floor level.

As you look around the church, you'll no doubt be drawn to the beautiful stained glass, most of which is modern with the exception of some small pieces of old glass surviving in the Boleyn Chapel. Above the rector's seat is a replica of the Boleyn arms emblazoned in the stained-glass window. A list of past rectors dating back to 1200 is displayed on the west wall of the church. Take note of the names from the first half of the sixteenth century, as these may well have been familiar to Anne.

Thomas's brass may be the main attraction, but he is not the only Boleyn buried in the church. Henry Boleyn, son of Sir Thomas, thought to have died in infancy, is buried near his father; a simple brass cross marks his tomb. A similar cross marks the final resting place of his brother, Thomas, at Penshurst church.

Apart from the brass of Sir Thomas and Henry Boleyn, the church is also home to another beautiful brass in memory of Margaret Cheyne, who died in 1419. Margaret's husband, William, was a landowner in the area and gave his wife a fine memorial.

As you absorb the serene mood of the church, and contemplate the lives of those in whose footsteps you walk, picture Anne admiring Margaret Cheyne's brass, perhaps imagining that when her time came she too would come to rest in the family chapel.

As a side note, there is an interesting legend attached to the nearby King Henry VIII inn, a name adopted in the 1830s. Originally the inn was called The Bull, and local legend has it that after 'their Anne' was brutally executed the local people renamed the inn The Bull and Butcher to show their anger towards the king. This story may be apocryphal, but its true merit lies in the satisfying opportunity it provides to imagine the local people of Hever showing their indignation at the violent and unjust judicial murder of Anne Boleyn.

Visitor Information
For information on prices, location and opening times, please visit the Hever Castle website at www.hevercastle.co.uk, or contact the castle on +44 (0) 173 286 5224.

The King Henry VIII inn is situated on Hever Road (postcode: TN8 7NH) opposite the entrance to Hever Castle and St Peter's church. A pub has occupied the site since the late sixteenth century, but the half-timbered pub you see today dates from 1647. To find out about opening times and menus, visit the King Henry VIII website at http://www.shepherdneame.co.uk/pubs/edenbridge/king-henry-viii, or telephone: +44 (0) 173 286 2457.

Postcode for Hever Castle: TN8 7NG.

Mechelen, Flanders

I find her so bright and pleasant for her young age that I am more beholden to you for sending her to me than you are to me.

> Margaret of Austria referring to Anne Boleyn in a letter to
> Sir Thomas Boleyn following her arrival at the Hapsburg court in 1513

In the summer of 1513, a young Anne Boleyn took leave of her parents in England, boarded a ship from Dover to Calais, and in the process set out on an adventure of a lifetime. We cannot know what was in Anne's heart when she first left her homeland; of what kind of future did she dream? What were her hopes and aspirations? Whatever was the case, one can easily imagine that she never anticipated that she was taking the first steps in an apprenticeship that would set her on the road to immortality.

She was headed for the seat of power of the Hapsburg court. At the time, this was Mechelen in the Low Countries, in what is known today as Belgium. Earlier in the year, while on embassy to the very same court, Sir Thomas Boleyn had secured a position for his youngest daughter as a *fille d'honneur* in the household of the indomitable Margaret of Austria, Regent of the Netherlands. It was a valuable prize to secure. The thirty-three-year-old Duchess of Savoy, thrice married and by then widowed, was not only a paragon of femininity, captivating *joie de vivre* and Renaissance accomplishments but was also a powerful *femme sole*, exercising absolute power rather astutely in her role as regent for the future Charles V.

It is interesting to learn about Margaret's character, for we quickly see mirrored in it so many of the attributes that would later be ascribed to Anne herself. In Jane de Longh's biography, *Margaret of Austria*, she writes of the impression that the young duchess made upon her second husband in 1501: 'Margaret's Flemish ways, her zest for life, her inclination to luxury and show, her robust humour, her straightforward sensuality found satisfaction in this gay companion.'

Although Anne was only to stay with Margaret for a year, one senses that the impact of the regent, known to all as *Madame*, upon the impressionable young English girl was profound. In time, when Anne reached the zenith of her power, we would see her emulate her erstwhile mistress in artistic and architectural taste, as well as in setting the same tone in the guidelines laid out for maintaining inscrutable morality within her own royal household.

Margaret was clearly delighted with her new charge as, having received her at court, she wrote the following to Sir Thomas:

> I have received your letter by the Esquire [Claude] Bouton who has presented your daughter to me, who is very welcome, and I am confident of being able to deal with her in a way which will give you satisfaction, so that on your return the two of us will need no intermediary other than she. I find her so bright and pleasant for her young age that I am more beholden to you for sending her to me than you are to me. (Translation from the original French)

There has been some suggestion that Claude Bouton travelled to England initially on some kind of errand related to the infant Princess Mary, who had recently become betrothed to the thirteen-year-old Charles. At some point, he returned to the Low Countries with Anne as his charge. We should remember that Anne was Charles's contemporary, being just one year younger than the child who would become one of her future husband's greatest rivals.

In thinking about the city that Anne first became acquainted with upon her arrival in the Low Countries, we can once again turn to Jane de Longh; she paints an evocative picture of Mechelen at the time:

> [The people of Mechelen] lived withdrawn and peaceful behind its ramparts

and canals. Across the drawbridges, through the gates, a rural traffic moved all day long of carts and wagons, pedestrians and horsemen ... in the centre of the intimate little town, along the quays of the Dijle, there was always a flapping of sails, a rattling of cranes and pulleys. Outside the walls, meadows and farmlands stretched toward the hazy Flemish horizon, the ditches which bordered them drawing strips of light through the ever moist green land while countless windmills turned industriously in the Flemish breeze.

As we shall see shortly, whereas the streets of sixteenth-century Paris have long been swept away, Mechelen is an altogether more resilient survivor, noted even today for its abundance of Renaissance architecture in typical Flemish style. It is not so hard to see through the veneer of time in Mechelen and recreate in your mind's eye the city that once greeted the young Anne Boleyn.

The Shaping of a Renaissance Queen

Once at court, it seems that Anne's introduction to the ducal household was a gentle one, for Jane de Longh goes on to point out that 'in the peaceful privacy of this modest palace she, [Margaret] in whose hands converged the threads of every European political intrigue, was able to create for herself a setting of feminine comfort and quiet harmony ... [in which] ... the spirit of courtesy and culture ... contrasted favourably with the loose and drunken manners of so many other courts'.

It was the beginning of Anne's introduction to Renaissance culture, which would be matured and refined in the coming years at the French court. Although Margaret would never set aside her widow's cap, she continued to surround herself with the finest artists, poets, philosophers and musicians of the time, delighting in painting, illumination, books and, of course, music. With Anne's sharp intelligence and capacity to absorb knowledge and wisdom from those who surrounded her, she learnt quickly. After her execution some twenty-three years later, the French poet Lancelot de Carles wrote of this earlier time: '*La Boullant* [Anne Boleyn], who at an early age had come to court, listened carefully to honourable ladies, setting herself to bend all her endeavour to imitate them to perfection, and made such good use of her wits that in no time at all she had command of the language.'

It seems that Anne was all too aware of her parents' high expectations for her education. In her sole surviving letter from her early years away from the English court, she wrote,

Sir,

I understand by your letter that you desire that I shall be of a worthy woman when I come to Court and you inform me that the Queen will take the trouble to converse with me, which rejoices me greatly to think of talking with a person so wise and virtuous. This will make me have greater desire to continue to speak French well and also spell, especially because you have so enjoined it on me, and with my own hand I inform you that I will observe it the best I can. Sir, I beg of you to excuse me if my letter is badly written, for I assure you that the orthography is from my own understanding alone, whereas the others were only written by my hand, and Semmonet tells me the letter but waits so that I may do it myself, for fear that it shall not be known unless I acquaint to you, and I pray you that the light of (?) may not be allowed to drive away the will which you say you have to help me. For it seems that you are sure (?) you can, if you please, make me a declaration of your word, and concerning me be certain that there shall be neither (?) nor ingratitude which might check or efface my affection, which is determined to (?) as much unless it shall please you to order me, and I promise you that my love is based on such great strength that it shall never grow less, and I will make an end to my (?) after having commended myself right and humbly to your good grace.

Written at five o'clock by your very humble and obedient daughter,

Anna de Boullan

The Ducal Palace

The palace in which Anne was to spend her time was another reflection of Margaret's artistic tastes, rooted in the heart of Franco-Flemish style. Having arrived back in the Low Countries from Savoy, where she had been widowed, Margaret initially lodged in Margaret of York's palace, located directly opposite the regent's later residence.

By the time Anne had arrived at Mechelen the city had built Margaret a new palace that was to be Anne's home for the following year. It was an unpretentious place, fashioned from brick and stone, giving rise to a distinctive style that historians such as Eric Ives have linked to the palace that would be remodelled for Anne some twenty years later at Whitehall. It was structured around a central courtyard; a pretty loggia, with flattened arches supported by stone pillars, ran around its perimeter. Although modest in size, the interior was resplendent, adorned with lavish fabrics and with rooms devoted to the regent's collections of art and priceless objects.

As you wander through the palace courtyard today, perhaps you might pause awhile and imagine Anne's voice floating down to you from an open window as, along with other ladies of the court, she learned the art of setting prose to music, cultivating the 'sweet singing voice that would make bears and wolves attentive'.

However, before long the wheel of fortune turned yet again. Mary Tudor, Henry VIII's youngest sister, was to be married to the King of France, and Anne was required as part of the new queen's household. After gaining her release from the ducal court, Anne packed her bags and headed overland to one of the most glamorous and bustling cities in Christendom. She was heading for Paris and her new life at the dazzling French court.

Visitor Information

Mechelen remains a relatively small city, less well known perhaps than nearby Brussels, Antwerp and Bruges. However, it more than makes up for its diminutive size with its many historical sites and superb Renaissance architecture.

The city is roughly fifteen minutes by train from Brussels. There are two train stations in Mechelen; Mechelen-Nekkerspoel will deliver you closest to the town centre, although the station is a little run down and, according to locals, not so safe at night. If you arrive here, head toward the bell tower of St Rumbold's Cathedral along Keizerstraat and just at the intersection on the left with Korte Maagdenstraat you will find Margaret of Austria's ducal palace.

Alternatively, if you arrive at the more modern Station Mechelen, it is best to take bus number 552 from the railway station, and get off four stops later in the Keizerstraat. There is no metro or tram in Mechelen, so getting around on foot is the best way to explore the city.

The old palace now serves the courts of justice, and although you cannot go inside the building, you can wander round the picturesque courtyard, allowing your imagination to indulge itself. The southern face (constructed of red brick and stone) is contemporary to Anne's time in Mechelen and would have been much as she had known it as a young girl, around five hundred years ago. You can also visit the Crown Hall, a really beautiful building (no photos allowed).

Opening times for the palace are: 9 a.m. – 5 p.m. from Monday to Friday. Note: the building is not open on Saturday.

On leaving the palace, continue in the same direction toward the Grote Markt (central marketplace). Almost immediately on your right after leaving the palace is a white stone building called the Stadsschouwburg. This was once Margaret of York's palace, and again is a building Anne certainly would have known. Today, only the former entrance hall remains, and this is now the city's cultural centre and theatre.

Finally, do continue on toward the marketplace, taking time to enjoy the many cafés, admiring the magnificent bell tower, part of St Rumbold's Cathedral, whose outline dominates this part of the city.

If you need more information on how to get to the city, opening times and places to stay, please contact the local tourist information centre via their web site at http://toerisme.mechelen.be/en/.

Château d'Amboise, Indre-et-Loire

> Le cinquiéme jour de juin 1515, mon fils, venant de Chaumont à Amboise, se mit une espine en la jambe, dont il eut moult de douleur et moi aussi; car vrai amour me contraignoit de souffrir semblable peine.
> On 5 June 1515, my son, while moving from Chaumont to Amboise, got a thorn in his leg, which caused him much suffering. And so did I suffer too, for true love compelled me to feel the same pain (as him).
>
> Recorded by Louise of Savoy in her journal

On 5 June 1515 the redoubtable Louise of Savoy, mother of the new king, Francis I, recorded the above entry in her diary. Earlier that year, on 15 February, her beloved son had made his triumphant entry into Paris following the death of his distant cousin Louis XII on New Year's Day 1515. The king and court had remained in Paris for the first half of the year, before finally leaving the city on 24 April and beginning a 90-mile journey south-west of the capital. Their destination was the Château d'Amboise, in the Loire Valley; this was the much-loved childhood home of France's virile new king, who had been installed there with his mother and sister by Louis XII back in 1501.

Anne Boleyn was among only six English ladies allowed to remain in the service of his wife, Queen Claude. The rest had been sent home to England with Mary Tudor, the dowager French queen. By that time, Anne had been away from Hever for around a year and a half. The slender fourteen-year-old girl with dark, beguiling eyes and lustrous auburn-coloured hair must have been teetering on the brink of womanhood; her impressionable young mind had already been exposed to the powerful female role model of Margaret of Austria, and once in France, she must have soon met Louise of Savoy and her daughter, the future Marguerite of Navarre. Over the next few years, Anne would no doubt meet visionaries like Leonardo da Vinci (who lived at Amboise from 1516 until his death in 1519) and be exposed to the thinking of French reformist writers like Jacques Lefèvre d'Étaples and Clément Marot, who was in residence at the French court during Anne's stay in France.

We must imagine her arriving at Amboise virtually fluent in conversational French and much at home in the sophisticated French court; it was a court that would soon become the epicentre of the Renaissance in Europe and would profoundly shape Anne's thinking and character, carving out her destiny as England's future queen.

The Château d'Amboise is situated now, as it was then, on top of a high plateau overlooking the Loire. Travelling from the north with the rest of the court, Anne would have seen its silhouette painted dramatically against the sky. It was June; the days long and warm, the light, airy rooms of the castle filled with the sweet scent of summer carried in through open windows on a gentle breeze. Perhaps Anne was struck, as the author was, by the marked difference between the homes of the English nobles, built to keep out the weather and keep warm, and those of their French counterparts, which seem to have been designed to let in the more benign weather of significantly warmer climes. Even today it is clear how the chalky stone and white marble interiors create bright, open spaces while the exterior walls literally gleam in the summer sunshine.

Touring the Château

The original entrance to the palace was not as it is today, which was once the tradesman's entrance, but via the *Porte des Lions*, a small defensive fort whose remains still stand on the eastern side of the plateau. A long and winding road, stretching for 4–5 kilometres, once made its way up to this entrance, and it is through this gateway that we can imagine Anne having her first glimpse of the place which would become her home for the next three years.

Sadly, only approximately 20 per cent of the sprawling complex of palatial buildings that Anne would have come to know intimately still exists today. However, luckily for us, two of those buildings are the Gothic and Louis XII wings. The latter is erroneously named as it was in fact built largely by Charles VIII but completed by King Francis during the first few years of his reign. These wings were subsequently used as the main royal lodgings for both Francis and his queen. Thus we can be quite sure that when we walk through the surviving rooms of the château we are walking through rooms that Anne once knew well.

The authors were there during a fine day in early September, when the château was set against a flawless sky and swallows swooped and dived from their nests tucked along the length of the string course beneath the château's pitched leaden roof. It was easy to imagine the splendour and insouciant nature of the French court. There is something about the place which speaks of carefree days, idle banter and playful flirtation. One can well imagine Anne dallying with the many *gentilhommes* of the court and honing the feminine guiles that would later so enrapture the King of England.

As you wander first around the Gothic wing and then the Louis XII, bear in mind the following.

The wonderful Grand Salle in the Gothic wing seems to have served a combined function equivalent to the English council chamber and presence chamber. So here, Francis would consult and hold audiences with wider members of the court. It is also here that the banquet following the wedding of the Duc de Lorraine and Renee de Bourbon-Montpensier took place (see below). This is an authentic sixteenth-century room and would have been largely as Anne would have known it.

The private chambers of Francis I are situated on the ground floor of the same wing, just off the Grand Salle. In a similar vein to the arrangement of rooms in Henry VIII's palaces, we move from the largest room (similar to Henry's privy chambers – although this room also seems to have been accessible to wider members of the court) through to a slightly smaller room that was the king's privy bedchamber, and finally we reach a much smaller privy dressing room (the English equivalent of a raying chamber). These ground-floor apartments looked out over beautiful Italian Renaissance vegetable gardens, arranged by Dom Pacello da Mercogliano, who went on to work at the Château de Blois in 1517.

The ground floor of this wing has been restored to its sixteenth-century glory and is packed with Renaissance architecture, furniture and interior decoration. Thus, it provides a strong sense of how the château would have been experienced by the young English *demoiselle d'honneur*. However, you will need to take this memory with you as you head upstairs to the first floor. The suite of rooms that you find there follows the same pattern as the king's below, and was once occupied by the diminutive Queen Claude. However, they have been restored to a later period. Thus, we need to see past the nineteenth-century interiors and imagine the queen surrounded by her ladies, doing their embroidery, reading or catching up on court gossip. It is likely that a good deal of Anne's time at the château was spent in these rooms.

Events at Amboise

As mentioned earlier, sadly we cannot state with exact certainty any specific events which involved Anne directly during this period of her life. However, we do know of a number of notable events that occurred at the Château d'Amboise during Anne's tenure at the French court. It is likely that she was present to witness the following.

On 26 June 1515, great celebrations were held as Francis claimed his right to the Duchy of Milan and began preparations for his campaign in Italy later in the year. The marriage of Antoine de Lorraine and Renee de Bourbon-Montpensier took place on the same day in the church of Saint-Florentin. This church once stood in the middle of the plateau, where the current bust of Leonardo da Vinci commemorates his initial resting place. The chapel was later destroyed during the French Revolution. Banquets, masques and tournaments followed. In one famous incident, a wild boar that had been set loose in the grand courtyard for entertainment broke free and threatened the spectators watching in the galleries of the Seven Virtues. The king managed to kill the beast with his own dagger. It must have been quite a spectacle for the young Anne to witness.

Soon came the birth of three royal children: Princess Louise on 19 August 1515; Princess Charlotte on 22 October 1516, and then finally the long awaited birth of the new *dauphin*, Francis, on 28 February 1518. Fabulous revels followed the baptism in the church of Saint-Florentin on the evening of 25 April 1518, with yet more dancing, masques and banquets. It was a double celebration, for the nephew of Pope Leo X, the Duke of Urbino, married a French princess, Madeleine de la Tour D'Auvergne, one week later on 2 May in the same church.

When we visit places like Amboise and begin to understand the key characters and events that surrounded Anne, we catch intriguing glimpses of those strong early influences that shaped her thinking in later life. We see her famed allure and grace forged amid the sophistication of the French court; we see her courage, strength and determination influenced by the formidable women that surrounded her; we see her flair for visionary thinking, perhaps inspired by the likes of Leonardo da Vinci; and we see Anne's interest in the new religion, undoubtedly ignited by reformist writers, whose works were widely read at the French court.

Website: http://www.chateau-amboise.com. Telephone Number: +33 (0) 247 57 00 98.

Hunsdon House, Hertfordshire

Anne Rocheford, one of the daughters and heirs of Thomas earl of Wiltshire and Ormond, keeper of the Privy Seal, created marchioness of Pembroke by charter 1 Sept. 24 Hen. VIII. Annuity of 1,000l. for life out of the issues of the honor, manor, or lordship of Hunnesdon [Hunsdon], Herts, and of the manors of Stansted Abbot, Roydon, Bourehouse, Pisso, Filolls, and Coxhall, Herts and Essex; and of all Crown lands in co. Pembroke …

Letters and Papers of Henry VIII, September 1532

In June 1528, a love-struck Henry VIII penned a moving letter to his 'entirely beloved' Anne Boleyn from his chamber at Hunsdon House, where he and his wife of nineteen years, Queen Katherine of Aragon, had sought temporary refuge following an outbreak of the 'sweat' in London:

> The uneasiness my doubts about your health gave me, disturbed and alarmed me exceedingly, and I should not have had any quiet without hearing certain tidings. But now, since you have as yet felt nothing, I hope, and am assured that it will spare you, as I hope it is doing with us. For when we were at Walton [Waltham Abbey], two ushers, two valets de chambres and your brother, master-treasurer, fell ill, but are now quite well; and since we have returned to our house at Hunsdon, we have been perfectly well, and have not, at present, one sick person, God be praised; and I think, if you would retire from Surrey, as we did, you would escape all danger. There is another thing that may comfort you, which is, that, in truth in this distemper few or no women have been taken ill, and what is more, no person of our court, and few elsewhere, have died of it. For which reason I beg you, my entirely beloved, not to frighten yourself nor be too uneasy at our absence; for wherever I am, I am yours, and yet we must sometimes submit to our misfortunes, for whoever will struggle against fate is generally but so much the farther from gaining his end: wherefore comfort yourself, and take courage and avoid the pestilence as much as you can, for I hope shortly to make you sing, la renvoyé. No more at present, from lack of time, but that I wish you in my arms, that I might a little dispel your unreasonable thoughts.
>
> Written by the hand of him who is and always will be yours,
>
> Im-H.R-muable

The king signed off his uncharacteristically handwritten letter – penned in a slanting, anxious hand – with his customary decorative monogram. However, on the left of the signature, in tiny writing, are the letters *im* and on the right of the signature *muable*, meaning *immuable*, or unshakeable. Henry was obviously concerned about Anne's health but comforted by the fact that she'd not yet shown any symptoms.

Henry's relief, though, was short lived, within days a messenger arrived at Hunsdon in the dead of night, with the 'most afflicting news'; Anne had fallen ill with the sweating sickness. As the French ambassador Du Bellay reported, the 'sweat' was a perilous disease: 'One has a little pain in the head and heart; suddenly a sweat begins; and a physician is useless, for whether you wrap yourself up much or little, in four hours, sometimes in two or three, you are despatched without languishing, as in those troublesome fevers.'

It's no wonder that this devastating news left Henry in shock. He penned a frantic letter of support to Anne, who was presumably now in quarantine at Hever Castle, stating that he 'would gladly bear half your illness to make you well'. The king lamented the fact that his best physician, 'in whom I have most confidence', was absent at the time 'when he might do me the greatest pleasure; for I should hope, by him and his means, to obtain one of my chief joys on earth – that is the care of my mistress'. Instead, Henry sent Anne his second-best doctor, William Butts and implored her to listen to his advice. He closed by saying that he hoped to see her again soon, 'which will be to me a greater comfort than all the precious jewels in the world'.

Henry's prayers were answered. On 23 June, Brian Tuke, the king's secretary, reported to Cardinal Wolsey that both Anne and her brother George had fallen ill but that, thanks to the ministrations of Dr Butts, they had made a 'perfect recovery'.

In May 1530, the court was again in residence; no doubt on this occasion Anne Boleyn was by the king's side. An entry in the *Privy Purse Expenses* records a payment of £5 made to George Boleyn, 'my Lord of Rocheforde', for 'shooting at Hunsden', a pastime Henry greatly enjoyed. The court returned again in 1531 and 1532, and made the most of all the diversions on offer, namely hunting, shooting, hawking and fishing.

In September 1532, Henry conferred on Anne the title of Marquess of Pembroke and granted her lands worth £1,000 a year, including the manor of Hunsdon. Over the next few years, Henry and Anne made several visits to Hunsdon, the royal couple clearly drawn to the beauty of this airy rural retreat.

A Short History

According to the antiquary Sir William Worcester, Hunsdon House was originally built in about 1447 by Sir William Oldhall, chamberlain of Richard, Duke of York, at a cost of 7,000 marks, nearly £5,000, with its principal feature being 'a brick tower 80 feet square and 100 feet high, crowned by gilded vanes', where Henry VIII is said to have enjoyed dining in private. This description suggests that Oldhall's tower would have been comparable to the extant great tower built at Tattershall in Lincolnshire by Ralph Cromwell, Lord Treasurer of England, between 1434 and 1447.

The house was luxurious and one of the most important residences of fifteenth-century England, as reflected by the string of illustrious owners that called Hunsdon home, including Edward IV, Richard III, Sir William Stanley and Margaret Beaufort. After Margaret's death, the house passed to Thomas Howard on his elevation to the dukedom of Norfolk, and then to his son and heir, Thomas, and finally into the hands of Henry VIII, who embarked on a program of building that would transform Hunsdon into a house of palatial proportions.

A Royal Residence

Between August 1525 and February 1534, Henry spent around £2,900 enlarging and modernising the existing manor at Hunsdon. While the surviving accounts do not paint a clear picture of the layout of the house that Anne visited, we know that the work appears to have been focussed on new apartments for the king, which stood at first-floor level and were accessed via a watching chamber. To complement the sumptuous panelled interiors, the king's glazier, Galyon Hone, was employed to repair all the old windows and glaze the windows in the king's new lodgings, gallery and closets with stained-glass windows displaying 'the king's armes, poises [mottoes], badges and bendis'.

Like many grand Tudor houses, Hunsdon also boasted an orchard, fishponds, gardens and a well-stocked deer park. It's no wonder then that in 1532 it was described as a 'palayes royall', to where 'his highness has great pleasure to resort for the health comfort and preservation of his most royal person'.

From 1536 onwards, Hunsdon was largely used as a residence for Henry's three children. Mary spent much time there before her accession to the throne, as did Edward, who was in residence at Hunsdon from May to July 1546, when he had his portrait – the famous image depicting the pre-adolescent Prince of Wales mimicking his father's haughty stance – painted with the house visible in the background.

In early 1536, Mary was moved from Eltham to Hunsdon. Since she was, at this time, in the words of historian David Starkey 'a mere appendage of her younger sister's household', it seems likely that the two-year-old Princess Elizabeth was also in residence. It's therefore entirely possible that on 19 May 1536, as Anne Boleyn drew her last breath, with her final thoughts on the fiery-haired daughter she was leaving behind, Elizabeth was miles away in Hunsdon, in the very house where her father, once so enamoured with Anne, was shaken to the core at the fear of losing her mother.

Visitor Information

It is hard to believe that Hunsdon was once such an important location in the lives of several Tudor protagonists, most notably Henry VIII, Anne Boleyn, Edward, Elizabeth and Mary. Today, the quaint, sleepy village is well kept and clearly prosperous but is otherwise unremarkable. There is nothing to hint at its historic past.

The house itself lies some way out of the village. You must take the turning into Acorn Street from the high street. This eventually becomes Church Lane. You will be driving for perhaps a couple of miles, leaving the village behind you, until the entrance to Hunsdon House appears suddenly on your left, just before a bend in the road. Immediately adjacent to this is St Dunstan's church. Opposite the entrance to the churchyard, on the far side of the road, is a car park. You may pull up here if you wish. Walking around the church (which was locked when we visited) reveals tantalising glimpses of the current house through trees and over hedges. Even though it is greatly changed as a result of being almost entirely rebuilt in the nineteenth century, Hunsdon is clearly still a splendid house that hints at its once great and illustrious past. Unfortunately though, the house is privately owned and there is no access.

Rest and refreshment can be found back in the village at one of its two public hostelries, The Crown or The Fox and Hounds.

Postcode: SG12 8PP.

Haseley Court, Oxfordshire

> Master Barentyne hath a right fair mansion place [with] marvellous fair walks, *topiarii operis [topary]*, and orchards and pools.
>
> John Leland, Tudor antiquarian

In August 1529, Henry VIII and Anne Boleyn stayed in Haseley for two days as they made their way toward the most northerly destination of that year's progress, Grafton Regis in Northamptonshire.

The beginning of that month had witnessed momentous events unfolding in London. The Legatine Court had been sitting in Blackfriars in judgment on the legitimacy of the king's marriage to his first wife, Katherine of Aragon. Dramatic scenes had seen the queen drop to her knees in front of the entire court and plead with her husband to be recognised as his true wife. In the end, Cardinal Campeggio deferred the decision to Rome. Henry and Anne found themselves no further forward in their pursuit of the king's divorce; furious, they had left the capital, beginning a two-month progress that would take in swathes of Essex, Bedfordshire, Berkshire, Oxfordshire and Northamptonshire.

Given the recent debacle in London, we might imagine that as Anne Boleyn arrived at Haseley Court, situated in the tiny village of Little Haseley near Oxford, she was experiencing a kaleidoscope of emotions ranging from frustration through to anger. No doubt tensions ran particularly high at times, since there is no reason to believe that Katherine of Aragon was anywhere but with her husband and the court at the time – although one imagines she was very much *persona non grata*. It was a tense *ménage a trois*, which would continue until 1531, when Katherine would finally be abandoned by Henry at Windsor Castle.

En route from Reading Abbey to the Old Palace of Woodstock (see also *In the Footsteps of Anne Boleyn* for more information on both these locations), contemporary *geists* indicate that as part of the progress, the court was due to lodge at Haseley on Monday 23 and Tuesday 24 August. Royal household accounts in the National Archives verify that the visit took place, with payments made to various royal offices for expenses incurred while at Haseley:

> Die Lune xxiij die Aug[ustus] ap[u]d hasley
> D[ispensaria] vj li[bre] v s[olidus] Buti[lleria] xj li[bre] x s[olidus] viij d[enarius]
> Monday 23 day of August at Haseley,
> Steward 6 pounds 5 shillings, Buttery 11 pounds 10 shillings 8 pence

Haseley – A Tale of Four Manor Houses

Identifying the exact house in which the royal couple stayed while at Haseley is a little more vexing as, at the time, Haseley was divided into four: Latchford, Rycote, Great Haseley and Little Haseley. All possessed manor houses of one form or another. According to the *Victoria Country History of Oxfordshire* online, with regards to Latchford, 'The chief house for the estate appears to have been

Latchford House, which was built, or rebuilt, in the 16th century presumably for the Lenthalls. Probably this was the house in Latchford taxed on seven hearths in 1665.' 'Seven hearths' suggests a small house, and set against other contenders, seems the least likely.

Rycote would come to pre-eminence only later in the sixteenth century, after it was acquired by the royal courtier Sir John Williams in 1539. He subsequently rebuilt the manor there. Sir John set about creating a grand house with adjacent park, and according to *Time Team*, in an episode entitled 'A Palace Sold for Scrap, Rycote, Oxfordshire', the house was visited by Henry VIII and Catherine Howard as part of their 'honeymoon' in 1540.

Great Haseley, on the other hand, once had a fine manor with illustrious royal connections. However, around the time of the visit, Leland describes 'the present farmhouse, which belongs to Windsor College [and which] stands next to the church and on the site of the [previous] manor house'. The description of the 'manor' at Great Haseley as a 'farmhouse' is a little at odds with an image which is in existence of the house drawn pre-1729, before its eighteenth-century remodelling. This image comes from a map in St George's Chapel Windsor (CC 11232) and shows a three-storey 'C'-shaped house, adjacent to the parish church and surrounded by gardens, yards and barns. However, perhaps the house was already occupied by tenant farmers (as was recorded in the late seventeenth century), and a 'farmhouse' hardly seems appropriate for a royal visit.

Our main evidence that Little Haseley was in fact the site of the royal stay comes from a thesis written by Neil Samman entitled 'Henry VIII & Wolsey: The Tudor Court & Royal Progresses, 1509–1547'. This extensive piece of work details all of Henry's progresses through this period and Samman notes Haseley Court, 'Sir William Barentyne's House', as being the lodging used by Henry and Anne during their brief stay in the parish. Additional circumstantial evidence adds weight to this theory.

Sir William Barentyne – A Likely Host

Barentyne was clearly well known at court and was obviously deemed worthy of patronage at the highest level. By the time of Anne's visit, Sir William, born in December 1481, was head of the household and would have played gracious host to the king, queen and Mistress Boleyn. He had served in the king's army during the campaign to take Tournai in 1513, during which he was knighted. In 1520 he was again in royal service, present at the Field of Cloth of Gold. Barentyne would go on to be present at the christening of Prince Edward in 1537, and be appointed as part of the reception party greeting Anne of Cleves on English soil in 1539–40.

Not only do we see Sir William embraced as a loyal subject by the king, but we have evidence that he was also on good terms with a number of the prominent men at court. Firstly, just three years earlier, in 1526, the dukes of Norfolk and Suffolk, the Marquis of Exeter and Anne Boleyn's own father, Viscount Rochford, were guests of Sir William at Haseley, attested to by an extant letter signed by all four gentlemen to Cardinal Wolsey and dated 'Sir Wm. Barington's house, St. Bartholomew's day [24 August]'. Thus, in terms of a royal visit, we see that the house already had 'form'.

Furthermore, Barentyne clearly had another influential friend at the pinnacle of Tudor Society – Thomas Cromwell. In December of 1529, Sir William penned a letter to Cromwell. This is summarised in *The Parliamentary History of the County of Oxford*: ' ... his heartily beloved friend, Master Cromwell. Hope to have seen him in those parts before Christmas. Will make him welcome if he will come to his house. Ask his favour in his suit for the ferme of the parsonage of Churchyll.' He goes onto request that Cromwell prevent another local landowner taking its possession, which Master Cromwell duly did, suggesting that Sir William did indeed hold sway at court.

Finally, almost immediately following the royal visit, in October 1529, Sir William was appointed 'knight of the shire' for Oxfordshire, only one of two gentlemen appointed to represent Oxfordshire in Parliament. Was this in recognition for hosting a successful visit? Perhaps, although this is supposition on our part.

In short, Sir William Barentyne seems to have been a man of some standing, and certainly well connected enough to secure the honour of a royal visit.

The Barentynes and a 'Right Fair Mansion Place'
Some fifteen years after the visit, John Leland was appointed rector at nearby Great Haseley church. He clearly passed through the village on his travels, for Leland's Itinerary states that 'Master Barentyne hath a right fair mansion place [with] marvellous fair walks, *topiarii operis [topary]*, and orchards and pools (Note: clipped yew hedges in the form of birds and chess pieces are mentioned in records dating to 1580, and later replacements survive to this day).'

The Barentynes had been resident at Haseley Court since the late fourteenth century or early fifteenth century. According to J. Blair in *The Manorial History of Chalgrove*,

> in 1391, with his brother Thomas Barentyne II, Drew [Barentyne] (a Lord Mayor of London in 1398 an 1408) had bought the Oxfordshire manor of Little Haseley. The sumptuous manor house at Haseley Court, much of which still remains, must have been built soon afterwards, and Leland's statement that `Barentyne the gold-smythe buylded the Manor Place at Little Haseley' is easily accepted.

The Appearance of Haseley Court
Leland describes that the approach to Haseley from Ewelme (the probable direction of travel for the royal party) as 'V [5] miles by chaumpaine ground sumwhat plentiful in corn but most layid to pasturage'. Unfortunately for the Tudor enthusiast, the house itself was remodelled significantly in the eighteenth century and little detail survives of the overall appearance and layout of the original medieval house. However, one wing contemporary to that period has

survived relatively intact – although much remodelled and Gothicised in the eighteenth and nineteenth century. According to *The Victoria County History of Oxfordshire*,

> Part of the fourteenth- and fifteenth-century house survives in a two-storeyed wing, running back from the main eighteenth-century block. The range retains some high-quality fifteenth- and possibly late fourteenth-century windows ... the complete reworking of the interior makes it difficult to judge what function the range may originally have fulfilled. A converted fifteenth-century barn with slit windows and original buttresses survives a little way north-west of the house.

Pevsner postulates that this wing may have been used as a first-floor hall; others have cited a chapel. Indeed, according to the current owners it is still called the Chapel Room to this day. In summary, an account by C. Hussey for *Country Life* magazine in 1960, states,

> If, as seems to be the case, Sir William Barentyne about 1520 erected so handsome a barn ... his 'right fair mansion place' must have been correspondingly imposing. There is no sign of this [house] now, or how it lay in relation to the 14th-century or 18th-century buildings. If it consisted of a quadrangle, these [extant ranges] would represent its north and west sides; and a vanished east range would have been quite close to a length of a straight 'canal' running north and south ... presumably a survivor of Sir William Barentyne's 'pooles'.

Accounts show the king and his riding court were still present at Haseley on 24 August but by the following day, they had reached the Old Palace of Woodstock.

Visitor Information
Little Haseley lies just a few miles south-west of Thame. To reach the village, you are likely to pass through Great Haseley, with its large manor house standing adjacent to the church – of which John Leland was once rector. Haseley Court is privately owned today, although the owners, Mr and Mrs Heyward, kindly allowed us to view what remains of the medieval house, its buttresses, doorways and windows giving tantalising glimpses into its early origins. However, the house is not open to the public. The gardens surrounding Haseley Court are renowned among horticulturalists, having been created in the mid-late twentieth century by the famed Nancy Lancaster. They are opened to special-interest groups on appointment only.
    Postcode: OX44 7LL.

Buckingham, Buckinghamshire

> The Progresse of K. Henry the VIIIth made in the XXIth yeare of his reigne.
> September 1st, at Langley; 4th, at Woodstock; 9th, at Buckingham; 10th, at

Grafton; 24th, at Buckingham; 25th, at Notley; 28th, at Byssham; 29th, at Windsor.

Letters and Papers of Henry VIII, 1529

On 9 September, and again on 24 September, the court overnighted in Buckingham, as recorded in Sir Henry Guildford's account book. While Sir Henry, the Comptroller of the Household, did not record exactly where in Buckingham the royal party lodged, we believe the available evidence points to the Buckingham home of Henry Carey, the son of William Carey and Mary Boleyn, who was three years old at the time of the visit.

The young Carey had inherited his father's property after his sudden death of the sweating sickness the previous year. However, as Henry had not yet reached his majority – twenty-one for a male – his wardship was granted to his maternal aunt, Anne Boleyn, 'one of the daughters of Viscount Rocheford'. While the exact date of the grant is unknown, the wording places it firmly before December 1529, when Anne's father, Thomas Boleyn, formerly Viscount Rochford, was created Earl of Wiltshire and Ormond. In fact, it's likely that the bill was signed not long after William Carey's death in June 1528.

The king had not visited Buckingham on any of his previous progresses and so the timing suggests that Anne had influenced the itinerary. It's possible that she'd simply wished to see her recently widowed sister, Mary.

The Dreaded Sweat

In the summer of 1528, the sweating sickness swept through the streets of Tudor London, claiming as many as two thousand souls before spreading across the English Channel to Calais. This was the fourth recorded outbreak of this enigmatic and virulent disease, which more frequently affected men than women and did not discriminate between the rich and the poor. Sufferers often experienced symptoms typical of a viral infection or the flu: a sense of apprehension, headaches, cold shivers, muscle aches and great exhaustion. This was followed by fever, accompanied by headaches and delirium. Chest and abdominal pain and difficulty breathing were also common.

Of those who contracted 'the sweat', the elderly, frail and very young were often spared; while for men in the prime of their lives, like William Carey, death came frighteningly swiftly – at times within a few hours of the first symptom. Understandably, any reported cases caused widespread panic, as noted by John Hoker in *Holinshed's Chronicles*: 'The greedie riddance of life procured by this sickness did so terrifie people of all sorts, that such as could make shift either by monie or friendship, changed their soile, and leaving places of concourse, betooke them (for the time) to abodes though not altogether solitairie yet less frequented ...'

Those who could fled at the first sign of illness, which is exactly what Henry VIII did in the summer of 1528, travelling from house to house in search of refuge. Mary Boleyn's husband was not the only member of the royal household to die during this outbreak; William Compton and Francis Poyntz also perished. Several others contracted the disease and survived, including Anne Boleyn.

The Story of the Two Manor Houses of Buckingham

The question of where Anne and Henry stayed during their visit to Buckingham in September 1529 is anything but straightforward. As stated, we believe that it's likely the couple stayed at Henry Carey's house in Buckingham. However, the exact location of the property is disputable. One possibility is that the modern-day privately owned Manor House, which lies opposite the old churchyard, the site of Buckingham's first church at the bottom of Church Street, is the manor house once owned by the Careys. The half-timbered residence, with its twisted chimneys, was built in the sixteenth century. Though altered subsequently, it was originally the house for the prebend of Buckingham and is visible on John Speed's map of the area from 1610. However, was this residence built at the time of Henry and Anne's visit to the area in 1529? And if so, was it spacious enough to host a royal visit? Local historian Ed Grimsdale is not convinced; he believes the house may in fact date from around 1560 and notes that a much larger house existed further south of the surviving manor house.

As Ed points out, the situation is complicated by the presence of this second, grander house on the river, again clearly visible on Speed's map. Although sometimes highly stylised, if we take the map at face value, we see that the house appears to comprise of two two-storey wings, one oriented east, the other west. These are connected by a single-storey gallery/building that faces south over the gardens and river. The entire complex is surrounded by a wall to the east, north and west (with the entrance to the compound in the north-west corner), while the River Great Ouse forms its southernmost boundary. Unlike the aforementioned smaller house, it is identified by name, presumably denoting its greater importance. This house, known as Prebend House, disappears from the records after the English Civil War, and there is no sign of it on Thomas Jeffreys' map of the area made in 1770. Thus at some point between 1610 and 1770, this grand house, perhaps the very house where Anne spent quiet moments walking by the river with her sister, was demolished. It's possible that this occurred during the English Civil War, or in the aftermath of a great fire that tore through the town in March 1725. It's recorded that 138 of the 387 houses that made up Buckingham at the time were destroyed. This tragedy left over 200 families homeless and desperate. While some effort was made to house the displaced townspeople, it appears that some took matters into their own hands, destroying several large houses to sell the materials to build small tenements. It's possible that this marked the end of Prebend House.

A Gift from a Tudor Queen

It's possible that Katherine of Aragon was staying at Castle House in Buckingham, the home of Edward Fowler, in September 1513, when she received news of the English victory against the Scottish at Flodden Field. King Henry was away on a military campaign in France at the time. In his absence, Katherine had been appointed 'Regent and Governess of England, Wales and Ireland'. According to the Chronicler Edward Hall,

> after this noble victory the earl [of Surrey] wrote first to the queen which had raised a great power to resist the said king of Scots, of the winning of the battle … and she yet being at the town of Buckingham had word the next day after that the king of Scots was slain and a part of his coat armour to her sent, for which victory she thanked God …

The queen penned a triumphant letter to her husband from Woburn Abbey on 16 September: 'Your grace shall see how I can keep my promise, sending you for your banners a king's coat.'

Local tradition claims that Katherine, so overjoyed at news of the victory, showed her gratitude to the people of Buckingham by giving them her ivory cross, which can still be seen today in Buckingham's Old Gaol Museum.

Visitor Information

Although Buckingham has suffered at the hands of fire and war, it still retains a pleasant charm. This is particularly true of the old town, now entirely residential, its streets containing their fair share of historic houses and landmarks. The old town is contained within a peninsula of land around which the river, called the Great Ouse, has flowed since time immemorial. We visited during an Indian summer, when the late September sun made the ancient streets and leafy banks of the river an entirely agreeable place to wander and soak up a time when two queens of England visited what was, at the time, the county town of Buckinghamshire.

We advise parking in the town's central car park (signposted as you enter the town). Head to the main high street, where the Old Gaol dominates the square. Here you will be able to view the ivory crucifix mentioned in the text above. It was easy to imagine Katherine on her knees, giving thanks to God for the victory at Flodden; how she might then have gifted this item, which had such emotional significance for this proud warrior queen, to the town. The tourist information centre, located on the ground floor, will also be able to give you a street plan of the town. This will help you find your way to the sites of relevance to us.

We recommend heading for Brackley Road (just beyond the convergence of West Street and School Lane), where you will find Castle House (the frontage since remodelled in the Queen Anne style). As noted above, it is thought that Katherine of Aragon was lodged here in 1513 as guest of the Fowler family. Using the map, retrace your steps down School Lane making your way toward Well Street. This leads down to the old town from the current centre. Notice the spire of the eighteenth-century church, sitting proudly atop of what was once the motte of the original Norman castle. It is the highest area of land in the town. At the bottom of Well Street, just before you enter the old cemetery (the site of the original church in Buckingham, before its demolition in the eighteenth century) you will find the Old Manor House on your left. Take note of the beautiful twisted chimney at the rear of the property, which can be easily seen from the road. This is one of the two contenders for the home of Mary Boleyn and her son, Henry (the less likely one).

To complete the tour of our locations, walk through the old cemetery and down Hunter Street. Just after the bridge over the river take a left down Station Road, filtering off immediately to your left down a path that leads through the trees. Follow the path a little way forward and take a left turn over the next wooden bridge. This brings you onto a car park, the likely site of the original Prebend House.

Having finished the tour, you do not need to retrace your steps. Using the map you can walk through Chandos Park, back toward the central car park. Alternatively, we can recommend Looby Lou's tea room on West Street, gloriously kitsch, cosy and charming; a perfect place to reflect on the glorious history of this little town.

The Old Gaol: Market Hill, Buckingham, MK18 1JX. Tel No: + 44 (0) 128 082 3020.

Looby Lou's Tearoom: 4 West Street, Buckingham MK18 1HL. Tel No: + 44 (0) 128 082 2787.

Chertsey Abbey, Surrey

> I went with eager steps to view the Abbey, [or] rather the site of the Abbey; for so total a dissolution I scarcely ever saw; so inveterate a rage against even the least appearance of it, as if they meant to defeat even the inherent sanctity of the ground. Of that noble and splendid pile, which took up four acres of ground, and looked like a town, nothing remains; scarcely a little of the outward wall of the precinctus.
>
> Dr Stukeley, October 1752

Chertsey Abbey once ranked among the greatest abbeys in England, rivalling the likes of Reading, Glastonbury and Bury St Edmunds. Its noble pre-eminence stretched back to the seventh century, when it was founded by the much-venerated St Erkenwald. This future Bishop of London established a Benedictine monastery on the site in the year 666.

Bede was the first to mention its existence, describing an abbey built upon a raised area of land known as the Ceroti Insula, surrounded by flood plains and adjacent to the River Thames. Nearly a thousand years after its foundation, the abbey's position, around 7 miles from Windsor Castle to the west, and a similar distance again from Hampton Court to the east, made it a very convenient staging post for Henry and the royal court.

Female Rivals

Over a period of thirty years, both Katherine of Aragon and Anne Boleyn would lodge within its walls in a quirk of fate that would be difficult to imagine. Thus in 1501 (strangely the same year in which Anne Boleyn was probably born), the Spanish Papers record that Katherine rested overnight at Chertsey on her way from Plymouth to London following her arrival from Spain. A contemporary account written shortly after the death of Katherine's first husband, Prince Arthur, called the

The Receyt of the Ladie Kateryne, states, 'Upon the morow, the vijth day of the rehersid moneth of Novembre, the Princesse on her bihalve toke her journey to Chartsey and ther lodged all that nyght, and from thens towardes Lamehith [Lambeth].'

The fifteen-year-old Spanish princess, with 'her titular name (Princess of Wales), her rosy cheeks, her light blue eyes, reminded people of her English blood'. It was a time of youth, hope and celebration. Seven days later, on 14 November 1501, Katherine was married to Prince Arthur in the old abbey of St Paul's in London. Such carefree times, witnessed within the walls of this now vanished abbey, were in stark contrast to the desolate pain that Katherine would endure some thirty years later. And indeed, thirty years later, Anne Boleyn's time had come. On 14 July 1531, Henry VIII finally abandoned Katherine at Windsor. Anne was at his side as they rode toward Chertsey. Historian David Starkey follows the trail of Henry and Anne left behind in the *Privy Purse Expenses of Henry VIII*, describing what happened next:

> Instead of starting out boldly to distant Woodstock, he [Henry] shifted only a short way to Chertsey Abbey, a mere seven miles to the east of Windsor. And there he and Anne (Boleyn) remained for at least ten days, crossing and recrossing the river by the ferries at Hampton Court and Datchet, and hunting in the neighbouring parks which clustered round the great forest of Windsor: they were at Mote Park on the 17th, at Ditton Park near Windsor on the 19th and at Byfleet Park on the 22nd.

On 23 July the couple were back at Chertsey Abbey, where the same expenses record payment to a servant of the Abbot of Westminster for bringing 'Relyke (Relic) water to Chartsay for the king's grace'.

This was Anne's first taste of life beyond Katherine's seemingly ever-present shadow. It must have been exhilarating and a time of carefree pleasure. Yet Anne Boleyn was not done with Chertsey; if her first sojourn was one of celebration, the second would capture a famous moment in history. After being created Marquess of Pembroke at Windsor Castle on 1 September 1532 (see entry on Windsor Castle), Chertsey Abbey would be the first destination to receive the 'Lady Marquess' as she rode with Henry toward London in preparation for their forthcoming visit to Calais. This time Anne's stay was relatively brief. By 18 September Henry and Anne were lodged at Chertsey, where the *Privy Purse Expenses* record that the king was brought pears and peaches, his hounds following behind from Windsor. On the following day, George Taylor, Anne's receiver, took delivery of 'stuf' from the 'Robes' (Great Wardrobe) for 'my Lady Marquess of Pembroke'; no doubt Anne was being suitably attired for her new, elevated status as the king's intended consort. By 21 September the royal couple had reached nearby Hampton Court.

The Medieval Abbey of Chertsey – Layout and Appearance
The abbey of Chertsey was the first to be dissolved, being surrendered to the Crown on 6 July 1537. Subsequently, much of the stone and other suitable materials would be carried just over a mile and a half eastwards to be reused in the construction of

Oatlands Palace (see entry for Oatlands Palace). What was left was used to build Abbey House (an early seventeenth-century house, demolished around 1810), or claimed by the citizens of the town of Chertsey to raise up the roads above the level of the flood plain. As a result, there was so little left that Dr Stukeley, visiting in the eighteenth century, lamented,

> I left the ruins of this place, which had been consecrated to Religion ever since the year 666, with a sigh for the loss of so much national magnificence and national history. Dreadful was that storm which spared not, at least, the churches, libraries, painted glass, monuments, manuscripts; that spared not a little out of the abundant spoil, to support them for the public honour and emolument.

However, fortunately, several archaeological digs have taken place over the last two hundred years, including two of particular significance – in the 1850s and 1950s. These have produced consistent findings, gradually adding to our understanding of the site and its appearance before the Dissolution.

There is only one contemporary image of the abbey and its surroundings, contained within a fifteenth-century manuscript called the Chertsey Chartulary. However, a number of seals of the great abbey survive, each showing a slightly variable representation of the abbey church. Stukeley gives us a wonderful impression of the surrounding site as it appeared in the eighteenth century:

> The domains of the Abbey extend all along upon the side of the river for a long way, being a very fine meadow. They made a cut at the upper end of it; which, taking in the water of the river, when it approaches the abbey, gains a fall sufficient for a water-mill for the use of the abbey and of the town. Here is a very large orchard, with many and long canals, or fish-ponds; which, together with the great mote around the abbey, and deriving its water from the river, was well stocked with fish.

A rule of the Benedictine order states that 'a monastery ought to be so arranged that everything that is necessary – water, a mill, a garden and a bakery – may be made use of, and different arts be carried on within the monastery so that there shall be no need for the monks to wander about outside, for this is not good for their souls'.

And so it was at Chertsey Abbey, with the map of the demesne showing the abbey church surrounded by meadows, mills and a large barn, called the Great Burway Barn. Antiquarian archaeologist W. Pocock, who undertook the first major excavations on the site in 1858, stated that from the stone debris, the abbey itself was most likely built from Caen stone. The design was cruciform, with a central tower surmounted by a spire and, as would be usual, with a main entrance located on the west side of the building. The church was around 275 feet in length, with the nave divided into three aisles by two ranges of Purbeck marble columns.

The habitual arrangement of buildings in a Benedictine monastery placed the cloisters and its attendant claustral buildings, such as the chapter house, abbot's lodgings, and refectory, directly to the south of the nave to catch the sun. However, Chertsey seems to have been different, with this complex of buildings sited to the north of the abbey church; the abbot's lodging and private chapel lying to the east of the Chapter House, which was in turn usually located on the eastern side of the cloister. Although we have no record of where Katherine, Henry and Anne stayed while at the abbey, the abbot's lodgings were the usual suite of rooms used by royal visitors to any abbey; sadly, nothing of these buildings survives today.

However, we do know that as Henry and Anne came and went from their lodgings, they would have passed beneath the gatehouse into and out of the heart of the monastic compound. We know something of the appearance and position of this as Pocock writes, 'The principal gate-house at Chertsey is said to have had a chapel over it … This I believe to have stood opposite the end of Guilford-street, on or near the site of the present church … and which was evidently built out of its ruins.'

As Anne left Chertsey for the final time, it would have been inconceivable to her that in a little over four years she would be dead at the hands of a man who professed to love her, and that just over a year on from her demise the abbey too would be dismantled, thus ending nine hundred years of religious devotion upon the site.

Visitor Information.

The slight remains of this once noble building are located in the town that grew up on account of the abbey's presence: Chertsey, in Surrey. It is a pleasant district of suburban London that lies just within the M25 orbital of the capital, brushing close to the edge of the Surrey countryside. Of course, five hundred years ago Chertsey Abbey would have stood proud atop its elevated insula, surrounded by peaceful meadows and through which meandered the mighty Thames. No such topographical landmarks are visible today. However, nothing has changed its geography, placing the ruins of Chertsey Abbey within easy reach of the sites of the lost palace of Oatlands, Syon Abbey and the rather more substantial remains of Windsor Castle and Hampton Court Palace. Thus, if you wish to go off the tourist trail and rediscover some of the more forgotten buildings of Henry's Tudor England, then a little pre-planning to encompass these additional locations might be in order.

We parked in the local Sainsbury's (supermarket) car park (Postcode: KT16 9AG), which is a pay-and-display car park on all but Sundays and Bank Holidays. Take a left out of the entrance to the car park and walk a short distance to the junction and turn left into Windsor Street. Walking ahead, you will soon come across the church, which Pocock states was probably built out of the remains of the abbey gatehouse that once stood close to this site. The sheer distance you have to walk along Windsor Street to reach the site itself indicates just how substantial the original monastic complex was. On the left you will shortly pass Chertsey Museum. It was closed on the day we were there (Sunday and Bank Holidays) and so we were unable to pay a visit. However, it does house additional information on the abbey and the history of the town.

Upon reaching the playing fields, turn right into Colonel's Lane and walk to the end. On your left is Abbey Gardens, cast in dappled shade. Here lie the rather paltry remains of part of a wall and the site of the abbey's kilns. An information board helps you orientate yourself. As you stand reading it, you will realise that the abbey church and claustral buildings were behind you, across the lane and underneath some rather fine-looking houses. Cast a glance over your right shoulder from this point and you will also see an ancient barn. Its masonry creates a chequerboard effect. Rob Poulton of the Surrey Archeological Society states in his book entitled *Archaeological Investigations on the Site of Chertsey Abbey* that the building is likely to be part early sixteenth century in date with some components possibly relating to the period after the dissolution of the abbey. Before you finish, do continue to walk through the park by the river, until you find the remains of the substantial medieval fishponds – quite a sight!

Although very little remains of Chertsey Abbey, it is a pleasant spot where the paths of two indomitable women crossed in time. It may be all but gone but somehow the imprint of its once mighty presence remains.

For rest and refreshment, make your way back to Windsor Street. Here there are plenty of pubs and shops to meet your needs.

Postcode: KT16 8RF.

Berkeley Castle, Gloucestershire

> Mark the year and mark the night,
> When Severn shall re-echo with affright,
> The shrieks of death through Berkeley's roof that ring,
> Shrieks of an agonizing king.
>   Gray's Bard referring to the murder of Edward II at Berkeley Castle

In the summer of 1535, with Sir Thomas More's body barely cold in its grave, Henry VIII and Anne Boleyn set out on a momentous summer progress. It was to be one of the longest and most politically significant of Henry's reign. Men of the reformed faith would be honoured by visits from the royal couple as they travelled from Windsor Castle through Oxfordshire, Gloucestershire, Wiltshire and Hampshire. While at Winchester, three of Anne's bishops would be consecrated in Winchester Cathedral in a carefully orchestrated piece of Henrician propaganda.

About one month into the progress, the king and queen left behind the priory of Leonard Stanley, where they had stayed overnight as guests of the prior, John Rodley. They began to snake their way across the English countryside amid a patchwork of golden fields, the crops ripened by the late-summer sun. Above their heads, the sound of nature's symphony filled the air, as skylarks warbled on the wing. Henry and Anne were heading toward their next stop, at Berkeley Castle.

On 8 August, the royal couple rode into the cool shadows cast by Berkeley Castle's gatehouse and took up residence in a medieval fortress that Leland would later rather disparagingly label in his itinerary as 'no great thinge'. It was the first and last time that Henry and Anne would visit Berkeley, but clearly they were determined to enjoy its pleasant charms as provision had been made in the *geists* for them to stay there for the entire week. On 9 August there is confirmation that the royal party are lodged at Berkeley on account of the opening line of the following letter, written by Thomas Thacker to Cromwell: 'This Wednesday, 11 Aug., I received your letter dated Berkley Herons, the 9th.' Cromwell was clearly keeping up a stream of letters for, in a second letter dated 18 August, Sir William Fitzwilliam made a reply to a letter also received from Master Secretary, saying, 'I received at Dover your kind letter, dated Barkley Herons, the 11th.' (Note: 'Barkley Herons' is probably a corruption of Berkeley Harness, which is the ancient name for the estate.)

Thomas Cromwell was obviously still close to the king's side, and from the profusion of letters recorded in *Letters and Papers* that continue through the first half of the progress, we can see Master Secretary busily overseeing the 'visitations' already being made to a number of monastic houses. Yet, perhaps this stay at Berkeley was even sweeter for Cromwell, for at the time he was the castle's constable, receiving income from its lands – a position he was to retain until his execution in 1540.

A Brief History

Berkeley Castle had fallen into Crown hands back in 1492 as a result of a bargain struck between William, Viscount Berkeley, and Henry VII. Viscount Berkeley received a marquessate and the title of Earl Marshal of England, while Henry VII would inherit Berkeley Castle upon the marquess's death. Thus, when Anne and Henry visited, the castle belonged to the king.

In appearance Berkeley did not dominate the local town as did some of the mightier Norman fortresses, such as Ludlow or Dover. Instead, the less political Berkeleys had focused on residential development within a pre-existing buttressed curtilage. In fact, the castle is well screened by the church and trees, such that its full glory can only be appreciated from the south, across the marshy meadows of the diminutive River Avon.

The Privy Apartments at Berkeley Castle

Berkeley Castle sits perched on a plateau that overlooks fields stretching away below it. Built on a typical Norman motte-and-bailey design in the eleventh, twelfth and fourteenth centuries, it is also highly distinctive, constructed from local pink, grey and yellow Severn sandstone with its roofs mainly fashioned in Cotswold stone, slate or lead. It has been described as being in an 'original and good state of preservation' and one of the 'supreme residential survivals of the fourteenth century'. It retains most of its original features down to doors, arrow slits and windows and even iron catches. The interiors remained largely unaltered from the sixteenth century until the 1920s, when the 8th Earl of Berkeley modernised and extensively altered the internal décor, installing many artefacts from elsewhere.

However, distinctive as it might be, the castle is also austere in its presence. Perhaps it cannot shake off the legacy of royal murder referred to in the quote above, an event for which the castle is probably best known in English history. It is at Berkeley that Edward II most likely suffered an ignominious end at the hands of his captors within the walls of the Norman keep.

On account of its exceptional state of preservation, the rooms used by Henry and Anne still survive in the 'great suite' that fronts the south-west facade of the building, although David Smith, chief archivist at Berkeley, adds a note of caution:

> The layout of the main apartments of the castle, as they were in the time of the visit, is still visible, i.e. the Great Hall, the chapel (now the Morning Room) and large parts of the keep, some of which are now in the private wing. But the interiors have been altered in the intervening centuries, and hardly any of the furniture dates from before about 1660.

However, in Emery's *Greater Medieval Houses of England and Wales, Volume III* a description is given of how the privy apartments would have been accessed from Edward III's great hall, allowing us to imagine more clearly the layout of the rooms that would have greeted Anne upon her stay at the castle:

> Access from the hall dais to the residential range is by a 1925 replacement Berkeley arch. It opened into a stair bay, presumably rectangular to balance the entry porch, but rebuilt in 1637 when the present stair was inserted … In its early form, the stair would have risen to a rectangular ante-chamber above the ground-floor lobby, possibly with a ribbed ceiling. This was the prelude to the three first-floor family apartments, the chapel at the angle, and the great or outer chamber followed by the inner chamber filling the remainder of the courtyard range.

Today we also leave the great hall from the high end, passing up the later staircase, as described in the quote above. At the top of the stair, we reach a lobby with the entrance to the chapel on your left. This was not the original entrance; that would have been at the other end of the chapel. It was swapped by the 8th Earl of Berkeley in the early twentieth century.

What is of note here is the sumptuous wall decoration. The authors have heard two versions of a story about its origins; both are of interest to us. The first is that the wall hangings were made for Anne and Henry's bedroom but somehow found their way to Berkeley. Did the royal couple leave them behind here after their visit? The other is that they once adorned the royal apartments in Henry's temporary palace at the Field of Cloth of Gold. Whichever version is true, they are clearly of exceptionally high status, fit for a king, and have been dated to be around five hundred years old.

Next, head into the fourteenth-century private chapel; this has been described as 'one of the most gloriously preserved in England'. Sadly, the 8th earl converted the chapel to a morning room by reversing the entry to the opposite end of the chamber, inserting a fifteenth-century French doorway, fireplace and overmantel, and removing the private pew to the adjacent room. However, its character is still recognisable in is generous proportions, 39 feet by 23 feet, with an apse located at its east end. The braces and ribs retain early painted decoration with an inscription added by John Trevisa, chaplain of the castle between 1379 and 1402. This is certainly something Anne would have read for herself. Emery states that 'the text is that of a thirteenth-century Anglo-French manuscript of the Apocalypse, the only surviving example of such an extended medieval Bible translation on a ceiling in France or England'. However, we have to admit that we found it difficult to make out this inscription ourselves as the paintwork is so faded.

Beyond the chapel we access the two delightful privy apartment rooms, which are fourteenth century in their rectangular shaping. Intercommunication between the two rooms was by the charming open-sided turret lobby spanning the courtyard end of the partition wall (currently containing a statue of the Madonnna and Child), with a garderobe located in the opposite corner. These rooms are wonderfully warm and welcoming. It is easy to imagine the king and queen whiling away the hours at Berkeley in the evenings, playing cards or dice. In our minds' eye, we might see Anne reading one of her many devotional texts in front of the window, facing out across the fields below.

In accordance with the usual layout of other royal residences, it is highly likely that the first room functioned as a privy/dining chamber, with the second as a bedroom. Make sure you take note of the wooden gallery that was once the privy gallery in the chapel. Undoubtedly, Anne would have attended Mass on a regular basis during her stay at the castle, looking down on the body of the church from this elevated position.

Events at Berkeley
Although the archives for the Berkeley family are extensive, very few records remain from the sixty-year period when the castle was in Crown hands. Thus, frustratingly, we have no record of what came to pass during the six or so days that Anne and Henry stayed there. No doubt they were hawking in the glorious countryside of southern Gloucestershire, while evenings were filled with gambling, conversation, music and dance.

Sir William Paulet's household accounts confirm that on Saturday 14 August the court moved on to the beautiful and historic castle of Thornbury.

Visitor Information
For opening times and other visitor information, please visit the Berkeley Castle website at http://www.berkeley-castle.com/index.php. Telephone number: +44 (0) 145 381 0303.

Postcode for Berkeley Castle: GL13 9BQ.

Thornbury Castle, Gloucestershire

The house or Castle of Thornbury aforesaid, is standing, and being within two miles of the river Seaverne which runeth on the north thereof, and is bounded and adjoyned unto the Church-yard of the Parish Church of Thornbury aforesaid on the south part; the Park there, called New Park on the North and East part; and one small parcel of ground called the Petties, on the West part.

Extract from a survey of Thornbury made in the reign of James I

Thornbury Castle, on the edge of the Cotswolds in south Gloucestershire, is the only Tudor castle to be opened as a luxury hotel, and as such offers guests the unique opportunity of staying in rooms where royalty and nobility sought shelter and hospitality hundreds of years ago.

A Brief History of Thornbury

In July 1510, Edward Stafford, 3rd Duke of Buckingham, obtained a licence to crenellate his large, double-courtyard mansion, built on the site of an earlier manor house at Thornbury. The licence also allowed him to enclose a park of 1,000 acres, extended in 1517 by a further 500.

He was the eldest son of Henry Stafford, 2nd Duke of Buckingham, and Katherine Woodville. Through his mother he was a nephew of King Edward IV, and on his father's side he was descended from the Plantagenet prince Thomas of Woodstock, son of Edward III. After his father's death, his mother married Jasper Tudor, King Henry VII's uncle. They resided together at Thornbury, where Jasper died in 1495.

Buckingham's Unfinished Palace

Thornbury was to be one of the most magnificent building projects of the time, comparable only with Thomas Wolsey's Hampton Court Palace and inspired by contemporary royal palaces like Richmond. It intended to serve not as a fortress but rather as a majestic and comfortable family home, although it could certainly have been defended if necessary.

Unfortunately, only part of the duke's grand plans for his new house were realised before his distant cousin King Henry VIII ordered his execution for alleged treason in 1521. Following the duke's demise, the king confiscated the castle and stayed with Anne at Thornbury from 14 August 1535 until their departure for Acton Court on 22 August.

On arrival, the royal party would have entered the spacious base court, covering almost 2.5 acres, through an imposing gatehouse in the south protected by a portcullis and flanking towers, with the great stable likely occupying the remainder of this range. Directly ahead would have stood the remains of Buckingham's north gate and the partially completed north lodgings, and to the left the west lodgings, both originally intended to house servants and men-at-arms, all but lying abandoned.

Their attention would have no doubt been drawn to the unfinished (yet still impressive) west front of the castle. Only the south-western tower and adjacent turret were completed as per the original plan, the remaining buildings only rising to two-storeys rather than the intended four. Had Buckingham's design been realised, the west front would have consisted of a central gatehouse four storeys high, flanked by two four-storey towers and two intermediate turrets.

Passing through the gatehouse – decorated with Buckingham's coat of arms – into the smaller inner court constructed of fine ashlar, Henry may have noted the scrolled inscription above the gateway:

Thys Gate was begon in the yere of owre Lorde Gode MCCCCCXI (1511) the ii yere of the reyne of Kynge Henri the viii by me Edw. Duc. of Bukkyngah' Erlle of Herforde Stafforde ande Northampto': Dorene savant.

The duke's motto, 'Dorene savant', means 'from now on, henceforth or hereafter' and was interpreted by some as signifying his ambition for the throne.

Opposite the inner gateway stood the east range, dominated by the great hall, behind which stood a chapel and a range of lodgings probably erected by Jasper Tudor. The chapel consisted of an outer chapel where the household could stand to hear the services, and at a higher level were two rooms, each containing a fireplace, where the duke and duchess once sat to hear the Mass. These buildings were part of the old manor house but had been retained and incorporated into Buckingham's new building.

On the ground floor of the double-storey north range were the larders, bakehouse, boiling house, great kitchen and privy kitchen, with lodgings above. To the south were the main apartments. This range originally housed Buckingham's own lavish suite on the upper floor, and on the ground floor were those of his wife, Eleanor Percy, Duchess of Buckingham, whose nephew Henry Percy, 6th Earl of Northumberland, was at one time romantically linked to Anne. The stacked lodgings consisted of three large chambers in the main body of the range and a bedchamber in the south-west tower, with the duke's on the first floor and the duchess's directly below.

It was in these apartments that Anne and Henry stayed during their visit. The rooms were lit by magnificent and complex oriel windows, those on the first floor more intricate than the ones below. The grand suite overlooked the privy gardens, described by Henry's commissioners as being surrounded on three sides by a 'goodly gallery', accessible from the rooms at either end of the duke's suite; it consisted of a loggia on the ground floor and a gallery built of timber and covered with slate at first-floor level: 'Conveying above and beneath from the principal lodgings both to the Chapel and Parish Church, the outer part of the said gallery being of stone embattled and the inner part of timber covered with slate.'

An extension from the south side of the gallery led from the castle to a pew by the north chancel window of the adjacent parish church (St Mary's church), where there was found 'a fair room with a chimney and a window into the said church, where the duke sometimes used to hear service'.

To the east of the privy garden was another garden, described by Henry's commissioners as 'a goodly gardeyn to walke ynne'. There was also an orchard set out with covered alleys and planted with hazel and whitethorn, a bush said to have been a favourite of Buckingham's:

Beside the same privie gardeyn is a large and goodly orchard full of younge grafftes well loden wt frute, many rooses, and other pleasures and many goodly alies [alleys] to walke ynne oppenly; and rounde aboute the same orcharde is covered on a good height, other goodly alies with roosting places covered ... From out of the said orcharde ar diver posterns in sundry places, at plasur to goe and entre into a goodly parke newly made, called the New Parke, having in the same no great plenty of wood, but many heggsrowes of thorne and great Elmes. The same Parke conteynneth nigh upon iii myles about, and in the same be vii^c (700) der [deer] or more ... Nigh to the said Newe Parke there is another parke called Marlwood, noething being between them but the bredth of an high waie ...

In the early sixteenth century, Thornbury had been called upon to accommodate a household of up to five hundred personnel, and so no doubt Henry and Anne were comfortable during their stay. The original plan was to remain at Thornbury for a week before moving to Bristol, but an outbreak of plague prevented the royal party from visiting the town. Instead, a delegation of townsmen came from Bristol on 20 August to pay their respects and presented Henry with ten 'fatte oxen' and forty 'sheepe towardes his moost honorable household'. To 'the right excellent Quene Anne' they gave a parcel-gilt cup with cover, containing a hundred 'marks of gold'. Anne responded by 'promising to demand or have none other gift' other than being able to return to Bristol in the future.

Visiting Thornbury Today
Today, Thornbury Castle offers guests the rare opportunity of sleeping in the very room where Henry VIII laid down his head. The Duke's Bedchamber is reached via the original circular stone staircase that both Anne and Henry used during their stay. It is wonderfully atmospheric, spacious, tastefully furnished and boasts a beautifully carved Tudor fireplace and four-poster bed. The chamber overlooks the privy garden and is a perfect blend of history and the modern conveniences that you would expect to find at a luxury hotel. The experience is all the more enhanced by welcoming touches like the decanter of sherry you'll find on arrival.

Aside from the grand Duke's Bedchamber, there are another twenty-six rooms to choose from, including some that now occupy the site of Buckingham's former chambers.

The rooms where Anne would have spent much of her time, once the apartments of the Duchess of Buckingham, today serve as the library and lounge, and the octagonal bedchamber where Anne slept during her stay is now the restaurant; all areas are freely accessible to guests of the hotel.

Don't miss the many copies of famous drawings and paintings of notable Tudor personalities that line the castle's walls, in particular a modern painting of Anne commissioned by the previous owner that depicts her in a stunning crimson gown with her famous 'B' necklace adorning her delicate neck.

You may also wander, at your leisure, in the breathtaking grounds of the castle for the duration of your stay, so take your time exploring the ruins of the partially completed outer court. Although the south range has long since disappeared, the remains of the north and west lodgings offer tantalising glimpses of what might have been – notice the fireplaces and the arrow-loop windows on the outer walls.

The inner court is much as Anne would have known it except that the east range, where the great hall once stood, and all the buildings beyond it, are now vanished. The building on your right as you enter the court is the inner face of the southern range, where Henry and Anne were lodged. Take note of the fine oriel window and impressive double chimney of brick constructed in 1514 that, together with the similar example on the other side of the range, are described as 'unequalled in England'.

The opposite face of this range is breathtaking, with its intricate oriel windows that once flooded Anne and Henry's rooms with light. This was the only building in the castle to be fitted with such spacious windows. Elsewhere, the lower rooms were lit by unglazed arrow loops, examples of which can still be seen in the ruined western range of the outer court.

As you traverse the well-trodden garden paths, note the remains of the embattled walls of the gallery where Anne once walked and lose yourself in the ancient yew-hedged garden, which is particularly atmospheric at dusk, when the past seems to descend with the first hint of night. Staying at Thornbury is like hurtling into the past without compromising on the comforts of today. The castle is a gift to guests who can appreciate the treasures it holds.

Visitor Information

To book a room at Thornbury Castle call +44 (0) 145 428 1182
Email info@thornburycastle.co.uk or visit http://www.thornburycastle.co.uk/
Non-guests are welcome to dine at the restaurant; however, it is strongly recommended that you book ahead to avoid disappointment.

Postcode for Thornbury Castle: BS35 1HH.

Acton Court, Gloucestershire

> Acton mannor place standithe about a quartar of a myle from the village and paroche churche in a playne grounde on a redde sandy soyle. Ther is a goodly howse and 2 parks by the howse, one of redd dere, an othar of fallow.
>
> John Leland, Tudor antiquarian

In the dying days of summer, Anne and Henry departed Thornbury Castle, followed in turn by a long train of courtiers. They journeyed for 7 miles across the Gloucestershire countryside, now tinged russet, to Acton Court, the home of Nicholas Poyntz, on the outskirts of the village of Iron Acton.

Despite his grandfather having been vice-chamberlain to Katherine of Aragon, twenty-five-year-old Poyntz favoured reform and so was honoured with a two-day royal visit, originally scheduled for the weekend of 21–22 August but in actuality taking place on 23 and 24 August.

The house that greeted Anne was constructed from local pennant sandstone covered in off-white render and was a mix of the old and the new. It was not a traditional quadrangle-courtyard house (although it would become more like one in the future), as there were only three distinct wings arranged quite tightly at oblique angles.

The East Wing at Acton Court: A Unique Tudor Survivor

Poyntz, eager to impress and clearly unfazed by the brevity of the visit, had spent the previous nine months, and a great deal of money, adding a magnificent new east wing to the existing moated house. The rectangular, two-storeyed addition, built on the site of the medieval kitchens, measured 32.4 by 8.7 metres and contained three grand state apartments at first-floor level (a presence chamber, privy chamber and bedchamber), each containing a fireplace and an adjacent garderobe (en suite) and decorated in the latest Renaissance style.

The first of the three chambers was hung with expensive tapestries, adorned with vibrant painted friezes and lit by an enormous rectangular window. Henry's throne and cloth of estate stood directly opposite the entrance and no one but the king was permitted to stand or sit beneath it. As the presence chamber was the setting for all major court ceremonials, it's almost certain that within its walls Poyntz was knighted as a reward for his extravagant hospitality. Henry and Anne may also have chosen to dine publicly here, as ushers and waiters bustled to and fro, or they may have preferred instead to dine more privately in the chamber next door.

The privy chamber was guarded by the king's gentlemen ushers. It was only accessible to those whose job it was to attend Henry around the clock, or to courtiers who were guests of the king. According to the Eltham Ordinance of 1526 (a set of rules designed to regulate the functioning of the king's privy chamber), there were six gentlemen, two ushers, four grooms, a barber and a page, all under the direction of the Groom of the Stool, who since 1526 had been Sir Henry Norris.

In this central room, Anne no doubt admired the exceptional painted frieze on the south wall, which was almost certainly painted by a French or Italian artist. It was comparable to contemporary friezes found in the palaces of the Loire Valley where Anne spent several years in service to Queen Claude, and similar in style and quality to decorative work seen at Whitehall Palace. Robert Bell described the frieze in his article 'The Renaissance Comes to Gloucestershire':

> The frieze is divided into three panels by balusters and capped by a trompe l'oeil cornice. The panels contain three different schemes of grotesque ornament executed in grey, white and ochre with touches of red and green on a black background. The centerpiece is a roundel, containing a female bust with braided hair in profile ... At the time, this type of design was known as 'antique work'.

The mastermind behind the original design may have been Hans Holbein, as the quality and inclusion of some of his favourite motifs, including pendant jewellery and dolphins, indicates. Holbein's portrait drawing of Nicholas Poyntz dates from 1535, and may have been made to commemorate the success of the royal visit, making Holbein's connection to the frieze more plausible. The remaining wall was panelled and painted in yellow ochre, a popular colour for internal walls and woodwork in Tudor palaces.

The final room in the series served as Henry's bedchamber and only Sir Henry Norris was permitted access. As in the south room, it was lit by a vast window and overlooked the formal gardens, which were surrounded by a gallery and accessible directly from the house. The walls were panelled and adorned with a painted frieze. The ceiling, like in the king's privy chamber at Greenwich Palace, was painted with false ribs and may have had gilded rosettes or another motif at the intersections. Poyntz wanted his guests to feel at home and spared no expense when it came to the interiors, even commissioning sets of Spanish and Italian ceramic plates and fine Venetian glass vessels to ensure that the rooms were not only magnificent but also well equipped.

A covered gallery led from Henry's bedchamber to the chapel and additional lodgings, presumably used to accommodate other members of Anne and Henry's entourage. From this wing, the royal couple could also enjoy the gardens by means of a covered gallery that spanned the moat. Henry, a voracious hunter, would have made the most of the sport on offer in Acton's two deer parks.

In the sumptuous new wing we can imagine Anne, clad in rich velvets and splendid silks, sipping wine from a fine Venetian glass, listening to the court musicians and dancing with her ladies. But once the revelries came to an end, to where did the queen retire?

Unfortunately, the arrangement of the rooms directly below those occupied by the king is unknown, as all clues to its original appearance and function were swept away when Poyntz had the ground floor completely remodelled some years after the royal visit. So it is uncertain as to whether or not, like at Thornbury, Anne had use of a suite of rooms directly below the king's. It is hard to imagine her being housed elsewhere, especially after Poyntz went to such extremes to please the royal couple and to demonstrate his unyielding loyalty.

It has, however, been suggested that the ground floor may have consisted of a single reception area, in which case Anne would then have stayed in the great chamber, located in the south range and connected to the new wing by a pentice.

The south wing had been rebuilt in the fifteenth century and refurbished by Sir Robert Poyntz, Nicholas's grandfather, who in 1479 married Margaret Woodville, an illegitimate daughter of Anthony Woodville, Earl Rivers, whose sister was Edward IV's queen.

Sir Robert had installed new sculptured fireplaces, glazed floor tiles and an impressive oriel window that projected out over the moat, possibly in anticipation of the house's first royal guest, Henry VII, who visited Acton Court on 23 May 1486. These rooms may have accommodated Anne and her ladies during their fleeting visit.

Visiting Acton Court Today

Acton Court survived until the seventeenth century, at which time it was sold and several of the ranges demolished. The remaining buildings were converted into a farmhouse and used as such until 1984. Fortunately for us, the range still standing is the east range, which, together with half of a north wing built in the 1550s, forms the L-shaped house that welcomes visitors today.

From the moment you step foot on the grounds of Acton Court, it is clear you have arrived somewhere very special. The raw beauty of the house is formidable; it has not been smothered by layers of Georgian and Victorian alterations, like so many other properties, and so is free to speak to us of its Tudor past.

On the ground floor there are many Tudor gems worth looking out for, like a section of softwood panelling originally from one of the upper-floor rooms, impressed-plaster motifs depicting Tudor roses, ancient floor tiles and even Tudor graffiti hurriedly scratched into a windowsill and dated 1589.

But the climax of any visit is the first floor; Poyntz's superb state apartments, although now devoid of their two enormous windows and most of their internal decoration, still retain their ability to impress. Although Acton Court was never a Tudor palace, the apartments built by Ponytz were equal in quality and magnificence to those found in places like Hampton Court. As you walk from one room to the next you get a real sense of their function, the progression from the public to the private. There is also something very satisfying about being able to walk in Anne's steps without being interrupted or re-routed by a Victorian wall!

The most spectacular survivor of Poyntz's Renaissance decoration is the frieze on the south wall of the central room. The symmetrical black-and-white design, with its beautiful gold and metalwork and touches of red and green, is breathtaking and hints at the room's opulent past. As you stand there admiring its intricacies, remember that it was likely designed by Hans Holbein and undoubtedly seen by Henry and Anne.

During Acton Court's restoration, what was left of the panelling was gathered and put in the north room. It is also possible to see some of the original floorboards, distinguishable from the more modern ones by their greater width. Henry's garderobe is also accessible, uncovered during conservation work in 1994 and today hidden behind a door. The second blocked doorway once opened on to a spiral staircase that led to the garden.

The surviving segment of Poyntz's long gallery, in the north range, built around 1550, is home to a painted frieze of elegant biblical text and moralising verses in Latin and a splendid classical mantelpiece.

Acton Court remains an outstanding monument to the extraordinary lengths that one courtier went to in order to impress his king and queen. The house, as far as possible, has been left in its original state. The absence of furniture, portraits or collections of antiques adds to the mystery and magic of a building frozen in time.

Visitor Information

We recommend combining a trip to Acton Court with a visit to Bristol City Museum, where artefacts found during archaeological excavations at Acton are displayed in the Curiosity Gallery and the front hall balcony. These include examples of expensive Venetian glass, Spanish ceramics and a polyhedral sundial attributed to the royal horologist Nicholas Kratzer.

Acton Court opens to the public on selected days during summer; please check their website for dates at www.actoncourt.com or telephone: +44 (0) 145 422 8224. Full access to the house and grounds is with a professional guide only. Tour times are available on the website. The house also regularly hosts Tudor-themed special events, so be sure to check their site for full details.

Postcode for Acton Court: BS37 9TL.

Winchester, Hampshire

The King and the Queen is merry and hawks daily, and likes Winchester and that quarter, and praises it much.

Sir Richard Graynfeld, 2 October 1535

Set amid majestic rolling countryside and ancient woodlands, the capital of Anglo-Saxon England has long been associated with kings and queens. For Anne and Henry, approaching the city gates of Winchester after an overnight stay at Hurstbourne Priors, it would have felt like coming home as aromas of wood fires, baking bread and roasting game scented the golden dusk of an early-autumn evening.

As backdrop to the culmination of the progress, the ancient city staged a ceremony which David Starkey has deemed 'one of the most extraordinary scenes of the Reformation', the public consecration of three newly appointed reforming bishops – Edward Fox, Hugh Latimer and John Hilsey – at Winchester Cathedral on 19 September 1535. Thomas Cranmer, Archbishop of Canterbury, performed the ceremony in the presence of the king and Anne, who'd worked tirelessly to solicit their appointments and was almost certainly by her husband's side to lend her support.

Although we cannot be certain where the court was lodged during their stay, as no records survive, it's likely to have been at the Bishop's Palace of Wolvesey, positioned next to the cathedral, as Winchester Castle had long since ceased to be used as a royal residence after an extensive fire destroyed the royal apartments in 1302. By the sixteenth century, it had declined in importance.

The intended plan was to stay at Winchester for four or five days, as specified in the original *geists*, before moving the 7 miles to Bishop's Waltham. However, the royal couple were so delighted with the sport on offer in the area, particularly the hawking, that they extended their stay to at least two weeks, moving to Bishop's Waltham around 18 or 19 September, before returning to Winchester on Saturday 25th. (It is also possible that the court was split between Winchester and Waltham, as we know that Henry and Anne were present at the consecration on Sunday 19 September.)

Not long after the royal party had arrived, Jean de Dinteville, a French diplomat, was granted an audience with the king and queen. On 15 September he wrote to Marguerite de Navarre, sister to King Francis I and wife of King Henry II of Navarre: 'Madame, the first time I saw the king and queen of England, I made your recommendations to them, and they were glad to hear of your recovered health. The Queen said that her greatest wish, next to having a son, is to see you again.'

Anne's strong expression of affection appears to be evidence of a close friendship between her and Marguerite. The two women certainly knew each other from Anne's time in service to Queen Claude, Marguerite's sister-in-law. However, the true nature of Marguerite's feelings towards Anne and the extent of their 'friendship' is the subject of debate and remains somewhat of a mystery. What the evidence does seem to suggest is that Anne viewed Marguerite as a role model and that, overall, Marguerite was pleasant in return.

While at Winchester, Henry and Anne received word that Catherine Willoughby, Duchess of Suffolk, had given birth to a son, Henry Brandon. (He would die tragically during an epidemic of the sweating sickness in 1551, just shy of his sixteenth birthday and within an hour of the death of his younger brother from the same disease.) While news of his birth was joyous, it must have left Anne and Henry hoping that they too would soon be blessed with the son they so desperately wanted.

Yet there were other matters occupying Henry's thoughts, as reported by Chapuys in a letter to Charles V on 25 September:

> The King having arrived at Winchester, where he is at present, caused an inventory to be made of the treasures of the church, from which he took certain fine rich unicorns' horns (licornes), and a large silver cross adorned with rich jewels. He has also taken from the Bishop certain mills, to give them to the community in order to gain favour. Cromwell, wherever the King goes, goes round about visiting the abbeys, making inventories of their goods and revenues, instructing them fully in [the tenets of] this new sect, turning out of the abbeys monks and nuns who made their profession before they were 25, and leaving the rest free to go out or to remain. It is true they are not expressly told to go out, but it is clearly given them to understand that they had better do, it, for they are going to make a reformation of them so severe and strange that in the end they will all go; which is the object the King is aiming at, in order to have better occasion to seize the property without causing the people to murmur.

Cromwell had not ventured too far from the king's side since joining the progress at Winchcombe, but he is not the only familiar name that we find accompanying Henry and Anne at Winchester. The correspondences of the Duke of Norfolk, Anne's uncle, reveal that he too intended to join the progress. On 24 September he wrote to Cromwell to ask him to 'speak to some of the harbingers for room for 24 horses in my company, and beg my servant to make my chamber ready against my coming [to Winchester]'. Charles Brandon had left his wife and newborn son to join the progress as well, where we find him on 25 September.

Wolvesley Palace

The complete plan of the buildings where Anne and Henry probably stayed is not known for certain, but we do know that Wolvesey was a luxurious palace, largely constructed in the twelfth century by the powerful Bishop Henry of Blois, brother of King Stephen and grandson of William the Conqueror. It was extended and refurbished over the centuries by its subsequent owners. The original approach to the palace was through a gate in the city wall which led to an outer courtyard containing stables and barns. The palace buildings were arranged around an inner courtyard and included a great hall, chapel, domestic buildings and kitchens, a tower and a gatehouse, surrounded on three sides by a moat.

It is possible that the royal guests were accommodated in rooms in the west range, as this was used throughout its life as the principal residence and private apartments of the Bishop of Winchester, who at the time of Anne's visit was Stephen Gardiner. These lodgings would certainly have been grand enough to house royalty.

From the early fourteenth century, the palace was used primarily for state occasions rather than as a permanent residence. In 1554, a feast was held in the east hall to celebrate Queen Mary's marriage to Philip II of Spain, which took place in Winchester Cathedral on 25 July 1554.

Today, all that remains of the palace that Anne would have known are ruins and a fifteenth-century chapel incorporated into a Baroque palace built for Bishop George Morley in the seventeenth century, on the site of the original one. This building is presently the private residence of the Bishop of Winchester. However, the ruins are in the care of English Heritage and are opened to the public. Look out for the graphic panels that tell the history of the palace and illustrate what the medieval buildings may have looked like.

Winchester Cathedral

Winchester Cathedral, where Anne witnessed the consecration of three new bishops, still stands as a glorious testament to the city's illustrious royal connections, its power and wealth. It is home to many treasures, including exquisite fourteenth-century oak choir stalls; seven chantry chapels, added between the fourteenth and sixteenth centuries; medieval floor tiles and wall paintings; over a thousand beautifully carved roof bosses and a sixteenth-century chair, said to have been used by Queen Mary during her wedding ceremony, now housed in the Triforium Gallery.

The nave is breathtaking and a perfect place to stop and imagine Anne walking regally and triumphantly, beneath the fine vaulted ceiling towards the high altar, to witness the consecration of 'her' bishops. The queen's gaze perhaps fell on the painted statues adorning the ornately carved stone screen soaring up behind the high altar, now replaced with modern statues, as the originals were destroyed during the Reformation. Luckily, there are a few unique survivals on display in the aforementioned gallery.

Apart from the cathedral and ruins of Wolvesey Palace, now known as Wolvesey Castle, the authors also highly recommend a visit to the only surviving part of

Winchester Castle – its great hall. It is home to King Arthur's round table, made in the thirteenth century and painted during the reign of Henry VIII. But perhaps more importantly, the hall was built at the same time as the now lost great hall at the Tower of London, where Anne feasted before her coronation and where the queen and her brother were tried on 15 May 1536. This extant hall gives visitors an insight into what the great hall at the Tower may have looked and felt like. Find a quiet spot and try to picture the special stands that were erected to cater for up to 2,000 spectators. Imagine each of the twenty-six peers delivering their verdict, one by one – 'Guilty, guilty, guilty …' – their judgments reverberating around the room. Think about the Duke of Norfolk, who cried as he condemned his niece to 'be burned here within the Tower of London, on the Green, else to have thy head smitten off, as the king's pleasure shall be further known of the same' and Anne's composed response echoing throughout:

> I do not say that I have always borne towards the king the humility which I owed him, considering his kindness and the great honour he showed me and the great respect he always paid me; I admit, too, that often I have taken it into my head to be jealous of him … But may God be my witness if I have done him any other wrong.

That such was her destiny would have been unimaginable to Anne as she enjoyed the hospitality in Winchester. Today, visitors will also be captivated by the city's rich history, the myriad of historic buildings and the raw beauty of the landscape. In this city of kings, queens and bishops, the past finds its voice, eloquently speaking of days gone by.

Visitor Information

With so much to see in Winchester, we recommend that before you visit you download a Winchester Explorer Map from www.visitwinchester.co.uk, which includes a city map, opening times and admission prices, and a suggested circular walking trail around the town covering all the locations associated with Anne and many more. Among the many additional locations is the Westgate Museum, which houses an interesting collection of artefacts, including a Tudor ceiling from Winchester College, and the City Museum, home to a number of fascinating exhibitions about Winchester's intriguing past.

For the Old Bishop's Palace, please check the English Heritage web site for opening times (which are seasonal) at http://www.english-heritage.org.uk/visit/places/wolvesey-castle-old-bishops-palace. It is not possible to park next to the old palace. The nearest car park is about a five-minute walk away at Colebrook Street (Postcode: SO23 9LH).

Postcode for the Old Bishop's Palace: So23 9NB.

The Vyne, Hampshire

> The King and Queen came to my poor house on Friday the 15th of this month, and continued there till Tuesday.
>
> William, Lord Sandys, to Thomas Cromwell, written from The Vyne, 22 October

On Friday 15 October 1535, Henry VIII and Anne Boleyn arrived at The Vyne, the home of William, Lord Sandys, one of Henry's leading courtiers and Lord Chamberlain of the Royal Household. This was not Anne's first visit to the house, as she had been by Henry's side when the court spent at least two days there in August 1531; however, it was her first sojourn as queen.

It is possible that Anne conceived for the final time at The Vyne. There is a suggestion that this child was the son Henry and Anne had so desperately wanted. Had he lived, he would have become heir to the Tudor throne and almost certainly saved his mother and uncle from the horrors of the scaffold.

But on this crisp autumnal day, the future would only have yawned brightly for Anne, as she returned to The Vyne, trotting on horseback through medieval parks and formal gardens as the royal retinue approached the grand moated house. Described by Leland in around 1542 as, 'one of the Principale Houses in all Hamptonshire', in its heyday The Vyne possibly even rivalled Hampton Court Palace in size. It was rebuilt primarily of brick on the site of a medieval house, with much of the work carried out between 1524 and 1526. It consisted of multiple ranges that made up a series of courtyards. In this palatial house, surrounded by acres of lush greenery, Sandys entertained his monarchs and the court for four days.

Anne and Henry were provided with their own suites of rooms on the first floor, which were connected by a gallery and may have been arranged around a courtyard. A full inventory of The Vyne taken after Lord Sandys' death in February 1541, describes the contents of some sixty rooms, including 'the king's chamber', 'the Quenys grete chamber', 'the Quenys lying Chamber' and 'quenes pallet Chamber'. Interestingly, the queen's rooms appear to have been more richly furnished than the king's, and as there exists no evidence of any subsequent visits by Henry VIII, it can be safely assumed that these rooms were appointed for Henry and Anne's visit. They were presumably occupied later on by Sandys and his wife, Margery, as the inventory records no other rooms for them in the house. We should though be mindful of the fact that the inventory was taken more than five years after the royal visit, and so some of the contents may well have changed. Nonetheless, it paints a vivid picture of the level of luxury to which Anne and Henry were accustomed.

The queen's great chamber was a riot of colour and texture, dominated by a bed of green-and-crimson velvet, dressed in a valance fringed with silk, and a gold-and-red satin quilt. There were also eight fine tapestries, a black velvet chair, four red-and-yellow satin curtains, a large pair of andirons (metal stands for holding logs in a fireplace) and a gilded 'loking glass'. In her 'lying Chamber' were found, among other items, five tapestries, a bed of cloth of gold and russet velvet with a matching valance fringed with silk and gold, a quilt of russet and yellow satin, two curtains and a medium-sized pair of andirons. The king's chamber had five small hangings, a pair of andirons, a green velvet bed and matching valance fringed with silk and gold. To the modern eye, such interiors might have appeared garish but to the Tudor observer, this was the height of opulence.

The queen's lodgings were followed by 'a great dining chamber', which served as the 'chief ceremonial room', during the visit. There, Anne and Henry spent time with their hosts and courtiers, eating, drinking and, as described in a letter by Francis Bryan to Thomas Cromwell on the day of their departure, being 'mery'. The walls were decorated with panelled or painted plaster and lined with a set of nine magnificent hangings, the floor covered with the most expensive Turkish carpet in the house. The furniture included one chair of black velvet, trimmed and garnished with gold, a large table, a pair of trestles and a cupboard. In addition, cushions of varying sizes appear in large quantities, with more than forty recorded! Some were made of crimson velvet, others of red and blue damask and a dozen cushions described as 'very sore worn' depicting roses and pomegranates – a device adopted by Katherine of Aragon – perhaps these were stored away by the hosts during Anne's visit ...

Moving further east through additional first-floor chambers, Anne would have arrived at the closets for Lord and Lady Sandys, 'over' and 'next' to the chapel respectively. Both closets were furnished with 'hangings of great flowers with my lord's arms in the garter' and were used to hear Mass privately, while the rest of the household stood in the body of the chapel below. Outside those found in royal palaces, it was one of the most lavish private chapels of its time, richly appointed with embroidered altar cloths, hangings and vestments for a priest, a deacon and a sub-deacon.

In the base court there were many other rooms relatively comfortably furnished, and presumably used to accommodate members of the court. Also recorded in the inventory are stables and kitchens, rooms for the schoolmaster, yeomans and cooks and an armoury where there was kept 'a pavilion conteyning iii chambers and a hall new with all their appurtenances'. Such pavilions were used for ceremonial or military purposes, as seen at the Field of Cloth of Gold. However, they were probably also erected to supplement a house's permanent accommodation and may have been used to house some of Anne and Henry's entourage during their stay.

As was the fate of so many grand Tudor houses, The Vyne was drastically reduced in size, altered and modernised by subsequent owners, and thereby much of Lord Sandys' house lies today buried beneath the lawns north of the present house. Of the sixty or so rooms included in the 1541 inventory, only a few survive.

Among the most extraordinary is a richly decorated first-floor oak gallery, almost certainly part of the gallery recorded in the inventory as connecting Anne and Henry's rooms and one of only a handful of long galleries surviving from the early sixteenth century. At the time of Anne's visit, it was sparsely furnished and, unlike the majority of the other rooms in the house, contained no hangings. The showpiece was the exquisite floor-to-ceiling linenfold panelling installed between 1518 and 1526, which still lines the walls today. Sandys had the coat of arms of many of his contemporaries carved into the panelling, creating a Who's Who of early sixteenth-century Tudor England. Keen eyes will notice, among other devices, the pomegranate and castle of Katherine of Aragon; the 'TW' initials and cardinal's hat for Thomas Wolsey; and Sandys' own coat of arms and insignia, including a ragged cross, the initials 'WS', a winged half-goat and his badge of a rose merging with a sun. The panelling was painted in the early nineteenth century and some years later the bay window in the south end of the gallery was added. Before leaving, take note of the carving of the royal arms supported by cherubs above the east door, as it is believed to mark the entrance to Henry's suite of rooms.

Next you come to a space presently occupied by the Gallery Bedroom and South Bedroom. If you could travel back in time to 15 October 1535, you would find yourself standing in Henry's lodgings, where gentlemen of his privy chamber, like Sir Francis Bryan, whom we know was present on this occasion, kept the king company, dressed and undressed him and performed a variety of other tasks. Sadly, nothing remains of the rooms where Anne once held court, although we can get an idea of the panelling that would have lined the walls in her chambers by visiting the Dining Parlour on the ground floor.

Although not original to the room, the linenfold panelling is Tudor. The room is also home to a number of paintings of interest, including a beautiful portrait of Chrysogona Baker, Lady Dacre, aged six, and a portrait of Charles Brandon after Hans Holbein. Mary Neville, Lady Dacre and Henry VIII can also be found among the sea of faces.

The final remarkable survival of Sandys' Tudor mansion is the magnificent chapel. Although the Ante-Chapel is today a separate room, in the sixteenth century it formed part of the chapel itself. Most of the interior decoration is of a later date. However, there are a few important exceptions; the beautifully carved choir stalls are Tudor and largely unaltered, as is the stained glass in the east window, which is among the finest examples of painted glass of the Renaissance period in England. On the top row is depicted the Passion of Christ and on the bottom row, left to right, Queen Katherine of Aragon kneeling with St Catherine; Henry VIII, shown at about thirty years of age with his name saint St Henry of Bavaria; and finally, Queen Margaret of Scotland, Henry's sister, with St Margaret of Antioch. The glass was originally commissioned by Sandys for the Chapel of the Holy Ghost in Basingstoke, where he and Margery were later buried. They were probably moved to The Vyne during the English Civil War. At the time of Anne's visit, the window was probably glazed with some form of heraldic glass.

The exquisite chapel tiles were imported from Antwerp in the early sixteenth century but only moved to their present position in the nineteenth century. They are glazed in four different colours – lemon yellow, cobalt blue, orange and bright green – a luxury only available to the wealthiest in Tudor times, and are striking to behold. Similar tiles were ordered for Hampton Court Palace and The More, Cardinal Wolsey's manor house in Hertfordshire in the 1520s and 1530s. It remains unclear, however, whether Anne saw them during her visit, as they are only first recorded in the chapel in the eighteenth century.

The surviving interior features of Lord Sandys' Tudor house are a potent reminder of a time when The Vyne was one of the greatest houses in Hampshire and Queen Anne Boleyn, possibly in the first bloom of pregnancy, was still hopeful of living up to her motto – the Most Happy.

Visitor Information
The Vyne is managed by the National Trust. For more information on how to reach The Vyne and its opening hours, which are seasonal, visit the National Trust website at http://www.nationaltrust.org.uk/vyne, or telephone +44 (0) 125 688 3858.
   Postcode for The Vyne: RG24 9HL.

The Tower of London, London

It comes to a thousand days – out of the years. Strangely just a thousand. And of that thousand – one – when we were both in love. Only one when our loves met, and overlapped and were both mine and his.
                    Anne's fictional speech from the Tower in Maxwell Anderson's
                                      Anne of the Thousand Days, 1948

Of all places associated with Anne's story, there is perhaps nowhere more poignant than the Tower of London, that mighty Norman fortress first constructed by William the Conqueror, shortly after the said Duke of Normandy invaded England in 1066. Situated in central London, on the north bank of the River Thames, it has looked over the City of London for over nine hundred years and has served as a royal palace and fortress, a prison and place of execution, an arsenal and royal mint, a royal menagerie and a jewel house.

   Within the shadows of its walls, Anne experienced both the pinnacle of her triumph – as she lodged at the Tower with Henry in sumptuous splendour prior to her coronation in 1533 – and the darkest days of her cataclysmic downfall, almost a thousand days later in May 1536. The only other time that we know of when Anne visited the Tower was during the first week of December 1532, shortly after she and Henry had returned from Calais.

   During that visit, the king and Anne, then Marquess of Pembroke, inspected the new queen's lodgings, which were being constructed for Anne in advance of her coronation the following year. At the same time, the king showed Anne the interior of the Jewel House, which once abutted the southern wall of the White Tower. This was a great honour indeed. Many items of gilt and partially gilt plate were transferred to adorn Anne's increasingly lavish household during that December; did the royal couple select the items from here? We can only begin to imagine what sights Anne laid eyes on for the first time that day, as the Jewel House was then used to house the Crown Jewels and coronation regalia, later to be used in her own coronation ceremony on 1 June 1533.

   And so no Tudor pilgrimage is complete without a visit to the Tower, but with its complex and varied history spanning almost a thousand years, it's easy to miss some important Anne connections. Let's explore these highlights together!

St Thomas's Tower

Much of the medieval palace was restored in 1532, in preparation for Anne's coronation the following year. St Thomas's Tower was at this time largely rebuilt and provided accommodation for two of Henry's senior household officials, the Lord Great Chamberlain and Lord Chamberlain, who were responsible for orchestrating the magnificent coronation ceremonies. It's still possible to see the fortified beck-and-timber walls that Henry had installed for this extravagant event. They certainly needed to be strong to withstand the weight of the ceremonial guns. According to Tudor chronicler Edward Hall, Anne's arrival was marked by the firing of a thousand cannons!

The Wall Walk

You exit the Wakefield Tower via a spiral staircase, which leads you to the South Wall Walk. Continue along this stretch of walk towards the Lanthorn Tower and pause about halfway to look out towards the open, grassy area in front of the White Tower; this area was once enclosed and contained a great hall where Anne and George Boleyn were tried in 1536, along with the Queen's Lodgings, specially built for Anne's coronation (see below, the Royal Apartments). In a merciless twist of fate, she would spend her final days and darkest hours in the very same apartments that only three years earlier had played host to such revelry and lavish celebrations.

Continue along towards the Salt Tower, used as a prison in the Tudor period, and follow the wall walk until you reach the Martin Tower.

The Martin Tower

As you enter, look out for the carving that reads 'boullen'. George Boleyn may have carved it, as tradition has it that he was imprisoned here. Although there is no conclusive evidence to prove it, it's plausible, considering the Martin Tower did house prisoners in Tudor times.

From 1669, it's where the Crown jewels were displayed and today houses an exhibition – *Crowns and Diamonds: The Making of the Crown Jewels*. Sadly, none of the jewels have an Anne connection.

From the Martin Tower, descend into the inner ward. From here, make your way towards the Beauchamp Tower and another Boleyn carving.

The Beauchamp Tower

This time the carving is of Queen Anne's falcon badge – minus its crown and sceptre – and can be found etched in a first-floor cell of the thirteenth-century Beauchamp Tower. There it competes for space with a sea of graffiti left by Tudor prisoners.

The Beauchamp Tower's spacious accommodation and proximity to the constable and his deputy made it a perfect place to house prisoners of high rank. In Mary I's reign, John Dudley, Duke of Northumberland, and his five sons were all imprisoned here.

This tower is also home to another important Tudor graffito: the name 'Jane' is roughly carved into the stone of the upper chamber. It is thought that Lady Jane Grey's distraught husband, Guildford Dudley, inscribed it during his imprisonment in 1553–4. But what of Anne's carving?

Did one of the men arrested alongside her hastily scratch her uncrowned falcon badge into the wall as a final display of loyalty to a queen they knew to be innocent? It's possible. And the fact that Anne's falcon has been stripped of its royal regalia, like its mistress, is most poignant.

As you leave the building and cross Tower Green, take note of the scaffold site on your left but keep in mind that although it's a touching memorial, it is not the site of the scaffold upon which so many notable Tudor personalities, including Anne, lost their lives (see Anne's Final Walk to the Scaffold Site below). Make your way now to the oldest of all the medieval buildings and perhaps the most imposing, the White Tower.

The White Tower

There is much of interest for the Tudor enthusiast in this ancient structure, begun by William the Conqueror in the 1070s, including a wonderful display from the Royal Armouries collection on the ground floor (don't miss the suits of armour belonging to Henry VIII and his son, Edward).

Much of the interior was refurbished for Anne's coronation, as the White Tower played an important role in the coronation ritual. On Friday 30 May 1533, eighteen Knights of the Bath were created, with each candidate required to take part in an overnight vigil in various chambers of the tower.

On the first floor, the Chapel of St John the Evangelist is a must-see, as it's said to be one of the best-preserved Norman chapels in the world. It's not known whether Anne visited the chapel for certain, but it remains a distinct possibility.

Let's now turn our attention to these once grand apartments that saw both triumph and tragedy.

The Royal Apartments

From Thursday 29 May to Saturday 31 May 1533, and from Tuesday 2 May – Friday 19 May 1536, Anne was accommodated in the queen's lodgings, part of the royal apartments, situated in the south-east corner of the Tower. She was not, as a Victorian myth later propagated, accommodated during her imprisonment in the Queen's House, which was built several years after Anne's execution (and which can still be seen overlooking Tower Green today). Like her cousin and predecessor, Catherine Howard would also spend the days before her execution, in February 1542, in the same luxurious queen's lodgings.

There had been royal apartments on that site, in one form or another, since 1220. During the reign of Henry II a permanent inner ward was created, and separate lodgings for both the king and queen were constructed, including a great hall (later to bear witness to the trials of Anne and George Boleyn). At the turn of the sixteenth century, Henry VII significantly enlarged the king's lodgings, with the addition of a tower (containing the king's library and closet) in 1501, with a gallery bisecting the new privy gardens following in 1506.

Then, in 1532, Henry VIII ordered Cromwell to organise the construction of a whole new suite of rooms in order to honour Anne as his queen-to-be. The additional space was also necessary to house the entire court during the two days of festivities, and provide a majestic backdrop to the opulent ceremonies that took place in the Tower prior to Anne's ceremonial entrance to the City on Saturday 31 May.

An engraving of the Tower made in 1597 shows the lodgings as Anne would have known them. Unfortunately, today they are all but lost save for a few foundation stones that give us an inkling of their former existence. However, if you find the south lawn, directly south of the White Tower, you will be looking over what was once the Tower's inner ward, as described below. Here, once again, you will need your imagination!

The entrance to the inner ward was through the mighty Cold Harbour Gate. Remnants of the gate can still be seen abutting the west wall of the White Tower today. Once inside the inner ward, in front of you would have been a complex of buildings arranged around an irregular triangular 'courtyard'. Running diagonally from the Cold Harbour Gate toward the great hall was a line of brick-built Tudor lodgings/offices; the thirteenth-century great hall occupied the southernmost aspect of the courtyard (roughly where the modern-day café and bookshop are situated), while a series of buildings ran at right angles from the hall toward the south-east corner of the White Tower and the Wardrobe Tower, thereby completing the far side of the courtyard. These latter buildings formed the newly built queen's apartments. Finally, abutting the southern wall of the White Tower was the Jewel House, mentioned above.

Anne's new suite of rooms was palatial, consisting of six chambers, including a great watching chamber measuring 70 feet by 30 feet, a presence chamber, privy chamber, closet/oratory, bedchamber and another large chamber (possibly a dining chamber). All rooms were decorated in the most fashionable Renaissance style. A flight of stairs led down directly from Anne's privy rooms into the courtyard. It seems that it was down those stairs that Anne was led to first her trial, and then, four days later, to her execution.

Read more about Anne's final walk to the scaffold in the Myths section below and let's now proceed to where Anne's physical remains were buried.

The Chapel Royal of St Peter ad Vincula

On the morning of 19 May 1536, Anne Boleyn went bravely to her death in a private execution at the Tower of London.

It took only one stroke of the executioner's sword to sever her delicate neck, the very same neck that the poet Thomas Wyatt had once praised as 'fair' in one of his admiring verses. It was then left up to her ladies to move and prepare her body for burial.

Anne's head was covered in a white cloth and carried by one of her attendants.

Her body was undressed and 'wrapped in a white covering' and placed in an old elm chest that had been used to store bow staves. Although only a short while ago Anne had been queen, loved and desired by a king, no provision had been made for a proper coffin.

Anne's women carried her body approximately 65 metres to the royal chapel of St Peter ad Vincula, passing the newly filled graves of Norris, Weston, Brereton and Smeaton, whose bodies had been buried in the churchyard adjacent to the chapel only two days earlier. There, Anne's ladies buried their mistress in the earth beneath the chancel pavement in an unmarked grave (see Myth Five below).

Only three years and thirty-seven days after she'd first dined lavishly as Queen of England, Anne now lay dead and all but forgotten by those at the English court, who now chose to turn their back on the past.

It's possible to visit Anne's final resting place and pay your respects. The chapel can be accessed through a yeoman warder tour (check the daily programme on arrival) or in the last hour of standard opening time, usually from 4.30 p.m.

Other notable Tudor personalities are also buried within the chapel, including Catherine Howard, George Boleyn, Jane Grey, Lady Rochford, Thomas More, John Fisher and Edward Seymour.

Before exiting the Tower complex, head to the Bell Tower. Though not open to the public, it is nevertheless important as it's here that the poet Thomas Wyatt spent his imprisonment in May 1536.

The Bell Tower

The Bell Tower was another place regularly used to house important prisoners. Notable personalities like Sir Thomas More and the Princess Elizabeth were at one time imprisoned here. Tradition has it that the poet Sir Thomas Wyatt witnessed the gruesome execution of the men accused alongside Anne from his prison in the Bell Tower (or somewhere nearby). He was so deeply affected by what he saw from his cell that he responded by writing a poem about the fate of those who rise and fall at court, 'Innocentia Veritas Viat Fides Circumdederunt me intimici me', where he emphasised that

The Bell Tower showed me such sight
That in my head sticks day and night.

What exactly was the 'sight' that so affected Wyatt? To follow this trail we need to exit the Tower and visit the site of the scaffold on Tower Hill.

The Scaffold on Tower Hill

On the morning of Wednesday 17 May 1536, George Boleyn, Henry Norris, Francis Weston, William Brereton and Mark Smeaton were led out of The Tower under close guard and beheaded on a high scaffold on Tower Hill. Large crowds had gathered to see the bloody end of these once great men, including many courtiers.

It was reported that all five men died in a dignified manner and observed scaffold etiquette by confessing their faults and confirming the justness of their punishments in their farewell speeches. What they did not allude to, though, were the specific crimes that brought them to this terrible fate.

The highest ranking, George Boleyn, faced the axe first, but only after he had delivered a very long speech, of which several versions survive, which commenced:

> Christian men, I am born under the law, and judged under the law, and die under the law, and the law hath condemned me. Masters all, I am not come hither for to preach, but for to die, for I have deserved to die if I had 20 lives, more shamefully than can be devised, for I am a wretched sinner, and I have sinned shamefully.
>
> I have known no man so evil, and to rehearse my sins openly it were no pleasure to you to hear them, nor yet for me to rehearse them, for God knoweth all. Therefore, masters all, I pray you take heed by me, and especially my lords and gentlemen of the court, the which I have been among, take heed by me and beware of such a fall.

Norris, Weston, Brereton and Smeaton soon followed.

Smeaton, a low-ranked musician, was the last to die. The sight that lay before him must have been horrendous, the block floating in a sea of red surrounded by butchered bodies and heads. Yet still he managed to find the courage to utter a few words before laying his head on the blood-soaked wood.

The mutilated corpses remained there until Tower officials stripped them of their clothes and piled them on to a cart that transported them to their final resting places: the Chapel Royal of St Peter ad Vincula for Lord Rochford, and the adjacent churchyard for Norris, Weston, Brereton and Smeaton. In the sixteenth century, the churchyard extended out to the area now occupied by the Waterloo Block.

Today a small square marks the spot of the scaffold on Tower Hill where more than 125 prisoners, including five of Anne's loyal subjects, lost their lives.

The court attempted to turn its back on these bloody events, but two poems attributed to Thomas Wyatt (although not all historians agree with this attribution), 'In Mourning wise since daily I increase' and 'Innocentia Veritas Viat Fides Circumdederunt me intimici me', ensured that they would not be forgotten.

In the latter, Wyatt reflects on the fate of those who rose high at court and experienced a reversal of fortune. He ends each verse with a Latin phrase that roughly translates as 'Thunder rolls around the throne'.

Verse three speaks for itself:

> These bloody days have broken my heart.
> My lust, my youth did them depart,
> And blind desire of estate.
> Who hastes to climb seeks to revert.
> Of truth, *circa Regna tonat.*

Common Myths about Anne Boleyn and the Tower
Myth One: Anne Boleyn and Traitor's Gate

On 2 May 1536, Queen Anne was arrested and transported from Greenwich to The Tower of London in full daylight. It is often said that Anne entered the Tower via Traitor's Gate, the gate below St Thomas's Tower, but this is incorrect.

In Charles Wriothesley's *A Chronicle of England during the Reigns of the Tudors, from A.D. 1485 to 1559 Vol. 1*, he states that

> Anne Bolleine was brought to the Towre of London by my Lord Chauncelor, the Duke of Norfolke, Mr. Secretarie, and Sir William Kingston, Constable of the Tower; and when she came to the court gate, entring in, she fell downe on her knees before the said lordes, beseeching God to helpe her as she was not giltie of her a accusement, and also desired the said lordes to beseech the Kinges grace to be good unto her, and so they left her their prisoner.

Court Gate was also referred to as Towergate, and if we look closely at the plan of the Tower of London labelled 'A True and Exact Draught of the TOWER LIBERTIES, survey'd in the Year 1597 by GULIELMUS HAIWARD and J. GASCOYNE' and compare it to contemporary plans, it is clear that the building labelled 'The Tower at the Gate' is today known as the Byward Tower. In the fifteenth and sixteenth centuries, royalty often used this private entrance when arriving at the Tower, it giving access via the wharf. Although originally constructed by Edward I, the gate through which Anne passed dates from the fifteenth century; both this and the drawbridge can still be seen today.

After disembarking the boat and climbing the stairs (today called the Queen's Stairs) on to the wharf, Anne would have crossed the aforementioned drawbridge. This was necessary as the moat surrounding the Tower was filled until 1843. She would have entered the Byward postern gate, exiting onto Water Lane. From here it is unclear exactly what route she took, but it would have only been a short walk to the entrance of the royal lodgings where she would spend her imprisonment.

Anne was not the only high-ranking prisoner said to have entered via this gate. Her daughter, Princess Elizabeth, followed in her mother's footsteps when she arrived at the Tower as a prisoner on 18 March 1554. Her mind must have been plagued with thoughts of her mother's dreadful end only eighteen years earlier.

Myth Two: Where Was Anne Imprisoned in the Tower?

Contrary to recent popular films and television series about Anne and the Tudors, Anne Boleyn was not kept in a cell during her imprisonment. Quite befitting her status as queen, she was housed in the same considerable splendour she had known in 1533, occupying the same queen's lodgings as have been described above, for the entire duration of her stay at the Tower.

Myth Three: Anne's Final Walk to the Scaffold Site

When Anne emerged from her lodgings, early on the morning of 19 May 1536, resplendent in a grey damask gown lined with fur, her head covered with an English gable hood, she was probably led down a flight of steps that appears to have stood in the north-east corner of the inner ward, leading directly down from Anne's privy rooms. Headed by Sir William Kingston – and with a guard of two hundred of the king's bodyguard in attendance – Anne made her way along a path in front of the Jewel House, (this no longer exists, but once abutted the south wall of the White Tower), toward the Cold Harbour Gate. Swinging right and passing under the shadow of the gate, Anne continued her walk northwards to the scaffold site.

Again Victorian myth leads many visitors to believe that the original scaffold site is on the current site of Tower Green, in front of the Beauchamp Tower. This is erroneous and not helped by a poignant monument to the executed, which was unveiled there in 2006. However, to stand on the site of the original scaffold, you need to head across the parade ground (on the north side of the White Tower), toward the entrance to the Waterloo Barracks and the exhibition of the Crown Jewels. There, roughly in front of the entrance to the barracks, was the site of the place where Anne died at the hands of the Sword of Calais, the French executioner from St Omer.

Myth Four: Anne Saw George's Execution

As we have already established, Anne Boleyn was detained throughout her imprisonment at the Tower in the queen's lodgings, situated in the south-east corner of the Tower precinct. Given the topography of the place, and the position of the scaffold on Tower Hill to the north-west of the fortress, it becomes clear that it would have been impossible for Anne to witness the execution of her brother and the other four men who suffered with George Boleyn on the scaffold that day. The only way this might have been possible would have been if Anne had been escorted to one of the towers on the north or west side of the Tower, specifically to watch the men die their bloody deaths. The only hint we have that the condemned queen might have been forced to watch the spectacle comes from Chapuys in one of his dispatches. However, in his biography of Anne, Professor Eric Ives dismisses this on account of the logistics involved in moving such a high-profile prisoner.

Myth Five: Is Anne Buried Beneath Her Memorial Plaque?

There exists some debate as to exactly where in the chancel Anne's body was buried. In October 1876, the chancel was restored with Queen Victoria's approval as part of a larger restoration project that hoped to address the dilapidated state of the chapel and bring it back to its original condition.

It was known that Queen Anne Boleyn, George Boleyn, Lady Rochford, Catherine Howard, the dukes of Somerset, Northumberland and Monmouth, and the Countess of Salisbury were buried there, and so work proceeded with great care, under the supervision of a team of six people. This included the Resident Governor of the Tower. The findings were documented by Doyne C. Bell in *Notices of the Historic Persons Buried in the Chapel of St. Peter Ad Vincula in the Tower of London* (1877).

The team claimed to have consulted various historical sources, and from these documents produced a plan showing where they believed the persons had originally been buried.

On 9 November 1876, the pavement above the spot marked on the plan as the final resting place of Queen Anne was lifted and the earth removed to a depth of 2 feet. Here the bones of a female were found. After a thorough examination, all present were convinced that the remains they had uncovered were those of Anne Boleyn, who, according to Bell, was recorded as being buried in front of the altar by the side of her brother George. George Boleyn's remains were not discovered during the restoration and so were either removed or buried further towards the north wall, an area that remained undisturbed.

The description offered by Dr Mouat (Local Government Inspector), who examined the bones, is very much in keeping with what we know of Anne's appearance with the exception of one comment – 'a rather square full chin'. The bones were also identified as belonging to a female of between twenty-five and thirty years of age. This is perhaps another discrepancy; however, the debate about Anne's year of birth is not one to explore here!

In addition, the committee also recorded that they had uncovered the remains of Lady Rochford and Margaret, Countess of Salisbury, near the south wall. Bell recorded that the bones believed to belong to Lady Rochford were of a female of 'rather delicate proportions' of between about thirty and forty years of age.

Catherine Howard's remains were not found. The explanation offered was that because she was so young at the time of death, her bones were not yet hard, and so the lime used in the interments turned her bones to dust.

Historian Alison Weir offers an alternative explanation. She believes that the bones identified as belonging to Anne Boleyn might in fact be those of Catherine Howard who was aged between sixteen and twenty-three years when she was executed, and whose miniature by Holbein may show her with what could be described as a square chin. Weir also argues that the remains identified as Lady Rochford by the Victorian committee are in fact those of Anne Boleyn. It's an interesting theory. However, as this has only been intended as a brief overview of the case, you can examine it in more detail by reading Doyne C. Bell's findings and Alison Weir's arguments in *The Lady in the Tower: The Fall of Anne Boleyn*.

Anne's demise did not bring about an end to the controversy that surrounded her in life, and after almost half a millennium, intrigue continues to trail her in death. What is certain is that in the end, on 13 April 1877, the remains of those exhumed from the chancel were reinterred where they had been found, and there they remain until this day, marked only by a Victorian memorial plaque. Each year on 19 May, the muted hues of the marble pavement in front of the altar accentuate the beauty of the red roses sent by anonymous admirers to commemorate the life of this remarkable woman.

Authors' Note

Before visiting, we strongly urge you to watch a brilliant video on YouTube by Historic Royal Palaces; it will help you visualise Anne's apartments at the Tower.

It charts the process of the digital re-creation of Anne Boleyn's lodgings (search on YouTube for 'Anne Boleyn's apartments – HM Tower of London').

Sadly, you cannot actually walk in Anne's footsteps from the site of her lodgings to the scaffold. However, do find the real site of the scaffold and go and stand there. Take a look around and you will see, almost unchanged, the last sight that met Anne's eyes before she was executed.

Finally, if you ever get chance, travel to the City of Winchester and see an extant great hall, built at the same time as the one at the Tower by the same king, Henry III. It probably looks very similar to how the great hall at the Tower once looked. Standing under its cavernous vaulted roof gives you a very good idea of the size, grandeur and acoustics of the hall and how Anne might well have felt at her trial in 1536.

Visitor Information
The Tower of London is managed by Historic Royal Palaces. For more information on how to reach the Tower and its opening hours, visit the Historic Royal Palaces website at http://www.hrp.org.uk/TowerOfLondon, or telephone +44 (0) 203 166 6000.

Postcode for the Lower Thames Street Car Park (Tower of London): EC3R 6DT.

Part Four
Jane Seymour

'BOUND TO OBEY AND SERVE'

Introduction

The year 1536 was 'the year of marvels' according to poet and chronicler Lancelot de Carles. He was writing about the incredulity felt across London at the savage turn of events that swept Anne Boleyn – and her accused paramours – from the pinnacle of Tudor society to the shallow, unmarked grave of a traitor. At the dawn of that New Year, nobody could have believed that within six months England would see the first execution of an anointed queen. Yet, driven by Henry's faithlessness and his all-consuming need for an heir, the wheel of Tudor justice had turned inexorably against his once beloved wife, ending with the judicial murder of six people, including Anne herself.

Yet, it was not just Anne's fall from grace which had been so shocking, but the lightning speed with which Henry was ready to replace her. Initially, few outside the Tudor court knew anything of what was transpiring behind the scenes with 'Mistress Semel' [Seymour]. Almost from nowhere, the pale and apparently insipid figure of the twenty-seven-year-old emerges from this blood-soaked episode, willingly stepping over Anne's bloodied corpse to take the prize. As historian David Starkey points out in his biography of Henry's six wives, she had accomplished in six weeks what it had taken Anne six years to achieve. And if the letter sent by Anne Boleyn to Henry from the Tower of London on 6 May 1536 is authentic, then we certainly know where Anne herself pointed the finger of blame for her predicament:

> ... your grace may be at liberty, both before God and man, not only to execute worthy punishment on me as an unfaithful wife but to follow your affection already settled on that party for whose sake I am now as I am, whose name I could some while since have pointed unto – your grace being not ignorant of my suspicions therein.

Looking unkindly upon Jane's wilful blindness, we meet a ruthless, cold-hearted woman. The pinched facial features, so clearly captured in Holbein's portrait of her, leave the impression of a joyless heart and a woman who is far from endearing. Yet judged in context of the times, and bearing in mind Jane's upbringing, her alliance to the Aragonese faction, family duty and clear observance of the Catholic faith, one can easily conclude that she probably did not see Anne as a legitimate queen. Perhaps she even shared Katherine of Aragon's view of Anne as a whore and fledging heretic. If Jane had also suffered physical assault at the hands of Henry's second wife – as would be accepted as part of a mistress's right to discipline those who displeased her – then surely Mistress Seymour could have easily overlooked the disgraced queen's suffering – and the part she herself played in Anne's death. Perhaps Jane even felt a sense of righteousness that God had delivered England from the heretical ideas of the 'putain'. If she did, then she was certainly not alone.

In physical appearance and intellectual capacity, there was apparently little to commend the king's new wife. Chapuys describes Jane as being 'of middle height, and nobody thinks that she has much beauty. Her complexion is so whitish that she may be called rather pale.' The ambassador also noted that she was 'not very intelligent, and is said to be rather haughty'. In short, she had neither brains nor beauty. However, Jane was everything that Anne Boleyn was not, and next to a son, this seems to have been all that Henry desired at this point in his life.

And so Jane was married to Henry VIII on 30 May 1535, just eleven days after Anne's execution. She would triumph and give Henry his legitimate son, but only after an uncomfortable wait of around six months before the pregnancy appeared. Yet, of course, her hour of glory was fleeting. Jane Seymour's life was extinguished on 24 October 1537 as a result of puerperal fever, just twelve days after giving birth to the future Edward VI.

One of the challenges for us in writing this book is that Jane Seymour's tenure as queen was short-lived. Apart from one brief and abbreviated progress from London to Dover in the summer of 1536, Jane undertook no other summer progresses at Henry's side; nor, in fact, does she appear to have strayed far from London. Thus, we are left with fewer entries to include in this book for Henry's third wife in comparison to all his other, more well-travelled, consorts.

In this section, we naturally begin by tracing Jane back to her childhood home at Wolfhall, a place located amid the peaceful countryside of rural Wiltshire. We are delighted to present new information that has recently come to light on the location and appearance of the Seymours' ancestral home. However, we must stress that Jane's presence at Wolfhall can only be assumed – although it is fair to say we are standing on fairly solid ground here. Indeed, it is hard to imagine her anywhere else before her appointment at court as maid of honour to Katherine of Aragon around 1528.

Thereafter, our first incontrovertible evidence of Jane Seymour's presence as a principal protagonist is her appearance at Beddington Place in May 1536. At this point Anne's downfall seems to have become inevitable in Henry's eyes, and as a consequence Jane was moved out of Anne's household and into the home of Sir Nicolas Carew. From this point forward, Jane Seymour was attended evermore as if she were already queen. Beddington Place has been visited before in our first book, *In the Footsteps of Anne Boleyn*. However, because of its significance to Jane's story, we have revisited the location with Mistress Seymour foremost in our minds.

Subsequently, events move at a pace, as we follow in Jane's footsteps to the king's manor at Chelsea, then known as Chelsea Place. Here, Jane and Henry were most probably betrothed on 20 May 1536. This fascinating residence, which played host to all of Henry's queens thereafter, is described in full. However, the site of Jane's wedding – Whitehall Palace – and the place where Jane was first presented publicly as queen and presided over her first Christmas – Greenwich Palace – is acknowledged in the Principal Royal Residences section.

The summer of 1536 was a whirlwind of celebration for the newlyweds; Henry had Jane at his side when he went in procession to hear Mass and give thanks at Westminster Abbey on 15 June. This was followed shortly thereafter, on the 29 June, by a reception at the Mercers' Hall on Cheapside. It seems that Henry wanted all of London to see his new queen. Both are detailed in this section.

Thence followed the short summer progress referred to above. This is not specifically covered in this book as several of the locations are included in other, more relevant, sections. However, for completeness, here we include a brief summary of Jane's travels during those summer months.

Rochester was the first stop after the royal party left London. We cover this location in the Anne of Cleves section, where we chose to focus on the fateful meeting with Anne's husband-to-be on New Year's Day 1540. Sittingbourne followed. At the time, this was a bustling town straddling the main London to Dover road. In the sixteenth century Sittingbourne was famous for its notable hostelries, used to accommodating kings and princes. Again, no location is recorded for the 1536 visit, although the most likely contender is the inn known as the Red Lion. It was the largest inn in the town, and had often accommodated royal visitors, including Henry V on his way back to London following the Battle of Agincourt in 1415. Henry VIII himself had also lodged there previously with both Charles V in 1520 and Anne Boleyn in 1532. The history and appearance of the inn is covered in *In the Footsteps of Anne Boleyn* and is not revisited here.

Finally, the royal couple lodged at Canterbury before moving on to their final destination at Dover. There is no documented evidence of where Jane and Henry resided while in Canterbury. It is possible that the royal couple stayed at the abbot's lodgings in St Augustine's Abbey (which had yet to be dissolved). This specific location is covered in the section relating to Anne of Cleves, who did lodge there, in the King's Manor (post-Dissolution), in the dying days of 1539. The progress terminated at Dover Castle, a location which is also included in the Anne of Cleves section.

Our final fully documented location for Jane is Chester Place, Edward Seymour's first London residence after relocating his family from rural Wolfhall. As Jane's star hurtled across the sky, so honours were heaped upon her family. As we shall hear, the new Viscount Beauchamp needed to be closer to court to capitalise on his good fortune. Therefore, at some point – and definitely by February 1537 – he and his second wife, the heavily pregnant Anne Stanhope, took possession of the house from the Bishop of Chester. Shortly thereafter a daughter was born. We have uncovered that the girl was named after the queen, and Jane Seymour herself stood as godparent to her niece at the now lost London residence on 22 February 1537.

By this time, the queen was with child. To safeguard the health of mother and baby there was no grand summer progress that year. Jane stayed lodged close to Henry in the London area until taking to her chambers at Hampton Court on 16 September. She died in her privy chambers five weeks later, having been successfully delivered of a son. The scene of both her triumph and demise is covered in the Principal Royal Residences section of the book.

Wolfhall, Wiltshire

> The Manor of Wulfhall, as appears from an old Survey, consisted at that time of about 1270 acres ... About the house, which is said to have been timber-framed, there were several gardens, 'the Great paled garden', 'My Old lady's garden' and 'My Young Lady's garden'. There was a Long Gallery, a Little court, a Broad chamber: and a Chapel.
>
> Reverend J. E. Jackson, 1875

Perched peacefully atop a crest of undulating farmland stands an unassuming red-brick house, all that remains of a building whose name has been recently immortalised in popular literature. Wolfhall, or Wulfhall as it was known in the sixteenth century, was the ancestral home of the Seymour family. Of Norman descent, the Seymours were the ancient wardens of Savernake Forest; through Jane's maternal line they were descendants of King Edward III of England, and her mother, Margaret Wentworth, was half-cousin to Elizabeth Howard and Edmund Howard, parents of Anne Boleyn and Catherine Howard respectively.

Nobody knows the exact date or place of Jane's birth. The local registers of the parish are not old enough to reveal the truth of the matter. However, most historians agree that this was almost certainly at Wolfhall, around the year 1508. Four brothers preceded her – John, Edward, Henry and Thomas – with Jane being the eldest daughter in a household of ten children. Mistress Seymour would end up staying at home with her mother and siblings until she was around nineteen years old (a mature woman by Tudor standards), when she secured a place at court as a maid of honour to Katherine of Aragon. However, before we rush forth to consider the events for which Wolfhall is perhaps most famous, we should pause awhile and recreate once more the environment in which Jane was raised. In doing so, we might understand more clearly the forces that shaped her quiet, but steely, character.

The 'Seymour's Beautiful Mansion of Wolfhall'

Wolfhall itself was situated on the edge of the forest, and by the time Jane's father became Lord of the Manor in 1491 it was a fine, double-courtyard, timber-framed house. Leland describes it simply as a 'beautiful mansion' ('*villa splendida*'). By

1672, a visitor to the area, John Aubrey, noted that a great part of it had already been demolished. In more recent times, local historian Graham Bathe has 'devoted much of his life' to studying Wolfhall and the Seymours. As a result, we now have a clearer picture than ever of the place Jane knew as home. In a recent article published in *British Archaeology*, he states that

> Wolfhall was a house with two or more courtyards (one known as the little court) set in a range of garden and orchards, barns and outbuildings. There was probably a gatehouse, as one of the gates had a garrett room above. There was a hall … kitchen, two galleries, a broad chamber, a great chamber with a chimney, the king's chamber (reserved for royal visits), a chapel, treasury house, evidence room (presumably for deeds relating to the substantial landholding) and an armoury.

He goes onto argue that for a house of this size and importance, there must have also been 'substantial family rooms, sleeping and servants quarters, offices, washing facilities, laundry and service buildings'. Wolfhall, it seems, was indeed a fine country manor, made all the more pleasant for the young Seymour siblings on account of a grand outdoor space that included around 2.5 acres of orchard and gardens (of which there were no fewer than eight). Six of them were specifically identified in inventories as the Primrose Garden, the Box Garden, My Young Lady's Garden, My Old Lady's Garden, an arbour and a 'paled garden' of one acre. It is not hard to imagine the sound of Jane and her nearest siblings, Thomas and Elizabeth, playing in Wolfhall's formal parterres, or learning vigorous courtly pursuits such as riding, hunting and hawking in the nearby Savernake Forest.

A 'Flower of Goodlihead' – The Influence of Margery Wentworth

Looking back on the evidence available to us, Jane seems fortunate to have enjoyed an extremely stable childhood in the heart of rural Wiltshire. While her father attended to his numerous obligations and duties to the Crown, Jane's mother remained largely at Wolfhall, her hands clearly full fulfilling her role as chatelaine in her husband's absence. Without doubt, Margery Wentworth was a constant presence in Jane's life and must surely have been influential in shaping Jane's own character.

Lady Seymour was a very mature thirty years of age when she gave birth to her eldest daughter. Already an experienced mother, she was immortalised in her youth by John Skelton's late fifteenth-century poem 'The Garland of Laurel', in which he says of her, 'Benign, courteous and meek, with your words well devised; in you, who list to seek, be virtues well comprised.'

Margery, he eulogised, was the 'flower of goodlihead'. It is not hard to see such sentiments echoed some fifty or so years later by Jane's own admirers. Mistress Jane's adherence to the conservative faith probably stemmed from her parochial upbringing by Catholic parents, away from the reformist doctrine that was inveigling its way into Henry's court at the time.

The scene is reminiscent of Katherine Parr's equally stable upbringing at Rye House in Hertfordshire (see entry for Rye House, Hertfordshire), a long period of continuity, surrounded by siblings, enjoying all that their rural idyll could offer. Both would watch the eldest male child leave home to serve in royal households: Edward Seymour in the retinue of Mary Tudor as she headed to France to become France's new queen in 1514, and William Parr to become part of the Duke of Richmond's schoolroom a decade later in 1525. We can imagine the family receiving letters from Edward at Wolfhall, with Jane hearing her mother recounting them aloud as the younger siblings listened with wide-eyed wonderment to tales of the French court. It must have seemed impossibly glamorous to the young girl, who was eight years Edward's junior. However, unlike Katherine Parr, there is no firm documentary evidence of Jane Seymour's education. It is highly unlikely from Jane's accomplishments as an adult that it was anywhere near as extensive as that of Henry's sixth wife, which embraced new humanist ideas of female education. Instead, as would be typical of the period, there was a focus on feminine pursuits. One of Jane's biographers, Elizabeth Norton, states that

> whilst she received little in the way of formal education, she was taught more traditional feminine accomplishments by her mother [and] would have learnt music with Margery, an important accomplishment for any young woman in search of a husband. Jane was also an expert needlewoman, and well after a hundred years after her death, her embroidery work was still preserved in the royal collection.

It is clear that the woman who would eventually choose to 'Obey and Serve' was a traditionalist. She embodied none of the fancy, new-fangled ways of her predecessor, Anne Boleyn – and for this Henry VIII seems to have been eternally grateful.

Wolfhall: The Scene of 'Une Nouvelle Amour'?

As we have already mentioned, Jane was appointed at court as a maid of honour to Katherine of Aragon around the year 1528. It was the year in which Henry first seriously declared an interest – or should we say obsession – with Anne Boleyn. Without doubt, Henry would have known Jane from this period. However, eclipsed by Anne's charisma and 'struck by the dart of love', he no doubt paid scant attention to the entirely forgettable Jane Seymour. This would change; it is often claimed that the pivotal moment in which Henry first truly noticed Jane was at Wolfhall during the summer of 1535.

That year saw a momentous royal progress, one of the longest and most politically significant of Henry's reign. The royal couple had travelled through Berkshire, Oxfordshire and Gloucestershire before reaching Wiltshire in early September. On 3 September 1535, Henry VIII and Anne Boleyn left Sir Edward Baynton's house at Bromham and rode east to nearby Wolfhall. They would stay at the manor for nearly a week (quite a considerable period of time for a royal progress), enjoying the generous hospitality of Sir John and Lady Seymour. The king and queen would have taken over Wolfhall itself, Sir John and his family decamping to nearby Tottenham Park. At that time, this was a mere hunting lodge belonging to the Seymours, about one mile distant from Wolfhall. But where was Jane in all of this? By 1535, Mistress Seymour was back at court, serving this time as one of Anne's ladies. It may well be that she arrived with her royal mistress, although we should stress that there is no firm documented proof of her presence at Wolfhall. It is though difficult to think of her being anywhere else, and as eldest daughter of the hosts, she certainly would have played a prominent role during the stay. However, it was not until the following year, in February 1536, that Chapuys first noted that the king was paying special attention 'to a lady of the Court, named Mistress Semel' and on 18 March refers to the relationship as *une nouvelle amour*.

The Myth of Wolfhall

It is 'oft claimed that Wolfhall was the scene of Henry's nuptials with Jane, the wedding feast taking place in 'a very long barne' on the site. Antiquarian John Britton was one of the first to write down what had clearly become a local oral tradition. From here the myth thrived for at least the next two hundred years. Writing in 1875, the Reverend J. E. Jackson recorded that at that time 'there [were] still to be seen, against some of the beams and walls, nails or hooks to which were attached the tapestry and hanging used to smarten it up for the dancers at Queen Jane's wedding'. Of course, contemporary evidence laid out in the *Letters and Papers of Henry VIII* has since shown this to by entirely untrue. Henry and Jane weren't married at Wolfhall, but rather in the queen's closet at Whitehall. That inveterate gossip of court, John Husse, wrote to his master, Lord Lisle, on 31 May 1536, confirming that 'the King was married yesterday in the Queen's closet at York Place or Manor, whose Grace is determined to see the watch on Midsummer night. London, 31 May'.

However, it may be that time has distorted real events at Wolfhall. There is an item recorded in Edward Seymour's account book for 1539 (when the king next visited Wolfhall), which indicates that a barn existed and that it was indeed used for royal visits:

Paid to Cornish the paynter for dyvers colours by him bought, for makyng certeyn frets & antiques on canves for my lord's Barn and house at Wulf Haull agenst the King's coming thether. 9th Aug.

A later entry suggests that the Earl of Hertford moved into the barn while Henry VIII occupied the main house. So it is conceivable that the said barn existed, and there may be some truth to the story of a family celebration having taken place there to mark Henry and Jane's wedding in 1536, although it was certainly not the site of the nuptials and the royal couple cannot have been present.

Visitor Information

The authors started their adventure at the church of St Mary in Great Bedwyn. Park the car with the churchyard on your left (this means you are pointing in the right direction to head on toward Wolfhall after your visit). Inside the church, stained glass that shows Jane's phoenix badge, the Tudor rose and Prince of Wales feathers can be seen. These were originally installed at Wolfhall but were discovered and moved to St Mary's church in the nineteenth century. Nearby is Sir John Seymour's impressive tomb (moved there from its original site at Easton Priory), along with a number of other memorials to the Seymour family, including Jane's eldest brother, John.

The Seymours' ancestral home has long since disappeared and for a long time, even its exact location was uncertain. However, following Graham Bathe's recent examination of underground structures, we can say with certainty that the current Wolfhall Manor House is on the site of (part of) the Tudor house. After years of neglect, the original stately manor became a humble farmhouse. Bathe writes of the house today:

> The present manor is an intriguing mix of periods and styles, much of which is Victorian, but with elements from at least four centuries. The west face shows the oldest features, constructed of brick with a prominent, black timber frame. There are stone hearths and the upper floor contains original timbers. The steep tiled roof supports tall chimneys, reminiscent of Tudor stacks, inviting the possibility that the house may have Seymour remnants.

In order to reach the house, get back in the car, drive ahead (if you parked with the church on your left) and down Church Street, but where this veers left over the canal, keep straight on along Crofton Road. Follow the winding country lanes alongside the river and canal, keeping your eyes open for a sign pointing to Wolfhall. You may seem to be snaking your way along for some time, before a sharp bend in the road to the right on the crest of a hill brings you between farm buildings with a rather run-down red-brick farmhouse on the left, and cow sheds on the right. A sign saying Wolfhall Farm tells you that you have arrived in the right location. It is the farmhouse and cow sheds, perched atop the plateau, which was the site of the old Wolfhall. The road which bisects them probably cuts through the site of the original great courtyard.

Please note that many cite the house that lies in the adjacent valley as being part of the original Seymour property. It is easy to see why; it has grand chimney stacks surmounting a relatively modest red-brick building. This building is called The Laundry. However, a recent architectural study by Graham Bathe and Tim Tatton-Brown has revealed that the house was constructed slightly later, being built by Jane's nephew, the Earl of Hertford.

Visiting a site now shrouded in myth, where so many believe Henry's attentions first seriously alighted upon Jane Seymour, cannot fail to pull at the heartstrings. This lost location still has the power to evoke emotion. Despite ourselves, we couldn't shake off the feeling that a long time ago something of significance occurred here, so far away from the bustle of London in this sleepy little valley. We came away with many ghostly voices keeping us company and found ourselves haunted for some time by a place that refuses to pass into obscurity.

Great Bedwyn church is opened to visitors on most days from between 9 a.m. and 4.30 p.m. The actual site of Wolfhall is not accessible, but it can be viewed from the road at any reasonable hour.

Postcode for Wolfhall: SN8 3DP.

Beddington Place, London

A fair house (or palace rather) ... which, by advantage of the water, is a paradise of pleasure.

Thomas Fuller, *The History of the Worthies of England*
(published posthumously in 1662)

On 2 May 1536, Queen Anne Boleyn was arrested at Greenwich Palace and taken to the Tower of London. To shield his new amour from the taint of scandal, Henry VIII had Jane moved from Greenwich Palace to Beddington Place, the home of Sir Nicholas Carew, one of Henry's young favourites and a member of his privy chamber. There, while his wife awaited trial in the Tower of London, he paid court to Jane.

Secret Trysts

On the day of Anne's execution, John Husee wrote in a letter to Lord Lisle that he'd been unable to gain access to Henry because for the past fourteen days the king had remained virtually shut away at his palace in Whitehall, only venturing out 'in the garden, and in his boat at night (at which times it may become no man to prevent him)'. It seems probable that Henry was visiting Jane at Beddington on these late-night boat trips. According to historian Eric Ives, these 'romantic night-time assignations and river trips ... actually began to win popular sympathy for Anne'.

Interestingly, this was not the first time the king had used Carew's country house for a romantic rendezvous. In 1528, Anne Boleyn had been sent, for propriety's sake, to her house at Hever, but the besotted king, unable to withstand the separation, organised for the would-be lovers to meet at Beddington Place. Their host was none other than Nicholas Carew, a relative of Anne Boleyn's and the man who would later encourage the king's affections for Jane.

A Fair House

At Beddington, Carew built a 'fair house (or palace rather) ... which, by advantage of the water, is a paradise of pleasure'. A grand deer park was attached to the manor and, according to John Phillips, at its peak 'occupied almost all the land between London Road, Wallington and Beddington Lane. Its northern edge adjoined Mitcham Common and its southern edge ran along Croydon Road and then around Carew Manor and its gardens to Beddington Lane.' Thomas Coryat in his *Crudities* of 1600 praised the water gardens, as did the seventeenth-century diarist John Evelyn. In *The Diary of Baron Waldstein*, recorded in 1600, the lush grounds of Beddington are brought to life in some detail:

> We made a four mile detour via Beddington in order to see a most lovely garden belonging to a nobleman called Francis Carew. A little river runs through the middle of this garden, so crystal clear that you see the water plants beneath the surface. A thing of interest is the oval fish pond enclosed by trim hedges. The garden contains a beautiful square shaped rock, sheltered on all sides and very cleverly contrived: the stream flows right through it and washes all around. In the stream one can see a number of different representations: the best of these is Polyphome playing on his pipe, surrounded by all kinds of animals. There is also a Hydra out of whose many heads the water gushes. The garden also contained orange trees that were covered by a removable wooden shed, or sheds, each autumn and heated with stoves over the winter to keep the frost at bay.

And so it was there, in Carew's grand moated manor house, surrounded by a fine deer park and picturesque gardens, the predecessor to his son's famous Elizabethan gardens, that Jane remained until 14 May, the day before Anne Boleyn's trial, when Jane was moved to a house on the river 'within a mile of his [the king's] lodging'. Again it appears that the king wanted his mistress nearby. According to Eustace Chapuys, at this new house, Jane was 'splendidly served by the king's cook and other officers', and also noted that Jane was 'most richly dressed'. There could be no doubt now of the king's intentions, Jane Seymour was being prepared for queenship.

The house that Jane knew no longer stands; the present house was rebuilt in the early eighteenth century and is today home to Carew Manor School. The only substantial remnant of the original house is a splendid Tudor hall, which boasts a fine early sixteenth-century arch-braced hammerbeam roof that rivals the magnificence of the great hall at Hampton Court Palace, although on a smaller scale.

While the interior of the hall has been much altered since Tudor times, it remains an imposing space. Although the Tudor house has long since disappeared, the fact remains that it was while at Beddington that Jane heard of the unprecedented and sudden fall of her rival, and contemplated her own imminent rise to the throne.

Visitor Information
The Grade I listed hall is open on select days. Tours run only on Sundays a couple of times a year and must be booked in advance. Telephone number: +44 (0) 208 770 4781.
Postcode for Carew Manor School: SM6 7NH.

Chelsea Place, London

> Also on the 20th daie of Maie, the king was married secreetlie at Chelsey, in
> Middlesex, to one Jane Seymour, daughter of Sir John Seymour.
>
> Charles Wriothesley, chronicler

In May 1536, gossip raged like wildfire across London. From the stews of Lambeth
to the dining rooms of society's elite, there was only one topic of conversation: the
iniquitous behaviour and fall of the king's second wife, Anne Boleyn. However, as
Anne's execution approached, the tide of popular sympathy was beginning to turn
in favour of the discarded queen. In a letter written by Ambassador Chapuys on
the day before the 'putain' was put to death, he warned, 'everybody begins already
to murmur by suspicion, and several affirm that long before the death of the other
[Anne Boleyn] there was some arrangement which sounds ill in the ears of the
people'.

The following day, Chapuys goes further and explains the reason for the
groundswell of mutiny:

> Although everybody rejoices at the execution of the putain, there are some who
> murmur at the mode of procedure against her and the others, and people speak
> variously of the King; and it will not pacify the world when it is known what has
> passed and is passing between him and Mrs. Jane Semel [Seymour].

In short, people were beginning to question if Anne was indeed guilty or perhaps
a victim of the king's capricious fancies. It is undoubtedly on account of these
sensitivities that the betrothal, and subsequent wedding, of Henry and Jane
was shrouded in secrecy. Thus, accounts of this narrow window in Jane's life are
somewhat conflicted, and her exact whereabouts in the run-up to her wedding
sometimes unclear. In a letter dated 19 May, Chapuys wrote, 'The day before the
putain's condemnation, he [the king] sent for Mrs. Semel by the Grand Esquire
and some others, and made her come within a mile of his lodging, where she is
splendidly served by the King's cook and other officers.'

At the time, Henry VIII was resident at Whitehall. Some have assumed that
at this point Jane was moved from Beddington Place to Chelsea Place. However,
even superficial inspection reveals that the king's manor at Chelsea was nearly
3 miles upstream from Westminster, and so does not fit the above description.
Perhaps a more obvious choice would have been one of the palatial buildings
fronting the river along the Strand. This was indeed only one mile downstream
from the Palace of Whitehall. At the time, these were largely occupied by eminent
noblemen and a number of Henry's bishops. In due course, two such houses,
Chester Place and Seymour Place, would come to be owned by Edward and
Thomas Seymour respectively, although evidence suggests that their occupancy
postdates Jane's marriage to Henry.

On 20 May 1536, Chapuys wrote, 'Mrs. Semel came secretly by river this morning to the King's lodging, and that the promise and betrothal [*desponsacion*] was made at 9 o'clock.' Sadly, he does not specifically mention the location in which the 'promise' was made. The key source for the information that this was the king's house, known as Chelsea Place and not Whitehall itself, comes from the sixteenth-century chronicler Charles Wriothesley. He states that the king 'was married secreetlie at Chelsey' on 20 May 1536. Jane's biographer Elizabeth Norton and historian David Starkey accept this account. Norton has Jane travel to meet Henry at Chelsea. Starkey says Jane resided at Chelsea for a full ten days, for the period between the engagement and her marriage at Whitehall on 30 May. Presumably, the king also went to Chelsea Place by barge from Westminster, allowing the ceremony to be conducted away from the prying eyes of court. (Note: in Tudor times, it was sufficient for the couple to consent to be married in front of witnesses to be considered 'married' in the eyes of the Church. Usually, another formal ceremony would then take place a later date. This may explain why Wriothesley talks of the couple been 'married' at Chelsea, when in today's parlance, what took place at Chelsea would be called an 'engagement' or 'betrothal'.)

The Royal Manor at Chelsea

Far from the well-heeled, suburban sprawl of modern-day Chelsea, at the turn of the sixteenth century the 'village' was but a sleepy hamlet, lying nearly 3 miles south of Westminster. Set apart from the dirt and grime of the city, and surrounded by arable pastures, Chelsea soon became a fashionable spot for the Tudor elite.

When visiting the area today, we must allow the concrete jungle of modern living to melt away and instead envisage a quiet, green haven, adjacent to the northern bank of the river. Populated by only 160 people in 1528, Chelsea consisted of a parish church (which still survives), surrounded by a smattering of houses, all set against a backdrop of open fields. Prominently, the pasture land was mainly divided into two adjacent fields, called Eastfield and Westfield. These two fields, which covered most of the parish, were separated by a thoroughfare known as Church Lane. To the south of these fields and along the riverside, were the fine residential properties of the well-to-do (including that of Sir Thomas More). These houses abutted the water's edge, providing easy access by barge upstream to Hampton Court and downstream to Westminster.

In 1536, Henry VIII acquired the manor house at Chelsea, called 'Chelsea Place', through an exchange with William Sandys (later Lord Sandys, of The Vyne). The house was probably only around twenty years old at the time, replacing an earlier medieval mansion that remained standing (for an undetermined period) about a fifth of a mile to the west. The new courtyard house covered around 5 acres and, according to *The History of the County of Middlesex*, a '1706 plan shows a house between 100 and 150 feet wide with space on the east for access to the gardens'.

Sadly, nothing is known of the arrangement of the interiors at Chelsea Place, except that when it was surveyed in 1674 the Tudor house contained twenty-three hearths. However, with regards to its external appearance, the same source states that 'the Tudor front appears from this to have been two-storeyed, with a battlemented parapet and bold chimneystacks as regular punctuation to five unequal bays. A plan of Chelsea village, drawn in 1706 … [shows] a courtyard-plan house with external stacks on the north and south fronts.'

It seems that Henry did little work to the house. *The History of the King's Works, Volume IV* notes only that in 1536–7, he had 'all the framed timber of the Kyngs clossett and the qwhyenes [queen's] new made at the Kyng's manor of Chelsaye'. One imagines that if the betrothal did indeed take place at Chelsea, then according to usual practice this most probably occurred in one of these chambers.

However, what most marked out Chelsea Place as a desirable residence were the peaceful environs and sumptuous gardens. These wrapped around the manor to the east and north of the building. To the south, a further courtyard gave access to the riverfront. The 1706 plan shows the enormity of the walled Great Garden lying to the east of the building. This is bisected by crossed paths (alleys) running east–west and north–south with a water feature at the centre. If drawn to scale, then from the plan it is easy to see that if the house measured 100–150 feet wide, then the dimensions of the Great Garden were some 500–600 feet by 300–400 feet.

As we shall hear shortly, Katherine Parr was granted the manor at Chelsea for life as part of her dower in 1544. Accounts dating from this period give us a glimpse into the singular beauty of the English garden created during its Tudor heyday. Some 64,000 privet plants created the hedges defining the structure of the garden; boarders were filled with scented plants, all at their most glorious during the summer months. These included lavender, rosemary and damask roses. The latter was considered a symbol of beauty and love, its edible pink petals being used to create rosewater for perfume or to flavour food. Indeed most, if not all, of the plants used in the gardens had the dual purpose of providing not only a breathtaking vista and sweet fragrance to enhance pleasant summer walks but also a practical purpose, including providing sustenance for the table. In the orchard to the north of the property, cherry, hazelnut, damson and peach trees all flourished.

Married in May, Jane Seymour would have briefly glimpsed the delights of the manor and its garden at its most prolific before being whisked away back to her residence of seclusion. However, if Starkey is correct, then perhaps she even spent ten giddy days there preparing herself for married life and her role as Queen of England.

Yet while Jane Seymour may have been the first of Henry's consorts to sample the delights of Chelsea Place, she would certainly not be the last.

Chelsea Place: A House of Queens

It must surely be testament to the agreeable nature of the manor and its gardens that all of Henry's final three wives visited, or resided, at Chelsea for various lengths of time. The most significant was, of course, Katherine Parr. She chose Chelsea as her main residence following the death of the king in 1547. It was here, between January and June 1547, that the dowager queen conducted a passionate and clandestine affair with the man who would soon become her fourth husband, Thomas Seymour. Katherine clearly enjoyed Chelsea's charms, writing in one of her love letters to Thomas that 'how be it, the time is well abbrevyated: by what means I knowe not, except the weaks be schorter [shorter] at chelsey than in other places'.

Two contemporary letters indicate that rather than travelling to Chelsea openly by barge to meet with Katherine, the couple tried to keep their assignations a secret, with Thomas arriving from the north of the house, across the aforementioned fields. In March, Seymour wrote to Katherine explaining that he had been seen by one of her brother-in-law's men: 'Yesterday in the morning I had written a letter unto your highness, upon occasion that I met with a man of my Lord Marquess as I came to Chelsea, who I knew not. Who told Nicolas Throckmorton that I was in Chelsea fields.'

In a subsequent letter, Katherine urges caution: 'When it shall be your pleasure to repair hither, ye must take some pain to come early in the morning, that ye may be gone again by seven o'clock ... I pray you, let me have knowledge near night at what hour ye will come, that your portress may wait at the gate to the fields for you.'

Katherine seems to have left Chelsea after her secret wedding in late May/early June 1547. There is no evidence that she ever returned. She died the following year at Sudeley Castle (see entry on Sudeley Castle).

Some six years earlier, on 4 May 1541, Catherine Howard is recorded as having travelled by barge from Chelsea to Baynard's Castle, returning on the 6th. Latterly, in the spring of 1557 and under less happy circumstances, Anne of Cleves arrived at Chelsea. Already unwell, the last surviving consort of Henry VIII would die at the manor on 16 July of the same year. The diarist Henry Machyn wrote, 'The xvi day of July died the lady Anna of Cleves, at Chelsea ... she was seyryd the nyght folohyng.'

It seems that Anne must have lain in state at Chelsea for around eighteen days, having been 'seyryd' (covered in wax cloth/embalmed), for Machyn goes onto say that 'the iij day of August my lade Anne of Cleyff, sumtyme wyff unto kyng Henry the viij[th] cam from Chelsey to be [buried] unto Westmynster'.

It had been a long, and sometimes arduous, journey from her home in the Rhine Valley so many years earlier, but after rejection by Henry, then near abandonment by the Privy Council of the day, Anne's struggles against the English were finally over. The last of Henry VIII's wives was dead. The house survived until around the 1750's when it was eventually demolished to make way for the genesis of modern day Chelsea.

Visitor Information

Today, Chelsea is one of the most affluent areas of the country. Although now engulfed by the sprawl of London, it remains, as it was in the sixteenth century, a highly desirable place to live. The King's Road, once a dirt track used by Henry VIII to access his manor from Westminster, has transformed into a bustling smorgasbord of trendy boutiques and cafés.

The manor itself, though, is completely lost, dismantled in 1755 after the death of its last occupant, Sir Hans Sloane. Its site is marked only by a blue plaque at the end of Cheyne Mews and next to Nos 19-26 Cheyne Walk, adjacent to Chelsea Embankment and the northern bank of the Thames. Apparently, the only remains of the once extensive gardens lie beyond the end of Cheyne Mews. Here Mulberry trees planted by Elizabeth I are said to survive. However, we were unable to find access to these gardens during our visit. Subsequently, the Chelsea Society confirmed that many Tudor bricks have been found in these gardens over the years. However, there is no public access.

Postcode for Cheyne Mews: SW3 5RH.

Westminster Abbey, London

On Corpus Christi day the King and Queen [Jane] rode from York Place to Westminster Abbey ...

Charles Wriothesley, chronicler

The origins of the collegiate church of St Peter in Westminster, or Westminster Abbey, are obscure. Nobody knows exactly when this mighty building was founded. However Edward the Confessor certainly built a magnificent Saxon church upon the site, and William the Conqueror sealed its place in English history by having himself crowned at the abbey following the conquest of England on Christmas Day in 1066. Subsequently, virtually every English monarch has been anointed and crowned here, including Katherine of Aragon in 1509 and Anne Boleyn in 1533.

The abbey is arguably one of the most historic and important buildings in England. It is steeped in centuries of English history and has steadfastly borne witness to profound social and religious change. Thousands of notable figures have passed through its doors and many now lie buried within its grounds. These include Henry VII, the founder of the Tudor dynasty, and his wife Elizabeth of York, who lie in eternal repose at the heart of the sumptuous Henry VII Chapel. Nearby, Edward VI is buried beneath the altar of the Lady Chapel, and his great-grandmother, the indomitable Margaret Beaufort, is buried in the south aisle of the aforementioned chapel. Indeed, there is much to be seen by the Tudor enthusiast, not least the grave of Anne of Cleves, who lies interred to the right of the sacrarium close to the high altar. Then, of course, there are the fabulous marble tombs of Mary I, Mary, Queen of Scots, and Elizabeth I.

However, as we are following in the footsteps of Jane Seymour, we will leave you to explore in full the delights of Westminster Abbey in your own time while we turn our attention to the events that unfolded beneath its soaring vaulted ceiling on 15 June 1536.

Stepping Back in Time: 15 June 1536
On Thursday 15 June 1536, the newly proclaimed Queen Jane rode from York Place, where she'd been lodged for a week, to Westminster Abbey. As Charles Wriothesley commented in his chronicle, the king's 'lordes, spirituall and temporall' rode at the head of the party, followed by the king, behind which rode Jane and

her ladies. According to Wriothesley, when they arrived at the abbey they formed a procession:

> First, all the abbottes quire following after the crosse in rich copes of cloath of goulde, the abbott himself following with his miter; then all the Kinges chappell in rich copes of cloath of gould; after them followed all the abbottes, being Lordes of the Perliamente, in their habettes, without copes; after them all the bishopps in their habettes, without copes; then the two Archbishopps of Canteberie and Yorke in their habettes, without copes, with the crosses afore them; then followed the Bishopp of Chichester, being also Deane of the Kinges Chappell, in a rich cope and mytred, bearing the sacrament of the alter, the sub-deane bearing it with him also, under a rich cannopie of cloath of gold, fower [four] of the gromes of the Privie Chamber bearing the cannopie, and fower other gromes of the Privie Chamber bearing fower staffe torches; then followed the King, the Earle of Sussex bearing the swerde, the Duke of Norfolke bearing the golden staffe as Marshall of Englande, and my Lorde Chauncelor with the Kinges Great Seale borne before him, the cheiffe peeres of the realme following the Kinge …

Wriothesley then records that after the king came Queen Jane, her train carried by 'my Ladie marye', probably a mistake on the chronicler's part as historians agree that the king's niece Lady Margaret Douglas in fact carried Jane's train. Following the queen were the lords and ladies of the court, who all assembled to hear High Mass before returning to York Place.

One can only guess at what Jane must have been feeling while walking up the abbey's central nave toward the high altar, where just three years earlier her predecessor and former mistress Anne Boleyn – whose body was barely cold in the grave – had been anointed and crowned Queen of England. Did she feel any guilt for the role she played in Anne's demise? Or was she simply basking in the joy of her own elevation and unconcerned by those who had been trampled to make way for her?

It's not too much of a leap of imagination to suggest that as Jane processed through the abbey on that summer's day her thoughts were firmly fixed on her own coronation, which everyone expected would take place without delay. Jane must have felt delighted at finally being the centre of attention, but perhaps she also felt the vulnerability of her position, as she well understood Henry's changeable nature. While she had managed to win the king's affections, to maintain them she needed to fulfil a queen consort's most important duty, and give Henry sons.

The birth of Prince Edward at Hampton Court Palace on 12 October 1537 cemented Jane's position. However, she would never sit upon the ancient coronation chair of Edward the Confessor, where all English monarchs since Edward II (except the boy king Edward V), had been crowned, as death soon claimed her.

Visitor Information

While there is much for the Tudor visitor to discover at Westminster Abbey, a definite highlight is the coronation chair of St Edward the Confessor. This precious artefact is currently kept behind glass at the west end of the abbey and was made on the orders of Edward I in 1300–1. Anne Boleyn is one of many English monarchs to have been anointed and crowned in that very chair.

Remember to pause a moment in front of the high altar and admire the medieval *cosmati* pavement upon which the coronation of Katherine of Aragon and Anne Boleyn took place.

Visit the Pyx Chamber and undercroft and see a number of precious Tudor artefacts, including the head of Mary I's funeral effigy and the so-called 'Essex ring' belonging to Elizabeth I. However, the Westminster Retable is perhaps one of the most precious items. It was painted in about 1270 and donated to the abbey by Henry III. It is thought that the Retable was set upon the high altar up until the Dissolution of the Monasteries.

Westminster Abbey is usually open to visitors from Monday to Saturday throughout the year. On Sundays and religious holidays, such as Easter and Christmas, the abbey is open for worship only. All are welcome to services. For more information visit http://www.westminster-abbey.org/visit-us/opening-times/general-opening-times.

Postcode for Westminster Abbey: SW1A 3PA.

Mercers' Hall, London

> Before this hospital, towards the street, was built a fair and beautiful chapel, arched over with stone, and thereupon the Mercers' Hall, a most curious piece of work.
>
> John Stow, Tudor antiquarian

It is St Peter's Eve, 1536. Anne Boleyn has been dead just six weeks and Jane Seymour proclaimed queen at Greenwich on 4 June. Two days earlier, Lancelot de Carles wrote of the life and death of Henry's once beloved second wife, stating that after Anne's execution

> the ladies were then as sheep without a shepherd, but it will not be long before they meet with their former treatment, because already the King has taken a fancy to a choice lady. And hereby, Monseigneur, is accomplished a great part of a certain prophecy which is believed to be true, because nothing notable has happened which it has not foretold. Other great things yet are predicted of which the people are assured. If I see them take place I will let you know, for never were such news. People say it is the year of marvels.

Yet despite this unprecedented and murderous turn of events, during midsummer, Henry VIII was in an ebullient mood. Sir John Russell wrote to Lord Lisle on the

3 June that 'the king hath come out of hell into heaven for the gentleness in this and the cursedness and the unhappiness in the other'. Thus, following the royal wedding, great pageantry surrounded the court, as we have heard a little about in the previous entry. Looking back, it seems that Henry was determined to press home to his people that a new dawn had finally broken across England – again. So when Jane Seymour accompanied her husband to witness the spectacle of the Great Marching Watch (see below for more details) at the Mercers' Hall on 29 June, on the surface all appeared rosy in the Tudor garden. However, we should not forget that despite all the 'baubles', in all likelihood it did not take long for Jane to feel the weight of responsibility, uniquely carried by a medieval queen, beginning to bear down upon her. Behind the scenes Chapuys had already been informed that

the coronation of this Queen has been delayed till after Michaelmas. Suspicious persons think it is to see if she shall be with child; and, if not, and there is danger of her being barren, occasion may be found to take another. I am told on good authority that this King will not have the prize of those who do not repent in marriage; for within eight days after publication of his marriage, having twice met two beautiful young ladies, he said and showed himself somewhat sorry that he had not seen them before he was married.

It seems that Jane was already under tremendous pressure to deliver to her royal master and husband his longed-for heir.

Tudor Cheapside

In Tudor England, Cheapside was one of the great thoroughfares of London. The road ran west from St Paul's in an easterly direction for about 300–400 metres. The end of Cheapside was marked by The Great Conduit, situated in the centre of the street, opposite the Mercers' Hall. So wide was the thoroughfare that during the medieval period, jousting tournaments were held there in stands erected for the viewing pleasure of the nobility.

In order to reach the hall, Henry and Jane must have ridden along its length from St Paul's, passing first the Cheap Cross. This was an ornately carved monument, erected in the centre of the street. It marked one of the twelve resting points of Queen Eleanor's body as it was conveyed from Lincoln to Westminster Abbey following her death in 1290. A little further along was one of the two conduits in Cheapside. Traditionally, wine would flow from these conduits during great state occasions, such as during the coronation procession from the Tower to Westminster. As Jane rode past, she would have been able to see the central conduit, still relatively newly gilded from the coronation of Anne Boleyn three years earlier – a reminder, perhaps, of how quickly it was possible to fall from grace in Henry's eyes.

While the street was wide, the stone and timber-framed houses and shops that lined Cheapside would have towered over the royal procession, their pitched, gable roofs and the dominating spire of St Mary-le-Bow soaring above the street below. John Stow, writing toward the end of the sixteenth century, speaks of how the buildings in Cheapside had developed since 'former times':

> From the great conduit west be many fair and large houses, for the most part possessed of mercers up to the corner of Cordwainer street, which houses in former times were but sheds or shops, with solers [solars] over them, but those sheds or shops, by encroachments on the high street, are now largely built on both sides outward, and also upward, some three, four, or five stories high.

The Mercers' Hall

At the end of the street, on its northern side, was the newly built Mercers' Hall. From medieval times, mercers, who were essentially dealers in cloth, had lived and worked in the Mercery, a district in Cheapside between Friday Street and St Mary-le-Bow. Over time, the traders formed a livery company, their meetings initially taking place in the Hospital of St Thomas of Acon. This building was located opposite the great conduit on the north side of Cheapside. It was on this site that the revered St Thomas à Becket had been born in 1118 and a commemorative chapel subsequently raised in his honour to mark the location. Within this first and ancient chapel, Thomas Butler, 7th Earl of Ormonde, was buried. He was the great-grandfather of Anne Boleyn.

After the dissolution of the monastic hospital, the Company of Mercers bought the rest of the buildings. However, prior to this, in 1517, they began building a second chapel between the hospital and the front of the street. This was situated on the ground floor with the Mercers' Hall above. The project to build the new hall was masterminded by Sir John Allen, founder of the Mercers' Hall Company. A sculptor from Antwerp (a town which had close ties to the Mercers through the Merchant Adventurers – see also the entry on the English House, Antwerp) was employed to carve a stone altar. Imray's comprehensive history of the Mercers' Hall concludes, 'This may indicate that the architecture of the new building had a general Netherlandish origin [and] made a distinctive public statement.'

She goes onto summarise the appearance of the building, stating that it measured about 100 feet in length, having five bays and a centrally situated porch. There was a handsome doorway which led to the chapel (on the ground floor) and the hall directly above it. The hall itself rose through two storeys and measured about 54 feet by 30 feet. Two images exist of the Mercers' Hall. The first is from the Agas Map of around 1560. This crude drawing shows a grand building with a pitched roof surmounted by a central louvre. Two floors are lit by the aforementioned bays, each one apparently separated by a projecting buttress. *The History of the Twelve Great Livery Companies in London* sets out to interpret this map, alongside 'other authorities', so as 'to afford a more correct idea of what must have been the appearance of this particular spot at the date mentioned'. This shows a great stone hall with beautiful mullioned windows, reflecting elements of the Continental style mentioned above.

St Peter's Eve – 29 June 1536

There are two pieces of evidence for Jane's presence at the Mercers' Hall during the midsummer celebrations of 1536. The first is a notice of the intention of 'his grace' to attend 'the Wache', or watch, accompanied by 'his mooste gracioues ladye the Quene'. Addressed to the 'Maister' of the Mercers' Hall, the entry (*Acts of Court of the Mercers' Company*, Vol. 2 1526–1560 – 29 June 1536) goes on to say,

> Desyrrynge [desiring] the Compenye to knowe theire myndes, yf theye wolde a banket [banquet] shulde be prepayred for his grace, yf he fortune to comme, as hathe ben done afore this tyme at the charges of this house. The Compenye willed Maister Wardeins yf his grace dyde comme, to prepayre a banket for hym at the costes & charges of this Compenye, in the beste maner they can devyse [devise] unto his graces pleasure.

Interestingly, it seems that this was not Henry's first visit to the hall. On this second visit, it seems the royal couple were to be lavishly entertained at the company's expense.

The second piece of retrospective evidence comes from John Stow's *The Survey of Old London*. In it we hear that 'in the year 1536, on St Peter's night, King Henry VIII and Queen Jane his wife, stood in this Mercers' Hall, then new built, and beheld the marching watch of this city most bravely set out, Sir John Allen, mercer, one of the king's council, being mayor'. Sir John Allen was clearly not only within the king's inner circle, but a highly influential man in the city. Henry seems to have chosen the spot in order to enjoy the culmination of the traditional spectacle of the week-long festivities of midsummer. From within the hall, Jane stood at Henry's side, peering out of one of its great windows, observing the Marching Watch on the street below. This celebration took place across the land, but in London the procession was particularly spectacular. It could involve up to four thousand people parading through the streets of the city. There was often a military flavour. However, other entertainment included the presence of Morris dancers, giant models and pageants.

It was just a brief moment in time. Jane would have her hour of glory, although she would have an agonising six-month wait before she fell pregnant with the future Edward VI. Although it endured for another 130 years or so, the Tudor hall perished in the Great Fire of London, probably on the second day of the fire, Monday 3 September 1666. Lying around one-third of a mile north-east from the original source of the fire, the hall was entirely consumed, along with much of the City. The Mercers rebuilt the hall, only for it to be destroyed by another fire during the Blitz in the 1940s. The current incarnation was opened in 1958.

Visitor Information

Cheapside must have once been a most fascinating street, with its wide thoroughfare, tall timber buildings, conduits and cross. It was a place of trade and spectacle, housing some of the finest goldsmith workshops in London. It was here, in a long-lost cellar, that the fabulous Cheapside Hoard (a fine collection of Tudor and Jacobean jewellery) was uncovered in 1912.

Today, though, there is little to inspire even the most enthusiastic of time travellers. Modernity has swallowed any evidence of bygone times. There is nothing left to see of the original Mercers' Hall. Indeed the current entrance is tucked away rather innocuously back from Cheapside on Ironmonger's Row. There is generally no access to the public. This is certainly one location where you must bring with you a vivid imagination as your travelling companion.

However, if you do make the odyssey to visit this location, perhaps your disappointment will be assuaged by walking just a couple of minutes around the corner to visit the Guildhall. This grand dame of the City's past was completed in 1440. It was the site of the trials of Anne Askew, Francis Dereham, Thomas Culpeper, Henry Howard, Lady Jane Grey, Guildford Dudley and Thomas Cranmer among others. For its lofty magnificence and poignant history, it is a must for any Tudor time traveller.

Guildhall is located just off Gresham Street. Entry is free.

Postcodes for the Mercers' Hall: EC2V 8HE.

Postcode for Guildhall: EC2V 7HH.

King's Place, London

The Ladye Mary, daughter to the Kinge by Queene Katheryn, was brought rydinge from Hunsedonne secretly in the nyght to Hacknaye, and [that] after-none the Kinge and the Queene came theder, and there the Kinge spake with his deare and wel beloved daughter Marye ...

Charles Wriothesley, chronicler

Just one week after enjoying the spectacle of the Great Watch in the City of London, on the afternoon of 6 July 1536, King Henry VIII and Queen Jane Seymour arrived at a royal house in Hackney. The property once stood north-west of the junction of Lea Bridge and Upper Clapton roads, now occupied by part of BSix Sixth Form College. The house was the scene of the king's reconciliation with his eldest daughter, twenty-year-old Mary, who'd finally been persuaded to swear the Oath of Supremacy, recognising her father as Supreme Head of the Church of England, and acknowledge her own illegitimacy. According to Jane Seymour's biographer David Loades, Henry's new consort played a part in bringing about an end to the years of estrangement by penning a letter to Mary in the days preceding her formal submission. While Jane's letter does not survive, Loades notes that Mary's response suggests that the queen may have advised her to submit to her father's wishes on the grounds that 'such cruel pressure', as Mary had long endured, 'would surely absolve her conscience'. Mary thanked Jane for her 'most prudent counsel' and within a few days gave in to her father's demands.

In Mary's submission, thought to date from 22 June 1536, she beseeches the king 'whom I have obstinately and inobediently offended ... to forgive mine offence therein, and to take me to his most gracious mercy'. Henry, obviously relieved by Mary's unconditional surrender, organised to meet his daughter at Hackney. According to the Tudor chronicler Charles Wriothesley,

> the Ladye Mary, daughter to the Kinge by Queene Katheryn, was brought rydinge from Hunsedonne secretly in the nyght to Hacknaye, and [that] after-none the Kinge and the Queene came theder, and there the Kinge spake with his deare and wel beloved daughter Marye, which had not spoken with the Kinge her father in five yere afore, and there she remayned with the Kynge tyll Frydaye at nyght, and then she roode to Hunsdone agayne secretelye.

News of Mary's return to favour quickly spread. On 8 July 1536, Eustace Chapuys reported the good news in a missive to Charles V:

> The day before yesterday, the 6th instant, the King and Queen left this with a small and secret company to visit the Princess three miles from here, where they remained till yesterday about vespers. The kindness shown by the King to the Princess was inconceivable, regretting that he had been so long separated from her. He made good amends for it in the little time he was with her, continually talking with her with every sign of affection, and with ever so many fine promises.

The ambassador goes on to relay that during the family reunion, Queen Jane gave her stepdaughter a 'beautiful diamond' and Henry gave her 'about 1,000 crowns in money for her little pleasures'. The show of affection continued, with the king promising Mary that she'd no longer have to worry about money because he would ensure she'd have 'as much as she could wish'. The family dined together sumptuously and on leaving the king informed Mary 'that he would send to her in three or four days Mr Secretary Cromwell and other persons to appoint her estate, and begged her to have patience and to remain at the lodging where she was before [Hunsdon]'.

A Short History

Henry acquired the house in Hackney in 1535 from Henry Percy, 6th Earl of Northumberland, who in the early 1520s had been romantically linked with Anne Boleyn. The oldest part of the house was probably built for William Worsley, the Dean of St Paul's, who owned the estate from 1479 until 1496, at which time he sold it to Sir Reginald Bray of London. From there, the estate passed through the Southwell family before being sold to Henry Percy in around 1532.

The king visited the house, known from 1621 onwards as Brooke House, in April 1535, and in September of that year granted the manor to Thomas Cromwell, who already owned another estate in the parish. Between 30 July and 23 September 1535, there are a number of letters written to Cromwell by his servants, reporting on the progress of building works at his house in Hackney. Since the majority of the letters predate the king's grant, it's possible that they are referring to Cromwell's other Hackney estate and not to the house that Jane Seymour visited. There is, though, one other possibility.

In May 1535, an order was issued to the keepers of Enfield Chase and Enfield Park to deliver a hundred oaks to James Nedeham, Surveyor of the King's Work, 'to be employed towards our buyldyngs at our place of Hakney', and so in a survey of London originally published in 1960 the authors suggested that 'the timber ordered by the King may have been a present to Cromwell and the grant of the house may have been delayed until the alterations were finished'. Either way, Cromwell's ownership of the house was short lived, and there is no evidence to suggest that he ever visited the house. By May 1536, the Hackney estate was back in Henry VIII's possession.

Interestingly, Henry Percy's connection to the house did not end when he relinquished ownership of the estate to the king. In May 1537, the earl wrote to Thomas Cromwell asking him 'to helpe me to the kinges hous of hakency wherby I trust the sonner to recover my helth'. Financial troubles, an unhappy and childless marriage to Mary Talbot and the burdens of his position had rendered thirty-five-year-old Percy ill and weak. By the end of May he was residing again at Hackney, where he died on 30 June. The earl's body was carried in procession to Hackney Church and buried in the churchyard the following day. It's tempting to wonder what might have become of Henry Percy and Anne Boleyn had their romance been allowed to flourish. How very different would the story of the Tudors be?

Other Notable Owners

From February 1548, Brooke House was owned by three successive generations of the Carew family. However, there is no evidence to suggest that they ever lived there. Instead, towards the end of the family's ownership we find it occupied by Lady Margaret Douglas, Countess of Lennox and granddaughter of Henry VII and niece of Henry VIII. Her close connection to the Crown, and her dynastic ambitions, occasionally incurred the displeasure of Henry VIII and his daughter, Elizabeth I. On more than one instance, Margaret's behaviour landed her in the Tower of London. Elizabeth imprisoned her in the Tower in 1566 after the marriage of her eldest son, Henry Stuart, Lord Darnley, to Mary, Queen of Scots, and again in 1574 after her younger son Charles Stuart's secret marriage to Elizabeth Cavendish, daughter of the indomitable Bess of Hardwick, Countess of Shrewsbury. It has been suggested that Charles Stuart and his wife Elizabeth may have lived at Brooke House during Margaret's imprisonment, and that their daughter Arbella (or Arabella) may have been born there. Charles Stuart died in 1576, presumably at Brooke House. His mother followed him to the grave two years later.

Three months after the death of the Countess of Lennox, the house and 43 acres of land were sold to Henry Carey, 1st Baron Hunsdon, the son of Mary Boleyn and thus cousin of Elizabeth I.

From 1597 to 1609, the house was owned by Elizabeth de Vere, Countess of

Oxford, before being sold to Sir Fulke Greville, the poet and dramatist, who in 1621 was made Baron Brooke. From this point on, the name Brooke began to be associated with the house.

In the eighteenth century it ceased to be a private residence, and from 1758–9 until 1940 served as a private mental asylum.

The Tudor House

Brooke House was damaged by bombs during the Second World War and the parts of the house that were still standing were demolished in 1954–5 to make way for a secondary school. With no trace left of the house above ground, and the earliest illustrations of the house dating to the eighteenth century, we must turn to contemporary descriptions and surveys to get an idea of what the house that Jane Seymour knew looked like.

In March 1535, an inventory was made of the furnishings in the house at Hackney on the king's behalf. The rooms mentioned are a gallery, a little chamber next to the gallery, the chief bedchamber, a closet, a dining chamber and a chamber of estate hung with a cloth of estate of blue velvet embroidered with flowers of gold – Azure and Or, the colours of Percy's coat of arms. Other furnishings included a chair and cushion matching the cloth of estate and seven 'arras' or wall hangings described as 'counterfett', a cheap substitute for real arras, and often painted or stained instead of woven. Also recorded are various carpets, stools, a table and a cushion of russet velvet lined with black damask.

Not long after the accession of Edward VI, the estate at Hackney was granted to Sir William Herbert, a gentleman of the Privy Chamber, who as the husband of Anne Parr, Katherine Parr's sister, had been a brother-in-law to the late King Henry. In the particulars of his grant, we have recorded the most detailed description of the Tudor house as it stood before it was subsequently altered, and so is worth duplicating here in full:

> There is a Manor place whiche is a Fayre House all of brick havinge a Fayre Hall and a parlor a Faire ketchyn a Pastory a drye larder with Buttry Pantery and all other houses of Office necessary and many Fayre Chambers a Faire long Galerye a proper Chapell and a Closet commynge out of the great Chamber over the Chappell a proper lybrarye to laye bokes in many other proper Roomes wythin the same Place And also a Fayre barne to ley haye a Faire Stable Roome able for stabling for horses And the said house is inclosid upon the backeside wyth a greate brode dyche and without that a Fayre large garden inclosid to the sayd House with a pale necessary for a garden or an Orcharde And at the furder ende of the sayd house [an] Orcharde havinge but Fewe trees of Frute therein wiche conteynyth di' acre or theraboutes And at the Hither end of the House comynge From London ys a Faire large garden grounde inclosyd with a bricke wall.

The diarists John Evelyn and Samuel Pepys both visited the estate in the seventeenth century, and both were hugely impressed with the gardens, which according to Evelyn were 'one of the neatest, and most celebrated in England'. Pepys too was delighted and wrote in his diary, 'The gardens are excellent; and here I first saw oranges grow ... Here were also great variety of other exotique plants and several labarinths, and a pretty aviary.'

So in this fair and well-appointed house, we can imagine Jane and Mary walking in the enclosed gardens, and savouring the long summer days, both women now buoyed by a sense of unity and purpose.

Visitor Information
Postcode for BSix Sixth Form College: E5 8BP.

Chester Place, London

> My lady Beauchamp's child was christened in the chapel in Chester Place ... The sponsors are the Queen, my lady Mary, and my lord Privy Seal.
>
> John Husee, February 1537

February 1537 must have been a month of both relief and celebration in the Seymour family. Jane was finally pregnant and her eldest brother, Edward, and his second wife, Anne Stanhope, would christen their new offspring on the 22nd of the month in their newly acquired and prestigious London home, Chester Place. The future surely could not have looked brighter for the Seymour bloodline.

The service took place in the chapel there, and as John Husee tells us, the baby's godparents were his aunt, Queen Jane, the Lady Mary and Thomas Cromwell. The latter would become related to Jane by marriage, when on 3 August 1537, Jane's widowed sister, Elizabeth, married Thomas' son, Gregory.

Chester Place: Seymour's New Power Base in London
After the Dissolution of the Monasteries, palatial properties, or 'inns' as they were often known, that were located on the north bank of the Thames between the City of London and Westminster, became the target for the 'new' men at Henry's court. Hitherto, they had been the property of a number of key bishoprics that had served the Crown as officers since the Middle Ages. With the changing times, Henry began to place increasing pressure on these bishoprics to exchange these valuable properties, close to Whitehall, with other lands and properties elsewhere. The king wanted his new officers at court to be close at hand. One such property belonged to the Bishop of Chester (also called the Bishop of Coventry and Litchfield). This was the aforementioned, Chester Place. According to Simon Thurley in his book, *Somerset House: The Palace of England's Queens*:

> Although they could have simply leased the inns in the past, the transfer of the freehold was needed in order to allow rebuilding, which was desirable to provide more suitable accommodation for secular and aristocratic families to obtain the architectural expression of their power and influence, as well as for dynastic

reasons. This is the context in which Edward Seymour acquired his first property in the Strand, Chester Inn.

Household accounts for Edward Seymour (created Viscount Beauchamp on 5 June 1536) show that the Seymour's main household seems to have transferred from Wolfhall to Chester Place on or around the 14 February 1537. The Seymour Papers, Volume 14, has an entry which confirms this: 'Paid for diverse accats [groceries] bread, whiting, plaice, butter, milk and other things for the nursery at Chester Place, 2 days ending 16 February, before my Lord began house there.'

This shift in power base must have been just in time for the birth and christening of the new child. It is interesting that both of Viscount Beauchamp's first two children are recorded as being born/christened at Chester Place (1537 and 1539 respectively), although according to the *Letters and Papers of Henry VIII*, Seymour was not formerly granted the property from the Bishop of Chester until April 1539. The Act states that 'a grant of Chester Place, in the parish of St. Mary of Stronde [Strand] without Temple Bar, (is made to) to Edw. earl of Hertford and Anne his wife, by Rol[and bp. of Coventry and Lichfield] made 14 April 28 Hen. VIII., and confirmed by the cathedrals of Coventry and Lichfield by deeds dated 16 April'.

However, also contained within the *Letters and Papers of Henry VIII* are a series of letters penned over two days by the then Bishop of Chester, Rowland Lee, in April 1537, a full two years earlier. In these letters we see the struggle between the bishop and his royal master and the pressure he was coming under to surrender his house to Viscount Beauchamp. We read of the bishop's manifest reluctance to do so and the inconvenience he envisages from losing his fine London house, so conveniently situated close to court:

Of late I received a letter from my lord Privy Seal, whereby it appeareth your Majesty desires to have my house, &c. at the Stronde [Strand], for lord Beauchampe, in exchange for a house of his at Cewe (Kew) foranempst Brayneforde (Brentford). When I attend on your Majesty at London, I have no other house there save that. And if I should take a house of that distance it should be tedious for me so far to seek my lodging. I beg your Majesty to suffer me to enjoy my said house. 2nd April.

Rowland Lee's pleas were in vain. A month later, on the 5 May, he concedes:

I have received, 1 May, the King's letters and yours for exchange of my house in Stronde with lord Beauchamp. I am content to gratify my Prince, but marvel your Lordship makes so little of my party that I should deliver my deed and know nothing of my recompense. I send it on your promise not to deliver it till I am recompensed, otherwise I have protested it shall never be my deed. Please give credence to my servant the bearer.

Therefore, when Jane visited Chester Place to stand as godmother in February 1537, we are assuming that the family must have already been leasing (or borrowing) the property before taking full ownership in 1539.

The Strand – Residence of the Elite

As we have already heard, Chester Place was situated on the Strand. In the sixteenth century this was the Mayfair/Kensington of its day. According to *Somerset House: Past and Present* at that time, the Strand was 'the residential quarter of the nobility':

> Indeed, [it] became a street of palaces, those of York, Durham, Exeter, Savoy, and Arundel being notably magnificent. Each had a special landing-place upon the Thames, which provided all classes of society with a highway for excursions of business and pleasure. Traffic between the Court and the City was carried by means of wherries from Whitehall to Blackfriars or London Bridge.

Thus, whether travelling by land or barge, situated halfway between Whitehall and the City, the Strand was the ideal location for Seymour's burgeoning aspirations.

The History of Chester Place

According to the sixteenth-century antiquarian John Stow in his *Survey of London*, 'a parcel of land and buildings lying in the parish of St Mary le Strand' was granted to the Bishop of Chester in 1257. It is presumed that Chester Place, the bishop's London residence, was built upon this spot by a certain 'Walter Langton, Bishoppe of Chester, treasurer of England in the raigne of Edward the first'. Stow goes on to add that the building was sited 'adioyning to the sayd church [St Mary Le Strand] betwixt it and the river of Thames'.

Sadly there are no clear images of the house that survive. A 1520 plan of London reproduced from the *British Atlas of Historic Towns, Vol III*, shows the plan of a courtyard house accessed by a central gateway from the Strand with a large garden fronting onto the river. Part of the grant giving Chester Place to Edward Seymour also tells us that it stood outside Temple Bar (which straddled the Strand) and came with gardens, an orchard, court and 'other buildings'. Wyngaerde's view of the Strand dated 1543 (before the demolition of Chester Place to create Somerset House) shows us something of the district and the palatial buildings that were wedged tightly along the north bank of the River Thames at the time. It is not possible, though, to confidently make out exactly which of these buildings was Chester Place.

Jane: A Royal Godmother

It has long been stated by reputable sources including *The Complete Peerage* that the first child of Viscount and Viscountess Beauchamp, christened in February 1537, was another Edward Seymour. However, in collaboration with Graham Bathe (see entry on Wolfhall), we discovered that this child was actually a girl called Jane, clearly named in the queen's honour. (Note: there is evidence that Mistress

Jane was actually the Seymours' second child, the first also being a girl. Please read Susan Higginbotham's excellent blog article 'It's a Boy! No, It's a Girl! Some Seymour Birth Dates'.)

The contemporary sources we unearthed during research for this book relating to this child irrefutably confirm its gender. An entry on 16 February in the Seymour Papers states, 'Linen cloth: Paid for 3 ells of Holland at 20d to line the font the day of christening of mistress Jane and after delivered to Roger Cotton, Yeoman of the Vellum [?] for a cupboard cloth 22 February. 5s.' This is further validated by the selection of two female godparents against one male, a typical arrangement for a female child. The reverse would be chosen for a boy.

It seems that in the days running up to the christening, throughout the house workmen were busy making repairs in preparation. The chambers and items upon which the work was undertaken shed a little more light upon the interior of the house. These include mentions of the 'bakehouse, kitchen, larder, buttery, pantry, nursery, an altar in my lady's chamber, the wardrobe, the jaques (toilet) in my lord's chamber, two doors in the garden, the great chamber, a lantern in the stair head, hooks to hang the plate in the great chamber and middle chamber'.

With regards to the chapel itself, Richard Williams was paid for 'making the porch against the christening of Mistress Jane, 22 February'. According to custom, the church porch was the scene of the first stage of the baptismal ritual. At Chester Place, the Seymour Papers state that in preparation for the christening, a glazier was paid for inserting 'windows at the stair head going into the chapel'. Thus we can say that the chapel was indoors and at first-floor level, accessed by a processional staircase. Because of this pre-existing arrangement, no porch existed and so had to be built; again, the accounts reveal a payment for this work. In his book *Medieval Children*, Professor Nicolas Orme gives a detailed account of the usual baptismal ritual and the significance of the church porch. This is summarised below.

It was a requirement that the child be 'instructed' before being christened. This had to take place outside the chapel; not yet a Christian, the child was ineligible to enter the sacred space. Accordingly, the baptismal party, including the midwife and godparents, would meet with the priest within the porch of the chapel or church. Often this was richly decorated, as means allowed.

For the christening of Frances Brandon, daughter of Mary Tudor, dowager Queen of France, in 1517, 'the church porch [was] hung with rich cloth of gold and needlework'. So we may think of Jane Seymour, perhaps dressed in one of her favourite black velvet or damask gowns (this was the most frequent fabric and colour recorded in the 1542 inventory of the queen's dresses), taking the instruction and answering on behalf of her niece.

Inside the chapel, the font, which John Husee states had (probably) been brought from the King's Chapel, would also have been lavishly decorated and lined with the Holland linen already described. Often a canopy was hung above the font. For the nobility, this too would be richly embellished. As godparent to the child, Jane would have stood (or indeed sat, as footstools are mentioned in the

Seymour accounts), around the font, playing an active part in the service. Cressy's *Birth, Marriage and Death* states that 'the Primary business of godparents was to answer on behalf of the child when the minister asked about forsaking the devil and all his works, on the reasonable assumption that the child was too young to answer itself'.

However, it was also the ties of kinship, issues of patronage and social standing that determined who was selected as a godparent. According to Cressy, often it was 'as much a matter of honour for the parents as a favour to the child' as to who stood around the font. Clearly, born into the highest echelons of Tudor society, this new child – and her parents – were blessed with three of the most powerful and wealthy godparents in the land.

The Birth of Somerset House and the End of Chester Place

While there is no evidence that Henry VIII attended the christening alongside his wife, the Seymour Papers record his presence there only one month after her death in November 1537. At this point in time, Chester Place appears to have been renamed Beauchamp Place, possibly after Seymour's elevation to the title of Earl of Hertford in October of the same year. The king was there again the following March. On this occasion, it may well have been associated with the christening of another child. We have found that this child is not usually recorded in modern accounts of the Seymour family, but he is clearly referred to in the following inventory item: 'Paid in reward to the lord of the wardrobe with the king for hanging of the chapel and porch at Beauchamp place for the christening of my lord's son, called Henry [some damage here] Lord Beauchamp, 14 March, who was born the 12 day of the same month at or between 4 and 5 of the clock in the forenoon. 20s.'

This was the earl and countess's first-born son (*not* Edward) and was undoubtedly Henry's namesake. Possibly this time the king stood as godparent. Whatever is the case, both little Henry and his sister, Jane, appear to have died in infancy and have all but been forgotten.

In time, Chester Place could not house the outsized ambitions of the man who would effectively rule England during the minority of Edward VI. According to Stow,

> All which, to wit, the Parish of St. Mary at Strand, Strand Inn, Strand Bridge with the lane under it, the Bishop of Chester's Inn, the Bishop of Worcester's Inn, with all the Tenements adjoining, were by commandment of Edward, Duke of Somerset, uncle paternal to Edward the Sixth, and Lord Protector, pulled down and made level ground in the year 1549. In place whereof he builded that large and goodly house, now called Somerset House.

Visitor Information

Today, not a brick remains of the once fine medieval town house visited by Jane Seymour in 1537. Although the Strand itself remains a wide and busy thoroughfare connecting Whitehall to the City, even the current Somerset House is an eighteenth-century replacement for the palatial residence commissioned by Lord Protector Somerset in 1549.

Travelling toward the city from Charing Cross, you will encounter the gateway leading into the huge quadrangle of Somerset House on your right. Before turning into the gateway, though, note the reconstructed church of St Mary le Strand in the centre of the road. Somerset had the original church demolished to make way for his new lodgings. We know that the original church was sited somewhere in the region of the north-east corner of the present quadrangle of Somerset House (the far left-hand corner as you enter the courtyard), as the original church vaults have been discovered in that location. According to Simon Thurley's *Somerset House*, Chester Place was overlaid roughly underneath the current buildings and courtyard of the current incarnation of Somerset House.

If you wish to take rest here, a pleasant café overlooks the said courtyard, which plays host to open-air cinema in the summer, and a very popular ice rink during the winter months.

Postcode for Somerset House: WC2R 1LA.

1. Reconstruction of Eltham Palace, Kent, *c.* 1605. Eltham Palace was one of Henry VIII's 'great houses', capable of lodging the entire court of around a thousand people. This reconstruction shows the palace largely as it would have appeared through the Tudor period. Key: A=gatehouse; B=green court; C=Chancellor's lodgings; D=inner courtyard; E=courtier lodgings; F=chapel; G=queen's lodgings; H=gallery; I=king's lodgings; J=great hall.

2. Greenwich Palace, Kent. The king's lodgings face the River Thames, with the king's kitchen on the ground floor to the right, then the massive central donjon containing some of Henry's most private chambers, including a library on the top floor. Moving to the left, after the donjon tower and at first-floor level, is the privy chamber, presence chamber and finally the chapel. This is on the far left-hand side of the range, distinguished by its pitch gabled end.

3. Whitehall and the Holbein Gate by Thomas Sandby, *c.* 1750. The Tudor tennis play is on the left of the gate, the later Banqueting House on the right. Anne Boleyn is said to have married Henry VIII in an upper chamber of the Holbein Gate in January 1533.

Above left: 4. Richmond Palace Gatehouse, 2012. The gatehouse, with Henry VIII's coat of arms, and part of the outer range of Richmond Palace are all that survive above ground of the palace, which was Anne of Cleves' primary residence from June 1540 until June 1548.

Above right: 5. Anne Boleyn's Window, the Dean's Cloister, Windsor Castle. Illustration by E. W. Haslehurt, 1910. Anne Boleyn's weeping ghost is said to have been seen on numerous occasions at this window.

Below: 6. The Lower Ward, Windsor Castle. Illustration by E. W. Haslehurt, 1910. This shows the lower ward of Windsor Castle, including the Round Tower in the distance and St George's Chapel on the left, burial place for Henry VIII, Jane Seymour and Charles Brandon.

Above left: 7. In the great fortified palace of Alcalá de Henares, Katherine of Aragon was born late on 15 December or in the early hours of 16 December 1485. *Above right:* 8. This lovely bronze statue of Katherine was installed in 2007, in the Plaza de las Bernardas, adjacent to the Archbishop's Palace in Alcalá de Henares, Katherine of Aragon's birthplace.

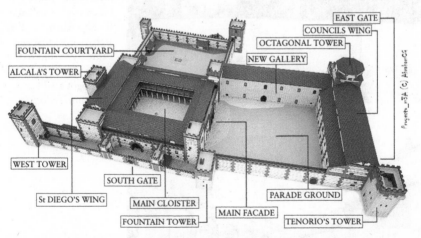

9. A reconstruction of the Archbishop's Palace, Alcalá de Henares, by Abraham Consuegra Gandullo. It shows the palace as it may have appeared in the late fifteenth century, at the time of Katherine's birth. Her family's apartments were probably situated around the main cloister, overlooking the Jardin de Bosque, or Forest Garden.

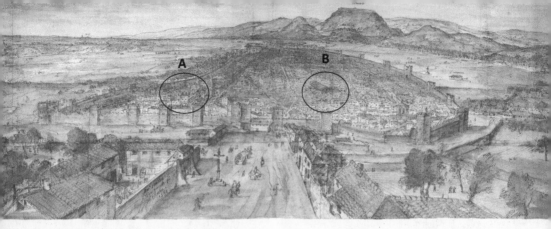

10. View of Alcalá de Henares by Anton van den Wyngaerde, 1565. The palace where Katherine was born is circled and marked A. Also visible is the church where the infant Katherine may have been baptised, circled and marked with a B.

11. La Plaza Mayor, Medina del Campo, 2015. The Testamentary Palace, home to the Museum of Isabel la Catolica, is situated in the Plaza Mayor de la Hispanidad, and stands on the site of the former royal palace where Isabella I dictated her will and died. It's also where the English ambassadors first laid eyes on a three-year-old Katherine, future Queen of England, and negotiated her marriage to Arthur Tudor.

12. Alcazar of Seville, Spain. The main facade of the Mudejar Palace of Peter I and the Renaissance gallery of the House of Trade, as seen from the Courtyard of the Hunt.

13. The Patio de las Doncellas, Alcazar of Seville, by night. This was the centre of the public area in the Mudejar palace and a place Katherine would have known well. Her family's rooms were situated on the first floor of the palace and many overlooked this courtyard.

14. View of Cordoba by Anton van den Wyngaerde, 1567. The fortified gate seen in the foreground is Calahorra Tower, which today houses the Al-Andalus Living Museum. Beyond the bridge and to the right is Cordoba's extraordinary Mosque-Cathedral, and to the left stands the Alcazar of the Christian Monarchs.

15. The Alhambra, 2014. A view of the Alcazaba taken from the Generalife gardens. Charles V's Renaissance Palace and the Nasrid palaces, where Katherine lived before moving to England, can also be seen.

Left: 16. Platerias Facade, Santiago de Compostela, 2015. While much of the exterior of the Cathedral of Santiago de Compostela has undergone significant remodelling over the years, the Platerias Facade is the church's oldest and most accurately reflects the Romanesque church that Katherine would have seen.

Middle: 17. Ludlow Castle Gatehouse, 2013. The arms of Sir Henry Sidney, Lord President of the Council of the Marches from 1559 to 1586, can be seen over the gatehouse, surmounted by the royal arms of Elizabeth I.

Bottom: 18. Ruins of Ludlow Castle, 2013. On the left are the remains of the Solar Wing, later called Prince Arthur's block, where Katherine and Arthur stayed while at Ludlow. To the right of the Solar Wing are the ruins of the Great Hall, where the newlyweds, along with their households, would have dined and entertained important guests on ceremonial occasions.

Top: 19. Leeds Castle, Kent, from an early twentieth-century book. Henry VIII and Katherine of Aragon overnighted at the castle in May 1520, en route to meet Francis I, King of France. The historic meeting between the two young Renaissance princes became known for its magnificence as the Field of Cloth of Gold.

Middle: 20. Buckden Palace, 2015. View of the Great Tower, curtain wall and part of the inner gatehouse range at Buckden Palace.

Bottom: 21. Reconstruction of Kimbolton Castle, *c.* 1683 by Stephen Conlin based on research by Simon Thurley. This reconstruction gives a good indication of how the house appeared during Katherine's stay in the 1530s. Key: A=Main entrance; B=Great Hall; C=South Wing (Privy apartments, including the Withdrawing Chamber and Gallery); D=the site of Katherine's most private chambers, including the bedchamber in which she died; E=the Chapel.

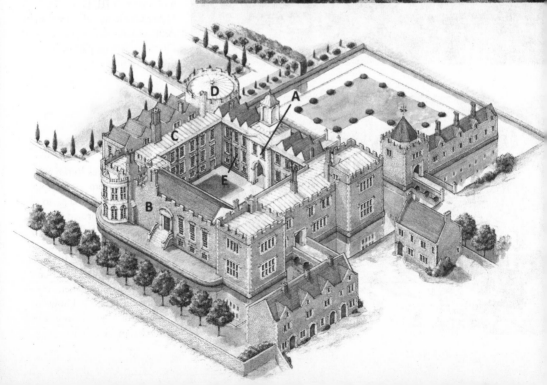

22. The Queen's Room, 2015. Although the interiors at Kimbolton were greatly altered in the eighteenth century, this room survives from the original Tudor building. It was here that Katherine of Aragon died on 7 January 1536.

23. Hever Castle and moat from a watercolour by C. Essenhigh Corke, 1910. Famously the childhood home of Anne Boleyn and the site of her courtship with Henry VIII. However, Hever Castle was also lived in by Anne of Cleves. She was granted Hever to lease as part of her divorce settlement.

24. Anne of Cleves Room at Hever Castle from a watercolour by C. Essenhigh Corke, 1910. This room once formed (part of) the solar, the Boleyn family's main living quarters on the first floor of the castle. It would have served a similar function for its eponymous owner, Anne of Cleves. Today it is known as the Book of Hours Room. The tapestry remains in situ.

Left: 25. St Peter's church, Hever, 2009. The church, which dates back to the twelfth century and is located in the centre of Hever next to Hever Castle, is best known for being the final resting place of Anne's father, Sir Thomas Boleyn. On 12 March 1539, he passed away at Hever Castle.

Right: 26. The Palace of Margaret of Austria, Mechelen. 2013. The Renaissance palace built for Margaret of Austria was home to Anne Boleyn for around a year, following her arrival there in the summer of 1513. The building now functions as the city's courts of justice.

27. Courtyard of the Palace of Marguerite of Austria in Mechelen, by Francois Stroobant, 1855. The picture shows the Renaissance interior of the courtyard. The architecture remains largely unchanged today and would have been familiar to Anne Boleyn.

Above: 28. The Gothic and Louis XII wings of the Château d'Amboise, in the Loire Valley, 2013. Anne Boleyn arrived here with the French court in May 1515. On the left is the gothic wing, containing the sixteenth-century Grand Salle on the ground floor. On the right is the Louis XII wing, containing the restored Renaissance lodgings of Francis I on the ground floor, and those of Queen Claude stacked directly above.

Middle: 29. Haseley Court, Little Haseley, 2015. The east wing containing the so-called 'Chapel Room' is the only obvious surviving fragment of the earlier medieval mansion at Haseley Court.

Bottom: 30. Buckingham's Manor House, 2015. The half-timbered residence with its twisted chimneys was built in the sixteenth century, though altered subsequently, and was originally the house for the Prebend of Buckingham. While it is visible on John Speed's map of the area made in 1610, it is not known for certain whether this was the manor house owned by the Careys in 1529.

31. Katherine of Aragon's ivory crucifix. Local tradition claims that while staying in Buckingham, Katherine of Aragon, so overjoyed at news of the English victory against the Scottish at Flodden Field, showed her gratitude to the people of the town by giving them her ivory cross, which can still be seen today in Buckingham's Old Gaol Museum.

32. Hundson House, 2015. Glimpses of the remains of Hunsdon House, as seen from St Dunstan's church. Henry VIII and Anne Boleyn visited the house on a number of occasions and in September 1532, after Henry conferred on Anne the title of Marquess of Pembroke, he granted her the Manor of Hunsdon, along with other lands.

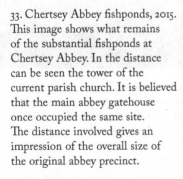

33. Chertsey Abbey fishponds, 2015. This image shows what remains of the substantial fishponds at Chertsey Abbey. In the distance can be seen the tower of the current parish church. It is believed that the main abbey gatehouse once occupied the same site. The distance involved gives an impression of the overall size of the original abbey precinct.

Left: 34. Berkeley Castle. The west range of Berkeley Castle today looks much as it would have done when visited by Anne Boleyn in the summer of 1535. The privy apartments run from right to left at first-floor level.

Right: 35. Thornbury Castle. On the edge of the Cotswolds, Thornbury Castle is the only Tudor castle to be opened as a luxury hotel. Pictured here is the double-storey south range of the inner court, which originally housed the Duke of Buckingham's own lavish suite on the upper floor and on the ground floor those of his wife, Eleanor Percy, Duchess of Buckingham. It was also in these apartments that Anne Boleyn and Henry stayed during their visit in 1535. Anne's bedchamber was on the ground floor of the south-west tower and Henry's directly above; both overlooked the magnificent privy garden.

36. The west front of Thornbury Castle, south Gloucestershire. This range was only partially completed at the time of the Duke of Buckingham's execution in 1521. The south-western tower and adjacent turret were finished as per the original plan, the remaining buildings only rising to two storeys, rather than the intended four.

Right: 37. Acton Court, Gloucestershire. In the sixteenth century, Acton Court, on the outskirts of the village of Iron Acton, was home to Nicholas Poyntz who spent nine months – and a huge sum of money – adding a new wing to his moated manor house in anticipation of a royal visit that would last just two days. Today, Poyntz's extravagant east range comprises much of what remains of Acton Court. *Below right:* 38. The 'Holbein Frieze', Acton Court. This frieze is found in the central room of the royal apartments at Acton Court and is named so because it is believed that Hans Holbein was the mastermind behind the design.

39. On 19 September 1535, Winchester Cathedral witnessed the consecration of three newly appointed reforming bishops, Edward Fox, Hugh Latimer and John Hilsey. Henry VIII and Anne Boleyn were present for the ceremony, which was performed by the Archbishop of Canterbury, Thomas Cranmer.

Above: 40. The Tower of London, as seen from the River Thames with a view of 'Traitor's Gate' and the White Tower, where eighteen knights of the Bath were created on 30 May 1533 as part of Anne Boleyn's coronation ceremonies.

Middle: 41. Site of the Scaffold on Tower Hill, 2013, on or near the spot where George Boleyn, Henry Norris, Francis Weston, William Brereton and Mark Smeaton were executed on 17 May 1536.

Bottom: 42. Byward Postern Gate, Tower of London, 2013. On 2 May 1536, Anne Boleyn was arrested and transported from Greenwich to the Tower of London. After disembarking the boat and climbing the stairs to the wharf, Anne would have crossed the drawbridge and entered the Tower via the Byward postern gate, pictured here, exiting onto Water Lane. In Anne's time the moat was filled and so the bridge was needed to cross into the Tower.

43. Wolfhall Farm. Extract from the 1820 estate map. Ref: WSA 1300/375L. Most surviving buildings associated with the farm are barns. However, their arrangement is distinctly reminiscent of the double-courtyard house recorded in the Tudor period. The modern-day road is shown running through what appears to be the larger of these two courtyards.

44. Wolfhall Farm, painting by Gillian Bathe. The painting shows the west face of the current Wolfhall Farm. According to historian Graham Bathe, it may contain elements of the Seymours' original country home.

45. Beddington Place. In the sixteenth century, Beddington Place was the home of Sir Nicholas Carew. The only substantial remainder of the original house is a splendid Tudor hall; the rest of the house was rebuilt in the early eighteenth century and is today home to Carew Manor School.

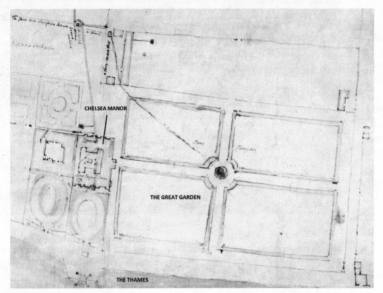

CHELSEA MANOR

THE GREAT GARDEN

THE THAMES

46. Detail from a plan of Chelsea Place's water supply, 1706. This shows the original Tudor house set around an 'H'-shaped inner courtyard. To the east lies the Great Garden. The Thames can be seen to the south and is accessed via a jetty. The building adjoining it to the left (and set around a larger courtyard) is a later addition and not part of the original Tudor house.

47. The North Front of Westminster Abbey, 2013. Virtually every English monarch has been anointed and crowned here, including Katherine of Aragon in 1509 and Anne Boleyn in 1533. While Jane Seymour died before she could be crowned, she heard High Mass at the abbey on 15 June 1536. Thousands of other notable figures have passed through its doors and many now lie buried within its grounds, including founders of the Tudor dynasty Henry VII and his wife Elizabeth of York, plus Edward VI, Elizabeth I, Mary I and Henry's fourth wife, Anne of Cleves.

Left: 48. Anne of Cleves panel (A). The first of three panel designs. This one shows the initials 'AC' set with an oval cartouche, a coronet above and swags below.

Middle: 49. Anne of Cleves panel (B). The second of three panel designs. This one shows a lion's head.

Right: 50. Anne of Cleves panel (C). The third of three panel designs. This one shows the emblem of the dukedom of Cleves with the eightfold fleur-de-lis.

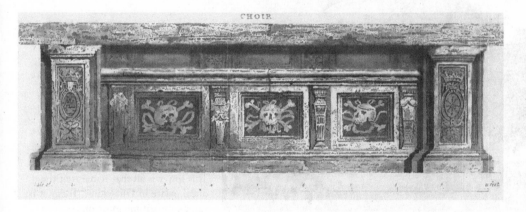

51. Anne of Cleves's tomb, Westminster Abbey. The Purbeck marble tomb clearly shows two of the three forms also depicted in the Anne of Cleves panels in Old Warden church; the 'AC' initials are surmounted by a coronet on the far left and the emblem of Cleves, also crowned, is seen on the far right. This gives definitive proof that the Old Warden panels are associated with Anne herself and not any other member of the Cleves dynasty.

52. The Ducal Palace, Düsseldorf. Copper engraving by Laurenz Janscha, 1798. Düsseldorf was the principal seat of the Duchy of Jülich-Kleves-Berg during the sixteenth century. It was in this palace that Anne of Cleves was born on 22 September 1515.

53. The Schlossturm, Düsseldorf, 2011. This tower is all that remains of the ducal palace in Düsseldorf. Today, it is run as a maritime museum.

54. The Rittersaal, Burg Castle. The Rittersaal, or Knight's Hall, was the main ceremonial chamber in the castle, similar in function to the great hall of England's castles and palaces. It was here that the celebrations were held for the betrothal of both Anne's parents and elder sister.

55. The Kemanate, Burg Castle. The Kemanate was the principal private living chamber of the family during Anne of Cleves' day. Here the duchess and her children would spend much of their time when indoors during daylight hours.

56. Schloss Düren (Hambach), Niederzier. An exterior view of the remains of Schloss Hambach (as it is known today), showing the round south tower and the appended south-eastern and south-western ranges.

57. Schloss Düren (Hambach), Niederzier. A view of the castle from the interior courtyard. The building has been much renovated in recent times following years of destruction through war, fire and neglect.

Left: 58. Amelia of Cleves. Some have argued that this image, by Hans Holbein, is of Amelia of Cleves, the younger sister of Anne. The likeness is thought to have been captured by the artist during his trip to the Duchy of Cleves in 1539, as part of the marriage negotiations between Henry VIII and Duke William, Anne and Amelia's brother.

Above: 59. *Die Hirschjagd* (*The Stag Hunt*), Lucas Cranach, 1540. A typical hunting scene of the day, painted with the Castle of Torgau, Saxony, in the background. Hunting was generally not deemed a suitable pastime for ladies of the German court at the time.

60. Schwanenburg, Kleve. View of part of the reconstructed castle. The view is taken from the southern side of the original entrance. This once stood roughly to the right of the building shown.

Left: 61. Schwanenburg, Kleve. View of the inner range that once bisected the outer from the inner courtyards of the castle. The famous Schwanenturm is seen rising above the building in the background.

Right: 62. The English Quay, Bruges, 2014. This view of Bruges looks eastwards toward what was once known as the 'English Quay' during the medieval period. Here ships would load and unload their cargo; at the far end of the picture, beyond the tree, was the original position of the Carmelite monastery, used for worship and lodgings by the English merchants living in Bruges.

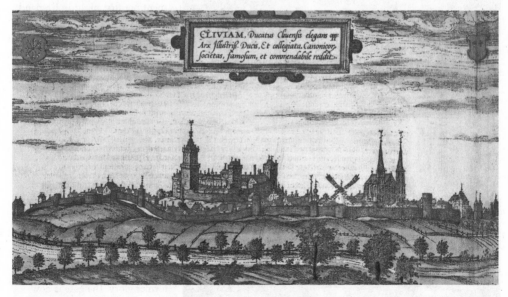

63. Kleve painted by Braun and Hogenburg, *c.* 1580. Alongside the medieval cathedral, Schwanenburg and the Schwanenturm dominate this perspective of the walled town of Kleve.

64. Deal Castle, Kent, 2013. Within its stone walls, Anne of Cleves dined on arrival in England in December 1539, before being taken to nearby Dover Castle, where she spent the night.

65. Dover Castle, Kent, from an early twentieth-century book. After dining at Deal Castle, Anne of Cleves was escorted to Dover Castle, where she spent her first night in England. The medieval castle had been guarding Dover Harbour, and welcoming visitors and returning Britons alike, for hundreds of years.

66. The Fyndon Gate, St Augustine's Abbey, Canterbury, 2015. This was the principal gateway into the abbey precinct during the sixteenth century. Built at the beginning of the fourteenth century, it was virtually destroyed during the Blitz but rebuilt afterward to its former glory. The gate is now part of the King's School, which occupies part of the original monastic site.

67. Bletchingley Place Farm, 2015. All that remains today of the manor house that Anne of Cleves was so fond of is a section of the principal gatehouse now converted into a private residence called Place Farm. Clearly visible is the Tudor arch, now blocked up except for a Georgian-style door case.

68. The King's Manor, Dartford. All that remains of the King's Manor today is one of the gatehouses, its adjoining Keeper's Hall and lodgings. It is used by the local council for civil marriages.

69. Old Paradise Gardens, Lambeth, 2015. These gardens occupy part of the site of the gardens of the once palatial home of the dukes of Norfolk, Norfolk House.

Above: 70. Oatlands Palace as recreated in its heyday by Stephen Colin based on research by Simon Thurley. A=Outer Gatehouse; B=Outer Courtyard; C=Inner Gatehouse; D=probable site of the medieval great hall and the entrance into the main public chambers of the palace; E=the queen's side; F=the king's side; G=the queen's privy gallery; H=the tower containing one of the queen's privy closets; I=the Prospect Tower; J=the queen's privy garden; K=the inner courtyard.

Below: 71. The Inner Courtyard of Oatlands Palace and the Outer Wall, by Anton van den Wyngaerde. Note the splendid inner gatehouse with the privy chambers of the king (thought to lie to the right of the gatehouse) and queen (extending to the left away from the gatehouse). The queen's bedroom is thought to be behind the great bay window to the left of the gatehouse, on the first floor. Facing south, these rooms would have been flooded with light.

72. South facade, Grimsthorpe Castle. Henry VIII and Catherine Howard stayed at the castle as guests of Charles Brandon, Duke of Suffolk, and his wife Katherine Willoughby in 1541 while on progress to Yorkshire.

73. Lincoln Cathedral, 2014. Henry VIII and Catherine Howard came in procession to the cathedral on arrival to Lincoln in August 1541. They alighted at the west end of the church, pictured here, where they knelt and reverently kissed a crucifix before proceeding inside.

74. Old Bishop's Palace, Lincoln, 2014. Pictured are the remains of the great hall, the main public space of the palace. The blocked doorway, just visible to the right, once led up to high-status guest lodgings where Henry VIII may have been lodged during his visit. Where Queen Catherine and her ladies slept is unknown; however, we can safely assume that she did not share the king's bedchamber, as one of Catherine's indiscretions with Thomas Culpeper is said to have taken place here.

75. Lincoln Castle, 2014. Henry VIII viewed the castle during his stay in Lincoln in August 1541.

76. Pontefract Castle, Pontefract. Oil on canvas by Alexander Keirincx, 1640–1. Access from the town to this mighty fortress can be seen spanning a deep gully on the left of the picture. The main gatehouse dominates the centre ground. The tower on the far right of the painting is the King's Tower, the Queen's Tower being partially hidden behind the Constable Tower in the foreground to the right of the gatehouse. The church to the right of the picture survives.

Left: 77. The gatehouse of Cawood Castle, interior view. This shows the main entrance into and out of the castle from what was once the inner courtyard. The likes of Richard III, Henry VIII, Catherine Howard and Cardinal Wolsey have all passed under this gateway. It is now preserved by the Landmark Trust and can be reserved as a holiday let.

Right: 78. The same gatehouse seen from the original approach to the castle. The so-called 'Banqueting Hall' can be seen forming the attached range. It occupied the front range of the outer court and therefore probably provided stabling and accommodation.

Top: 79. The King's Manor, 2015. It was converted from the abbot's lodgings of St Mary's Abbey after its dissolution in November 1539. The building subsequently became the headquarters of the Council of the North. It is often surmised that it was in this building that Catherine Howard stayed alongside her husband during the 1541 progress.

Middle: 80. The ruins of St Mary's Abbey, York, 2015. This picture shows all that remains standing of the main abbey church. The claustral buildings in which Henry VIII and Catherine Howard lodged during their stay in York have been lost. They now lie underneath the Yorkshire Museum, part of the current Abbey Gardens.

Bottom: 81. Thornton Abbey gatehouse, 2015. On 6 October 1541, Henry VIII and Catherine Howard arrived at the former Augustinian abbey of Thornton, where they remained for three days. Today, much of the abbey lies in ruin but the imposing fourteenth-century gatehouse survives. The quality and detail of the surviving sculptures and decoration attest to the magnificence and wealth of the abbey in its heyday.

82. Aerial view of the inner court of Chenies Manor, Buckinghamshire. The south range with its wonderful twisted Tudor chimneys was built around the summer of 1550. While this building was not standing at the time of Henry VIII and Catherine Howard's visit in the autumn of 1541, the smaller west wing was. This range would have originally extended further north, and contained the great hall.

83. Aerial view of the glorious sunken gardens of Chenies Manor, Buckinghamshire. The brick building just glimpsed in the bottom-left corner of the photo was standing at the time of Catherine Howard's visit in the autumn of 1541.

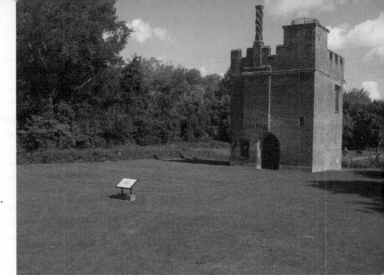

84. Rye House Gatehouse, 2015. The gatehouse is all that is left of Rye House. The imprint of the house and courtyard can just be made out, marked in the grass.

85. Gainsborough Old Hall, 2015. In the late spring of 1529, Katherine Parr travelled north to Lincolnshire to begin her new life as the wife of Edward Borough. For a period of about two years the young couple lived with Edward's family at Gainsborough Old Hall.

86. Snape Castle, Bedale, Yorkshire, 2015. This photograph shows the south-east corner of the building, including the original chapel, once used by the Latimers for worship, on the right of the picture. Behind the chapel is the ruinous north-east tower.

Top left: 87. Church Stowe Manor, Northamptonshire. This handsome building is all that remains of the medieval house inherited by Katherine Parr on the death of her second husband, Lord Latimer. The parish church, just captured to the right of the photo, would have been standing during Katherine's visits to the manor.

Middle left: 88. Reconstruction of Woking Palace as it would have looked in the sixteenth century. Entrance into the courtyard across the moat remains the principal access point to the site today. The great hall lies directly opposite the gatehouse, while the royal apartments are shown in the background, at the top of the picture. Service buildings are shown in the foreground.

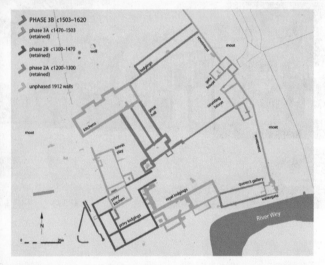

Below left: 89. Woking Palace plan. This plan is based on the most recent excavations at the site of Woking Palace. It shows the main entrance across the moat, via the gatehouse, leading to an outer courtyard. Directly across from the gatehouse stands the great hall, with the royal privy apartments in the south, adjacent to the River Wey.

Bottom left: 90. Reconstruction of Otford Palace. Created by Rod Shelton, this model shows what the sprawling palace complex may have looked like in the sixteenth century. Queen Katherine Parr and Henry VIII were reunited there in October 1544, after the king returned from a military campaign in France.

91. A model of Nonsuch Palace created by Ben Taggart. This view shows the south wing and the Privy Garden, as it appeared in 1610.

92. A model of Nonsuch Palace by Ben Taggart. This view shows the exterior of the south wing from the Privy Garden, as it appeared in 1610.

93. Aerial view of Sudeley Castle, Gloucestershire. To the left of the formal gardens once stood the lavish east range, where it's almost certain Katherine Parr spent her final summer. The now vanished south range would have contained the Great Hall, and a cross range, now lost, once separated the two courts. The refurbished fifteenth-century church north of the formal gardens is the final resting place of Katherine Parr.

94. Katherine Parr's tomb, St Mary's church, Sudeley Castle. The magnificent canopied tomb, with a recumbent effigy of the queen, was designed by George Gilbert Scott and carved by John Birnie Philip in the middle of the nineteenth century.

Right: 95. An illustrative picture of a medieval banquet held in the Great Hall of Eltham Palace, *c.* 1365. Drawn by G. F. Sargent, engraved by J. Godfrey.

Below: 96. Eltham Palace, ground-floor plan. Note the outer or 'Green Court' with the Lord Chancellor's Lodgings in the north-west range. This building still survives today. Around the Great Court, the surviving great hall is clearly marked, along with the chapel which is now lost. The royal lodgings run along the north-west range, while courtier lodgings wrap around the north-east angle of the Great Court.

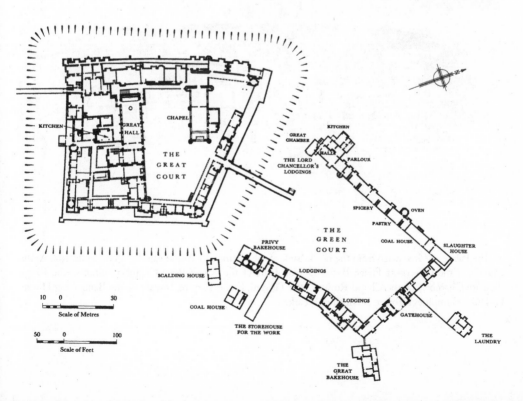

KITCHEN

GREAT HALL

CHAPEL

THE GREAT COURT

GREAT CHAMBER

KITCHEN

THE LORD CHANCELLOR'S LODGINGS

PARLOUR

SPICERY

OVEN

PASTRY

THE GREEN COURT

COAL HOUSE

SLAUGHTER HOUSE

PRIVY BAKEHOUSE

SCALDING HOUSE

LODGINGS

COAL HOUSE

LODGINGS

GATEHOUSE

THE STOREHOUSE FOR THE WORK

THE GREAT BAKEHOUSE

THE LAUNDRY

10   0   30
Scale of Metres

50   0   100
Scale of Feet

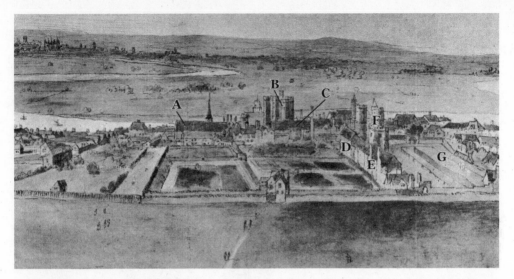

97. The Palace of Greenwich from Observatory Hill, with the spire of St Paul's in the background, by Anton van den Wyngaerde. A=the Church of the Observant Friars; B=the Donjon (part of the King's Privy Chamber suite); C=the Queen's Privy Lodgings; D=the Disguising House; E=the Banqueting House; F=the Tiltyard Towers; G=the Tiltyard.

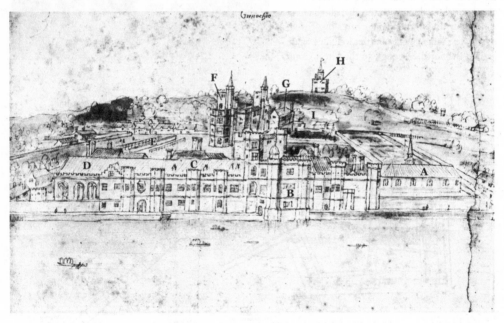

98. The Palace of Greenwich from the north bank of the Thames, by Anton van den Wyngaerde, 1558. A=the Church of the Observant Friars; B=the Donjon (part of the King's Privy Chamber suite); C=the King's Presence Chamber; D=the Chapel Royal; E=the Tiltyard; F=the Tiltyard Towers; G=the Banqueting House; H=Duke Humphrey's Tower; I=Greenwich Park.

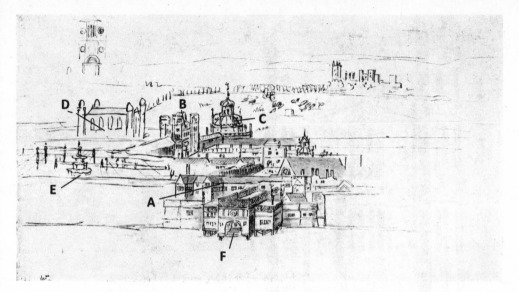

99. The Privy Stair, Whitehall Palace, by Anton van den Wyngaerde. The Privy Stair allowed direct access to the palace from the waterfront. Although the relative position of some of the buildings is distorted, we can clearly make out: A=the Queen's Gallery; B=the Holbein Gate; C=the Cock-pit; D=the Tennis Play; E=the Great Garden; F=The Privy Stair.

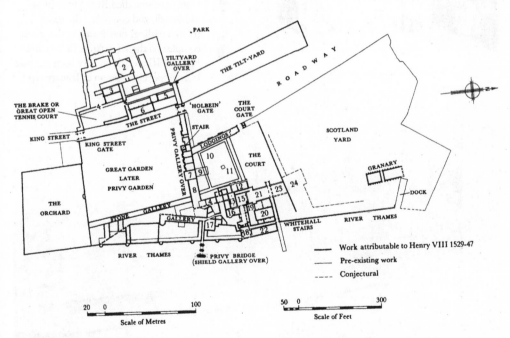

100. Floor plan of Whitehall. At first-floor level, the queen lodgings are located close to the Thames and are marked by No. 16, the queen's presence chamber and No. 17, the queen's bedchamber. The queen's gallery is adjacent to this overlooking the river. No. 19 is the royal pews overlooking No. 20, the chapel.

Sumptibus Societatis Antiquaria Lond: 1745.   B. 7. I. 777

101. The Holbein Gate, taken from *Vestusa Monumenta*, Volume 1, 1806. The Holbein Gate once straddled King Street (now Whitehall) and connected the main palace buildings on the east to the leisure complex on the west. Anne Boleyn and Henry VIII are said to have been married in an upper chamber on 25 January 1533.

102. View of the south of Hampton Court Palace made by Anton van den Wyngaerde in 1558.

103. View of the north of Hampton Court Palace made by Anton van den Wyngaerde in 1558.

104. Richmond Palace by Anton van den Wyngaerde, c. 1558. Richmond Palace is perhaps best known to the Tudor enthusiast as the place where the first and last Tudor monarchs – Henry VII and Elizabeth I – took their last breaths, but it was also well known to Henry's queens, in particular Anne of Cleves, whose primary residence it was from June 1540 until June 1548. Pictured here, from left to right, are the chapel, royal lodgings with gatehouse in foreground, hall and kitchen.

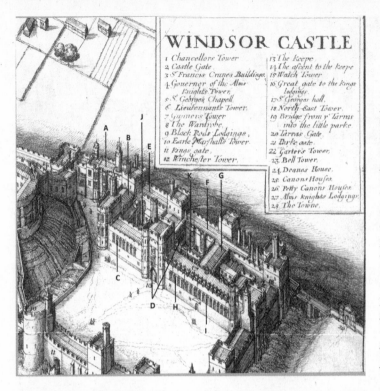

WINDSOR CASTLE

1 Chancellors Tower
2 Castle Gate
3 S:t Francis Cranes Buildings
4 Gouernor of the Alms Knights Tower
5 S:t Gerorges Chapell
6 Lieutennants Tower
7 Gunners Tower
8 The Wardrobe
9 Black Rods Lodgings
10 Earle Marshalls Tower
11 Kings gate
12 Winchester Tower

13 The Keepe
14 The ascent to the keepe
15 Watch Tower
16 Great gate to the kings lodgings
17 S:t Georges hall
18 North-East Tower
19 Bridge from y:e larms into the little parke
20 Tarras Gate
21 Parke gate
22 Garter's Tower
23 Bell Tower
24 Deanes House
25 Canons Houses
26 Petty Canons Houses
27 Alms Knights Lodgings
28 The Towne

105. Detail of Royal Apartments at Windsor Castle, adapted from an engraving by Wenceslaus Hollar, unknown date. A=the Henry VII Tower (Henry's library and other 'secret rooms'); B=the queen's bed and privy chamber; C=the queen's presence chamber; D=the queen's watching chamber; E=Henry VIII's privy chambers; F=Henry VIII's presence chamber; G=the great watching chamber; H=the chapel; I=the great hall; J=Brick Court; K=inner court (now the Waterloo Chamber).

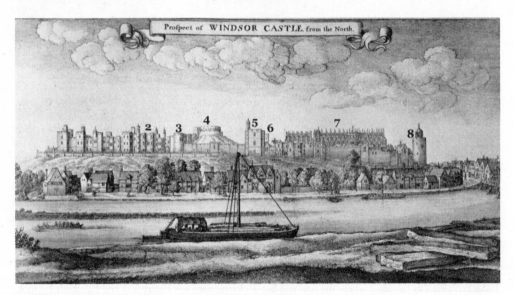

Prospect of WINDSOR CASTLE. from the North.

106. The view of Windsor Castle from the north, engraved by Hollar, 1667. The king's royal apartments stretch away from the left (labelled '2' on the etching) via 3=the gatehouse to the upper ward; 4=the keep; 5=Winchester Tower; 6=the Lieutenants' Tower; 7=St George's Chapel; to '8', which is the Bell Tower.

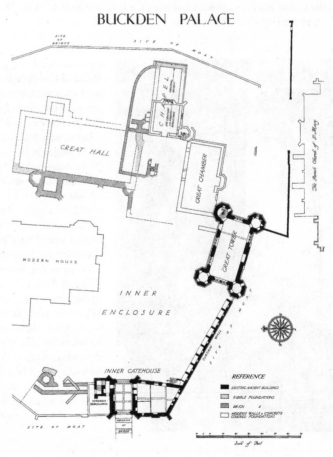

Above: 107. The interior of the Chapel Royal at Windsor Castle, by Hollar. This shows the chapel in the upper ward following the refurbishment of 1570–1.

Right: 108. First-floor plan of Buckden Palace. This plan clearly shows the arrangement of the great hall, chapel and Great Chamber (all now lost), sited around a small garth, or courtyard. Attached to this is the Great Tower, the site of Katherine's private chambers. This is still standing today in a much-altered form.

BUCKDEN PALACE

REFERENCE

EXISTING ANCIENT BUILDINGS

RUBBLE FOUNDATIONS

BRICK

MODERN WALLS & CONCRETE COVERED FOUNDATIONS

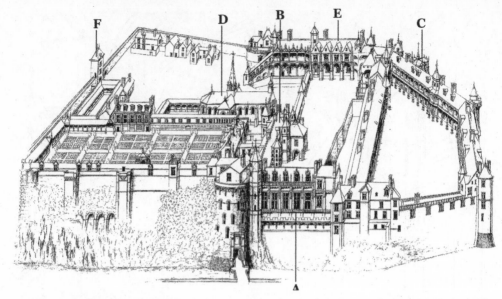

109. Engraving of the Château d'Amboise from the sixteenth century by Jacques Androuet du Cerceau. This is how the chateau would have appeared to Anne Boleyn during her time at the French court. A=Grand Salle; B=Louis XII wing; C=St Hubert Chapel; D=Saint-Florentin church; E=Logia of the Seven Virtues; F=Porte des Lions. The Château d'Amboise fell out of favour and into a gradual state of decay after it was all but abandoned as a royal residence following the untimely death of Henri II in 1559. It is now preserved and cared for by the Foundation Saint-Louis.

Left: 110. Detail of a portrait of Prince Edward at Windsor Castle, probably showing Hunsdon House in the background, from where, in June 1528, Henry VIII penned a moving letter to his 'entirely beloved' Anne Boleyn. The king and his first wife, Queen Katherine of Aragon, were staying at the house following an outbreak of the plague in London. *Opposite top:* 111. Chertsey Abbey. This reconstruction of the plan of Chertsey Abbey shows the entire abbey precinct as it appeared during the later Middle Ages. It is most likely that any high-status visitor would be lodged in the abbot's lodgings. The exact location of this building is not known, although it may have been located around the Cloister Garth. *Opposite middle:* 112. The south-east view of Berkeley Castle in the county of Gloucestershire, Samuel and Nathaniel Buck, 1732. Henry VIII and Anne Boleyn probably lodged in the main privy apartments, shown here in the foreground of the picture. Where the south-facing wing (left) joins the east-facing wing (right) was the chapel (now the morning room). The earlier medieval keep is in the centre background, as is the parish church of St Mary (background left). *Opposite bottom:* 113. The Old Manor House, Chelsea. By J. Barlow, 1810. The north front of Chelsea Manor House (left of picture) from an old drawing published in Faulkner's *Historical and Topographical Descriptions of Chelsea*.

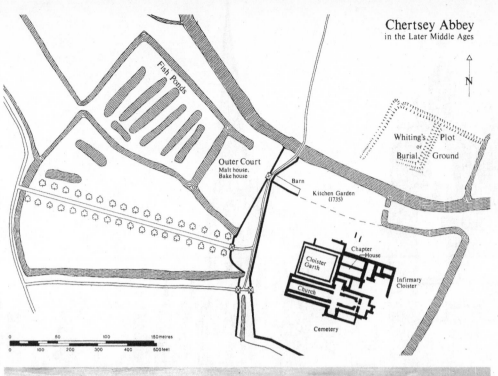

Chertsey Abbey
in the Later Middle Ages

N

Fish Ponds

Whiting's Plot
or
Burial Ground

Outer Court
Malt house,
Bake house

Barn

Kitchen Garden
(1735)

Cloister
Garth

Chapter
House

Infirmary
Cloister

Church

Cemetery

| 0 | 50 | 100 | 150 metres |

| 0 | 100 | 200 | 300 | 400 | 500 feet |

114. View of Tudor Cheapside, looking east to west and toward St Paul's Cathedral. In the centre of the street stands the Cheap Cross in the distance. The central conduit can be seen in the foreground. The church of St Mary-le-Bow is on the near left-hand side of the picture. The Mercers' Hall is not visible in this picture.

115. Two views of the Mercers' Hall from the Tudor period. The bottom shows the hall as it is represented on the Agas Map of London from 1560. The second is a reconstruction of the hall taken from *The History of the Twelve Great Livery Companies in London*. This shows a little more of the detail of the building as described in contemporary accounts.

116. 'Panorama of London from the River: The Strand' by Anton van den Wyngaerde, *c.* 1544. This shows the area of the Strand that was occupied by the inns of the bishops of Chester and Llandaff in the 1530s. Wyngaerde's illustrations were not always dimensionally accurate and, according to Simon Thurley, 'definitively untangling the buildings shown is now probably impossible'. However, we have circled the rough location of Chester Place, as it existed before its demolition to make way for Somerset House.

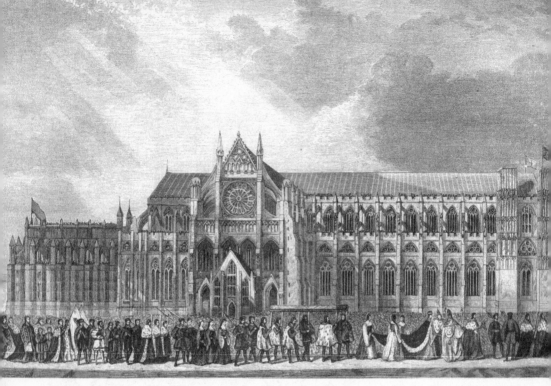

Above: 117. 'The Coronation Procession of Anne Boleyn' (originally from a drawing by David Roberts in the Tyrrell Collections, 1872–8). In this nineteenth-century engraving, we see Anne walking in procession toward the great west doors of Westminster Abbey for her Coronation on Whit Sunday, 1 June 1533.

Below: 118. The Tower of London viewed from the south, from *Old London Illustrated*, 1921. A=the Great Hall; B=the Queen's Lodgings; C=the Queen's Gallery; D=Inner Courtyard; E=Coldharbour Gate; F=the White Tower; G=Martin Tower; H=the Chapel of St Peter ad Vincula; I=the Bell Tower.

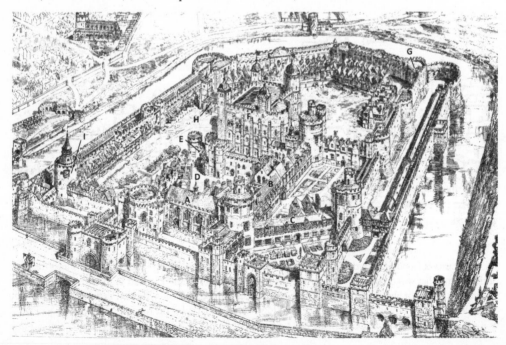

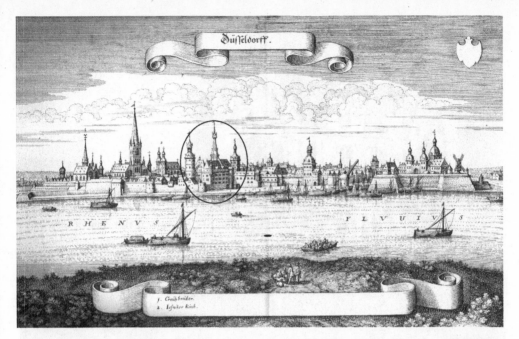

119. The Old City of Düsseldorf by Matthäus Merian, 1647. The City Palace of Düsseldorf is circled. This was where Anne of Cleves was born on 15 September 1515. Note the two towers on either side of the central building, one of which (on the left) still stands today as the Schlossturm (Palace Tower).

120. Schloss Burg an der Wupper as it appeared in the sixteenth century.

121. The English House, Antwerp. It was at the English House in Antwerp that Anne of Cleves was first officially received by the English nation. The building was located in the heart of the city, next to the Old Bourse.

122. 'The Reception of Quentin Metsys into the Guild of St Luke of Antwerp in 1520', by Edouard de Jans (1855–1919). Although not directly related to Anne of Cleves, this image does illustrate the interior of a high-status building in Antwerp during the first half of the sixteenth century. Similarly, the clothes are typical of the period. It recreates for us an idea of the type of reception that might have greeted Anne upon her celebrated arrival into the city.

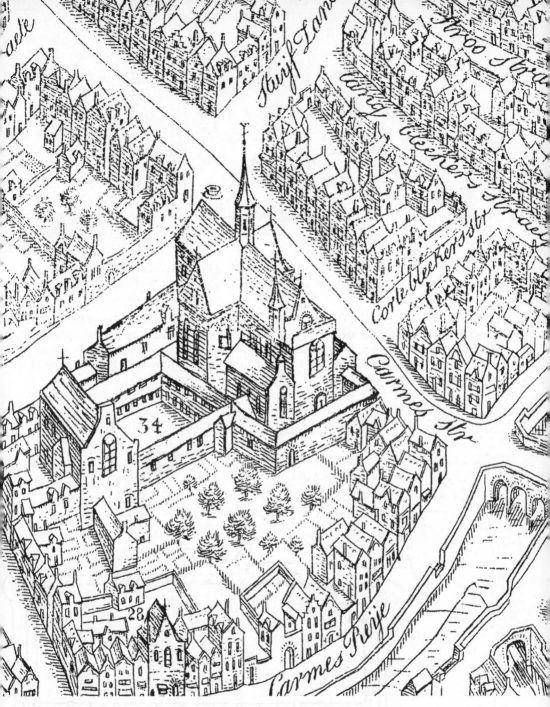

123. Detail of Carmesstraat and the Carmelite monastery from a sixteenth-century engraving of the city. The monastery had links to the English mercantile community in Bruges. Thomas More was lodged here during his six-month stay in the city in 1515.

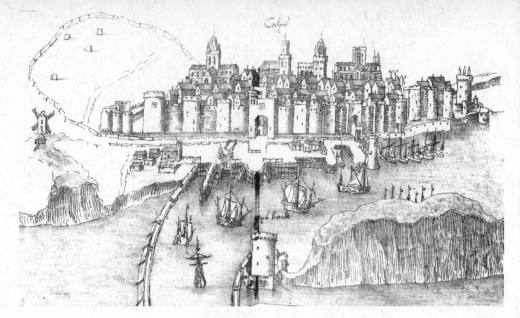

124. View of Calais in the time of Henry VIII from *The Chronicle of Calais in the Reigns of Henry VII and Henry VIII*, 1846. In this contemporary drawing of sixteenth-century Calais, the port is clearly visible, defended by the Rysbank Fort. The main Lantern Gate is seen positioned centrally. On the skyline we can see (from left to right) the church of St Mary (still standing today), the Town Hall, the Staple Hall and, on the far right, St Nicolas's church.

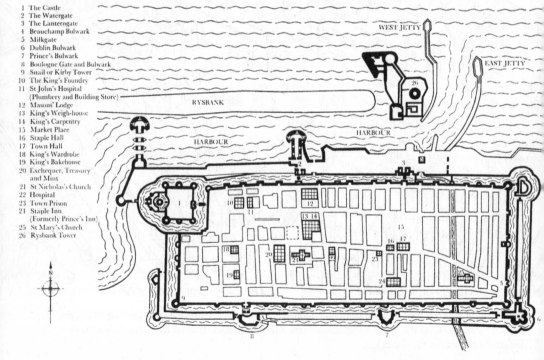

1   The Castle
2   The Watergate
3   The Lanterngate
4   Beauchamp Bulwark
5   Milkgate
6   Dublin Bulwark
7   Prince's Bulwark
8   Boulogne Gate and Bulwark
9   Snail or Kirby Tower
10 The King's Foundry
11 St John's Hospital
    (Plumbery and Building Store)
12 Masons' Lodge
13 King's Weigh-house
14 King's Carpentry
15 Market Place
16 Staple Hall
17 Town Hall
18 King's Wardrobe
19 King's Bakehouse
20 Exchequer, Treasury
    and Mint
21 St Nicholas's Church
22 Hospital
23 Town Prison
24 Staple Inn
    (Formerly Prince's Inn)
25 St Mary's Church
26 Rysbank Tower

125. Street plan of Tudor Calais, based on a map held in the British Library. The grid-like system of the streets of old Calais is largely preserved in the modern-day town. Note that the Exchequer once stood at position 20, on the western side of the town.

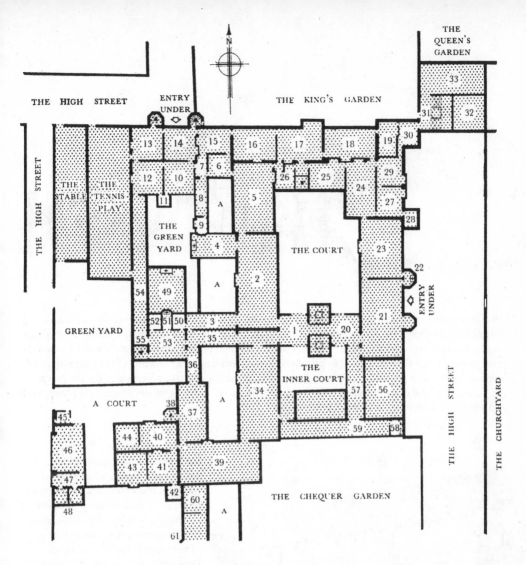

THE QUEEN'S GARDEN

N

THE HIGH STREET

ENTRY UNDER

THE KING'S GARDEN

THE HIGH STREET

THE STABLE

THE TENNIS PLAY

THE GREEN YARD

THE COURT

GREEN YARD

THE INNER COURT

ENTRY UNDER

THE HIGH STREET

THE CHURCHYARD

A COURT

THE CHEQUER GARDEN

126. This floor plan shows the Exchequer as arranged for the meeting between Henry VIII and Francis I in 1532. Anne of Cleves probably occupied the apartments used by Anne Boleyn during that visit, as denoted by Nos 20–33.

127. Seventeenth-century view of Deal Castle by Wenceslaus Hollar.

Deale Castle

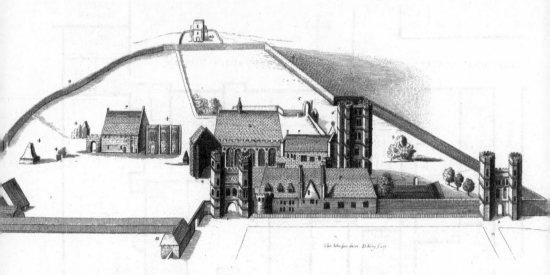

128. The remains of St Augustine's Abbey, Canterbury, as seen from the tower of the cathedral, 1655. This illustration shows the King's Manor following its conversion from the original monastic buildings. During the sixteenth century, these buildings were as follows: 1=the Principal Gate; 2 and 7 formed the main part of Henry VIII's lodgings; 6=Ethelbert's Tower standing at the junction of the king and queen's lodgings (at the time it was the only surviving part of the abbey church); 7 (as seen in the foreground of the picture)=the site of the queen's outer chambers. The queen's privy chambers would have connected 6 and 7 but do not seem to be shown in this image.

129. The Old Bishop's Palace, Rochester. Little remains of the old Bishop's Palace today. However, medieval brickwork of a much earlier time can be seen forming the fabric of a surviving building. This illustration of 1886 apparently shows one range of the original building, although little descriptive evidence is left of the palace's original arrangement.

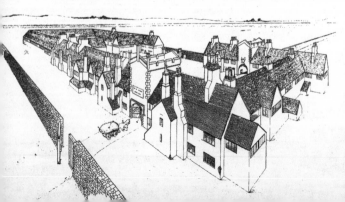

130. The King's Manor, Dartford. This conjectural drawing shows the King's Manor of Dartford during its zenith in the sixteenth century. There is a good deal of debate about its layout and orientation. The gatehouse and building shown in the near right-hand side of the picture are the only parts of the manor still standing today.

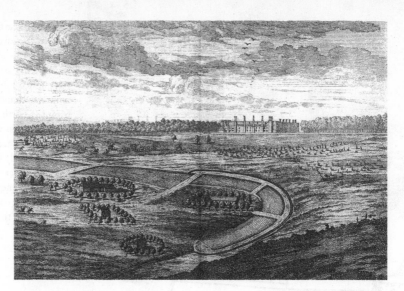

131. Grimsthorpe Castle. This engraving of Grimsthorpe Castle predates the major remodelling work of the eighteenth century and so gives some idea of the appearance of the house that Catherine Howard visited in August and October 1541.

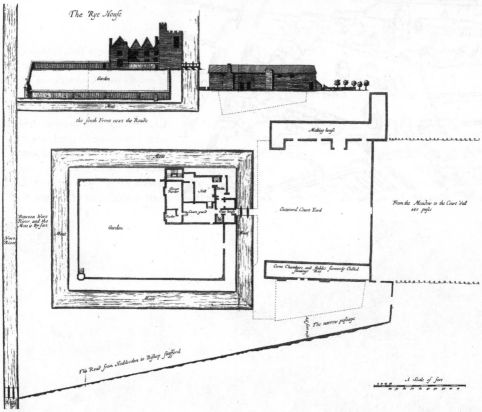

132. Rye House Plan and Elevation. Taken from *A true account and declaration of the horrid conspiracy against the late King, his present Majesty, and the government as it was order'd to be published by His late Majesty*, this image shows both the plan and the elevation of Rye House in 1683. Little would have changed from the house that Katherine Parr knew as a child. The image clearly shows the moated manor house, with outer court and attendant service buildings. Within the moat, the large garden wraps around the manor buildings, labelled as the gatehouse, kitchen, hall, great parlour and parlour, all arranged around three sides of a courtyard.

133. Snape Castle, Bedale, Yorkshire. One of the earliest representations of Snape Castle, although the grand towers and castellated parapets were added after Katherine Parr's tenure as chatelaine. The view is from the north-west. This simple courtyard house is shown from the rear and is clearly already partly in decay. Only the south range remains intact (as it is today). The two standalone ruinous towers were once connected to complete the four sides of the courtyard.

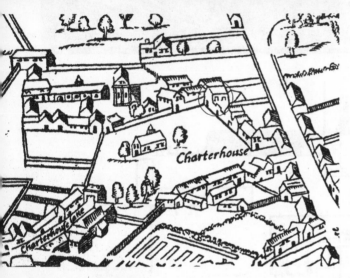

134. Charterhouse Yard, London. Detail taken from the Agas Map of 1561 showing Charterhouse Yard with the buildings of the dissolved Carthusian priory of the Charterhouse sited along its northern edge. Fine houses fronted onto the 'square' along its eastern and southern sides. The Latimers' Charterhouse residence is circled, lying in the most north-easterly part of the yard.

135. Nonsuch Palace, c. 1620. Approaching from the north, Henry VIII's Nonsuch Palace was not unlike any other. The entrance-front was dominated by a wide three-storey gatehouse with polygonal corner turrets made of a brick core and faced in stone, as seen in this painting made by an unknown Flemish artist.

Part Five
Anne of Cleves
[Anna von Jülich-Kleves-Berg]

'GOD SEND ME WELL TO KEEP'

Introduction

On 4 August 1557, Anne, 'daughter of Cleves', former Queen of England and fourth wife of King Henry VIII, was laid to rest in a stone tomb adjacent to the sacred heart of Westminster Abbey. Unlike the flamboyant memorials sculpted for her Tudor in-laws, Henry VII and Elizabeth of York, or those of her stepchildren, Edward, Mary and Elizabeth, Anne's tomb is so unassuming that it might be easily missed by the casual time traveller. Thus, as in death, so Anne was in life: understated yet dignified.

Of all Henry's wives, Anne of Cleves is probably the most easily dismissed. Her story has none of the drama attributable to the redoubtable characters of Katherine of Aragon and Anne Boleyn, their titanic battle forging a white-hot crucible of religious and societal change. The German princess possessed nothing of the vivacious sex appeal of the rather tragic figure of Catherine Howard; she could not claim to be an outstanding paragon of intellect, such as Katherine Parr; nor could her memory be aggrandised by the legacy of a Tudor heir, as was the case with Jane Seymour. A brief and unsuccessful marriage, overshadowed by strong, charismatic giants of the age, has eclipsed her virtues. As we shall hear shortly, such virtues were forged from the principles of female propriety at the German ducal court in which she was raised, modesty, subtlety, devotion to faith and purity being first among them.

Unfortunately, it is probably still true to this day that Western society venerates masculine qualities of leadership over the kind of feminine attributes associated with Anne of Cleves. Even the iconic female figures of the Tudor court, such as Katherine of Aragon, Anne Boleyn and her daughter, Elizabeth, stand out for their warrior-like qualities of courage, determination and dazzling charisma. They forged their way into the nation's history through sheer force of personality and by proving themselves to be as formidable an adversary as any man. However, this was not Anne. Furthermore, Henry's infamous distaste for his new bride's personal appearance and bodily odour (he is alleged to have said that she 'had unsavoury smells about her'), as well as the posthumous ravaging of Anne's memory as the 'Flanders mare' does nothing to help us appreciate her many worthy qualities.

Of course, whether Anne was attractive or not must surely be a matter of personal taste, to which even Henry, as capricious as he was, was entitled. It is not the place or purpose of this book to explore the queen's relative physical merits. Anne's biographers have done so at length elsewhere. However, it is appropriate to paint a picture of the woman that we shall follow from her birthplace in Düsseldorf to her dower properties in England.

There are several contemporary accounts of Anne's appearance, as well as a number of portraits, including the most famous, painted by Holbein, from which we might draw our own conclusions. Perhaps the most illuminating physical description of 'Madame Anne of Cleves' comes from the French ambassador, Monsieur Marillac, who was present at Anne's first formal meeting with the king on Blackheath, just outside Greenwich on 3 January 1540. According to his letter to the French king, Francis I, 'she looks about 30 years of age, tall and thin, of medium beauty, and of very assured and resolute countenance. She brought 12 or 15 ladies of honour clothed like herself – a thing which looks strange to many.' In a second missive, written on the same day to Anne, Duc de Montmorency, Marillac provides further details of Anne's appearance:

> The Queen of England has arrived who, according to some who saw her close, is not so young as was expected, nor so beautiful as everyone affirmed. She is tall and very assured in carriage and countenance, showing that in her the turn and vivacity of wit supplies the place of beauty. She brings from her brother's country 12 or 15 damsels inferior in beauty even to their mistress and dressed so heavily and unbecomingly that they would almost be thought ugly even if they were beautiful.

It is widely accepted that Anne's heavy Germanic dress did little to flatter what looks she did possess. Other than her nose, which might have been slightly longer than desirable for a woman, it seems that Anne was middling in her beauty, tall and slim, of swarthy complexion but with fair hair. However, what is clear is that her behaviour was impeccable, 'like a princess', and in this Anne of Cleves won many admirers.

If we follow Anne back to her childhood home along the banks of the Rhine in Germany, as with Anne Boleyn's early days in the Low Countries and France, we begin to appreciate more clearly the forces that melded that character. Travelling silently alongside Anne in her gilded chariot from her birthplace in Düsseldorf to her fateful first meeting with her husband-to-be in Rochester, we witness a young woman emerging from the shadow of her brother. From her first official reception by the English nation at Antwerp, through towns and cities such as Calais, Dover and Canterbury, again and again we read fulsome accounts of Anne's kind and temperate nature, as well as her earnest desire to please her new husband and learn the ways of her adopted homeland.

Researching Anne's early life gave insight into the genesis of this most kind-hearted and agreeable of women. As we shall hear in the entry for Schloss Burg an der Wupper, Anne came from an apparently warm and loving home. Never far from her mother's side, she must have been keenly aware of her parents' devotion to each other. In short, we believe Anne of Cleves learnt how to love with a generous heart. It is not hard, therefore, to imagine her having high expectations of married life, of a husband not unlike her father, who doted on her mother and seems to have lavished her with gentle affection. Indeed, Anne never seemed to come to terms with Henry's rejection of her, always seeing herself as his rightful wife, ever hopeful that he would return to the marital fold. Perhaps her idealised version of a 'happy ending' could never be completely extinguished.

However, regardless of her heartfelt feelings on the matter, Anne of Cleves remained ultimately deferential to her husband's wishes, never seeking to raise arms, either literal or metaphorical, against him. Instead, she yielded and her reward was Henry's bountiful thanks in lands, properties and position as the 'king's sister'. Perhaps most tellingly of all, though, was the fact that Anne won the hearts of her two stepdaughters, Mary and Elizabeth. Mary was perhaps the most difficult character to conquer, being almost exactly the same age as Anne when the latter arrived in England in January 1540; Elizabeth was but a child of seven. With the exception of a difficult period early in 1554, following the Wyatt rebellion, both royal ladies were to remain on good terms with Anne of Cleves until her death. This won her a royal burial, as befitted Anne's status, following her death on 16 July 1557.

In this section, we will begin by taking you on a journey to the Rhine Valley in Germany, presenting in detail for the first time to an English audience the palaces and castles which Anne called home during her childhood. By working with local historians, archivists, guides and native German and Dutch speakers, we have recreated the buildings as Anne would have known them, as well as describing the cultural milieu which forged her famed manners and deportment. From here, we will follow Anne on her journey to England, a gruelling trek through the harshest of northern European winters to reach her new homeland. Sometimes covering only 5 miles a day, the journey from Düsseldorf to Greenwich took around five weeks. During that time, Anne and her train lodged in many places. However, we have decided to focus on eight of the most significant, either because there are substantial remains to be visited, or because of the intriguing story and/or accounts associated with the location in question.

Because of the relative paucity of information hitherto explored in texts of Anne's life relating to her early years, we actively took the decision to devote a significant portion of this segment of the book to Anne of Cleves's time in modern-day Germany, as well as her travels through the Low Countries en route to England. Of Anne's dower properties, Bletchingley and Dartford are described in full in this section. For Richmond Palace please see the section on the Principal Royal Residences. Finally, Anne's time at Hever Castle is touched upon in the section devoted to Anne Boleyn.

Interestingly, it has been our research into Anne, the woman most easily dismissed from history, which has brought forth our greatest discovery. As you shall read in the next section, a most unexpected turn of events has led us to 'discover' a lost Tudor interior, described by eminent Tudor historian Jonathan Foyle as a 'nationally important historic collection' associated with Henry's fourth wife (see below, the Anne of Cleves Panels).

History has indeed been unkind to this most amiable of characters, who, like all of Henry's wives, was thrust into an impossibly demanding and difficult situation. Our earnest wish is that in following in the footsteps of the 'daughter of Cleves' you will appreciate afresh this most warm-hearted and gracious of women.

The Anne of Cleves Panels

During the course of our research into the entry for Bruges, we turned our attention to a set of carved panels, currently installed in Old Warden Church in Bedfordshire. Tradition had it that these carved oak panels had originally come from 'Anne of Cleves' chapel in Bruges'. If this legend were true, then we assumed that they must have come from the lodging in Bruges that accommodated Anne overnight as she made her brief passage through the city. Sadly, the exact location of these lodgings has been lost to time (see entry on Bruges), but how these panels ultimately ended up housed in a parish church in Bedfordshire is summarised by Jonathan Foyle in the introduction to a report, commissioned by the authors in 2015, in order to investigate the provenance of the carvings. In it, he states that 'they were collected by Robert Henley Lord Ongley (1803–77) who refurbished Old Warden church in 1841–2, amid a range of salvaged Continental carving'.

The carvings themselves are crisp and are of remarkable workmanship. From the mid-nineteenth century through to the early twenty-first century, antiquarians and historians alike have commented on the likely nature of the panels, with disparate conclusions being reached as to their true age and probable geographic origin; everything from the Jacobean period through to the eighteenth and nineteenth centuries has been cited over the years, while origins have been given as widely as England, France or the Low Countries. It seems that we had an enigma on our hands – and one which was not going to yield its secrets easily. However, we were determined to bring modern techniques to bear in an effort to resolve this mystery once and for all. Little did we appreciate at the time the twist and turns that lay ahead.

Therefore, in conjunction with architectural historian Dr Jonathan Foyle, conservator Helen Hughes and local historian and Ongley biographer Christine Hill, an original research project was commissioned to undertake physical, forensic and historical analysis of the panels.

The Appearance of the Panels

Three different types of panels survive. All are carved in oak. The first has the initials 'AC' set with an oval cartouche, a coronet above and swags below; the second a lion's head; the third an emblem which looks like a spoked wheel without the rim. We soon identified this as being the emblem of Cleves. At the outset of our investigation it was clear that much of the attention and commentary had hitherto focused on the initialled 'AC' panels. The other two had largely been ignored, such that we found that there had never been the accurate identification of the panel bearing the Cleves emblem as such. This was our first discovery. It led us one step closer to establishing a link with our protagonist. A much more exciting and definitive discovery would soon follow.

During our investigation, a review of Anne of Cleves's much-overlooked tomb in Westminster Abbey led to another surprising – and pivotal – find. The exact same three panels were also represented on Anne's sixteenth-century tomb – this time carved in marble. We could find no evidence that this link had been recorded before. There was no doubt; for the first time we had incontrovertible evidence that the panels in Old Warden Church were linked to our Tudor queen. Furthermore, on detailed inspection it was clear that the two sets of panels, the ones on the tomb and the oak panels at Old Warden were not just similar but *identical*, including minor flaws in the carving that had been transferred from one to the other. The significance of this we will return to later. However, this find meant there was now no doubt – the panels in Old Warden Church were definitely linked to Henry's fourth wife. But the question remained: were they contemporaneous to her life, or simply later copies?

Contemporary or Copies?

Anne's tomb was known to early antiquarians. However, there was a revival in interest relating to all things Tudor in the first half of the nineteenth century due to the opening of Hampton Court Palace to the public for the first time in 1838. Enter Robert Henley-Ongley, 3rd Baron Ongley of Old Warden. He had inherited his title and his estate in Bedfordshire from his father in 1814. Upon reaching his majority he remodelled his village of Old Warden in the Picturesque style and created a romantic Swiss garden. In 1841 he turned his attentions to the parish church of St Leonard's, furnishing it with carvings, panelling and box pews salvaged from the Low Countries and England. It is clear that this project coincided with the surge of interest in the Tudor period. It was at this point that the Anne of Cleves panels are recorded as being assembled in the church alongside a range of other fine carvings. Had the carvings simply been copied from the tomb, made to order to furnish Ongley's project in Old Warden, or did they represent authentic sixteenth-century panels originally commissioned by Anne of Cleves herself and used to adorn a high-status room in one of her residences? Had these panels survived the subsequent loss of that property, only to be salvaged and used elsewhere, thus preserving them over the centuries? This was now the question we needed to answer.

Back in the twenty-first century, initial visual and scientific investigation of the panels produced disappointing results. Physical examination of the panels showed that they had been cut down in size, almost certainly at the point that they had been fitted *in situ* into Old Warden Church. This was not a problem in and of itself. However, the crisp appearance of the wood was worrying. In order to date the panels to the Tudor period, we had hoped to see two key pieces of evidence; the first was appropriately aged wood. Secondly, it was expected that forensic examination would also show up microscopic flecks of paint (as we believed at the time that the original panels would have been painted in vivid colours, according to the fashion of the day). The type of paint pigments used would make the paint, and therefore the panels, traceable to the sixteenth century. Unfortunately, our initial forensic analysis revealed no evidence of paint at all. Combined with the fresh appearance of the panels, this seemed to be the end of our quest. We were forced to conclude that the Anne of Cleves panels in Old Warden Church were nineteenth-century replicas, commissioned and installed by an eccentric English gentleman with a love of fine old carvings and a developing interest in the Tudor period.

A Surprising Find ...
Then, quite unexpectedly, just a couple of months later an additional panel came to light which caused us to completely re-evaluate our findings. In May 2015, Bonhams auction house put another panel, with the same carved 'AC' initials, up for sale. We could not believe our eyes! However, the panel was presented with a provenance which dated it to the Jacobean period: 'circa 1610, possibly installed at Suffolk House, a Jacobean palace on The Strand.' However, we knew that this could not be correct. As Foyle observed, 'It does not date from the reign of James I (1603–25) but matches Anne of Cleves' tomb sculpture of *c.* 1557: its style is Counter-Reformation classicism. There is no realistic scenario of an early Anne of Cleves revival, so given its evidently considerable age, this panel must relate to her directly.'

This was not the end of our discoveries. Included in the Bonhams write-up was mention of another carving, this time of the lion's head panel belonging to the Museum of London (held in storage and again with an incorrect, but similar, Jacobean provenance associated with it). These two panels exactly matched those on both the tomb and those in Old Warden Church. It seems we had identified two more panels from the original set of carvings.

According to Jonathan Foyle, 'the match to her tomb sculpture presupposes that it [the Bonhams panel] came from a late domestic environment, a pattern that was copied by her workshop for the tomb. This is confirmed by the tomb's fictive timber moulding details.' Interestingly, the Bonhams panel was partially covered in plaster (gesso). It was this fact which led us to fundamentally question our original conclusions about the authenticity of the panels. Foyle describes the state of the panel in his report: 'The plaster is not original, as the carved central field of the panel is darker than the surround, suggesting a wax treatment to the oak in its first iteration. The plaster seems to be a gesso, typical of Flemish panels more than English, applied when it was salvaged.'

Foyle concluded that, rather than being painted, the panels had originally been gilded (see the gilded carved panelling in the background of the painting *The Family of Henry VIII* from around 1545, held in the Royal Collection at Hampton Court Palace), with plaster being applied at a later date. Gilding does not leave traces of pigment behind, but is completely worn away over time. This finally explained why we had not been able to identify any medieval paint during our first forensic examination. However, Foyle also states in his report that 'the southern panel [in the church] appears to have a crusty deposit in the tassels. This would match the secondary gesso seen on the Bonhams panel.'

It seems that the Bonhams panel and the ones located in Old Warden Church had originated from the same original set of carvings. The effect of the plaster had been to preserve the integrity of the wood. This also explained why the panels had appeared to be of a later date. In conclusion, Foyle states, 'At least some, and possibly all of the panels at Old Warden are by the same hands and probably from the same source as the Bonhams panel.'

Some months after our official investigation into the panels was concluded, we had the opportunity to submit the Bonhams panel for carbon dating. This would be the final test, one that would ultimately confirm or refute our hypothesis that the panels were contemporary to Anne's life. The results of the dendrochronological testing, conducted by Professor Dr Peter Klein, concluded that the oak had originated in the West German/Netherlandish region. In other words, the wood originated from Anne's homeland; a window into Anne's sentimental and enduring connection with happier times perhaps? The most likely date for the creation of the panels was given as '1544 upwards'. This dating fits perfectly with the style of the carving (counter-Reformation classicism), and our theory that the panels would have adorned one of Anne's dower properties. Finally, the puzzle of the Old Warden panels was solved.

The Truth about the Anne of Cleves Panelling

And so, from the evidence to date, we can draw together our final summary. At some point, probably in the 1550s, and therefore toward the end of Anne of Cleves's life, the panels were commissioned by Henry's fourth wife. The design reflected not only Anne's heraldry but the decoration and style that are typical of a period known as 'counter-reformation classicism', in essence the short period of time in which Catholicism flourished again under Mary I (1553–8). The carved images bear no reference to religious iconography, and thus we were able to dismiss the legend that they had come from 'Anne of Cleves' chapel in Bruges'. These interiors were commissioned to grace one of Anne's residences, probably in a high-status room such as a long gallery or closet. As you will read about later in this section, the dating of the panels to the 1550s leaves us with two primary contenders: the King's Manor at Dartford or Chelsea Place in London. As we shall hear in this section, it is widely held that Anne lived at Dartford between 1553 and the spring of 1557, when she moved to Chelsea Place (see entry on the King's Manor, Dartford). This was Anne's final dower property before her death in July of the same year (see entry on Chelsea Place).

With Anne's death, the same workshop which had carved the original wooden panels was commissioned to decorate the old queen's tomb. The fact that the wooden panels are identical, including flaws in the design, mean that the same template must have been used in both instances. In this way, we can be sure that the Westminster Abbey carvings and the Old Warden panels originated in the same workshop. However, it seems highly unlikely to us that the master mason generally accredited with Anne's tomb, Theodore Haveus of Cleves, was in fact responsible for carving the panels; the gentleman in question did not arrive in England until five years after Anne's death. Thus, the name of the workshop currently remains a mystery.

With the death of Mary I, artistic tastes changed. Perhaps the style of the carvings fell out of fashion, or simply a new owner wished to reflect their own personal tastes, or the original house was demolished, but at some point the carvings were removed from their original position. There is a suggestion from the Bonhams catalogue that the panels may have ended up in a grand Jacobean property, such as Suffolk House (later Northumberland House) on the Strand. We have not been able to refute or verify this fact. There is currently a 300-year gap during which their whereabouts remains unknown.

A Twentieth Century Twist to the Tale

However, there was one final piece of our jigsaw to put into place with regards to the two separate panels – the so-called 'Bonhams Panel' and the Museum of London specimen. We were able to establish that they had been loaned to the fledging museum around the time of its creation in 1912 by a Mr James Dowell Phillips. Mr Phillips turned out to be an antiques dealer and manager at Owen Grant Ltd. The company had a particular interest in salvaging rare pieces of antique furniture and their shop at 3 Clifford Street in London's West End was arranged like a home, with each room appearing as though lived in. Rooms included in a surviving catalogue for the business include, rather aptly, the Henry VIII Room and the Elizabethan Staircase. An entry describing the firm in the *American Art News* of February 1913, states,

> Although it may justly be claimed that there is little on view that may not be termed a 'museum piece,' one special room is set aside as a museum for a number of unique and historical examples of very early work, destined to remain permanently in the possession of the firm, and not intended for sale. Among the exhibits are a number of fine chairs of the reign of Henry VIII and the bellows belonging to Queen Elizabeth ... A fine panelled room of the early Tudor period is at present on view at Clifford St.

Records discovered at the Museum of London, following our enquiry about the lion's head panel, identified that while two panels had been loaned to the museum by Mr Phillips, one had subsequently been returned. We have assumed that this was most likely the Bonhams panel that was sold by a 'gentleman of Spitalfields' in May 2015, some 100 years later. Why the two panels were split up is unknown. Our theory is that Mr Phillips acquired a set of salvaged panels from an unknown source – possibly left-over panels from Lord Ongley's project, or possibly through another source. We certainly know that Owen Grant made 'a specialty of the restoration of old mansions and many a fine historical house', and so the panels would have been of particular interest to them. A letter in the archives of the Museum of London indicates that initially the panels seemed destined to be used as decorative panelling for a door being commissioned by Lord Esher. However, this never transpired. For some reason, one of the panels was recalled at some point from the Museum of London, while the other, the lion's head, remained in its safekeeping – as it still is to this day.

A Rediscovered, 'Nationally Important Historical Collection'

It was an unbelievable case of synchronicity that led to our re-evaluation of the provenance of the Anne of Cleves panels. The forces that moved behind the scenes to cause a panel that had been separated from the original set at least 150 years earlier to come up for sale within weeks of our investigation into the Old Warden artefacts defies imagination. Yet, it did – and it changed everything. According to Jonathan Foyle, these panels now comprise a 'nationally important historic collection' and that the set 'illuminates [one of] the finest interiors in the Counter Reformation age of Queen Mary, of whose personal environment nothing remains'. Anne of Cleves once gazed upon their beauty, as they adorned one of the grandest chambers in her lodgings. We are blessed that they have survived and that now they can be appreciated once more, taking their place alongside other Tudor relics associated with Henry VIII's fascinating wives.

Visitor Information

If you wish to view the Anne of Cleves Panels in situ in St Leonard's church, Old Warden, you must first make an appointment to do so via the current vicar or church warden. Please find up-to-date details via the church's website, http://www.ivelsouthbenefice.co.uk/OldWardenIndex.htm. The Lion's Head panel in the Museum of London is currently on display in the War, Plague and Fire Gallery (ref.: 1092). In 2017, the Bonhams panel was placed on permanent exhibition at Hever Castle in Kent.

Schloss Düsseldorf, Düsseldorf

> [The town of Düsseldorf] is famous for two things; the one is a magnificent palace belonging to the Duke: the other the residence of the Duke's Court here.
> Thomas Coryat, English court jester, traveller and chronicler

A Childhood on the Banks of the Rhine

On 22 September 1515, the Duchess Maria of Jülich-Berg gave birth to her second daughter, Anna (hereafter referred to by her anglicised name, Anne), in the city palace of Düsseldorf. To understand the location of this auspicious event, we must first understand a little about the Duchy of Jülich-Kleves-Berg in the early sixteenth century. The principality would eventually occupy a region covering roughly 5,500 square miles in the north-west territory of modern-day Germany. Over time, four separate, but adjacent, dominions – those of Jülich, Kleve, Berg and Mark – had been united through a series of dynastic marriages. Anne's father, Johannes (John) III, did not inherit his patrimony until 1521, but by the time his second daughter was born he had been serving as the Duke of Jülich-Berg since 1511, following his father-in-law's death.

Situated on the east bank of the mighty River Rhine, at the time Düsseldorf was the capital of the principality. A mid-seventeenth-century etching records the now lost medieval city in glorious detail. Looking across at the town from the west bank of the river, we see, as we might expect, a substantial city wall encircling the citadel. The skyline is pricked by spires of imposing Gothic churches. Dominating the foreground are numerous turreted buildings, surmounted by cupola- and onion-shaped domes, weathervanes and flags apparently being tugged by a south-westerly breeze. In the centre of the picture, several boats are moored alongside the main quay; to the left of this, a large, four-storey building, set at an angle to the quay, supports its own central spire atop a pitched leaden roof. This was the palace in which Anne, England's future queen, was born.

The Appearance and Layout of the City Palace

The early seventeenth-century English traveller Thomas Coryat, who chronicled his journey through Europe in 1607 in *Coryat's Crudities*, stated that the palace 'was the most sumptuous building of any dwelling house that I saw in the Netherlands' (from where he had just arrived). Fortunately for the eager time traveller, a number of engravings survive of the building, alongside a late eighteenth-century floor plan of the ducal residence. What these reveal is that the main palace complex was essentially arranged in a U shape around a central courtyard. At each end of the parallel (north and south) ranges that formed the sides of the U were two four-(originally three-) storey round towers, surmounted by cupola. These are significant, as today the north tower is the sole survivor of the entire palace complex. Flanking the palace on either side were two further, irregular-shaped courtyards enclosed by walls, and a gallery looking onto the quay, as well as further lodgings.

A more detailed engraving of the main palace courtyard from 1585, showing gentlemen of the court practicing their fencing, records the key architectural features that would have become so familiar to Anne: the grey, tiled roof; the crenulated string course with scalloped mouldings on the underside; the irregularly shaped windows situated without symmetry into the north and south ranges; and finally, the tower dominating the western range. This separated the gallery and loggia, both of which fronted onto the spacious inner courtyard.

On 23 December 1510, five years before Anne was born, the City Palace of Düsseldorf was badly damaged by a fire that tore through the north-eastern part of the building. However, according to Fimpeler-Philippen and Schürmann, the authors of *Das Schloss in Düsseldorf*, despite the destruction there seems to have remained satisfactory living quarters, for the ducal family remained in residence.

Rebuilding of the palace would continue until 1521 – that is until the union of the territories of Kleve-Mark and Jülich-Berg. However, 1521 did not see the end of the palace's development. Builders were employed again from 1528 to 1530, in 1534, in 1538 and again in 1540. Thus, during her time in Düsseldorf, the young Anne must have grown accustomed to the sound of sawing and hammering that accompanied these ongoing works.

In terms of the internal layout of the palace, Fimpeler-Philippen and Schürmann go on to state that the most likely arrangement of the privy apartments was that the duke occupied the northern part of the first-floor range, fronting onto river. This would, of course, have given admirable views up and down the Rhine. The duchess would be lodged either directly above the duke's chambers on the second floor, or more likely occupied the southern part of the first-floor range. Both sides would be linked through a shared room or hall, and in each instance, the main privy living area would be positioned overlooking the river, while the bedchamber faced on to the courtyard.

Life in the Palace

It is unclear exactly how much time Anne spent at the ducal palace in Düsseldorf. We know that the family moved around the various palaces and castles owned by Anne's father and that a fair amount of her early years was spent at Schloss Burg an der Wupper, near Solingen (see entry on Schloss Burg an der Wupper, Solingen). However, as we also know that Anne was brought up 'never [far] from her mother's elbow', we can be fairly sure that she visited the city palace regularly as the itinerant ducal court normally lodged at Düsseldorf over the winter months. Indeed, Anne and her sisters, Sybille and Amelia, would have spent much of their time in the duchess's apartments, surrounded and educated by women. As we shall hear a little more of later, the Duchess Maria was an ever-present influence in the girls' lives.

However, unlike the gay licentiousness of the French court, life at the ducal court of Cleves appears to have been considerably more reserved and orderly. We see glimpses of this in various official documents that describe the rules governing court life. Thus, for example, a proclamation issued in 1521 sets out to strictly control who could eat where at court, with the young princes and princess confined to eating meals in their privy chambers. Later, in 1534, when Anne was nineteen, a second diktat set forth requirements for 'daily quiet and orderliness', with no 'spontaneous parties'; at nine o'clock in the evening, the last glasses of wine were poured before being locked away for the night by the *hofmeister* (master of the palace). After this time, 'playing, drinking or sitting together' by members of the court was strictly prohibited!

A Marriage Treaty Arranged

No doubt Anne was present at the city palace to witness the departure of her beautiful elder sister, Sybille, when she left behind her family to wed the Electoral Prince Johann Friedrich of Saxony in 1527. A little over a decade later, it was Anne's turn to be in the spotlight. Of course, by this time her father had died, with her brother Wilhelm inheriting the title of 'duke' in February 1539. Thus it was Wilhelm who oversaw the negotiations of his sister's hand in marriage to the King of England. Recorded in the *Letters and Papers of Henry VIII*, on 4 September 1539, the duke dispatched a delegation of ambassadors bound for London in order that they might finalise the marriage contract between Henry and Anne. The letter simply states, 'Desires credence for William ab Harff, prefect of his court, and Dr. Henry Olysleger, whom he sends with John a Doltzk, knight, and Francis Burchart, vice-chancellor, the ambassadors of John Frederick, duke of Saxony. Düsseldorf.'

As we can see, the commission is signed from Düsseldorf. One cannot help but imagine Anne, aware of what was transpiring, watching the gentlemen of her brother's court ride out from the palace gates and wondering if soon she would be following in their wake. Certainly, she would not have to wait long. After being lavishly entertained by an ebullient king at Windsor and Hampton Court, the ambassadors from Cleve had returned to their homeland by the beginning of October. Shortly thereafter, the marriage treaty was signed by both parties, and on 26 November 1539, Anne finally left the City Palace of Düsseldorf for the final time. Surely she must have sensed that a far greater destiny awaited her, but that the price of it would be that she would never see the place of her birth again.

The City Palace of Düsseldorf Today

Sadly, virtually nothing remains today of medieval Düsseldorf. At the turn of the twentieth century, areas of the Rhine Valley, including Düsseldorf itself, became an industrial powerhouse for Germany. Thus, during the Second World War the area was targeted and heavily bombed by Allied forces. What medieval treasures had not been swept away by Germany's industrial revolution were therefore destroyed by conflict. However, not all the destruction was man-made. In fact, the old City Palace had been lost some seventy years earlier as a result of another catastrophic fire that virtually burnt it to the ground in 1872. Numerous photographs taken during and after this period (see *Burg und Schloss Düsseldorf* by Kuffner and Spohr, for example) show both the palace as a heap of charred ruins, as well as illustrating the subsequent development of what would become known as Burgplatz (Castle Place); this marked the site of the old palace after it was torn down. Today, only one of the two towers that once abutted to the end of the palace's northern and southern wings remains standing as the Schlossturm (Palace Tower). Thus, at least there is an identifiable marker to help the time traveller orientate themselves in space.

When you visit Burgplatz in the Altstadt (Old Town), you must imagine the northern wing of the palace running toward the river from the Schlossturm, joining to the now lost west-facing wing that once looked out over the Rhine, and then turning again toward the end of the current Burgplatz to form the southern wing. As mentioned earlier, this second tower has been lost to time. Thus, the centre of Burgplatz forms the bulk of what was once the inner courtyard of the palace.

Visitor Information

Perhaps rather unfairly for the City of Düsseldorf, the authors visited on a very dreary, wet morning in mid-August. Much of the Aldstadt was still sleeping.

Generally this area of the city is known colloquially as the 'longest bar in Germany' on account of the string of bars that line its streets. While you will find these streets humming with activity later in the day, it seems that through the morning Aldstadt is still sleeping off its collective hangover. Ill-prepared for such gloomy weather at the height of summer, it was a fairly thankless task to make our way through virtually deserted streets with soggy feet and a decrepit umbrella that barely sheltered us from the rain. However, armed with a map of the city that can be picked up at any hotel, it is straightforward to find the promenade that runs alongside the River Rhine. This eventually spewed us out onto Burgplatz. To add to the gloom of the morning, we were thwarted from visiting the interior of the Schlossturm (which normally houses a maritime museum) as it was locked up and deserted. We later found out that the museum was closed for redevelopment. No timeline could be given by the city marketing office of Düsseldorf for its reopening.

Amid the casual tourists, we spent a while looking out over the expanse of the Rhine, large cargo vessels chugging their way north and south, much as ships must have done for countless centuries. Eventually chilled, and beaten back by the rain, we retreated to a wonderful café that we found just around the corner from the main plaza called Gut and Gerne. Here we took refuge in a steaming mug of hot chocolate and allowed ourselves to reflect on the sad decline of this once great palace.

For more information about Düsseldorf and places to stay, please contact the tourist information office. Website: http://www.duesseldorf-tourismus.de/en/tourist-information-offices/. Tel No: +49 (0) 211 17 202844.

Gut and Gerne is situated on Burgplatz 3–5, 40213, Düsseldorf. Tel No: +49 (0) 211 86 39 96 96. The café specialises in chocolate drinks and the hot chocolate was to die for!

Schloss Burg an der Wupper, Solingen

> Wo kom een Lank do butten
> Em groaten dutschen Riek
> Wall usser aulen Heemoth,
> Dam 'Lank der Berge' gliek?
> Where is a land out there
> That is equal to our old home,
> The big German Kingdom,
> The land of the mountains?

Friedrich Storck, 'Die Berg'sche Heemooth'

About 20 miles south-east of the city of Düsseldorf, in the heart of the heavily forested Wupper Valley, lies Castle Burg, a medieval, fortified hunting lodge. The castle was once the principal home of the counts of Berg before Düsseldorf took up pre-eminence as the capital of the newly unified duchy. Here it is said that the young Anne spent significant periods of time during her childhood in the company of her mother and siblings.

Castle Burg began its life in the first half of the twelfth century, the buildings being constructed with defence in mind. Perched high up on top of a forested plateau, the sheer drop to the west provided an almost impenetrable western facade of wooded, but craggy, rock. The east, on the other hand, was more vulnerable to assault, and thus was protected by a moat, at least 15 metres deep (now filled in and serving as the road that sweeps by the entrance to the castle), a drawbridge, a series of gatehouses leading from the outer to the inner ward and commodious walls. If these fortifications were breached, a huge square defensive tower sited at the centre of the castle's inner ward provided the last bastion of defence. Here the early medieval counts and their families could retreat if the castle was ever laid to siege. Thankfully, this never happened. As greater security settled over the land with the dawning of the Renaissance, the castle's architecture was adapted to be more like a comfortable manor than a fortress, with aggrandisement of spacious private apartments for the duke, duchess and their guests taking place at the end of the fifteenth century and the beginning of the sixteenth century.

We know that while Duke Johann, Anne's father, was away attending to the business of the duchy, the duchess and her children were installed at the castle. (At some point Anne's brother, Wilhelm, was removed from the company of his sisters to begin his instruction as the future Duke of Jülich-Kleves-Berg.) It is not hard to imagine why. The castle afforded greater protection than the undefended palace in Düsseldorf, while its isolated position in the countryside must have been deemed a healthier environment in which to bring up children. And isolated the castle must have been. The guide who showed us round Anne's erstwhile home said that once all visitors have left, all that can be heard is the wind blowing across the hilly peaks of the valley. It is not hard to strip away these sounds of modernity and imagine instead the noises of medieval life, providing the muted harmony to a life of quiet, yet privileged, domesticity.

Within the inner ward, the main staircase still leads up to the first floor of the 'palace', a part of the castle that incorporates both the key ceremonial rooms, as well as the private chambers used by the family and honoured guests. At the end of the fifteenth century, this part of the castle was widened southwards by 4 metres in order to build a new kitchen on the ground floor. At the same time, the raising of the palace walls in the fashionable style of the day gave the castle its romantic appearance, since captured by generations of painters who have fallen for its fairy-tale charms. New guest accommodation was also added on the upper floors. On account of the building's commanding position, the family and guests must have enjoyed stunning views of the surrounding hills and countryside; views which can still be enjoyed to this day.

A Germanic Renaissance Education

It is likely that much of Anne's time at the castle was spent following a predictable routine, incorporating her education into those pastimes deemed suitable for a noble woman of the day. According to Retha Warnicke in her book *The Marrying of Anne of Cleves*, Anne's father was 'known for his splendid clothing, and his estates were pivotal in the adoption of new ideas and social patterns, since the Lower Rhine was the principal route by which the French culture penetrated into Germany'.

In fact, the cultural milieu that existed around Anne as she grew into adulthood seems to perfectly reflect the schism between old and new, so thematic of the time. While the court might be looking to such 'new ideas', the Duchess Maria was a conservative Catholic, educating her daughters according to a curriculum that traditionally included reading, writing, some geography and rudimentary Latin. From Nicolas Wooton, an English ambassador sent to Germany to report on Anne's attributes in 1539, we hear something of Anne's education and accomplishments: '[The duchess had raised her] in a manner never far from her elbow, the Lady Duchess being a wise lady and one that very straightly looks to her children'. But that other than her accomplishment at needlework, 'which occupieth most of her time', Anne could not speak any language other than German, or 'sing or play any instrument, for they take it here in Germany as a rebuke and an occasion of lightness that great ladies should be learned or have any knowledge of music'.

In England and France, reformist thinking had begun the advancement of female education, with instruction in pastimes such as hunting, hawking, dancing, singing and even musical composition being viewed as essential to one's marriage prospects and family advancement at court. Although the ducal court was profoundly Erasmian and liberal, it is clear that such social accomplishments were not valued as part of female education. Thus, socially Anne was hopelessly unprepared for her position as queen of her adopted country, and it is not hard to imagine her being a figure of ridicule to some less generous members of Henry's aristocracy.

In terms of religion, Anne herself would always acquiesce to Henry VIII's views on the Church, but ultimately she was born into and died in the Catholic faith. She maintained her distance from reformist thinking, quite in contrast with her elder sister, Sybille. As the Electress of Saxony, Sybille ruled over a land which was at the epicentre of the Reformation. She would eventually leave the Catholic fold entirely and, influenced by her new husband, become a zealous convert to the reformist cause and a close personal friend of Martin Luther and Erasmus. An interesting family tension perhaps? Maybe, but a far more real and less discussed aspect of Anne's upbringing was her exposure to the intimate and loving relationship between her parents. This is relevant as it likely provides us with clues about Anne's attitude toward marriage.

Anne's parents, the future Duke and Duchess of Jülich-Kleves-Berg, were betrothed in Castle Burg in 1510. The ceremony took place in the Rittersaal (Knights' Hall), or possibly on the ground-floor chamber beneath it. The event is captured in a nineteenth-century mural adorning the wall of the former chamber. It was a dynastic match that brought Anne's parents together, and yet poems apparently exchanged between the duke and duchess makes it clear that love sustained them. Interestingly, a similar story is true of Sybille and her husband, Johann Friedrich. Once more, correspondence that pours forth sentiments of love, exchanged during her husband's imprisonment during the Schmalkaldic War, reveals a devoted couple. In the end, they would die natural deaths within one month of each other.

It is not hard to imagine Anne and her sisters brought up surrounded by warmth, exposed to the close and affectionate relationship shared by her parents, which was perhaps more uncommon in the sixteenth century, in a time when love within marriage was not deemed to be essential. When we understand this about Anne's upbringing, we can easily envisage the high hopes Henry's future queen consort must have had for her impending nuptials; dreams of a kind, considerate and affectionate husband with whom she might share the rest of her life. Sadly, Henry had long since lost these noble attributes. In the end, Anne would be bitterly disappointed in the life that awaited her in England. In time, she would come to yearn for home.

Touring Anne's Childhood Home

Driving out from Düsseldorf along the scarily high-speed autobahn toward Solingen, the flat industrial plains soon give way to a more interesting terrain. Winding, wooded roads eventually led us out of suburbia and into the mountains, as we penetrated deep into the Wupper Valley. Approaching from the west, a final turn in the road revealed the steep escarpment upon which the castle is perched.

We chose to park at the foot of the escarpment in one of the free car parks, catching the chairlift that takes you right up into the heart of the castle's old outer ward. (Note: The car parks get very busy in the height of summer, so perhaps best to plan to arrive early. Also, if you do not fancy the chairlift, there is a second car park at the top of the hill, adjacent to the castle's gatehouse entrance.)

Despite the fact that the castle was almost completely rebuilt around the turn of the twentieth century, the architect G. A. Fischer writes in his book *Schloss Burg an der Wupper: Die Burgen des Mittelalters* that 'because of images, archaeological digs and contemporary documents, the castle can be quite accurately recreated as it was in the middle of the sixteenth century'. Thus, the time traveller can relax and know that we are indeed following in the footsteps of Anne of Cleves, passing through the building that she once called home. While there is much to see in the castle, we will focus on those areas most directly related to Anne: the palace, with its grand Rittersaal (used for great occasions such as the marriage of Anne's parents in 1510, and the betrothal of her elder sister, Sybille, in September 1526), as well as the family's private living quarters.

We were lucky enough to have a guide for our visit. His knowledge and clear passion for the castle's history truly brought the castle, Anne and her family to life. You can choose to book a guide for your visit too, but if you don't then you must make for the main flight of stairs heading up from the principal part of the inner ward to the first floor. You first enter an antechamber, the walls painted in the nineteenth century to tell the story of the counts of Cleve and their later descendants. The Rittersaal is the grand room leading off this chamber. This great chamber, used for state celebrations, is dominated by a row of central pillars supporting a vaulted ceiling. Once, at least two great fireplaces warmed the space against the icy northern European winters. As you wander around, you will enjoy the murals and brightly decorated walls, but bear in mind that in Anne's day the walls would have been whitewashed, decorated only with tapestries, with solid, unfussy wooden furniture lending a hand only to practicality.

Moving back through the antechamber from the Rittersaal, you will enter perhaps the most moving room in the castle. It was here, in the Kemenate, that Anne would have lived her everyday life, alongside her mother and sisters. During the daytime, this room served as the main communal living space. Perhaps you might pause a while as we did, seating yourself in the window and imagining a young Anne, attending to her needlework or gazing out over the treetops, dreaming of where life might take her.

The chapel of the castle has been much restored, and the interiors are not contemporary to Anne's time. However, it is thought that the original chapel was likely to have been sited roughly in the space where it is found in today. Finally, climbing the staircase leads you into the attic. You will find an exhibition of life at the castle filling glass-fronted cabinets, but once upon a time it was here, probably alongside her parents, that Anne would have laid her head at night.

Castle Burg is a satisfying location to visit, stimulating the senses and enriching our picture of the life of the German nobility in the sixteenth century. Although we were unlucky enough to visit on a cold day, as we dropped back down to our starting point on the chairlift, assaulted again by driving rain, we could not help but feel that finally we had gotten just a little closer to one of Henry's most enigmatic queens.

For more information, visit the castle's website on http://www.schlossburg. de, or email them on info@schlossburg.de. Although the website is in German, courteous staff will be quick to respond to emails. If you wish to have your own personal guide for your visit, we can highly recommend Cevin Conrad, an American who has been living with his German wife and family near the castle for the last twenty-six years. Please contact the castle and ask for Cevin directly.

The castle is well provided for by food kiosks within the castle precinct, and by a number of excellent restaurants adjacent to the castle, just outside the main gatehouse.

Schloss Düren, Niederzier

Your Grace's servant Hanze Albein[Hans Holbein] hathe taken th'effigies of my ladye Anne and the ladye Amelye [Amelia] and hath expressyd theyr imaiges verye lyvelye [lively]. Düren, 11 Aug. 1539.

Nicolas Wooton, English diplomat

The Portrait of a Bride

During the summer of 1539, a frenzy of communication streamed back and forth between London and the ducal principality of Cleve. Henry VIII of England had been scouring the courts of Europe for a suitable bride, and his eye had fallen upon the two remaining unmarried sisters of the new Duke of Cleves, Wilhelm

V. Ambassadors were dispatched from the English court to conduct the delicate negotiations that were intended to culminate in a marriage treaty; one of these ambassadors was Nicolas Wooton. It is from one of Wooton's letters, penned to King Henry VIII on 11 August 1539, that we derive our strongest proof of Anne's presence at the Palace of Düren:

> Hit [It] maye please your Highness to be [advertised that on the ... [day] of July I received your Grace's most ... [letters of] the 12th of the same month, and shortly afterwards addressed myself to the Duke [of Cleves, of whom], 31 July, I had audience at Düren, in the high parts of the duchy of Juliers.

The letter captures one of the most well-known moments of Henry's courtship with the Princess of Cleves. Unable to see his future bride for himself, Henry requested that the two potential candidates, Anne and her younger sister, Amelia, should be painted so that he might see their likeness. According to German accounts, the task should have fallen to Lucas Cranach the Elder, the famed German court painter of the Renaissance age. However, Cranach was ill. Instead, the sisters were painted by Henry's own court painter, Hans Holbein. In the same letter Wooton goes on to describe the resultant images as 'verye lyvelye [lively]', i.e. lifelike.

One sketch survives by Holbein, thought to be derived from this sitting. Although whether this is Anne's image, or indeed that of her younger sister, is debated. Much like the final and undisputed oil-on-canvas painting of Anne, the sitter in the sketch stares out impassively at the viewer. However, in contrast, the face is more oval, the cheekbones more prominent, the eyes fuller and the chin more pointed than that of the face of the sitter in the oil painting. In character too, when one looks carefully, there is a sense of a different woman portrayed; the gaze is just a bit more penetrating, the corners of the mouth showing no hint of the enigmatic smile playing lightly across the lips of the woman that we know to be Anne. However, perhaps more telling is that the sitter in the Holbein sketch very clearly has dark-brown hair. If we look very closely at Anne of Cleves in the oil painting, if anything, there is a sense of a lighter, sandy-brown colour to the hairline. The evidence for this is strengthened by the only description that we have of Anne's hair colour. It comes from the near-contemporary chronicler Edward Hall, who reported that on her wedding day Anne wore 'her here hangyng downe, which was fayre, yelowe and longe'. There is indeed a good chance that time has left us with an oil painting of Anne and a preliminary sketch of the twenty-one-year-old Amelia.

Düren: A Medieval Hunting Lodge

It is difficult to even conceive of the emotions these two sisters must have felt as Holbein's flair for realism captured their likeness: trepidation, pride, excitement, sadness? Of course their presence at Düren for this event can be inferred only through association, i.e. that the sisters were also present in the castle at the same time that the letter was written, alongside their brother, the English ambassadors and the rest of the ducal court. This would not be unusual, since Anne and Amelia were mature women who, by 1539, might appropriately take up their position there. However, in our discussions with the current owners of Schloss Hambach (as the Palace of Düren is now known), it has been suggested that Anne and Amelia may have been lodged elsewhere when the pictures where painted, notably at the Schloss Burg an der Wupper. It is impossible to say definitively with the evidence currently available.

However, we can say that August would have been a typical time for the Duke of Cleves, his close family and the court to be resident at this location. At some point during mid-summer, the court habitually transferred from Schwanenburg in Kleve (see entry for Schwanenburg, Kleve), travelling some 90 miles south into the territory of Jülich. Here, the Palace of Düren was located about 30 miles south west of the great medieval city of Cologne. Thus, if Anne was not present there in 1539, we can confidently expect that she would have visited there at some point during her younger years.

It seems that Düren was particularly favoured for the rich hunting to be found in the forest surrounding the castle. This must have been plentiful in the height of summer. Although we have not found any specific source relating to such activity at Düren, a 1540 painting by Lucas Cranach called *Die Hirschjagd* (*The Stag Hunt*), shows hunting in the forest surrounding the castle at Torgau in nearby Saxony (home to Anne's elder sister, Sybille, when she was Electress of the region). Predominantly, we see gentlemen both on foot and on horseback, dressed in skirted coats. There is carnage, as copious numbers of deer and bears are slain using hunting dogs to bring down the prey, else spears and crossbows are wielded as weapons of choice. Our research in Germany revealed that hunting was not generally considered a particularly popular pastime for ladies. However, two female figures can be seen enjoying the hunt from a boat on the river, and in one case, a woman takes aim with a crossbow at a stag. We have no accounts of Anne hunting, but if she did, this place and this painting must surely conjure up a portrait of a scene with which she would have been familiar.

The History of the Palace of Düren

There had been a modestly sized castle on the site since the early Middle Ages. The original structure burnt down in 1278, only to be replaced by a more substantial fortress, commissioned by Count Walram of Jülich in 1317. Yet, like the other royal residences at Düsseldorf and Kleve, it seems that this castle too was to be beset by repeated tragedy. Indeed, it is a miracle that anything at all has survived to this day! In 1512, just three years before Anne was born, careless handling of gunpowder caused an explosion which destroyed the gunpowder 'mill' and some adjacent buildings. Eighteen people lost their lives. However, the main living quarters seem to have remained intact. *Die Geschichte Der Feste Hambach*, written by Claessen in 1960, states that the palace accounts, dated 1513, indicate that subsequent repairs to the castle buildings were undertaken at a reasonable cost. The same report also states that in 1526 a much larger building programme was undertaken. This seems to have been largely on account of the growing prominence of the ducal family and its expanded household.

Up until that point, three separate towers were noted to be in existence: the Duke's Tower, the 'large' tower and the Chancellery Tower, sited probably at three corners of a large courtyard, which was in turn surrounded by a moat. After 1525, a fourth tower was constructed. This was intended solely to house the living quarters of the duchess, her children and other female members of the court. There is a wonderful account of a large bay window being inserted in the tower. It was so ornate that it took around one and a half years to complete, becoming renowned as a work of art in its own right. It is a fanciful figment of the imagination, but rather lovely nonetheless, to imagine Anne and her sister being painted by Master Holbein, illuminated by the light that flooded through its inset glass.

However, Düren was not yet the grand Renaissance palace that it would later become, as we shall hear shortly. The palace would be burnt to the ground for the third time in 1543, before rising to its zenith in the latter part of the sixteenth century.

A Palace Destroyed

In 1543, the Holy Roman Emperor and his army marauded into the Rhine Valley, invading the territories of the Duke of Cleves. It seems to have been a terrifying episode for the ordinary folk of the land. Nicolas Wooton, who was clearly once more in the duchy on behalf of Henry VIII (who was in temporary alliance with Charles V), reported on 1 September 1543 that

> after the taking of Düren, the men of Gulik all fled, except a prisoner of this country and a fool, and the women sent the keys to the Emperor, who willed them to send for their husbands and promised to preserve their privileges. It was well fortified and furnished, and is now garrisoned by the Emperor; as also is Düren, which, however, is mostly burnt ... the town of Cleves and all the country on this side the Rhine will be at the Emperor's commandment. This taking of Düren has made them all afraid.

Thus, the castle at Düren was once more destroyed. According to *Die Geschichte Der Feste Hambach*, Anne's mother, the Duchess Maria, had been resident there at the time. She had had to flee for her life and died shortly thereafter. Surely, it was with a heavy heart that Anne of Cleves, four years on and now living over 500 miles from home, learnt of the humbling of her native homeland and of her mother's death on 29 August 1543. From Louvain on 6 September, Nicolas Wooton describes how 'the old lady Duchess of Cleves is departed this world raging and in a manner out of her wits [as it is reported] for spite and anger of the loss of her country'.

As we have intimated, this was not the end for the castle. Once more, it would rise like a phoenix from the proverbial ashes. In 1558, one year after Anne's own death, her brother began the restoration of the place with the construction of a fabulous Renaissance palace with courtyard, consisting of four red-brick ranges with circular, turreted towers in each corner. Through much of the seventeenth and eighteenth century, Düren went onto serve as a pleasure palace, but again, its glory days were numbered. By the end of the eighteenth century, the castle was falling into ruin and the building and its contents were sold off by its French owners between 1801 and 1804. What was left was subsequently used as farm buildings. Unsurprisingly, the old palace fell further into decay as a consequence. Over 100 years later, Düren was once more caught up in heavy fighting, this time between German and American troops during the Second World War. Finally, Wilhelm's Renaissance masterpiece fell into utter ruin.

However, thanks to the efforts of its current owners, two of the four wings and three of the four towers still survive in various states of repair. Restoration is ongoing with parts of the building now fully renovated and being occupied as private residences.

So it seems that, despite everything, this place, which once saw a young woman's fate sealed as a future Queen of England, is determined to survive no matter what Father Time throws its way. Truly it can be said that the Palace of Düren is a survivor.

Visitor Information

There is no doubt that the ruin of the Palace of Düren is a peculiar location to visit. Having turned off the main road, the visitor finds themselves progressively engulfed in pleasant German suburbia. There is no lofty plateau upon which the palace is perched, nor is there any long, sweeping driveway announcing a grand dame of history that is hidden away behind an avenue of ancient trees. No, instead, one final turn into Schlosstrasse (Palace Street), in the midst of a well-manicured housing estate, brings you suddenly upon the ruins of this most noble of buildings.

The south-eastern and south-western ranges and two of the large, circular towers of the Palace of Düren are easily visible from the roadside. Fronting onto the road, directly in front of where the main palace gatehouse would have once stood, is the modern entrance to the complex. Two stately red-bricked pillars faced by broken remnants of carved stone display an understated sign that indicates you have arrived at 'Schloss Hambach'.

While most of the south-western range lies torn apart and open to the elements, progress on restoration of what remains of south-eastern range is complete, as is the work to restore the western and eastern towers. Of course, having sustained such considerable damage and endured centuries of neglect, the building must be a shadow of its former self. Almost barrack-like in its appearance, the fragmented, scalloped decoration on the towers is the only ornamentation that tells of a more illustrious past.

Perhaps, though, the most impact comes from the obvious scale of the place, hinted at by that which remains. As you stand before the entrance, or wander through the courtyard, it is not hard to touch once more a time when one woman's future hung in the balance, a time when the ducal principality of Jülich-Cleve-Berg held the balance of power in an epoch in which a handful of alpha males utterly dominated the Christian world.

The current owners of Schloss Hambach have kindly indicated that if you are visiting the site, you may enter the courtyard to view the interior of what remains of the castle. You may also gain access to certain areas inside the building (the south and west towers) but to do this you must first book an appointment with the owners by calling: +49 (0) 2428/2566 (German-speaking only). Please note that Schloss Hambach is a private residence. Do be respectful of this at all times and note that there are no amenities on-site.

Address: Schlossstrasse 117, 52382, Niederzier-Hambach.

Schwanenburg, Kleve

> Oh land so richly blessed,
> Oh land so beautiful and strong,
> How you smile towards us,
> From the stream of the Rhine to the Mark.
>
> Friedrich Storck, 'Die Berg'sche Heemooth'

Schwanenburg in Kleve was the principal seat of the dukes of Cleve from the eleventh century, the name 'Kleve' being derived from the lower Germanic word *cliff*, meaning 'steep slope', indicative of the high plateau upon which the fortress was founded. By the early sixteenth century, with the union of the territories of Jülich, Kleve, Mark and Berg, the ducal dynasty reached its zenith. Schwanenburg took its place alongside the City Palace of Düsseldorf and the Palace of Düren (see entries on the City Palace of Düsseldorf and Schloss Düren, respectively) as principal residences of Anne's father and his family. As such, we can be sure that Anne knew Schwanenburg well. It is likely that the one-year-old was present in the nursery when her younger brother, the future Duke of Cleves, was born at Schwanenburg on 28 July 1516. However, the only definitive placement we have of the future Queen of England at the castle is in relation to her departure to England, as we shall hear shortly.

The medieval fortress that Anne would have known was usually visited in the springtime, as part of the annual itinerary of the ducal court. It was built in a sickle shape, atop a lofty promontory overlooking the River Rhine. Access to the outer ward, or courtyard, was from the south. A causeway spanned a defensive ditch that led through a medieval gateway, both of which have long been lost. Adjacent to the main entrance and adjoining the great hall at its southern end was the Johannisturm. This contained a bell that chimed every quarter of an hour. It must have been a familiar sound to Anne, conducting the rhythms of everyday court life when the duke and his family were in residence. In an increasingly dilapidated state, the tower was sadly demolished in 1785, along with the adjacent hall.

Once inside the courtyard, a curved wall ran along the promontory to the west.

This seems to have merely served a defensive function and incorporated another of the four towers of the castle, the Spiegel Tower, built in the early fifteenth century to contain the ducal archives. Opposite this was the straight eastern range, beginning with the grand ceremonial rooms in the south, of which we have already mentioned the great hall. In a similar design to the arrangement of rooms encountered in Henry's great houses, a successive series of chambers of decreasing size and increasing intimacy stretched northwards, ending in the ducal family's privy apartments.

In addition, a substantial wall separated the southern from the northern parts of the castle, as it still does to this day. Other than through the eastern range, access to a smaller, inner courtyard was thus through an internal gateway sited in the middle of this intermediate range. Once inside, the courtyard would have been dominated by the great Schwanenturm, or Swan Tower, which contained the final rooms in the ducal lodgings. At around 180 feet tall, the Schwanenturm is perhaps the most iconic feature of the castle. Its square walls, domed cupola and aerial weather vane, shaped symbolically as a swan, are very clear from Braun and Hogenburg's 1572 etching of Kleve. From this drawing we can also cast our imagination beyond the castle walls to recreate the town which must have served it, and which Anne inevitably passed through on her historic journey to England. Here we see a typical medieval walled citadel, the castle dominating a sea of red roofs; only the cathedral (which still stands today, albeit a later replacement) and a windmill built into the town's defensive wall compete in scale and grandeur for the observer's attention.

A Marriage Train Assembles

On 7 November, Anne's brother, the Duke of Cleves, issued a decree ordering all men who were appointed to accompany Henry's bride to England to assemble at Schwanenburg on the twenty-fifth day of the same month. A day later, on 26 November, Anne herself left the City Palace of Düsseldorf with her attendants – and, one imagines, her mother and younger sister – alongside her. Records of the travel itinerary, now housed in the National Archives, state that Anne's first stop was 'Burg', about 20 English miles from Düsseldorf. The authors believe that this most likely refers to modern day Duisburg, which is en route to Kleve. However, we have been unable to confirm this.

The following day, Anne continued her journey to Kleve. There she was to rendezvous with the rest of the royal party. There must have been excitement at the prospect of the great adventure ahead, as well as deep sadness at the anticipated farewell to her family.

Other than the fact that Duke Wilhelm had ordered all the men to be appropriately attired in clothing and armour, no German records survive of Anne's departure. However, understanding the layout of the castle and the type of ceremonies associated with such significant events, it is not hard to imagine a grand gathering in the great hall, each and every person powdered according to their degree; Anne herself standing before her younger brother as he spoke to the gathered audience of the great alliance to be made between England and his territories, of wealth, honour and solidarity, and a young woman, whom the chronicler Edward Hall later described as being so 'fayre a lady, of so goodly a stature and so womanly a countenance', receiving his blessing. As the royal party made its way out into the chilly courtyard, no doubt festooned with colourful banners, did Anne maintain her composure as her mother embraced her for what they both must have feared might be the final time?

Sadly, although we have no details of Anne's departure, or of her appearance that day, Hall provides an evocative account of her arrival in England and of her official reception on Blackheath, near the royal palace of Greenwich. His meticulous account leaves us with a glimpse into Anne's trousseau at the time and how she might have appeared at her final appearance in Kleve:

> When her Grace was aduertysed [advertised] of the Kynges cdmyng [coming], she issued out of her tent beyug [being] apparelled in a ryche goune [gown] of cloth of golde reised, made rounde without any trayne [train] after the Dutche fassyon [fashion], and on her head a kail, & oner that a rounde bonet or cappe set full of Orient Perle [pearl] of a very propre fassyon, & before that she had a cornet of blacke veluet [velvet], & about her necke she had a partelet set full of riche stone which glystered all the felde.

What is more, from the same account, we also know that Anne travelled the whole of her journey from Germany to England not on horseback but in a chariot, which Hall describes as being decorated with 'well carued gylte [carved gilt] with armes of her coutrey [country] curiously wrought & couered [covered] with cloth of gold'. Although this chariot no longer exists, it is very similar in description to the one which carried Anne's elder sister, Sybille, to Saxony for her wedding in 1527. This survived until the Second World War, when it was destroyed in an Allied bombing raid. Luckily for the time traveller it had been photographed by that time and clearly shows a vehicle that is ornately gilded, as described by Hall above (as seen in Fimpeler-Philippen and Schurmann's *Das Schloss in Düsseldorf*).

We also know from a letter written around one week later by Nicolas Wooton, a principal member of the English delegation travelling with Anne, that her train totalled 263 persons with 228 horses. Accompanying the soon-to-be queen were eighty-eight of Anne's country folk, mostly younger ladies and gentlemen who intended to stay with her in England after her arrival. These included Anne's steward, secretary and chaplain, but perhaps most interesting of all was a certain Mrs Susannah Gilman, whose maiden name was Hornebolt (anglicised from *Horenbout*). She was famously the first female artist at Henry VIII's court, having come to England with her parents in 1522. Her talent was exceptional. In 1567, Guiccidardini stated that her 'excellence in painting, particularly in the art of miniatures and illumination, was beyond believing.' However, for Henry, it was not Susannah's artistic talents that were of value. Instead, the thirty-seven-year-old must have been one of the few ladies at the English court who spoke

Anne's native tongue, Susannah herself originating from Flanders, close to Anne's German homeland. She was also the wife of John Gilman, a long-term servant of King Henry VIII. Susannah was Gilman's second wife. They married on the 22 September 1539 at St Margaret's church in Westminster. Around two weeks later she was dispatched to Düsseldorf on the king's orders, no doubt to prepare Anne for the great honour, and challenge, which lay ahead. Susannah Gilman was to be the 'first of her [Anne's] gentlewomen', taking precedence over all her other ladies.

It must have been a glorious sight, the colourful cavalcade snaking its way gently northwards, accompanied by the thirteen trumpeters lent to Anne by her brother-in-law, the Duke of Saxony. Perhaps as we stand at the heart of Schwanenburg today, we can still sense the last moments of Anne's departing and hear the ghostly echoes of those trumpeters sounding Anne's moment of triumph.

Visitor Information
We visited Kleve from our base in Düsseldorf, an easy drive one hour to the north west of the city. It is a pleasant, provincial town, although due to exceptionally heavy bombing during the Second World War, when around 90 per cent of the town's buildings were destroyed, virtually nothing survives of Kleve's original pre-1945 fabric. This included Schwanenburg, the once mighty medieval fortress lying at the heart of the ancient Duchy of Kleve. However, luckily for us, from the ashes of its virtual annihilation Anne's ancestral home was partially rebuilt and it now stands towering over the town, much as it has done for generations.

On arrival, we looked to park the car in a small car park directly adjacent to the castle. This seems to fill quickly, so if you wish to park there, it is probably best to arrive early. However, we got hopelessly lost in Kleve's one-way system, eventually abandoning our vehicle in a car park located near the top of the main pedestrianised high street. We made our way to the castle on foot. If you find yourself in the same situation, do not fear as the castle is easy to find and is well signposted from the main street, which runs downhill toward the river.

A significant amount of the castle was reconstructed in the late 1940s. This includes the western range and the buildings surrounding the castle's inner ward, incorporating the site of the original privy apartments of the duke and his family. The majority of the public state apartments, including the great hall, which once ran parallel to the eastern edge of the promontory and across the modern-day car park, have been lost.

Even though only partially rebuilt, Schwanenburg is an impressive sight, perched high up on a rocky outcrop overlooking the town, its substantial walls and lofty position indicative of the turbulent times in which it was originally constructed. Today, the entrance to the castle from the south is a pleasant spot, with lawn and flowerbeds planted at the foot of its south-facing walls. The lie of the land hints at a defensive ditch, but nowadays only a tarmac drive leads you through where the main outer gateway once stood into what would have been the castle's outer ward. To your right, beginning with the great hall, ran the state rooms in a northerly direction, toward the ducal family's private apartments. Helpfully, there are a number of information boards dotted around that help you orientate yourself in space, including pictures of the castle at various times in its history. To your left are some immaculately kept buildings that are used today as offices serving the county and district courts. These include the rebuilt Spiegel Tower. We understand that the ground floor is still accessible to the public, although as this is not signposted we completely missed this fact at the time and failed to pay a visit! Perhaps you will have more luck?

Through the gateway ahead of you is the smaller inner courtyard, dominated by the Schwanenturm, the second of the four towers, which survives from Anne's time. Unfortunately, when the castle was eventually abandoned in the eighteenth century, part of it was converted to a prison. This heralded the end of its fine interiors, which have been irrevocably lost to circumstance. None of the original private rooms of the ducal family remain intact, but the Schwanenturm remains open to the public and is the castle's main tourist attraction. It is possible to climb the tower for a modest fee. Beware, though, that there is a stiff ascent, although the fabulous 180-degree views across the town, the River Rhine and surrounding countryside are evocative of a sense of power and dominance of the duchy of Jülich-Kleves-Berg at its zenith in the early sixteenth century. Books pertaining to the history of the castle are available in the small shop at the base of the tower (although they are in German); toilets are also on-site. If you wish to take your ease and enjoy some refreshments after your ascent of the tower (believe us, unless you are exceptionally fit, you will need to!), make your way to the nearby high street, where you will find plenty of cafés and restaurants.

Opening times for the Schwanenturm: April–October, daily 11 a.m. – 5 p.m.; November–March, Saturday and Sunday only 11 a.m. – 5 p.m.

The English House, Antwerp

My lady of Cleves is to be at Antwerp on the 2 Dec., and does not mean to stay there more than one day; so that she may be expected in Calais six days later. Antwerp, 29 Nov
> Extract from a letter from Stephen Vaughan to Lord Lisle, 1539

At the beginning of December 1539, Anne entered Antwerp. In the mid-sixteenth century, the city was one of the pre-eminent centres of trade and commerce in Europe. By this stage in her journey, Henry's future bride had left behind her brother's dominions. To everyone's surprise, the Holy Roman Emperor, Charles V, had granted safe passage to Anne and her train through his territories in the Low Countries. Henceforth, Anne would travel under his protection until reaching the town of Gravelines, near the English enclave of Calais. Apparently, as we hear from Stephen Vaughan in a letter to Lord Lisle on 26 November 1539, this arrangement was overseen by the Queen Regent, Mary of Hungary, then governor of the Netherlands on behalf of her elder brother: 'The Queen intends sending a noble person to the lady of Cleve to see her well treated in the Emperor's dominions till she pass Gravelyng [Gravelines].' This assurance of safe passage overland meant that Anne did not have to suffer a gruelling and potentially dangerous sea voyage to reach her future home, much to the relief of the Cleves embassy.

Antwerp marked a significant stage in Anne's progress. For not only did England's future queen meet with her Imperial escorts in the form of Floris d'Egmond, Earl of Buren, and Ferry de Melen, Charles V's Master of the Horse, but it would be here that the first formal English reception of 'my lady of Cleves' would take place. This was hosted by the Company of Merchant Adventurers, whose governor, Stephen Vaughan, was a friend and agent of Thomas Cromwell. In this capacity, Vaughan was to personally host Anne's brief visit at the Merchant Adventurers' headquarters in Antwerp, also known as the English House.

Medieval Antwerp

Until the middle of the fifteenth century, Bruges had dominated as the centre of trade in Continental Europe (see also the entry on Bruges). From the early part of the century, the River *Zwin* began to silt up. This had a catastrophic impact on the financial prosperity of the town. Eventually, this precluded great sailing ships from penetrating directly into the heart of the city from the sea. As a result, by the beginning of the sixteenth century Bruges went into decline and key trading groups, such as the Italians, Germans, English, Spanish, French and Portuguese, moved the centre of their activities to Antwerp.

At the time of Anne's visit, Antwerp was nearing the pinnacle of its prosperity. In *The Flemish School of Painting* by Professor Wauters, there is a wonderfully evocative picture of Antwerp in the first half of the sixteenth century:

> As early as 1503, the Portuguese, and then the Spaniards, had sent to Antwerp the produce of their new colony; the English followed, so that in 1516 this city numbered more than a thousand, foreign commercial houses … Innumerable sails covered the Scheldt, and at times, as many as two thousand five hundred ships, laden with merchandise from all parts of the world, thronged the river; about five hundred vessels daily entered and left the port, and sometimes ships might be seen at anchor for more than a fortnight, without being able to reach the quays to either load or unload. By land the traffic was not less great; more than two thousands wagons every week arrived from Germany, France and Lorraine.

At the time, the city was estimated to have had in the region of 150,000–200,000 inhabitants, while the 1566 census confirms the presence of twenty-two public squares, 212 streets and 13,500 houses. Antwerp must have been a colourful melting pot of cultures and tongues, woven into a vibrant trade in commodities, money and ideas. In terms of the latter, the city had become a magnet for controversial thinkers on religious reform such as William Tyndale. Tyndale had been arrested at Antwerp, prior to his execution, just four years before Anne's brief visit. It was into this thriving citadel that Anne of Cleves was welcomed by the English nation as the new queen.

The English House

The company's headquarters in Antwerp was established in 1474, when the local government granted a house to the English nation. Such gestures were a common practice at the time and were viewed as an effective way to bind the economic future of the city with the nation in question. The English House was located in the heart of the city 'beside the Old Bourse' (identified in a letter from Dymock to Stephen Vaughan on 26 May 1546). 'The Old Bourse', which still exists today in a somewhat unkempt state, was the place in which goods were traded between nations. For the English merchants, this predominantly meant wool. In homage, the street upon which the Old Bourse was located was renamed in the fifteenth century from Bullinckstraat to Woolstraat (Wool Street). Specifically, this was on account of the wool stored by the English merchants in several warehouses situated adjacent to the old exchange.

According to *De Engelse Natie Te Antwerpen*, the main entrance to the English House was located on the north side of Woolstraat (today known as Oude Beurs), between a house called Calais, which was located on the corner of the Predikherenstraat (today Lange Doornikstraat) and another house by the name of De Pelikaan, located on the corner of the Hofstraat (which was at that time not more than an alley). The plot, which was about 100 metres long but only 25 metres wide, extended back from the main entrance to run the whole length of the block, with a back gate and a barn adjacent to Zirkstraat. Around 1510 a gallery was built in the garden. This contained stalls and booths for the sale of English cloth.

Luckily for us, a front elevation entitled *English House (The Old Facade), ca. 1460–1542* still exists, revealing a three-storey property decorated in the Gothic style, with typical Flemish/Dutch crowstep gables containing cusped arches and three-centre-arch door surrounds. Floor plans also exist in Antwerp's archives; however, as stated in the *Historiek der Straten en openbare plaatsen van Antwerpen*, at the end of the fifteenth century, the English nation had planned to renovate/rebuild the property. These plans never materialised. Therefore, it is possible that the drawings were just plans and were never actually executed. Interestingly, they do show well over 100 stalls at the back of the property, at least some of which must have already been in existence from 1510 (as described above). The lifeless two-dimensional plans can only hint at how the English House must have been a bustling hive of activity, with traders and buyers daily bartering over the produce of Henry's green England, set among luxurious Renaissance lodgings.

An Official Reception in Antwerp

Having travelled from Cleves via Ravenstein, Bertinburg, Tilburg and Hoogstraaten, in the end, perhaps one day later than expected, Anne finally approached the city of Antwerp. It was 3 December 1539. *Letters and Papers of Henry VIII* describes how

many English merchants met her grace four miles without the town, in fifty velvet coats and chains of gold, and at her entering into Antwerp she was received with twice four score torches, beginning in the daylight, and so brought her to her English lodging, where she was honourably received, and they kept open household one day for her and her train.

Although not a contemporary drawing, we have included a nineteenth-century picture of the reception of the artist Quentin Matsys by the Guild of St Luke in Antwerp in 1521. We are assured by the archives in Antwerp that this depicts a good likeness of both the fashions of the day and the likely interior of a high-status sixteenth-century lodging in the city, the type of reception that would have welcomed Anne on her arrival. What is more, the city archives afford us a glimpse of how the royal party were entertained during their brief stay, with Lord Buren feasting Anne's attendants while Stephen Vaughan played host to Henry's future bride.

However, Anne's relationship with Antwerp was fleeting; 'the next day the English merchants brought her, on her way to Stetkyn, and gave her a gift and so departed'. After Anne and her attendants had departed from the town, Nicolas Wooton put pen to paper, and in a footnote of a long letter to Cromwell urged that 'Mr Vaughan and the merchants should be thanked for my lady's entertainment at the English house here. Lord Bure[n] says he never saw so many people gathered in Antwerp at any entry, even the Emperor's. What with my lady's train, and Mr Vaughan, and the merchants, it was a goodly sight. Antwerp, 4 Dec.'

Visitor Information
Five hundred years after Anne's brief sojourn through Antwerp, the city still remains a thriving metropolis, although as one might expect much of the medieval town has been lost to relentless modernisation and the destructive aftermath of the Second World War. However, the Grote Markt (Market Place) is a fine open space dominated by the late sixteenth-century town hall and several fine examples of sixteenth-century guild houses, built in typical Flemish style. At the heart of the city's old quarter, this is a good place to begin your adventure and leaves the time traveller with an excellent impression of the types of building that Anne would have seen as she passed through the city.

Find Wisselstraat, which leads off the central marketplace to the north. You will soon come across Oude Beurs. To your left, on the north side of the street, and on a site now occupied by Nos 17 or 21, was the front entrance to the English House. Sadly, nothing remains of this once great building. It was razed to the ground during the infamous Spanish Fury in the late sixteenth century. You must use your imagination to recreate the impressive facade in your mind's eye before wandering straight ahead into Hofstraat (once Wolstraat), bearing in mind that the plot occupied by the English House ran along the whole length of the street on your left-hand side. About halfway along this road, on the right, is a tall, green doorway (No. 15). Through this inconspicuous nineteenth-century entrance you will find yourself stepping back into a rather neglected, cobbled courtyard of sixteenth-century design. You are now standing in the Old Bourse, the place where traders of all nations once gathered to conduct their business. This little space once hummed with lively conversation as nations bartered their wares. Today, however, you are likely to find yourself alone, the stonework blackened with centuries of grime, the masonry crumbling above your eyeline; the pretty spherical design of the cobblestones beneath your feet is assaulted by weeds that threaten to take over a surface polished by centuries of wear. But despite its appearance, the Old Bourse is a hidden treasure.

The loggia that runs around the courtyard was created in 1515, with the large, octagonal tower, or Pagaddertoren (Pagadder Tower), dating from 1533. This was used by merchants to watch for the arrival of ships into the nearby port. The Old Bourse is now used as municipal offices, and thus the courtyard is open to the public during normal working hours.

If you wish to see more of the medieval city, make your way to the nearby Butcher's Hall on Vleeshouwersstraat. Its sixteenth-century exterior is a fine example of a grand trading hall of the period. Completed in 1504, it is one of the oldest surviving buildings in Antwerp, although at the time of writing, frustratingly, it was not open to the public.

Finally, to see two fascinating Tudor artefacts, be sure to visit the Cathedral of our Lady next to the Grote Markt. Directly outside the main entrance you will find an ornate well. It is here – while he was exiled in the city – that William Tyndale is known to have met secretly with fellow reformers. Step upon the small stone steps that run about the base of the well and trace your hands over its surface, knowing that you are standing on a spot where history played out a revolution that would change the fabric of English society.

Once inside the fourteenth-century gothic Cathedral of Our Lady, head to St Antony's Chapel. Here you will find the most surprising survivor of the Tudor age. It is a beautiful stained-glass window, commissioned by English merchants during the reign of Henry VII but finally installed some thirty years later in 1539, the year of Anne of Cleves's visit. One assumes that this must have been done to commemorate the event, although we have not come across any direct proof that this was indeed the case. This 500-year-old survivor of some of the heaviest bombing in the Second World War depicts the king (Henry VII) kneeling in prayer opposite his wife, Elizabeth of York. Rich with Tudor imagery, this little-known artefact is a wonderful and surprising find, so far as it is from English shores. Be sure to sit for a while and imbibe its many charms.

Website for the Cathedral of Our Lady: http://www.dekathedraal.be/en/.

The areas described are surrounded by shops, cafés and restaurants, so you will not be short of refreshments. We stopped for lunch in a wonderful vegetarian restaurant right next to the cathedral called De Rosenobel. Although a little quiet during the day, the service and food was excellent, making for a pleasant change from the usual tourist fare. Their website is http://www.rosenobel.be/. Address: Blauwmoezelstraat 2, 2000 Antwerpen.

Bruges, Belgium

To-day she leaves Antwerp, and trusted to be at Bruges on Saturday, but as the horses could not be put over the Schelde yesterday because of the low water, it will be Sunday before she gets there.

Nicolas Wooton, Antwerp, 4 December 1539

Of all the locations covered in this book, Bruges' story and its relationship to Anne of Cleves has been perhaps the most enchanting – and frustrating. The city has teased us with real and beguiling possibilities for the location of Anne's lodgings, but like a clever seductress, she never completely yielded herself, or her secrets, to our persistent probing. Yet the city is, without doubt, one of the fairest medieval cities in northern Europe, and the story drew us evermore into an enigma just too intriguing to cast aside without retelling. Thus, while we know with certainty that Anne did indeed lodge briefly in Bruges overnight on Sunday 7 December 1539, our journey in search of her will take us through many of its charming streets but will ultimately leave us, at least for the time being, with an unresolved Tudor quandary.

Medieval Bruges and the English Nation
Through the Middle Ages, Bruges was a powerhouse of European economy, such that it has even been called 'the cradle of capitalism'. Before Antwerp took up the mantel of the premier trading centre in Europe toward the end of the fifteenth century, the English Merchant Adventurers based themselves in the city, alongside several other key trading nations. Furthermore, ties to the English nobility through the mid-fifteenth century were significant; Margaret of York, the younger sister of King Edward IV, was married to Charles the Bold just outside Bruges in 1468. The following day, Margaret would make her joyous entry into the city, among lavish celebrations. Just two years later, Edward was usurped from his throne and took temporary refuge at the Burgundian court; part of his time in exile would be spent lodged alongside his brother, the future Richard III, at the Gruuthuse in Bruges, which can still be visited today.

Much as in Antwerp, the English merchants carved out a small enclave for themselves within the city. Just east of the central Grote Markt we can still see their ancient legacy in the street names that cluster around a small area fronting on to one of Bruges's inner waterways: Engelsestraat (English Street), Koningstraat (King Street, leading to English Square) and the Spinolarei (English Quay). Today, tourist boats regularly power past the place where English sailing ships unloaded their cargo of fine English wool. The relevance of this English niche will soon become apparent.

Anne in Bruges – A Tudor Mystery
Our aim was to identify 'Anne of Cleves' chapel' (and lodgings), a turn of phrase which came from the local legend of the Anne of Cleves panels, described at the beginning of this section. This has never been done before – and with good reason.

With the exception of a single entry in Bruges' archives (expense archives dating from September 1539 to September 1540) stating that a merchant had been paid by the City to deliver wine to 'the daughter of Cleves being within the city to travel to England in December', no further mention of her lodgings are made, either in the city's archives or within the English correspondence at the time. However, the fact that no expenses are listed by the city adds weight to the fact that it was not the city of Bruges that hosted her stay. So, as possible options for Anne's lodgings, we are left considering either a high-status hostelry of some description or a private house with noble connections.

Identifying 'Anne of Cleves' Chapel in Bruges'

Firstly, we should not take any historical reference to 'Anne of Cleves' chapel (and any associated lodgings) in Bruges' to mean that she owned a property there. There is no evidence of this being the case. It merely seems to point to her overnight lodging in the city. It is clear that as soon as she left her homeland, Anne was beginning the transmutation from a German noble lady to an English queen. She had recently been officially received by the English in Antwerp and would again be so as she approached Calais. It seems most likely to us that this pattern would have continued. So, a lodging with an English connection, like the English House in Antwerp (see entry on the English House, Antwerp) is a very plausible contender. Unfortunately, the English House in Bruges was only established in the latter part of the sixteenth century (and still exists today in a much remodelled form). Up until that point, it seems that the English Weigh House on English Street had served the English mercantile community. According to Murray in *Bruges, Cradle of Capitalism, 1280–1390*, this 'weigh house' was actually 'a cluster of buildings that the city leased out'. Whether this 'cluster of buildings' provided a suitable lodging for a queen-to-be we do not know, only that the actual weigh house consisted of a cellar (with the scales for weighing wool) and a room on the first floor for meetings of the English merchants.

During our *In the Footsteps* travels over the past three years, we have come to appreciate the predictability of the English nobility, particularly in terms of their travel itineraries and lodgings. With this in mind, we were also intrigued by a chance finding: a reference in *Les Marchands de la Hanse et la Banque des Médicis* to a chapel dedicated to Thomas à Becket in the local Carmelite monastery. This monastery was located just a stone's throw away from the English quarter mentioned above. It was apparently 'requisitioned' during the medieval period by the English for worship. The monastery gave a little piece of ground to the English merchants to build a small chapel next to the church. This was the chapel dedicated to Thomas à Becket. In addition, in exchange for thirteen burial plots and Masses said for the dead, the merchants paid for repairs to the church walls. We know from our previous research that it was common practice for English royalty to lodge in religious houses, the abbot ceding his personal lodgings to his honoured guests as part of the monastic tradition of providing hospitality to travellers. What is more, during our research in the archives in Bruges we uncovered the fact that some twenty years earlier another notable Englishman had also lodged at the same monastery during his six-month stay in the city. This man was Thomas More. He is thought to have written *Utopia* while staying in Bruges, possibly at this very same monastery. In other words, we have a location with form; it was a building with a previous history of lodging English 'notables'.

Of course, there could be other contenders for the location of Anne's overnight stay. However, their case is not as compelling. For instance, it is possible that Anne lodged at Charles V's palace in the city (part of which survives today a five-star hotel called the Princenhof). He had, after all, provided safe passage for Anne through his territories. However, despite this act of graciousness, the relationship between Henry and Charles was poor at the time and, according to the archivist in Bruges, such a level of hospitality seems unlikely. There is perhaps also a case for Anne lodging at the House of Ravestein in a street called Molenmeers (now a hotel). This had been owned by one of Anne's kinsmen, but by the 1530s the building was no longer in the possession of the family, and so again this makes such a visit far less likely.

And so, while we are able to debunk one myth associated with Anne of Cleves – that of the panels which were supposed to have originated in the city – the final truth about her lodgings remains tantalisingly inconclusive. However, we sincerely hope that one day, someone somewhere will finally unearth that truth and that maybe, just maybe, by recording our research to date we will have assisted in that happy outcome.

Visitor information
While we cannot deliver you with certainty to the doorstep of Anne's lodgings in Bruges, the time traveller interested in medieval history will immediately be seduced by the city's ancient charms. On a fine summer's day in particular there can be no fairer place in the world to lose oneself, either wandering through its maze of medieval streets and grand squares, or by taking a boat trip along one of its inner waterways, as one architectural gem after another floats by. Time slips through your fingers here, both because there is so much to see and because it is all too easy to lose yourself in a time warp, forgetting the modern world as you explore such historic buildings as the Gruuthuse, the Holy Blood Basilica in Burg Square or the Belfry Tower in the Grote Markt.

If, on top of the usual tourist destinations, you are in search of some of the locations mentioned in this entry, we recommend arming yourself with a tourist map picked up at any hotel or at the local tourist information office. Head from the Grote Markt toward Jan Van Eyck Plein (where there is a fine statue of the fifteenth-century artist), then walk along the right-hand side of the canal that you will find there; you are now walking along the Spinolarei (English Quay). Six centuries ago, English boats would be moored alongside the quay, goods being unloaded amid the sound of English tongues. Further along, you will come across Engelsetraat, first recorded as such in 1330. Here was sited the 'English weigh house', containing scales in the cellar for weighing the wool arriving from England. There was also a meeting room for gatherings of the English merchants on the first floor. A little further on still is Koningstraat. Continue past the end of this street, onward to where the canals merge. Cross a pretty little bridge that will lead you to the corner of Potterierei and Carmestraat. In addition to a few houses fronting the street, in the sixteenth century this corner block was the location of the Carmelite monastery, still indicated by the eponymous street name.

Refreshment is never far away in Bruges. It is a paradise for any beer or chocolate lover, and while beer is not our fare we set aside plenty of time to sample the local chocolate in many of its different guises, the strawberries dipped in chocolate being a particular favourite of ours! We were lucky enough to stay in one of the finest hotels in Bruges, the Hotel de Tuilereen, a fifteenth-century patrician house overlooking the famous Dijver Canal. If you can afford it, Bruges is certainly the place to indulge yourself, and we can highly recommend the Tuilereen's elegant rooms – particularly one fronting on to the waterway. After a full day of following in the footsteps of English royalty, it was heavenly to lie on the four-poster bed with the windows thrown wide, being lulled by the melodic chimes of Bruges' famous belfry singing to us of a 'Stranger in Paradise'.

Bruges Tourist Information: Markt, 8000 Brugge, Belgium. Telephone No: +32 50 44 46 46.

Hotel de Tuilereen website: http://www.hoteltuilerieen.com. Telephone No: +32 50 34 36 91.

The Exchequer, Calais

> And before the Staple hall stoode the Merchauntes [merchants] of the Staple well apparelled, which lykewyse presented her with an. C [100]. souereyns [sovereigns] of golde in a ryche pursse, which hertely thanked them, & so she rode to the kings place called the Checker, & there she laye. xv. [15] dayes for lacke of prosperous wynde.
>
> Edward Hall, chronicler

In the first half of the sixteenth century, Calais was the only jewel of English sovereignty that remained as part of the French mainland. It was a remnant of the vast empire of England's Plantagenet dynasty; a dynasty that had once reigned across not only England, but much of northern and western France, and as far south as Aquitaine.

Calais was part-garrison, part-trading town, the last outpost of English soil before reaching the rest of the Continent and beyond. Within its fortified walls was a grid-like network of narrow streets, packed tightly with fine medieval houses owned by affluent Calais merchants. Every so often, these streets would open up into spacious squares used for trading, recreation and the gathering of townsfolk.

In the dying days of 1539, Calais had been holding her collective breath, waiting for the arrival of Henry's soon-to-be fourth wife. Even across the centuries, it is still possible to sense the palpable air of expectation in those who patiently tarried there. A steady stream of letters crossed the Channel between London and the Continent, hinting at the busy preparations for, and growing anticipation of, the arrival of England's queen. One such witness was Thomas Cromwell's son, Gregory, who had landed in Calais on 2 December. He was in the service of the Lord High Admiral, William Fitzwilliam, Earl of Southampton. On 9 December, Gregory wrote to his wife, Elizabeth (Jane Seymour's sister),

> Bedfellow,
> The day before the making hereof we received the just news of lady Anne's repair hither, the same being appointed upon Thursday next coming … After she once entereth the English Pale both she and her whole train shall be at the king's charge … The lord Deputy, with all the spears and officers of the town, will receive her at the English Pale; my lord Admiral, with all us accompanying him, a little without the town. My Lady Lisle and all other ladies and gentlewomen, at the town gates.
> At Calais, the 9 December, Your loving bedfellow,
> Gregory Cromwell

The Arrival of Anne of Cleves in Calais

Thanks to the writing of the chronicler Edward Hall, and the contents of documents held in the National Archives, we have a detailed account of Anne's reception into the town a few days later than originally anticipated, on Thursday 11 December. On what must have been a chilly winter's morning, around dawn, Anne entered the English Pale. England's new queen and her train must have travelled through the quiet hours of the night to reach Gravelines from Dunkirk. One can only imagine her relief at the sight of the English delegation after nearly two weeks of being incessantly jolted this way and that, as the royal train pushed through the depths of a northern European winter. We will turn to Hall to describe what happened next:

> … at the turnepyke on thys side of Gravelyng [Gravelines], was the lady Anne of Cleve received by the lorde Lisle, duputie of the town of Calice [Calais], and with the speres and horsemen belonging to the retinue there, all being fresh and warlike apparelled, and so marching toward Calice, a myle and more from the towne, met her grace the earle of Southampton, gret admiral of England, and apparelled in a coate of purple velvet cut on cloth of golde, and tyed with great agelttes and treifoiles of golde, to the nombre of iiiiC (four hundred), and baudrick-wise he ware a chayne, at which dyd hang a whystle of golde set with ryche stones of a great value.

Accompanied by thirty gentlemen of the king's household, including Sir Francis Bryan and Sir Thomas Seymour – both resplendently dressed with 'gret and massy chaynes' – the Earl of Southampton welcomed his queen with 'low obeysaunce' before bringing her 'into Calyce byt the Lanterne gate, where the shippes laye in the haven garnyshed with their banners, pencelles, and flagges, pleasauntly to beholde'.

Tragically, the bombing of Calais during the Second World War destroyed virtually every remnant of the town's medieval grandeur. However, due to the efforts of English antiquaries in the nineteenth century, we do know something of the buildings that had survived over the intervening three hundred years, including the Lantern Gate, which is mentioned in Hall's account above. Combined with contemporary accounts of the town and its history, the modern-day time traveller can yet walk in 'my Lady of Cleves's footsteps and gain some satisfaction by seeing beyond its unexciting modern-day facade to once more recreate the sixteenth-century town in their mind's eye.

A view of the town as it was in the sixteenth century, taken from the *Chronicle of Calais in the Reigns of Henry VII and Henry VIII*, shows the skyline of Calais as Anne would have seen it as she approached the town. The citadel was fortified by enormous city walls. Along its length, a series of towers provided a mixture of both accommodation and defence. The Lantern Gate, in the centre of the picture, stands roughly at the point of the intersection of the modern-day Boulevard des Allies, the Boulevard de la Resistance and the Rue de la Mer. It was the principal gate of the town. Beyond the city walls, one can see the long-lost outline of four key buildings which made up the town's impressive skyline; the churches of Our Lady to the left and St Nicholas to the right, while the exquisite medieval structures of the Town Hall and Staple Hall stand centrally, directly to the south of the Lantern Gate.

In the *Letters and Papers of Henry VIII*, further details of Anne's arrival at this gate are recorded as follows:

> When she [Anne] came to the Lantern Gate she stayed and viewed the King's ships, the Lion and the Sweepstake, decked with 100 banners of silk and gold, wherein were 200 master gunners and mariners and 31 trumpets, and a double drum that was never seen in England before; and so her Grace entered into Calais. At her entry, 150 pieces of ordnance let out of the said two ships made such a smoke that one of her train could not see another. Where stood in order on both sides the streets, like a lane, with 500 soldiers in the King's livery of the retinue of Calais, and the mayor of Calais with his brethren, and the commons of Calais, and the merchants of the Staple, stood in like manner in array, and made a lane wherethrough she passed to her lodging. There the mayor and his brethren came to her and gave her 50 sovereigns of gold, and the mayor of the Staple, 60.

The Exchequer at Calais

We know from Hall's account that Anne was lodged at the king's Exchequer for fifteen days when she remained at Calais due to an 'unhappy wind'. This was situated directly adjacent to the long-lost church of St Nicolas, west of the main marketplace (today the Place d'Armes). Thanks to a plan of the Exchequer, thought to have been drawn up in the early or mid-1530s, we know exactly the arrangement of its rooms.

As a principal royal lodging, the Exchequer was substantial, with around sixty separate chambers. At least two external entrances passed under two separate gatehouses to access a series of inner courtyards; the plans themselves allocated rooms to 'the king's apartments', 'the queen's apartments' and 'the French king's apartments'. *The History of the King's Works* states that this allocation was most likely devised in anticipation of the 1534 visit of Henry VIII and Anne Boleyn, which sadly never materialised. However, the royal couple had stayed there two years earlier, in 1532, and it is likely that Anne of Cleves was lodged in the very same suite of rooms that Anne Boleyn once occupied (for further information on this visit, please see *In the Footsteps of Anne Boleyn*).

On the queen's side are listed fourteen separate chambers. Principal among these are the queen's great chamber; the queen's dining chamber; the queen's raying chamber; the queen's bedchamber; the gallery; and the queen's garden chamber – the latter, of course, leading out into the queen's privy garden. Anne was now mistress of her own considerable household and was afforded every courtesy and luxury that money could buy. Perhaps she had never before known such freedom as she kept open house, her daily pastimes, which were the 'best that could be devised', overseen by her hosts, Lord and Lady Lisle. It is indirectly through Honor Lisle that we learn more of Anne's agreeable character. In reply to an earlier correspondence from the said lady, Anne Basset, who was in London at the time, wrote, 'I humbly thank your ladyship of the news you write me, of her Grace that she is so good and gentle to serve and please. It shall be no little rejoicement to us, her Grace's servants here, that shall attend daily upon her, and most comfort to the King's majesty, whose highness is not a little desirous to have her Grace here.'

Through a veiled shroud of time, we intermittently catch glimpses of Henry's twenty-four-year-old queen, and each time we find ourselves faced with a dignified woman, gracious, gentle and eager to please her new king and subjects. It is easy to visualise Anne at Calais amid a whirl of vibrant celebration, sometimes enjoying the many lavish banquets and jousts laid on in her honour, other times patiently learning to play card games that might please her husband. It seems somehow poignant, and perhaps even bittersweet. The loving husband that Anne may have dreamed of from her childhood waited impatiently for her on the other side of the Channel. She had left only a short time to enjoy her innocence and happy dreams before being confronted by the reality of Henry's cold-heartedness and fickle moods.

Visitor Information
From a historical perspective, we find Calais a fascinating town. However, the destruction left in the wake of the Second World War and the modern-day realities of a border town besieged by immigrants wishing to cross the Channel to England does not make this an easy place to visit. It is one location where you may not wish to travel alone. However, Calais may well be your point of arrival on

the Continent, or of your crossing to England. We enjoyed wandering its streets in search of the town that Anne once knew. If you feel the same, make your way to the site of the now vanished Lantern Gate, adjacent to the old harbour (its exact position is as described above). To enter the town, follow in Anne's footsteps and make your way down Lantern Street, now the Rue de la Mer, and you will find yourself standing in what was once the footprint of the main marketplace, now the Place D'Armes. Only two ancient buildings remain to be seen today in Calais. The first of these is on the south side of the Place D'Armes. The Tour de Guet is a rare survivor from the Middle Ages; it once stood behind the thirteenth-century town hall, destroyed during the Second World War. The surviving tower certainly would have been a building seen by Anne, albeit not quite in this derelict state!

On arriving in front of the Staple Hall, the royal party would have then turned right and headed down what was once called the 'High Street', the main road heading east–west through the town. This is now called the Rue d'André Gerschel. Sadly, both the church of St Nicolas and the Exchequer are long lost and their precise location is difficult to fathom. However, they were oriented facing each other, perhaps somewhere close to where the Rue d'André Gerschel intersects the Rue de la Victoire.

If you are interested in another extant remnant of medieval Calais, you might also wish to visit the Church of Our Lady (now called the 'Eglise Notre Dame'). This was being refurbished during our visit, and therefore was not open to the public. However, one assumes that the renovations will eventually be complete. It is a veritable time capsule. Built during the height of the English occupation, it is renowned as the only surviving English-style church in France. Many kings and queens have passed through its doors, and from a Tudor perspective it contains the tomb of John Bourchier, 2nd Baron Berners, half-brother to Anne Boleyn's mother, Elizabeth.

Deal Castle, Kent

> On 27 Dec., St. John's Day, she [Anne of Cleves] took ship, and landed at the Downs, between 6 and 7 p.m., where she was met by the duke and duchess of Suffolk, who, with their train, accompanied her to Deal Castle. There she banquetted, and proceeded to Dover, where she tarried till Monday, and then set forth to Canterbury, where she was received by the Archbishop with other bishops and the gentlemen of Kent.
>
> *Letters and Papers of Henry VIII*, January 1540

Two days after Christmas 1539, Anne awoke to the news she'd been eagerly awaiting. The winds had eased, and the conditions were favourable enough for her to sail to England.

England's New Queen Arrives

By all accounts, this was Anne's first sea journey, so we can imagine her feeling nervous at the prospect of the crossing but elated to be finally leaving Calais, where she'd spent the last fifteen days waiting for a break in the weather. At around noon she embarked with her retinue, the salty sea air filling her lungs as she set off on her 20-mile voyage across the Channel to Deal.

The fleet of around fifty painted ships 'trimmed with streamers, banners and flags' was under the command of William Fitzwilliam, Earl of Southampton and Lord Admiral of England, whom Henry had appointed to escort Anne safely, and 'in all solemnity and triumph', to her new home. The king was impatiently awaiting the arrival of his new bride, so luckily for Fitzwilliam and Anne, the weather turned temporarily in their favour, and a remarkably swift passage ensued.

A winter crossing of the English Channel could take more than twenty-four gruelling hours, and travellers often arrived at their destination seriously ill, so Anne's arrival at Deal, in good health, in the early evening of the same day was a blessing. As there was no pier at Deal at the time, Anne, along with all the baggage, would have been rowed to shore. From the Tudor chronicler Edward Hall we hear that the party landed at Deal about 'v. of the clocke', while another contemporary document records the arrival time, as 'between 6 and 7'. Either way, night had fallen by the time Anne set foot on English soil.

There to greet her by torchlight were Thomas Cheyney, Lord Warden of the Cinque Ports; Charles Brandon, Duke of Suffolk, and his wife, Catherine Willoughby; Richard Sampson, the Bishop of Chichester; and 'a great number of knights and esquires and ladies of Kent', who escorted Anne to Deal Castle to dine. Darkness perhaps masked the fact that the castle was not yet quite finished. Hall described it as 'newly built' at the time of Anne's visit but in reality, it was not completed until around September 1540. This and the fact that the accommodation was fairly spartan – being purely a garrison fortress designed to accommodate a captain, thirty-four soldiers, a trumpeter and a drummer, is why, after a short rest, the royal newcomer was taken to nearby Dover Castle, where she spent the night.

Castles in the Downs

In June 1538, Charles V and Francis I of France signed a peace treaty. Later the same year, Pope Paul III announced that Henry VIII had been excommunicated from the Catholic Church. This was enough motivation for Henry to build Deal, Walmer and Sandown; known as the three 'castles in the Downs', they were designed to protect the Deal coastline from a feared Catholic invasion.

The 'Downs' refers to a stretch of water located between the coastal town of Deal and the notorious and greatly feared Goodwin Sands, a 10-mile-long sandbank where, over the centuries, at least a thousand ships have been wrecked. While this natural feature provided some protection from would-be invaders, especially in fog and storms, the 'Downs' offered local mariners and hostile forces alike a safe anchorage place sheltered from most winds and within easy access to a long beach. It became a haven for ships and a popular landing and embarkation point in the sixteenth century and beyond. Thus it was a much more attractive alternative than the cliffs of Dover to the south or the inhospitable Sandwich flats to the north, turning the sleepy fishing village of Deal into one of England's busiest ports.

Its proximity to mainland Europe also posed a significant concern for Henry, who in February 1539 devised a plan for its fortification. In the 'device by the King', Henry proposed the building of 'three new bulwarks [forts] to be made in the Downs and other places on the frontiers of the sea'. In addition to the three stone castles, Henry also built four smaller earthen 'bulwarks'. As H. M Colvin explains in Volume IV of *The History of the King's Works*, 'all seven fortifications appear to have been linked by a trench or covered way to form a single defensive line extending along two and a half miles of coastline'. The king appointed two local men, Sir Edward Ryngeley and Thomas Wingfield, to oversee the new works, which were underway by April 1539. Unfortunately, the Tudor building accounts for the 'castles in the Downs' were lost, but the good news is that two of the three castles, Deal and Walmer, still survive.

The Tudor Castle

The castle where Anne dined on arrival to England was by far the largest of the three fortresses built in the Downs. Enclosed by a dry moat and curtain wall, its only entrance from the landward side of the castle was protected by a drawbridge and portcullis. Its strong central tower, which served as a gun platform, dominated the design and was surrounded by six small semi-circular bastions, which were situated on a further six enormous rounded bastions, one of which served as the gatehouse.

Heavy guns could be mounted from four different levels: the roof of the central tower, inner bastions and outer bastions, and from a 'gun-room' below the outer bastions. Handguns or arrows could also be fired from a narrow gallery that ran around at basement level. In all, there were at least 145 openings for weapons. However, there's nothing to suggest that the castle was ever so heavily armed, and luckily for Henry the feared Catholic invasion never came.

Visitor Information

Today, Deal Castle is owned by English Heritage and opened to the public throughout the year. Free parking is available in the large car park next to the castle. If you happen to arrive early, as we did on the day of our visit, we recommend a stroll along the shingled beach to admire the beautiful scenery.

The castle can be comfortably explored in one to two hours. Be sure to take advantage of the free audio tour available on arrival, as this will give you a good overall history of the site. Things to look out for: the massive oak doors with their iron studs at the entrance are almost certainly original; Anne and her welcoming party would have crossed the drawbridge, today replaced by a stone causeway, and passed through these doors into the entrance hall. The first floor of the keep was the domain of the captain of the castle and any distinguished guests; while there is no documentary evidence to prove it, this may have been where Anne dined. On this floor you'll also find examples of Tudor wattle-and-daub partitions and a sixteenth-century garderobe. The ground floor of the keep was home to the thirty-four soldiers of the Tudor garrison; note the remains of an original Tudor fireplace and brick oven. From the keep's basement, originally the principal storage area of the castle, visitors can access 'the Rounds', a series of atmospheric passageways that run right round the outer bastions, but be warned, they are dark and occasionally flooded. The basement is also home to an exhibition on Deal Castle.

Those of you interested in learning more about Deal's maritime history might like to combine your visit to the castle with a visit to the Deal Maritime & Local History Museum, situated in the heart of Deal, just off the High Street and behind Deal Town Hall. The energetic among us might also like to take advantage of the walking trail from Deal to Walmer Castle. This easy 2-mile walk along the coast gives you unsurpassed views of the English Channel and opportunities to rest along the way on one of the benches provided. Perhaps as you do so, you might imagine the hive of activity that would have preceded the future Queen Anne's arrival at Deal.

For more information on the walk, please visit the Kent County Council website at http://www.kent.gov.uk/leisure-and-community/parks-and-outdoor-activities/find-a-walk/walks-for-all-walmer-castle-to-deal-castle.

For Deal Maritime & Local History Museum opening times and visitor information, please visit http://www.dealmuseum.co.uk/Deal_Museum/Home.html.

For castle opening times and other visitor information, please visit the Deal Castle website at http://www.english-heritage.org.uk/daysout/properties/deal-castle, or telephone +44 (0) 130 437 2762.

Postcode for Deal Castle: CT14 7BA.

Dover Castle, Kent

> On her arrival at Dover the duke of Suffolk and lord Warden of the Cinque Ports, with the other lords appointed to wait upon them, and the duchess of Suffolk and other ladies, shall receive her at her landing, and convey her to the castle, attend upon her during her abode there, and at her departure conduct her to Canterbury, and so forth till her meeting with the King.
>
> *Chronicle of Calais*

On the evening of Saturday 27 December 1539, the Lady Anne, accompanied by the Duke and Duchess of Suffolk, Sir Thomas Cheyne and a large number of knights, esquires and ladies, travelled by torchlight from Deal Castle – where Anne had rested after arriving from Calais – a short distance down the coast, to Dover Castle. No doubt exhausted from the day's events, Anne must have been eager to retire. The queen-in-waiting spent the following day and night at the castle, before moving onto Canterbury, where another grand reception, this time led by the Archbishop of Canterbury, Thomas Cranmer, awaited her.

On Monday 29 December, at around eleven o'clock, after the last of Anne's baggage and 'necessaryes' had arrived at the castle, the party rode out amid torrential rain and battering winds. The Duke of Suffolk and Thomas Cheyne were anxious not to lose another day to the foul weather; after all, King Henry VIII was not one to be kept waiting.

Later that evening, a relieved Suffolk and Cheyne reported from Canterbury in a letter to Thomas Cromwell that Anne, unperturbed by the wind and hail that blew 'contynuelly in her face', was so 'desirous to make hast to the King['s Highness] that her Grace forced for no nother, which [we] perceyvyng were very gladde to set her G[race] furthwarde'. Anne's perseverance and amiability were winning her admiration.

A Short History

By the time of Anne's visit, the medieval castle perched atop the gleaming White Cliffs of Dover had been guarding the harbour, and welcoming visitors and returning Britons alike, for hundreds of years. Its mighty great tower, visible for miles out to sea, along with the castle's curtain walls and inner bailey, were built by Henry II in the 1180s. In the thirteenth century, King John and Henry III completed the outer defences started by their predecessor; however, these were not the first structures to occupy this commanding position over the town.

The Romans constructed a *pharos* or lighthouse to guide ships into the harbour in the first half of the second century AD, which still stands, and the Saxons built a church that was probably part of a fortified settlement. Soon after his victory at the Battle of Hastings, William the Conqueror built a timber-stockaded castle on the site and from then on Dover Castle was continuously garrisoned until 1958.

Preparations for the Arrival of Anne of Cleves

In the latter part of 1539, Thomas Cromwell was busy finalising arrangements for Henry VIII's marriage to Anne and overseeing the preparations for her impending arrival. In his remembrances of November 1539, the following note is included: 'The sending of such officers as shall furnish the houses and farres [ferries] at Calais and Dover for the receiving of the lady Anne, with all apparel for the same.'

Then in early December, Thomas Cheyne penned the following letter to Cromwell:

I thank you for your letter of this day's date; be assured that I have taken such order for provision to be made at Dover of all things necessary for our mistress [Anne] that shall be that there shall be no lack. I have already sent not only to Dover but all along the way Her Grace shall come. From my poor house, Thursday, 4 Dec.

Henry's chief minister had enthusiastically promoted the match with the German princess, and so had a vested interest in seeing that all went to plan and that no detail was overlooked. It's no surprise, then, that according to the research of Dr Gordon Higgott, an independent architectural historian, 'the longest recorded campaign of refurbishment works under Henry VIII [at Dover] was for the intended reception of Anne of Cleves in 1539', at which time, a crown of iron was erected over the king's lodgings in the keep. Interestingly, this feature is visible in a drawing of the castle made by the surveyor John Bereblock in 1570.

The Royal Apartments

While we know that Anne spent her first two nights in England at Dover Castle, no documentary evidence exists detailing exactly where Anne was lodged during her stay. It is thought likely that it was one of two possibilities: the first was that, like many queens and distinguished guests before her, including Charles V in 1520, Anne was lodged in a suite of rooms in the great tower; the second was that Anne occupied a chamber in a range of royal lodgings situated along the north-east side of the inner bailey and connected to the keep by a covered passageway or pentice.

In around 1480, King Edward IV modernised the keep in order to use it as a royal residence. On the first floor were the queen's apartments, and on the floor above, the entrance level, were the king's rooms. Each floor had an 'outer' room and an 'inner' room; the outer functioned as a hall or presence chamber, where the king and queen dined publicly or held audience, while the inner served as a privy chamber, where monarchs could enjoy some level of privacy. The second floor also housed a private chapel. In addition, each floor had a series of smaller 'mural chambers' opening off the main rooms, which over the centuries served a variety of purposes, including something akin to modern bedrooms in the fifteenth century.

We know from the work of Dr Higgott that the four main chambers at the time of Anne's visit were as follows:

> On the first floor the 'outer' (NE) room was the Queen's 'Reigning Chamber', while the 'inner' SW room was her Privy Chamber; on the second floor the 'outer' NE room was the King's Great Chamber or Watching (i.e Guard) Chamber, while the 'inner' SW room was variously styled his Privy or Presence Chamber. This general arrangement seems to be confirmed by several references in the accounts for the refurbishment of 1625-6 to the king and queen's 'Presence' and 'Privy' chambers, which confirm that the first floor was regarded as the Queen's, and the second floor as the King's.

If Anne and her ladies were not accommodated on the first-floor of the great tower, then they may have stayed in one of the chambers that made up a range of royal lodgings on the north-east side of the inner bailey known as the King's Lodgings. These buildings were constructed in the thirteenth century as accommodation for Henry III. When his wife, Queen Eleanor of Provence, was in residence, she stayed in her own suite of rooms in the great tower. The king's new range included a great hall named Arthur's Hall, presumably after the legendary king, plus a series of royal chambers and a chapel. Edward IV refurbished these buildings in the fifteenth century, installing new windows. In Bereblock's drawing of Dover, the range is clearly visible to the north of the keep.

The Modern Time Traveller

While very little remains of the King's Lodgings, the apartments in the great tower survive. They are presented as if Henry II and his court were in residence, and are a fascinating evocation of a medieval court in all its splendour.

Next to the Princess of Wales' Royal Regiment Museum is Arthur's Hall, which today is home to an exhibition on the royal history of the castle. At the south-east end of the hall are three blocked doors excavated in the 1970s. The central door originally gave access to the kitchen, while the doors on either side led to the buttery and pantry.

Be sure to visit the church of St Mary in Castro, situated beside the Roman lighthouse, as both were standing at the time of Anne's visit. While the church was heavily restored in the nineteenth century, the outer shell is largely original.

As you walk the grounds of this great English landmark, imagine Anne and her entourage riding out on that wintry morning in December 1539. After weeks of travelling across land and sea, Anne had only three more days to wait until she'd come face to face with England's king.

Visitor Information

Dover Castle is managed by English Heritage. Please visit their website for visitor information at http://www.english-heritage.org.uk/daysout/properties/dover-castle. Telephone number: +44 (0) 130 421 1067.

The authors recommend combining a visit to the castle with a visit to Dover Museum & Bronze Age Boat Gallery to learn more about the fascinating history of this historic port town and view the remains of a large prehistoric boat thought to be 3,000 years old!

Why not also join a tour of Dover's Town Hall, the Maison Dieu, built in 1203 by Hubert de Burgh to provide temporary accommodation for travelling pilgrims on their way to the shrine of Thomas à Becket in Canterbury. If that wasn't enough to keep your senses occupied, Deal and Walmer Castle are within 7 miles of Dover. Visit http://www.dovermuseum.co.uk to find out more about Dover Museum. To find out how to join a tour of Dover Town Hall visit http://www.visitkent.co.uk/attractions/dover-town-hall-maison-dieu-/8436.

Postcode for Dover Castle: CT16 1HU.

St Augustine's (Austin's) Abbey, Kent

> ... on whych day, for all the storme that then was, she marched toward Caunterbury, and on Baram downe met her the Archbishop of Canterbury accompanied with the bishop of Ely, Saynt Asse, Saynt Dauyes & Douer, a great company of gentlemen well apparelled, so brought her to St Austens without Canterbury, where she lay that nyght.
>
> Edward Hall, chronicler

A Royal Reception on Barham Down

The 'incommodius' weather that blighted Anne's arrival in England continued to ravage the Kentish countryside as Henry's new bride doggedly pushed on toward

Greenwich. After leaving Dover behind, Anne's train travelled around 16 miles in a north-westerly direction toward the venerable city of Canterbury. As we hear above from the chronicler Edward Hall, she was to be lodged in the (by then dissolved) abbey of St Austin's, also known as St Augustine's.

On Barham Down, a point roughly halfway between Dover and Canterbury, Anne was met by Thomas Cranmer, archbishop of the aforesaid city, accompanied by the bishops of St Asse [possibly St Asaph], St David's and of Dover, along with a 'great company of gentlemen'. We can only imagine the scene: upon an exposed land whipped up with gusty winds and icy rain, the leading cleric of the land makes his obeisance to a young woman wrapped in furs but flinching against the hail that constantly pricks at her uncovered face. Outwardly, all ran smoothly. However, the fierce weather took its toll on those prepared to ride out and greet their new queen. Cranmer wrote to Thomas Cromwell on the day before the reception was due to take place, declaring,

> [He] has received, by his servant, Eaton, 50 'sufferans' from Cromwell, which he will present to Lady Anne tomorrow. If he can compass it, the town of Canterbury shall add 50 angels, and all to be presented in one cup. Asks him [Cromwell] to excuse the bearer, Mr. Pheneux, for his absence here. If he and other gentlemen had not assisted, would have received her with but a slender company. The whole number appointed to him, beside his own company was not six score, and some of them failed. Canterbury, 29 Dec. Signed.

Having presented Lady Anne with her cup of gold, the soggy train must have reformed and continued on its miserable journey toward the medieval city of Canterbury. With winter holding England in its chilly grip the days would have been short, and given the distance to be covered in horrendous conditions it is not surprising that we hear of Lady Anne being received by the mayor and citizen of Canterbury 'with torchlight and a good peel of guns'. It must have been pitch-black by the time Anne arrived at her lodgings.

The Medieval City of Canterbury and the Abbey of St Augustine

Even today, Canterbury retains an abundance of medieval charm and is a magnet for tourists and pilgrims alike. In this regard, little has changed over the centuries; the late eighteenth-century *Kentish Traveller's Companion*, first published in 1776, gives us a splendid account of the topography and appearance of the pre-industrialised, walled city that Anne would have seen on that stormy day in December 1539:

> The city is seated in a pleasant valley, about one mile wide, between hills of moderate height and easy ascent, with fine springs rising from them; beside which the river Stour runs through it, whose streams, often dividing and meeting again, water it the more plentisully [sic], and forming islands of various sizes, in

one of which the western part of the city stands, make the air good and the soil rich.

To the west of the city, directly outside Burgate and the city walls, stood the Abbey of St Augustine. After around nine hundred years of monastic presence, the abbey had been surrendered to the king's commissioners on 30 July 1538. Once in Crown possession, Henry VIII eventually set about transforming part of the monastic complex into a fine new palace. This conversion was specifically stated to have been undertaken 'against the coming of the Lady Anne of Cleves', the work being entrusted to James Needham, Surveyor of the King's Works. His accounts survive in the Bodleian Library, and therefore we can describe in some detail the lodgings which awaited Lady Anne upon her arrival.

Work began on 5 October 1539, just the day before the marriage treaty between Henry of England and Anne was signed. With just weeks to convert the old abbot's lodging to the so-called 'king's side', and build an entirely new queen's range, time was most definitely of the essence. Consequently, according to the fulsome account in Colvin's *History of the King's Works, Volume IV*, 'during November, he [Needham] had 350 craftsmen and labourers on the site, with the purchase of 31 dozen candles showing that work must have gone on after dark'.

The new queen's lodgings consisted of two ranges. The first range contained the principal privy chambers, which ran perpendicular to the king's in an east–west direction and were sited at first-floor level. Both these sides joined each other at the old abbot's chapel, positioned directly north of the defunct abbey church (which was demolished 1541–53). This would henceforth be known as the chapel royal. Adjacent to this chapel was a 'little chamber' that appears to have separated the king and queen's bedchambers. The second range contained the queen's public chambers (these being the outer great chamber and the great chamber). Running on a north–south axis, parallel to the king's side, this second range joined the main gatehouse in the north to the queen's privy apartments in the south. It formed the final wing of the new complex, all of which fronted on to the renamed 'palace courtyard'. In all, Anne's new lodgings included an outer great chamber, a great chamber, a watching chamber, a presence chamber (which probably doubled up as a dining chamber), privy chamber, bedchamber, closet and chapel. According to the *History of the King's Works*,

> the main building was a timber-framed structure 13 feet 6 inches high standing on brick basement walls ... apart from the basement walls, the principal features built in brick were five chimney stacks, some gable ends and two jakes. The fireplaces were provided with ... mantles of stone. The roofs were tiled ... .The buildings were finished inside and out by plasterers who lathed and ceiled the roofs [and] pargetted the internal partitions.

The account of the plasterers 'whitening the outside of the hall' on the king's side, along with painting the king's lodgings with yellow ochre and his privy lodgings with 'pencilled' red ochre, conjures up images of Whitehall Palace. This part-timber, part-brick building had been similarly decorated several years earlier in the height of Renaissance fashion.

Finally, Anne was to be honoured with the placement of her badges alongside the king's in the new windows glazed by the master glazier, Galyon Hone. At the same time, four representations of her arms were painted by John Hethe of London, 'one in the waiting chamber and ii [2] in her chamber of presence', the final one being executed in oil and set over the half-pace stair going up to the queen's lodging. Perhaps it was the first time that Anne had seen her badge so proudly displayed on English soil.

In a letter written to Lady Lisle, we hear how Anne entered her 'grett chamber' upon arrival at the abbey. Charles Brandon, Duke of Suffolk, and Sir Thomas Cheney go on to say in their joint missive, written to Cromwell from the abbey that very evening, that in that chamber 'were 40 or 50 gentlewomen [who waited] in velvet bonnets to see her, all which she took very joyously, and was so glad to see the King's subjects resorting so lovingly to her, that she forgot all the foul weather and was very merry at supper'.

The following day, Anne pressed on toward Rochester, stopping overnight in Sittingbourne, a Kentish town situated on the London to Dover road, famous for its inns. Some of these inns were formidable in size and had, for generations, hosted kings and princes on their way to and from the capital (see also the introduction to this section). Although the King's Palace at Canterbury survived into the eighteenth century, it changed hands a number of times before finally falling into ruin.

Visitor Information
A little like York, Canterbury is a complete destination for the time traveller in its own right. While our focus is trained on a relatively small area lying outside the city walls to the west of Canterbury Cathedral, the cathedral itself, its monastic ruins and charming medieval streets make for a perfect weekend getaway. (Perhaps also consider combining your visit with Leeds Castle; see the Leeds Castle entry in this book for further information.)

The ruins of St Augustine's and the King's Palace are well tended by English Heritage. There is a large visitor centre on-site which includes an exhibition of the abbey through the ages. We visited on a crisp January afternoon, when the sinking sun set the crumbling remains in sharp relief against a vibrant blue sky. Until the Dissolution in 1538, men had been worshipping on this site for nearly a thousand years following the consecration of St Augustine as the first Archbishop of Canterbury in 597.

Despite the almost total dereliction of the abbey for nearly five hundred years, a tangible spiritual presence remains. It is a joy to meander among the imprint of the ruins, stumbling across small plaques set into the ground; these mark the final resting places of generations of Saxon archbishops, including St Augustine himself. There are several benches placed here and there so that you may take your rest. If the English weather is kind to you, on a fine day the views across the ruins toward Canterbury Cathedral are stunning.

Make your way down into what remains of the cloister, heading over to the wall on the far side. Two wrought-iron gates set into the wall allow the visitor to peer through into what was once the palace courtyard. However, in the sixteenth century this view would have been impossible, for the king's lodgings ran from the wall of the nave, northwards toward the current library of King's School (which itself looks like a medieval hall), directly in front of where you are standing. Retrace your steps back into the ruins of the nave; you cannot miss the single largest segment of standing wall, built largely from medieval stone but incorporating tell-tale red Tudor bricks. This is the only surviving segment of the original King's Palace. Sadly, nothing more remains of the range built specifically for England's new queen.

To view the only other remains of the buildings that Anne would have seen, you must leave the abbey site, retracing your steps through the visitor centre and back out onto the street. Turn right and head along to the end of the road, and then turn right again onto Monastery Street until reaching the original, principal gatehouse to the King's Palace. We can be certain that when Anne was met by torchlight and brought to her lodgings at St Austin's, she would have passed underneath this gateway. The Fyndon Gate, as it is known today, was almost destroyed during a bombing raid in 1942. However, thankfully it was subsequently restored to its former glory, as was the adjacent thirteenth-century hall that was once used for receiving the abbey's guests.

Of course, there are numerous cafés, bars and restaurants to choose from in Canterbury. However, our particular favourite for eating is Pinocchio's on Castle Street – one of the best Italian restaurants we have ever had the pleasure to dine in. We are still dreaming about the garlic bread and tiramisu! During your visit to St Augustine's, toilets, a limited range of snacks and gifts are available from the visitor centre. A large car park is situated directly across the street from the abbey site on Longport. Information can be found at http://www.english-heritage.org.uk/daysout/properties/st-augustines-abbey. The telephone number for the visitor centre is +44 (0) 122 776 7345.

Postcode for St Augustine's Abbey: CT1 1PF.

St Andrew's Priory, Kent

On New Year's Eve the Duke of Norfolk with other knights and the barons of the exchequer received her grace on the heath, two miles beyond Rochester, and so brought her to the abbey of Rochester where she stayed that night and all New Years Day.

Eustace Chapuys, Imperial ambassador

A Fateful Meeting

No account of Anne of Cleves could leave out the pivotal moment which probably sealed the fate of her personal relationship with Henry before it had even started. For it was at Rochester, on New Year's Day 1540, that Anne would be 'ambushed' by a monarch rejuvenated, apparently impatient at the prospect of meeting his future bride. The encounter is well known and recorded in more than one contemporary source. Here, the Imperial ambassador, Eustace Chapuys, gives his second-hand account:

> And on New Year's Day, in the afternoon, the king's grace with five of his privy chamber, being disguised with mottled cloaks with hoods so that they should not be recognized, came secretly to Rochester, and so went up into the chamber where the said Lady Anne was looking out of a window to see the bull-baiting which was going on in the courtyard, and suddenly he embraced and kissed her, and showed here [*sic*] a token which the King had sent her for [a] New Year's gift, and she being abashed and not knowing who it was thanked him, and so he spoke with her. But she regarded him little, but always looked out the window ... and when the King saw that she took so little notice of his coming he went into another chamber and took off his cloak and came in again in a coat of purple velvet. And when the lords and knights saw his grace they did him reverence ... and then her grace humbled herself lowly to the king's majesty, and his grace saluted her again, and they talked together lovingly, and afterwards he took her by the hand and led her to another chamber where their graces amused themselves that night and on Friday until the afternoon.

A similar account is detailed in Charles Wriothesley's *A Chronicle of England During the Reigns of the Tudors, From A.D. 1485 to 1559*, although neither of these descriptions give any hint at the repulsion that Henry claimed he felt on meeting his new bride. Up until this point, praise for the Lady Anne's appearance and countenance had been fulsome from all sides, and Henry had expressed no qualms on seeing Holbein's earlier portrait of Anne. The adverse testimonies of this event seem mainly to be dated to June and July of 1540, when evidence to be used during the divorce proceedings was being gathered from eyewitnesses and courtiers close to the king. This included the by-then disgraced Thomas Cromwell, Earl of Essex. Languishing in the Tower at the king's mercy, Cromwell recorded his recollections of the king's first impressions of his bride-to-be:

> After that your Majesty heard that the lady Anne was arrived at Dover and that her journeys were appointed towardes Greenwich and that she should be at Rochester on New Year's eve. At night your Highness ... *** [perhaps a line lost] Grace repaired towards night to Greenwich, where I spake with your Grace and demanded of you how you liked the lady Anne. Your Grace, being somewhat heavy, as I took it, answered and said she was no such manner of woman as she had been declared to you, with many other things.

So what is the truth of the matter? In an excellent exposition detailed by Retha Warnicke in her book *The Marrying of Anne of Cleves*, the interwoven complexities of sixteenth-century royal etiquette, cultural difference, personal taste and political tensions are explored in detail. It is these issues that make getting to the bottom of what actually occurred during that fateful January afternoon difficult to fathom. It is certainly not within the scope of this book to repeat it here. For those who are interested in understanding more about the interplay of these forces, we encourage you to read the aforementioned account.

Instead, we will turn our attention back to the city that greeted Anne as she rode forth from Rainham Down in seasonally torrid weather, accompanied by the Duke of Norfolk, Lord Dacre of the South, Lord Mountjoy and other barons of the Exchequer.

The City of Rochester and the Priory of St Andrew

In the mid-sixteenth century, Rochester was a typical medieval walled city, situated adjacent to the banks of the River Medway. *The Kentish Traveller's Companion* of 1776 states that 'in point of antiquity, [Rochester] is inferior to few cities in England; as a see, she yields only to that of Canterbury'. At this point, the river is both deep and wide as it nears its estuary. William Smith, a Rouge Dragon Pursuivant with the Royal College of Arms, helpfully recorded his impressions of Rochester just forty years after Anne's brief visit, in 1588.

> Rochester ys [is] but a litle cittie, but very ancient, as may appeare by the walles thereof, which now in many places are gone to decay. Also the Castell [castle], which seemeth to be builded when the Tower of London was, and is lyke [like] ye [the] same building. The cheiffest Church is called St Andrewes. There is a very Fayer [fair] Bridge of stone, Founded by Sr Rob Knolles, knight, with a Chapell at ye est [east] end therof, which Bridge is builded upon pyles [piles], lyke as London Bridge is … The River of Medway passeth under the said Bridge … It is of such depth that all the Quenes Mattes shippes do ryde there, at a low water, all along the River from Rochester to Upnor Castell [castle].

Within the city walls, and adjacent to the great Norman castle, was the priory of St Andrew, historically home to the bishops of Rochester. Like any medieval monastic complex, the thriving community was centred about the cathedral. Within its extensive boundary walls were the usual arrangement of claustral buildings: the cloister, chapter house, frater, dorter, kitchens, infirmary, etc. Several medieval gateways led into the grounds, the principal of which was the Cemetery Gatehouse, which gave access from the high street through the lay cemetery, in front of the west doors of both St Nicolas's church and St Andrew's Cathedral, before reaching the Priory Gate, or Great Gatehouse. This latter structure gave entry into the outer court, or *curia*, of the monastery. Directly ahead of the visitor, across a courtyard that must have measured in the region of 150 square feet, was the Bishop's Palace, last regularly inhabited by Bishop John Fisher. He had been executed for treason in 1535. An inventory taken after Fisher's death lists his goods by room, and so we hear of the principal chambers in the house:

His owne bed chamber, the great study within the same chamber, the north studye, the South Galorye [gallery], the Chappell in the ende of the South Galory, the brode galary [broad gallery], the old galary, the lytle [little] study beside the Warderobe, the great Chappell within the same house, the little chamber nexte the same Chappell, the great chamber next the same, the olde dynyng chamber, the halle, the parlor, the chamber nexte the same, the Clerk of the Kytchyns [kitchens] chamber, William Smadle's Chamber, Master Wilson's chamber, the Brewhous, the Cooke's chamber, the keching [kitchen], the entre besides the keching.

This was clearly a substantial building, but we know that its fabric had been sorely neglected, such that by the mid-1520s, when Erasmus visited his great friend at the palace, it was a cold and uncomfortable habitation. In a later letter sent to Fisher, the former laments of the bishop's want of attention to his health by residing at this house in Rochester. The *Archeologica Cantiana* (Volume XII) precised the contents of this letter, in which Erasmus says,

[He] suspects that the Bishop's ill health is mainly attributable to the situation (*'ex loco'*) of his Palace; the sea is near, and the shore muddy; the Bishop's library – his 'paradise'! – is surrounded with glass windows (*'bibliothecam undique parietibus vitreis'*), which let in the air at every chink, and are very injurious to people of weak health. He adds that if he (Erasmus) were to stay in it three hours he should be sick. A boarded and wainscoted room would be much better than bricks and mortar (*'lateres et calx'*), which exhale a noxious vapour.

The exact layout of the Bishop's Palace is unknown. Perhaps all that can be said with certainty is that it ran along almost the entire south side of the curia. However, an etching by John Harris of the remains of the building in 1717 is described in St John Hope's *Cathedral Church and Monastery of St Andrew at Rochester*:

... the Bishop's Palace is shewn with a western wing, standing at right angles to the existing block, but not overlapping it, against the wall bounding the street. The same view apparently shews a similar wing on the east. From the enumeration of chambers in the inventory it is possible that they were arranged around three sides of a courtyard which faced north, with the bishop's garden behind.

Certainly there is nothing in this description that does not fit with the account of Anne meeting with Henry, how the king 'went up into the chamber where the said Lady Anne was looking out of a window to see the bull-baiting which was going on in the courtyard'.

The Bishop's Palace and the King's Palace
Yet we cannot close this story without saying that we cannot definitely state that this is where Anne actually lodged during her two days in Rochester. In our

reading, there seems to be confusion about exactly where the historic encounter between Henry of England and Anne of Cleves actually took place. When the priory – rather than the castle – is correctly identified as the location in question, most historians place Anne in the Bishop's Palace. However, detailed accounts of the history and layout of the priory reveal that there is another, sometimes cited, contender – the King's Palace. The 1887 edition of *Archeological Cantiana* (Volume XVII) states that 'it was in this King's Palace, doubtless, that King Henry VIII had his first interview with Lady Anne of Cleves'.

We know that prior to the Dissolution, rooms to the east of the cloister, near the infirmary, were used by royalty. So, the Close Roll for 1321 states that the then queen was 'in her chamber in the infirmary of the Priory of Rochester'. It seems that there were rooms reserved for the king and queen in existence at the priory for some time prior to the sixteenth century. Quite how extensive those lodgings were is difficult to tell, as is whether this collection of chambers was initially referred to as 'the King's Palace'. It is possible that only after the aggrandisement of these lodgings in 1541–42 did this term became common parlance.

The palace was designed to provide lodgings for the king and other notables travelling between London and Dover. *The History of the King's Works, Volume IV*, gives an excellent account of the monastic buildings requisitioned by Henry VIII for this purpose. However, to be clear, the priory was not dissolved until 20 March 1540, and the works to convert buildings centred on the cathedral's cloisters, only beginning in February 1541. Obviously, this post-dates Anne's arrival at Rochester. There is a chance that she was lodged in a suite of medieval rooms, in the priory complex, rather than in the Bishop's Palace. But we can rule out that she lodged in the King's Palace, as it was later known. It simply did not exist at the time.

Finally, we should note that Jane Seymour also visited Rochester with Henry VIII during the short summer progress of 1536. The location of the royal lodgings is not recorded in contemporary records. Presumably, these were the same ones that Anne of Cleves would make use of four years later. (Although we stress there is no documentary proof of this and it remains only a working hypothesis).

Visitor Information

Quite at odds with some of the neighbouring Medway towns, the very centre of Rochester at least has retained a good deal of its ancient charms. Certainly, if you approach the city from across the river you will still see the ruins of the tallest keep in Britain dominating the skyline, just as it did when it was constructed around nine hundred years ago.

Rather conveniently, there is a public car park just a stone's throw from the beginning of our trail – Cathedral Car Park (postcode ME1 1LX). From the car park, turn left and head up the hill to the high street. Directly ahead of you is Cemetery Gate, one of the original gatehouses leading into the abbey precinct. Pass underneath the gatehouse and walk directly forward along College Yard. In the past, this walkway led through the lay cemetery of the abbey; a wall once ran to your right, and soon you will pass the now deconsecrated St Nicolas's church on your left. In the sixteenth century, this place acted as the lay church for the local community. A short distance forward brings you to the main west doors of the cathedral. In 1539, Anne may well have paused at this spot, the church to her left and the Great Gate ahead of her. As we have heard, this led through to the curia of the priory. The gate and adjacent almonry are long gone. However, conjure it up once again in your mind's eye as you follow the path forward, passing beneath its ghostly shadow. Five hundred years ago you would now be standing in the inner courtyard of the priory. Directly ahead lies a small green, and behind that a wall and a building whose stonework hints at its medieval past. This building is all that remains of the Bishop of Rochester's lodgings. If you are in any doubt, a stone plaque fixed to the aforementioned wall reminds those who care to look that

> Here lived for thirty one years, John Fisher Bishop of Rochester, Chancellor of the University of Cambridge and cardinal, who lay down his life for his faith on Tower Hill, June 22, 1535.

If this is indeed the remains of Anne's lodgings in Rochester, then by deduction you are quite possibly standing in the courtyard where 'my Lady of Cleves' watched the bear being baited while Henry unsuccessfully vied for her attention. It is a strange feeling indeed to be in the place where a future Queen of England's fate was sealed before she had hardly even uttered a word.

Back over to your left, behind iron railings and adjacent to the south side of the church lies a pretty garden. Due to repairs being undertaken to the cathedral, it was closed when we visited and so we could not explore the sunken grassy area, once covered by the priory's cloister. However, even through the railings the remains of the eastern side of the claustral buildings can be clearly seen. The edifice you can see once formed part of the monk's dorter. Somewhere nearby, on the far side of the dorter, were the lodgings once used by medieval royalty – and possibly Anne – before the king's palace was built, post-1541. At the end of the path, directly in front of you, stands the Prior's Gate; at one time this was the rear entrance and exit to the priory precinct.

Of course, although not directly linked to Anne's visit, you will no doubt want to visit the cathedral church and adjacent castle. It is easy to spend two to three hours in the city at least, and probably more if the weather is fine. The nearby high street offers a bountiful supply of restaurants and cafés where you can take rest and refreshment. If you are looking for a cosy, dog-friendly café, try The Deaf Cat coffee bar (www.thedeafcat.com), also on the high street. Alternatively, on a fine day, the grassy moat surrounding the castle would be the perfect place to unfurl a blanket and enjoy your own packed lunch. You can easily rest a while and admire the eleventh-century facade of the cathedral opposite, or imagine the arched causeway that once spanned the moat, connecting the castle with its erstwhile medieval companion.

Postcode for Rochester Cathedral: ME1 1SX.

The Manor of Bletchingley, Surrey

> We have appointed you two houses, that at Richmond where you now lie, and the
> other at Bletchingley, not far from London that you may be near us and, as you
> desire, able to repair to Court to see us, as we shall repair to you.
>
> King Henry VIII in a letter to Anne of Cleves

The King's Entirely Beloved Sister

When Anne of Cleves discovered that it was the king's wish to have their marriage
of six months dissolved, there was little she could do but acquiesce. Anne feared
that if she resisted she might be mistreated and exiled like Henry's resolute
first queen, Katherine of Aragon. Even worse, perhaps she might face the same
brutality that cut short the glittering life of Anne Boleyn. Instead, on 11 July 1540,
Anne wrote to the king from her apartments at Richmond Palace:

> It may please your majesty to know that, though this case must needs be most
> hard and sorrowful unto me, for the great love which I bear to your most
> noble person, yet, having more regard to God and his trust than to any worldly
> affection, as it beseemed me, at the beginning, to submit me to such examination
> and determination of the said clergy, whom I have and do accept for judges
> competent in that behalf. So now being ascertained how the same clergy hath
> therein given their judgement and sentence, I knowledge myself hereby to accept
> and approve the same, wholly and entirely putting myself, for my state and
> condition, to your highness' goodness and pleasure; most humbly beseeching
> your Majesty that, though it be determined that the pretended matrimony
> between us is void and of none effect, whereby I neither can nor will repute
> myself your Grace's wife … yet it will please you to take me for one of your
> most humblest servants, and so to determine of me, as I may sometimes have the
> fruition of your most noble presence; which I shall esteem for a great benefit, so,
> my lords and others of your Majesty's council, now being with me, have put me
> in comfort thereof; and that your highness will take me for your sister; for the
> which I most humbly thank you accordingly.

In a final declaration of acceptance, Anne signed the letter, 'Your Majesty's most
humble sister and servant Anne dochtter the Cleyffys'. Henry, delighted to not
be faced with another drawn-out divorce settlement, responded the very next day
from Westminster:

> Right dear and right entirely beloved sister,
> By the relation of the lord Master, lord Privy Seal and others of our Council
> lately addressed unto you we perceive the continuance of your conformity, which
> before was reported, and by your letters is eftsoons testified. We take your wise
> and honourable proceedings therein in most thankful part, as it is done in respect
> of God and his trust, and, continuing your conformity, you shall find in us a

perfect friend, content to repute you as our dearest sister. We shall, within five or six days, when our Parliament ends, determine your state after such honourable sort as you shall have good cause to be content, we minding to endow you with £4000 of yearly revenue. We have appointed you two houses, that at Richmond where you now lie, and the other at Bletchingley, not far from London that you may be near us and, as you desire, able to repair to Court to see us, as we shall repair to you. When Parliament ends, we shall, in passing, see and speak with you, and you shall more largely see what a friend you and your friends have of us.

The king ended the letter by asking, or perhaps demanding, that Anne be 'quiet and merry' and signed it, 'Your loving brother and friend, H. R.' Henry indeed proved himself a generous 'brother' and magnanimous friend, making provisions for the former queen to be recognised as 'the king's sister', and granting her 'precedence over all ladies in England, after the queen and the king's children'. As stated in his letter, he also granted Anne a generous annual income, as well as Richmond and Bletchingley, described as having 'splendid houses and parks', and offered her hangings, plate, jewellery and furniture to soften the blow. While Anne was no longer Queen of England, the final grant of lands made to her in January 1541, on the condition that she remain in England and follow 'the laws of this realm', made her a very wealthy woman.

The Story of Three Executions

In the fifteenth century, the manor of Bletchingley was held by Henry Stafford, Duke of Buckingham, until his attainder and execution for treason in 1483, at which time it became Crown property. Thus it remained until Henry VII granted it to Buckingham's widow, Catherine Woodville, in 1485. Through her it passed to her eldest son, Edward Stafford, 3rd Duke of Buckingham – who entertained Queen Katherine of Aragon there in 1519 – until his attainder and execution for treason in 1521. At this time the house again reverted to the Crown. Henry VIII entertained Cardinal Wolsey there in November 1521 before granting it to Sir Nicholas Carew and his wife the following year. Uncannily, Carew met the same end as the two previous male owners of Bletchingley, attainted and beheaded for high treason in March 1539.

His widow, Elizabeth, petitioned the king through Cromwell to be permitted to keep Bletchingley, but her pleas fell on deaf ears. In 1540, Bletchingley was granted to Anne of Cleves, who lived there on and off until around 1547, when she somewhat reluctantly surrendered the property to Sir Thomas Cawarden, a gentleman of the privy chamber and a member of her household, as instructed by King Edward VI's council.

We find a touching testament to Anne's fondness of Bletchingley in her last will and testament, where, among other things, she declared that 'we will and bequeath to the poor of Richmond, Bletchingley, Hever and Dartford, 4 l. [pounds] to each parish'.

Bletchingley Place

All that remains today of the manor house at Bletchingley is a section of the principal gatehouse, now converted into a private residence called Place Farm. The highlight of the facade, according to Rod Wild, Data Secretary of the Domestic Buildings Research Group (Surrey), is 'a fine four-centred-arched entranceway, with five ribs of moulded bricks. This is now blocked up except for a Georgian-style door case. The rest of the frontage is a splendid patchwork of old bricks, pierced with windows in a similar Georgian style. An angular fragment of foundation, outside one of the end walls, hints that an earlier footprint may have had towers.'

Recent dendrochronology tests undertaken on the roof of the building concluded that it was likely built in 1547 or shortly thereafter, thus indicating that Cawarden made repairs to the original house that had been somewhat neglected under Anne's ownership. By examining a contemporary description, and a surviving sketch, of the house taken from a map of Pendell Manor made in 1622, it's possible to get a sense of the layout of the original residence.

In an account of Edward Stafford's lands taken after his execution in 1521, it's stated that 'the Manor House, within a mile of the town of Blechingligh, is properly and newly bilded, with many lodgings and offices. The hall, chapel, chambers, parlours, closets and oratories, be newly ceiled with wainscot roofs, floors and walls, to the intent they may be used at pleasure without hangings.'

While there is no record of when this house was built, its description as 'newly bilded' suggests that it was probably constructed in the early sixteenth century. Like so many grand houses of the time, it comprised two quadrangles, north and south, as shown in the aforementioned sketch, and was surrounded by parkland.

By 1403, there were two enclosed parks known as the North and South Parks, later also known as the Little and Great Parks, respectively. In 1540, Sir Thomas Cawarden was appointed keeper of the parks and master of the hunt of deer there.

The sketch of 1622, while not detailed, clearly shows that the main entrance was an arched gateway in the southern quadrangle. It also depicts a number of chimneys on the north range of the upper quadrangle, likely denoting the location of the principal apartments. This fits perfectly with what we know of the layout of Tudor double-courtyard houses; the outer or lower courtyard usually housed the administrative offices, while the upper or inner courtyard was home to the principal apartments.

When we piece together all the available information, what emerges is the image of a sprawling house, one luxurious enough to attract royalty and distinguished guests alike, and as we've seen, one worth fighting for.

The Holbein Mantelpiece

The house at Bletchingley was partially dismantled at some point before 1655, at which time John Evelyn records in his *Diary* on 21 June 1655, 'I went to Rygate to visit Mrs. Cary at my Lady Peterboro's in an ancient monastery well in repaire but the parke much defaced; the house is nobly furnish'd. The chimney-piece in the great chamber carved in wood was of Henry 8, and was taken from an house of his in Blechinglee.'

This splendid mantelpiece Evelyn speaks of is thought to have been designed by Holbein, and survives to this day at Reigate Priory. It stands as a beautifully carved reminder of the opulent interiors of Bletchingley's heyday. Unfortunately, the remainder of the house did not fare as well; in the seventeenth century it was all but demolished. The only building left standing was the gatehouse, to which a second storey was added in order to convert it into a comfortable farmhouse – the present-day Place Farm.

Visitor Information
Bletchingley is a small village lying just south of the busy London Orbital (M25). The main Bletchingley Road runs through its wide high street, connecting the pretty little village of Godstone in the east with the town of Reigate to the west. Arriving from Godstone (which you are likely to do if you drive via the M25), look out for the Bletchingley Arms on your right. Soon after this, there is tight turn on the right (Church Lane). Take this road and follow it for a little over a mile or more. It will take you past Bletchingley Golf Course until, about 100 metres before the road ends in a T-junction, you pass a driveway on your right. Keep your eyes peeled, for once you see the farmhouse at the top of the drive you will recognise it immediately – the strangest arrangement of a facade you are likely to see! The iconic Tudor-style archway that once led under the gatehouse is now bricked up, the later Georgian doorway inserted apparently randomly and off-centre, completely ruining the building's symmetry.

The road is narrow at this point, so parking is not easy. We pulled up a little after the driveway, leaving on our hazard lights as we peered at all that remains of this once great Tudor mansion from the bottom of the drive. Clearly, this is private property, so it is here you must stay. Sadly, upon the rising ground, not more than a mile or two north of the farmhouse, the constant drone of traffic makes it almost impossible to conjure up the once peaceful surroundings of Anne's life here at Bletchingley.

We did not stay long, but turned the car around and headed back the way we came to pause a while at the local church, St Mary the Virgin. Inside is the tomb of the man who managed to wrest Bletchingley away from Anne of Cleves: her steward, Sir Thomas Carwarden.

After concluding your visit to Bletchingley, it is an easy five to ten-minute drive on to Reigate Priory Museum in Reigate, where ordinarily one can view the fireplace reputedly designed by Holbein that once graced the interior of the Manor of Bletchingley. However, unfortunately, due to structural issues with the building the museum is closed until further notice. If you wish to get an update for yourself on the museum's website, go to http://reigatepriorymuseum.org.uk/.

Should you visit around lunchtime, there is a fine pub in the village of Bletchingley itself (the Bletchingley Arms, mentioned above) should it be convenient to stop for some refreshment: http://www.baronspubs.com/bletchingleyarms/. Finally, other locations within easy reach of Bletchingley are Hever Castle and the ruins of Otford Palace (see entries on Hever Castle and Otford Palace respectively).

Postcode for Place Farm: RH1 4QR.

The King's Manor House, Kent

[The King's Manor at Dartford] remained in the possession of the crown till King Edward VI. In his second year, in consideration of the surrender of lands in Surrey, granted to the lady Anne of Cleves, the repudiated wife of King Henry VIII, his manor of Dartford, with its appurtenances, belonging to the late priory; his park, called Washmeade in Dartford; the site of the late monastery or priory of Dartford, together with the houses, buildings, gardens and orchards belonging to it, with all waters, fisheries, wears, courts-leet, views of frank-pledge, liberties, warrens, &c. with other premises therein-mentioned ... to hold for her natural life, or so long as she should reside within the realm.

Edward Halstead, *A History and Topographical Survey of Kent*, 1797

Dartford: A Priory Dissolved and a Manor Born

On Friday 2 January 1540, Anne of Cleves arrived in Dartford. It was to be her final stop on the roughly 500-mile trip from her birthplace of Düsseldorf to her new home as queen consort in Greenwich. On this occasion, Anne's visit to Dartford was fleeting, a brief overnight stay before her official reception by the king and court on Blackheath the following morning.

At Dartford, we are dealing with not one but two locations. For in the space of a little over ten years, Anne herself would witness the transformative hand of time. The medieval priory that hosted her first visit would soon be torn down and in its place would rise up a new lodging, henceforth known as the King's Manor. Little could she have suspected back in January 1540 that Dartford would come to serve as her principal residence in the final years of her life. It would be a time when her hopes and dreams of a satisfying marriage and place as the premier lady of the land would lie in tatters; a time when she longed to see her homeland of Cleves and be reunited with the family of her childhood, no more to be a 'stranger in a foreign land'. Such notions must have been inconceivable as Henry's bride approached the east of Dartford, along the London–Dover road, on that cold day in January.

The town's position on the pre-eminent medieval thoroughfare to the Continent from the capital city was, in part, responsible for its prosperity. According to Dartford Town Archives,

Most towns in southern England at this time had an average population of 500–600 residents. Dartford, with its population approaching 1,000, was larger than average. [However,] by twenty-first-century standards, Medieval Dartford was more like a village than a town; the countryside penetrated almost into the town centre, where timber-framed properties occupied a long thin strip of land and often had gardens, orchards and vegetable plots adjoining.

However, it was the Dominican nunnery (also referred to as 'priory') founded by Edward III in 1349 for which Dartford was perhaps best known. The development of the town also owed much to its influence, and a number of young aristocratic ladies 'took the veil' at the priory, including Bridget, the youngest daughter of King Edward IV and Elizabeth Woodville. Bridget was buried in the priory church after her death in 1507.

The Priory at Dartford (1349–1541)

Although of some eminence, there are no contemporary records that provide us with an insight into the appearance and layout of the original medieval nunnery. However, during excavations undertaken in 1913, two main buildings were revealed. In his write-up of these works, entitled *The Priory of Dartford and the Manor House of King Henry VIII*, A. F. Clapham records,

> The first [building runs] E. and W. and the second at right angles to it and extending toward the N. Both were substantially built of rag-stone rubble, with square projecting buttresses, and whilst the first showed no evidence of having been included in Henry VIII's manor-house, the second had various Tudor additions, indicating that it had been incorporated in that building.

He surmises that the building orientated east–west was, as we might expect, the priory church, with its dimensions measuring 102 feet by 20.5 feet. The second he proposed to be the eastern alley of the cloister. Unfortunately, Dartford was the only Dominican nunnery in England, so there were no comparable monastic houses against which Clapham could test the theory of his proposed layout.

During her overnight stay in Dartford Priory, one imagines that Anne would have lodged in the highest-status rooms; no doubt these would once have belonged to the prioress. However, this is supposition on our part, based on the usual practice of an itinerant royal court. Sadly, there are no further clues to the nature of these lodgings at Dartford. Thus, we shall not dwell further upon the 1540 visit. Instead, we will turn to Anne's later encounter with Dartford some thirteen years on, when the manor house became her principal residence in the year 1553.

The King's Manor at Dartford

Following the surrender of the priory to the Crown as part of the Dissolution of the Monasteries in 1539, Henry set in motion plans for its demolition, which was 'spedely to be done'. In its place a manor house was to be constructed, henceforth to be known as 'the King's Manor at Dartford'. The royal abode was to be just one of a series of houses sited along the main London–Dover road. The intention was to utilise Dartford and other monastic properties, such as St Andrew's at Rochester and St Augustine's at Canterbury (see entries for St Andrew's Priory, Kent and St Augustine's Abbey, Kent) as convenient staging posts along the way. Once more, the Surveyor of the King's Works, James Needham, was placed in charge and once more detailed accounts (located at the Bodleian Library and the National Archives) furnish us with considerable information regarding the layout and appearance of the new manor. Sadly, no contemporary floor plans exist and there continues to be some debate about the exact layout and orientation of the manor.

The first book of accounts for the building of the King's Manor is headed, 'The Boke[book] of Dartford beginning from Sunday the 19th day of June in Anno 33 regni H. VIII (1541) and ending the 30th day of April in Anno 36 (1544) regni H. VIII prediciti.' Located on the western side of the town, The King's Manor was to retain the existing boundary wall of the priory, enclosing several acres of land. It is unclear exactly how much of the original priory was reused. Certainly much of it was dismantled and the materials recycled for the new works, including the 'breaking uppe of toumes [tombs] and tome stones in the church.' These tombstones would later be uncovered forming part of the palace drains during the twentieth century excavations described above. Presumably, one of the tombs dismantled included that of Princess Bridget of York.

However, it is clear that some parts of the original priory were incorporated into the new building, including the 'steples [steeple]' which became an office of the waiters of the queen's privy chamber. It also seems that the cloister was indeed retained. The *History of the King's Works, Volume IV*, states that the evidence for this was that the 'ironwork in the cloister was to be repainted at a later date'. However, Simon Thurley's *The Royal Palaces of Tudor England* goes further, saying that the royal lodgings were located 'around the monastic cloisters', indicating in his account that these chambers were approached directly from the great court (previously the cloister court) via the new, principal staircase. Thurley is one of the most recent architectural historians to write about the manor at Dartford. However, in our sources, he seems to be alone in explicitly suggesting that the central courtyard, known as the 'great court' in the building accounts, is in fact the original monastic cloister; an arrangement which mirrors that used in the new building work of the King's Palace at Rochester. Thus the suggestion is entirely credible. However, Dartford remains one of those locations where there still seems to be considerable debate and disagreement on the exact orientation of the buildings.

Like all the great, modern houses of the day, Henry's manor was arranged around two courtyards; at Dartford these are referred to in the building accounts as the 'great court' and the 'little court' respectively. The latter contained a number of service offices and seems to have been located to the west of the great court. The former comprised the principal royal apartments, other lodgings and service offices. The king and queen's 'sides' probably encompassed all of the northern range and at least part of the western, and possibly, eastern ranges. The apartments were situated at first-floor level, with subsidiary offices located below.

Exploring the Tudor Manor House
As a time traveller arriving at the King's Manor after the mid-1540s, you would approach the royal lodge from the east, passing beneath the eastern gatehouse

directly into the great court. According to A. F. Clapham's scale drawing from his 1913 paper, this measured some 180 feet by 150 feet. Dartford Manor, it seems, was no small building! Although the entire place appears to have been built largely of brick (two million of them according to the building accounts), ragstone, hardstone and free stone from the nearby dissolved Barking Abbey was also utilised. It also seems that some of the ranges facing into the courtyard were constructed of timber; large, glazed, timber-framed windows at first-floor level lit all the principal royal apartments. On the exterior walls, galleting with flint was applied for decorative purposes, and as with the king's new lodgings at St Augustine's in Canterbury, extensive external decoration with 'pencilling and okering' in red, black and white covered at least the southern and eastern ranges.

Raising your eyes, you would notice the pitched, tiled roofs of the king's side (which probably covered part of the northern and adjacent western range), one measuring 134 feet long and the other 110 feet. Extending across the eastern side of the northern range was (probably) the queen's side, covered by three separate roofs (one presumes covering three separate chambers), with respective dimensions of 110 feet by 30 feet, 92 feet by 30 feet and 70 feet by 30 feet. These measurements give us some idea of the dimensions of the royal lodgings, which, as might be expected, contained the usual chambers on each side. However, what marks out Dartford as being a house of its time is the absence of a great hall or a 'great kitchen', both normally expected to serve an entire household. Thus we see that this manor house was intended to serve only the king, queen and a select number of courtiers. This was typical of houses that Henry had built later on in his reign.

To enter the royal apartments, you would have used one of the best documented processional staircases of Tudor England. According to Colvin's *History of the King's Works*,

> as one mounted the stairs in the 'halpase' [antechamber or vestibule], leading to the royal apartments, one was confronted by freestone figures of a lion and a dragon set on pillars and holding weather vanes displaying the king's arms. They were gilded by John Heath of London, painter, who also gilded numerous vanes which turned in the wind on roofs and battlements.

At the head of the stair, the 'halpas' led off in different directions, to the left and right; in one direction lay the king's great chamber, in the other the queen's. It is here that visitors patiently awaited their audience with their royal masters. Finally, for pleasure, there were extensive gardens and orchards adjoining the property, accessed by way of separate, privy vice-stairs from both the king's and queen's sides.

Anne's Changing Fortunes

The King's Manor at Dartford was clearly far from the palace that Anne must have become accustomed to at Richmond, her principal home after her divorce from Henry. Yet it was obviously a sizable property (over a hundred rooms), constructed in the height of English Renaissance fashion, and so befitted well her status. After all the drama of her disastrous marriage to Henry, having been supplanted as queen before seeing herself sidelined during the reign of her stepson, Edward VI, Anne initially arrived in Dartford once more as a prominent persona at court. Mary Tudor had ascended the throne and Anne was much in favour with her erstwhile friend, making (as it would turn out) her final public appearance at Mary's coronation on 1 October 1553. At some point during this same year, Anne moved to Dartford, where she would spend all but the last few weeks of her life.

Anne of Cleves, Chatelaine of the King's Manor at Dartford

Although the King's Manor at Dartford had been granted to Anne for life by Edward VI in 1548, she did not finally take up residence there until 1553; this followed the forced surrender of her manor house at Bletchingley in Surrey. By then, of course, the work at Dartford was complete. By the same account, a good deal of water had passed under the bridge for Anne, who like all of Henry's wives had had to contend with a considerable amount of adversity and danger since arriving in England. Yet in some ways, while Henry had lived, he had been her protector, sheltering her from the harsh financial realities of the inflation which was rampant in England at the time. With Henry gone, this state of affairs did much to undermine Anne's intrinsic wealth, and, unable to maintain her principal residence at Richmond Palace, the Privy Council had forced her to surrender it back to the Crown in 1548. A separate dispute had also resulted in the loss of Bletchingley, another of Anne's favourite residences, a year earlier; it was just months after Edward ascended the throne.

Traditionally, it is believed that Anne lived at Dartford between 1553 and 1557. However, we have found it difficult to find much evidence of her time there. The only verifiable reference to Anne at the manor comes in *The Loseley Papers*, in which it is stated that 'all which premises were provided for by the seide Sir Thomas Carwerdan, at her Grace's request before her officers at her howse at Dartforth'.

The time that Anne spent at the King's Manor certainly proved to be eventful. Within a year of Anne's triumphant appearance at Mary's coronation, she would fall out of favour with the queen for her friendly association with the Princess Elizabeth. This followed the tenuous implication of Elizabeth's involvement in the Wyatt Rebellion in early 1554. Indeed, those first few months of 1554 must have been trying, for on 14 March Anne's brother William, Duke of Cleves, wrote to inform Mary that his councillor, Dr Herman Cruser was returning to England 'to convey to Lady Anne the melancholy intelligence of the death of their sister Sybil, Duchess of Saxony'. It is likely that such news was conveyed to Anne at Dartford.

During the course of our research, we also came across references in current literature to Anne hosting visits from the princesses Mary and Elizabeth at Dartford. However, we could not find any contemporary sources to verify this story. Rusticated from court for the remainder of Mary's reign, geographically isolated, homesick and approaching the end of her life, one is left with the impression that Anne's time at Dartford was not particularly happy. In April 1557, already unwell with the illness that would carry her to the grave, Anne left the King's Manor behind and moved to Chelsea (see also the entry Chelsea Manor). Here she would die on 16 July of the same year.

Visitor Information

It is always thrilling to visit any Tudor survivor, even if what remains is a mere fragment of the original building. However, that said, on more than one occasion we have arrived at a location only to be confronted by a treasured Tudor jewel engulfed by scruffy suburbia. Sadly, Dartford is one such location. Clinging on for dear life remains just one of the principal gateways that once led into, and out of, the manor complex, along with its adjacent Keeper's Hall and lodgings. Today the building contains offices, the ground floor being used by the local council for civil marriages.

On a normal day you can only visit the outside of the building, while inside the main doors there are some information boards that tell of the manor's illustrious past. Since the building is now situated adjacent to a large shopping complex, parking is easy. Head for the Prospect Place Retail Park (Postcode: DA1 1DY). Once parked, take a look around and you will see a red-brick building with tiled roofs on the edge of the car park. It is the only building in sight that looks to have any age or character. Make your way round to the front, where there is a small but well-tended garden. You can wander around outside, and dip inside to read the information boards – although you will already have much more information at your fingertips with this book in your hands! Outside, along Priory Road, you will see the white stone of the original wall that enclosed first the priory, then the manor complex. Some way along it, a crumbling Tudor arch sits over a gateway that is sorely neglected. The town itself is run-down and has little to commend itself to the time traveller, so you may find your trip fleeting, perhaps combining it with some of your other Kentish *In the Footsteps* locations.

You can find a little more information on open days, where we understand guided tours of the Manor Gatehouse are given; contact details and location here: http://www.akentishceremony.com/kcc-register-offices/the-manor-gatehouse.

Postcode: DA1 2BJ.

Part Six
Catherine Howard

'NON AUTRE VOLONTE QUE LA SIENNE'
'No other will but his'

Introduction

Wrapped against the chill of the February morning, Catherine made her way past the sombre crowd of men that had gathered at the Tower of London, by invitation of the king, to watch her final moments on earth. She climbed the few steps to the straw-strewn scaffold, perhaps still stained with the blood of her cousin Anne Boleyn, who'd been beheaded on its wooden platform less than six years earlier. With the help of her four female attendants, Catherine calmly prepared for her end. As custom dictated, she paid the executioner and forgave him for what he was about to do, before briefly addressing the hushed onlookers. The former queen played her part perfectly, acknowledging her faults and the just punishment she'd received, reaffirming her belief in Christ and asking all present to pray for her and for the king. She then knelt in prayer, before being blindfolded, and was beheaded with a single blow of the axe.

Otwell Johnson witnessed Catherine's execution, and shortly afterwards wrote a letter to his brother about what had transpired. In it he noted Catherine's 'steadfast countenance' and 'wonderful patience and constancy' on the scaffold. Contrary to popular belief, there were no hysterics and professions of love for Thomas Culpeper, no recriminations and no protestations of innocence. This young woman, who was probably no older than about twenty-one at the time, faced her brutal end with dignity and courage. A few months after being stripped of her title as queen, Catherine put on her most regal performance.

The Early Years
Very little is known about the early life of Catherine Howard; her date of birth is open to speculation, with some historians favouring a date around 1521 and others around 1525. What is certain is that she was one of a number of children born to Jocasta Culpeper (also known as Joyce) and Lord Edmund Howard, who was a younger brother of the irascible Thomas Howard, 3rd Duke of Norfolk.

Her paternal aunt Elizabeth was Anne Boleyn's mother. When it comes to where Catherine was born, the evidence is again scanty and contradictory, with some suggesting the Howard home at Lambeth, and others Oxenheath in Kent, the home of Catherine's maternal uncle.

In the first decade of Catherine's life, her mother, Jocasta, died and so young Catherine was sent to live with her step-grandmother, the Dowager Duchess of Norfolk, who divided her time between her residences at Horsham and Lambeth. Virtually nothing is known of Catherine's life in the dowager's household, with the exception of a number of lurid tales extracted during the interrogations that took place in the late autumn and early winter of 1541/2, at which time it was revealed that while in the care of the dowager, Catherine became romantically involved with Henry Manox and Francis Dereham; it appears the latter replaced the former in Catherine's affections.

Regardless, the lovers were soon parted, because some time in the autumn of 1539, Catherine's influential uncle, Thomas Howard, found his niece a position in the household of Anne of Cleves, soon to be Henry's fourth wife and Queen of England. Not long after, the vivacious Howard girl caught the eye of the ageing and disillusioned king.

Catherine the Queen
Henry VIII's marriage to Anne of Cleves lasted only six months. On 9 July 1540 the marriage was annulled, and less than three weeks later, on 28 July 1540, a forty-nine-year-old Henry married Catherine Howard at Oatlands Palace in Surrey. On the very same day, Thomas Cromwell was executed on Tower Hill for advocating the king's disastrous marriage to the German princess. For the first few months of Henry and Catherine's married life the king enjoyed a renewed sense of vigour, besotted with his young bride. Catherine spent her one and only Christmas and New Year as queen at Hampton Court Palace, where Henry showered her with lavish gifts, including 'a Jesus of gold containing 32 diamonds having three pearls hanging at the same', 'a purse of gold enamelled red, containing 8 diamonds set in goldsmith's work, with also hinges and button of wire gold' and a 'carcane for the neck [necklace], of goldsmith's work, wherein is set in gold 6 very fair table diamonds, and 5 very fair rubies, and betwixt every of the same stones is two fair pearls'.

With the exception of Norfolk House and Syon Abbey (now Syon House), where Catherine was confined for almost three months following the discovery of her premarital affairs and her private meetings with Thomas Culpeper, this section of the book focuses on locations that Catherine would have known as queen. After Norfolk House we journey to Oatlands Palace, the aforementioned site of Catherine's nuptials. From there, we join Henry and Catherine on their progress north.

The Progress of 1541
In April 1541, it was confirmed that the king and his young wife Catherine Howard would make a royal progress to the north of England in the hope of

meeting Henry's nephew, James V of Scotland. The aim was to reassert the king's authority in the parts of his realm that had recently been torn by rebellion, hence the thousand-strong armed contingent that accompanied the progress. This was to be one of the longest and most magnificent progresses of Henry VIII's reign, with the king intent on overawing subjects who had never seen him in person. Up until this point, Henry had not ventured further north than Boston. Apart from the escort of soldiers, more than 4,000 horses were used as mounts and transport for the king's finest tapestries, plate and his and Catherine's most sumptuous clothing. Around 500 members of Henry and Catherine's household accompanied the royal couple on their journey north, including Jane Boleyn, Viscountess Rochford, the queen's chief gentlewoman, and Thomas Culpeper, a gentleman of the Privy Chamber whom it appears Catherine had begun seeing privately before the progress commenced. Because many of the places where they would be staying along the way were too small to house the entire royal escort, 200 tents were taken along as well.

They departed Westminster on the last day of June. However, the weather was so horrendous that by mid-July the vast entourage had only reached Grafton. According to a letter written on 18 July, by the French ambassador Marillac, who accompanied the king on his progress, along the way Queen Catherine fell ill:

> Reckoned that this King, who left London on the 30th June, would be, by this time, about Lincoln; but the rains have since been so great and incessant, and the weather so unseasonably cold and stormy, that, besides damage to the crops and increase of contagious diseases, the roads leading to the North, which is all marshy country, have been flooded and the carts and baggage could not proceed without great difficulty, so that the said King is as yet only a short journey from this town. Owing to some indisposition of the Queen and the weather not being yet settled, some say the journey is in terms of being broken, and that if it goes forward it will be on account of the great preparations made by the dukes of Suffolk and Norfolk, who have gone before; at all events they will not go far before the end of this month, and the Court will not be at Lincoln till the 10th or 12th of next month.

Marillac's estimation was not far off; after a short stay at Grimsthorpe, the home of the Duke of Suffolk, Henry and Catherine reached Lincoln on 9 August, where they were magnificently received. The royal couple were at Gainsborough Old Hall on the evening of the 12 August and at Pontefract on 24 August. They overnighted at Cawood, the palace of the Archbishop of York, on 4 September before reaching York on 16 September, the official entry not taking place until 18 September. Writing to Francis I from York on 16 September, Marillac confirmed that the king was waiting 10–15 miles outside of the city walls 'for this town to be ready to receive him'.

The court remained in York until 27 September, where the king was graciously received. Those who had been less than loyal to the Crown during the uprising known as the Pilgrimage of Grace, prostrated themselves and begged the king's forgiveness in a carefully choreographed submission, the sincerity of which is open for speculation. The king's nephew James V, though, failed to show up, greatly wounding Henry's pride.

This affront did not mark the end of Henry's troubles. On 25 October the court was at Chenies Manor in Buckinghamshire, and the following day it was at Windsor Castle. By late October, we find Catherine and Henry at Hampton Court Palace, where just a few days later Henry learned of his wife's premarital sexual relations and, not long after, of her private meetings with her alleged lover Thomas Culpeper at Lincoln, Hatfield (in Yorkshire), Pontefract and York.

By 22 November 1541, details of Catherine's relationships with Manox and Dereham, and her late-night trysts with Culpeper, were in the open, and Marillac reported that a 'proclamation was made at Hampton Court that she had forfeited her honour, and should be proceeded against by law, and was henceforth to be named no longer queen, but only Katharine Howard'. The former queen's friends and Howard relatives quickly dissociated themselves from her and, while many of them were interrogated and imprisoned for a time, only Catherine, Lady Rochford, Francis Dereham and Thomas Culpeper bore the full brunt of the king's wrath, paying for their actions with their lives.

We close this chapter of the book at Syon Abbey with a heavy heart, for it's there that Catherine spent the last few months of her life, ricocheting between acceptance of her fate and utter despair, before making her final journey to the Tower of London. She no doubt prayed for the king's mercy, but he would never forgive her, because, in the words of Lacey Baldwin Smith, 'she had taken from him the image of his youth'.

Norfolk House, London

That Katharine queen of England, formerly called Kath. Howard, one of the daughters of lord Edmund Howard, before her marriage with the King, led an unlawful, carnal, voluptuous, and licentious life with divers persons, in the house of Agnes duchess of Norfolk, at Lambeth, Surr. [where she was brought up], especially with Francis Derham, of Lambeth, and Henry Manak, of Streteham ...
Letters and Papers of Henry VIII, December 1541

Almost nothing is known about the early life of Catherine Howard, daughter of Lord Edmund Howard and Jocasta Culpeper. Her date of birth and birthplace are up for debate, as are the details of her childhood. The tales of sexual promiscuity preserved in relation to Catherine's trial shed some light on her upbringing. However, it should be remembered that those colourful stories were extracted during interrogations that took place in the late autumn and early winter of 1541/2, years after the events had allegedly taken place. Furthermore, the terrified witnesses were all desperately trying to absolve themselves of any wrongdoing and only too eager to tell lurid tales of the young queen.

What is certain, though, is that before her marriage to the king, Catherine spent years in the care of her step-grandmother, Agnes Tilney, Dowager Duchess of Norfolk (second wife of Thomas Howard, 2nd Duke of Norfolk, who died in 1524), during which time Catherine became romantically involved with Henry Manox and Francis Dereham. She was probably in her early teens when these relationships began, leading some modern historians to label the events as child abuse and the men involved child abusers. While we won't be exploring this idea further here, we acknowledge that, while it is shocking to our modern sensibilities, the boundaries were not as clear in Tudor times, when the legal age of marriage for a girl was twelve and a boy fourteen.

Catherine's relationships with Manox and Dereham played out at the Dowager's estates at Horsham and her London residence in Lambeth, Norfolk House (not to be confused with the nearby Lambeth Palace, the London residence of the Archbishop of Canterbury).

The Allegations

The stories that emerged from late October 1541 told of late-night trysts and unbridled lust. By Manox's own admission, he had joined the duchess's household in 1536 – the same year that Catherine's cousin Queen Anne Boleyn was beheaded at the Tower. He was employed to teach Catherine how to play the virginal and the lute, but before long found himself in love with his young pupil, and she with him. On one occasion, Duchess Agnes found the couple alone together and gave Catherine 'two or three blows' and 'charged them never to be alone' again. Clearly this did not perturb the two, who continued to meet in secret and used a maid to carry love tokens back and forth. It was even rumoured that the two had become engaged.

One Mary Lascelles testified to having remonstrated with Manox over his arrogance at aspiring to marry a Howard lady, and warned him of the trouble that would come his way if the duchess found out about the affair. Catherine eventually made it very clear that she would not marry her music teacher; she was, after all, the niece of a duke. The affair appears to have ended soon after, but not before the couple were seen walking alone in the duchess's orchard at Norfolk House. Whether the relationship was ever consummated is unclear, for Manox swore 'upon his damnation' that he 'never knew her carnally', a fact that in the end may have saved his life.

By all accounts, Manox was soon replaced in Catherine's affections by one Francis Dereham. The jilted and jealous musician testified to all-night 'banquets' taking place in the maidens' chamber at Norfolk House, corroborated by the testimony of one of the duchess's former employees, who told of how Catherine would steal the keys to the girls' chamber from the duchess's bedchamber once she'd fallen asleep, presumably to let Dereham in. A servant of the duchess testified to having seen, on three separate occasions, Dereham lying in Catherine's bed 'suspiciously in his doublet and hose'. However, Francis was not the only young man frequenting the girls' dormitory; his cousin Edward Waldgrave is also mentioned. If there were others, their names have not been preserved.

Under interrogation, Manox confessed to having written a letter to the dowager, revealing the goings-on in the maidens' chamber and of the dishonour being brought to her house. However, it appears that the warning was dismissed as of no great importance, even though on one occasion an outraged duchess stumbled upon Catherine and Dereham herself, embracing and kissing. She is reported to have given Dereham 'a blow, and also beat the Queen [Catherine] and gave Joan Bowmar [Bulmer] a blow because she was present'. That the duchess knew something of what was going on under her roof appears obvious. What is less certain is whether or not she was aware that Catherine and Dereham had consummated their relationship, and had even taken to calling each other husband and wife.

It was later alleged that after discovering that Catherine and Dereham had been apprehended, the dowager opened one of Dereham's coffers that had been left in her keeping at Lambeth, reading and destroying a number of documents that she found there. A foolish act on the dowager's part and one that the Crown would pounce on, for why would the duchess destroy any papers unless she thought that the writings contained words of treason? By concealing them, she had become an accessory to treason, and if charged and found guilty, would face the grisly consequences.

The young couple paid the ultimate price for their youthful romance, and while the dowager escaped the charge of treason, she was severely punished for her involvement, enduring a month of exhausting interrogations before being found guilty of misprision of treason (knowing of a treason and not divulging it to the proper authorities) along with other members of the Howard clan, including her son Lord William. Her goods and possessions were forfeit to the Crown, including her beloved Norfolk House. This was followed by almost five months of imprisonment in the Tower of London – a harrowing ordeal for any person, but especially one in their mid-sixties!

The Sixteenth-Century House

The Tudor mansion where Catherine entertained her paramours once stood amid extensive gardens and orchards across the river from Westminster Palace, and opposite the archiepiscopal residence of Thomas Cranmer. It was constructed in around 1514, around the time when the fortunes and power of the Howard family were rising. In 1513, Thomas Howard, Catherine's grandfather, and his eldest son led King Henry VIII's army to victory over the Scots at Flodden Field. The following year, the title of Duke of Norfolk was bestowed on Thomas. His eldest son and namesake succeeded him as 3rd Duke of Norfolk in 1524, around the time of Catherine's birth.

Nothing remains of Norfolk House, and, surprisingly for a residence that belonged to one of the most prominent families of the Tudor reign, very little is known of its appearance and layout. There are no known images of the house dating from the sixteenth century. While the buildings that formed part of the Duke of Norfolk's London residence appear in the background of Wenceslaus

Hollar's etching of Lambeth Palace, and in the foreground of his *Prospect of London and Westminster taken from Lambeth* (both made around 1647), the perspectives and artistic licence used makes it difficult to make any firm conclusions about its appearance.

However, we can glean something of the look of the buildings from archaeological reports based on excavations of the site made in the late 1980s and early 1990s. Surviving documentary evidence points to a large courtyard house, built along the street frontage, with an orchard to the south. The northern wall facing onto the street had diaper patterning, typical of brick houses of the period, with the main entrance through a timber-built porch. Further details appear in documents pertaining to its sale in 1608. These were reproduced in a survey of London published in 1951:

> From the details contained in this sale some idea can be gained of the size of Norfolk House and the disposition of the buildings. There was a great gate from 'the King's highway leading from Lambeth Town to St. George's Fields' [i.e. Lambeth Road] leading into a paved yard. On the west was the Duke's chapel which, by 1590, had been partitioned to make a hall, buttery and parlour, and a number of small rooms; on the east were the kitchen offices with 'a greate chamber' on the first floor, a gallery, oratory and several closets and the hall opening on to the garden on the south. The total width of the garden was 125 feet, and it is a reasonable assumption that the street frontage was approximately the same.

Author and historian Marilyn Roberts, who has carried out extensive research on the history of Norfolk House, believes that the house may have resembled the still-extant Gainsborough Old Hall in Lincolnshire, where Katherine Parr lived after her marriage to Sir Edward Borough.

Towards the end of the sixteenth century the property was divided into three, with further divisions taking place in the seventeenth century. The buildings suffered as a result of multiple occupancy and the numerous divisions that had taken place over the years. By the mid-eighteenth century Norfolk House had been largely demolished. The gardens and orchards that once surrounded the grand house, where Catherine strolled with her lover arm in arm, were reduced to nothing more than wasteland.

Visiting the Site Today

Norfolk House once stood on what is now Lambeth Road, roughly where the Novotel London Waterloo Hotel stands today. If you wish to visit all that remains of the gardens of the once palatial home of the dukes of Norfolk, head to Lambeth Road, which runs in front of Lambeth Palace and St Mary's church. Opposite one of the two entrances to St Mary's church, across the road, lies Lambeth High Street. Turn onto this road and you will see the gated entrance to Old Paradise Gardens ahead of you. We visited on a sunny June day, when plenty of locals were out exercising their dogs or simply sitting and watching the world go by. However, other than the rather peculiar arrangement of old tombs and tombstones around the perimeter walls, this modest garden speaks little of 'paradise' – or its illustrious connections to the past. Around it high-rise hotels loom over the green space, and we found it nigh impossible to reconnect with the fine pleasure gardens that once graced this part of Lambeth.

While in the area, we recommend a visit to the Garden Museum, housed in the medieval and Victorian church of St Mary, where several members of the Howard family were laid to rest in the floor beneath the Howard chapel (now the museum's café), including Catherine's step-grandmother Agnes Tilney and her aunt Elizabeth Boleyn, mother of George, Anne and Mary Boleyn.

It's also possible to arrange a guided tour of Lambeth Palace, the historic London residence of the archbishops of Canterbury.

To book a guided tour of Lambeth Palace visit http://www.archbishopofcanterbury.org/pages/about-lambeth-palace.html.

Postcode for the Novotel London Waterloo Hotel: SE1 7LS.

Oatlands Palace, Surrey

After the marriage, the said Katharine [Howard] and Francis [Dereham] confessed, alleging in excuse a secret contract of marriage between them; which evil life and contract they did, 31 May 32 Hen. VIII., and at other times, traitorously conceal from the king, until the said Katharine (the king believing her to be chaste and free from other matrimonial yoke), at Otelands, 28 July 32 Hen. VIII., arrogantly contracted and coupled herself in marriage with the king.

From an account of the trial of Lord William Howard 'and others' for misprision of treason, 22 December 1541

Unusually, the evidence for Catherine Howard's presence at Oatlands Palace (often referred to in contemporary texts as 'Otelands') does not come from the usual flurry of letters that one might expect, dating to the summer of her marriage to Henry VIII. Instead, the true date and location of this most understated of affairs appears only as a passing mention, recorded during the trial of Lord William Howard, Catherine's uncle, on 22 December 1541, some seventeen months after the event. If not for the existence of this document, we would undoubtedly believe instead that the ceremony took place at the beginning of August 1540 at Hampton Court, as stated in the near-contemporary chronicles of Edward Hall and Thomas Wriothesley. The former declares that 'the eight day of August, was the Lady Katheryn Haward, niece to the duke of Norfolk and daughter to the lord Edmond Haward, shewed openly as Quene at Hampton Curt'. Note that Hall does not actually mention the wedding itself, which is inferred (correctly) to have occurred at some earlier point. However, Wriothesley states, 'This yeare the eight daie of Awgust, being Sondaie, the King was maried to Katherin Hawarde, daughter of the late Edmond, deceased, and brother to the Duke of Norfolke, at his mannor of Hampton Court, and that daie she dined in her great chamber under the cloath of estate, and was there proclaymed Queene of Englande.'

This date of 8 August, when Catherine first appeared as Henry's queen, has led to contradictions regarding the date and place of Catherine's nuptials, as seen in accounts penned by later historians. However, as the trial documents are truly contemporary, we believe we must take this as our primary evidence.

The reason for such discretion over the king's fifth marriage is graven in letters plain elsewhere in the *Letters and Papers of Henry VIII*. During the summer of 1540, the delicate matter of the day was the annulment of Henry VIII's marriage to Anne of Cleves. Henry had to tread carefully, ensuring no offence was taken by Anne's brother, Wilhelm, Duke of Cleves, having seen his sister cast aside after just over six months of marriage. State papers are painstaking in recording 'the Lady of Cleves' complicity in the proceedings and her gracious acceptance to become the 'king's sister', not to mention a wealthy *femme sole* to boot. At the same time, all that the French ambassador was able to report on the matter to his master, King Francis I, on 21 July 1540 was that 'it is commonly said that this King will marry a lady of great beauty, daughter of Norfolk's deceased brother', and in a separate letter of the same date that

> [He/Marillac] must not omit that the cause of this sudden settlement of so important an affair [the annulment of Henry's marriage to Anne of Cleves] is said to be that this King has already consummated marriage with this last lady, relative of the duke of Norfolk, and it is feared she is already enceinte. Cannot affirm this otherwise; for these are things which are kept secret.

Clearly, even Marillac himself knew that he was being kept well and truly in the dark. However, he was not alone. In a rather gossip-laden letter, written only after Catherine and Henry's marriage was made publicly known, the French ambassador retrospectively explains what little he knew of the events unfolding behind closed doors. He reports that while at Hampton Court, the king had left to go 'to the chase' with a small hunting party and that 'most of the lords [had] retired to their houses'. Our supposition must be that almost as soon as the annulment of Henry's marriage to Anne of Cleves was granted, the king dismissed the wider court and took off to nearby Oatlands, with only a small and trusted circle. Here the young Catherine Howard was married to the King of England on 28 July 1540.

Oatlands – the Queen's Palace

By the mid-1530s, the principal country seat of the English monarchy had moved westwards from Greenwich to Hampton Court. According to Simon Thurley's contribution in Poulton's *Excavations at Oatlands Palace*, the acquisition of Oatlands in 1537 from the wealthy Reed family was 'part of a project masterminded by Thomas Cromwell, to provide the new palace [Hampton Court] with the ancillary lands and subsidiary houses necessary for its status'.

At its peak, the Honour of Hampton Court consisted of a huge area covering 40,000 acres. This included the palaces of Oatlands and, later, Nonsuch. The transformation of Oatlands was closely linked with the development of Henry's principal out-of-town residence; the same master craftsmen oversaw its remodelling, and a road was built directly between the two in the summer of 1537. It has been proposed by Thurley that the intention was that Hampton Court would be assigned as the king's residence, Oatlands the queen's and Nonsuch reserved for the use of Edward, Prince of Wales. Thus, the hypothesis is that the manor of Oatlands was originally intended as a palace for Anne of Cleves. In the inventory of the king's goods at Oatlands, made upon his death in 1547, a handful of notable items are listed which relate to Henry's consorts. One identifies a sheet with the initial 'K', whereas two significant items were undoubtedly made for Anne of Cleves. The first is a bed, identified as 'Quene Anne's bedd':

> … having Ceeler Tester vj vallaunces [valances] and thre[e] bases of Crymsen Clothe of goulde [gold] with works paned with white clothe of Siluer [with] works richely embrawdered [embroidered] with borders of purple vellat [velvet] upon the semes [seams] and with C and Viij badges of the kings and Quene Annes with Crownes ouer the badges and two grete / Armes of the kings and queen Annes joined together in a garlonde [garland] with a crowne imperyall [imperial] …

The second is a carpet 'wrought with the kings Armes in the Myddes and Roses and Quene Annes Cognisaunce [emblem]'. Whether Anne was able to enjoy these luxuries we do not know, as sadly there is no evidence that she spent any time at the palace during her short tenure as queen.

A Manor House Transformed

The Tudor manor house that Henry acquired in 1537 seems to have been a fine property indeed. The Reeds were wealthy London merchants whose city residence was renowned as being the finest in London: Crosby Place (a former residence of Richard III, whose great hall still survives in Chelsea to this day). Their country home can surely have been no different. According to Thurley, the relatively modest amount of money (£17,000) required to remodel the house in order to accommodate a reduced royal riding court implies its pre-existing grandeur. Thankfully, a handful of drawings of the Tudor palace survive from before its demolition in 1650. These, combined with extensive excavation of the site in the twentieth century, provide a fairly comprehensive picture of the palace that welcomed Catherine as queen during that heady summer of 1540.

The building of the palace was phased over six to seven years (1538–44/5) and it is uncertain exactly how much of the work had been completed by the time Catherine first laid eyes on this jewel in Henry's crown. However, it is clear that the entire privy apartment complex surrounding the inner courtyard, the inner gatehouse and part of the middle court (possibly including the outer gatehouse) would have already been standing. As the royal party approached along the road from Hampton Court during that exceptionally hot summer, surely Catherine must have marvelled at the tall, timber-framed Prospect Tower. It was the most unusual and outstanding feature of the palace. With its jettied upper storey and mullioned and transomed windows, the tower would have soared above the palace's many gabled roofs, the glazing glinting in the morning sun and setting it ablaze like a beacon.

The Royal Apartments at Oatlands

Initially, Oatlands was a traditional courtyard house surrounded by a moat. Within this moat the first phase of development focused on the creation of the principal private apartments of the king and queen. This involved 'the translating and taking down of divers chambers', including the great hall (which was lost) and the original chapel (which was 'translated' into new chambers for the queen). Although the royal lodgings are known to have occupied the north-eastern and south-western wings of the original manor house respectively, the exact layout of the rooms remains unclear, as most of the excavations that have taken place on-site have focused on the buildings sited in the outer courts. Therefore, according to the *Excavations of Oatlands Palace*, 'all that can be deduced is informed conjecture'. However, the pattern is clear. Having passed underneath the inner gatehouse to enter the inner courtyard,

> it is likely that the entrance to the royal apartments was in the north range of the inner court [directly ahead of any visitor to court] where the great hall had been ... This would suggest that the two suites of lodgings were entered at the north and then continued round the east and west sides of the court meeting at the south. Although it is unusual for the innermost royal apartments to be in an entrance range, it was normal for them to be south facing. Thus at Oatlands the existing configuration of the house required a non-standard response from Henry VIII's architects.

The sketch of the privy court gatehouse range made by Anton van der Wyngaerde in 1559 clearly shows the most privy of the royal chambers, running across the front of the range at first-floor level. According to Colvin's *The History of the King's Works, Volume IV*, this inner gatehouse, 'with its diapered brickwork and turreted gateway [to] the new range, formed an imposing entrance to the king's house'. Current thinking is that the queen occupied the western range, shown to the left of the gatehouse. When viewing the aforementioned image, Catherine's bedchamber was positioned where the large bay window projects outwards from the frontage of the range.

The inventory taken after the death of Henry VIII provides us with a glimpse into the lavish interiors of Oatlands. Unfortunately, there is little if anything that connects us with Catherine directly; perhaps this is to be expected given her ignominious end. However, maybe for the briefest time, she sat upon one of two chairs of 'carnacion vellat [carnation velvet] fringed with carnacion silke[. A] throne for the kinge having two knoppes [?knobs] of copper and gilte[,] thither for the queen having two knoppes of Ankomy silvered.' Or perhaps she loved, as we do, the 'cheire[chair] of clothe of goulde [gold] reyzed [raised] with Roses and flowers [flowers] of grene [green] and red vellat [velvet] with Swnnes [swans] of white vellat fringed with grene silke'.

The Queen's Lodgings at Oatlands

Seventeenth-century inventories suggest that the queen's lodgings were larger than the kings, though there is a note of caution here. Once more, Poulton's *Excavations of Oatlands Palace* states,

> It is very unusual for a royal palace to have more extensive accommodation for the queen than the king and the layout at Oatlands either demonstrates that Henry VIII had always intended the queen's side to be larger, as Oatlands was to be the queen's palace, or that in the Jacobean period the sides were swapped.

Along with the usual rooms one might expect to find in royal lodgings, it seems that the queen's sides had a series of smaller rooms, or 'cabinets', including a closet positioned in a tower off the queen's garden gallery. Perhaps it was here, or in the newly built chapel close to the queen's bedchamber, that the second female member of the Howard clan was joined in holy matrimony with one of the most fickle and dangerous men in all of England.

Tragically, the records reveal that Catherine was never to return to the palace. According to the *Letters and Papers of Henry VIII*, by the time Henry visited again it was early December 1541. The queen had fallen from grace and her relatives were being interrogated in London. It was from Oatlands on 8 December that the 'Council with the King' wrote to the council acting in London that

> the King directs them [the Council in London] to commit the duchess of Norfolk, lord William, and his wife, lady Bridgewater, and the others noted to be in the case of misprision of treason, to the Tower, and put their houses and goods in safe custody … As for Culpeper and Deram [Dereham], if the latter can tell no more, they are (with convenient warning to prepare their souls) to be executed.

A New Bride at Oatlands – July 1543

Henry was nothing if not a man of habit, and Catherine Howard not the only 'Katherine' to grace Oatlands' chambers. Having wed Katherine Parr at Hampton Court Palace on 12 July 1543, the king quickly whisked his new bride away to the relative seclusion of Oatlands. We know this on account of the letter that Katherine penned there to her brother, just eight days after becoming Henry's sixth consort. Part of this letter is reproduced here:

> Right dear and well beloved brother, we greet you well. Letting you with that when it hath pleased Almighty God of His goodness to incline the King's

majesty in such a wise towards me, as it hath pleased his highness to take me of all others, most unworthy, to his wife, which is, as of reason it ought to be, the greatest joy and comfort that could happen to me in this world …
Given at my lord's manor of Oatlands, the twentieth of July, the thirty-fifth year of his majesty's most noble reign.
Katherine the Queen.

Perhaps we might imagine Katherine, secluded in the queen's closet and overlooking her privy garden, thoughtfully composing this letter to her younger brother, the sweet scent of summer wafting in through the open window. Outside that window, Henry's building programme at Oatlands was coming to an end. The palace would remain a favoured royal residence for another hundred years before it essentially became a casualty of the English Civil War, being sold by the order of Parliament and subsequently demolished in 1650.

Visitor Information
A visit to the site of the lost palace of Oatlands must surely be reserved for only the most diehard of Tudor enthusiasts. During the course of writing our *In the Footsteps* books, on several occasions we have been confronted merely with earthworks in the ground, the only surviving clue to a lost Tudor mansion. In these instances, the quiet surrounding fields give a moment's repose to imagine the glorious edifice that might have still stood to this day, if not for a quirk of fate intervening to reduce it to its foundations. However, the time traveller is afforded no such luxury at the site of this, one of Henry's most impressive palaces. The whole area is now covered with a modern-day housing estate. Yet strangely, in among the uninspiring twentieth-century architecture, the visitor will notice sections of wall, standing around eight foot high, constructed of small, uneven-looking red bricks typical of the period. It is the tell-tale sign that you are in the right spot.

If you wish to visit the most prominent feature of the site, make your way to Old Palace Road. Park at the far end and go on foot, ahead to Rede Court. This pedestrian-only footpath leads to Gate Court, which is straddled by the Tudor gateway that once gave access to the palace compound. You will not be kept long, so you may wish to include this on your own progress from Hampton Court Palace (see Hampton Court Palace), along to nearby Chertsey Abbey (see Chertsey Abbey), and possibly on to Windsor Castle (see Windsor Castle) if time allows. There are no amenities on-site.

The local museum at Elmbridge houses a collection of artefacts recovered during excavations of the palace over the year. Occasionally these are exhibited. If you wish to find out more, go to the museum website at www.elmbridgemuseum.org.uk.

Postcode for Old Palace Road: KT13 8PQ.

Grimsthorpe Castle, Lincolnshire

> But Grimsthorpe I may term an extempore structure, set up on a sudden by Charles Brandon duke of Suffolk, to entertain King Henry the Eighth, in his progress into these parts ...
>
> Thomas Fuller (1608-1661),
> Church of England Clergyman

Set amid expansive rolling pastures and historic woodland, Grimsthorpe Castle in Lincolnshire is thought to have been built in the thirteenth century by Gilbert de Gant, Earl of Lincoln, and has been the home of the de Eresby family since 1516. Henry VIII and Catherine Howard stayed at the castle as guests of Charles Brandon, Duke of Suffolk, and his wife Katherine Willoughby in 1541, while on progress to Yorkshire.

The Tudor Period

In 1516, Henry VIII granted the reversion of the manor to William Willoughby, 11th Baron Willoughby de Eresby, after his marriage to Maria de Salinas, a lady-in-waiting and close confidante of Henry's first wife, Katherine of Aragon. After William's death in October 1526, the couple's only surviving child, Katherine Willoughby, aged seven at the time, inherited her father's title and estates, with the exception of those lands entailed to male heirs, and eventually obtained possession of Grimsthorpe after the death of the Countess of Oxford in 1537.

As custom dictated, the young heiress who'd not yet reached the age of majority – fourteen for a female and twenty-one for a male –became the king's ward, who in turn sold the wardship to his brother-in-law, Charles Brandon, for a considerable sum.

The sale of wardships was a lucrative business for the Crown in Tudor times, and those wardships seen as particularly advantageous, like Katherine's, attracted multiple bidders all eager to prosper, as not only did the guardian pocket the rents of the ward's lands and property, they also had control over whom they married. It's not surprising, then, to find that in order to keep this significant source of income in the family, the ward was often married to one of the guardian's own children. In the case of Katherine Willoughby, some historians suggest that she was intended as a bride for Henry Brandon, Earl of Lincoln, the youngest son of Charles Brandon and his third wife, Mary Tudor, the former Queen of France. However, three months after Mary's death in June 1533, the widowed duke took his fourteen-year-old ward, Katherine, as his fourth wife. In 1540, he set about enlarging and rebuilding his wife's house at Grimsthorpe, in order to host a royal visit the following year.

A Royal Visit

On 30 June the court left Westminster and began making their way north to York. The incessant rain and unseasonably cold and stormy weather made travel difficult, and the flooded roads became almost impassable. By mid-July, the vast royal entourage had only gotten as far as Grafton, about 60 miles from Westminster. After passing through Northampton, Pipewell, Liddington and Collyweston, Henry and Catherine reached Stamford.

On the evening of 5 August, the royal party arrived at Grimsthorpe in south Lincolnshire, where they stayed until 8 August, as guests of the Duke and Duchess of Suffolk, returning once more on 14 October for an overnight stay on the return trip from York. The house that greeted Henry and Catherine was of late thirteenth-century origin but had been enlarged and extensively rebuilt using stone from the dissolved abbey of Vaudey, granted to Brandon in 1539 and situated just across the valley from Grimsthorpe. While no sixteenth-century drawing of the house survives, Grimsthorpe is mentioned in John Leland's *Itinerary*:

> From Coly Weston to Grimsthorpe, about an 8 miles or 9, most by playn ground, good corn and pasture, but little wood saving about toward Vaudey Abbey and Grimsthorpe itself. It appearith by the ruins of Vaudey Abbey a good ½ mile this side of Grimsthorpe that it hath been a great thing. There is in the wood by Vaudey Abbey a great quarry of a course of marble, whereof much belikelihood was occupied in the Abbey. There is a fair Park between Vaudey and Grimsthorpe. The place of Grimsthorpe was no great thing, before the building of the second court. Yet was all the old work of stone and the gatehouse was faire and strong and the walls on each side of it embattled. There is also a great ditch about the house.

This second court mentioned by Leland is thought to have been the buildings built in great haste by Charles Brandon to receive Henry and Catherine. According to *Pevsner*, 'he built three small towers and four ranges to form a courtyard, all of which survives, and later added a second court which was mentioned in the late C 16 by Leland'.

Thomas Fuller, writing in the seventeenth century, noted that 'the hall therein was fitted to a fair suit of hanging, which the duke had by his wife Mary the French queen'. It's also recorded that after Charles Brandon's death, 'bedding for nearly 100 individuals was removed from Tatershall Castle to Grimsthorpe and Eresby, with thirteen Turkish carpets and numerous varied tapestries'. It's safe to assume that the interiors and furnishings of Grimsthorpe at the time of the royal visit would have been just as luxurious. Unfortunately, alterations made to the castle in the seventeenth, eighteenth and nineteenth centuries, and the absence of contemporary drawings or detailed descriptions, make it almost impossible to make any conclusions about the layout of the Tudor house.

What we do know is that while at Grimsthorpe, Catherine exchanged secret letters with Jane Rochford, asking her for 'that thing which was promised her', which appears to have been a private meeting with Culpeper.

While the queen entertained herself by arranging late-night trysts, none of which are known to have taken place at Grimsthorpe, the Privy Council sat on 6 and 7 August. However, no business was recorded. Those present at the meeting included Charles Brandon, Duke of Suffolk; Catherine Howard's uncle Thomas Howard, Duke of Norfolk; William Fitzwilliam, Lord Privy Seal; Robert Radcliffe, Lord Great Chamberlain; Thomas Wriothesley, Earl of Southampton, one the king's principal secretaries; Anthony Browne, Master of the Horse; and Sir John Gage, Comptroller of the Household, who also held the post of Constable of the Tower. In less than six months' time, he would be called upon to supervise the arrangements for the execution of young Queen Catherine.

A Royal Orphan

After the death of Katherine Parr in September 1548 and Thomas Seymour in 1549, their orphaned baby daughter, Mary Seymour, was sent to live at Grimsthorpe with her governess, Elizabeth Aglionby, with around twelve attendants, including maids and servants. While this was her father's dying wish, presumably because his late wife and Katherine Willoughby had been close friends, it proved too much of a financial burden for the Duchess of Suffolk. She complained of receiving none of the allowance she'd been promised by the Duke of Somerset, and likened the burden of looking after the former queen's daughter to having a 'sickness'. In late August 1549, she wrote to William Cecil from Grimsthorpe informing him of her continued troubles caused by the fact that 'the queen's child hath layen, and still doth lie at my house, with her company about her, wholly at my charges'. On 22 January 1550, an Act of Parliament made Mary eligible to inherit the property belonging to her father that had not been returned to the Crown after his attainder. However, she never did claim any of her father's estate. From this point on, we hear nothing more of Mary in Katherine's correspondences with Cecil, and so can only assume that, tragically, the unwanted orphan died before her second birthday, probably drawing her last breath at Grimsthorpe.

Visitor Information

For opening times and visitor information please visit Grimsthorpe Castle's website at http://www.grimsthorpe.co.uk/. Telephone number: +44 (0) 177 859 1205.

Postcode for Grimsthorpe Castle: PE10 0LZ.

Lincoln, Lincolnshire

> The King and Queen came riding into their tent, which was pitched at the furthest end of the liberty of Lincoln, and there shifted their apparel, from green and crimson velvet respectively, to cloth of gold and silver ...
>
> Frederic Madden (ed.), *Account of King Henry the*
> *Eighth's Entry into Lincoln in 1541*

After spending several nights with the king's trusted friend Charles Brandon at Grimsthorpe, the royal party travelled via Sleaford to Lincoln, where they arrived on Tuesday 9 August 1541. Thankfully for us avid time travellers, a herald was on hand to record the king and queen's entry in great detail. This vivid account allows us to peer through the veil of time and experience the pomp and ceremony that accompanied all royal entries, and come face to face with Henry and Catherine in all their magnificence.

The King and Queen's Entry into Lincoln

From the account we know that on Tuesday 9 August, Henry and Catherine were at Temple Bruer, 7 miles from Lincoln, where the mayor of Lincoln, burgesses and other citizens were on hand to meet them. We're told that, near to the king's tent, the gentlemen and yeomen of Lindsey and their servants lined up on horseback on one side, and the mayor and other citizens on foot on the opposite side. The archdeacon, dean and clergy then 'made a proposition in Latin, presented a gift of victual, and then passed the nearest way to the Minster'. The herald then continues,

> The King and Queen came riding into their tent, which was pitched at the furthest end of the liberty of Lincoln, and there shifted their apparel, from green and crimson velvet respectively, to cloth of gold and silver. Behind that tent was one for the ladies, and, some distance off, a 'hayle' where the six children of honor, dressed in cloth of gold and crimson velvet, and the horses of estate were prepared. When the King and Queen were set on horseback, the heralds put on their coats, the gentlemen pensioners and train rode according to the ancient order, then came lord Hastings bearing the sword, then the King, then his horse led by the Master of the Horse, then the children of honor 'each after other' on great coursers, then the earl of Rutland, Queen's chamberlain, then the Queen, then her horse of estate, then all the ladies, then the Captain of the Guard and the Guard, then the commoners. Proceeding in this order, they found, at the entry into the liberty, Mr. Myssleden, serjeant at law, being recorder of Lincoln, with gentlemen of the country, the mayor and his brethren ... who kneeled and cried twice 'Jesus save your grace'; and the recorder read and presented a proposition in English (which the King handed to the duke of Norfolk) with a gift of victual. The mayor then presented the sword and mace and was placed beside Clarenseaux king of arms, behind the dukes, while his brethren and the burgesses, followed by the gentlemen of the country and knights, were placed before the train.

Church bells pealed and crowds gathered as the procession made their way through the decorated town. Catherine and Henry alighted at the west end of the cathedral, where there was 'a carpet and stools and cushions of cloth of gold, with crucifixes laid thereon for the King and Queen'. There, the royal couple dismounted and knelt. The Bishop of Lincoln, John Longland, handed them each a crucifix, which they reverently kissed before proceeding into the church 'under the canopy to the Sacrament', where they prayed while the choir 'melodiously' sang a *Te Deum*. The formal proceedings over, 'his grace went straight to his lodging, and in like case all the train for that night'.

The following afternoon, Henry rode to the castle and 'viewed it and the city', and on Friday, trumpeters heralded the king and queen's departure for Gainsborough.

The Bishop's Palace

His Grace's lodging was almost certainly the grandiose palace of the bishops of Lincoln, which boasted spectacular views over the city and surrounding countryside from its commanding hillside position adjacent to the cathedral. It was built in the mid-twelfth century by Bishop Robert de Chesney as a residence for himself and his large household of officials and servants, and later enlarged and altered by subsequent bishops.

As the administrative centre for one of the largest diocese in medieval England, the palace was impressive, and reflected the enormous power and wealth of the bishops. It was therefore perfectly suited to host a royal visit.

Henry and Catherine remained for three nights as guests of Bishop Longland, who honoured and entertained his royal visitors by holding great feasts in the west hall, the palace's public and ceremonial heart. We can imagine the king and queen dressed in all their finery, sitting on a raised dais with the bishop and their highest-ranking nobles, feasting on local delicacies served on glittering silverware, while the rest of the travelling court dined at wooden trestle tables below. The royal entourage was kept warmed by an open hearth situated in the centre of the hall and the space lit by large paired windows detailed in black Purbeck marble, matching the lofty marble piers and arcades.

At the opposite end of the hall, in the south-west corner, a door led to a spiral staircase which led to the bishop's great chamber above. This appears to have been where the king was lodged during his stay. Where the queen and her ladies slept is unknown. However, we can safely assume that the queen did not share the king's bedchamber, as one of Catherine's indiscretions with Thomas Culpeper is said to have taken place at Lincoln. It's possible that the queen and her ladies were allocated rooms in the east hall range, modernised in the fifteenth century by Bishop Alnwick.

'The Lady Shall Be No Longer Queen'

Under interrogation, Francis Dereham confessed that he'd known the queen carnally many times 'in a naked bed' before her marriage to the king. However, he was adamant that they'd not resumed sexual relations after her marriage because Thomas Culpeper had replaced him in her affections. This new revelation led to Catherine's ladies being questioned about the queen's relationship with Culpeper.

Under examination, Catherine Tylney revealed that at Lincoln the queen 'went two nights to lady Rochford's chamber, which was up a little pair of stairs by the Queen's chamber'. She and Margaret Morton had accompanied the queen upstairs on the first night but were promptly sent away. Soon afterwards, Margaret returned to Lady Rochford's chamber and Catherine Tylney went to bed. According to Catherine's confession, Margaret returned to her chamber at two o'clock in the morning, by which time the queen had not yet retired. On the second night, the queen sent her ladies to bed but took Catherine Tylney with her to Lady Rochford's chamber, where she was allegedly ordered to wait in a room with 'Lady Rochford's woman', and so was not able to see whom the queen was meeting. Tylney also admitted to conveying messages between the queen and Jane Rochford, although she claimed not to have known the content of the messages.

On one occasion at Lincoln, the queen and Jane were at the 'back door' at eleven o'clock at night waiting for Culpeper to arrive when 'one of the watch came with a light and locked the door'; Culpeper was forced to pick the lock of the queen's suite to gain access!

Under interrogation, Lady Rochford claimed that at Lincoln, 'when the Queen was with Culpeper, she was asleep until the Queen called her' and so, conveniently, did not see what went on between the two. Even still, she maintained that Catherine and Culpeper's relationship had been sexual. Culpeper, however, would admit to nothing more than talk and desire. He claimed to have spent the long nights at Lincoln talking to Catherine, and confessed only that he'd professed he loved her 'above all creatures' – but more dangerously, he admitted that he'd 'intended to do ill with her'. Talk and intent were just as damning as action. Under the Treasons Act of 1534, traitors were those who 'do maliciously wish, will, or desire by words or writing, or by craft imagine' the king's death or harm. Catherine and Culpeper had sealed their fates.

Visitor Information

Lincoln is a bustling city; its suburbs tumble down the south-facing hillside from the high plateau upon which the Roman city was originally founded. We arrived by car from the south-west, the flat lowlands of Lincolnshire ensuring that the Norman cathedral is clearly visible at some distance from the city. It is a breathtaking sight, the near-thousand-year-old building standing regally against the raised skyline. Indeed, there is something comforting in the sense of continuity it invokes, connecting us over millennia to the dawn of medieval England.

In many ways, Lincoln is a tale of two cities. You may find yourself enjoying the low-lying harbour and surrounding shops, but if your delight is found among historic buildings, then you are most likely to find your ease in the Cathedral Quarter. However, if you have any issue with mobility, we strongly urge you to find accommodation close to the cathedral; otherwise, the strenuous climb up the charming but aptly named 'Steep Hill' may prove a challenge.

At the top of the plateau, the Norman castle, the old abbey gatehouse, the cathedral and the old Bishop's Palace are within a stone's throw of one another, the medieval central marketplace being a daily hub of activity that connects them all. Here you will also find the local tourist information centre, located in a typical wattle-and-daub house that was built just two years after Henry and Catherine visited Lincoln, in 1543.

Entry to the cathedral is free of charge. From just inside the great west door, you can enjoy a fine view of the nave. It is also permissible to visit the Morning Chapel for private devotions, or the cathedral shop. But if you want to explore further, there is a fee. At the time of writing this was £8 per adult. All tours of the cathedral are included in the entry charge. On Sunday there are no tours, but equally there is no charge.

While in the cathedral, make sure you visit the tombs of Katherine Swynford and her daughter Joan Beaufort, Countless of Westmoreland. These medieval noblewomen were both ancestors of Henry VIII; through his mother, Elizabeth of York, Henry was the great-great-grandson of Joan, and on his father's side he was the great-great-grandson of Katherine's son John Beaufort. Henry VIII's sixth wife, Katherine Parr, was also descended from Joan Beaufort. Sadly the tombs were stripped of the brass effigies and decorated shields during the English Civil War. Only the plain stone sarcophagi remain behind.

Website for the cathedral: http://lincolncathedral.com. Telephone: +44 (0) 152 256 1600.

Adjacent to the cathedral, on its south side, lies the now ruined Bishop's Palace, currently owned by English Heritage. There is an excellent audio tour of the ruins, along with helpful information boards whose illustrations are useful in bringing the once-luxurious splendour of the rooms to life.

For those of us following in the footsteps of Catherine Howard, the key areas are the ragged remains of the once great west hall – the main public space of the palace – and the adjacent building located running perpendicular to its south end. A blocked doorway in the south-west corner of the west hall once led up to high-status guest lodgings on the first floor. The on-site guide related to us that it was in these rooms that Henry was lodged while at the palace. In the nineteenth century this building was converted into a Victorian chapel, the first floor being stripped out, creating one large space from floor to ceiling. It is possible to visit the interior of the chapel by going next door to a hotel that is owned by the cathedral. If the chapel is not in use, you will be allowed to venture inside.

At the first-floor level there is little to see that recreates the splendour and comfort that the king must have enjoyed, although on the ground floor you will clearly see the three doorways (most now blocked up) that once led from the great hall at its low end through to the kitchen, pantry and buttery. As you stand silently in the aisle of the chapel, it is not so hard to let your mind slip away from the present and to imagine the ghostly commotion around you as servants come and go from the kitchen, bearing aloft a plethora of fine dishes to be served to Bishop Longland's royal guests, feasting in the great hall beyond.

Details of opening times and entrance fees for the Old Bishop's Palace can be found by visiting the English Heritage website at http://www.englishheritage.org.uk/daysout/properties/lincoln-medieval-bishops-palace. Telephone: +44 (0) 152 252 7468.

Cafés, restaurants and toilet facilities abound both at the locations mentioned, and in the vicinity of the market square. Our favourite tea room was the quintessentially English Mrs Bunty's (18 Steep Hill; Postcode: LN2 1LT. Telephone:

+44 (0) 152 253 7909), which recreates the flavour of 1940s England; tea is served in old-fashioned china alongside a variety of delicious cakes. Just make sure you leave room to indulge yourself after all your sightseeing!

Finally, while in Lincoln, you may wish to plan a visit to nearby Gainsborough Old Hall (15 miles), Thornton Abbey (39 miles) or Grimsthorpe Castle (40 miles).

Please note that parking is very limited around the cathedral. Castle Car Park is the closest, but only has twenty-seven spaces (postcode: LN1 3AA). Alternatively, just five minutes' walk away is Westgate parking, with around a hundred spaces (postcode: LN1 3BG.)

Postcode for Lincoln Cathedral: LN2 1PX.

Pontefract Castle, West Yorkshire

O Pomfret, Pomfret! O thou bloody prison!
Fatal and ominous to noble peers!
Within the guilty closure of thy walls,
Richard II here was hack'd to death;
And for more slander to thy dismal seat,
We give to thee our guiltless blood to drink.

William Shakespeare, *Richard III*

When the brightly coloured, royal cavalcade crossed beneath the grey barbican of Pontefract Castle, Catherine Howard must have been well aware of its murderous history. Aside from the Tower in London, it is hard to think of a more foreboding, or grisly, fortress in England. As the quote above states, it was at Pontefract (often referred to in the sixteenth century as Pomfret) that Richard II met an untimely end, one that remains shrouded in mystery to this day. Several other nobles followed suit over the next couple of centuries. Perhaps most notably were the brother and son of Elizabeth Woodville, Anthony Woodville, Earl Rivers, and Richard, Lord Grey, respectively.

We only have to look at surviving etchings and oil paintings, which capture the castle as it appeared before its destruction shortly after the English Civil War, to know that Pontefract's reputation as the key fortress of the north was well deserved. According to Ian Roberts, principal archaeologist with the West Yorkshire Archaeological Society, 'the oil painting [of Pontefract Castle] of 1625, variously attributed to Joos de Momper or Alexander Keirincx ... [although] a bit stylised, almost certainly [gives] the most realistic image of the exterior'. What is immediately striking when we look at these images is the sheer enormity of the defences. Arriving at Pontefract on the afternoon of the 23 August 1541, from nearby Hatfield (not to be confused with Hatfield House in Hertfordshire, which is some 100 miles away), Catherine would have found the castle 'built on an elevated rock, commanding extensive and picturesque views'. An early nineteenth-century account of the castle (taken from *The Mirror of Literature, Amusement, and Instruction*), from which this latter quote derives, goes on to paint a vivid picture of the castle's environs:

The north-west prospect takes in the beautiful vale along which flows the Aire, skirted by woods and plantations. It is bounded only by the hills of Craven. The north and east prospect is more extensive, but the scenery is not equally striking and impressive. The towers of York Minster are distinctly seen and the prospect is only bounded by the limits of vision … To the south and southwest, the towering hills of Derbyshire, stretching towards Lancashire, form the horizon, while the foreground is a picturesque country variegated with handsome residences.

The main entrance to Pontefract Castle was from the south. Entering under the barbican and across a short bridge spanning a deep gully that connected the castle to the town, the royal couple would have ridden through an enclosed courtyard before reaching the main castle gatehouse, or Porter's Lodge. This substantial building comprised two stately towers and a portcullis. Beyond this gatehouse lay the main castle yard. According to Roberts, who has studied Pontefract Castle extensively, by the sixteenth century this area was probably mostly given over to pleasure gardens. What presented itself to Catherine on that day must have been an impressive sight.

Surrounding the castle yard were its defensive walls. The 1625 oil painting of Pontefract clearly shows how these walls pitched by various degrees, dictated by the contours of the plateau upon which the castle rested. The walls were topped by a crenulated parapet and interrupted at intervals by seven substantial square towers. The eighth tower made up the enormous and rather fanciful keep, perched atop the motte. In his contemporary *Itinerary*, Leland describes this keep by saying that it 'takes the form of three large and three small round turrets', with its walls said to be 21 feet thick.

The Royal Apartments at Pontefract Castle

By the sixteenth century, the keep's state rooms had been abandoned and were largely used as an arsenal, but according to Roberts they 'may have retained some accommodation'. Along with service buildings such as the great kitchen, privy kitchen, larder and scullery, the king and queen's lodgings had been moved and arranged around the entire northern wall of the defensive circuit.

The specific buildings of interest to those following in Catherine's footsteps are the great hall (which may also have been used as a presence chamber) and the king and queen's towers that flanked it at either end. These two towers can be seen in the 1625 painting of the castle, the tower on the far right of the painting being the King's Tower, with the queen's partially hidden behind the Constable Tower (in the foreground and to the right of the main gatehouse).

The evidence that we have for the arrangement of the royal apartments at Pontefract comes from a survey carried out in 1643. It appears that the hall was located at first-floor level, with an undercroft beneath; two separate passages linked it to the private royal apartments; the first to the Queen's Tower via the hall's west end, the second to the King's Tower in the east.

Both towers consisted of four floors and an underground cellar. On the queen's side, at first-floor level, the principal bedchamber connected directly with the passage from the great hall. From this room, there was an exit via one staircase to the nursery on the ground floor, and a second which ascended to the two rooms above (one situated above the other). One assumes that it was into one of these rooms that Lady Rochford, the queen's lady-in-waiting, managed to smuggle a rather foolish Thomas Culpeper for his late-night assignations with Catherine.

A Treasonous Affair

Having taken the submission of the insurgents in Lincolnshire, Henry crossed into Yorkshire during the third week in August 1541. Marillac, the French ambassador, who was travelling with the court during the progress, described how the king

> had been received in divers places by the gentlemen of the country, coming by bailiwicks and stewardships, to the number of 5,000 or 6,000 horse. Those who in the rebellion remained faithful were ranked apart, and graciously welcomed by the King and praised for their fidelity. The others who were of the conspiracy, among whom appeared the archbishop of York, were a little further off on their knees; and one of them, speaking for all, made a long harangue confessing their treason in marching against their Sovereign and his Council, thanking him for pardoning so great an offence and begging that if any relics of indignation remained he would dismiss them.

We can only imagine Catherine mounted atop her horse and looking down upon yet another set of the king's wretched subjects, grovelling for her husband's mercy, as one lone voice spoke up on behalf of all:

> We your humble subjects, th'inhabitants of this your Grace's county of York, ... confess that we wretches, for lack of grace and of sincere and pure knowledge of the verity of God's words ... have most grievously, heinously and wantonly offended your ... Majesty ... in the unnatural, most odious and detestable offences of outragious disobedience and traitorous rebellion.

With the submission complete, the court retired to the royal chase of Hatfield, near Doncaster, where, according to Marillac, the hunting was bountiful. Thereafter, Henry and Catherine removed to Pontefract. The king and queen were to stay there for twelve days. During this time, the Tudor court continued to turn as usual. No doubt an endless round of pleasantries such as hunting, hawking, gaming and dancing kept the lust of youth at least partially satiated, while the *Letters and Papers of Henry VIII* show that the Privy Council met almost daily, although no business was recorded for the days in question.

In the background, though, the king was embroiled in matters less usual; he had instigated the most private and delicate of negotiations, centred on meeting with his nephew, the Scots king James V, in York. Henry makes plain the discretion required in his letter, dated 29 August, to his Lord Chancellor, Thomas Audley. The entry summarises that 'an overture has been made by one of the King of Scots' most secret councillors for a meeting between the two Kings which is not unlikely to take effect … As this meeting is yet uncertain it is to be kept secret from the rest of the Council, and those who must be privy to the making of the safe conducts must be sworn to secrecy.'

Yet, if Henry thought he was the only royal person involved in subterfuge while at Pontefract, in a matter of months he would be rudely shaken from his delusional arrogance. For it is here, at Pontefract, that Catherine was continuing her clandestine affair with twenty-seven-year-old Thomas Culpeper. The one and only letter we have from Catherine to Thomas is poignant and dated 31 August 1541, while Catherine was residing at the castle; the last line, 'as long as life endures', speaking volumes about the depth of her feelings for this young gentleman of the king's privy chamber:

> Master Culpeper, I heartily recommend me unto you, praying you to send me word how that you do. I heard you were sick, and never longed so much for anything as to see you. It makes my heart die to think I cannot be always in your company. Come when my lady Rochforthe [Rochford] is here, for then I shall be best at leisure to be at your commandment. I thank you for promising to be good to that poor fellow my man, for when he is gone there is none I dare trust to send to you. I pray you to give a horse for my man, for I have much a do to get one, and therefore I pray send me one by him; and in so doing I am as I said afore; and thus I take my leave of you, trusting to see you shortly again, and I would you were with me now that you might see what pain I take in writing to you. Yours as long as lyffe [life] endures. – Katheryn.

Exactly what transpired between Catherine and Thomas at Pontefract we will probably never know. However, testimonies gathered as evidence against the queen in November of the same year certainly indicate that Pontefract was one of the locations specifically cited for the queen's infidelity, with Margaret Morton stating that 'at Pomfret, every night, the Queen, being alone with lady Rochford, locked and bolted her chamber door on the inside, and Mr. Dane, sent to the Queen from the King, one night found it bolted', while Culpeper himself confessed that 'the Queen would in every house seek for the back doors and back stairs herself. At Pomfret she feared the King had set watch at the back door, and lady Rochford made her servant watch in the court to see if that were so.'

As romantic as these liaisons might seem across the centuries, clearly tensions were running high for the young queen. We learn more of Catherine's mood during these twelve days, with Margaret Morton going on to report to her inquisitors that 'at Pomfrat the Queen was angry with Mrs Louffkyn and her [Margaret Morton] and threatened to put them away'. It is easy to visualise the tense encounter, the accusations and Catherine's intemperate mood. She must have known that she was treading on very dangerous ground indeed.

The Destruction of Pontefract Castle

The military might of Pontefract was notorious in England. Even Oliver Cromwell, leader of the Parliamentarian forces during the English Civil War, later Lord Protector, once wrote of Pontefract,

> [The castle] is very well known as one of the strongest inland Garrisons in the Kingdom; well watered; situated in rock in every part of it; and therefore difficult to mine. The walls are very think and high, with strong towers; and if battered, very difficult to access, by reason of the depth and steepness of the graft.

However, it did not stop the Parliamentarian forces besieging it three times. According to *The Mirror of Literature, Amusement, and Instruction*:

> This third siege was the most destructive to the castle: the tremendous artillery had shattered its massive walls; and its demolition was completed by order of Parliament. Within two months after its reduction, the buildings were unroofed, and all the materials sold. Thus was this princely fortress reduced to a heap of ruins.

Visitor Information

On the day the authors visited Pontefract Castle, brooding, grey skies rather fittingly reflected the dark reputation of this now ruined fortress. We drove from the south, toward what was once a highly strategic northern town; the gentle, undulating landscape of south Yorkshire pricked here and there with the brutalism of concrete towers, arising from nearby twentieth-century power stations. Although the town has emerged from the grime of the Industrial Revolution, Pontefract can hardly be designated a town of great natural beauty and therefore, tends not to be on the main tourist trail. Thus, on a typical day you are more likely to find yourself accompanied by locals walking their dogs than fellow time travellers seeking to reveal the castle's hidden history.

The climb to the castle is steady, reminding the visitor of the building's long-standing dominance over the surrounding countryside. However, today you will find that the view is almost entirely obscured by trees, except on top of the castle's motte, where the keep was once located. The visitor has access to all that remains of this once renowned behemoth, its innermost precinct, including some of the foundation stones making up the royal apartments. Information boards placed around the site will help you orientate yourself with the principal landmarks: the keep, the great kitchen, the great hall, the King's Tower and the Norman and Elizabethan chapels. Little, if anything, appears to have survived of the queen's lodgings in the Queen's Tower. Nevertheless, it is easy to sit awhile on the grass and imagine Lady Rochford's servant nervously watching the entrance to its back stairs, making sure the queen was free of suspicion; or within its walls, as darkness falls, the young queen being undressed by her virile lover. It is an evocative place, where the brutality of men, which saw noble blood spilt, contrasts starkly with the warmth of a young woman's love.

The car park for the castle is just adjacent to the foot of its walls. Parking is free for up to four hours, as is entry to the castle grounds. Next to the entrance is a modest visitor centre (apparently due to be upgraded in 2016 thanks to Heritage Lottery funding). This sells guidebooks for the castle, a limited range of snacks, drinks and gifts. Toilets are also on-site. The large, grassy area once covered by formal gardens is an ideal place to enjoy a picnic. The grounds are immaculate, making this a great place for children to run around freely. Also, for those of you who are dog lovers, your canine companions are welcome but must be kept under control.

Pontefract Castle is owned and run by Wakefield Council. A wide range of special events are held on-site throughout the year and guided tours of the underground artillery magazines currently run between Wednesday and Sunday at 3 p.m., for which there is a small charge. If you are planning a visit, we recommend that you check out the website at http://www.wakefield.gov.uk/residents/events-and-culture/castles/pontefract-castle. Telephone number: +44 (0) 197 772 3440.

Postcode for Pontefract Castle: WF8 1QH.

Cawood Castle, North Yorkshire

There lingers too 'neath fancy's eye that strangely blended scene
When Cawood's ancient halls become a palace of a queen ...
Go, Queen, from grandeur to despair, 'tis but an earthly doom,
The morning may rise in splendour yet the night set in black gloom.

Monody on the ruins of Cawood Castle

The Medieval History of Cawood

Today, Cawood (correctly pronounced *Cowud*) Castle is but a willowy shadow of the once great archiepiscopal palace that, during its zenith, was described as 'the veritable Windsor of the north'. Lying just 7 miles south of the City of York, and on the navigable banks of the River Ouse, its foundation can be traced to the year 930, when the Saxon king Athelstan granted land at Cawood to the diocese of the aforementioned city. Subsequently, the fortunes of the manor house at Cawood [later called 'castle'] waxed and waned 'first as a simple residence of the Archbishop, and then as an almost impregnable fortress', with the property being built up at various times, before apparently falling into decay, a cycle which seems to have repeated itself through Cawood's illustrious history.

Although essentially never owned outright by the Crown, this transmutation from palace to fortress was forged from necessity, for it was long used as a royal abode during periods of turbulence. During these periods, the Crown became Cawood's tenant-in-chief. For example, from 1299, during the five years that Edward I waged war against the Scots, the de facto capital of England became York. Edward's young queen, Margaret of France, resided at the castle, while her husband marauded across Scotland, visiting her at Cawood, mainly during the winter. The early medieval history of Cawood, festooned with visiting kings, queens, princes, triumph and treachery is fascinating in and of itself. However, such an exposition lies outside the scope of this book, but we agree with Wheater's *History of Sherburn and Cawood*, which states that the castle was always 'a place of far more than ordinary importance'.

In the mid-fourteenth century, Alexander Neville, then archbishop, is said to 'have bestowed much cost on his Castle of Cawood, building divers towers and other edifices about it'. Through the fifteenth century, in the hundred or so years before Catherine visited the castle, two successive archbishops also invested significantly in the fabric of the building. First Archbishop Bowet (1407–26) built the 'wall', presumably around the castle compound, and the great hall, which is specifically mentioned in George Cavendish's account of the arrest of Cardinal Wolsey at Cawood in 1530. However, it was Bowet's successor, Cardinal Kempe, whose hand can be most readily seen carved into the fabric of the castle that survives to this day. One of the cardinal's biographers states that 'we have no memorial of him in the See of York, but what he has left himself, which was the gatehouse of the palace of Cawood, adorned both inside and out with his arms and ensigns of a cardinal'.

The Site and Layout of Cawood Castle

Leland's *Itinerary* provides a short, but contemporary, account of the surroundings and location of Cawood Castle, stating that 'after another four miles, where the soil was good for pasture, corn and woodland, I crossed the river and arrived at Cawood. The Archbishop of York has a very fine castle here.'

The village of Cawood lies adjacent to a 90-degree bend in the River Ouse. Before the current steel swing bridge was constructed in 1872, the river was crossed by a ferry, its revenues controlled by the Archbishops of York. The silent highway of the Ouse was an important thoroughfare for traffic during the Tudor period. During the medieval period, a quay was constructed in an area adjacent to the river; this is still called the Jetty to this day, while the earliest known engraving of the ruins of Cawood, dated to after the English Civil War, show boats upon the river carrying people, livestock and other goods.

Logically, Catherine would have approached Cawood from the south-west, having ridden the roughly 14 miles from Pontefract. In Blood and Taylor's *Cawood: An Archiepiscopal Landscape*, we hear that 'the palace was clearly meant to be approached from the south corner of the village market place across the Bishop Dike, presumably by a bridge, alongside an assumed continuation of the gatehouse range and then left through the gatehouse into the palace proper'.

At around 130 metres long and 70 metres wide, the rectangular market place of Catherine's day was much larger than the rather paltry, triangular space we see today. Time has eroded its grandeur and status, buildings relentlessly encroaching on a space which once ran down to the river and extended southwards to form the main driveway up to the palace's gatehouse. It is this gatehouse and its range that are the only substantial remains of an earlier complex of buildings. Sadly, no floor plans or contemporary drawings of the palace survive from the medieval period, nor do any detailed descriptions of the palace buildings themselves. Thus, we simply do not know exactly how Cawood appeared to Catherine during her brief visit in the summer of 1541. However, all is not lost! The surviving gatehouse and range, plus an eighteenth-century etching, archaeological surveys of the surrounding area and a handful of key documents related to Cawood allow us to build up a reasonable picture of the palatial residence that once played host to England's young queen.

According to Alastair Oswald, landscape archaeologist at the University of York, who has studied Cawood Castle and its environs, the palace

> exhibits no defensive features, apart from its partially moated site, its high walls and strong gates. All these features are best interpreted as symbols of power and prestige, since all high-status medieval buildings, from abbeys to Henry's castellated banqueting house at Nonsuch, aped or borrowed from castle architecture.

In terms of the overall layout of the palace, he goes onto say,

> The overall design and layout of the individual rooms of the palace probably had much in common with, for example, the extant Archbishop of York's nearby palace at Bishopthorpe, or the now ruinous palace of the Archbishop of Canterbury at Otford in Kent (which Henry effectively rebuilt), or an Oxbridge College, or Henry's custom-built palace at Nonsuch in Surrey, to name but a few [such that] in Henry's time the palace almost certainly comprised two square courts back to back.

This dual courtyard arrangement was of course typical of fashionable, high-status houses of the day. On account of this, we can predict with a degree of certainty how the chambers of the palace were arranged. Two inventories complied toward the end of the castle's life help us to further reimagine its original appearance. The first is a report compiled for Cromwell in relation to 'the visitation of the Province of York on 12 Jan 1536'. Recorded in the *Letters and Papers of Henry VIII*, the report states that Cawood consisted of

> ... the hall, pantry, buttery, ewery, great kitchen, &c., porter's lodge, gatehouse chamber, upper chamber over the gatehouse [both still extant], and in all the different chambers, including the treasurer's chamber, Dr. Bonar's chamber, Constable's chamber, my lord's sleeping chamber, the great chamber, the chapel, the lodging of bishop Savage, the little gallery towards the water side, the library, Mr. Winter's chamber, the chamber in the tower, and Augustine's chamber; in all 49 chambers or apartments.

Then, in 1530, Cawood found itself as the setting for the dramatic final act in the life of the once omnipotent Cardinal Wolsey. Henry Percy, Earl of Northumberland, was dispatched to arrest his erstwhile master, who had retired to Cawood and his Archbishopric of York following his fall from favour earlier in the year. George Cavendish, at the time Wolsey's gentleman usher, gives us a tantalising glimpse of just a fragment of the castle's layout in this excerpt from *The Life of Wolsey*:

> They [Northumberland's men] stopped [blocked] the stairs that went up to my lord's chamber where he sat, so that no man could pass up again that came down. At last, one of my lord's servants chanced to look down into the hall ... and returned to my Lord, and showed him that my Lord of Northumberland was in the hall.

Clearly, ascending from the great hall was a flight of steps that led to some kind of dining, or presence chamber at the first-floor level. Here, we might expect that Henry and Catherine would have dined in the presence of the court during their two-day stay at Cawood.

Then, following Wolsey's death, an inventory was taken of all the late cardinal's goods. This is also detailed extensively in the *Letters and Papers of Henry VIII* and consists of a long list of plate, tapestries, valuable soft furnishings, including a 'cloth of estate of plain cloth of gold', chapel vestments, and contents of the many so-called *offices* serving the palace. However, little detail is given that provides us with any greater insight into the key public and private chambers, chambers where Catherine would have spent most of her time while at Cawood. To enrich the picture further, we must roll back time, to the so-called Great Feast of Cawood held in 1465. Perhaps one of the greatest medieval feasts ever recorded, it was staged to celebrate the enthronement of George Neville, brother of the Kingmaker, as Archbishop of York. The list of guests and of the food served survives in Leland's *Collectanea*. Of even greater interest is that the seating arrangements are listed by chamber, and so we hear of the great hall, the chief chamber, the second chamber, the low hall and the gallery.

While each of these contemporary documents contributes another fragment of the picture, Alastair Oswald synthesises these elements, leaving us with a visual impression of the palace that greeted Catherine as she arrived there at Henry's side on the 4 September 1541:

> The building known [today] as the Banqueting House (a tradition probably referring to the notoriously extravagant 'Great Feast of Cawood' in 1465) occupied the front range of the outer court and therefore probably provided stabling and accommodation. The real dining hall would have occupied the range between the two courts. A chapel would have stood on one side of the inner court and the Archbishop's private accommodation, which he would, of course, surrendered to any royal visitor, would have occupied the rear side of the inner court, or perhaps the eastern side, looking towards the gardens, the village church, and with an oblique view of the river unspoiled by any ungodly activities on the wharf.

The Demise of Cawood Castle

When Henry and Catherine visited Cawood in 1541, after several centuries of continuous occupation, the castle was nearing the end of its eventful history. Blood and Talyor state that 'after the fall of Wolsey, the palace was clearly in a poor state and subsequent archbishops seem largely to have abandoned Cawood in favour of their palace at Bishopthorpe, much closer to York. By the early seventeenth century most of the land ... had been leased out.'

However, it was the English Civil War which sealed the fate of this most noble of estates. Cawood was caught up in the fighting between Royalist and Parliamentarian forces. After the conclusion of the war, on 30 April 1646, Parliament resolved that Cawood, along with several other northern garrisons, be made untenable; and thus the old castle was reduced to a ruin, only the gatehouse and its adjacent range surviving the onslaught of demolition.

Visitor Information

Cawood is no longer the strategically important location it once was. This bustling medieval village, frequented by kings, queens, princes and archbishops now rests quietly amid relatively flat, open pasture land. It is almost as if this historic spot has seen too much drama at the centre of English affairs and now has gratefully taken its ease in a long awaited repose.

If you drive southwards from York to visit the village, you are likely to travel along the Fulford Road, passing the Fulford Cross (postcode: YO10 4PB; see also the King's Manor and St Mary's Abbey, York). This most historic of monuments has come to an ignominious end, the crumbling remains standing defiantly by the side of a busy thoroughfare, adjacent to a supermarket car park. However, perhaps you might still pause, pulling up in the car park as we did, to acknowledge this place where Catherine watched the submission of the humiliated citizens of York.

Heading further south on your journey, the woods surrounding Cawood that Leland mentioned in his *Itinerary* seem largely to have disappeared, and the old ferry, which for hundreds of years conveyed travellers across the river now replaced by a slightly archaic-looking, mid-nineteenth-century steel bridge. On the far side, the quay is long gone.

At the traffic lights, turn left; the stately remains of Cawood Castle will appear very quickly on your right-hand side. Unless you have booked to stay at the castle through the Landmark Trust, you will not be able to access its interior. However, having seen inside the gatehouse for ourselves, we can highly recommend staying in these once high-status rooms. Views from the rooftop are spectacular, and staying here must be very special indeed; everyday knowing the likes of Catherine Howard, Henry VIII, Thomas Wolsey, Edward I and a young Richard III travelled through the passageway beneath you. Take heed, though; this is a popular destination and is often fully booked well in advance. If you wish to stay there, you would be well advised to plan at least one year ahead, particularly if you intend to stay during the busy summer months.

If you are not staying at the castle, do not despair as there are excellent external views of the remains from both the road to the front, and from the Castle Garth (once the castles' gardens), both of which are fully accessible to the public. Do note, though, that when you are standing in front of the castle next to the road, you are standing inside the courtyard of the original building, or possibly on the site of the old banqueting hall, where the Great Feast of Cawood took place over five hundred years earlier. The castle covered most of the ground running down to the river from this point. The road, of course, was a much later addition.

For rest and refreshment, there is a pub adjacent to the bridge by the river. Sadly, we visited on a Monday, when it is closed through much of the day. However, there is a pleasant garden, the perfect place to ponder on the giants of English history who have passed this way before you.

You can contact the Landmark Trust who own and rent out Cawood Castle as a holiday let on +44 (0) 162 882 5925; email: bookings@landmarktrust.org.uk. Website: http://www.landmarktrust.org.uk/.

Postcode for Cawood Castle: YO8 3SG.

The King's Manor and St Mary's Abbey, York

[Thanks to] the King for appointing them the house, which of late was called St. Mary's Abbey without the city of York.

The Council of the North to Thomas Cromwell,
written on 17 December 1539

The ancient city of York is a medieval jewel; the gateway to the rugged, but poetic, beauty of North Yorkshire's dales and moorlands. After the Romans established the fortress town of *Eboracum* in the first century AD, the city went through periods of decline and revival, until, in the ninth century, it became firmly established as the Viking capital of the north, Jorvik. Situated on the banks of the navigable River Ouse, Jorvik soon became an important northern trading post, prospering through the Middle Ages as the port grew in importance. We can imagine sailing ships docking on the quay, bringing fine wines from Europe while increasingly craftsmen flocked to find work in a city that had become noted for its wool and leather trade.

By the time of Catherine's visit in 1541, the great medieval buildings of York, such as its Gothic minster and the once powerful Abbey of St Mary's, were established, and in the case of the latter, already in decline. However, they must have defined the skyline of a city whose cramped medieval streets had long ago begun to spill over its confining walls, such that York, as it was by then known, enclosed 'extensive areas of pasture, gardens and orchards'.

The city was to be the most northerly destination of the 1541 progress. In some ways, also its centrepiece, as it was here that Henry expected to meet with his nephew, James V, King of Scotland. The exact purpose of this meeting, and Henry's intentions toward Scotland, remains contentious. Some academic sources suggest that Henry was seeking to provoke conflict with the Scots and rally support in Yorkshire and the north for a military campaign, with others suggesting that the English king wished to close down the threat against his northern border so that he might turn his attentions toward waging war with France. Either way, the king's usually omnipotent will was to be thwarted; James would never materialise. However, just as at Lincoln, York provided another opportunity for the submission – and some might say humiliation – of Henry's rebellious northern subjects.

Wisely, the citizens of York recognised Henry's dark mood and his uncompromising stance toward the northern rebels, such that upon hearing of the impending visit, they, like other towns before them, set forth to demonstrate their absolutely loyalty to the Crown by planning a grand reception for the king and queen. This reception was to include a number of set pieces designed to convey not only their unconditional submission, but also a very specific message: that through the king's mercy, the townsfolk of York would receive his majesty's forgiveness and redemption. By the 12 July, the Lord Mayor, Robert Hall had commanded the erection of scaffolds around Micklegate Bar, where, according to tradition that stretched back as far as Richard II, it was assumed that the royal party would enter the city. Then, in August,

> It was agreed that Mr Recorder shall ride to Bolton to my lord archbishop, to desire his grace of his best advice and counsel, how and after what manner they should submit themselves to the king's highness on the coming of his majesty to the city, and whether the said presence in the name of the whole body of this city should confess themselves guilty in anything done in the time of the late rebellion, according as the Lincolnshire men had done …

In the end, perhaps in a deliberate act meant to further subjugate the citizens of York, Henry approached York from the south along the Fulford Road on 18 September, having travelled the roughly 15 miles from Wressel Castle. In his informative paper on Henry VIII's progress through Yorkshire, Tim Thorton of Huddersfield University describes how 'instead of entering through a carefully choreographed statement of the city's loyalty at Micklegate, in which the king would have been made complicit, the corporation, many of the leading citizen's and the gentry of the Ainsty were left to kneel ignominiously round the cross at Fulford, while the Recorder read out a submission'.

No doubt Catherine witnessed the whole affair, mounted upon her horse, alongside her husband. At the end of it, Henry was handed parchment upon which were scribed their words of repentance, their sorrow reinforced with a gift of a cup of double silver gilt and £100, while Catherine received 'another cup with £40 therein to the queen's grace for the worship of this city'.

From this point, the royal party moved northward to enter York through Walmgate Bar, the principal entrance from the east. It is clear from medieval maps of York that the most direct route would then have taken Henry and Catherine along Walmgate, Fossgate, Collergate and Petergate (all of which still exist), directly through the heart of the city, past the towering edifice of York Minster and onto the King's Manor, which lay just outside the city walls to the west. Before the Dissolution of the Monasteries, the manor had served as the abbot's lodgings, and therefore, was part of the mighty Abbey of St Mary. Catherine would lodge at the abbey with Henry for the next ten days, while all the while the court must have held its collective breath, anxiously awaiting the arrival of the King of the Scots.

The Development and Buildings of the King's Manor

The Benedictine Abbey had been one of the wealthiest in the north, but the Dissolution had seen its closure in November 1539. By the time of the 1541 progress, the church was being gradually demolished, its bells being taken down at some point in 1541–2. The other monastic buildings of the abbey were also being slighted, valuable building materials, such as the lead from the abbey's roof, gradually being sold off. However, in among the desolation, the medieval abbot's lodging was saved by royal decree; henceforth it was to be known as the King's Manor, and as such, became property of the Crown and the headquarters of the King's Council of the North, who as the quote above shows, formally took possession on 17 December 1539. Traditionally, it is in these lodgings that Henry and Catherine are said to have stayed during their time in York.

The original thirteenth-century abbot's lodgings were extensively rebuilt in the late fifteenth century, principally using brick and terracotta for the window mouldings, which, according to the Royal Commission for Historical Monuments (RCHM), was 'exceptional' for its time, remaining one of the earliest recorded uses of such material for structural work in England. The RCHM goes on to say that 'late 13th-century plinth mouldings, similar to those of the abbey church, still exist in enough places to suggest that the house was U-shaped and of the same extent as the later medieval rebuilding'.

It seems that the building that Catherine would have known had a lower storey built from white magnesian limestone ashlar, supporting a timber-framed first floor, with the public and private chambers arranged around three sides of an open, west-facing courtyard. Views would have been outwards, to the north-east, toward the nearby minster, or to the south-west across the courtyard to the abandoned abbey cloister and chapter house. Between 1539 and 1540, a modest amount of £58 3s 9d was spent on repairs to the palace. However, much more extensive alterations were required for the visit of the royal couple. To complete this work, Clement Throckmorton, an official of the Court of Augmentations was granted a staggering £400 to 'repair and beautify' the building. Given this equates roughly to somewhere in the region of £1 million, the results must have been impressive, its interiors the epitome of luxury. However, closer inspection of the records indicates that what exactly constituted 'the King's Manor' in the mid-sixteenth century is blurred even to those responsible at the time for its maintenance and upkeep. Colvin's *History of the King's Works* states that Throckmorton's accounts do not appear to have survived, but that 'a survey of the Palace of York made a few years later indicates that the "frater" was used as "the king's hall", while the "dorter" served as the queen's lodging'.

This suggests that the royal couple did not actually lodge in the abbot's lodgings, but in part of the old abbey buildings. Professor Christopher Norton, whose paper on *The Buildings of St Mary's Abbey, York and their Destruction*, published in 1994 in the *Journal of the Society of Antiquaries*, argues that this is indeed the case. In unpublished correspondence with Professor Norton, he states that 'the king stayed in the prior's apartments in the west range [of the cloister], the first floor refectory in the south range was used as his hall, while the queen was lodged in the ex-dormitory in the east range'.

A first-hand account of the preparations comes from the French ambassador. Writing from York on 16 September, Marillac had been able to view the extravagant preparations being made to receive the King of Scots. He gives us another precious glimpse into the hive of activity centred on reviving the crumbling fortunes of the once great abbey: 'This king is furnishing a great lodging of an old abbey, on which 1,200 or 1,500 workmen are night and day building, painting, etc., and adding tents and pavilions. Besides, he has had brought from London his richest tapestry, plate, and dress ... with marvellous provision of victuals from all parts.'

Professor Norton goes onto say that the abbot's lodgings were in a poor state. If this is the case, then given all the above, the £400 given to the Court of Augmentations must have gone toward the conversion, repair and beautification of these deserted abbey buildings.

A Belligerent King and a Scottish Snub

Despite the fact that Henry and Catherine remained in York for ten days, there seem to be very few details of how they spent their time. Thornton suggests that this is largely because 'the local predominant response [to the visit] was, strikingly, to choose to forget or at least largely ignore the fact that the event had occurred at all ... Henry's stock stood very low indeed as a king "with the terrible character of neither sparing man in his anger nor woman in his lust".'

However, we know that in terms of state business, two key edicts were issued by Henry during the time that the court resided in York. Both are recorded in the *Letters and Papers of Henry VIII*, the first dated 20 September, which states, 'Any one in these parts grieved for lack of justice from the Council resident in York or any other, might have free access to the King and Council and favourable audience to declare his grief during the King's abode in these parts.'

Despite complaints pouring in from all and sundry from the very next day, Henry appears to have remained recalcitrant and unyielding. The king and council 'examined these complaints, [and] declared them forthwith all to be false and untrue'. The second was a command to the Archbishop of York 'to cause all the shrines with their hovels to be taken down throughout his province'. Thus, several shrines that had remained hitherto untouched in a number of northern churches were dismantled and 'made plain'. Even five hundred years later, it is easy to sense Henry's belligerent mood during the summer of 1541, and it is difficult to imagine

Catherine, young and as yet unburdened by the harsh realities of the Tudor court, finding much carefree pastime in her husband's company. However, one interesting reference from an early twentieth-century publication by the then Dean of York called *Picturesque Old York* states that perhaps Catherine found an alternative source of entertainment: 'He [Henry] wiled away the time in making the abbey buildings more suitable for a royal palace, and Catherine Howard, finding the old city dull, went off with her ladies and courtiers to hunt at Pontefract.'

Such an idea is appealing. At around 20–25 miles from York as the crow flies, a further visit to Pontefract by Catherine would have required her to be away from York for probably at least three nights. Certainly, daily hunting excursions during a progress were the norm, and so this is a possibility. However, since we have not yet been able to validate this information with any other source, we remain sceptical that Catherine simply abandoned her husband at York for several days on end.

Whatever is the truth of the matter, by 26 September, Henry's patience had been exhausted. Rebuked, and possibly feeling humiliated by his nephew's failure to appear, the king and court departed. Neither Catherine, nor Henry, would ever see the city again.

Visitor Information

Like other great medieval cities of England, York is a treasure to be enjoyed in its entirety, containing far more than any single location. Therefore, if you are planning a visit to this one-time capital of the north, then take your time, for there is plenty to enchant the modern-day time traveller. If you wish to explore the city and its environs, perhaps you might absorb yourself completely in the experience of the 1541 progress and book yourself into Cawood Castle, using this as your base (see Cawood Castle). The gatehouse of Cawood is now rented out as a holiday let by the Landmark Trust.

Parking in and around York is plentiful (including a park and ride). However, the city is a tourist hotspot at all times of the year, particularly so in summer. The authors therefore recommend making a point of arriving early. On this occasion, we began our trail around 8 a.m., and were able to visit many of York's most popular outdoor tourist areas almost undisturbed up until about 9 a.m. This is a golden hour before many of the indoor attractions open and the streets rapidly fill with locals and visitors alike.

Walmgate Bar

Having parked on the west side of York (the Barbican Parking), we followed part of the city walls until reaching nearby Walmgate Bar. It is worth noting that, alongside Chester, York has the longest and best-preserved town walls in England, the stone and materials used to construct them estimated as weighing 100,000 metric tons. The walls are 3.4 kilometres long and there are five main 'bars' or gateways and forty-five towers. One of these 'gates' is Walmgate Bar, through which Catherine and Henry entered the city of York. Today, traffic streams past it incessantly, although only pedestrians are allowed to walk beneath it directly in the footsteps of the royal cavalcade. From here it is a fifteen-minute walk along Walmgate, Fossegate, Collergate and Petergate delivering you to the foot of the minster. All the time you might imagine the citizens of York, gathered to give a rather muted welcome to their sovereign lord.

As you go, you will find the streets narrowing progressively, medieval 'snickleways' (a local name for passageway) increasingly leading off in different directions; shops filled with a cornucopia of delights to fascinate and tempt the passer-by. Furthermore, there are so many ancient churches, landmarks and museums to see, and we defy you to pass them by and reach your destination without making several fascinating diversions. However, eventually, having enjoyed several such 'baubles', we arrived at the King's Manor, just outside Bootham Bar on the east of the city. At this point, it is easy to see how the original abbey of St Mary's and the manor lay outside the city's ancient walls.

The King's Manor

Rather fittingly, the King's Manor is now the Centre for Medieval Studies and is part of the University of York. The range that fronts to the entrance makes up the oldest part of the building and would certainly have been familiar to Catherine. Plans of the building, drawn up by the HRMC, show the right-hand side of the range was the part of the manor developed during the sixteenth century, and so may have made up part of the considerable redevelopment of the building prior to the 1541 visit.

You are free to wander around the grounds and even access the building. During week days, the students' refectory is open to the public. This was once part of the manor's great hall, and on this basis it is worth a visit, although its earlier charms have clearly been sacrificed over the years to practicality. We happened to visit on a Saturday, so there were no students around. Happily though, it was possible to wander around the building unimpeded, and although much of the interior has been remodelled, a number of exquisite survivors of earlier interior décor survive. If you are bold enough, you might be able to catch glimpses of them through open doorways, or you might make it your business to see them, as we did. When you have imbibed your fill, leave the building via the front entrance, immediately turning about on yourself to the right once out of the manor gates. This will take you down the side of the King's Manor (allowing you to enjoy more of its architectural charms), to the gardens of the Yorkshire Museum. Here you will find the remains of the Abbey of St Mary.

The Abbey of St Mary

The museum itself was essentially built on top of the abbey cloister, chapter house and other conventual buildings. The dorter and frater referred to in the earlier sections no longer exist. So, if indeed these abbey buildings were used during the visit, they have long since been lost, and remain only to be conjured up in our imagination. However, the gardens make a fine place to rest a while and ponder three remarkable weeks, almost five hundred years ago, when a belligerent king and his young consort were hosted by Henry's reluctant northern subjects.

Other Places of Interest

Sadly, there are no records of how the king and queen were entertained while in York; we know nothing more of who they visited, gifts they were given, or even if they attended the Mass in York Minster, as would have been usual when the sovereigns were received into a provincial city. However, it is almost unthinkable that they did not see the interior of what remains the largest gothic cathedral in northern Europe. We strongly urge you to do the same. There is a considerable entrance fee but it is, in our opinion, worth it.

If you wish to sample more of the city Catherine would have seen as she progressed through Tudor York, wander a while through its medieval streets; Stonegate and The Shambles are particular favourites of ours. In doing so, you will never be far from enticing coffee bars and English tea rooms, with Betty's (there are two, and we recommend the ancient charms of the one on Stonegate) being perhaps one of the most famous tea rooms in England. It is our absolute favourite place to go for breakfast or afternoon tea. Betty's telephone number: +44 (0) 845 600 1919; website: www.bettys.co.uk.

There are many other wonderful medieval/Tudor buildings in York. While these are evocative of the age, they are not directly linked with the 1541 progress, and therefore lie beyond the scope of this book. We strongly urge you supplement your visit with wider research of some of the best places to visit, although do not forget to walk the medieval walls. We can particularly recommend climbing up to them at Monkgate and walking in an anticlockwise direction. This will give you some of the most outstanding views of the minster you are likely to see. In all, the amateur historian can easily spend two days in York, so at least plan for an overnight stay, maybe two if possible. If you are not basing yourself there, you might also want to combine your visit with nearby Cawood Castle (see the entry on Cawood Castle), lying 8 miles to the south of the city.

Postcode for King's Manor: YO1 7EP.

Thornton Abbey, Lincolnshire

> This has been the finest place that ever I saw in my life. If the gaithouse be thus neate, undoubtedly the building of the college and the abby was one hundred times more excellent.
>
> Abraham de la Pryme, 1697

On 6 October, Henry VIII, accompanied by Catherine Howard and an extensive retinue, crossed the Humber from Hull to Barrow and made their way to the former Augustinian Abbey of Thornton, where they remained for three days. The royal couple were on their way back to London after having progressed through Lincolnshire and Yorkshire, and had, by this stage, been travelling for three months.

Layout and Short History of the Abbey

Founded in the twelfth century, Thornton Abbey was one of Britain's wealthiest Augustinian abbeys. Like other great monastic houses of the day, the abbey precinct was divided into an outer court and an inner court, with the principal access via a great gatehouse in the west. The whole complex was walled and surrounded by a moat. At the heart of the precinct, in the inner court, stood the monastic buildings arranged around a cloister on the south side of the church. The east range contained the dormitory block and a vestibule that formed the entrance to the chapter house. In the south range, the refectory and the western range served as the abbot's lodgings and guestrooms, where it's possible that Henry and Catherine were lodged during their stay.

There would also have been fishponds, workshops and stables and other domestic buildings, including an infirmary, a *reredorter* or communal latrine, a bakehouse, brewhouse and a kitchen somewhere near the refectory. A park of 80 acres and various gardens, cottages and barns are also mentioned in grants made during the reign of Edward VI.

By 1521, it was 'one of the goodliest houses of England of canons'. It was also one of only a handful of monasteries to survive the Dissolution by becoming a secular college, set up for 'the ministration of the sacraments, the observance of good manners, the care of the aged and those who had spent their lives in the service of the realm, and for the instruction of the young'.

Unfortunately, the abbey's unusual transition was short lived, and in 1547, Edward VI dissolved the college, the site of which was eventually granted to Henry Randes, Bishop of Lincoln, whose son sold it to Sir Robert Tyrwhitt of Kettleby in 1575. Sir Robert's grandson, Robert, in turn sold it to Sir Vincent Skinner of Westminster. The English antiquary Abraham de la Pryme, writing in 1697, relates that Sir Vincent pulled down some of the college buildings to build a 'large but somewhat low hall'. Pryme's description is one of the most helpful in understanding the appearance of the buildings at this time, and so is reproduced here, almost in full:

> From thence I went to Thornton. I was amazed to see the vast stupendious fragments of the buildings that have been there. There is all the gait-house yet standing, of a vast an incredible biggness, and of the greatest art, ingenuity and workmanship, that ever I saw in my life. There is four or five images, standing in the front thereof, of excellent simitry and workmanship, and upon every exalted or turrited stone in the battlements of the gatehouse, and on the top of the turrits, stands images, from the middle, of men with swords, shields, pole-axes, etc., in their hands, looking downwards; and I was told that upon the battlements of the whole college, when it was standing, was innumerable statues of the greatest ingenuity and workmanship imaginable, some in shape of soldiers, others of astronomers, others of carpenters, others of all trades and sciences, so that looking up, the battlements of all the whole building seemed to be covered with armed men. There are abundance of images yet, on various places of the

gatehouse, of dogs, bulls, bears, foxes, lions, etc. The passage all over a vast moat is of delicate workmanship and ingenuity, so that I cannot easy describe the same.

There is ther the hugest finest court that ever I saw in my life, with two rows of trees on each side, on both sides of which trees is the ruins of vast buildings to be seen, and the like almost all over. At the north side is the fragments of the chappel, of mighty fine stone, and curious workmanship, which, by the arches that is now stand[ing], appears to be above half buried in the ground in its own ruins … Out of part of the old buildings is built a large but somewhat low hall, not farr of the aforesayd chappel, which, with the whole estate, belongs to the Lady Skinner …

This has been the finest place that ever I saw in my life. If the gaithouse be thus neate, undoubtedly the building of the college and the abby was one hundred times more excellent.

He goes on to state that 'Skinner built another hall [the first house he built quickly fell into disrepair] out of part of the stones that the other was built of, which hall now stands on the east side of the court of the abby, and is all built on arches of some of the old building'.

This other hall is the 'low hall' mentioned earlier in his account and is today known as 'Abbot's Lodge'. This building incorporates the ground floor of a thirteenth- or early fourteenth-century monastic range, the first floor of which was entirely rebuilt in the seventeenth century. While the name points to this building having been the abbot's lodgings, where high-status guests, like the king and queen, would have traditionally been lodged, it's now thought that the abbot's lodgings were in fact in the west claustral range, as previously mentioned, or possibly in a separate building identified in a geophysical survey in 2011 that once stood south of the chapter house.

Remains of Thornton Abbey

The avenue of trees that so impressed the diarist is gone, as are the figures on the ramparts of the gateway. The 'chappel' mentioned in de la Pryme's account was in fact the chapter house, of which there are still some remains standing. Only the foundations remain of the western range, where the Tudor monarchs may have slept, and nothing at all above ground of the possible separate abbot's house discovered in 2011. Luckily, the imposing fourteenth-century gatehouse survives!

Above the entrance still stand the carved figures of the Virgin, St John the Baptist on the left and a bishop on the right, possibly St Augustine the Doctor. As you marvel at their intricacy and beauty, remember that Catherine too would have gazed upon these, and passed under the lofty archway, still hung with the original oak doors that visitors use to this day. The gatehouse would have originally been rendered with white mortar (so that the brick would not have been visible) and was probably administrative in function, possibly containing the abbot's court and exchequer.

The quality and detail of the surviving sculptures and decoration attest to the magnificence and wealth of the abbey in its heyday. It may go some way to explaining why Henry saved the building from total destruction, and chose this fairly isolated location as the site for the College of the Holy Trinity of Thornton.

Visitor Information

We have visited many locations associated with Henry's Tudor England. Each has a unique flavour, some standing out above the crowd – and for many different reasons. The ruins of Thornton Abbey is one such place; its isolated position on the edge of Lincolnshire means that the time traveller will never find themselves 'just passing by' in order to visit. For all but those who live locally, it is a destination requiring us to make the pilgrimage for the sole sake of visiting this once magnificent abbey. Its position is among the most restful places that you will encounter on your travels.

Having stayed overnight locally, we hopped in the car early, aiming to arrive for opening time. From a distance, the enormous abbey gateway can be seen towering above the flat Lincolnshire countryside surrounding it. Its reputation as one of the most awe-inspiring surviving medieval gateways does not disappoint. It is majestic. Arriving early meant that we virtually had the place to ourselves. This only added to the tranquillity of the place. The visitor can explore inside the gateway, as well as take a stroll across lush pasture land to the site of the ruined abbey itself. The site is managed by English Heritage and so information boards, placed here and there, do help you orientate yourself. Dogs are allowed on-site but not beyond the gate that leads to the abbey ruins. They must remain on a leash at all times.

You may wish to combine your visit with Lincoln (40 miles away) and/or Gainsborough Old Hall (35 miles away). If you wish to stay over locally, we would happily recommend Croxton House Bed and Breakfast (ask for the double room with the enormous en suite, facing out over the front gardens!). They can be contacted via their website: http://www.croxtonhousebedandbreakfast.co.uk/.

For more information about the abbey itself and opening times, visit the English Heritage web site on http://www.english-heritage.org.uk/visit/places/thornton-abbey-and-gatehouse.

Postcode: DN39 6TU.

Chenies Manor House, Buckinghamshire

> Beautifully mellow under the trees by the church, and archaeologically a fascinating puzzle.
>
> Nikolaus Pevsner, architectural historian, 1960

By late October 1541, the court had returned from their long progress north and was settling back into the routine of everyday life. Towards the end of the month, we find Catherine Howard at Chenies Manor in Buckinghamshire, the home of Sir John Russell, where a Privy Council meeting was recorded as having taken place on the 25th. While all appeared normal on the surface, Henry and his young wife were blissfully unaware that a cataclysmic storm was brewing, one that would end with the execution of four people, including Henry's 'rose without a thorn'.

A Storm on the Horizon

Sometime in October 1541, a courtier and Protestant fundamentalist, named Thomas Lascelle, whose sister had resided in the household of the Dowager Duchess of Norfolk alongside Catherine, approached Thomas Cranmer with a story about the queen's colourful past, including her alleged relationship with her former music teacher Henry Manox and one Francis Dereham. The news was worrying enough for the archbishop to take to Lord Audley and the Earl of Hertford, who all agreed that the king needed to be informed. This Cranmer did in writing, leaving a note for the king in the Holy Day Closet at Hampton Court Palace revealing the queen's alleged pre-nuptial sexual liaisons. While all involved expected Henry to react furiously, he instead calmly ordered an enquiry into the queen's conduct, primarily to protect her reputation, confident that the accusations were unfounded. The investigations, though, proved the king wrong, and revealed further damning details about Catherine's youthful folly and even more damaging allegations of a recent affair with a member of the king's household, Thomas Culpeper. During questioning, Alice Restwold, one of Catherine's attendants, mentioned the queen's recent visit to 'Cheyneys, the lord Admiral's house', so it's possible that one of the queen's illicit meetings with Culpeper took place there.

The Tudor House

The house that greeted Catherine was a sprawling complex of buildings surrounded by parkland and formal gardens. Originally constructed in the mid-fifteenth century, it was extended and refurbished in the late 1520s or early 1530s by Catherine's host, Sir John Russell, a rising star at the Tudor court. He inherited the house through his marriage to Anne Sapcote and set about transforming it into a residence worthy of hosting royalty. Leland, who visited Chenies not long after Catherine's visit, said,

> The olde House of the Cheyneis is so translated by my Lorde Russel, that hath that house on the right of his wife, that litle or nothing of it yn a maner remaynith untranslated: and a great deale of the House is even newly set up made of brike and timber: and fair logginges be new erected in the gardein. The house is within diverse places richely painted with antique workes of white and blak. And there be about the House 2 parkes, as I remembre.

While no sixteenth-century image of the house survives, it's thought that the luxurious state apartments were in the north, overlooking the splendid formal gardens. By 1541, Henry's expanding girth and badly ulcerated leg would have prevented the king from occupying the rooms on the first floor. Instead, he would have been accommodated in a chamber on the ground floor. A narrow passage connected the still-extant church in the east with the medieval great hall that intersected the north range at a right angle, beyond which stood the state apartments, forming a T-shape of sorts. The main entrance to the complex was in the west, where two flanking buildings marked the entryway. Sadly, little else is known about the house's appearance or layout during the reign of Henry VIII.

Visiting Chenies Manor Today

Very little is left of the house that Catherine and Henry visited in the autumn of 1541. Much of the vast complex disappeared over the centuries or was significantly altered, and so almost all of what you see today post-dates Catherine's visit. Nevertheless, it is still a site worth visiting, albeit with a good dose of imagination! When standing in the inner court, with the gated entrance to the house and church on your left, you're facing the south range with its wonderful twisted Tudor chimneys, built around the summer of 1550. While this building was obviously not standing at the time of Henry and Catherine's visit, the smaller west wing was. This range would have originally extended further north, and contained the great hall mentioned earlier.

If you turn now and face the opposite direction, you'll be facing a boundary wall, which separates the inner courtyard from the 'labyrinth' maze, Orchard and Kitchen Garden beyond, accessed via a gate in the northwest corner. Here, very close to the boundary wall, once stood the narrow passage that led from the church to the great hall and beyond to the sumptuous royal lodgings, of which nothing remains above ground. Take your time exploring these gardens, as they occupy part of the site of the original Tudor gardens. When standing with the 'labyrinth' on your right, try and imagine the striking north range, where Catherine and Henry slept, rising to the left of you, in the space today occupied by farm buildings.

While exploring the beautiful sunken garden, reminiscent of those at Hampton Court Palace, take note of the brick building in the far right corner as you enter, as it too was standing at the time of Catherine's visit. The guided tour of the house will reveal the building's interesting Elizabethan connections, including a room believed to be where Elizabeth I worked during her visits to Chenies.

It's difficult not to pity Catherine, who during her stay had no inkling of the danger she was in. Within a fortnight she would be confined to her apartments at Hampton Court Palace, and within a month she would no longer be England's queen. Catherine would pay the ultimate price for her youthful indiscretions, meeting her end on a scaffold in the Tower of London.

Visitor Information

For opening times and other visitor information, visit the Chenies Manor website at http://www.cheniesmanorhouse.co.uk/home, or telephone + 44 (0) 149 476 2888.

Postcode for Chenies Manor House: WD3 6ER.

Syon Abbey, London

> The Queen's departing to Syon shall be on Monday next or later. The ladies and others appointed to depart shall do so on Monday, and only such remain at Hampton Court as shall attend her to Syon.
>
> *Letters and Papers*, November 1541

On or near the site now occupied by the Georgian mansion Syon House, the London home of the Duke of Northumberland, once stood Syon Abbey, England's only monastery of the Bridgettine order, founded in 1415 by Henry V. It was originally built in Twickenham Park, across from Henry V's Shene Palace (later rebuilt and renamed Richmond Palace by Henry VII), but was moved to a new site (that of Syon House) in 1426, where it flourished until it was suppressed on 25 November 1539. The empty monastic buildings passed into the possession of the Crown and were used by Henry VIII as a royal house. Here Catherine Howard was confined for almost three months in the late autumn and winter of 1541/2 after the discovery of her pre-marital affairs and her private meetings with Thomas Culpeper. Then five years later, in 1547, the coffined body of Henry VIII rested in the abbey church on its way to burial at Windsor.

A Young Queen Imprisoned

In the middle of November 1541, the queen was moved from Hampton Court Palace, where she'd been confined to her apartments for a week, to Syon House. Catherine, as the French ambassador Marillac told Francis I on 11 November, 'has taken no kind of pastime but kept in her chamber, whereas, before, she did nothing but dance and rejoice, and now when the musicians come they are told that it is no more the time to dance'.

There were certainly no revelries at the former monastery of Syon. Catherine would spend the last few months of her short life hoping and praying for a royal pardon that would never arrive, although rather strangely, the Spanish ambassador Eustace Chapuys reported to the Emperor Charles V on 29 January 1542, that 'she [Catherine] is still in Sion House, making good cheer, fatter and handsomer than ever she was, taking great care of her person, well dressed, and much adorned [with jewels]; more imperious and commanding, and more difficult to please than she ever was when living with the King, her husband'.

Perhaps Catherine was in denial and unwilling to accept the danger she was in, or perhaps the stress of her imprisonment was causing her to ricochet wildly between hysteria and calm, not unlike the behaviour displayed by her cousin Queen Anne Boleyn during her imprisonment. As for Catherine's jewels, these had been confiscated before her removal to Syon House, so it's also possible that the ambassador's sources had got the story wrong. Furthermore, as we shall shortly see, Henry's instructions were clear: she was to be 'lodged moderately.'

The man in charge of this bleak household was Catherine's vice-chamberlain, Sir Edward Baynton. He was also Catherine's brother-in-law, through his marriage to her half-sister, Isabel, who had served Catherine since her elevation to queenship. On 11 November, Thomas Cranmer, who by this stage had conducted several interviews with the queen at Hampton Court Palace, received instructions from the Privy Council pertaining to her removal to Syon House:

She is to be removed to Syon House, and there lodged moderately, as her life has deserved, without any cloth of estate, with a chamber for Mr. Baynton and the rest to dine in, and two for her own use, and with a mean number of servants, as in a book herewith. She shall have four gentlewomen and two chamberers at her choice, save that my lady Baynton shall be one, whose husband shall have the government of the whole house and be associated with the Almoner.

Nothing is known about how Catherine spent her days at Syon. It's likely that she received at least two visits from lords of the Privy Council during her confinement. We hear from Chapuys that

immediately after Parliament had pronounced sentence, wishing to proceed with all moderation and justice in the Queen's case, had sent to her certain privy councillors and members of Parliament to propose that she should, if she wished, defend her own case in that assembly. This the Queen refused, submitting herself entirely to the King's commiseration and will, all the time admitting and owning that she deserved death.

Catherine would not have long to wait. In January 1542, a Bill of Attainder against her and Lady Rochford was introduced in Parliament, and, among other things, recorded that

the said Queen and lady Rochford are, by authority of this Parliament, convicted and attainted of high treason, and shall suffer accordingly; and the said Queen, lady Rocheford, Culpeper, and Dereham shall forfeit to the Crown all possessions which they held on 25 Aug. 33 Hen. VIII. The Royal assent to this Act shall be given by commission … To avoid doubts in future, it is declared that the Royal assent given by commission shall be valid in all cases hereafter, that any lightness of the queen for the time being may be revealed to the King or his Council, and that an unchaste woman marrying the King shall be guilty of high treason.

The clause inserted by Parliament, which stated that the royal assent would be given by commission, meant that Henry did not have to agree to the bill in person. Rather than having to attend a ceremony in which the whole text of the bill was read aloud, which 'might reopen a wound already closing in the Royal Bosom', the monarch could now appoint commissioners for this purpose.

On the afternoon of 10 February 1542, the Lord Privy Seal and members of the council arrived to escort Catherine to the Tower of London. All signs of the 'imperious and commanding' woman described in Chapuys' earlier report were gone. Instead, the lords were confronted with a panicked and frightened girl, who after some resistance boarded the barge with her ladies and began her final journey. Chapuys described the pitiful scene:

On the afternoon of the 10th, the Queen after some difficulty and resistance was conducted to the Tower by the river. The Lord Privy Seal, with a number of privy councillors and a large retinue of servants, went first in a large oared barge; then came a small covered boat with the Queen and four ladies of her suite, besides four sailors to man the boat. Then followed the duke of Suffolk in a big and well-manned barge, with plenty of armed men inside. On their arrival at the Tower stairs the Lord Privy Seal and the duke of Suffolk landed first; then the Queen herself, dressed in black velvet, with the same honors and ceremonies as if she were still reigning.

The site of the Tower only served to heighten Catherine's already fragile state. Marillac reported to the King of France that her execution was expected to take place without delay but 'as she weeps, cries, and torments herself miserably, without ceasing, it is deferred for three or four days, to give her leisure to recover'.

On the day following Catherine's arrival to the Tower, the attainder received the royal assent. The condemned former queen had only two days left to live.

The Fate of the Monastery Buildings

Very little is known for certain about the appearance and layout of the monastic complex at Syon. While most abbeys conformed to a basic layout – a large church surrounded by cloisters and other monastic buildings – Syon was a little different. It was a Bridgettine monastery, and so housed both men and women, who lived separately, necessitating double of many of the usual abbey buildings. The brothers had their own cloister and associated buildings, as did the nuns. The two groups came together for worship in the abbey church, but even then, the ingenious design was such that they could remain invisible to one another. While the brothers sat in the choir, the sisters occupied a mezzanine gallery above them. Recent archaeological investigations suggest that the church at Syon was one of the largest in medieval England; at around 80 metres long by 30 metres wide, it was double the width of King's College Chapel in Cambridge and comparable to Salisbury Cathedral.

Syon was also built to cater for the many pilgrims that flocked there from all over Europe. They would have been housed in the outer precincts of the abbey, where the monastic bakery, the brewhouse, grain mill, coal house and slaughterhouse would have stood. The spiritual benefits on offer at Syon were not the only attraction: the abbey housed one of the largest libraries in England, containing over 1,500 books that drew in scholars from all over the world, including Erasmus and Thomas More.

There would also have been accommodation for royal and aristocratic guests. Henry VI maintained his own chamber in the abbey precincts, and Margaret Beaufort and Katherine of Aragon were regular visitors. According to William Latymer, who served as chaplain to Anne Boleyn, Anne too visited the nuns at Syon, while staying at nearby Richmond Palace in early December 1535. This seems to have been part of an organised effort to try and persuade the community to accept the king as head of the Church. While the sisters had warmly welcomed

Henry's first queen, Anne's reception was much frostier. Despite this visit and others from Thomas Cromwell, the king's physicians, various academics and the Bishop of London, resistance against the Crown continued at Syon, and in November 1539 the abbey was finally suppressed.

Where exactly Catherine Howard was lodged during her stay is unknown. After Henry VIII's death, Edward Seymour, Duke of Somerset and Lord Protector of England, acquired the property and demolished some of the abbey buildings, reusing the materials to construct a grand Renaissance house, built partly on the footprint of the enormous abbey church. He laid out new gardens, including one established by his physician, William Turner, said to be the first botanical garden in the country. After the duke's execution in 1552, John Dudley, Duke of Northumberland, acquired the house. It was here that his daughter-in-law, Lady Jane Grey, learned that she was to become queen.

After a brief return of the nuns in the reign of Mary I, Syon again reverted to the Crown. It remained a royal residence until it was leased to the 9th Earl of Northumberland in 1594, by which time the house was essentially the one you see standing today. The earl eventually obtained the freehold of the estate in 1604, at which time it was reported as being in some disrepair. He spent a considerable amount of money refurbishing the house and may have been responsible for clearing away the remains of the abbey complex.

In the eighteenth century, the interiors of Syon House were completely redesigned by Robert Adam and the grounds transformed by the English landscape architect Lancelot 'Capability' Brown. In the following century the exterior of the house was reworked, the building being clad in Bath stone and a Porte Cochere added.

Today, Syon House is the home of the Duke and Duchess of Northumberland, who open it to the public throughout the year. Visitors are free to roam the beautiful grounds where Catherine Howard and other prominent Tudor personalities once walked, many of whom, by their own actions or those of their ambitious families, met their end under the executioner's axe.

Visitor Information

For opening times and other visitor information, please visit the Syon House website at http://www.syonpark.co.uk, or telephone +44 (0) 208 560 0882.

Postcode for Syon House: TW8 8JF.

Part Seven
Katherine Parr

'TO BE USEFUL IN ALL THAT I DO'

Introduction

Legend has it that Katherine Parr always knew her destiny was to be queen. There is a tale that originates in an annotated copy of John Bale's *Centuries* that, when she was a child, a fortune teller told Katherine that 'crowns not needles were in her future' and that her 'hands were ordained for sceptres'. Most historians now believe this tale to be apocryphal and indeed, if Katherine ever held such notions as a child then by the turn of her third decade of life, flighty imagination must have conceded itself to the realities of time and circumstance. By this time, Lady Latimer was a mature woman of thirty and twice widowed. Although her dowers had left her well provided for, during the course of her last marriage the Latimers had narrowly escaped the damning – and fatal – accusation of treason (associated with Lord Latimer's dubious role in the Pilgrimage of Grace). As 1543 dawned and Lord Latimer lay dying, Katherine had already proven herself to be a dutiful, loyal wife; her character was inherently kind and generous, her mind fiercely curious, her intellect sharp. However, through the lens of time, at least, there is no obvious indication that the sceptre which had been prophesied many years earlier was about to fall into her hands.

Indeed, to the time traveller looking back on Katherine's life, it is difficult to decide whether her story is a fairy tale, charting the rise of a simple gentlewoman to a noble (and much-admired) queen, or one that details a sequence of dramatic (and sometimes traumatic) events that outstripped the norm – and from which Katherine *almost* emerged triumphant. Yet fascinate it does, for Katherine Parr's story is of such enormous improbability that it is beguiling. The twists and turns captivate us, not least because at the centre of it all is a woman of formidable character and competence, steering not only herself, but those whom she loved, on a steady course, always constant and often self-sacrificing. In short, she is a woman one can easily admire.

Katherine Parr's Early Life

Katherine's date and place of birth are obscure, although it is widely accepted that she was probably born at Blackfriars in London around the year 1512. We can definitively place the whereabouts of Katherine Parr in her early years at Rye House in Hertfordshire. This became the family home when Katherine was around five years old in 1517. Here she seems to have stayed until her first marriage to Edward Borough in 1529. Unlike the itinerant royal households in which Katherine of Aragon, Anne of Cleves and, to a degree, Anne Boleyn were raised, Mistress Parr grew to adulthood in a highly stable family environment, surrounded by the companionship of her siblings and cousins. The effects of the clear maternal affection poured upon all the Parr children, the education received at Rye House and the protected constancy of her environment clearly forged a well-balanced young woman; such maturity shines through at all stages in Katherine's life.

A Married Woman

While the new Lady Borough remains in relatively sharp focus during her early adult years (in that she is easily placed at Gainsborough Old Hall, and later as mistress of her own household in Kirton-in-Lindsey), a set of fortuitous circumstances, common sense and an artefact left behind by Katherine at Sizergh Castle are our only guides to her movements following the death of her first husband in 1533.

However, with Katherine's remarriage around one year later, we find ourselves once more with a surer footing. The trials and tribulations of the Latimers during the turbulent uprising now known as the Pilgrimage of Grace shine a light on a brief period of Katherine's residence at Snape Castle as the second Lady Latimer. Frustratingly, however, there are only vague details of Katherine's whereabouts after the family left Snape in 1537. Probably for safety's sake, the Latimers moved south, mainly dividing their time over the next six years between Lord Latimer's residences in Yorkshire, Northamptonshire and London.

One can now sense Katherine moving toward the destiny which awaited her. And yet, the period between 1537 and 1543 lacks detail. Katherine seems to fade temporarily into the background; we infer her presence at the side of her husband, or managing his property while Lord Latimer travelled north on the king's business. We see glimpses of the people – family, friends and acquaintances – with whom she likely came in contact as a result of their physical presence close to the Latimers' various properties. This is particularly true in Northamptonshire and London. We know also of her familial ties to court through her younger sister and brother. And yet exactly when Katherine resided at these various properties, when she was introduced at court, how and when she met and fell in love with Thomas Seymour, how and why Henry VIII singled out Katherine as his new consort, and when her reformist ideas matured are simply left open to conjecture. We have, however, attempted to follow Katherine through these tumultuous years, recreating for the time traveller the very different places and social milieu that leads us closer to the heart of Henry's royal England and to Katherine's elevation to the pinnacle of Tudor society.

Katherine the Queen

After Katherine's marriage to Henry at Hampton Court on 12 July 1543, the new Queen of England once again moves into the spotlight and is easily traceable at the king's side. At no point is Katherine's presence in history more strongly felt though than during her period as Regent of England. Proclamations, declarations and correspondence allow us to follow her to two locations that are most strongly and specifically connected to Katherine: Woking Palace and Otford. Woking saw Katherine Parr at the zenith of her power, surrounded by Henry's three children, with the queen governing England alongside the Privy Council. At Otford, a victorious but ageing king was reunited with Katherine on English soil in early October 1544.

The final location included in this section is Katherine's last home, Sudeley Castle. This romantic Tudor location is nestled in a verdant Gloucestershire valley. It witnessed Katherine's only known pregnancy and her demise from puerperal fever just days later. She lies entombed in the tiny chapel in the castle's garden, the only Queen of England to be buried on private ground.

Katherine leaves us with a legacy of ideas and ideals expounded through her writing. In this way, of all Henry's wives, it is possible to get up close and personal to the mind of a Tudor queen. Her personal correspondence opens the door to look into a passionate life and a generous heart that finally – after so many years of tumult – united Henry's household in the winter of the king's life.

Rye House, Hertfordshire

> The house is an old strong building that stands alone, encompassed with a moat, and towards the garden has high walls, so that twenty men might easily defend it for some time against five hundred.
>
> *A True Account and Declaration of the Horrid Conspiracy Against the Late King, His Present Majesty, and the Government,* 1685

At some point during the first few years of Katherine's life, Rye House in rural Hertfordshire became the Parr children's permanent home. Here, Katherine and her younger siblings, William and Anne, would spend their formative years being educated alongside several cousins, including Maud, eldest daughter of Katherine's uncle, William Parr of Horton. It was the beginning of a lifelong friendship. Alongside Katherine's younger sister Anne, Maud would become one of Katherine's closest friends and confidantes, even serving the dowager queen during her final few months at Sudeley Castle (see entry on Sudeley Castle).

The Making of a Tudor Queen

The Parrs moved to Rye House after leasing it from Sir Thomas's cousin Sir Andrew Ogard. However, not long after establishing the household there, on 11 November 1517, Sir Thomas Parr died of the sweating sickness at his London home in Blackfriars. He was forty years of age. In death, Katherine's mother would be entombed next to her husband in the now lost church of St Anne's, Blackfriars, close to the family's city base. However, despite the obvious importance of this residence, it seems Sir Thomas and Lady Maud opted instead for a rural upbringing for their offspring, a common practice for wealthy Tudor families. It afforded a healthier environment for children with its abundant green open spaces and healthy fresh air.

Katherine was just five years old at the time of Sir Thomas's demise, so probably remembered very little about him. Quite in contrast, though, her mother would become a central, much-loved and highly influential figure in the young girl's life. At the time of her husband's death, Lady Parr was twenty-five years old. With three small children to care for, Maud divided her time between her duties at court as lady-in-waiting and close friend of Katherine of Aragon, and those of her role as chatelaine at Rye. It is here that Katherine's mother established a schoolroom for the younger generation of Parrs, and it is here that we can imagine Katherine receiving the avant-garde humanist education that was becoming fashionable at the beginning of the sixteenth century. Indeed, as an adult, Katherine's sister Anne would recall how their mother had modelled the Parr children's tuition on that prescribed by Sir Thomas More, the doyen of female Renaissance education. According to Janel Meuller, author of *The Complete Works of Katherine Parr*, 'a single tutor educated the three Parr children under a programme of study that included Latin, French, Italian and even some basic medical lore'.

As she goes on to point out, letters written to Katherine by her stepchildren when she was queen attest to a certain level of competence in the aforementioned languages. Her scholarly accomplishments later in life reveal her mastery of English, while the fact that Katherine always signed off her own household accounts make it likely that arithmetic was also on the curriculum. This latter skill may have been acquired as a result of Maud Parr's association with the renowned scholar, cleric, mathematician and humanist Cuthbert Tunstall. Although fatherless from an early age, Katherine was not bereft of male influence while growing up at Rye House. Clearly, Maud was an intelligent and formidable woman in her own right. Yet, as was customary for the day, Lady Parr consulted with close male relatives on key matters including the running of her estates and the education of the children. In this regard, two figures stand out: Katherine's uncle William Parr of Horton, and the aforementioned Cuthbert Tunstall. Both men would provide a constant and guiding presence throughout Katherine's life. However, it is Tunstall's hand that can perhaps be most keenly felt in his influence on the Rye House curriculum. It was this education, couched within the strong bonds of family affection, which would forge Katherine's virtuous and kind but self-assured character.

We do not know what aspirations Lady Parr had for her daughters, but a well-rounded education for an aspiring Tudor lady also included the mastery of certain accomplishments such as dancing, music, riding and hunting. While Katherine, her siblings and cousins applied themselves diligently in lessons, there must have been much free time and space to learn these additional pursuits.

According to Katherine's biographer, Linda Porter, 'outside the schoolroom, Katherine Parr developed other interests and enjoyed a variety of pastimes. She liked country pursuits and was a keen rider and hunter. She collected coins, played chess and loved music and dancing.'

And so, Katherine's idyllic life must have cycled from day to day, joyously punctuated by the return of Lady Parr from court. As the children began to mature, it is easy to imagine Katherine, William and Anne surrounding their mother's skirts, listening agog to tales from court: of the new French fashions brought back to England by Mary Tudor, the dowager French queen; of a chivalrous and handsome King Henry, his gracious Spanish consort and the little Princess Mary; of power, intrigue and endless merry disport. It must have seemed a glittering and fascinating world, so very far away from the quiet idyll of Rye House.

Rye House – A Moated Medieval Manor

Although only the gatehouse still stands, we know much about the appearance of the manor house that Katherine called home for around twelve years, thanks both to archaeological excavations and a seventeenth-century plot to assassinate the then king, Charles II (known as the Rye House Plot). The judicial papers prepared for the prosecution of the conspirators contains not only a description of the house, but a floor plan and illustrations that show the elevation of the building.

Construction of Rye House was begun in 1443 by the original Sir Andrew Ogard (grandfather of the aforementioned Sir Andrew). He was granted a licence to empark it, along with '50 acres of land, 10 acres of meadow, 80 acres of pasture and 16 acres of wood ... and to enclose the site of the manor with stone and mortar, and to turret, remellare, embattle and machicolate it'.

The manor itself took its name from the surrounding marshland, known in the sixteenth century as the Insula de Rye. To the south-east was the River Lea, which ran to the rear of the moated enclosure, while to the north-west, in front of the gatehouse, ran the toll road toward Newmarket. At the time of its construction, the park of Rye House covered a total of 156 acres, giving the Parr children plenty of space to practice the arts of riding, hunting and hawking.

The manor itself is of particular interest to architectural historians. According to the paper 'Rye House and Aspects of Early Brickwork' by T. P. Smith, 'Rye House must be regarded as an early instance of brick building in this country, after its re-introduction from the Continent'. Despite its modest size, from the moulded, decorative brickwork that remains today as part of the gatehouse, it is not hard to imagine what a splendid building this must once have been. Surrounded by a 20-foot-wide moat, the rectangular inner enclosure, which contained the manor and its gardens, measured some 230 feet by 160 feet. As the opening quote makes clear, this enclosure was in turn surrounded by a high wall, set back some 16 feet from the moat on three sides, only the gatehouse abutting the water's edge. Around four-fifths of this area was laid to gardens, the manor itself occupying only a small area in the north-west part of the enclosure. According to Emery's *Greater Medieval Houses of England and Wales*, the gatehouse was part of the residential accommodation at Rye House. It opened into a small court, 40 ft by 24 ft, with buildings on three sides and a low gated wall on the forth. Steps close to the gatehouse gave entry to the almost square hall, 32 ft by 26 ft, with the kitchen and offices at its lower end abutting the gatehouse ... Across the small court were two linked parlours.

These parlours adjoined the great hall at its high end, and would have made up the principal living chambers for the Parr family. Was it in one of these parlours, or maybe the large first-floor chamber of the gatehouse, that the children took their daily lessons? The manor was not grand in terms of the number of rooms it contained, so options for placement of the schoolroom are limited. With so little left of the original manor, it is delicious to think that maybe a room of such importance might have survived unrecognised through some quirk of fate.

The End of an Era
By 1525, Katherine's days of innocence were coming to an end. At the age of just twelve, her brother was sent away to be brought up in the household of Henry Fitzroy, the newly created Duke of Richmond. Two years earlier, Katherine herself had already been subject to a failed round of marriage negotiations with Lord Scrope of Bolton. However, four years on, a new set of negotiations had been successfully completed with a different suitor. Katherine was seventeen when she was contracted to become the wife of Edward Borough, the twenty-year-old son and heir of Sir Thomas Borough of Gainsborough in Lincolnshire. A new life awaited her in the northern shires of England. Katherine would surely need to draw upon all the learning she acquired at Rye to navigate the sometimes choppy waters that lay ahead (see entries on Gainsborough Old Hall, Sizergh Castle and Snape Castle).

Visitor Information
Today the remains of Rye House have been engulfed by the march of time. A little like a visit to Gainsborough Old Hall, as you approach you will find yourself wondering if you are in the right place at all! Surrounded by rather dull and tatty land in use for both domestic and commercial purposes, the time traveller emerges suddenly on the site, Rye's handsome gatehouse standing encircled by the moat as it has been for centuries. The grassy enclosure that once formed beautiful formal gardens is laid to lawn as a small park, used by locals. Free parking is on-site and you are likely to find yourself with plenty of space to wander round the gatehouse and admire its fine architectural features. Within the enclosure, and behind the gatehouse, the outline plan of Rye House is marked out in the lawn, each chamber helpfully labelled to help you identify where you would be standing in the house during its heyday. What is immediately obvious is just how compact and bijoux Katherine's childhood home was – certainly a far cry from the great palaces she would come to know as home. Yet as you wander round with your thoughts to keep you company, perhaps you might reflect on the fact that, small as it may be

Katherine's rise to the pinnacle of Tudor society is due in no small part to the accomplishments acquired and the character forged here at Rye House.

On a few days of the year, the gatehouse is open to view its interior chambers. Please see the website for further details at https://www.visitleevalley.org.uk/en/content/cms/nature/gardens-heritage/rye-house-gatehouse/. At all other times, only the exterior is accessible. If you are in the area, you might wish to combine your visit with a stop at Hunsdon (see entry for Hunsdon House).

Postcode: EN11 0LB.

Gainsborough Old Hall, Lincolnshire

I am indebted to Sir Thomas Borough, knight, for the marriage of my daughter.
Maud Parr's will, May 1529

In the late spring of 1529, Katherine Parr journeyed north to begin her life as the wife of Edward Borough, son of Sir Thomas Borough and his first wife, Agnes Tyrwhit. Among Katherine's possessions were two gold bracelets and a rosary of carved wooden beads, a wedding gift from her beloved mother. For a period of about two years, the young couple lived with Edward's family at Gainsborough Old Hall in Lincolnshire, one of the most isolated of English shires, mainly due to geographical factors and an inadequate transport network. The Great North Road, which entered the county at Stamford, was the only easy overland approach from the south. Most southerners viewed the county as unwholesome and uncivilised, opinions based largely on ignorance. Henry VIII later famously described its populace as 'one of the most brute and beastly of the whole realm'. This remote county, while still governed directly from London, was a world away from the lavish ceremonies and endless intrigues of the Tudor court; nevertheless, it was now Katherine's home.

The Borough Family

Not much is known about the character of Katherine's young husband, probably in his late teens or early twenties at the time of his marriage, apart from a suggestion that he suffered from a weak constitution. Health problems certainly ran in the family; his grandfather Sir Edward Borough, who died less than a year before his namesake's marriage, was pronounced in 1510 'a lunatic though with lucid intervals' and kept under lock and key in his own house, Gainsborough Old Hall.

Edward's father, Sir Thomas Borough, knighted on Flodden Field after victory over the Scots, was by all accounts, and even for his time, an overbearing and cantankerous man, who, according to Katherine's biographer Susan James 'ruled his family with an iron hand'. If his interactions with his son Thomas's wife, Elizabeth Owen, are anything to go by, then life at Gainsborough must not have been easy for Katherine. In 1537, Sir Thomas threw his son's pregnant wife, Elizabeth, out of the house and she was forced to live with a 'kinsman of her husband', where she gave birth to a premature son. In desperation, she wrote to Thomas Cromwell of her 'great travail' and of how her father-in-law had not permitted his son Thomas to see her, or his newborn baby, whose life was said to be in danger. She wrote again soon after, complaining of 'the trouble she is put to by Lord Borough who always lies in wait to put her to shame'. She informed Cromwell that she was aware that her father-in-law had complained about her to the Privy Council, 'declaring that her child is not his son's'. She begged Cromwell to intercede on her behalf, to prevent her baby from being disinherited and ended the letter by saying that 'her husband dare do nothing but as his father will have him'.

We get another glimpse of Katherine's father-in-law's character when, in 1533, while serving as Anne Boleyn's chamberlain, he is said to have been 'roughly rebuked' by Henry VIII for having unceremoniously removed from a barge – and mutilated – Katherine of Aragon's arms during the new queen's coronation celebrations. While there can be little doubt that Sir Thomas expected those under his roof to obey him, Linda Porter suggests that he was more flexible when it came to spiritual matters; 'indeed he was himself interested in the new religious ideas and kept a reforming chaplain in his household'. This passion and interest in the new religion must have had some effect on Katherine's own views, and she may have engaged in religious discussions with the Boroughs' chaplain.

Yet, with such a hard man as head of the house, it's only natural that the teenaged Katherine would have felt homesick and yearned for the familiarity and comfort of her childhood home in rural Hertfordshire, where she was raised and educated alongside her younger siblings, William and Anne (see entry for Rye House). After Katherine's father succumbed to the sweating sickness in 1517, her mother, Maud, was left with three young children to care for, and while it's clear that Maud Parr greatly valued education and discipline, she also furnished a good deal of motherly affection on her children, becoming a much-loved and influential figure in their lives.

The powerful mother–daughter bond continued to flourish during Katherine's years at Gainsborough. No doubt she wrote regularly to her mother, informing her of the challenges of living under Lord Borough's roof, and on at least one occasion, in the summer of 1530, the pair met in person. Maud was staying at her own manor of Maltby, approximately 20 miles west of Gainsborough, and it was perhaps at her suggestion that the following year, Katherine, with her husband by her side, moved out of the Borough family home and became mistress of her own house.

A Medieval Manor House

Constructed between 1460 and 1480 by Sir Thomas Borough (Katherine's first husband's great-grandfather) as a demonstration of his family's growing wealth and power, Gainsborough Old Hall is one of England's best-preserved medieval manor houses. The residence where Katherine spent around two years of her life remains much as it was when she lived there. Built partly of brick and partly timber-framed, it consists, as it did in the sixteenth century, of three ranges built around a courtyard and features a striking great hall in the north range; an ample kitchen block; a west range which originally contained three floors of lodgings, many of which featured their own fireplace and garderobe; an east range that in Katherine's day housed the large ceremonial chambers, and a three-storeyed polygonal tower, which formed part of the family's private apartments. An inventory made in 1496, after the death of Thomas Borough, lists Lord Borough's house as having 'a hall, a parlour, an inner parlour, a withdrawing room, a great chamber with another next to it, a chamber in the tower, and in the gallery'. Unfortunately, part of the document is missing and so there were likely other rooms listed that remain unidentified.

While not palatial in size, the house was deemed grand enough to host a number of visitors of note, including King Richard III who overnighted there in October 1483 while on his way from York to London, and King Henry VIII and Catherine Howard, who stayed at the Old Hall for three days during the return leg of their progress to York in August 1541.

During her two years spent under the roof of the irascible Thomas Borough, Katherine Parr probably occupied rooms in the east range. It was not too long before her father-in-law permitted her and Edward to set up their own household at Kirton-in-Lindsey, 12 miles or so from Gainsborough, where it was hoped Katherine would produce children – sons to carry on the Borough name. As it turned out, Sir Thomas's eldest son was dead by the early spring of 1533. Katherine would have to wait another fifteen years before she felt the warmth of her own baby in her arms.

Visitor Information
Half an hour's drive to the west of Lincoln lies the town of Gainsborough. We were informed by the curator of Gainsborough Old Hall that the majority of visitors who come to this most beguiling of medieval buildings base themselves in the city. Here you will find the best of the accommodation and amenities. A visit to the hall can be easily done in half a day. So, we recommend that you plan your morning or afternoon of sheer Tudor indulgence to coincide with your stay in Lincoln.

Swathes of open agricultural land define the county of Lincolnshire. In the middle of August, which was when we visited, the golden patchwork of fields, and the quiet simplicity of country life, allows the bustle of Lincoln's busy tourist centre to soon be forgotten.

I am not sure what we were expecting as we approached the town, but you may be perplexed, as we were, to find yourself being engulfed by scruffy modernity: terraced houses, supermarkets and even a McDonalds as we approached the supposed location of the hall. At one point, we began to think that our satellite navigation system had made a mistake. How could a thing of such beauty be located in the epitome of suburbia? Then all of a sudden, we turned into the most unassuming of urban streets and the hall was in front of us. Its once extensive parkland and gardens has clearly been sold off over the centuries, and this grand dame of history has been left holding on to the merest sliver of gardens, which enfolds it on all sides. However, these lawns embrace what is, without doubt, one of the oldest and finest medieval houses you will have the pleasure of seeing. We defy you not to say 'Wow!' several times over as you alight from the car and begin to appreciate what a miracle it is that this ancient house has survived, virtually intact, since its last Tudor owners vacated the premises.

The main entrance to the house will take you into the east wing of the hall. Today, the ground floor largely serves as the hall's restaurant and shop. Although there is an excellent audio tour of the house (which we encourage you to use), what you will not hear is that this part of the hall once comprised the ground floor of the family's private apartments, and thus held some of the most sumptuous chambers in the house. As Lady Borough, the young Katherine Parr would have spent much of her time in the private lodgings of the east wing, or dining in public for feasts held by the family in the great hall. With regard to the arrangement of lodgings for Henry VIII and Catherine Howard during the 1541 progress, they are sadly not known. It has been postulated, though, that on account of the king's size and infirmity by 1541, it is most likely that he was lodged on the ground floor, in the area now occupied by the shop. It is also thought this would make it likely that Catherine's rooms were located on the first floor, just a few turns away, up the vice stair, which is still part of the Old Hall's tower.

Note, though, that because the Old Hall is surrounded on all sides by houses, parking is limited (although on Sunday, when we visited, we had no problem pulling up just outside). You may find that you need to park in town at either the Market Place, or Marshall's Yard Car parks and take a five- or ten-minute stroll through the town to reach the hall.

For further information on opening times, special events and prices, please visit Gainsborough Hall's web site at http://www.gainsboroughholdhall.com/. Telephone: +44 (0) 015 227 8202.

Postcode: DN21 2NB.

Sizergh Castle, Cumbria

> Amongst the residences of the knightly families around Kendal none were of greater importance during the middle ages than Sizergh, the seat of the Stricklands.
>
> *The Manorial Halls of Westmoreland and Cumberland*, 1892

A Northern Widow

How Katherine Parr might have come to find her way to Sizergh Castle, situated in the remote north-west of England, is testament to the complex web of family relationships so common among the upper echelons of Tudor society. Blood ties, as well as bonds forged through matrimony, resulted in extended family networks that were often relied upon in the sixteenth century for security, protection and promotion.

Such was the case in 1533, when Katherine found herself widowed for the first time and at a crucial crossroads in her life. With the death of her mother around eighteen months earlier, there was no parental hand to guide Katherine in her next move. Furthermore, although her younger siblings were advancing at court (Anne Parr was already in Anne Boleyn's household and her brother, William, increasingly bound in friendship with cosmopolitan noblemen such as Thomas Wyatt and Henry Howard), they were not yet in a position to promote their sister's cause.

Katherine's biographer Linda Porter states that it was probably to the likes of Cuthbert Tunstall that the young widow turned for help in the spring of 1533. Tunstall was by then Bishop of Durham, as well as President of the Council of the North. Through him, therefore, we see another of Katherine's ties to the north of England emerging. In addition, during Katherine's marriage to Edward Borough, she had also developed a relationship with another key figure. Her name was Catherine Neville. This Catherine had become wife of Henry Borough, brother of Katherine's father-in-law Sir Thomas, sometime after 1526. Born around the turn of the sixteenth century, Catherine Neville was already connected to the eldest Parr sibling through her father's bloodline. She also happened to be the Dowager Lady Strickland through her first marriage to Walter Strickland of Sizergh.

There is a long held tradition that it was Catherine who invited her kinswoman to stay at Strickland's Westmoreland home following the death of Edward Borough. As Catherine's son by Sir Walter was still in his minority, Catherine remained mistress of Sizergh, and so would be perfectly placed to invite a young companion to join her at the family home. Indeed, it seems the women had much in common, not only through their shared familial connections but in how both of them were widowed by 1533 – Catherine Neville for the third time. Did the two women find some peace and solitude in the remote Westmoreland countryside? Once you have visited Sizergh, it is easy to imagine how this quiet location might have appealed to a woman like Katherine, a place for intelligent reflection and a chance to take stock on what direction to take next in life.

Katherine Parr's Westmoreland Legacy

Although Katherine Parr's stay at Sizergh Castle cannot be proven by irrefutable documentary evidence, most historians accept that there is a strong case for her presence there over a twelve-month period following the death of her first husband. Apart from the necessary familial connections that made such a stay possible, further evidence is drawn from the presence of a finely embroidered counterpane and toilet cover apparently still in the possession of the Strickland family. It is said to have been given by Katherine Parr as a gift and 'thank you' to the mistress of the house. For five hundred years this has remained at Sizergh as a 'precious heirloom and memorial of their [the family's] ancestral connection with Queen Katherine Parr'. This quote comes from *The Lives of the Queens of England* by Agnes Strickland, who also writes about the item itself, which in the nineteenth century was 'proudly exhibited' at the castle,

the material on which both the counterpane and toilet cover are worked is the richest white satin … The centre of the pattern is a medallion, surrounded by a wreath of natural flowers, wrought in twisted silks and bullion. A spread-eagle in gold relief, gorged with the imperial crown forms the middle. At each corner is a lively heraldic monster of the dragon class, glowing with purple, crimson and gold. The field is gaily beset with large flowers, in gorgeous colours, highly enriched with threads of gold.

Strickland goes on to say that 'the lapse of three centuries has scarcely diminished the brilliancy of the colours, nor tarnished the bullion; nor is the purity of the satin sullied, though both these queenly relics have been used on state occasions, by the family'.

When visiting Sizergh, we enquired about the whereabouts of this artefact today, as it was most certainly not on display. Unfortunately, the staff knew nothing about it. Despite follow-up, we were unable to verify its current presence at the castle.

Sizergh: A Northern Haven

Today Cumbria lies at the heart of the tourist map, encompassing the wildly beautiful and scenic Lake District. However, in the sixteenth century it must have been remote, with Sizergh Castle situated on rising ground on the right bank of the River Kent, 3 miles south of Katherine's ancestral home town of Kendal. Although not in residence there, her younger brother was still lord of the manor of Kendal Castle and its surrounding park. Indeed, for many years it was believed that Katherine was born and raised in Kendal. However, it is now widely accepted that by the early 1500s the castle was falling into disrepair; far away from the advantages offered at court and increasingly outdated as a residence, Kendal Castle was deserted by the Parrs. Katherine's grandfather is thought to have been the last of the family line to live there. Thus we can imagine that, heartened by the companionship of her friend Catherine Neville, nearby Sizergh Castle presented a comfortable residence for the young widow, close to her ancestral home.

The Origin and Appearance of the Medieval Castle

The Manorial Halls of Westmoreland and Cumberland states that the first deeds for Sizergh were granted during the reign of Richard I (1157–99). However, the house that Katherine called home was largely fourteenth century in origin. Since the mid-sixteenth century, there has been considerable remodelling and redevelopment of the house. The first of these redevelopments came just twenty years after Katherine's sojourn there, with the eighteenth and nineteenth centuries seeing further substantial changes. Of all the parts of the castle that stand today, the redeveloped great hall (now the entrance hall with dining room above) and the great tower, once called the Deincourt Tower, are the most relevant to our story.

The castle that greets the time traveller today is U-shaped. However, prior to 1555, Sizergh essentially only consisted of the central range: in the middle, the lofty great hall; to the right, an embattled and turreted four-storey tower containing the private living quarters of the family; and on the left, a medieval service block, aggrandised after 1555 to provide additional accommodation on the newly built upper floors. This was the house that Katherine would have known when she arrived at Sizergh in 1533.

A New Marriage

Katherine was a young and very attractive widow. No doubt brokered by her close family members and friends, a second marriage was soon arranged. In an article by Susan James, one of Katherine's recent biographers, she states, 'It was probably at Sizergh Castle in Westmoreland that Katherine met and married her second husband, the considerably older, twice widowed, John Neville, Lord Latimer of Snape in Yorkshire.'

John Neville was also a distant kinsman of Katherine's; he was a second cousin of her father. As a Neville, he was also a member of one of the most ancient and powerful lineages in the north. No image or likeness remains that might tell of his physical attractiveness to the beautiful twenty-year-old widow. However, in Tudor England, these considerations were secondary; Neville brought to the marriage a title, lands and property. Perhaps Katherine also found herself attracted to the idea of being protected by a 'man of the world'. At twice the age of his new bride, the proposition must have been very different to the boy to whom she had been wedded a few years earlier.

It is highly likely that Katherine had a free hand in choosing her second husband, as according to historian David Cressy, 'widows and widowers contemplating remarriage could do pretty much as they pleased'. Whether Katherine did indeed remarry at Sizergh, or in the chapel of her new home at Snape, we do not know. However, by 1534, Lady Latimer was ready to set out on a new adventure. Yet it would not be without peril, for Katherine would soon find herself in the heart of North Yorkshire and embroiled in one of the most dangerous uprisings of Henry VIII's thirty-eight-year reign, the Pilgrimage of Grace.

Visitor Information

Today, Sizergh Castle is a *tour de force* of panelled Tudor interiors, particularly the Inlaid Chamber, which is among the finest you are likely to see anywhere in England. Any lover of Tudor interiors will be enraptured by the fabulous carving, but please do remember that the majority of the panelling was installed during the second half of the sixteenth century. A notable exception to this is the oak linenfold panelling in the Linenfold Room, which is early sixteenth century in origin and, according to the National Trust, was probably reused during Elizabethan times. Thus, we can assume that in 1533, similar decoration adorned the grandest rooms in the castle.

As you explore the castle, pay particular attention to the entrance hall, which once formed part of the original great hall. It has been vastly remodelled down the centuries, so that it is now almost unrecognisable. The other rooms of particular interest to those travelling in the footsteps of Katherine Parr are contained within the medieval tower. At the first-floor level, two rooms (the Dining Room and the Queen's Room) were once fused into one to create the solar, the main living quarters for the family during daylight hours. The Queen's Room is named in honour of Katherine Parr, but again it is an Elizabethan creation and not contemporary with Katherine's time at the castle. Nevertheless, it is a charming room and of all the rooms at Sizergh, it is here on this first floor that it is easiest to imagine Katherine seated in front of the fire, reading from her beloved books or embroidering the intricate counterpane that would be a gift for her friend.

Today the National Trust cares for the castle, but the Stricklands continue to live there, as they have done continuously since it came into the family by marriage in 1239. There is a fabulous visitor centre on-site with all the amenities you could hope for, including a shop and café.

Website: http://www.nationaltrust.org.uk/sizergh/. Telephone: +44 (0) 153 956 0951.

When we visited Sizergh, we stayed overnight in nearby Kendal. (We can highly recommend a local bed and breakfast, the Sonata Guest House. It is small but perfectly formed! Attention to detail is second to none, the welcome as warm as you could hope for: http://www.sonataguesthouse.co.uk/. Telephone +44 (0) 153 973 2290.

Early the next morning, we took the opportunity to climb up to the ruins of Kendal Castle, which lie on high ground to the east of the town. The ascent is certainly a stiff climb requiring a degree of fitness. It is clearly a popular place, though, with walkers and dog lovers making the most of the open ground and fabulous panoramic views from the summit. We visited in November, when the ground was muddy underfoot and a fierce chill prevented our lingering there. However, on a warm summer's day this would be a wonderful spot to unfurl the picnic blanket. Surrounded by around a thousand years of English history, there couldn't be a more beautiful place to enjoy your refreshments. As you do, it would be hard not to reflect on the long and tortuous road that took the Parrs from obscurity in the north of England to the pinnacle of Tudor society at the heart of Henry's court, almost 300 miles to the south.

Postcode for Sizergh Castle: LA8 8DZ.
Postcode for Kendal Castle: LA9 7BL.

Snape Castle, North Yorkshire

A goodly castel in a valley belonging to the Lorde Latimer, and ii or iii parkes welle woddid [wooded] abowt hit [it].

John Leland, Tudor antiquarian

During what must be one of the most momentous years in English history, a twenty-two-year-old Katherine Parr arrived in Richmondshire as the new chatelaine of Snape Castle. It was the summer of 1534. In London, King Henry VIII and his principal minister, Thomas Cromwell, were driving through two Acts of Parliament, both of which would shape the very fabric of the kingdom: the Act of Supremacy and the Act of Succession. As a result of the former, no more would England bend her knee in submission to Rome. The latter confirmed that England had a new line of succession, with the infant Elizabeth displacing her bastardised half-sister Mary. Furthermore, in April of that year, Anne Boleyn, queen for almost a year, was described as having a 'goodly belly'; it seemed that Henry's second wife was once more pregnant with the great hope for the future of Henry's dynastic aspirations.

This surely must have seemed a far cry from the idyllic and verdant valley that Katherine first beheld as she approached Snape Castle. Surrounded by a cluster of modest dwellings that had grown up as a village around the original medieval manor house, the fifteenth-century castle had replaced an earlier mid-thirteenth-century hall. According to Emery's *Greater Medieval Houses of England and Wales*, the castle that Katherine came to call home for nearly ten years was 'essentially a medieval courtyard manor house', such that four ranges fronted into an interior courtyard measuring 180 feet by 140 feet.

No floor plans of the original house remain, but we do know that the house that Katherine knew was much remodelled later in the sixteenth century by Thomas Cecil (son of Elizabeth I's principal minister, William Cecil, Lord Burghley), after he inherited it through marriage to Dorothy, Katherine's step-granddaughter. Thus, the castellated exterior, still visible today, was actually added some forty or more years after Katherine was resident at Snape. Instead, to get a feel of the Tudor house, we must imagine a simpler structure, without the grand towers or crenulated parapets. *A History of the County of York, North Riding: Volume 1* points us toward those parts of the castle most relevant to Katherine's story: 'The oldest parts are the chapel in the south-east corner, part of the fabric at the east end of the south range, and the ruinous buildings on the east and north sides of the courtyard.'

These 'oldest parts' include the divided remains of the fifteenth-century great hall, situated in the south-east corner of the building, adjacent to the chapel. The height of the hall was apparently lowered at a later date by the insertion of a ceiling, creating an additional first floor. When the east side of the castle was put up for rent in 2005, in an interview with *The Telegraph* newspaper, the owner, Lady Parnaby, confirmed that in terms of the castle's interior 'the east wing is Tudor-Jacobean in style with flagged floors, skip-size inglenooks and low ceilings, whereas the rooms in the west are panelled, airy and well-proportioned and completely Georgian in style'.

It seems that little survives of the castle that Katherine called home. Other than the ruinous and ivy-covered north and eastern ranges, where barrel-vaulted chambers are entered from the courtyard via fifteenth-century pointed doorways, it is in the chapel where we may walk in the footsteps of England's erstwhile queen. This building served the family's religious needs during Katherine's tenure at Snape. Some suggest that this may well have been the site of her nuptials with Lord Latimer, although there is no proof of this. Today, the chapel is entered via an external staircase that was added during the nineteenth century. However, in Katherine's time, it is believed that an internal corridor connected the main castle apartments to the chapel at the head of the flight of stairs (today, tucked away behind an innocuous-looking door outside the chapel's entrance). Although the dimensions of the chapel are largely unaltered, the interior has been much remodelled, particularly in the eighteenth century. Only the southern windows, and the most westerly window in the northern range, are fifteenth century and therefore contemporary with Katherine's tenure at Snape. As you push open the chapel's heavy door, the stillness is enchanting and invites you to rest a while and imagine the Latimers coming and going in their daily devotions, Katherine's keen mind enquiring into the new faith that was inching its way across England's spiritual landscape.

The Lady of the Manor

After a short sojourn into widowhood (see Sizergh Castle), the future Queen of England had married into the powerful Neville family, whose fame and notoriety have been firmly established for many through the recent resurgence of interest in the Wars of the Roses. Indeed for a brief time Snape had been home to Cecily Neville and her daughter Anne, then queen of Richard III. The forty-one-year-old John Neville, 3rd Lord Latimer, had taken Katherine as his third – and, as it would turn out, final – wife in the summer of 1534. However, as the new Lady Latimer, not only was Katherine expected to fulfil her role as lady of the manor and chatelaine of the castle, but also to take on the role of stepmother to Lord Latimer's two children, the fourteen-year-old John and nine-year-old Margaret. While Margaret and Katherine soon developed a close relationship that would endure until Margaret's early death, John was altogether an entirely different proposition. Katherine's stepson would eventually turn into a wayward and violent adult, accused of rape and murder. As Linda Porter highlights in her book *Katherine the Queen*, Katherine herself gave an intimate insight into some of her parental challenges at Snape in her later writing:

> Younglings and unperfect are offended at small trifles, taking everything in evil part, grudging and murmuring against their neighbour … when [they] see that it is reputed and esteemed holy to commit sin … they learn to do that, and worse, and wax cold in doing good and confirm themselves in evil, and then they excuse their wicked life, publishing the same with the slander of their neighbour. If any man reprove them, they say such a man did thus and worse … their affections dispose their eyes to see through other men and they see nothing in themselves.

These reflections were recorded in Katherine's later composition, *Lamentations of a Sinner*. However, if the daily dealings with a truculent teenager were an ongoing challenge, they could not match the danger that swept into Snape in the winter of 1536/7, in the wake of the uprising that became known as the Pilgrimage of Grace.

Katherine Parr, the Hostage of Snape

Who would have ever known at the beginning of that fateful year how this idyll of rural Yorkshire life, which had gone unchanged for centuries, was about to be rent apart by the defiant subjects of Henry VIII's northern lands? Changes initiated far away in London were finally brought to bear upon the great abbeys of Yorkshire. For the deeply conservative and largely Catholic population of the north, the gathering momentum of the Dissolution was too much to bear. If you visit the nearby ruined abbeys of Fountains or Jervaulx during your travels, it is not hard to sympathise with this sentiment; such seismic change to such magnificent buildings threatened to destabilise the very fabric of everyday life, both spiritual and temporal. It must have been both frightening and intolerable.

Although the tumult of the initial uprising left Snape untouched, during the winter of that year, an angry mob of insurgents arrived at the castle, forcibly taking Katherine and Lord Latimer's children hostage 'as surety for Lord Latimer's continued commitment to the causes for which the northern men had risen'. There is no evidence to suggest that Katherine or her two stepchildren were harmed, although it is easy to imagine how terrifying such an incident might be. We can imagine this young woman, mature beyond her years, dealing ably with the aggressors, but nevertheless being enormously relieved to see her husband arrive at the gates of the castle. Lord Latimer had hurried back in all haste from London, having learnt that 'the commons of Richmondshire, grieved at my coming up [to London], have entered my house at Snape and will destroy it if I come not home shortly'.

Latimer's presence was sufficient to disperse the mob, his family, home and goods remaining unmolested. A full account of this period, detailing the involvement of John Neville with the Pilgrimage and the motivation for the incursion, is beyond the scope of this book. For our purposes, danger passed with the end of this episode and perhaps by the skin of his teeth John Neville managed to clear his name and remain in the good graces of the king. Sadly, though, the Pilgrimage of Grace sealed the fate of the abbeys of Yorkshire. They became seen not only as a hotbed of corruption, but dissent as well. It is fascinating to think that Katherine would have borne first-hand witness to their ruthless suppression, watching a way of life irreversibly destroyed and a new world emerge, a world in which Katherine would soon play a very significant role.

Visitor Information

Snape is a picturesque, sleepy village lying in the heart of one of the most rugged and romantic parts of England, the Yorkshire Dales. Rolling hills of lush pastures, divided up by dry stone walls, are the signature of this little piece of England. Here, summers are bountiful and winters harsh.

You are most likely to approach the castle along an avenue of lime trees that form a lugubrious canopy in the height of summer. Emerging from beneath it, the visitor almost immediately finds themselves upon the castle, situated on the left-hand side of the road. Sadly, it is not possible to access the interior of the remaining south wing, which since the nineteenth century has been divided into private residences. However, a well-marked path leads you from the main road in front of the castle to the entrance to the chapel on the south-east side. This is still used occasionally for services and is open to the public seven days a week. There is no fee for entry. On the way to the chapel, you will find excellent views of the south wing of Snape Castle and come up close to the ruins of the eastern and northern ranges. While ivy covering crumbling walls seems somehow romantic, we could not help but feel saddened by the messy disarray of the grounds. Cleary no effort is being made to preserve those parts of the building that are relentlessly being claimed by time.

Once you have finished, rest and refreshment can be found at the Castle Arms Inn, located about half a mile or so away at the other end of the village. This delightful pub serves excellent food and we loved its culinary delights, the warm welcome of the landlord and the charms of the fifteenth-century building. The inn also provides bed and breakfast, should you wish to stay in the village overnight. Telephone: +44 (0) 167 747 0270; website: http://www.castlearmsinn.com. If you prefer self-catering accommodation, Snape Mews, situated adjacent to the castle itself, is a history lover's idyll. Telephone: +44 (0) 167 747 0307; website: http://www.snapecastlemews.com.

Postcode for Snape Castle: DL8 2TJ.

Church Stowe Manor, Northamptonshire

The firtilitie [fertility], salutarie ayre [air]; pleasant perspects and conveniencie of this Shire in all things to a generous and noble mynde [mind] have so allured Nobilitie to plant themselves within the same that no Shire within this Realme can answere the like Number of Noblemen, as are Seated in those Partes.

John Norden's description of Northamptonshire, 1610

As we shall hear shortly, Lord Latimer died in late February or early March 1543 at the Latimers' London home in Charterhouse Yard (see entry on Charterhouse Yard). His will was proven on 12 March, and in it he bequeaths to 'Lady Katherine, my wife, [who] shall have and hold for term of her life the manor of Stowe with mine churches and Little Stowe with all and singular th' appurtenances to the same belonging in the county of Northampton'.

It is primarily from this document that modern historians surmise that Church Stowe Manor was once home to Katherine Parr and her family at some point between the years 1537–43. As mentioned elsewhere in this book, the perceived wisdom is that during these six years the Latimers had moved southward from their permanent residence at Snape in North Yorkshire (see entry on Snape Castle), travelling as circumstances dictated primarily between Lord Latimer's residences near and in York: Blackfriars, then later Charterhouse Yard (both in London), and Stowe Manor in Northamptonshire. Presumably, Lord Latimer, either with or without his wife, must also have returned to Snape Castle from time to time to oversee his estates and attend to essential business. This roving lifestyle was partly forced upon the Latimers as a result of the fallout of the Pilgrimage of Grace and John Latimer's poor relationship with Cromwell. During the years in question the family had their Charterhouse Yard property seized, with Lord

Latimer being regularly required to do service in the north of England on behalf of the Crown, the good graces of the family apparently upheld with a degree of fragility by regular payments to Cromwell, as recorded from time to time in the *Letters and Papers of Henry VIII.*

However, in our search (which included contacting the owners of the property and a well-known biographer of Katherine) we uncovered no proof of Katherine's definitive presence at Church Stowe Manor. Yet the theory that Lord and Lady Latimer settled in Stowe-Nine-Churches for a period of time is made more appealing by understanding that at Church Stowe, Katherine would no longer be the isolated chatelaine of a Catholic northern territory. Instead, she would take her place in loyal middle England, surrounded by her Parr relatives. As Linda Porter states, 'here at the heart of England, Katherine could exchange visits with her uncle William Parr, who lived at Horton Manor, near Northampton, and with her Vaux and Lane Cousins'.

As we have already noted (see the entry on Rye House), William Parr was one of the two significant male influences on Katherine following the death of her father when she was just five years of age. The now demolished Horton Manor lay within just one day's ride from Stowe, and after the turbulence of the preceding couple of years, having her uncle and mentor so close to offer support and guidance must have been a great comfort.

In terms of the 'cousins' mention above, the first two were through the paternal line. Maud, Lady Lane, who had been brought up with Katherine in the schoolroom at Rye, married Sir Ralph Lane of Orlingbury in 1523. They lived at Glendon Hall, around 30 miles to the north-east of Church Stowe. Fortuitously, Maud's sister, Anne Parr, lived but not one mile away from there at Rushton Hall, wife of Sir Thomas Tresham.

Her Vaux relatives were also linked as closely by blood ties, but this time through the maternal line; the then Lady Vaux was Elizabeth (*née* Cheney). She had also been raised alongside Katherine at Rye. It seems that once more the family intimacy of Katherine's childhood was recreated amid the peace of Northamptonshire's rich pastures.

Northamptonshire: A 'Most Pleasant Shire'

Thanks to antiquarian John Norden we have a wonderfully evocative record of Northamptonshire at the turn of the seventeenth century. This pre-industrialised landscape would have changed little in the sixty or so years after Katherine owned the manor at Stowe-Nine-Churches. He eulogises,

> This Northamptonshire is a most pleasant Shire, adorned both with salutarie and profitable Seates, manie [many] and notable Sheepe Pastures, rich feedings for Cattle, firtile Corne Groundes and lardge Feilds greatly inrichinge [enriching] the industrious Husbandman ... The Countrie [is] most comfortable for Travaylers [travellers] not only in regard of the open perspects which are delightfull to wayfaringe Men, But also in regarde of plentie of Townes, Parishes

and Villages, which are so univeriallie [universally] dispersed, that in every two or three Myles [miles] at the most, is found a Place of ease to the wearisome Travylour [traveller].

Still surrounded by unspoilt countryside, you will find yourself in complete agreement with Master Norden if you visit the village of Church Stowe for yourself. Norden also speaks to us about the pleasant pastimes that Northamptonshire nobility such as Katherine, her stepdaughter Margaret and her cousins might have enjoyed together:

> For Hawkinge both on Land and River it will hardly be matched, such pleasant Fields and lardge [large] perspects at will, to view the soaring Fawkon [falcon], and golden streames so interfaceinge the cheareful [cheerful] Hills and Dales replenished with Game of all sortes to delight the noble Mynde [mind]. Deare [Deer], Red and Fallow, both in Parks, Forests, and Chases are so plentifull as no one Shire yeeldeth [yielded the] lyke.

The Manor at Church Stowe

According to *British History Online*, the first mention of the manor and its surrounding park was in 1326 'when Gilbert de Middleton was granted the manor of Stowe "with the park" (Cal. Pat. 1324–7, 160). Its later history is unknown but Bridges (Hist. of Northants., I (1791), 88) records that in the late 17th century there were two contiguous parks, which had by his time "been converted to other use".'

However with regards to the house itself, most unusually for a building that holds such historical significance, it seems that almost nothing is known of its history or appearance. The medieval house was apparently built around 1420, but was almost entirely 'Georgianised' in 1732. According to its owners, the 'sash windows replaced the original mullioned windows' throughout. The 1968 listing of the house adds one fragment more to the picture: '[The] fine late medieval truss in [the] roof above; presumed former open hall with clasped principals, tie-beam, king-post, and arched collar braces'.

Photographs of these timbers can be seen on the website for Church Stowe Manor (http://churchstowemanor.com/) in the 'History' section. Thus, it seems all we can say with some certainty is that the house that Katherine called home had a large, open hall, as would be typical of a house of the time, and that it was almost certainly located on the site of the current building.

This period of Katherine's life is largely unrecorded; we do not really know where she went, who she met, or indeed when she first came to court. However, in following in her footsteps one certainly feels that this brief window in her life, surrounded by old friends and family members, was a moment of quiet repose and simple domesticity before a greater destiny called Katherine onward.

Visitor Information

Although the medieval house has long gone, when you visit the site today you will soon appreciate its location and understand what a thoroughly agreeable spot this must have been to Katherine. Situated high up on a ridge of land, the views to the north over the nearby village of Weedon Bec are breathtaking.

Church Stowe itself is a small village. You can park up near the village green, and then wander down to the church of St Michael, easily visible from the road. Standing facing the church at the entrance to the graveyard, diagonally over to the right and beyond the churchyard is a fine-looking house with Georgian-style windows. This is what remains of Church Stowe Manor. There are better views from behind the church, or indeed from the fields at the foot of the escarpment. Note that to reach these fields you must use the public footpath to the left of the churchyard. This leads downhill into an open field. Once here, the views ahead and the views back to the church and manor house really do fill the soul with a sense of ease. Despite the fact the mainline high-speed trains can occasionally be seen, and heard, hurtling north and south about a mile away to the north, this little piece of England has tranquillity and beauty enough to connect us back to a distant past.

The manor today is owned by Carole and Geoff Wood, who clearly take great pride in the house. Although it is not accessible to the general public, the website for Church Stowe Manor shares their love for the house: http:// churchstowemanor.com. Note that if you wish to visit the church, which contains a fine tomb of Elizabeth Carey (*née* Neville, the granddaughter of Lord Latimer), then please call ahead, for the church is usually kept locked. The number for the churchwarden is +44 (0) 132 734 0728. Note that there are no pubs in the village, nor any other amenities.

Postcode: NN7 4SG.

Charterhouse Yard, London

A little without the Barres of west Smithfield is Charterhouse lane, so called, for that [it] leadeth to the sayd plot of the late dissolued Monasterie, in place whereof, first the Lord North, but since Thomas Howarde late Duke of Norffolke, haue made large and sumptuous buildinges, both for lodging and pleasure. At the gate of this Charter house is a faire water Conduit, with two cockes seruing the vse [use] of the neighbours to their great commoditie.

John Stow, Tudor antiquarian

If the years 1536–7 had proven to be tumultuous for Katherine Parr, they must have paled into insignificance set against those circumstances that unfolded in Lady Latimer's life during 1542–3.

The previous two years had seen particularly dry weather in England; Europe baked during the 'Big Sun Year' of 1541. Soft fruits such as cherries and grapes were picked weeks earlier than usual, Parisians walked across the bed of the River Seine and in London the inhabitants died in their droves of the 'Auge'. The two sun-soaked summers of 1540 and 1541 also created an easy backdrop against which the king's infatuation with Catherine Howard had blossomed, ultimately culminating in the fateful northern progress of 1541. With Catherine's precipitous fall from grace at the end of that same year, the mood at court changed. Henry, the aggrieved husband, mourned his ill fortune while Catherine languished, awaiting her fate in Syon Abbey (see entry on Syon House). The young queen was eventually beheaded in the Tower, guilty of treason, on 13 February 1542. And so began an inconceivable series of life-changing events that would see Lady Latimer become England's new queen just under eighteen months later.

A Peculiar Turn of Circumstance

Following the Latimers' move south from Snape Castle at the end of 1537, it seems that the family divided their time between Shropshire, Northamptonshire, Yorkshire and London as Lord Latimer's business dictated. And by the time Katherine married her second husband in 1534, John Latimer was already in possession of a property located at roughly what is now No. 10 Charterhouse Square (then called 'Yard'), having leased it two years earlier from the adjacent Carthusian Priory, simply called The Charterhouse. Initially, this was the Latimers' principal London residence. However, as a result of John Latimer's ambiguous involvement in the Pilgrimage of Grace and poor standing with Thomas Cromwell, the Charterhouse Yard property was 'seized' around 1536–7 at the request of Cromwell's friend Sir John Russell. Latimer was much aggrieved by the turn of events. His complaint to Cromwell tells us something more of a property that he seems to have coveted for its charms and position in clean, open space outside the city walls. Latimer complains,

> Whereas your lordship doth desire ... of your friends my house within Chartreux Churchyard [Charterhouse Churchyard], beside so ... I assure your lordship that the getting of a lease of it [the property] cost me 100 marcs, besides other pleasures [improvements] that I did to the house, for it was much my desire to have it, because it stands in good air, out of press of the city.

However, there was little else that Latimer could do. As a result, for four years, the less salubrious Blackfriars became Lord and Lady Latimer's London base until Cromwell's execution in 1540. At this point the lodgings were returned to the family.

In January 1542, Lord Latimer was in London, serving as a peer in Parliament. Based in their Charterhouse Yard residence, Katherine – perhaps more than most – must have been familiar with every gory detail of the events unfolding at court. Her younger sister, Anne, had become part of Catherine Howard's intimate circle of ladies, entrusted with the queen's jewels and also attending the young girl during her incarceration and subsequent execution. It is not difficult at all to imagine the hushed conversations between the two sisters as Anne relayed her first-hand account of the whole sorry affair in the quiet privacy of the Latimers' house in Charterhouse Yard.

Yet, as Catherine's blood spilled to atone for her sins, another drama was unfolding a little closer to home. The disastrous marriage between Katherine's brother, William, and Anne Bourchier finally came to a very public and humiliating end during this period. From the beginning, the marriage had been an unmitigated disaster. Eventually, in 1541, Anne took a lover and became pregnant with his child. It was the last straw for William, who ultimately moved to end the marriage and disbar any of Anne's children from inheriting his estate. How much Katherine remained in London during this time, and was directly privy to each excruciating turn of events, is unknown. However, as William also had lodgings in Charterhouse Yard, this must have been an intimate family affair, bringing a good deal of embarrassment to all concerned parties.

A Return to Widowhood

As 1542 rolled on, disquiet erupted on England's border with Scotland and Lord Latimer was subsequently dispatched on the king's service. Perhaps by this time there was evidence of John Latimer's failing health, for on 12 September of that same year he made out his will prior to his departure for the north. As it turned out, Katherine's second husband survived the harsh winter, returning to London with the intention of sitting in the first term of Parliament. However, by this time he was dying. It seems that Katherine nursed him at home in Charterhouse Yard until sometime in late February/early March of 1543, when her husband finally 'shuffled off this mortal coil'. And so, aged thirty, Katherine became a widow once more. It must have been from the Latimers' Charterhouse Yard residence that the funeral cortege set off the short distance to St Paul's Cathedral, where John Latimer was finally laid to rest in a tomb that is now lost to time, but which Stow's *Survey of London* states was 'in a chapel by the north door of St Paule's'.

With the passing of one relationship was the blossoming of another. There is nothing to suggest that Katherine was living anywhere other than at Charterhouse Yard during those first few months of 1543, when two rival suitors vied for the hand of this most compelling of women. It is well beyond the scope of this book to chart the flourishing romance between Katherine and the dashing Thomas Seymour, or to describe how Lady Latimer might have come to the attention of the king. These contentious events are more fully debated by Katherine's biographers, but suffice to say that when we visit the modern-day Charterhouse Square, we might imagine the rollercoaster of emotions experienced by Katherine as she was plunged first from shock at the bloody end of Catherine Howard, through family shame, to grief at the loss of her husband, before finally experiencing the dizzy excitement of burgeoning love.

So, with these events in mind, now let us roll back the centuries and experience Charterhouse Yard, the Latimers' favoured London residence, through Katherine's eyes.

Charterhouse Yard: A Haven 'Out of the Press of the City'

Two maps of Tudor London are an invaluable aid for the time traveller wishing to recreate the landscape Katherine passed through on a daily basis. The first is a modern reproduction of a *Tudor Map of London: 1520*, taken from *The British Atlas of Historic Towns, Vol. III*. On it we see the Carthusian Priory of The Charterhouse lying no more than half a mile to the north-west of London's ancient city walls. Entry to the walled city was via a number of gateways whose names are familiar to Londoners to this day, although the gateways themselves have long since been lost: Ludgate, Newgate, Cripplegate, Aldersgate, Bishopsgate and Aldgate. Travelling from Henry's court at Whitehall toward the city, along the Strand and Fleet Street, the skyline was defined by the many, pulchritudinous spires of London's churches, with one dominating them all: St Paul's Cathedral.

By Katherine's time, the sprawl of London had spread beyond the confines of the city. Here, large areas of open ground – fields, orchards, fairgrounds and comely manor houses along with their gardens – continued to surround Katherine's route to and from Charterhouse Yard. The map shows that she must have regularly ridden by West Smithfield, where heretics perished at the stake (and which today is the largest meat market in the UK), and the Norman priory of St Bartholomew, whose priory church still stands in all its glory.

The second map of note is the Agas Map of 1561. This provides us with a clear picture of the area around Charterhouse itself, including Charterhouse Yard. On it we see that entry to the yard was via Charterhouse Lane from the west, or from what is now Carthusian Street to the east. The map shows that both entrances were gated; the former survived until 1775. Charterhouse Yard itself originally formed the outer precinct of the priory. According to *The Survey of London* (Volume 46), 'what is now Charterhouse Square [acted] as a buffer zone between it and the City'.

The modern-day square has retained the integrity of the original medieval precinct – an irregular pentagon of open ground. In the sixteenth century, the Agas Map shows how the yard was bounded on the northern side by the priory (which post-Dissolution became the grand private house first of Lord North, and then of the Duke of Norfolk) and on its eastern and southern perimeters with fine houses, occupied by many notables of the day. We have already heard that Katherine's brother owned (or leased) property there. In addition, according to Gerald Stanley Davies in his book entitled *Charterhouse in London: Monastery, Mansion, Hospital, School*, 'The French and Venetian ambassadors had houses in the square in Henry VIII's, Edward VI's, Mary's, and Elizabeth's reigns. Jean de Dinteville, who appears in Holbein's Ambassadors, lived there in 1533, (as did) his successor, Charles Solier, Sieur de Morette (also painted by Holbein), in 1534.'

Furthermore, the *Survey of London* also records that a regular contributor to our *In the Footsteps* books also lodged in the Yard as Katherine's immediate neighbour: 'John Leland, the topographer and "King's Antiquary", [is] recorded at a tenement adjoining Lord Latimer's mansion between 1538 and 1546.'

Entering the Yard from Charterhouse Lane, Katherine would have faced the old Carthusian Priory ahead of her to the north, the conduit described in the opening quote above to her left, and a medieval chapel to her right. This was cited on the centre of the green and marked the fact that during the fourteenth century, the yard had been the burial place of thousands of victims of the Black Death. The sixteenth-century historian John Stow describes his visit to Charterhouse Yard during the reign of Elizabeth I, recording the following:

> In this plot of ground there was in that yeare more then 50000. persons buried, as I haue reade in the Charters of Edward the third: Also I haue seene and read an Inscription fixed on a stone Crosse, sometime standing in the same churchyard and hauing these wordes: Anno Domini 1349. regnante magna pestilentia, consecratum fuit hoc Camiterium, in quo &infra septa presentis monasterii, sepulta fuerunt mortuorum corpora plusquam quinquaginta millia, prater alia multa abhinc usque ad presens, quorum animabus propitietur deus Amen [In the year of the Lord 1349. during the reign of a great pestilence, this Camiterium was consecrated, in which, within the precinct of the present & the monastery, the dead were buried the bodies of more than fifty thousand men, besides many other things from this time until the present, of which he may be merciful to the souls of the god Amen.]

The Rise and Fall of No. 10 Charterhouse Yard

The Latimers' home was situated in the far north-eastern corner of the yard; it was one of the largest tenements on the square (if not the largest), at least two storeys standing, being clearly visible on the Agas Map. *The Survey of London* states, 'Before 1690, the east side of Charterhouse Yard had the largest houses, with ample gardens stretching eastwards as far as the backs of houses in Aldersgate Street, with which some of them were connected.'

Interestingly, the north side of the house abutted the perimeter of the priory itself – and the residences of the Bassano brothers, who were staying at the priory. These five brothers were immigrants from Venice, musicians taken into the king's service during the 1530s. It seems that Katherine became acquainted with their talents during her time in Charterhouse Yard as they were later employed in her own royal household.

No. 10 Charterhouse Yard probably remained reasonably intact until the end of the seventeenth century, when it was 'acquired by Peter Ward of St Botolph without Aldersgate, brewer, who had demolished most of the group and erected six houses on the site'. *The Survey of London* goes onto say,

> At No. 10, Ward retained elements of the previous houses on these sites. These were brought to light by the inter-war owner of No. 10, Frank Daphne, a solicitor, who called it 'The Dower House' and claimed it as 'the house from which Henry VIII married Catherine Parr'. A description of the interior of No. 10 in 1933 mentions a vaulted brick basement (perhaps surviving from Lord Latimer's house here) … In 1938–9 during further renovations in the basement Daphne uncovered 'a great deal of Tudor work including a large fireplace, some 18ft. in width, similar to the fire places in the great kitchen at Hampton Court … This fireplace survived the Blitz and was drawn in 1942. But despite efforts to

incorporate it in the new building on the site, it was allowed to deteriorate and was eventually destroyed.

Today a mid-twentieth-century office block stands on the site that witnessed the final days of Katherine's provincial life before it was set to change forever.

Visitor Information

Perhaps because part of the medieval Carthusian priory and the later Tudor house survive, there is still a tangible sense of history to be felt as you wander round Charterhouse Square. We pulled up outside the site of the Latimers' townhouse in an iconic London black cab and immediately were assaulted with images of Katherine and her family coming and going on horseback. Glancing along the row of modern tenements and offices, it was easy to imagine bumping into John Leland, Katherine's neighbour, leaving his house to set off on one of his many travels around England, or catching a glimpse of the strapping figure of Charles Solier, ambassador, returning from his business at court.

If you stand with your back to the stretch of medieval wall fronting the Charterhouse on the north side of the Square and look south, you would have once seen the wall of London encircling the City beyond the far side of the green. The conduit and chapel at the centre of the square have long gone, but the substantial stone gateway to the priory remains, and the Tudor manor house can be seen from the road rising above the line of the wall.

The Charterhouse today is a trust which provides housing for a small community of men over sixty, all of whom have given service to the country. The good news is that the 'brothers' run tours of the Charterhouse on select days throughout the year. We booked on to one of the tours and can highly recommend doing so. You will see the Tudor great hall and great chamber – all part of the house in which the 4th Duke of Norfolk was held prisoner under house arrest as part of his involvement in the Ridolfi Plot to overthrow Elizabeth I in 1571. The tours are small, as this is well off the tourist trail – a welcome break from some of the more popular historic locations in London. Please check the website for tour dates and bookings: http://www.thecharterhouse.org/tours.

In all, this little haven of Tudor England, a backwater from the intensity of a modern-day global city of commerce, is a gem. No. 10 Charterhouse Yard may be lost, but the square remains in form much as it did in Katherine's time, the fabric of the most significant Carthusian priory in England.

Note: If you are visiting Charterhouse Square, you are but a stone's throw away from one of the most ancient churches in London: the Church of St Bartholomew the Great in West Smithfield. This was founded as an Augustinian priory in 1123. The church partly survived the Dissolution of the Monasteries and contains some exceptionally fine Norman and medieval architecture.

Outside, the main timber-framed gatehouse was built by Lord Richard Rich, by then Lord Chancellor of England. It is said that from that building Mary I watched the burning of heretics in the square below. It is a gruesome thought.

Postcode for Charterhouse Square: EC1M 6AN.
Postcode for St Bartholomew the Great: EC1A 9DS.

Woking/Oking Palace, Surrey

Her Highness straightly chargeth and commandeth that no manner of person
or persons, in whose houses the plague hath been [shall return] to court ...
upon pain of her grace's indignation, and further punishment at her highnesses
pleasure.
And of this, under applicable legal penalty, let nothing be omitted. By Katharine,
Queen of England and General Regent. From [W]Oking, the eighteenth day of
September, the thirty-sixth year of our reign.

> Royal proclamation issued by Katherine Parr on 18 September 1544

Katherine first visited Woking Palace as queen just days after her wedding. It was
the end of July, 1543. The *Letters and Papers of Henry VIII* chart the progress of
king and court through the last two weeks of that same month as the newlyweds
progressed from Hampton Court via Oatlands (see entries for Hampton Court
Palace and Oatlands) arriving at Woking by the 29 July. We know of the court's
presence there on account of a letter written by the Privy Council to the Deputy
and Council of Ireland on the same date. On this first occasion, Katherine's stay
at Woking Palace must have been fleeting, for by the 31 July the court had arrived
at nearby Guildford.

Katherine, the Queen and General Regent of England

However, more significantly, Katherine was to use Woking as her base through
much of September of the following year. By this time, she had been appointed as
General Regent in absence of her husband, who was laying siege to the town of
Boulogne on the French mainland; it was to be Henry's final military campaign.
With plague besieging London, it seems the queen decided to remove herself to
the heart of the quiet Surrey countryside, some 13 miles south-west of Hampton
Court Palace. Alongside her were the twenty-eight-year-old Princess Mary, the
eleven-year-old Princess Elizabeth and the seven-year-old Prince Edward.

A steady stream of letters between the 'Council with the Queen' (in Woking)
and the 'Council with the King' (in Boulogne) bears testament to Katherine's
assiduous application to her task as regent, ably supported at Woking by her
council of 'Canterbury (Thomas Cranmer), (Sir Thomas) Wriothesley, (Thomas
Thirlby, Bishop of) Westminster and (Sir William) Petre'. However, the queen's
expenses for the month make it clear that whilst Katherine may well have based
herself at Woking and relished her role as Queen Regent, she also took the
opportunity to visit a number of nearby properties in Surrey and Kent. According
to Katherine's biographer Susan James, 'with periodic returns to Woking to check
on the Council's work, Catherine and the children travelled to Mortlake, Byflete,
Catherine's brother's house at Guildford, Chobham, Beddington Place and

Eltham. She visited friends at Merewood, Sir Robert Southwell's home, and at Allington Castle, home of the Wyatt's'.

As the royal entourage travelled, they must have felt the premature chill of the encroaching winter nipping in the air, for the autumn of 1544 was unusually cold. Consequently, another item in Katherine's expenses around this time records payment to a 'Mr. Frytton [for] riding from Oking to London "for certeyn the Queen's Graces ffurde [fur] gownes from Baynardes [Castle]"'.

Suitably dressed in her furred winter gowns, the unseasonably cold weather did nothing to dampen spirits. Katherine was already proving to be a very effective, and much-beloved, stepmother. With Elizabeth recently welcomed back at court, the eleven-year-old must have delighted in spending her birthday alongside her surrogate mother, surrounded by her family and 'released' from Ashridge, where she had spent the last year. The latter was a place that Elizabeth herself seems to have had little warmth for, calling it 'this, my exile'. Although, as Susan James is at pains to point out, the exact nature or reason for this year-long absence from court remains unclear. But we can imagine Katherine and her stepchildren progressing at a sedate pace through the Surrey and Kentish countryside, enjoying the hospitality of good friends and the pleasure of hunting, which was plentiful throughout the month of September. The queen's expenses for the month (recorded in the *Letters and Papers of Henry VIII*) lists sundry gifts of venison being sent to favoured courtiers, including the Duchess of Richmond, Lady Hertford, Lady Heneage and indeed to the king himself, in Boulogne.

Katherine ably managed the affairs of state during this period and her letters reveal a woman who appears both clear-headed and confident in her authority. On 18 September, she issued a proclamation that effectively barred any person who had had contact with the plague from attending court. This was signed, 'From [W] Oking, the eighteenth day of September, the thirty-sixth year of our reign'. Then on the following day, after nearly three weeks of waiting, Katherine received news of the king's campaign from her brother-in-law, Sir William Herbert. He had ridden all haste from France, carrying the happy tidings that Henry was victorious and that Boulogne had fallen. In a letter from the queen and council to Francis Talbot, 5th Earl of Shrewsbury, written on the same day, the 19 September 1544, we hear that

> the Queen, having this night advertisement by Sir William Herbert, of the Privy Chamber, that Bulloign is in the King's hands without effusion of blood, Shrewsbury shall cause thanks to be given to God, by "devout and general processions" in all the towns and villages of the North, and also signify to the Wardens of the Marches this great benefit which God has 'heaped upon us'.

The Story of the Palace at Woking

The history of the old manor of Woking, or Oking, as it is often called by Tudor scribes, goes back to the thirteenth century. Woking Manor was granted to Margaret Beaufort and Henry Stafford in 1466 and it was their principal home until Stafford's death in 1471. It remained in Margaret's possession until 1483 and was re-granted to her in 1485 by Henry Tudor, upon his accession to the throne.

Henry VII took the manor into his own hands in 1503. In 1508, he commissioned the building of the Tudor great hall, which was subsequently completed in 1511 by Henry VIII. In time, Woking became a much-loved royal palace, often used by the king. It was visited in turn by Katherine of Aragon, Anne Boleyn, Catherine Howard, as well as Katherine Parr. An extract from a survey of the manor made in the second year of the reign of James, records that at Woking, there was 'a certain mansion there, sumptuously built with an orchard and garden, stables and other buildings adjoining the said mansion and its appurtenance'.

The royal residence lay surrounded by Woking Park, half a mile downriver from old Woking village. The earliest known view of the palace comes from Norden's map of Woking Park, made in 1607. Even though this later map does not show the full extent of the palace in its halcyon days (as certain ranges had already been demolished), what we see is a charming arrangement of several buildings, including a great hall, all surrounded by a moat and adjoining the River Wey. While the buildings themselves covered 4 acres, there were also extensive formal gardens, orchards and a fishpond that covered an additional 4 acres. However, according to the Friends of Woking Palace, who have done much research into the site in recent years, 'Woking does not seem to have been a large palace and the king and queen would generally be accompanied by a 'Riding Court' of perhaps forty to sixty people when they visited for a few days at a time.'

Nevertheless, a now lost fourteenth-century survey confirms that even in its early days, it was a manorial complex of some size including a hall, two chapels and many other rooms and offices. In the environs, there was also a corn mill and a fulling mill, separate stables for the king and queen, as well as an extensive deer park, which by the Tudor period had extended to cover around 590 acres. The landscape of the surroundings varied, no doubt contributing to its appeal for both hunting and hawking; it consisted of lightly wooded sections in areas that occupied the higher ground in the park, as well as large glades and 'lawns' for deer coursing. It seems that Katherine took full advantage of that park during that eventful autumn of 1544.

The Lodgings at Woking Palace

According to the Friends of Woking Palace, 'access to the Palace was invariably by horse, despite the number of erroneous modern histories that state royal access was by barge up the River Wey from the River Thames.'

Very little is actually known about the royal apartments at Woking. Archaeological evidence suggests that it is very likely that the royal chambers lay to the south and south-west of the great hall built in 1508–11, and incorporated buildings built over the preceding 250 years right up to the time of Lady Margaret Beaufort and Henry VII. We know from one reference that the queen's apartments were connected to the king's quarters by a gallery, an arrangement that was not uncommon in other royal palaces. Furthermore, all the principal chambers including the great hall seem to have been sited at first-floor level and accessed by three or four processional staircases.

The *History of the King's Works* gives us many more tantalising glimpses into the other state chambers and privy lodgings that could be found at Woking during the Tudor period. These included those of key courtiers, who frequented the palace alongside the king and queen. Among these accounts, on the king's side we hear of a watching chamber, bedchamber and raying chamber, while on the queen's, a dining room, the 'great bay window' in her privy chamber and a raying chamber. In 1540, 'the king's gallery was replastered and glass was repaired in various rooms, including the king's and queen's waiting chambers, the king's privy chamber, the king's closet, Mr Heneage's chamber, Sir Anthony Knyvet's lodgings, the Duke of Norfolk's lodging and the Lord Admiral's lodgings'. In 1543, the year in which Katherine Parr was married to the king, the newest additions were installed at Woking; these were the reframing of a window in the king's presence chamber, while 'an arbour (chiefly of birch branches) [was made] for the king to dine and sup in'.

During Katherine's tenure as queen, Woking was very often visited on the way to, or from, the king's lodgings at Guildford, which lay to the south-west (see entry on Guildford in *In the Footsteps of Anne Boleyn* for further details) and the newly built Oatlands Palace, lying just 7 miles north-east of Woking, en route to Hampton Court (see Oatlands Palace).

Long after both Henry and Katherine had departed this earthly realm, Elizabeth would once again return, this time as queen. Visited only once during the reign of Edward VI, and never by Mary I, it seems Elizabeth alone held fond memories of the place and a time when she once more felt the warmth of a mother's love. During the late 1570s, Elizabeth I poured money into refurbishing Woking Palace (to the tune of £2,027), adding new apartments and reroofing the entire complex while demolishing and rebuilding sections of the earlier building. But with the death of Elizabeth, the palace's glory days also died. Within fifty years Woking was utterly abandoned and lay in ruins. Memories of a triumphant three weeks in the autumn of 1544, when Katherine ruled as de facto General Regent of England, fell silently into their earthen graves.

Visitor Information

Only a few vestiges of this previously much-loved royal abode remain to be seen above ground. However, the surrounding moat and the River Wey mark out the footprint of the palace and its once tranquil gardens.

The Friends of Woking Palace has done a wonderful job in preserving what is left of the site. During the four years to 2012, they participated in an archaeological project led by Surrey Heritage and funded by the Woking and Surrey councils, Surrey Archaeological Society and supported by the universities of Reading, London and Nottingham. In March 2013, further funding was granted to the Friends by the Heritage Lottery Fund for a much wider three-year community project, including the surrounding area and its park. Evidence gathered from the seasons of excavations, together with research into the landscape and documents, have helped to shed more light on this fascinating site. An information board close to what was once the main entrance contains information and a reconstruction of the buildings that Katherine would have seen during her visits to Woking in the 1540s.

Across the moat from this main entrance, the royal apartments once extended away to your left, with the great hall directly in front of you. However, the large wall still standing was not part of this structure, but another building that sat behind the hall. Its function is unknown, although the most likely hypothesis describes its use as an indoor tennis court. The function of the building that stands directly to its left is also unknown. The current theory is that it was once a wine cellar; newly transcribed documents suggest that it sat below the king's presence chamber.

Beyond this wall lay the King's Gardens, with additional gardens and fishponds in the copse sited adjacent to the gardens. Today you can reach the fish pools through a wooden gate over to your right, beyond the remaining palace buildings.

It was a warm September day when we visited Woking Palace for the second time; this time to see first-hand the last archaeological dig that will be allowed to take place on the site for a generation. Seeing some of the palace's foundations uncovered, plus a highly decorated and rare fifteenth-century Venetian tile and a slender sixteenth-century pin close up, brought home this place's bustling and illustrious past. Although nearby electricity pylons and distant, modern farm buildings keep you firmly rooted in the present, the open countryside and lazy, meandering river, preserve something of the haven that once served a king and his court. Certainly, it was not too hard to see Katherine taking air in the gardens with princesses Mary and Elizabeth.

Woking Palace is owned by Woking Borough Council and it is surrounded by private land. Public access to the palace is restricted to three open weekends a year, held by the Friends of Woking Palace on behalf of the local council. Dates are set for May, July and September. During the open weekends, there are guided tours to learn about the history of the site and various displays. Full details are to be found on the Friends of Woking Palace website. Special group visits can also be organised via the same group.

Please note: No parking is available at Woking Palace or along Carters Lane leading to it, as this is private land. Access on open days is by foot and cycle via a signed route (about one mile from Old Woking). On some open days a free shuttle bus service is available (check Friends of Woking Palace website). Free long-stay parking is available in Old Woking in the larger car park (beyond the small short-stay car park) by the mini roundabout in the high street at the junction of the A247 and B382.

For more information on the palace and visiting the site please visit the Friends of Woking Palace website at http://www.woking-palace.org/. Telephone:+44 (0) 772 229 9026.

Postcode for High Street, Old Woking: GU22 9JH.

Otford Palace, Kent

> The said Manner [house] of Otford standeth all invironed with hill and
> champione [open] grounds whereuppon groweth woods greate plentye. Also, the
> Town standeth northe west side of the said sight in one strete partly buylded on
> both sides with some fayre houses which contayneth in lengh VIII hundred fete.
> Also, the Ryver is current through the said Towne whereuppon standeth a water
> mill and in the said Ryver be dyvers kynds of Fyshe as Troutte and other fyshe.
>
> From a survey of Otford Manor, *c*. 1541

In 1537, Archbishop Thomas Cranmer was forced to part with a number of his
Kentish properties that had caught the eye of King Henry VIII, including Otford
Palace. The sprawling Tudor complex was built by the Archbishop of Canterbury,
William Warham, around 1514, on the site of an earlier manor house and in its
heyday was larger than that of his rival Thomas Wolsey's house, Hampton Court
Palace, built around the same time.

Warham's episcopal mansion played host to royalty on a number of occasions;
Henry VIII visited in August 1519 and again on 21–22 May 1520. Alongside him
was his first wife, Katherine of Aragon. The royal couple and their vast entourage
of around 4,000 people were on their way to France to meet Francis I, a gathering
that would later become known for its magnificence as the Field of Cloth of
Gold. Clearly impressed by Warham's newly built palace, Henry returned in May
1522 and again in September 1527. In 1532, after the archbishop's death, the eleven-
year-old Princess Mary Tudor spent part of the winter months at Otford, and
in early October 1544 Queen Katherine Parr was reunited there with her ageing
husband the king, after his return from a military campaign in France, which had
seen the capture of Boulogne.

Queen Katherine, Regent of England

The campaign in France in 1544 was the last time Henry would personally lead his
army into battle. During his absence he appointed Katherine, his wife of barely
a year, as Regent-General of England, a testament to the high regard in which
he held her. Katherine did not disappoint her husband. She performed her role
capably and enthusiastically, ruling the realm for three months, with the help of a
regency council. The only other of Henry's wives to have been entrusted with such
a role was Katherine of Aragon, thirty-one years earlier. During Katherine Parr's
tenure, the 'council with the Queen' maintained a steady flow of correspondence
with Henry, updating him regularly on all the important news from home.
Katherine and her three stepchildren spent part of the summer at Hampton Court
Palace, from where she wrote to the king on 6 August that 'the Prince and the rest
of the King's children are well'. For much of the rest of the summer, the court was
based at Woking Palace (see entry on Woking/Oking Palace).

After the capture of Boulogne, Katherine went on a short progress through
Surrey and Kent, before moving to Eltham, where on 28 September her council

informed Henry that 'the Queen intends to remain here without going to Otforde until the King's further pleasure be known'. Within the next couple of days Katherine must have received word from Henry and travelled to Otford, because a record of an account of payments made by the queen's council reveals a payment to two yeomen and a groom for transporting '2 carts with the Queen's coffers' from Eltham to Otford.

After the joyful reunion, the victorious king and his queen travelled to Leeds Castle in Maidstone (see also entry on Leeds Castle), before returning to Otford, where they remained for over a week, eventually making their way back to London.

A House Fit for Royalty

Warham's grand brick palace was built on the site of a twelfth-century manor house and covered an area of about one hectare to the south of the present-day St Bartholomew's church. It was arranged around two main courtyards, separated by an ornamental moat and great gallery, with gate houses at the north and south ends. The main rectangular courtyard, enclosed on four sides, was accessed via a lofty red-brick gatehouse in the north range, similar in appearance to the surviving gatehouse at Hampton Court Palace. Adjoining the main gatehouse on either side, were two-storeyed galleries that led to two octagonal towers that marked the northeast and northwest corners of the immense outer court. Flanking this space was a gallery in the east that overlooked the kitchen garden, beyond which stood the domestic offices, and on the opposite side, in the west range, stood a gallery with twenty-one adjoining chambers used to house the archbishop's extensive household. This west range of lodgings overlooked the palace's splendid formal gardens, of which an excellent contemporary description appears in *Otford in Kent: A History* by Dennis Clarke and Anthony Stoyel. The garden

> wherein be four square alleyes sett with all manner of quicksett on both sides with dyvers knottes of herbes, and in the same be trees of dyvers Fruitts, and in the garden by three lytle houses of pleasure with seats, and in the said garden is Currant a Bryke of freshe water issuinge out of the aforesaid springe, and pondes wherein fyshe may be preserved and kept.

At the time of Katherine's visit, there were a number of fishponds in the gardens, with 'dyvers kinds of Fyshe as Bremes, Carpps, Roche and Dase'. There were also numerous rabbit burrows; the furry animals were raised on the estate for food, a common practice in sixteenth-century England. It's said that the magnificent gardens of Otford Palace inspired Cardinal Wolsey's grounds at Hampton Court.

Opposite the main gatehouse was the entry to the smaller second court and principal buildings of the palace that occupied the moated site of the pre-Tudor manor house. A wooden bridge connected the outer court to the great gallery, 'well edified and bilded of free stone with large oute caste of bay windows after an uniforme plan'. Beyond this great gallery was a complex of buildings and little courtyards, including the medieval great hall, chapel and the state apartments, where all royal visitors would have stayed, including Katherine Parr and Henry VIII in 1544. To the south of the estate, a great deer park no doubt added to the palace's appeal. It occupied 222 acres and in around 1541 contained around 140 deer. The park was also noted for the abundance of game that roamed its grounds, including 'mallard, heron, partridge, pheasant and other fowls'.

Despite its glorious attributes, and the prodigious amount of money spent on its construction, there was a significant flaw: the palace had been built on low land that was prone to flooding. On 12 January 1523, Warham wrote to Wolsey from Knole, another of the archbishop's residences, explaining how his physicians had declared him temporarily unfit to attend Wolsey due to the travel involved. He also thanked the Cardinal for his advice 'to live in high and dry grounds, like Knoll, and for his offer of lodging in Hampton Court'. Warham may have had the larger house, but Wolsey was implying that his house was still superior.

In 1537, when Cranmer was told that he'd have to hand over the mansions of Otford and Knole, the archbishop tried to persuade the king to allow him to keep the latter, even though it was smaller than Otford. He said it was, 'too small a house for his majestie'. Henry was not amused, he responded by saying that

> I had rather have it than this house [meaning Otford], for it standith of a better soile. This house standith lowe, and is rewmaticke, like unto Croydon, where I colde never be withoute sycknes. And as for Knoll [it] standeth on sounde, perfaite, holsome grounde. And if I should make myne abode here, as I do suerlie mynde to do nowe and than, I myself will lye at Knolle, and most of my house[hold] shall ly at Otteforde.

Between 1541 and 1546, Henry VIII spent large sums of money on repairing the buildings, and maintaining the fishponds, parks and gardens at Otford. Despite this injection of cash, within two years of Henry's death in January 1547, the mighty Otford Palace was in decay.

Visitor Information

The remains of Warham's once magnificent palace are located in the charming little village of Otford. Although nestled between the busy London Orbital (M25) and the M26, somehow the little patch of low-lying land, surrounded by a crescent-shaped ridge of upland, manages to retain its quiet splendour. The epicentre of the village is a large duck pond, around which cluster shops, a tea room, pubs, the parish church and a driveway that leads toward the remains of the palace. Here you will find (in order, from left to right, as you stand facing the ruins with the duck pond behind you) part of the main entrance gateway, and the north-west gallery of what was once the outer (or base) court (these are now converted into cottages); adjoining it are the gnarled remains of the north-west tower.

Beyond this range lay the outer court, delineated roughly by an area known today as Old Palace Field. If you look carefully at this expanse of grass, you can see the land raises slightly to form a level plateau, presumably marking out the site of the original courtyard. Beyond this, and across what is now a lane, lay the private apartments used by Henry and Katherine of Aragon in 1520, then later by her namesake, Katherine Parr in 1544. Sadly, these are all now entirely lost. Two information boards located nearby show the layout of the palace to help you orientate yourself and bring the place to life.

Little is left, and the remains are currently part of a campaign to prevent the ruined north-west tower from entirely collapsing. At the time we visited, the tower was covered in scaffolding and can only usually be viewed from the outside. If you wish to see a 3D representation of the palace at its zenith, make your way back to the duck pond, taking the second turning on the left into the high street. A little way along here, opposite the entrance to the main car park, is the Otford Heritage Centre, which has a model of the palace on display. To check opening times of the centre, please call +44 (0) 195 952 2384.

We also recommend a visit to St Bartholomew's church, where you'll find an ornate sixteenth-century Easter sepulchre. Note the Tudor roses, and on one of the spandrels, a pomegranate – the badge of Katherine of Aragon.

A tea room and a number of pubs provide rest and refreshment for the weary traveller. The main car park situated just off the high street makes it convenient to explore the village and its historic ruins.

Postcode for the main car park in Otford: TN14 5PG.

Nonsuch Palace, Surrey

> That which no equal has in Art or Fame, Britons deservedly do Nonesuch name.
> Comment made by a German visitor to Nonsuch in 1568

On 22 April 1538, the twenty-ninth anniversary of Henry VIII's accession, the forty-six-year-old widowed king began building a palace, the likes of which had never been seen before. While Henry was a prolific builder, this was the first time he would raze an entire village, along with its manor house, church and churchyard, in order to construct a royal house from scratch. Clearly, the king intended this to be something extraordinary. It was to be a house to celebrate the recent birth of his long-awaited male heir, Prince Edward, and to symbolise the power and magnificence of the Tudor dynasty. This nonpareil palace, justly named 'Nonnesuche', would take nine years to complete and cost in excess of £24,536 – over £10 million in today's money. Sadly, nothing today remains of Henry's Nonsuch.

'A Privy Palace'
Built on the site of the manor of Cuddington, located between Ewell and Cheam in Surrey, Nonsuch was sited conveniently close to London and only 6 miles from the king's riverside mansion at Hampton Court. In comparison to Henry's greater houses – Windsor, Beaulieu, Richmond, Hampton Court, Eltham and Woodstock – that could accommodate and feed the entire court, Nonsuch was 'a mere hunting-box', as described by architectural historian Simon Thurley. It covered

about two acres, compared with Hampton Court's six, Oatland Palace's ten and Whitehall's twenty-three! It was intended to be a place the king could retire to with a small group of favoured guests, or his riding party. Baron Waldstein, a young Czech traveller, visited Nonsuch in 1600 and observed,

> This is a place of such splendours that it overshadows the glory of all other buildings far and wide. That most illustrious King Henry VIII fixed upon this particularly healthy situation for it, intending it for his own pleasure and recreation, and he had it constructed with so much magnificence and splendour that you would think that he was striving for the very last word in sumptuous display, and at the same time cramming the sum total of all architectural skills into this one single building …

Nonsuch was built exclusively for the king's private entertainment, a 'privy palace', but in spite of this we find the court in residence in early July 1545. Henry was probably eager to show off his new and splendid house, which the English historian William Camden, writing in 1586 when Nonsuch was in the hands of John, Lord Lumley, described as being

> built with so great sumpteousnesse and rare workmanship that it aspire to the very top of ostentation for shew; so as man may thinke that all the skill of Architechture is in this one peece of worke bestowed and heaped up together. So many statues and lively images there are in every place, so many wonders of absolute workmanship, and works seeming to contend with Roman antiquities, that most worthily it may have and maintaine still this name it hath of Nonesuch …

Katherine Parr was undoubtedly by the king's side during the visit, where tents were required to accommodate the court and furniture and hangings were borrowed from Whitehall. This was not Katherine's first visit to Nonsuch; the previous year, while the king was away on a military campaign in France, the queen dined there while in residence at Hampton Court. On 20 December 1546, Henry wrote a letter to the 'Council of Scotland' from Nonsuch but it is unclear whether or not Katherine was with him on this occasion.

A House Without Equal

Like many important houses of the day, Nonsuch was arranged around two main courtyards of approximately equal size, and was surrounded by well-stocked parklands and formal gardens, which 'all make it seem as if Loveliness herself had selected this very place to live in unity with Health', in the words of Baron Waldstein.

Approached from the north, Henry's new palace was not unlike any other. The entrance was dominated by a wide three-storey gatehouse, with polygonal corner turrets made of a brick core and faced in stone, as seen in two paintings: one by an unknown Flemish artist in the early seventeenth century, in the Fitzwilliam

Museum, Cambridge, and the other painted by Henry Danckerts in around 1660, now held at Berkeley Castle.

Through this broad gatehouse the visitor accessed the enclosed outer court, flanked on the east and west by two-storey battlemented lodging ranges. A passage in the east range accessed a narrow court around which stood the kitchen and domestic buildings. Opposite the outer gatehouse was a second, much narrower and taller gatehouse, on either side of which were found the cellars. This central inner gatehouse was approached by a flight of eight steps and surmounted by a clock. It marked the end of the similarities between Nonsuch and other Tudor residences, and the commencement of Henry's fantasy palace.

The Inner Court

This internal stone gatehouse gave access to the remarkable inner court, where all four inward-facing walls were covered with Renaissance-style decorations that set it apart from any other palace ever built in England. John Evelyn, the English writer and diarist, noted the contrasting architecture between the two courts during a visit in January 1666:

> The Palace consists of two courts, of which the first is of stone, castle-like ...
> the other of timber, a Gothic fabric, but these walls incomparably beautified.
> I observed that the appearing timber-puncheons, entrelices, etc., were all so
> covered with scales of slate, that it seemed carved in the wood and painted, the
> slate fastened on the timber in pretty figures, that has, like a coat of armour,
> preserved it from rotting.

The walls of the three-storey ranges encompassing the inner court were mainly timber-framed, apart from those facing on to the court on the ground floor, which were built of stone. Plaster stucco panels, depicting scenes 'from classical history and mythology, the arts and virtues, floral and other designs' in high relief adorned the upper two levels, between borders of carved and gilded sheets of black slate, believed to be the work of Nicholas Bellin of Modena (a short time before, he'd been working on the decorations of Fontainebleau Palace in France). The contrast between the white stucco and the black slate must have been striking, not to mention the fact that many of the reliefs were near life-sized! Peter Reed, writing for *Epsom and Ewell History Explorer*, describes how the decorations were organised in three levels: 'Roman emperors at the top; gods and goddesses in the middle and various scenes at the bottom – the Labours of Hercules on the west side, the Liberal Arts and Virtues on the east side, and Henry VIII together with Prince Edward forming the centre piece of the south side of the inner courtyard.' Many of these decorations bore mottoes intended to teach Prince Edward the duties of a king-in-waiting.

Within this ornately decorated inner courtyard stood the entrance to the royal apartments; the king's rooms occupied the west range, while the queen's were in the east. These sumptuous first-floor lodgings were accessed via two similar doorways, which stood opposite each other in the inner court and led to a processional stair. The royal suites were comprised of the usual sequence of rooms, ranging from the public to the monarch's innermost private rooms. However, there was no great hall and the guard chamber was on the ground floor, meaning that the presence chamber was entered directly at first-floor level. This was different to the typical layout of royal houses and was probably a reflection of the fact that Nonsuch was never intended as a place to host great court festivities, and so one reception room, accessed directly from a stair in the inner court, was seen as sufficient. The south range was divided lengthwise: a luxurious gallery occupied the space overlooking the inner court, where a fountain stood at its centre, and on the other side, overlooking the privy gardens to the south, were the king's and queen's respective bedchambers.

While no detailed illustration of the inner court survives, we catch a glimpse of the upper part in John Speed's engraving of the south front of Nonsuch on his map of Surrey published in 1610. The elaborate decorative scheme continued on the three external walls of the inner court, which overlooked the privy gardens. The diarist Samuel Pepys, who visited Nonsuch on 21 September 1665, recorded in his diary that 'all the house on the outside [is] filled with figures of story, and good paintings of Rubens or Holbein's doing. And one great thing is that most of the house is covered, I mean the posts and quarters in the walls, covered with lead and gilded.'

The striking south front is also brought to life in a 1568 drawing by Joris Hoefnagel depicting the progress of Elizabeth I to the palace. In the forefront, we see the queen seated in a carriage, surrounded by soldiers with pikes, and in the background, the unmistakable south front of Nonsuch Palace, with its pair of octagonal towers surmounted by onion-shaped cupolas and weathervanes.

Beyond the south front was a walled privy garden, and to the west an orchard, beyond which stood a banqueting house on a hill. William Camden wrote,

> As for the very house it selfe, so environed it is about with Parkes full of Deare, such dainty gardens and delicate orchards it hath, such groves adorned with curious Arbors, so pretty quarters, beds, and Alleys, such walkes so shadowed with trees, that Amenitie or Pleasantnesse it selfe may seeme to have chosen no other place but it where she might dwell together with Healthfulnesse.

Waldstein was just as complimentary. After touring the house, he explored the garden, 'which is the finest in the whole of England, and exceedingly delightful it is. There are 3 distinct parts: the Grove, the Woodland, and the Wilderness, with a circular deerpark nearby … One of the most interesting things in the garden is a walk where one can stroll completely sheltered from the sun's heat; this is because the trees are curved in shape and therefore cast a deep shadow.'

Stories of Henry's legendary palace quickly spread around Europe and it became known for its unrivalled splendour. Tragically, less than 150 years after its completion, Nonsuch lay in ruins.

The End of Nonsuch

In 1682, Barbara Villiers, Duchess of Cleveland, was given permission to demolish the residence given to her by her paramour, King Charles II. Over the next decade, she had Nonsuch dismantled and its raw materials sold off to pay for her gambling debts. Almost three centuries later, in 1959, Oxford Professor Martin Biddle coordinated the first excavation of the site of Nonsuch, uncovering thousands of fragments of the carved and gilded slate and decorated plaster-stucco. Thanks to Biddle's extensive research and tireless work, and the surviving contemporary descriptions and pictorial representations of the royal residence, the ostentatious magnificence of Henry VIII's Renaissance masterpiece has been revealed.

Visitor Information

While no trace of the palace remains above ground today, it is possible to see a splendid model of the palace on display in the Nonsuch Palace Gallery at the Mansion House in Nonsuch Park. The elaborate model, commissioned by volunteer group, Friends of Nonsuch and built by model maker Ben Taggart, took 1,250 hours to construct and measures an impressive 2.2 by 1.2 metres. It is by far the closest we will ever come to experiencing the unparalleled extravagance of Henry VIII's palace.

A second, smaller model, also built by Ben Taggart, is on display at the Friends of Whitehall Museum in Cheam, alongside a number of artefacts from Nonsuch discovered during excavations in 1959, these include pottery, stucco, glassware and decorative slates.

Why not do as the authors did and view the intricate models before visiting the site of Nonsuch Palace, armed with mental images of what the palace looked like in its heyday, and a good dose of imagination? Today, three granite pillars in Nonsuch Park mark where the palace once stood amid beautiful parkland. We recommend reading 'The Nonsuch Trail' from the *Ewell and Epsom History Explorer* before your visit, and following the proposed route that begins at the London Road car park and covers a distance of about a mile. Refreshments and toilets are available at the Mansion House, situated at the centre of the park.

For Service Wing Museum opening times, visit http://www.friendsofnonsuch. co.uk/opening-times.html.

For Whitehall Museum opening times and other visitor information, please visit the museum's website at http://www.friendsofwhitehallcheam.co.uk, or telephone +44 (0) 208 770 5670.

Read 'The Nonsuch Trail' at http://www.epsomandewellhistoryexplorer.org.uk/ NonsuchTrail.html.

Postcode for Mansion House, Nonsuch Park: SM3 8AL.

Postcode for Whitehall Museum Cheam: SM3 8QD.

Sudeley Castle, Gloucestershire

There is a particular time in the evening when the light is at a certain level ...

there is this sense of timelessness here, I can't really explain it but one merges into it.

Lady Ashcombe, owner of Sudeley Castle

Nestled deep in the Cotswold Hills, close to the ancient town of Winchcombe, lies beautiful Sudeley Castle, perhaps best known as the final resting place of Henry VIII's erudite sixth wife, Katherine Parr. Within Sudeley's honey-coloured stone walls Katherine spent some of the happiest days of her life, awaiting and preparing for the birth of her first child, with her fourth husband, the debonair and ambitious Thomas Seymour.

Elation and Despair

In mid-June 1548, Thomas Seymour and his pregnant wife, Katherine Parr, made their way from Hanworth to Sudeley Castle in Gloucestershire. There, in Thomas's newly refurbished country house, Katherine hoped to escape the troubles she'd found herself embroiled in since the death of King Henry. She must have longed to begin a more peaceful life, surrounded by her family and friends, and the man she had been in love with since before her marriage to the king. The last eighteen months had been a trying time for Katherine. It had been marred by the growing disaffection and constant quarrelling between her and Edward Seymour, Lord Protector of England; the public disapproval and branding as 'hasty' of her marriage to Thomas; her brother William's ongoing marital dramas; and her husband's inappropriate and shocking behaviour towards her stepdaughter, the teenaged Princess Elizabeth, while she was in their care. The conflicts and scandals had taken their toll and caused significant emotional stress on the dowager queen, who now sought solace in the countryside.

According to historian Linda Porter, Katherine's 'entourage at Sudeley included her new almoner, Miles Coverdale, her doctor, Robert Huicke, a full complement of maids-of-honour and gentlewomen, as well as 120 gentlemen and yeomen of the guard'. Katherine also had the companionship of a learned young lady who shared the dowager queen's love of books and religion; her name was Jane Grey, and she had recently become her husband's ward.

Together they whiled away the long summer days reading and discussing their favourite books, and taking walks in the fine gardens when Katherine felt up to it. Her pregnancy had not been easy. However, she was comforted by the fact that over the summer she'd managed to mend her relationship with both her stepdaughters. The Princess Mary, who had not greeted the news of Katherine's marriage to Thomas Seymour well, wrote to her in August: 'I trust to hear good success of your Grace's belly; and in the meantime shall desire much to hear of your health, which I pray almighty God to continue and increase to his pleasure as much as your own heart can desire. '

The Princess Elizabeth, whom Katherine had been forced to part with due to the scandal involving the princess and her husband, responded to one of Katherine's letters:

Although your Highness' letters be most joyful to me in absence, yet considering what pain it is to you to write, your Grace being so great with child, and so sickly, your commendation were enough in my Lord's letter. I much rejoice at your health with the well liking of the country, with my humble thanks, that your Grace wished me be with you, till I were weary of that country ... God send you a most lucky deliverance.

The rooms that would serve as the baby's nursery, overlooking the gardens and the chapel, were hung with fine tapestries and decorated in crimson velvet and taffeta. The furniture and plate was the finest money could buy, as befitted the child's status. The English writer and poet Agnes Strickland, writing in the nineteenth century, described the rooms in some detail:

The outer apartment, or day nursery, was hung with fair tapestry representing the twelve months; a chair of state, covered with cloth of gold, cushions of gold, all the others being tabourets with embroidered tops: and a gilded bedstead, with tester curtains and counterpoint of corresponding richness. The inner chamber was also hung with costly tapestry, specified as 'six fair pieces of hangings', and besides the rich cradle, with its three down pillows and quilt, there was a bed with a tester of scarlet and curtains of crimson taffeta, with a counterpoint of silk serge, and a bed for the nurse, with counterpoints of imagery to please the babe. A goodly store of costly plate, both white and parcel-gilt, was also provided for the table service of the anticipated heir.

All that was needed now was a baby to fill the magnificent cradle.

On 20 August 1548, Katherine gave birth to a healthy baby girl and named her Mary after her elder stepdaughter. While Thomas had been expecting and hoping for a son and heir, he was clearly overjoyed at his wife's safe delivery, and no doubt smitten with his little girl. He proudly wrote to his brother, the Lord Protector, announcing the happy tidings and extolling his daughter's beauty. On 1 September, he received a letter of congratulations in return, written from Syon House:

After our hearty commendations, we are right glad to understand, by your letters, that the Queen, your bedfellow, hath a happy hour; and, escaping all danger, hath made you the father of so pretty a daughter. And although (if it had pleased God) it would have been to both of us and we suppose also to you, a more joy and comfort if it had, this the first-born, been a son, yet the escape of the danger, and the prophesy and good hansell [promise] of this, to a great sort of happy sons, which as you write we trust no less than to be true, is no small joy and comfort to us, as we are sure it is to you and to her Grace also, to whom you shall make again our hearty commendations with no less gratulation of such good success.

Tragically, Katherine had not escaped all danger. Within a few days she developed a high fever, which after childbirth was a clear sign of puerperal fever, the deadly bacterial infection that had claimed the life of her husband's sister, Jane Seymour, eleven years earlier. Lady Elizabeth Tyrwhit, one of Katherine's ladies-in-waiting, witnessed her final hours, and her account is included below. It should, though, be noted that Lady Elizabeth was no friend of Thomas Seymour and later gave evidence against him when he was arrested for treason.

Two days afore the death of the Queen, at my coming to her in the morning, she asked me where I had been so long, and said unto me, she did fear such things in herself, that she was sure she could not live: Whereunto I answered, as I thought, that I saw no likelihood of death in her. She then having my Lord Admiral [Thomas] by the hand, and divers others standing by, spake these words, partly, as I took it, idly [deliriously], 'My Lady Tyrwhit, I am not well handled, for those that be about me careth not for me, but standeth laughing at my grief, and the moregood I will to them, the less good they will to me:' Whereunto my Lord Admiral answered, 'why sweetheart, I would you no hurt.' And she said to him again aloud, 'No, my Lord, I think so'; and immediately she said to him in his ear, 'but my Lord you have given me many shrewd taunts.' Those words I perceived she spoke with good memory, and very sharply and earnestly, for her mind was far unquieted. My Lord Admiral perceiving that I heard it, called me aside, and asked me what she said; and I declared it plainly to him. Then he [Thomas] consulted with me, that he would lie down on the bed by her, to look if he could pacify her unquietness with gentle communication; whereunto I agreed. And by the time he had spoken three or four words to her, she answered him very roundly and sharply, saying, 'My Lord, I would have given a thousand marks to have had my full talk with Huicke, the first day I was delivered, but I durst not, for displeasing you': And I hearing that, perceived her trouble to be so great, that my heart would serve me to hear no more. Such like communications she had with him the space of an hour, which they did hear that sat by her bedside.

It's unlikely that Lady Tyrwhit fabricated the whole account, but it's possible that she coloured it to further taint Seymour's already sullied reputation. A short time later Katherine resigned herself to her fate, sending for her doctor and her chaplain, Robert Huicke and John Parkhurst, and dictated her will. She left all her property and possessions to her husband, 'wishing them to be a thousand times more in value than they were'. Of her beautiful baby girl, lying a short distance away in her splendid cradle, there is no mention, and no record of her mother having requested to see her in her dying hours. Perhaps this was one final goodbye that was too heartbreaking for the already broken queen to bear.

In the early hours of 5 September 1548, thirty-six-year-old Katherine Parr died. Her body was wrapped in layers of cere cloth to prevent decay and encased in a lead coffin before being buried in the chapel at Sudeley Castle. Anthony Martienssen stated that 'her funeral was conducted according to the simple doctrine of the New Faith. Lady Jane Grey was the chief mourner, and Miles Coverdale, whom Katherine had brought back from exile in Germany … preached the final sermon.'

Thomas Seymour was left stunned by his wife's sudden demise. With her died his last voice of reason and he spiralled out of control. Within six months, he was executed for treason and the infant Mary was left an unwanted orphan (see entry for Grimsthorpe).

The Discovery of Katherine Parr's Coffin

After the Civil War, Sudeley Castle was slighted and abandoned, and left to the mercy of weather, time and the local builders who plundered its stones. For over a century sheep and cattle grazed where kings and queens once walked, but even in its decrepit state, the magic of Sudeley, and its intriguing and romantic past, drew the occasional tourist.

In May 1782, a group of 'lady sightseers' discovered a marble panel on the wall of the ruined chapel. According to Agnes Strickland, they enlisted help to dig below the panel and discovered a lead coffin buried a foot beneath the ground. The inscription confirmed that they'd found the remains of Katherine Parr. Driven by curiosity, they made two openings in the 'leaden envelope' that encased Katherine's body and found that she was wrapped in layers of cere cloth. They were utterly shocked to discover that the queen's face, 'particularly the eyes, [were] in the most perfect state of preservation'. Unnerved by their finding, they ordered the leaden coffin reburied. Not long after, a Mr John Lucas, said to be the person who rented the land on which the chapel stood, again removed the earth from the leaden coffin and ripped up the top of the coffin. He claimed that Katherine's remains were 'entire and uncorrupted', and after making an incision in the layers of cere cloth covering one of the former queen's arms, found that her flesh was still 'moist and white'.

The story quickly circulated, and over the next fifty years Katherine's coffin was disturbed on several other occasions before her remains were sealed in the stone vault of the Chandos family in 1817. In the mid-nineteenth century, the architect George Gilbert Scott was employed to restore the chapel, which was completed and re-dedicated in 1863. Scott designed a magnificent canopied tomb with a recumbent effigy of the queen, made of white marble and carved by John Birnie Philip. Katherine's coffin, now containing little more than 'brown dust', was buried beneath this exquisite monument, where she remains in repose until this day, the only English queen to be buried in a private house.

The Tudor Layout of Sudeley Castle

The castle we see today is mostly Elizabethan, built in the later sixteenth century by Baron Chandos and partially restored by the Dent family in the mid-nineteenth century. However, the castle as Katherine knew it had been constructed in the mid-fifteenth century by Ralph, Baron Boteler, and in the 1470s by Richard, Duke of Gloucester.

Boteler constructed a large, double-courtyard residence between the years 1441 and 1458. It was constructed from the honey-coloured local Cotswold stone. He then added a private chapel outside the moat of the castle in the early 1460s, the shell of which survives today. The detached chapel was connected to the main building via a covered gallery that extended from the south side of the church.

The castle was approached through a gatehouse in the north, originally protected by a moat and drawbridge. The outer court of lodgings and perhaps offices gave way to an inner court, accessed via an internal gatehouse. On the opposite side stood a grand banqueting hall, flanked by square residential towers, one of which survives today. The west range of the inner court housed the kitchens, services and offices while the east range opposite probably housed the living quarters. The two courts were originally separated by a cross range that no longer exists, but the two towers which once stood at either end of the range still stand, albeit in a restored state. Part of Boteler's outer court – namely the gatehouse and a segment of outer wall – and a section of his inner court – a barn, now in ruins – and the chapel are all that survive from this first phase of construction.

The three ranges that today line the outer court were almost entirely rebuilt in 1572. It seems that the more lavish apartments, where it's almost certain Katherine spent her final summer, were in the now ruined east range of the inner court thought to have been built by Boteler's successor, Richard, Duke of Gloucester, to replace the original residential range. It's in these apartments that Henry VIII and Anne Boleyn also stayed, during their sojourn at Sudeley in the summer of 1535.

Gloucester's lavish east range overlooked formal gardens and consisted of a suite of three apartments on the ground floor and first floor, both similar in plan. The rooms were lit by a sequence of magnificent windows glazed with stained glass built into both the courtyard and outer walls, and warmed by elaborately decorated fireplaces. A spiral staircase connected the ground floor with the first-floor suite, which was even grander than the ground floor. In these sunlit rooms, decorated with fine tapestries and ornate ceilings, we can imagine Katherine spending time with her ladies and overseeing preparations for her baby's eagerly awaited arrival. The long summer evenings would have provided ample opportunity for Katherine to walk in the formal gardens, the Queen's Garden today occupying the site of the original Tudor parterre.

The now ruined east range, draped with clematis and roses, is a truly magical place. Look carefully and you may glimpse Katherine and Thomas, hand in hand, emerging from the romantic ruins.

Sudeley Castle exudes a sense of timelessness that is rarely felt elsewhere. Within its idyllic grounds the past and present merge, and we're left standing side by side with its former inhabitants.

A Tour of Sudeley Castle

Sudeley is by far one of our favourite places in the world because of its serene and magical atmosphere and also for the many Tudor treasures housed there.

To make the most of your day at Sudeley, begin at the Visitor and Plant Centre adjacent to the car park and make your way to the ruins of the fifteenth-century tithe barn built by Boteler and now home to a romantic garden, abundant with wild roses, hydrangeas and wisterias. In the summer you can breathe in their beautiful scent as you take in the stunning view of the castle.

From here, follow the path to the entrance to the exhibitions in the original fifteenth-century west wing of the castle to learn more about Sudeley's past residents, in particular Katherine Parr. Be sure to visit the 'Six Wives at Sudeley' exhibition, which houses replica Tudor costumes from David Starkey's television series *The Six Wives of Henry VIII*.

The 'Katherine Parr' exhibition is a must-see, as it offers a unique opportunity to see personal items belonging to Henry's sixth queen, including a signed prayer book, a love letter to Thomas Seymour and even a lock of her strawberry-blonde hair! Throughout the exhibition you can hear more about Katherine's story in a film presented by David Starkey – *The Life and Loves of Katherine Parr, Queen of England and Mistress of Sudeley*.

The story of Katherine's life continues in a new exhibition in the South Hall that begins in the Knot Corridor with a display of Tudor jewellery. There you have the opportunity to see a copy of the National Portrait Gallery's full-length portrait of Katherine, before visiting rooms that may have formed part of her private apartments.

From there, cross the garden to St Mary's church, which was left in ruins after the English Civil War and restored in the nineteenth century but which retains much of its original shell. This is where Katherine was buried in September 1548, in a simple ceremony conducted entirely in English, the first Protestant funeral service of an English queen. The interior of the church, including Katherine's grand tomb, is Victorian.

Be sure to leave yourself sufficient time to explore the medieval ruins and lose yourself in the numerous stunning gardens, including the Tudor physic garden.

We guarantee that Sudeley will haunt your imagination long after the visit has come to an end.

Visitor Information

For information on how to reach Sudeley Castle and its opening hours, which are seasonal, visit Sudeley Castle's website at http://www.sudeleycastle.co.uk, or telephone +44 (0) 124 260 4244 (during open season only).

Postcode for Sudeley Castle: GL54 5JD.

List of Illustrations

55. The Kemanate, Burg Castle. (© Schlossbauverein Burg an der Wupper e.V).
56. An exterior view of the remains of Schloss Hambach. (Author's collection)
57. Schloss Hambach. (By kind permission of Eheleute Ilse and Martin Müller)
58. Amelia of Cleves. (Wikimedia Commons)
59. *Die Hirschjagd* (*The Stag Hunt*), Lucas Cranach, 1540. (Wikimedia Commons)
60. Schwanenburg, Kleve. (Author's collection)
61. Schwanenburg, Kleve. (Author's collection)
62. The English Quay, Bruges. (Author's collection)
63. Kleve, Germany. By Braun and Hogenburg, *c.* 1580. (Author's collection)
64. Deal Castle, Kent, 2013. (Author's collection)
65. Dover Castle, Kent, from an early twentieth-century book. (Author's collection)
66. The Fyndon Gate, St Augustine's Abbey, Canterbury, 2015. (Author's collection)
67. Bletchingley Place Farm, 2015. (Author's collection)
68. The King's Manor, Dartford, 2015. (Author's collection)
69. Old Paradise Gardens, Lambeth, 2015. (Author's collection)
70. Oatlands Palace as recreated in its heyday. (© Stephen Conlin, based on research by Simon Thurley)
71. The Inner Courtyard of Oatlands Palace and the Outer Wall, by Anton van den Wyngaerde. (© Ashmolean Museum, University of Oxford)
72. South facade, Grimsthorpe Castle. (© Grimsthorpe Castle, by kind permission of Ray Biggs, Grimsthorpe Estate Office)
73. Lincoln Cathedral, 2014. (Author's collection)
74. Old Bishop's Palace, Lincoln, 2014. (Author's collection)
75. Lincoln Castle, 2014. (Author's collection)
76. Pontefract Castle, Pontefract. (© The Hepworth Wakefield/Wakefield Council Permanent Art Collection)
77. The Gatehouse of Cawood Castle, interior view. (© The Landmark Trust)
78. The Gatehouse of Cawood Castle, exterior view. (© The Landmark Trust)
79. The King's Manor, York, 2015. (Author's collection)
80. Remains of the Abbey of St Mary in York, 2015. (Author's collection)
81. Thornton Abbey gatehouse, 2015. (Author's collection)
82. Aerial view of the inner court of Chenies Manor, Buckinghamshire. (Photo © Peter Mukherjee, by kind permission of Mrs MacLeod Matthews)
83. Aerial view of the sunken gardens of Chenies Manor, Buckinghamshire. (Photo © Peter Mukherjee, by kind permission of Mrs MacLeod Matthews)
84. Rye House gatehouse, 2015. (Author's collection)
85. Gainsborough Old Hall, 2015. (Author's collection)
86. Snape Castle, Bedale, Yorkshire, 2015. (Author's collection)
87. Church Stowe Manor, Northamptonshire. (© Carole and Geoff Wood)
88. Reconstruction of Woking Palace as it would have looked in the sixteenth century. (© Lyn Spencer)
89. Plan of Woking Palace. (© Surrey County Archaeological Unit, part of Surrey County Council)

112. The south-east view of Berkeley Castle in the county of Gloucestershire, Samuel and Nathaniel Buck, 1732. (Author's collection)
113. The Old Manor House, Chelsea. (Author's collection)
114. View of Tudor Cheapside, looking east to west and toward St Paul's Cathedral. (Author's collection)
115. Two views of the Mercer's Hall from the Tudor period. (Author's collection)
116. 'Panorama of London from the River: The Strand' by Anton van den Wyngaerde, *c.* 1544. (Wikimedia Commons)
117. 'The Coronation Procession of Anne Boleyn' (originally from a drawing by David Roberts in the Tyrrell Collections, 1872–8). (Author's collection)
118. The Tower of London viewed from the south, from *Old London Illustrated*, 1921. (Author's collection)
119. The Old City of Düsseldorf by Matthäus Merian, 1647. (Wikimedia Commons)
120. Burg Castle as it appeared in the sixteenth century. (© Schlossbauverein Burg an der Wupper e.V)
121. The English House in Antwerp. (Author's collection)
122. The Reception of Quentin Metsys into the Guild of St Luke of Antwerp in 1520, by Edouard de Jans (1855–1919). (Author's collection)
123. Detail of Carmesstraat and the Carmelite monastery. (Author's collection)
124. View of Calais in the time of Henry VIII from *The Chronicle of Calais in the Reigns of Henry VII and Henry VIII*, 1846. (Author's collection)
125. Street plan of Tudor Calais, based on a map held in the British Library. (By kind permission of the Stationery Office)
126. Floor plan of the Exchequer. (By kind permission of the Stationery Office)
127. Seventeenth-century view of Deal Castle by Wenceslaus Hollar. (Wikimedia Commons)
128. The Remains of St Augustine's Abbey, Canterbury, as seen from the tower of the cathedral, 1655. (Author's collection)
129. Remains of the old Bishop's Palace, Rochester. (Author's collection)
130. The King's Manor at Dartford during its zenith in the sixteenth century. (© Dartford Borough Council)
131. Engraving of Grimsthorpe Castle. (Document reference: LLHS 48/3/4/2, by kind permission of Lincolnshire Archives)
132. Plan and elevation of Rye House in 1683. (© Hertfordshire County Council)
133. One of the earliest representations of Snape Castle. (Author's collection)
134. Detail taken from the Agas Map of 1561 showing Charterhouse Yard (© London Metropolitan Archives)
135. Nonsuch Palace, *c.* 1620. (By kind permission of the Stationery Office)

Further Reading

Primary Sources

The National Archives
E101/420/8 – ff. 27v, 28r, 28v, 29r, 29v, 30r.

Anon., *Book of Accompt of 'the expensis and provisions of thousholde' of Edward Seymour, Viscount Beauchamp, at Chester Place and (from 1 May, f.84) Beauchamp Place, 16 Feb. 28 Hen. VIII–28 May, 29 Hen. VIII*. Volumes 15 and 16. Longleat House: 1537.

Anon., *Chronicle of King Henry VIII of England*, trans. M. Hume. London: George Bell and Sons, 1889.

Baeza, G., *Cuentas De Gonzalo de Baeza Tesorero de Isabel la Catolica, 1477–1504*, 2 vols. Madrid, 1956.

Bergenroth, G. A., ed. Calendar of State Papers, Spain, Volume 1, 1485-1509. London, 1862.

Bergenroth, G. A., ed. Calendar of State Papers, Spain, Volume 2, 1509-1525. London, 1866.

Cavendish, G. *The Life of Wolsey*. Reprinted by the Folio Society. London, 1962.

Coryate, T., *Coryate's crudities: hastily gobled up in five moneths travells in France, Savoy, Italy, Rhetia commonly called the Grisons country, Helvetia alias Switzerland, some parts of high Germany and the Netherlands: newly digested in the hungry aire of Odcombe in the county of Somerset, and now dispersed to the nourishment of the travelling members of this kingdome*, Volume 2. 1611.

Dowling, M., ed., *William Latymer's Chronickille of Anne Bulleyne*. London: Camden Society, 1990.

Gairdner, J., ed., *Letters and Papers: Foreign and Domestic Henry VIII*, Volumes 5–13. 1880–93.

Gairdner, J. and Brodie, R. H, eds, *Letters and Papers: Foreign and Domestic Henry VIII*, Volumes 14–21. 1894–1910.

Gairdner, J., ed., Historia Regis Henrici Septimi. Includes the Journals of Roger Machado. London: 1858.

Groos, G. W., ed., The Diary of Baron Waldstein: A Traveller in Elizabethan England. London: Thames and Hudson, 1981.

Harpsfield, N., *Treatise on the Pretended Divorce Between Henry VIII and Catherine of Aragon*. Reprinted for the Camden Society. London: Nichols and Sons, 1838.

Kipling, G., ed., *The Receyt of the Ladie Kateryne*. Oxford: Oxford University Press, 1990.

Madden, F., ed., *King Henry VIII's Entry into Lincoln, in 1541*. London: 1831.

Munzer, H., *Itinerary and the Discovery of Guinea*, trans. J. Firth. London: 2014.

Nicolas, N. H., *The Privy Purse Expenses of King Henry the Eight from November MDXXIX to December MDXXXII*. London: William Pickering.

Pulgar, H, D., *Crónica de los Señores Reyes Católicos Don Fernando y Doña Isabel de Castilla y de Aragón / escrita por su cronista Hernando del Pulgar; cotexada con antiguos manuscritos y aumentada de varias ilustraciones y enmiendas (1482)*. Valladolid: Maxtor, 2011.

Smith, L. T., ed., *The itinerary of John Leland in or about the years 1535–1543*. London: G. Bell, 1907.

Sprat, T. A., *True Account and Declaration of the Horrid Conspiracy against the Late King, His Present Majesty, and the Government as It Was Order'd to Be Published by His Late Majesty*. Newcomb, 1685.

Starkey, D., ed., *The Inventory of Henry VIII: The Transcript*, Volumes 1 and 2. Society of Antiquaries & Harvey Miller, 1998.

Stow, J., The Suburbs without the Walls: A Survey of London. Reprinted from the text of 1603, ed. C. L. Kingsford. Oxford: 1908.

Wood, M. A. E., Letters of Royal and Illustrious Ladies of Great Britain, Volume II. London: Henry Colburn, 1846.

Wriothesley, C., A Chronicle during the Reign of the Tudors. London: Longmans, Green (etc.), 1838.

Secondary Sources

Aubrey, J., *Wiltshire: The Topographical Collections*. London: Longman and Co., 1862.

Baldwin Smith, L., *Catherine Howard*. Stroud: Amberley Publishing, 2009.

Bathe, G. and Holley, R., 'In Search of Wolfhall', *British Archaeology*, May–June 2015, pp. 48–55.

Blood, N. K. and Taylor, C. C., 'Cawood: An Archiepiscopal Landscape', *Yorkshire Archaeological Journal*, 64. 1992.

Boreham, P. W., *Dartford's Royal Manor House Re-discovered*. Dartford Borough Council, 1991.

Brook, R., *The Story of Eltham Palace*. London: George G. Harrop, 1960.

Brothers, C., 'The Renaissance Reception of the Alhambra: The Letters of Andrea Navagero and the Palace of Charles V', *Muqarnas: An Annual on Islamic Art and Architecture*, XI. Leiden: E. J. Brill, 1994.

Buckler, J. C., *An Historical and Descriptive Account of The Royal Palace at Eltham*. London: J. B. Nichols & Son, 1828.

Bray, W., ed., *The Diary of John Evelyn*. New York & London: George G. Harrop, 1960.

Brayley, E. W., *A Topographical History of Surrey, Volume 2*. Dorking: Robert Best Ede, 1850.

Britton, J., *The Beauties of Wiltshire, Volume II*. London: 1801.

Byrne, C., *Katherine Howard: A New History*. Made Global Publishing, 2014.

Calleja, R. H., *Granada and the Alhambra: Art, Architecture, History*, trans. N. J. Graham. Granada: 2005.

Chandler, J., *John Leland's Itinerary: travels in Tudor England*. Sutton Publishing, 1993.

Chilvers, A. *The Berties of Grimsthorpe Castle*. Bloomington: Author House, 2010.

Claessen, H., *Die Geschichte Der Feste Hambach*. Unpublished work, 1960.

Clapham, A. W., 'The Priory of Dartford and the Manor House of Henry VIII', *The Archaeological Journal*, 83(1), pp. 67-85. 1926.

Cloulas, I., *Les Châteaux de la Loire au Temps de la Renaissance*. France: Pluriel, 2010.

Collier, L. H., 'The English Sweating Sickness (*Sudor Anglicus*): A Reappraisal', *Journal of the History of Medicine Oxford*, 36 (4), pp. 425-45.

Colvin, H. M., *The History of The King's Works: Volume III 1485-1660 (Part I)*. London: Her Majesty's Stationery Office, 1975.

Colvin, H. M., *The History of The King's Works: Volume IV 1485-1660 (Part II)*. London: Her Majesty's Stationery Office, 1982.

Cressy, D., *Birth, Marriage and Death: Ritual, Religion and the Life-Cycle in Tudor and Stuart England*. Oxford: Oxford University Press, 1997.

Cross Standing, P., ed., *Memorials of Old Hertfordshire*. London: Bemrose, 1905.

Davies, G. S., *Charterhouse in London: Monastery, Mansion, Hospital, School*. London: J. Murray, 1921.

de la Tour, D., *Château d'Amboise*. Paris: Connaissance des Arts, 2004.

de Longh, J., Margaret of Austria. London: Jonathan Cape, 1954.

des Cars, J., *La Véritable Histoire des Châteaux de la Loire*. France: Plon, 2009.

De Smedt, O., *de Engelse Natie te Antwerpen in de 16e eeuw (1496-1582): Tweede deel*. Antwep: De Sikkel, 1954.

Emery, A., *Greater Medieval Houses of England and Wales: 1300–1500 Volume I, Northern England*. Cambridge: Cambridge University Press, 2006.

Emery, A., *Greater Medieval Houses of England and Wales: 1300–1500 Volume II, East Anglia, Central England and Wales*. Cambridge: Cambridge University Press, 2006.

Emery, A., *Greater Medieval Houses of England and Wales: 1300–1500 Volume III, Southern England*. Cambridge: Cambridge University Press, 2006.

Fimpeler-Philippen, A. and Schurmann, S., *Das Schloss in Düsseldorf*. Düsseldorf: Droste, 1999.

Fischer, G. A., *Schloss Burg an der Wupper: Die Burgen des Mittelalters und das Leben auf Denselben in Wort und Bild Dargestellt*. Germany: 1980.

Fuller, T., *History of the Worthies of England Volume II*. London: Nuttall, 1840.

Foyle, J., 'The "Anne of Cleves" Panels, St Leonard's, Old Warden Church, Bedfordshire. Unpublished report, 2015.

Fox, J., *Sister Queens: Katherine of Aragon and Juana, Queen of Castile*. London: Phoenix, 2011.

Fraser, A., *The Six Wives of Henry VIII*. London: Phoenix Press, 1992.

Gem, R., ed., *Book of St Augustine's Abbey, Canterbury*. English Heritage, 1997.

Gillman, A. W., *Searches into the History of the Gillman or Gilman Family*. London: Eliot Stock, 1895.

Guerrero, P. S., *The Real Alcazar of Seville*. Spain: Editorial Palacios y Museos, 2014.

Hicks, C., *The King's Glass: A Story of Tudor Power and Secret Art*. London: Pimlico, 2012.

Historic Towns Trust, *A Map of Tudor London: 1520*. Old House Books, 2008.

Hume, M., *The Wives of Henry the Eighth and the parts they played in history*. London: E. Nash, 1905.

Hunt, A., *The Drama of Coronation: Medieval Ceremony in Early Modern England*. Cambridge: Cambridge University Press, 2008.

Hussey, C., 'Haseley Court, Oxfordshire I&II', *Country Life*, 11 and 18 February 11 1960.

Hutchinson, W., ed., *Belgium the Glorious: Her Country and Her People, Volumes I and 2*. London: Hutchinson and Co., c. 1915.

Imray, J., *The Mercer's Hall*. London: The London Topographical Society, 1991.

Ives, E., *The Life and Death of Anne Boleyn*. Oxford: Blackwell Publishing, 2004.

Jackson, J. E., 'Wolfhall and the Seymours', *Wiltshire Archaeological and History Magazine*, XV, p. 140. 1875.

James, S., Catherine Parr: Henry VIII's Last Love. Stroud: The History Press, 2009.

Jones, E., A., *England's Last Medieval Monastery: Syon Abbey 1415–2015*. Gracewing, 2015.

Kent Archaeological Society, *Archaeologia Cantiana, Volume VI*. London, 1866.

Kent Archaeological Society, *Archaeologia Cantiana, Volume XVII*. London, 1887.

Kent Archaeological Society, *Archaeologia Cantiana, Volume XXI*. London, 1895.

Kent Country Council, *Kent Historic Towns Survey, Rochester: Archaeological Assessment Document*. 2004.

Kuffner, H. and Spohr, E., *Burg und Schloss Düsseldorf: Baugeschichte Einer Residenz*. Kleve: B.o.s.s-Dr.-und-Medien, 1999.

Lambert, U., *Blechingley: A Parish History*. London: Mitchell Hughes & Clarke, 1921.

Lane, P., *The Moors in Spain*. London: T. Fisher Unwin, 1888.

Lipscomb, S., *A Visitor's Companion to Tudor England*. London: Ebury Press, 2012.

Loades, D., *Catherine Howard: The Adulterous Wife of Henry VIII*. Stroud: Amberley Publishing, 2012.

Loades, D., *Jane Seymour: Henry VIII's Favourite Wife*. Stroud: Amberley Publishing, 2013.

Loades, D., *Mary Tudor*. Stroud: Amberley Publishing, 2012.

Mackenzie J. D., *The Castles of England: Their Story and Structure, Volume 1*. New York: The Macmillan Company, 1896.

Malden, H. E., ed., *A History of the County of Surrey, Volume 4*. 1912.

Maréchal, J., *Europese aanwezigheid te Brugge. De vreemde kolonies (XIVde–XIXde eeuw)*. Bruges: 1985.

Martienssen, A., *Queen Katherine Parr*. London: Sphere Books Ltd, 1975.

Morris, S., & Grueninger, N., *In the Footsteps of Anne Boleyn*. Stroud: Amberley, 2013.

Mueller, J., ed., *Katherine Parr: Complete Works and Correspondence*. Chicago: The University of Chicago Press, 2011.

Murray, J. M., *Bruges, Cradle of Capitalism 1280–1390*. Cambridge: Cambridge University Press, 2005.

Needham, R. and Webster, A., Somerset House, Past and Present. New York: Dutton, 1905. Nichols, J. G., ed., *The Chronicle of Calais in The Reigns of Henry VII & Henry VIII to The Year 1540*. London: The Camden Society, 1846.

Norden J., Speculi Britanniae Pars Altera: Or, A Delineation of Northamptonshire; Being a Brief Historicall and Chorographicall Discription of that County, Volume 3. London: 1720.

Norton, C., 'The Buildings of St Mary's Abbey, York and Their Destruction', *The Journal of the Society of Antiquaries of London*, LXXIV. 1994.

Norton, E., *Anne of Cleves: Henry VIII's Discarded Bride*. Amberley, 2010.

Norton, E., *Jane Seymour: Henry VIII's True Love*. Amberley, 2011.

Ogilvy, J. S., *A Pilgrimage in Surrey*. London: George Routledge & Sons Ltd, 1914.

Orme, N., *Medieval Children*. New Haven and London: Yale University Press, 2001.

Oswald, A., *Archaeological investigations on Cawood Castle Garth, Cawood, North Yorkshire*. Swindon: English Heritage, 2005.

Page, W., et al., eds, A History of the County Buckingham, Volume 3, pp. 471–489. London: 1932.

Page, W., et al., eds, A History of the County of Huntingdon, Volume 2, pp. 260–269. London: 1932.

Page, W., et al., eds, A History of the County of Huntingdon, Volume 3, pp. 75–86. London: 1932.

Pevsner, N., & Harris, J., Lincolnshire, 27. Penguin Books, 1973.

Pock, W. W., 'Chertsey Abbey', *Surrey Archaeological Collections: Relating to the History and Antiquities of the County*, 1, pp. 97–121. 1858.

Porter, L., *Katherine the Queen: The Remarkable Life of Katherine Parr*. London: Macmillan, 2010.

Poulton, R., 'Archaeological Investigations on the Site of Chertsey Abbey', *Research Volume of the Surrey Archaeological Society*. Guildford: Surrey Archaeological Society, 1988.

Poulton, R., *Excavations at Oatlands Palace 1968–73 and 1983–4*. Woking: Surrey County Archaeological Unit.

Poulton, R. and Pattinson, P., *Woking Palace; Excavating the Moated Manor*. Guilford: Spoilheap Publications, 2015.

Priestley, J., *Eltham Palace*. Chichester: Phillimore, 2008.

Purey-Cust, A. P., *Picturesque Old York*. 1909.

Roberts, I., *Pontefract Castle*. West Yorkshire Archaeology Service, 1990.

Robinson, J. M., *Windsor Castle: The Official Illustrated History*. London: Royal Collection Enterprises, 2001.

Royal Commission on Historical Monuments, *City of York, Volume IV: Outside the City Walls East of the Ouse*. London: Her Majesty's Stationery Office, 1975.

Royal Archaeological Institute of Great Britain and Ireland, *Memoirs illustrative of the history and antiquities of the county and city of York: communicated to the annual meeting of the Archaeological Institute of Great Britain and Ireland*. York: July 1816.

Samman, N., *The Henrician Court During Cardinal Wolsey's Ascendancy, 1514–1529*. University of Wales, Ph.D, 1988.

Sherwood, J. and Pevsner, N., *The Buldings of Oxfordhsire*. London: Penguin, 1974.

Smith, F. F., *A History of Rochester*. London: Daniel, 1928.

Smith, T. P., 'Rye House, Hertfordshire and Aspects of Early Brickwork in England', *The Royal Archaeological Journal*, 132. 1975.

Starkey, D., *Six Wives: The Queens of Henry VIII*. New York: Harper Collins, 2001.

St John Hope, W. H., *The Architectural History of the Cathedral Church and Monastery of St Andrew at Rochester*. London: Mitchell and Hughes, 1900.

Strickland, A., *The Lives of the Queens of England, from the Norman Conquest*. Philadelphia: 1848.

Strickland, A., *Memoirs of the Queens of Henry VIII and of his Mother, Elizabeth of York*. Philadelphia: Blanchard and Lea, 1853.

Stukeley, W., 'Caesar's Passage over the Thames', The Gentleman's Magazine, 1. March 1797.

Tatton-Brown, T., 'The Buildings and Topography of St Augustine's Abbey, Canterbury', *Journal of the British Archaeological Association*, 144, pp. 61–91. 1991.

Temple, P., 'The Charterhouse', Survey of London, Monograph 18. London: Yale University Press, 2010.

Temple, P., ed., 'Charterhouse Square area: Introduction; Charterhouse Square', Survey of London: South and East Clerkenwell, 46, pp. 242–65. London, 2008.

Thornton, T., 'Henry VIII's Progress through Yorkshire in 1541 and its Implications for the Northern Identities', *Northern History*, XLVI. 2 September 2009.

Thurley, S., *Somerset House: The Palace of England's Queens, 1551–1692*. London: The London Topographical Society, 2009.

Thurley, S., *The Royal Palaces of Tudor England*. London: Yale University Press, 1993.

Thurley, S., *The Whitehall Palace Plan of 1670*. London: London Topographical Society, 1998.

Thurley, S., *Whitehall Palace: An Architectural History of the Royal Apartments 1240–1690*. London: Yale University Press, 1999.

Thurley, S., *Hampton Court: A Social and Architectural History*. London: Yale University Press, 2003.

Thys, A., *Historiek der Straten en openbare plaatsen van Antwerpen*. Antwerp: 1893.

Tillet, P. M., ed., *A History of the County of York: The City of York*. 1961.

Tremlett, G., *Catherine of Aragon: Henry's Spanish Queen*. London: Faber and Faber, 2010.

Turner, M., *Eltham Palace*. London: English Heritage, 1999.

Vandewalle, A., *Les Marchands de la Hanse et la Banque des Medicis*. Bruges: Stichting Kunstboek, *c.* 2002.

Various, 'Pontefract Castle', *The Mirror of Literature, Amusement, and Instruction*, XIX(531). 28 January 1832.

Warnicke, R., *The Marrying of Anne of Cleves: Royal Protocol in Tudor England*. Cambridge, 2000.

Wauters, A. J., *The Flemish School of Painting*. London: Cassell & Company, 1885.

Wareham, J., *Three Palaces of the Bishops of Winchester: Wolvesey, Bishop's Waltham Palace, Farnham Castle Keep*. London: English Heritage, 2000.

Weir, A., *Henry VIII: King & Court*. London: Vintage Books, 2008.

Wheater, W., *History of the Parishes of Sherburn and Cawood*. London: 1865.

Wheeler, L., *Chertsey Abbey: An Existence of the Past*. London: Wells Gardner, Darton & Co., Ltd, 1905.

Williams, P., *Katharine of Aragon*. Stroud: Amberley Publishing, 2013.

Williams, W. R., *The parliamentary history of the county of Oxford, including the city and university of Oxford, and the boroughs of Banbury, Burford, Chipping Norton, Dadington, Witney, and Woodstock, from the earliest times to the present day, 1213-1899, with biographical and genealogical notices of the members*. Brecknock: Private printing for the author by E. Davies, 1899.

Willis, B., *The History and Antiquities of the Town, Hundred, and Deanry of Buckingham*. London: 1755.

Guidebooks
Deal Castle
Dover Castle
Gainsborough Old Hall (Sue Allan)
Grimsthorpe Castle (Tim Knox)
Leeds Castle
Medieval Bishop's Palace, Lincoln (Glyn Coppack)
Schloss Burg an der Wupper. (D. Soechting)
Sizergh Castle
Thornton Abbey

DVDs
The Vanished Palace of Otford

Internet Resources
Higginbottom, S., 'It's a Boy! No, It's a Girl! Some Seymour Birth Dates': http://www.susanhigginbotham.com/blog/posts/its-a-boy-no-its-a-girl-some-seymour-birth-dates/#comment-450359

'Excavations on the site of Norfolk House, Lambeth': http://archaeologydataservice.ac.uk/archiveDS/archiveDownload?t=arch-457-1/dissemination/pdf/vol06/vol06_13/06_13_343_350.pdf

'Plan General de Ordenacion Urbana de Medina del Campo': http://www.ayto-medinadelcampo.es/pgou/DOCUMENTOS/DOCUMENTACION%20 NORMATIVA/DN-CT%20CATALOGO/ANEXO%20PALACIO%20 TESTAMENTARIO/Anexo_P_Testamentario.pdf

'Syon House, Syon Park: An Archaeological Evaluation of a Bridgettine Abbey and an Assessment of the Results': http://www.wessexarch.co.uk/reports/52568/ syon-park

'TuristAlcala: El blog de Abraham Consuegra Gandullo': http://www.turistalcala. blogspot.com.es/

About the Authors

In recent years, both authors have dedicated many hours to researching and writing about Anne Boleyn and Tudor history in general. Dr Sarah Morris first became interested in the Tudors at school. Her passion remained largely a private hobby until she set pen to paper in 2010 and began writing *Le Temps Viendra: A Novel of Anne Boleyn*; the first of two volumes was published in the autumn of 2012, the second following in 2013. That same year, the first of the *In the Footsteps* series, co-authored with Natalie Grueninger, called *In the Footsteps of Anne Boleyn*, was also released and reached number one on the Amazon bestselling list in several categories.

For Australian-born Natalie Grueninger, it was a visit to the Tower of London on a wintery day in 2000 that ignited her curiosity about Anne and the world in which she lived, and set her on a path of learning that would eventually lead to the creation, in 2009, of *On the Tudor Trail*, a website dedicated to documenting historic sites associated with Anne Boleyn and sharing information about life in Tudor England. Although Natalie's interest in the Tudors was awakened in her early twenties, as a child she was fascinated with the past and the concept of time.

Having been drawn together initially by our love of Anne Boleyn, we soon realised that we shared an insatiable curiosity for the buildings and locations associated with the Tudor period, and in particular associated with the royal court. Both of us remain endlessly intrigued by the fact that when we stand in a building or space where someone from the past once stood, it is only time, and not space, which separates us. And so once more, we journeyed into Tudor England.

For further updates, author events and to contact the authors visit either:

For Sarah Morris: www.letempsviendra.co.uk or https://www.letempsviendra.wordpress.com/about/
For Natalie Grueninger: www.onthetudortrail.com or www.nataliegrueninger.com

We look forward to hearing about your adventures in following in the footsteps of the six wives of Henry VIII!

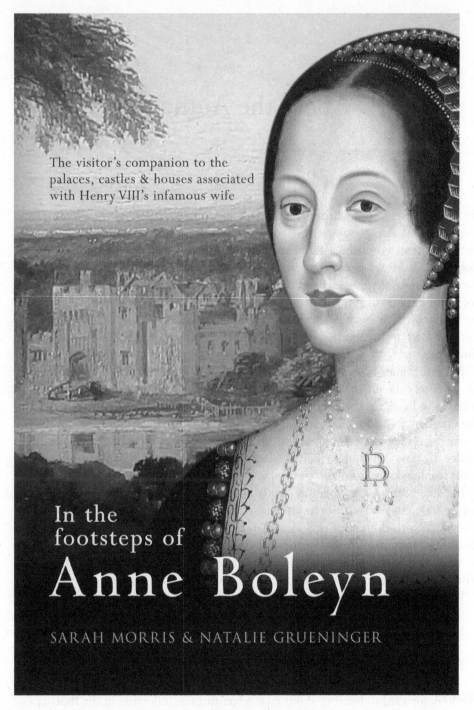

Also available from Amberley Publishing

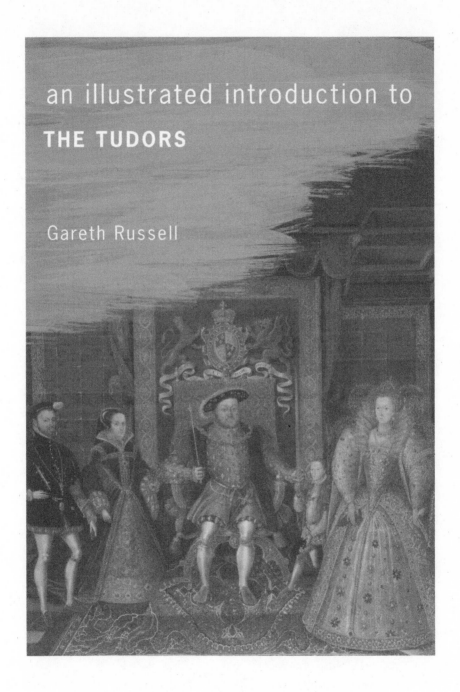

an illustrated introduction to

THE TUDORS

Gareth Russell